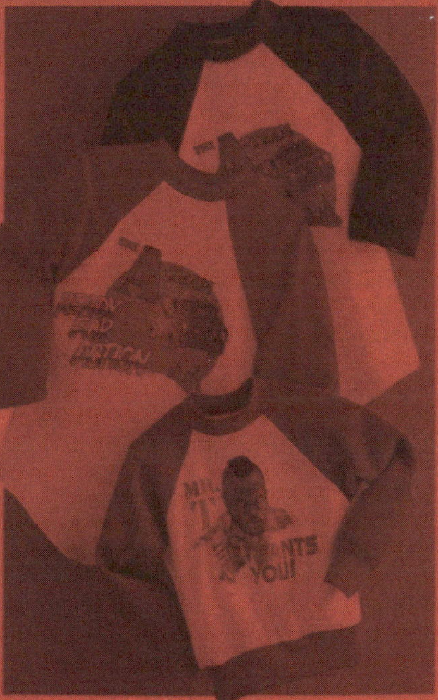

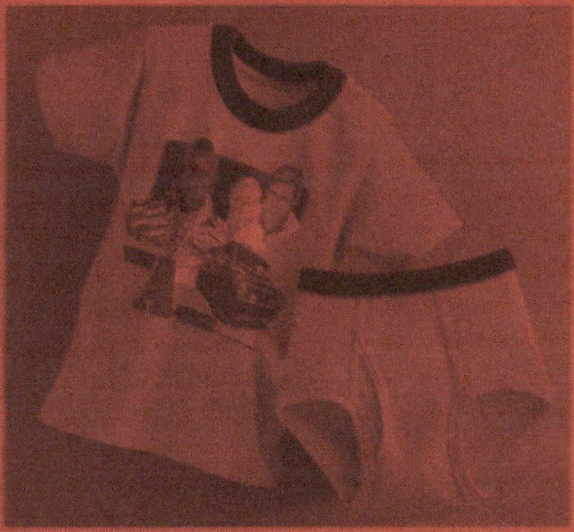

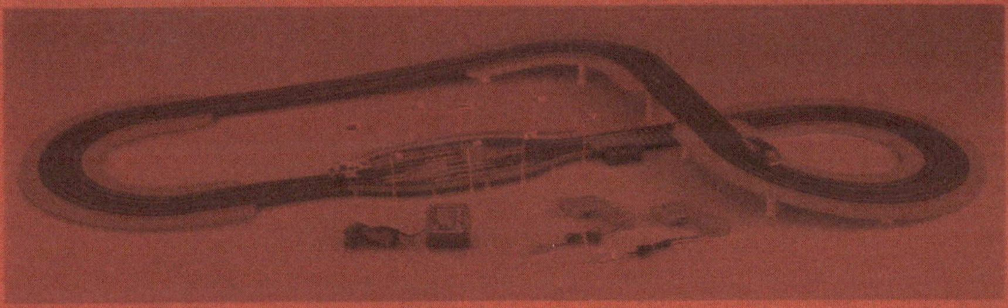

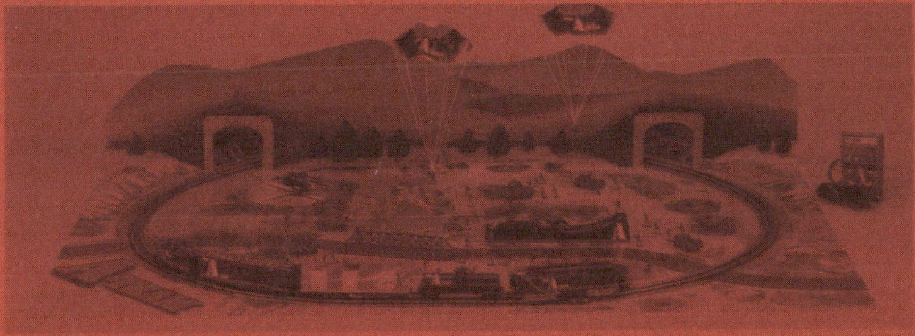

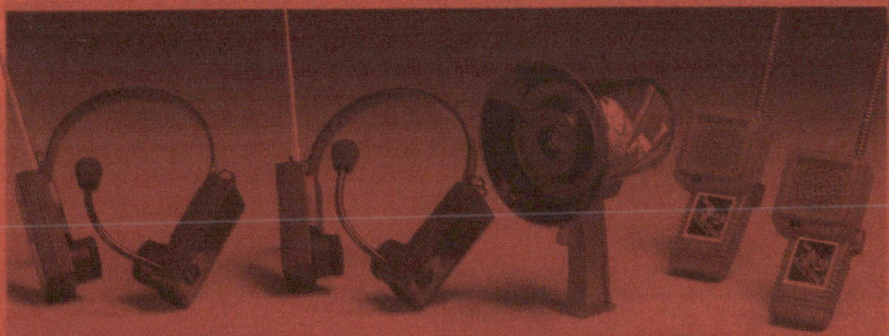

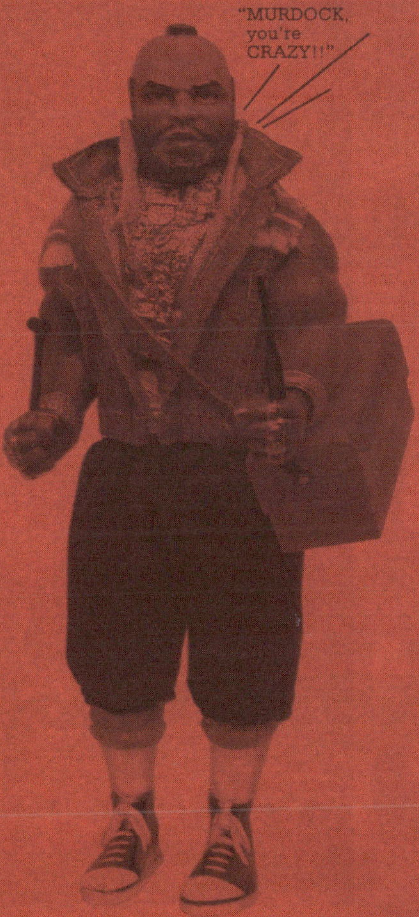
"MURDOCK, you're CRAZY!!"

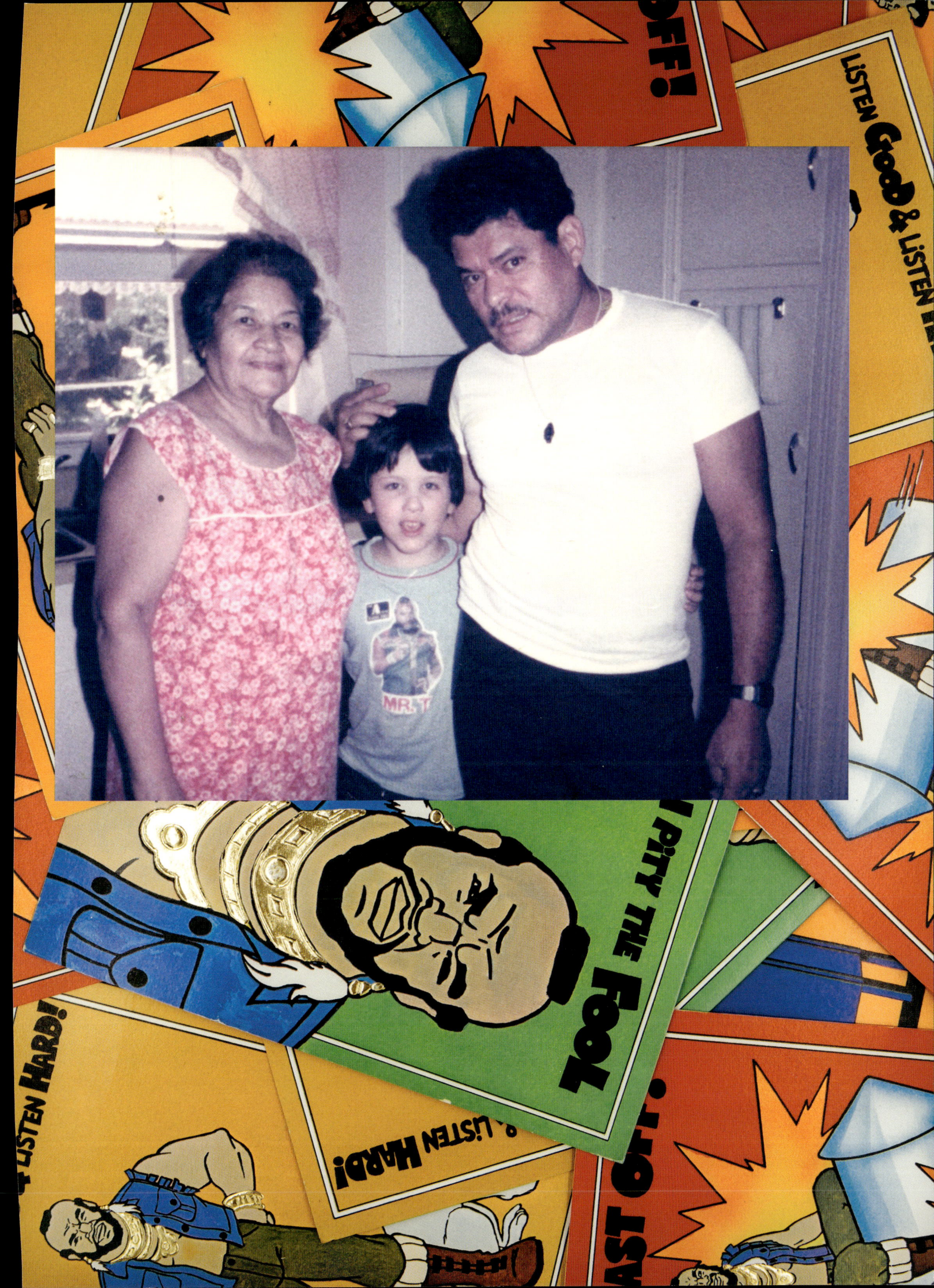

OFF!
LISTEN GOOD & LISTEN
MR. T
PITY THE FOOL
LISTEN HARD!
& LISTEN HARD!

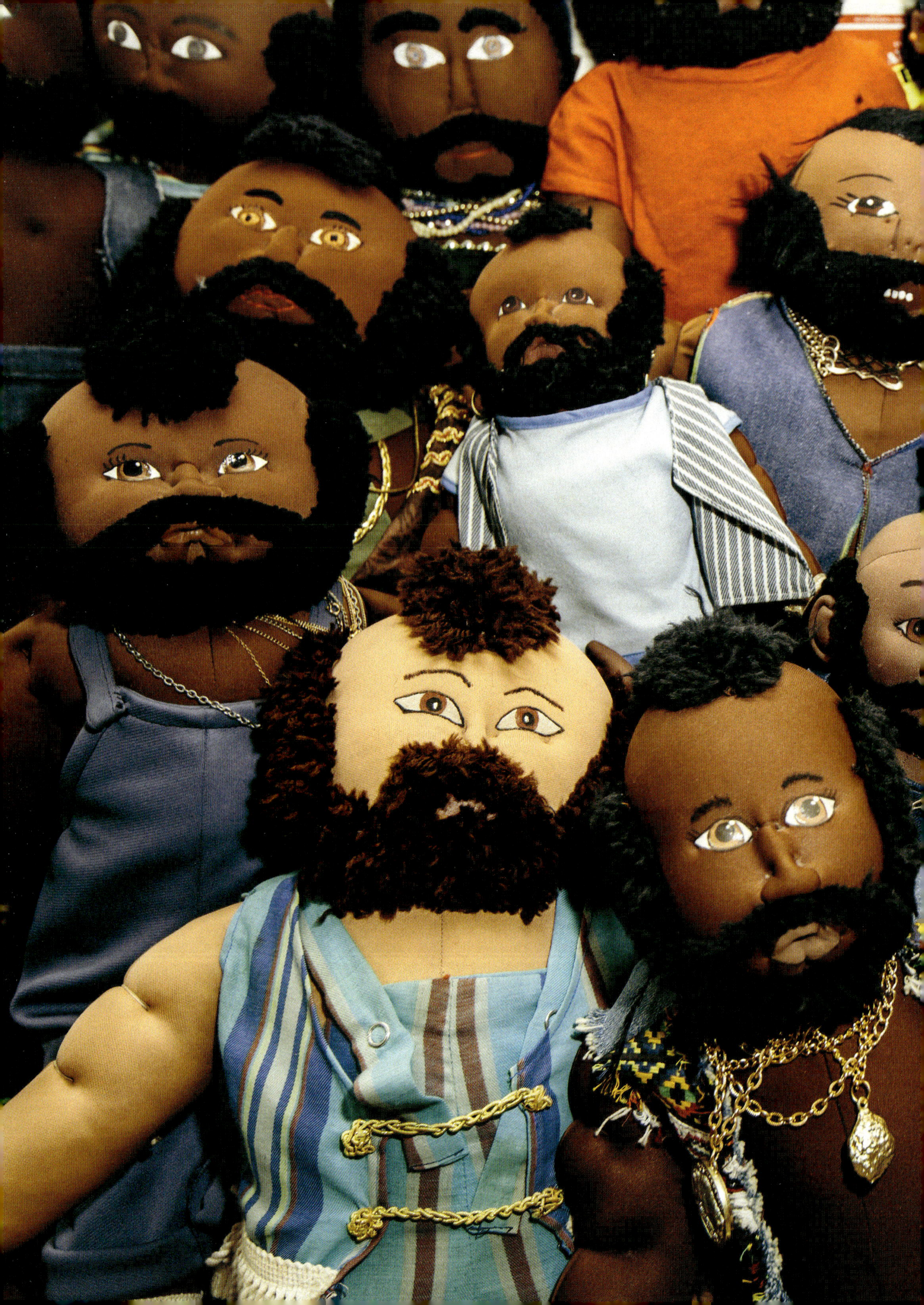

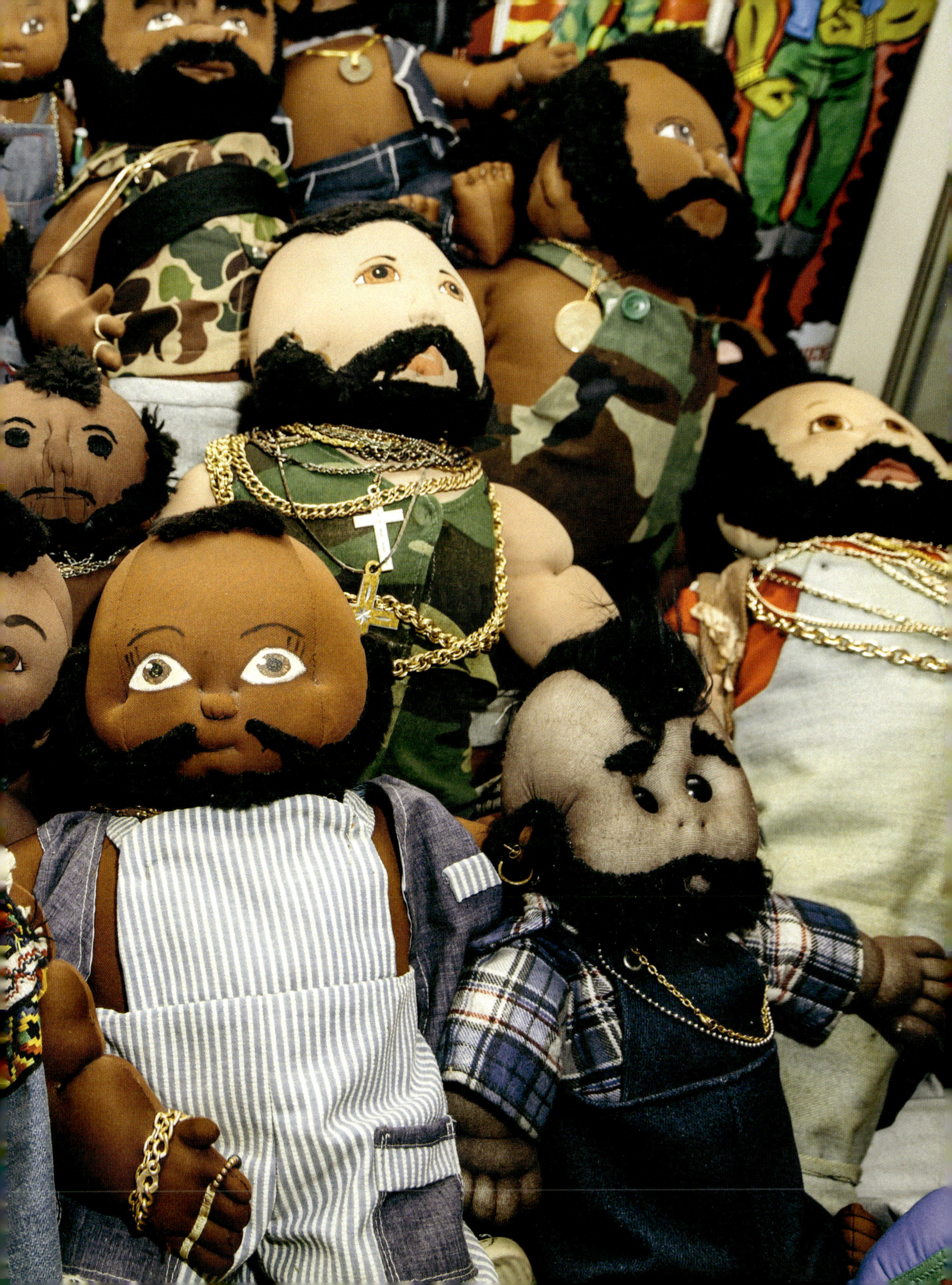

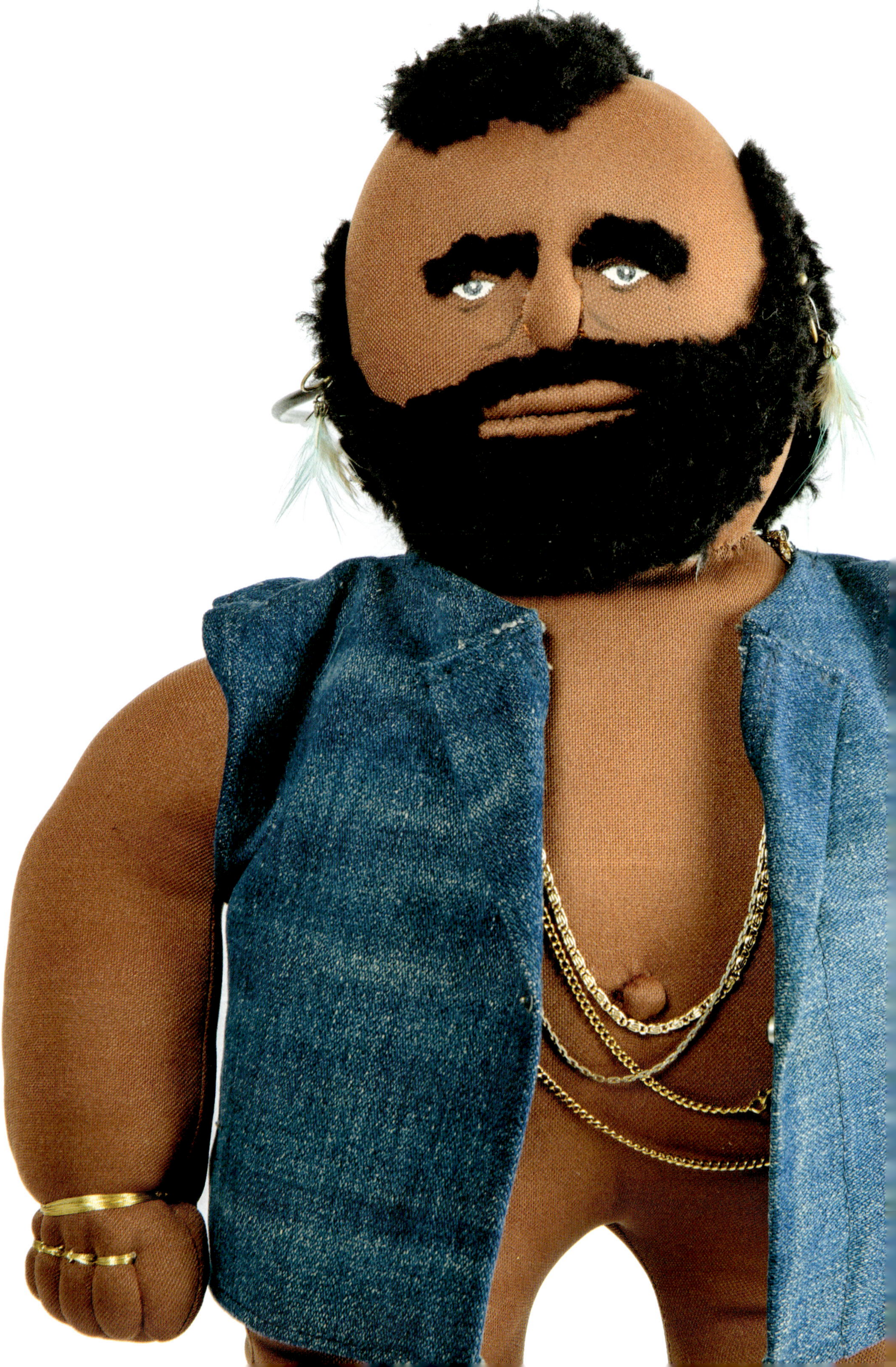

I PITY THE DOLLS

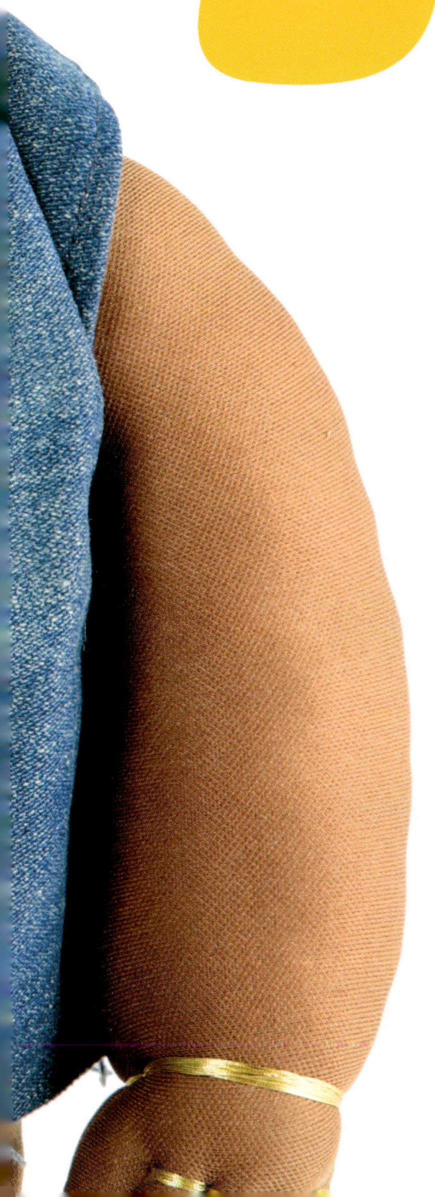

GREG RIVERA
QUANG LE

Design by MIKE ESSL

Schiffer Publishing Ltd
4880 Lower Valley Road • Atglen, PA 19310

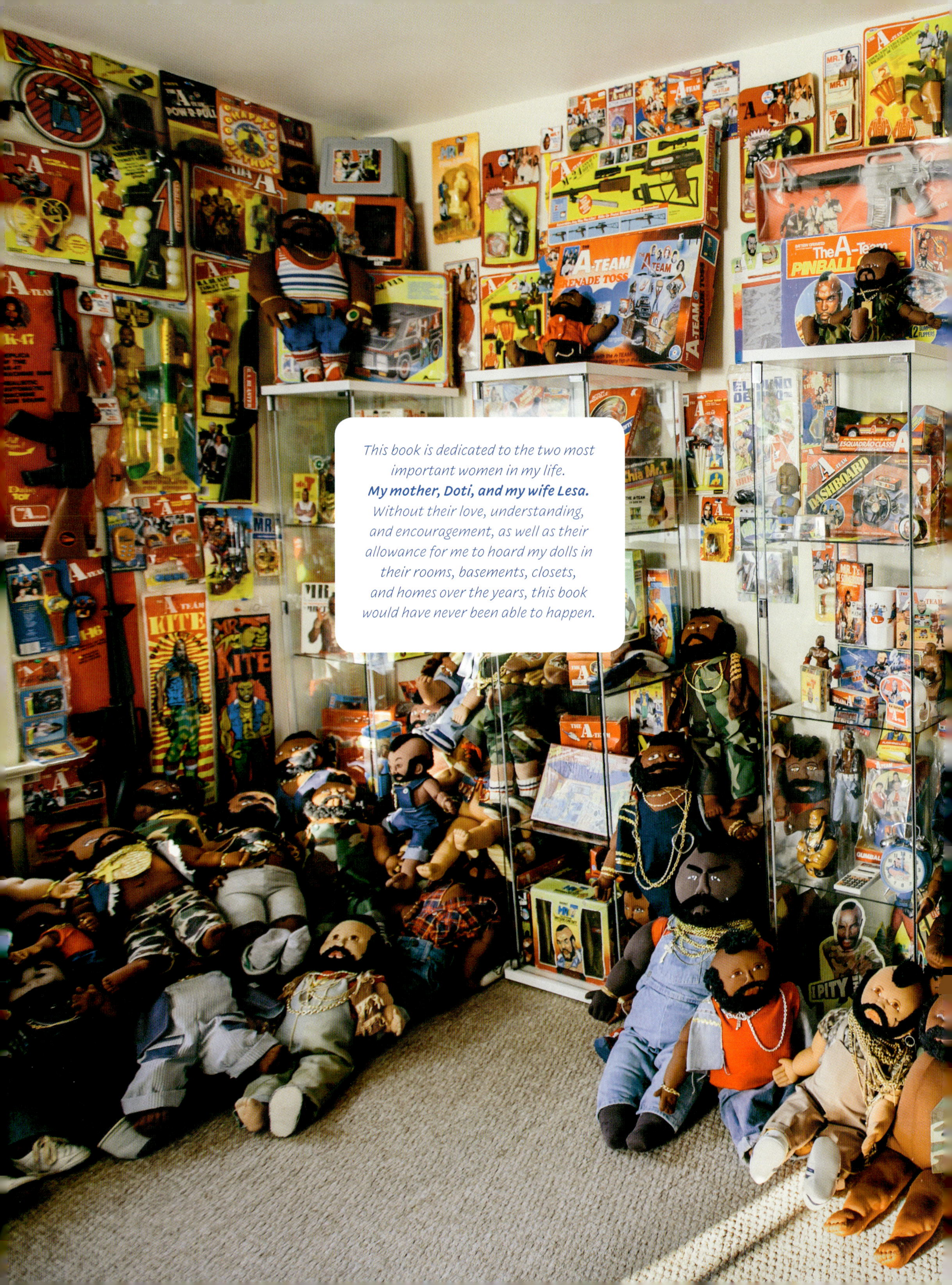

This book is dedicated to the two most important women in my life.
My mother, Doti, and my wife Lesa.
Without their love, understanding, and encouragement, as well as their allowance for me to hoard my dolls in their rooms, basements, closets, and homes over the years, this book would have never been able to happen.

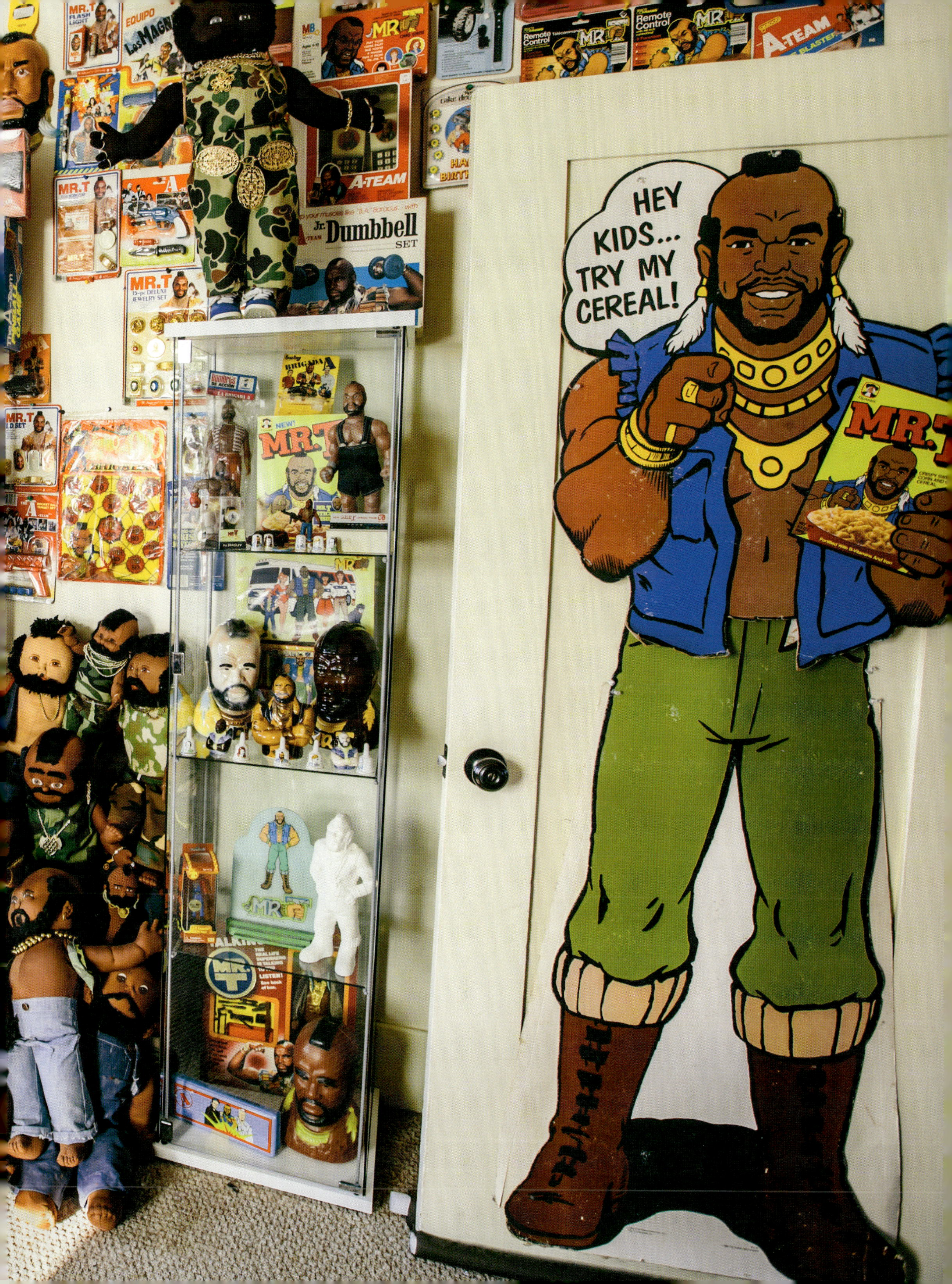
HEY KIDS... TRY MY CEREAL!
MR.T
Jr. Dumbbell SET
A-TEAM
Remote Control
MR.T 15-pc DELUXE JEWELRY SET
BRIGADA A
NEW! MR.T

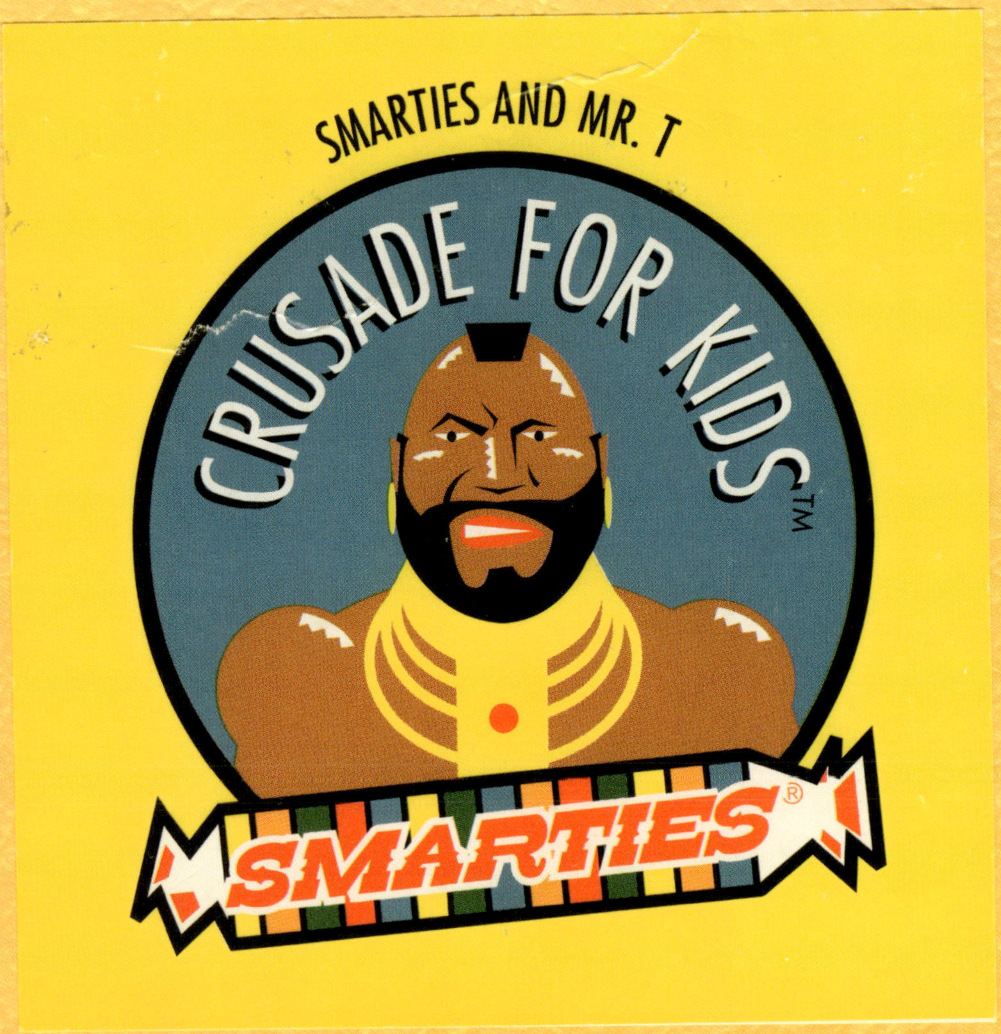

Library of Congress Control Number: 2018956477

Use of Mr. T Soft Sculpture Doll Pattern granted under permission by Martha Holcombe. All photography © Quang Le unless noted. Design by Mike Essl. Typeset in Inkwell by Hoefler & Co. and Cheee by OH No Type Co.

ISBN: 978-0-7643-5724-4
Printed in the United States of America

Published by Schiffer Publishing, Ltd.
4880 Lower Valley Road
Atglen, PA 19310
Phone: (610) 593-1777; Fax: (610) 593-2002
E-mail: Info@schifferbooks.com
Web: www.schifferbooks.com

For our complete selection of fine books on this and related subjects, please visit our website at www.schifferbooks.com. You may also write for a free catalog.

Schiffer Publishing's titles are available at special discounts for bulk purchases for sales promotions or premiums. Special editions, including personalized covers, corporate imprints, and excerpts, can be created in large quantities for special needs. For more information, contact the publisher.

We are always looking for people to write books on new and related subjects. If you have an idea for a book, please contact us at proposals@schifferbooks.com.

ABOVE *Smarties Crusade for Kids promotional folder.*

RIGHT *Mr. T ring cardboard display. Uruguay.*

PAGE 1 *Greg with his Padrino Benny and his wife in the early '80s. Mr. T birthday cards, Ruby Spears Entertainment, 1984.*

PAGES 4–5 *The doll nicknamed John Belushi.*

PAGES 6–7 *Quang's place during shooting.*

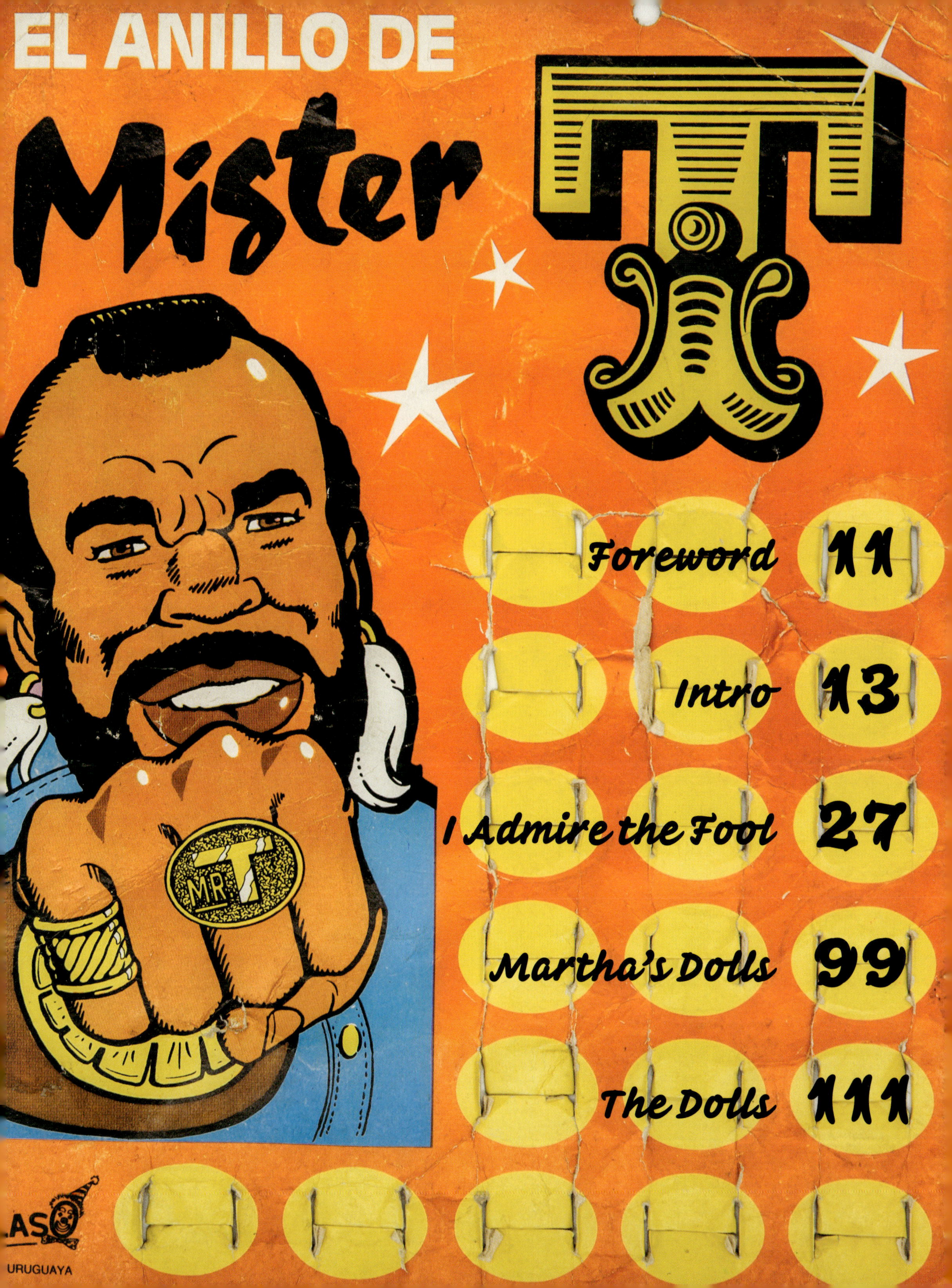

Foreword 11
Intro 13
I Admire the Fool 27
Martha's Dolls 99
The Dolls 111

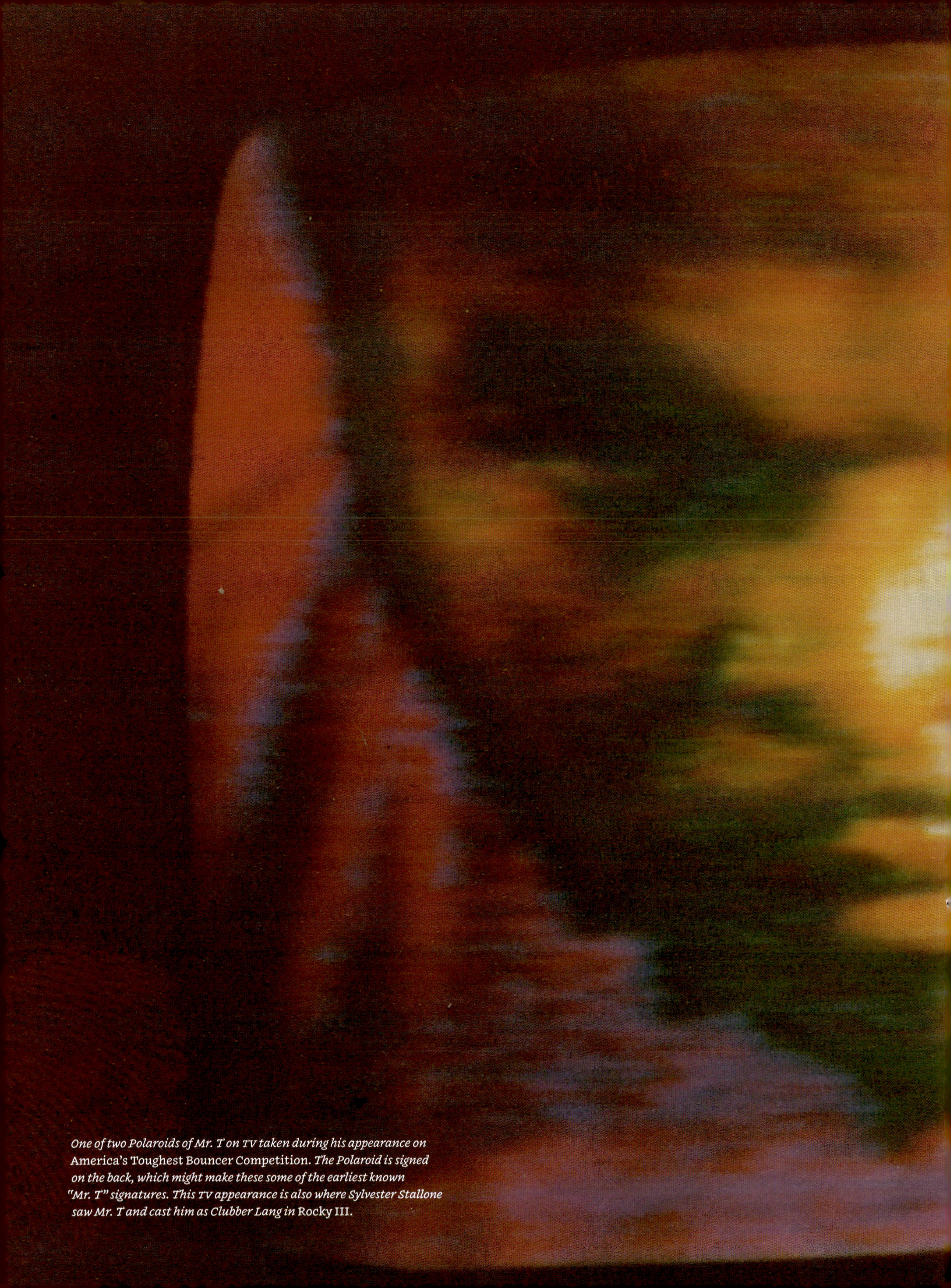

One of two Polaroids of Mr. T on TV taken during his appearance on America's Toughest Bouncer Competition. *The Polaroid is signed on the back, which might make these some of the earliest known "Mr. T" signatures. This TV appearance is also where Sylvester Stallone saw Mr. T and cast him as Clubber Lang in* Rocky III.

You were probably expecting a foreword by Mr. T. Sorry, fool! Instead you get me, owner of the world's SECOND largest Mr. T collection, and the designer of this book. I've been collecting Mr. T toys since I saw *Rocky III* as an eight-year-old in suburban Philadelphia. I've also known Greg Rivera for almost twenty years and can vouch for the *absoludicrous* size of his T collection.

The last time we tried to count, Greg had over 1,000 more pieces of T merch than I did, and that's not including the dolls. It would be impossible for me to catch up. He has things I could never get, like a one-of-a-kind prototype of B. A. that *haunts me* to this day. To his credit, Greg is incredibly cool about it all. If you show him something with Mr. T's face on it his response is usually, "Oh yeah I have that. I got it at a flea market in Florida for two dollars." Brutal. Greg has everything, but he's never met Mr. T.

That's the one thing I have on Greg. I met The Man. At a Planet Hollywood autograph signing, I stood in line for more than an hour and met my hero. Mr. T put his arm around me and said, "Hey there, big buddy." We took a photo together and I went outside and sobbed. There wasn't enough time to tell T his kindness and positivity inspired me to become a teacher. Mr. T famously preached, "stay in school and don't do drugs," and I became a college professor and didn't drink until I was in my late twenties. I'm the fool you should pity.

My love of T includes Greg's 200 creepy Cabbage-Patch-Kid-style Mr. T dolls. His dolls have lived in my apartments and taken over my storage spaces. I've had the misfortune of dragging huge bags of dolls as checked luggage on the way to the I Pity the Dolls show in San Francisco. All this, and I only own three dolls!

Each doll is unique and filled with the love it takes to hand-make a pint-sized T. I hope that our book, and Quang's incredible photos, fill you with the same joy that the dolls brought their original owners.

Mike Essl
BROOKLYN, NY
SEPTEMBER 17, 2018

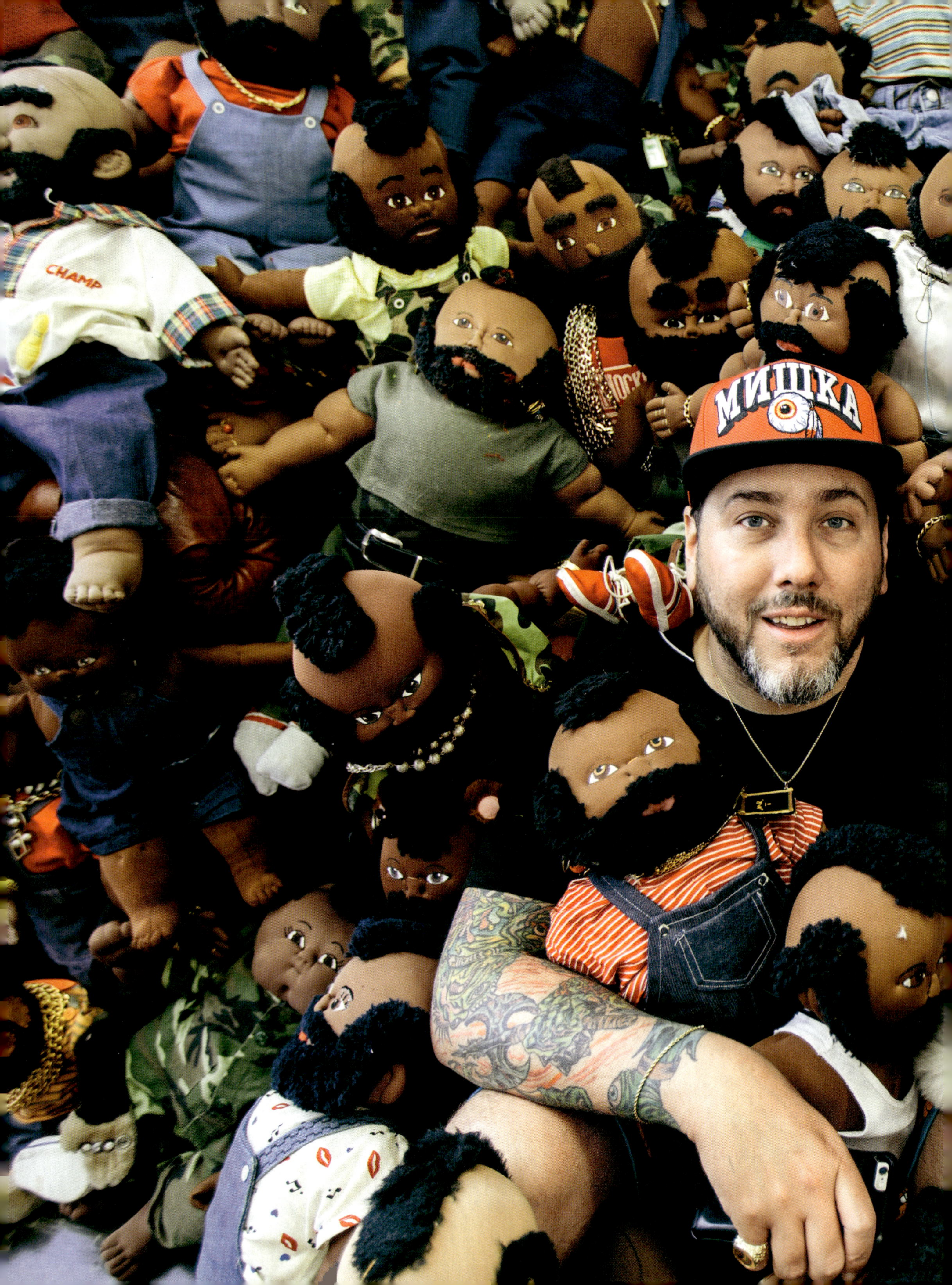
CHAMP
МИШКА

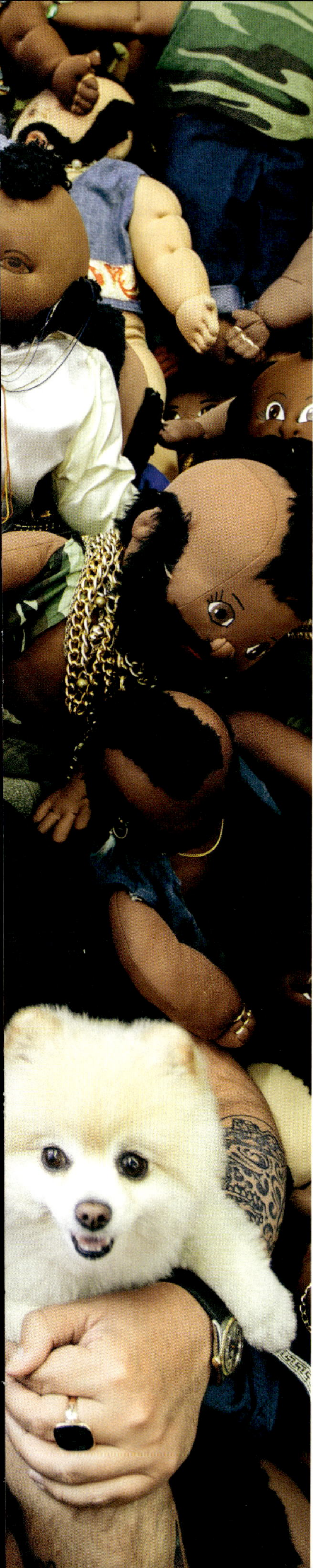

INTRO

This book represents the culmination of my life's work as the foremost Mr. T memorabilia collector in the world. If you are wondering how this all got started, I guess you would have to go back to my childhood. I was born in Bridgeport, Connecticut, in 1979. I remember watching *The A-Team* with my father as a kid in the mid-1980s. Whenever the theme song would come on I would run to the couch, waiting to see what crazy adventure the guys would be getting into. The guy I was most excited about, however, was **MR.T**! His gold chains, Mohawk, and "Bad Attitude" is what really got me excited! Mr. T was my hero! He was all over TV in the '80s. He had his own cartoon, his own cereal, and his own toys. I still remember my older brother getting me the Galoob 8" A-Team figure for Christmas as a kid. It was my favorite. I would have him wrestle Skeletor and get him in crazy adventures

We left Connecticut in 1988. My dad worked for the city and had retired after twenty-five years in the Parks Department. Bridgeport was pretty dangerous at that time. Violent crime was at an all-time high. My family decided to move to central Florida to be close to my godfather. Before we left, my mom made me sell all my toys at a tag sale, including my Mr. T action figure. Come to think of it, that's what might have started it all. Thanks, Mom!

My older brother was a big influence on my early collecting. He would bring me to flea markets, yard sales, antique malls, and auctions as early as I can remember. Florida had so many of these, it was pretty easy to start buying toys again. Some of the first and best pieces of my collection were found at the central Florida fairgrounds at their Wednesday morning markets, including one of my

Greg Rivera, Romy, and 200 Mr. T dolls.

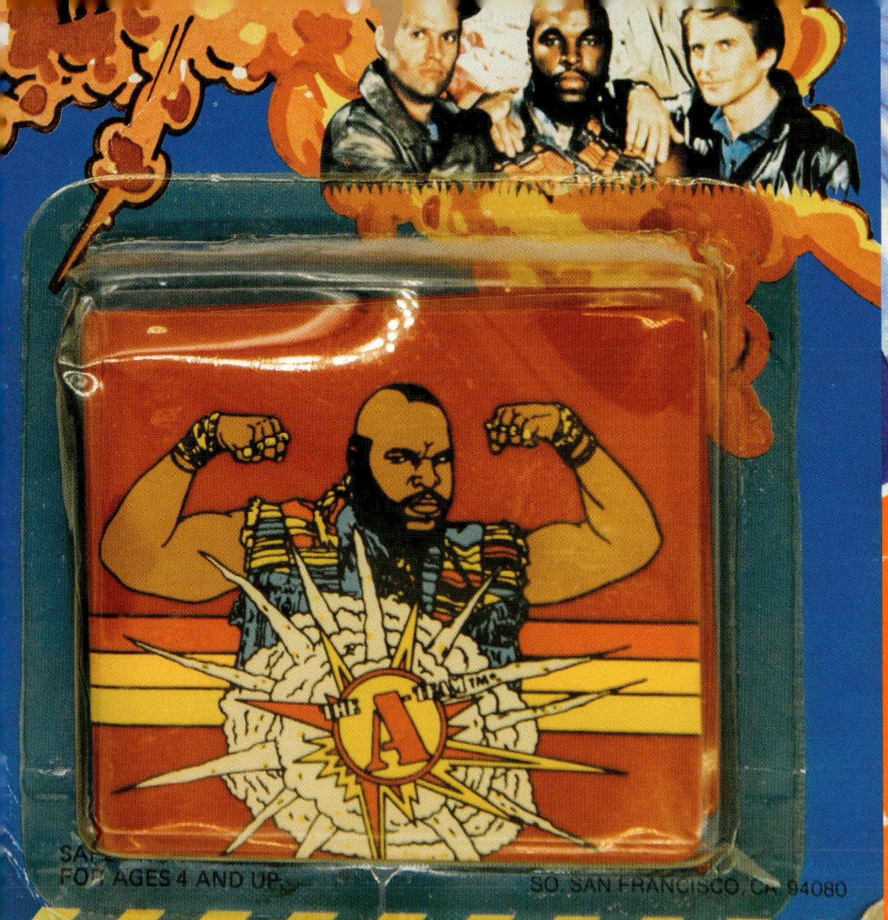
FOR AGES 4 AND UP
SO. SAN FRANCISCO, CA 94080

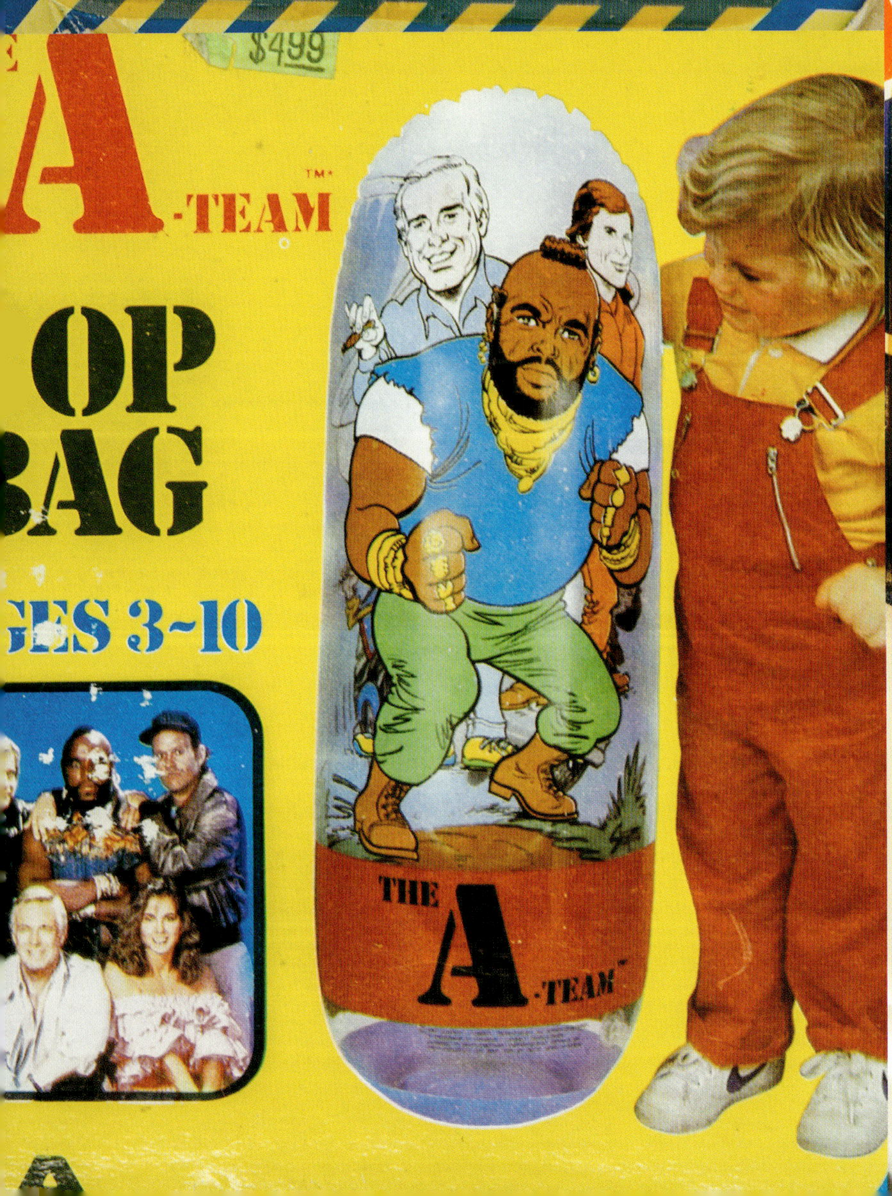
$499
A-TEAM
OP
BAG
GES 3~10
THE
A-TEAM

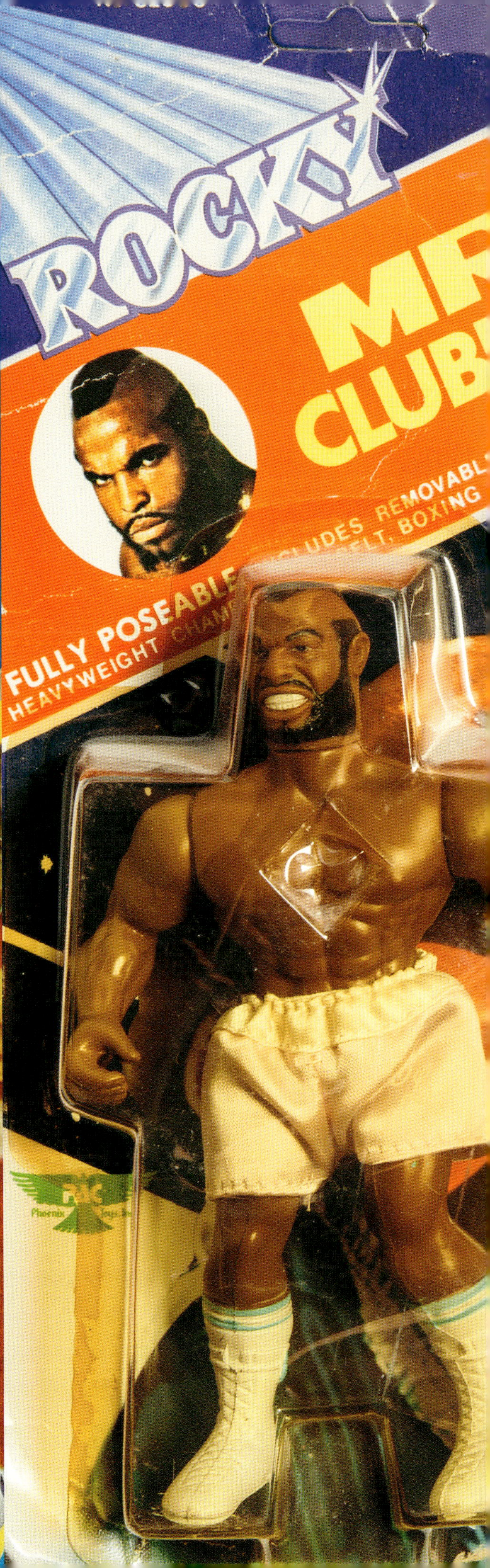
ROCKY
MR
CLUB
FULLY POSEABLE
HEAVYWEIGHT CHAM
REMOVABL
BELT, BOXING

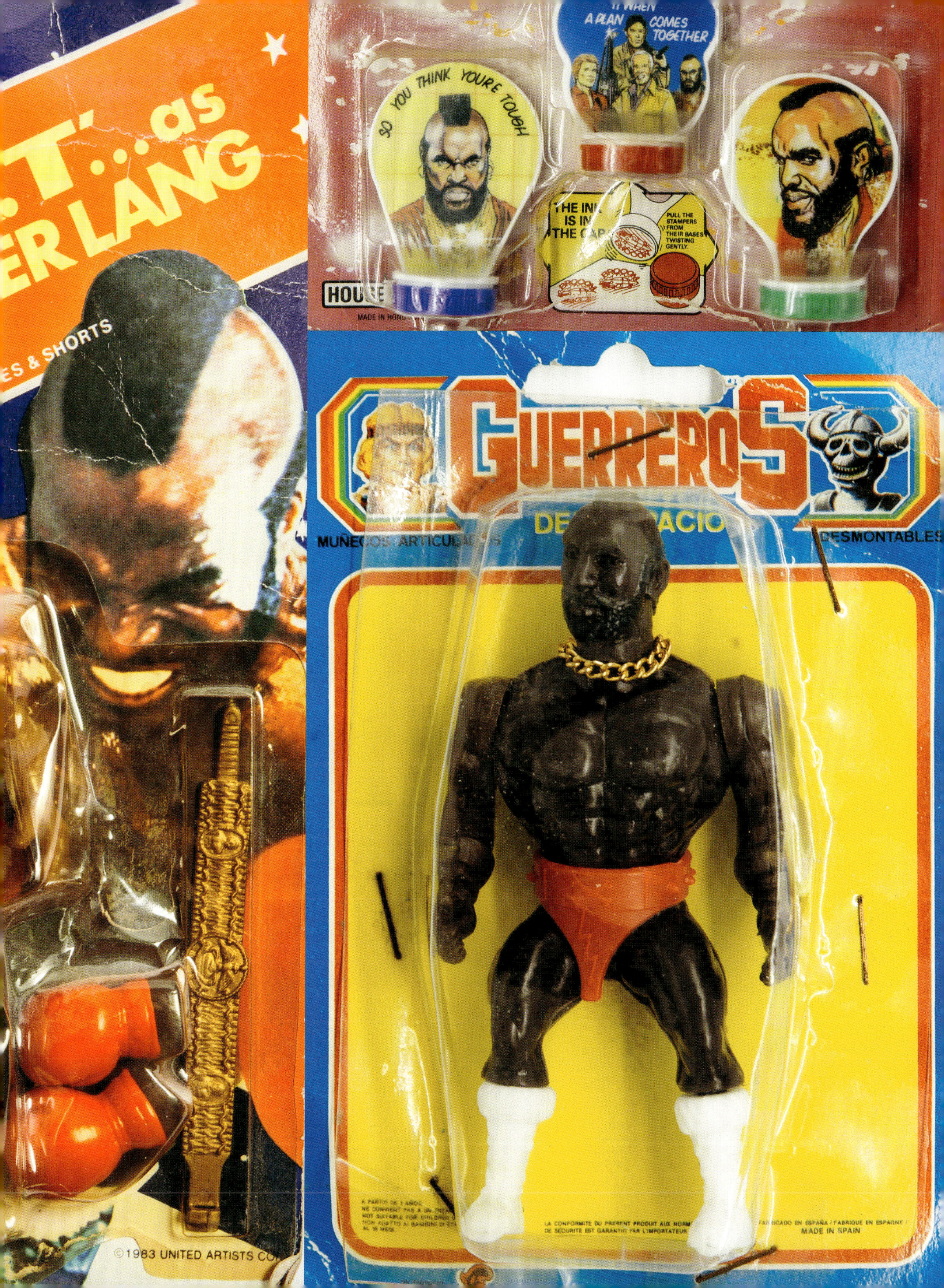

A PLAN COMES TOGETHER
SO YOU THINK YOURE TOUGH
THE INK IS IN THE CAP
PULL THE STAMPERS FROM THEIR BASES TWISTING GENTLY.
GUERREROS
DESMONTABLES
MADE IN SPAIN

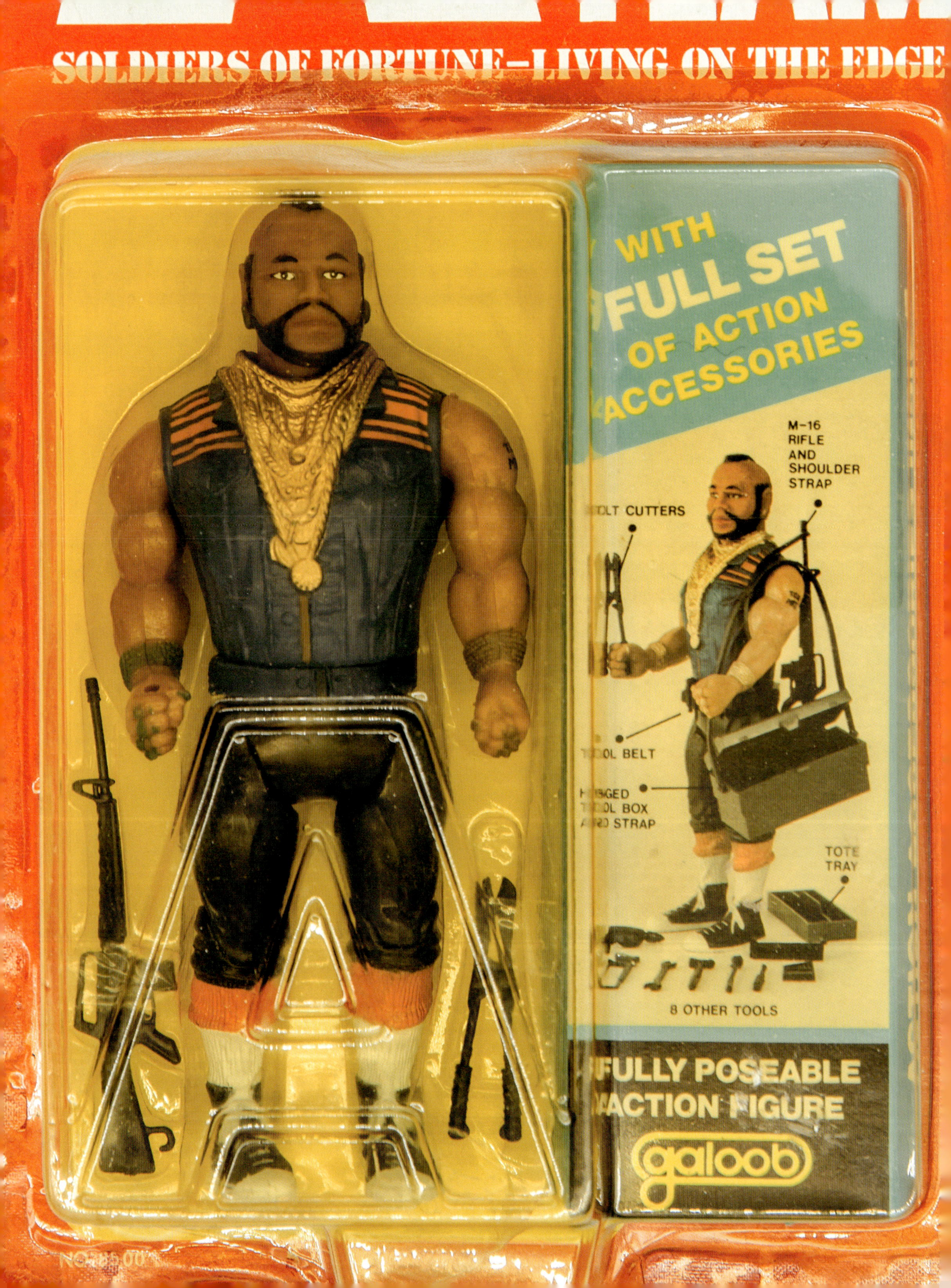
SOLDIERS OF FORTUNE–LIVING ON THE EDGE
WITH
FULL SET
OF ACTION
ACCESSORIES
M-16
RIFLE
AND
SHOULDER
STRAP
TOTE
TRAY
8 OTHER TOOLS
FULLY POSEABLE
ACTION FIGURE
galoob

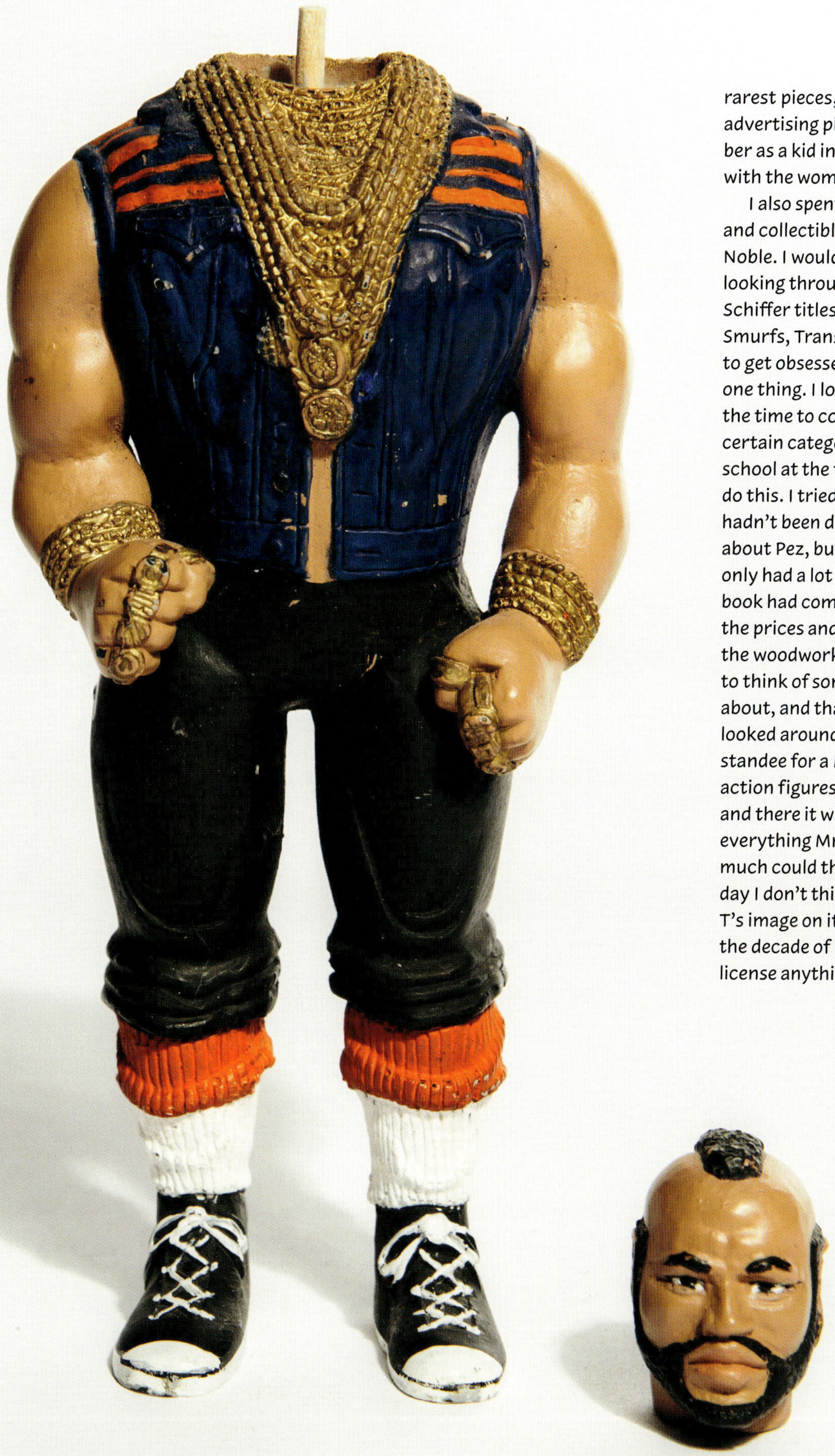

rarest pieces, my life-size cardboard advertising piece for Mr. T cereal. I remember as a kid in middle school negotiating it with the woman for five bucks!

I also spent a lot of time in the antiques and collectibles book section at Barnes & Noble. I would literally sit there for hours looking through the books. (A lot of them Schiffer titles!) McDonald's, lunchboxes, Smurfs, Transformers, Simpsons. I started to get obsessed with the idea of collecting one thing. I loved that someone had spent the time to collect as much as they could in a certain category. I was finishing up high school at the time and decided I was going to do this. I tried to think of something that hadn't been done before. Originally I thought about Pez, but pretty soon I realized that not only had a lot of people collected them but a book had come out soon after, skyrocketing the prices and bringing the collectors out of the woodwork. So I racked my brain. I needed to think of something that I was excited about, and that hadn't been documented. I looked around my room. I had my giant standee for a Mr. T cereal, a couple of books, action figures, and couple of other items, and there it was, Mr. T. I was going to collect everything Mr. T! At first I thought, how much could there be out there? Still to this day I don't think I have everything with Mr. T's image on it! I think the '80s really became the decade of licensing, and boy did Mr. T license anything he could.

Hand-painted resin protype, 1983.

LEFT *B. A. action figure, Galoob, 1983.*

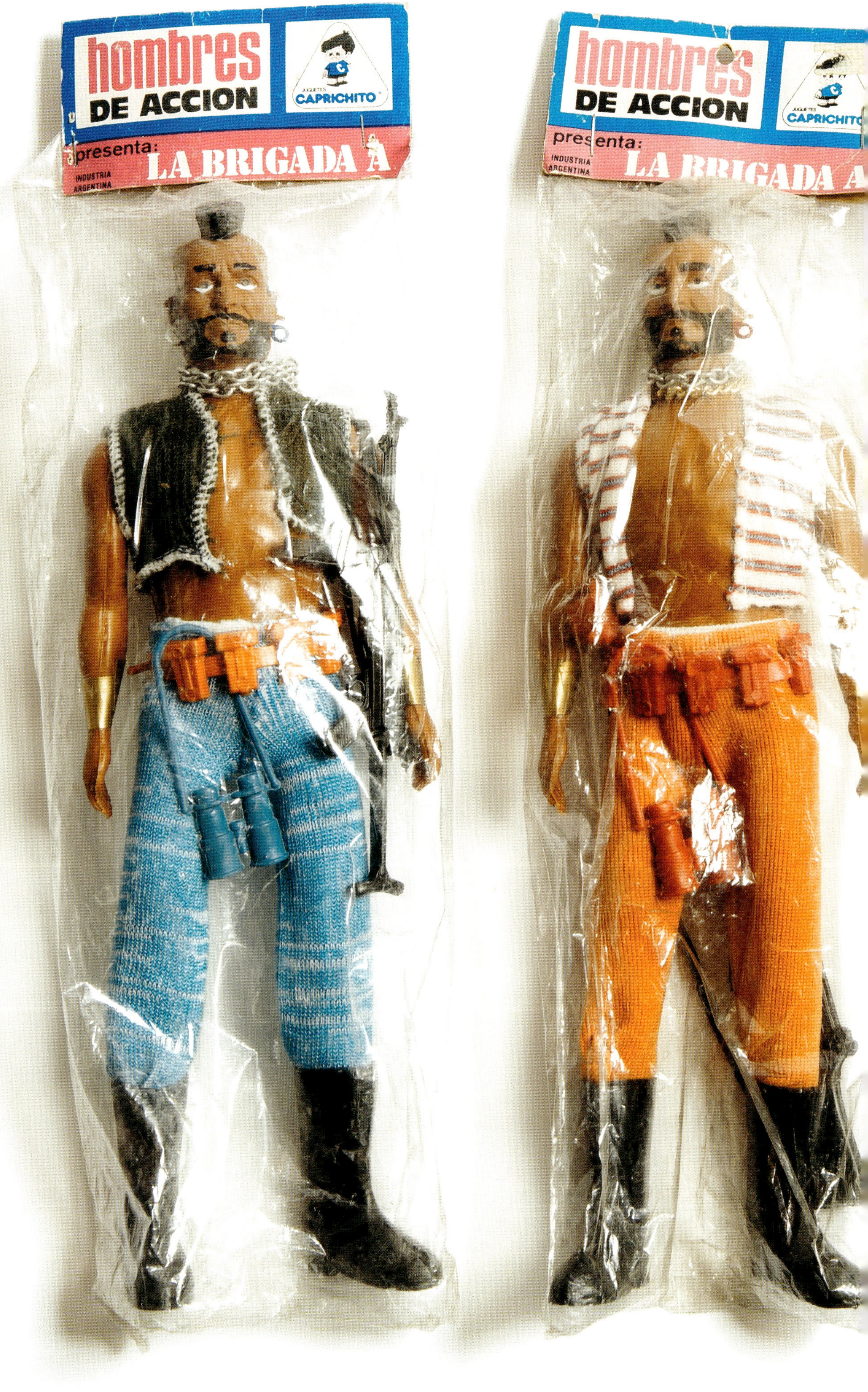
hombres
DE ACCION
JUGUETES
CAPRICHITO
presenta:
INDUSTRIA
ARGENTINA
LA BRIGADA A
hombres
DE ACCION
CAPRICHITO
presenta:
INDUSTRIA
ARGENTINA

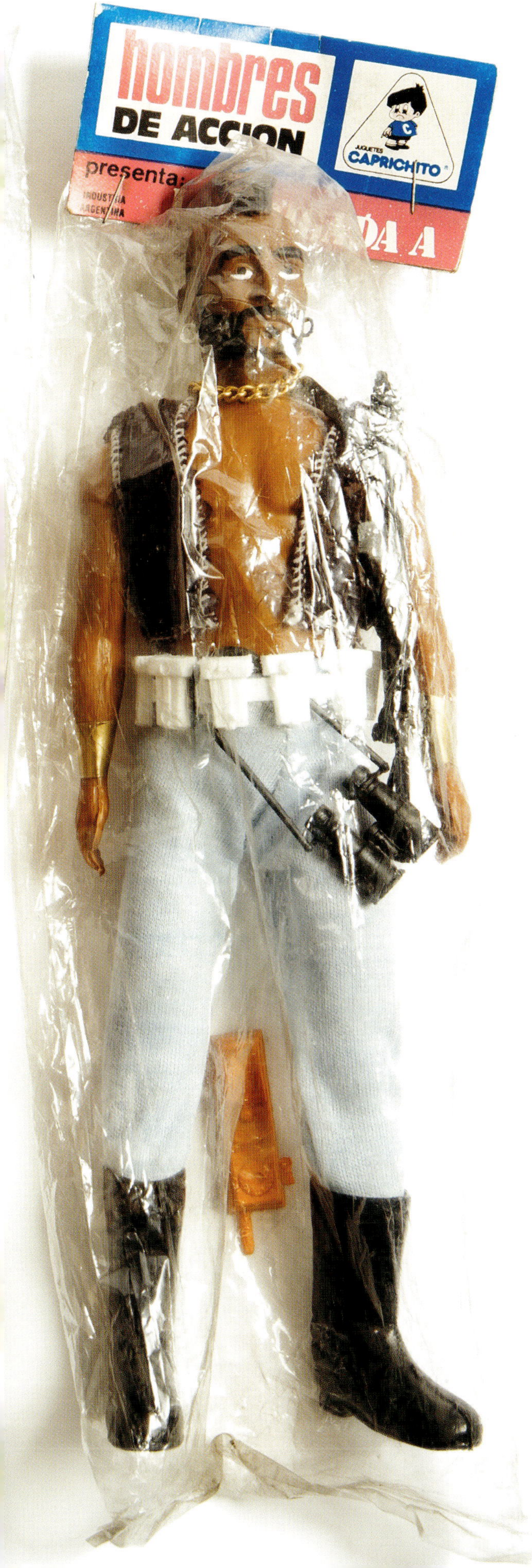

It wasn't until my second year of college at the University of Central Florida that my collection really started to take shape. I was driving down Mills Ave. in Orlando and saw a sandwich board outside of a shop with a painting of Mr. T. I made a U-turn and went into the shop. It was called Populuxe. I walked in and there were multiple shelves of everything Mr. T. I felt like I hit a goldmine. The owner of the store, Brian Cain, explained to me that he had just decided to sell his Mr. T collection. I couldn't believe it! Being a college student, I didn't have too much money, so I bought what I could. I started to come in so much that Brian asked me if I wanted a job (I think he secretly knew he could pay me in Mr. T!), so that summer I worked there. The majority of, if not all of, my paycheck went to my collection. This was 1998, so it's when I started to learn to sell (then buy) on eBay. This became the dark hole that became my collection. eBay opened up a new world or Mr. T memorabilia. I started to find things from the UK, Spain, and Argentina, and not to mention all of the stuff in the USA that they had licensed Mr. T's image on. From soap to air fresheners, games, flashlights, wallets, dolls, and banks, it was insane. This is also around the time I met my friend and designer of this book, Mike Essl.

Back when eBay first started, you could actually see who you were bidding against. For the first year or two I was winning anything and everything that I bid on. That's until I saw username "MikeEssl" beating me. After this happening a few times, I had to contact this guy. I remember our first conversations, and Mike telling me how big of a collection he had. So I sent him some photos of mine and he was blown away. Soon after, we decided to create a truce. We would let each other know if the other was going to bid on something. Also, Mike had a real job and more money than me, so I let him take the high-ticket items. At this point our combined collection was and still is, to my estimation, the largest collection of Mr. T memorabilia in the world!

RIGHT *Bragada A B. A. action figure, Galgo. Argentina.*

BELOW *Bootleg action figure.*

FAR RIGHT *El Invencible action figure. Uruguay.*

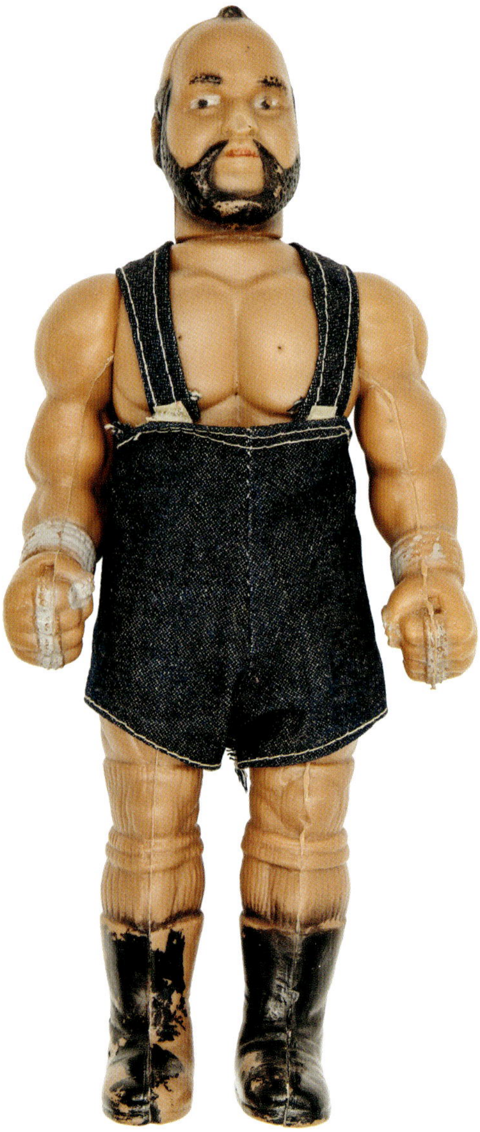

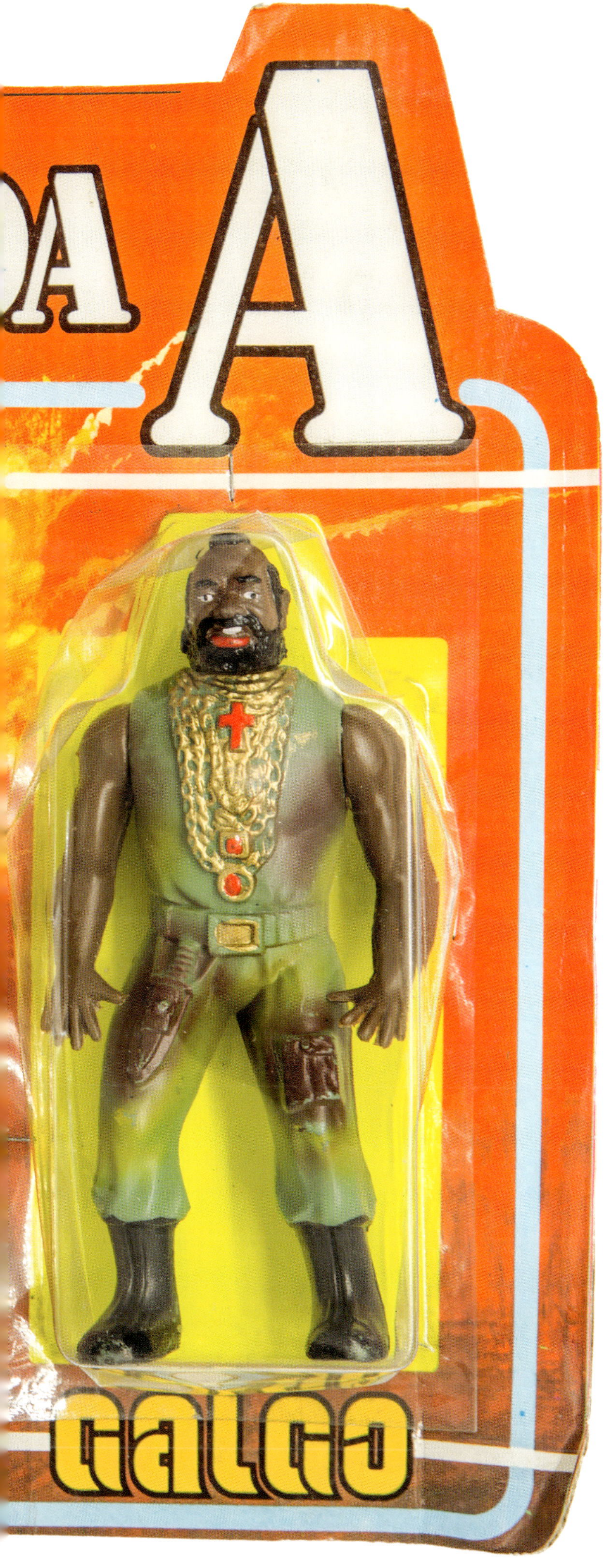
DA A
GALGO
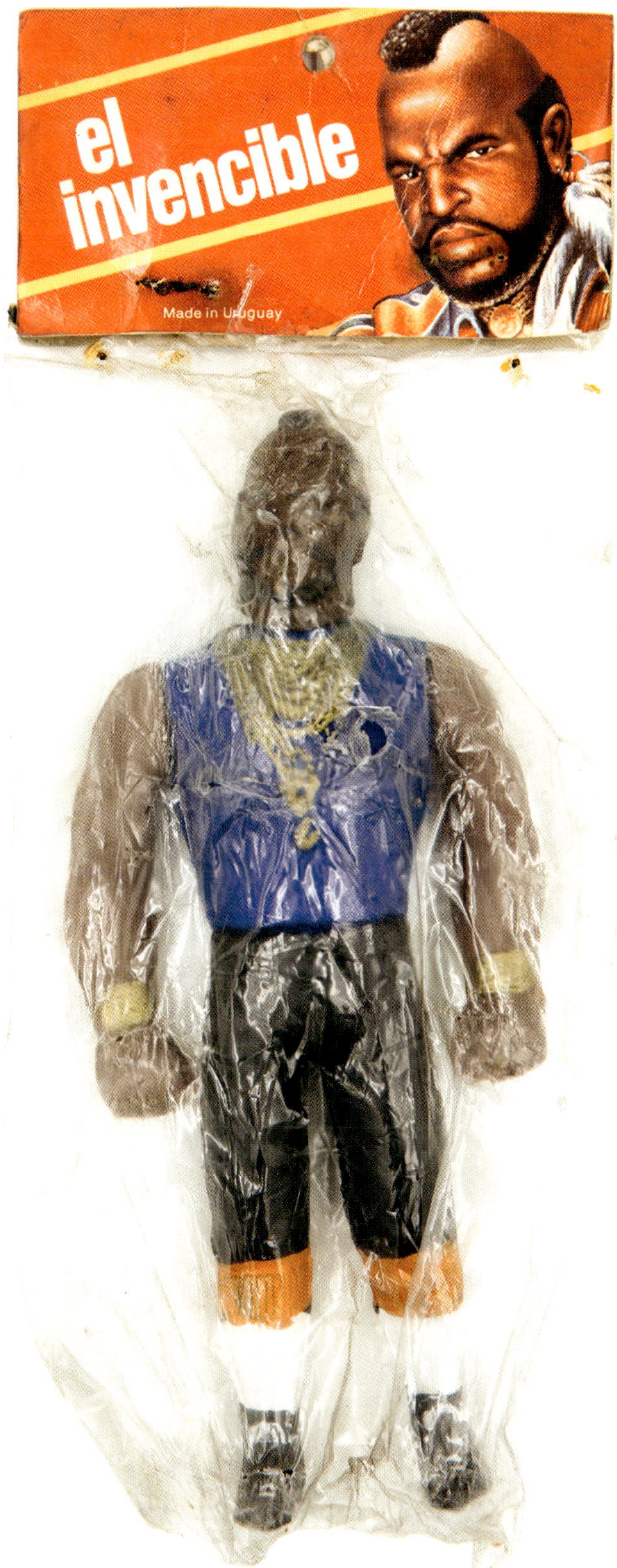
el invencible
Made in Uruguay

Mr. T-Rex by Andrew Heffron a.k.a Lab Monkey Number 9.

RIGHT *A-Team, B. A. action figure, Glasslite.*

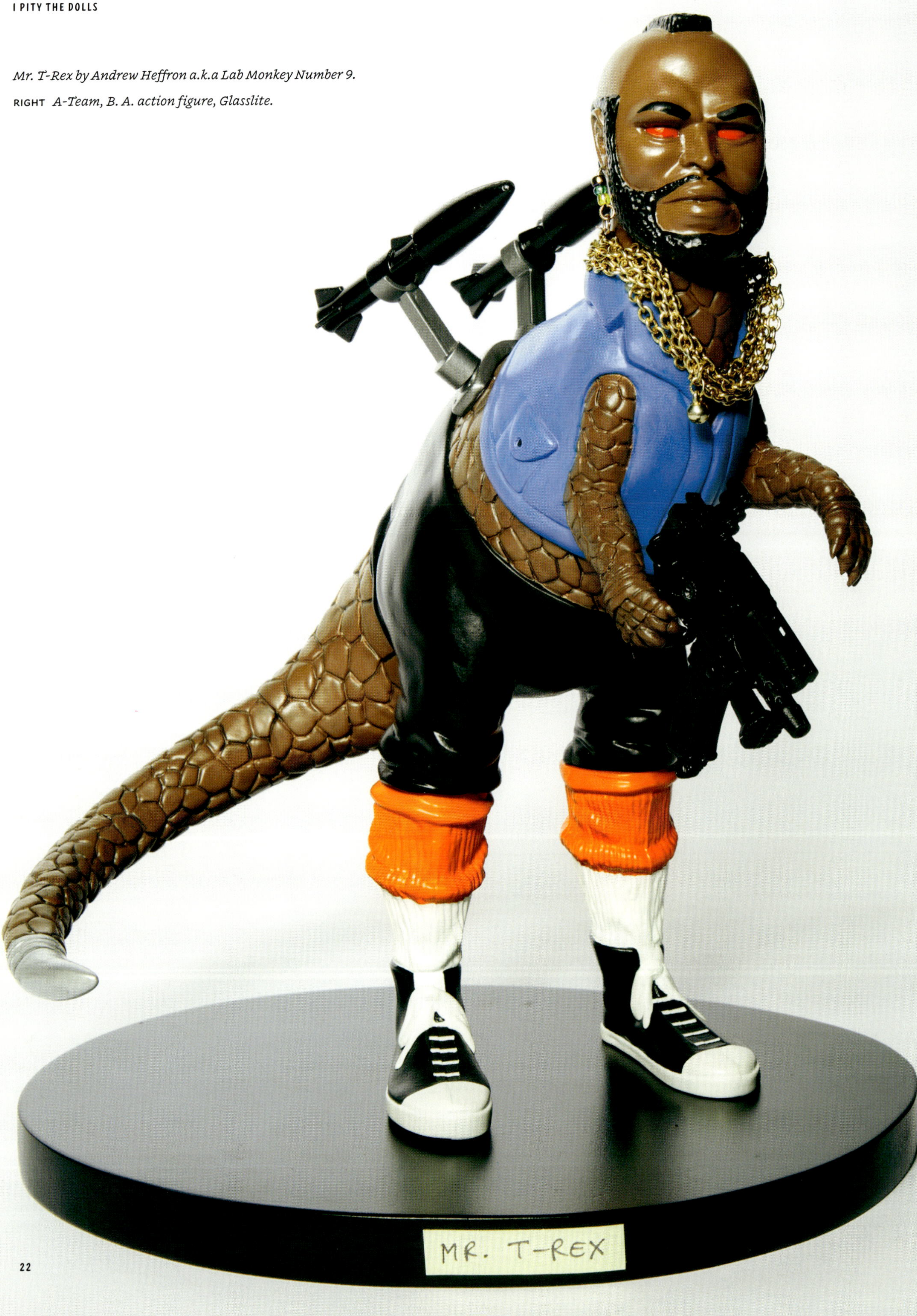

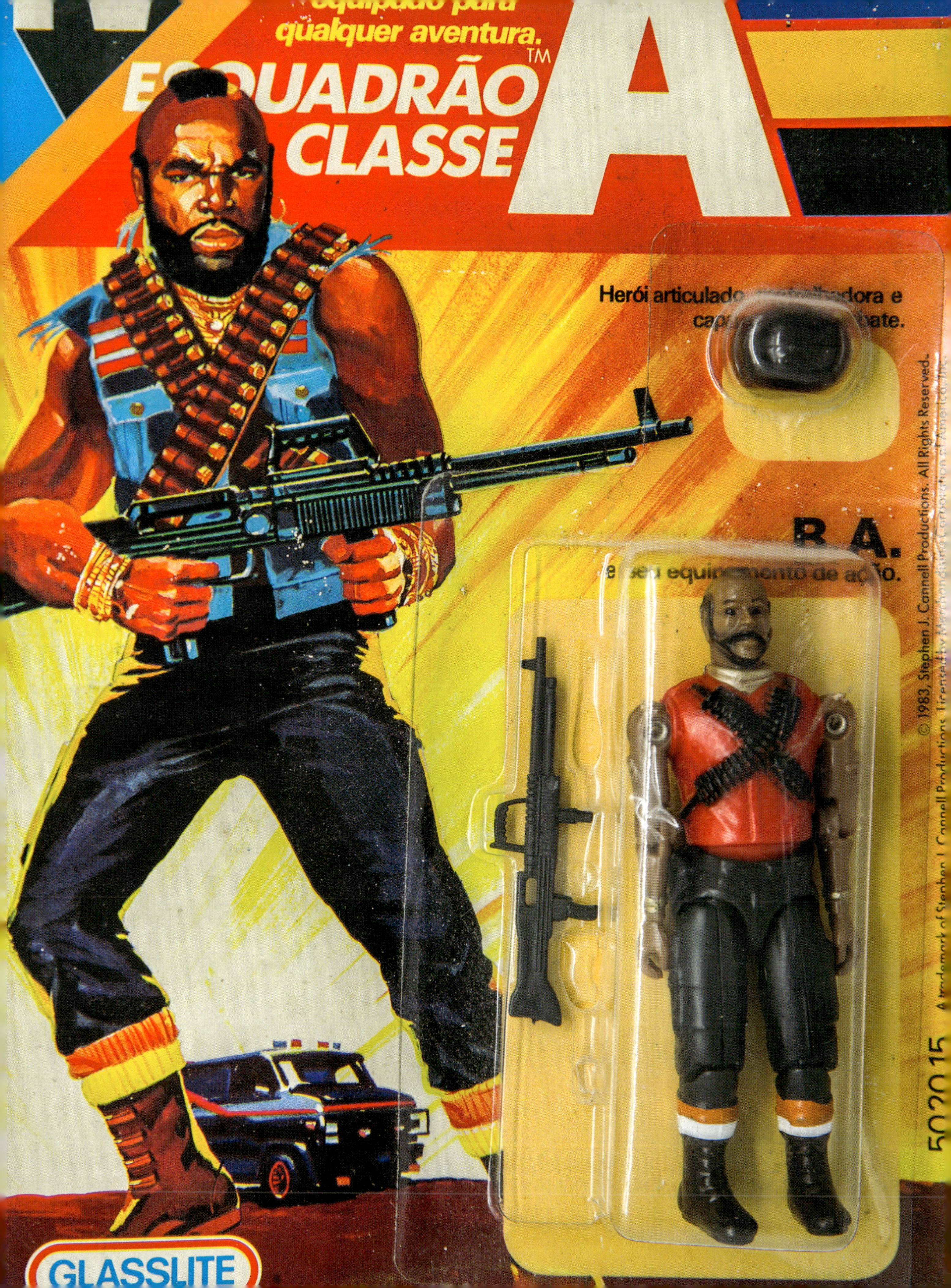
qualquer aventura.
CLASSE
A
Herói articulado
B.A.
© 1983, Stephen J. Cannell Productions. All Rights Reserved.
502015
GLASSLITE

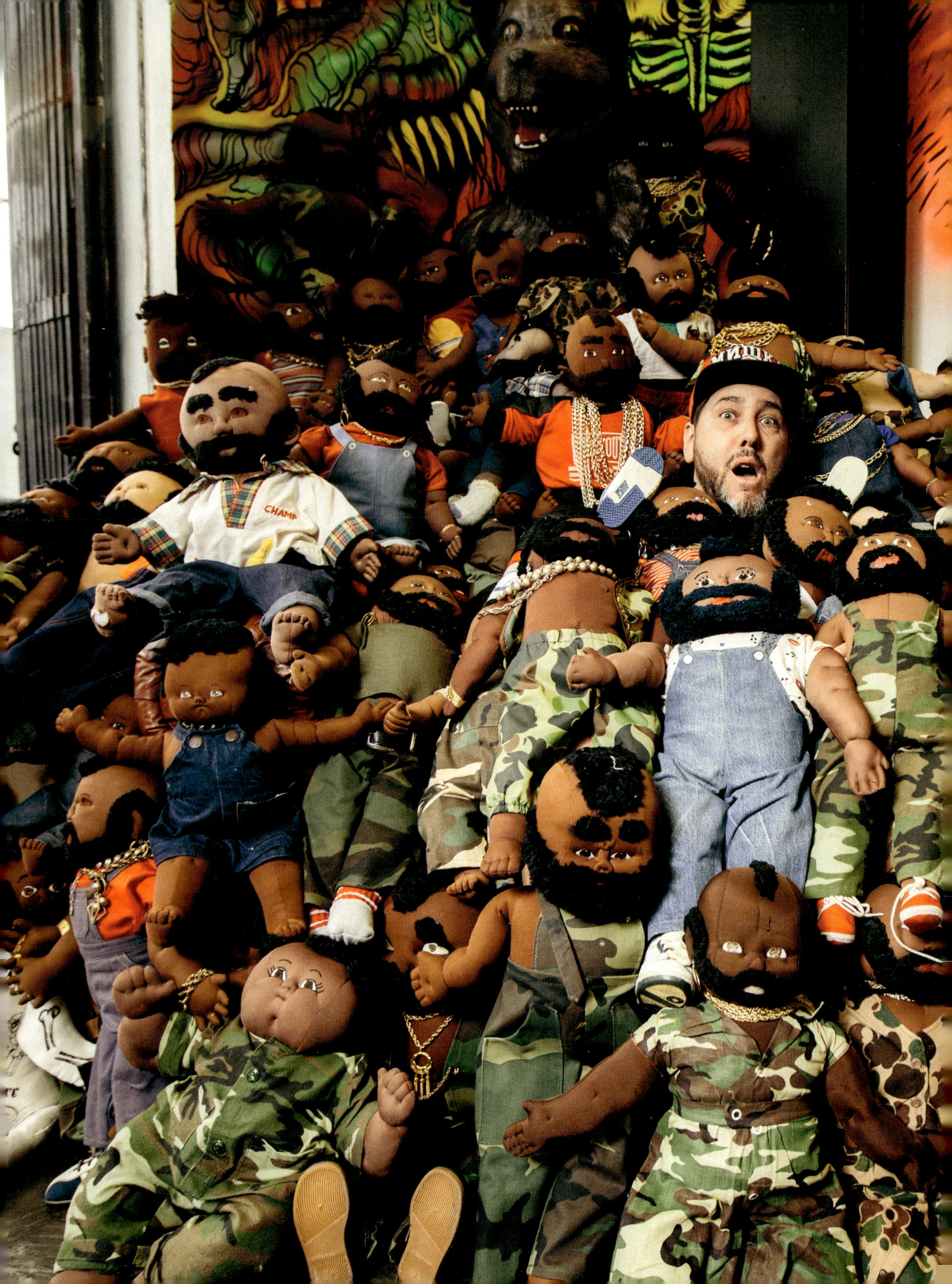
CHAMP

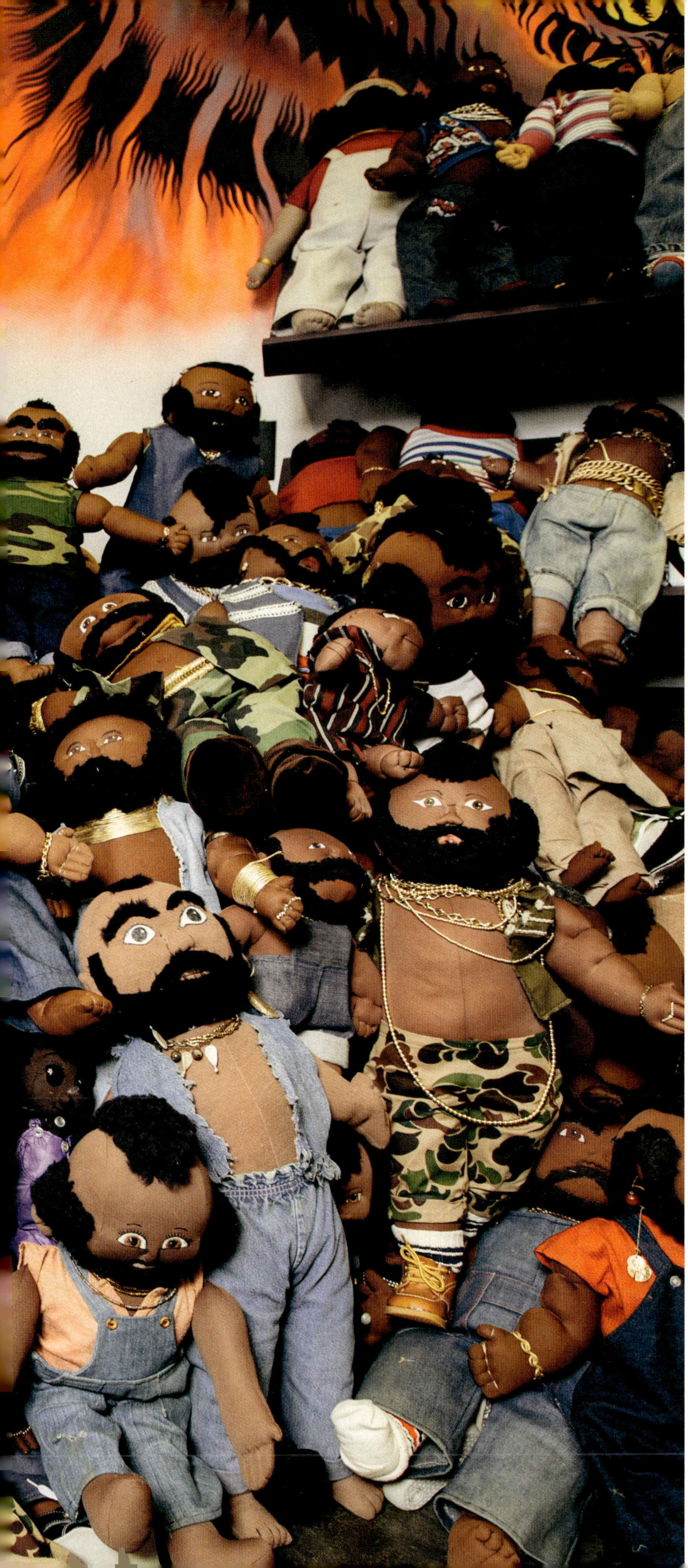

As my collection grew and became more refined, the aspect of my collection that started to intrigue me the most was these homemade Mr. T Cabbage-Patch-Kid-style dolls. Mike thought they were creepy. He had one and that was enough for him, but not for me. The one thing Brian from Populuxe would never sell me was his homemade Mr. T doll. It intrigued me more than anything else I had ever seen. What was this? Who made it? Why did it exist? Instead of selling me the doll, he gave me a pattern book by Miss Martha Originals.

I remember seeing the cover. "Mr. T Soft Sculpture doll pattern. Exclusive design by Martha Holcombe." He told me that here is the pattern this doll was based on, there has to be more out there. I accepted the challenge and found enough of these dolls that they could completely cover my body, with just my head popping out. (I think at last count it was a little over 200 of them!) Although some of the favorite parts of my collection are the mass-produced, knock-off and foreign items.

The dolls hold a really special place for me, as they represent a token of love created for a child. Each one made is completely different, its accuracy or its charm, dependent on the artistic level of each craftsman. Whenever anyone would see my dolls in person it would always make them smile. I think that's why I have enjoyed collecting them. Each one is unique. I have kept them as found. Some are naked, missing pants, or missing a shoe, or even have orange skin! I think it was important to show them how they survived as pieces of modern-day folk art. A tribute to black Americana, but made as a testament to a real-life superhero!

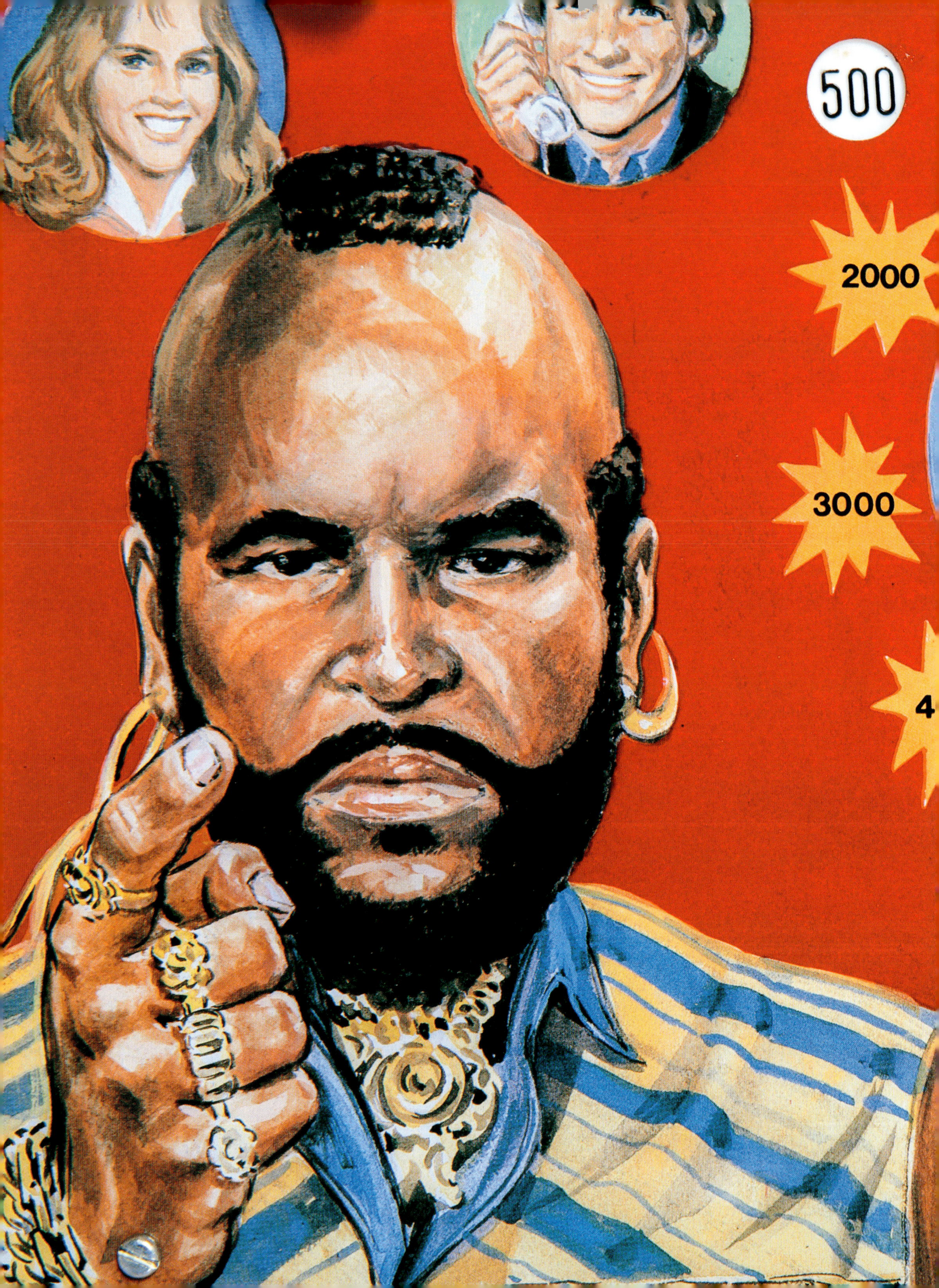

500
2000
3000
4

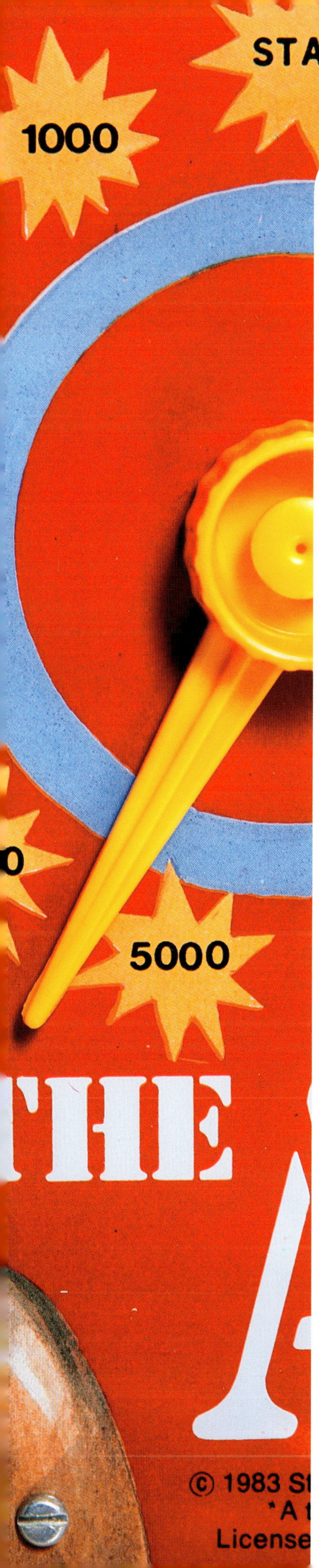

I ADMIRE THE FOOL

Mr. T collectors are few and far between, but in the early 2000s I was foolish enough to believe that I was one of them. I had some Mr. T children's books and assorted paltry treasures that gave my eighteen-year-old self a feeling of fulfillment, or maybe it was accomplishment. It's so long ago that it's hard to remember.

My self-image as a Mr. T connoisseur was shredded when I came across Greg Rivera's eBay profile. I didn't know who he was at the time but his profile photo showed a handsome and stylish-looking man only a little older than me drowning in a sea of Mr. T merchandise. I never bought another Mr. T item. What was the point? The man in the photo had already accomplished my goal.

Years later I began working for Greg's clothing company, Mishka, although it was at least a year before I realized where I'd first seen him. He told me how he'd begun collecting objects with Mr. T's image on them and how he met Mike Essl, his competitor turned co-collector, and how they exhibited their dolls in galleries. Every now and again I'd try to get to the heart of why Greg had amassed so much Mr. T stuff that it had become his identity, and I'd get unsatisfactory answers. Greg has said that his drive to collect Mr. T merchandise came from a desire to be the biggest collector

Mr. T wants you to play pinball! A-Team bagatelle desktop pinball game, 1983.

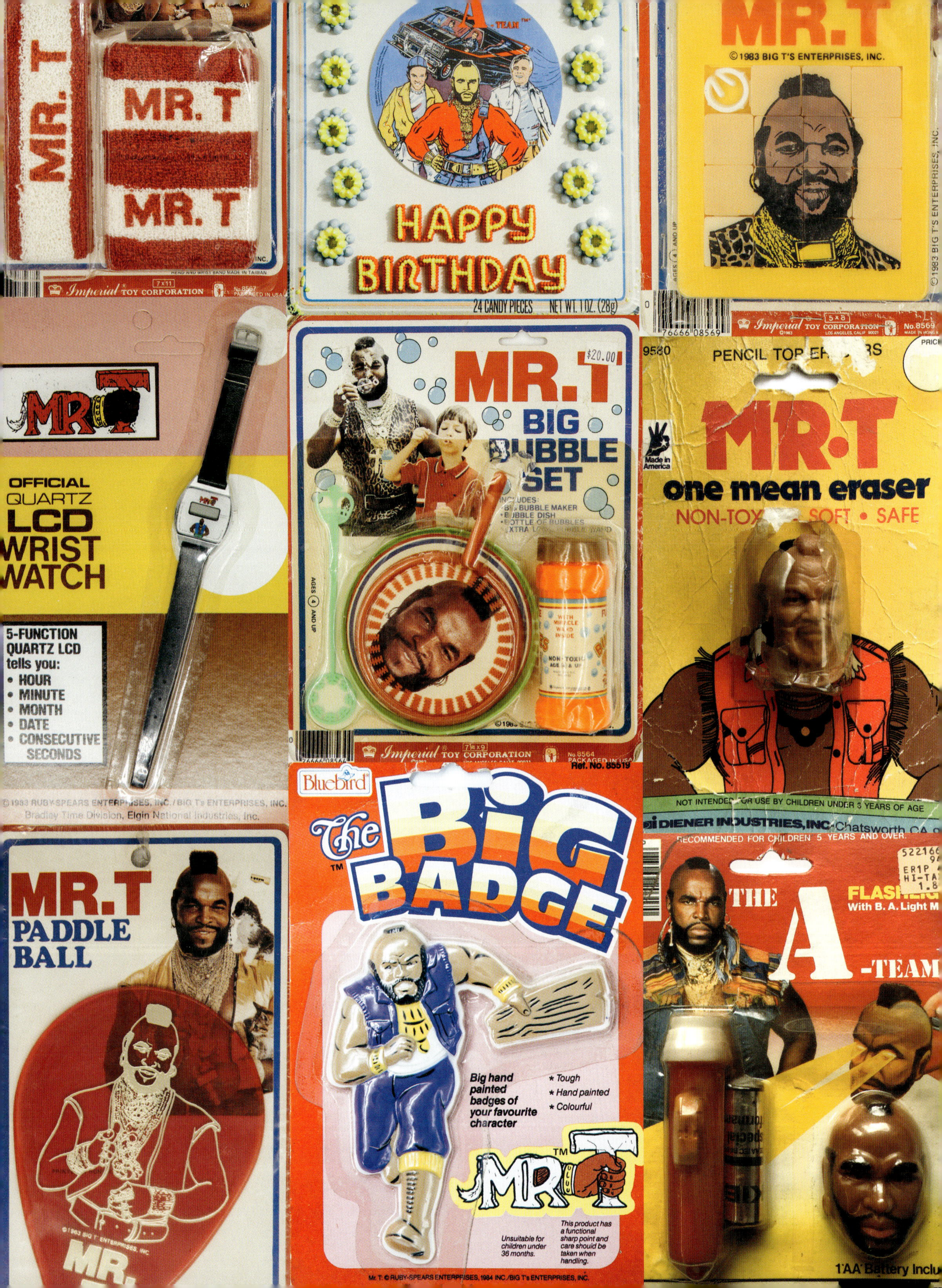

MR. T
MR. T
MR. T
Imperial TOY CORPORATION
HAPPY BIRTHDAY
24 CANDY PIECES NET WT. 1 OZ. (28g)
MR.T
©1983 BIG T'S ENTERPRISES, INC.
Imperial TOY CORPORATION
No. 8569
MR T
OFFICIAL
QUARTZ
LCD
WRIST
WATCH
5-FUNCTION
QUARTZ LCD
tells you:
• HOUR
• MINUTE
• MONTH
• DATE
• CONSECUTIVE SECONDS
©1983 RUBY-SPEARS ENTERPRISES, INC./BIG T's ENTERPRISES, INC.
Bradley Time Division, Elgin National Industries, Inc.
$20.00
MR.T
BIG
BUBBLE
SET
AGES 4 AND UP
Imperial TOY CORPORATION
No. 8564
PENCIL TOP ERASERS
Made in America
MR-T
one mean eraser
NON-TOXIC • SOFT • SAFE
NOT INTENDED FOR USE BY CHILDREN UNDER 3 YEARS OF AGE
DIENER INDUSTRIES, INC. Chatsworth, CA
RECOMMENDED FOR CHILDREN 5 YEARS AND OVER.
MR.T
PADDLE
BALL
Bluebird
The BIG BADGE
Big hand painted badges of your favourite character
* Tough
* Hand painted
* Colourful
MR T
Unsuitable for children under 36 months.
This product has a functional sharp point and care should be taken when handling.
Mr. T: ©RUBY-SPEARS ENTERPRISES, 1984 INC./BIG T's ENTERPRISES, INC.
THE A-TEAM
FLASHLIGHT
With B. A. Light
1 'AA' Battery Included

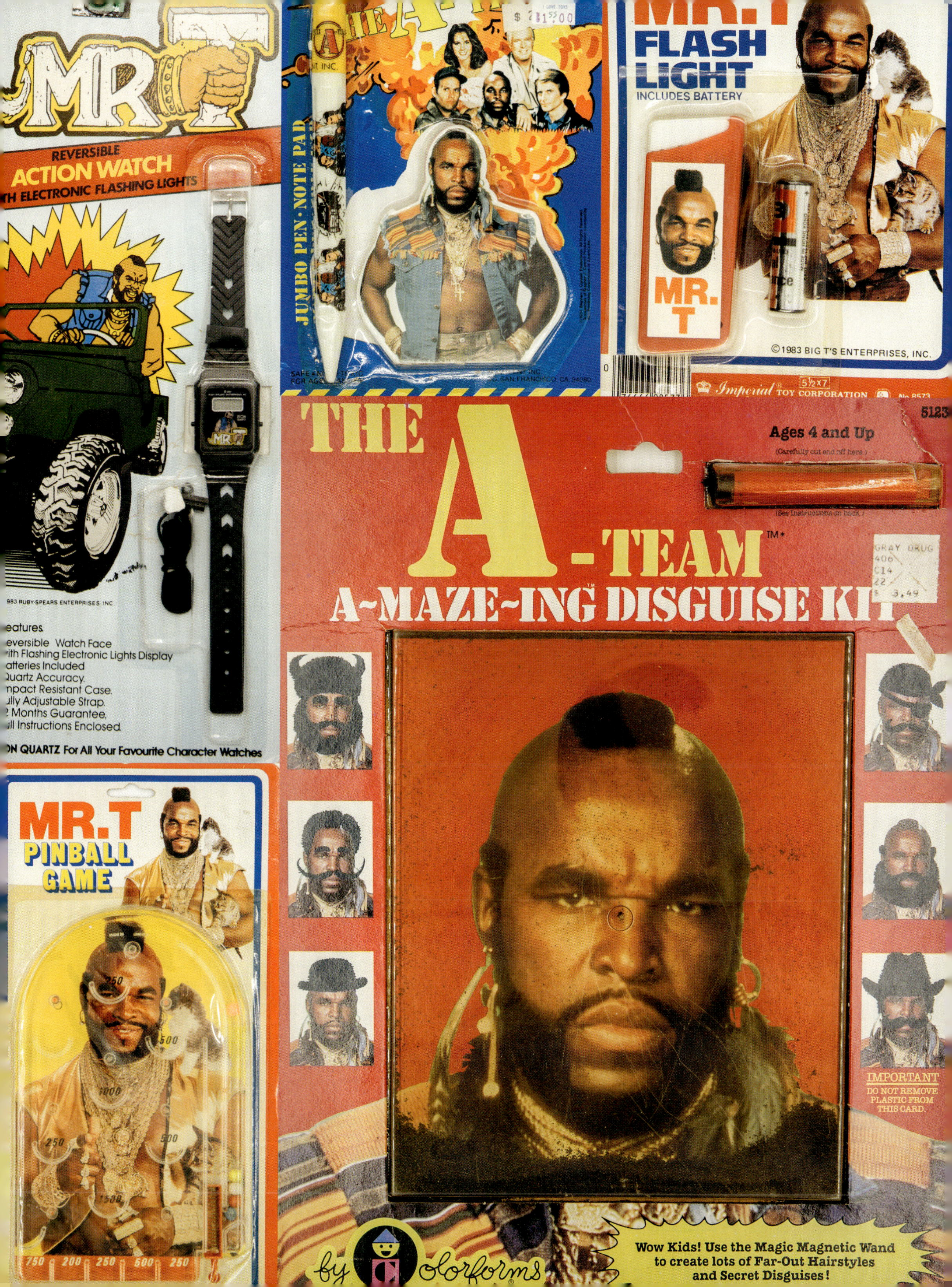

MR T
REVERSIBLE
ACTION WATCH
TH ELECTRONIC FLASHING LIGHTS
983 RUBY-SPEARS ENTERPRISES, INC
eatures
eversible Watch Face
ith Flashing Electronic Lights Display
atteries Included
uartz Accuracy
mpact Resistant Case
ully Adjustable Strap
Months Guarantee
ll Instructions Enclosed
ON QUARTZ For All Your Favourite Character Watches
JUMBO PEN · NOTE PAD
MR. T
FLASH LIGHT
INCLUDES BATTERY
MR. T
©1983 BIG T'S ENTERPRISES, INC.
Imperial TOY CORPORATION
THE A-TEAM
Ages 4 and Up
A-MAZE-ING DISGUISE KIT
IMPORTANT
DO NOT REMOVE PLASTIC FROM THIS CARD.
MR.T
PINBALL GAME
by Colorforms
Wow Kids! Use the Magic Magnetic Wand to create lots of Far-Out Hairstyles and Secret Disguises!

of something, and there didn't seem to be much competition to be the best Mr. T collector. I think that a quest for identity is part of why Greg has become the world's biggest Mr. T collector, but I don't think it's the only one.

I enjoyed the character that Mr. T presents himself as. Although I liked Mr. T, I didn't love him. Greg admires Mr. T and talks about him being a real-life superhero. Through Greg's passion for all things T, I gained a wider appreciation of this icon of 1980s entertainment. You may find Mr. T's appearance and demeanor foolish, but it is you who plays the fool. Mr. T is a true individual and, behind the barked catchphrases and chains, is an admirable person. Mr. T is a true individual who defies categorization. He dresses outlandishly, but every element of his iconic outfit has significance, from his mohawk, which is to honor the Mandinka people, to his boots, which were his father's. Despite his gruff vocal delivery and tough image, Mr. T is a devout Christian who cared about inspiring kids to stay on the straight and narrow. He also rose to prominence as a formidable black man at a time when it seemed like America wanted its black stars to be cute and nonthreatening like Gary Coleman. Peewee Herman similarly became a character who brought aspects of queer culture into the mainstream in a way that wasn't consciously recognized by the viewers.

In many ways my friend Greg is similar to Mr. T. Instead of gold chains, he often wears a lot of flashy rings. Instead of a bodybuilder's physique, he's covered in tattoos. Like Mr. T, he's a very sweet man with a lot of empathy and a Christian

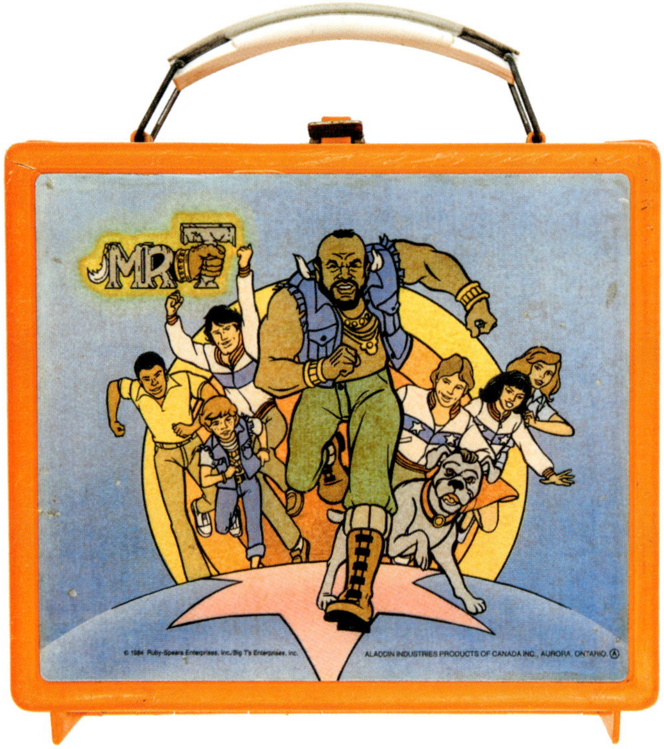

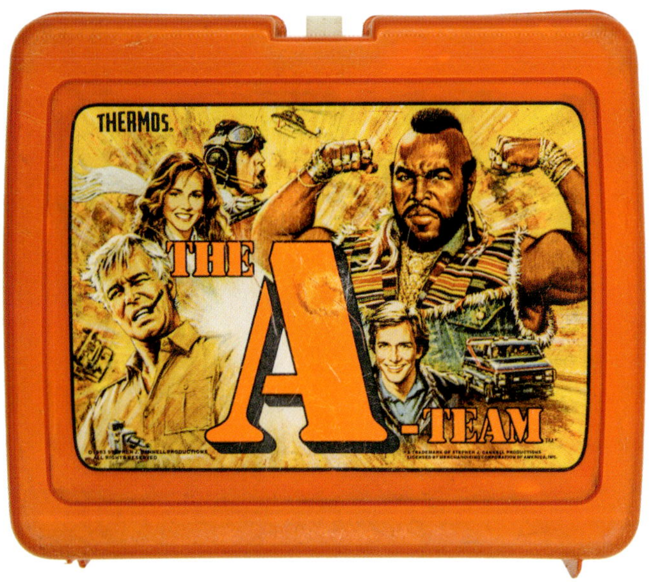

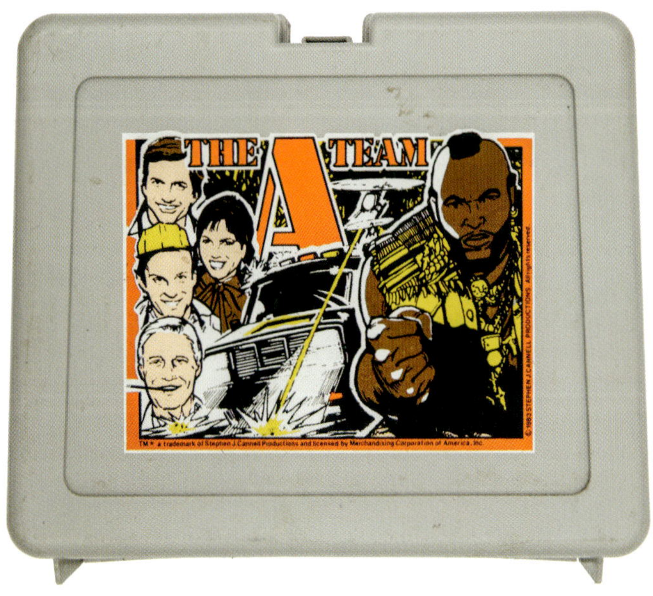

An assortment of Mr. T lunchboxes from the US, UK, and Canada.

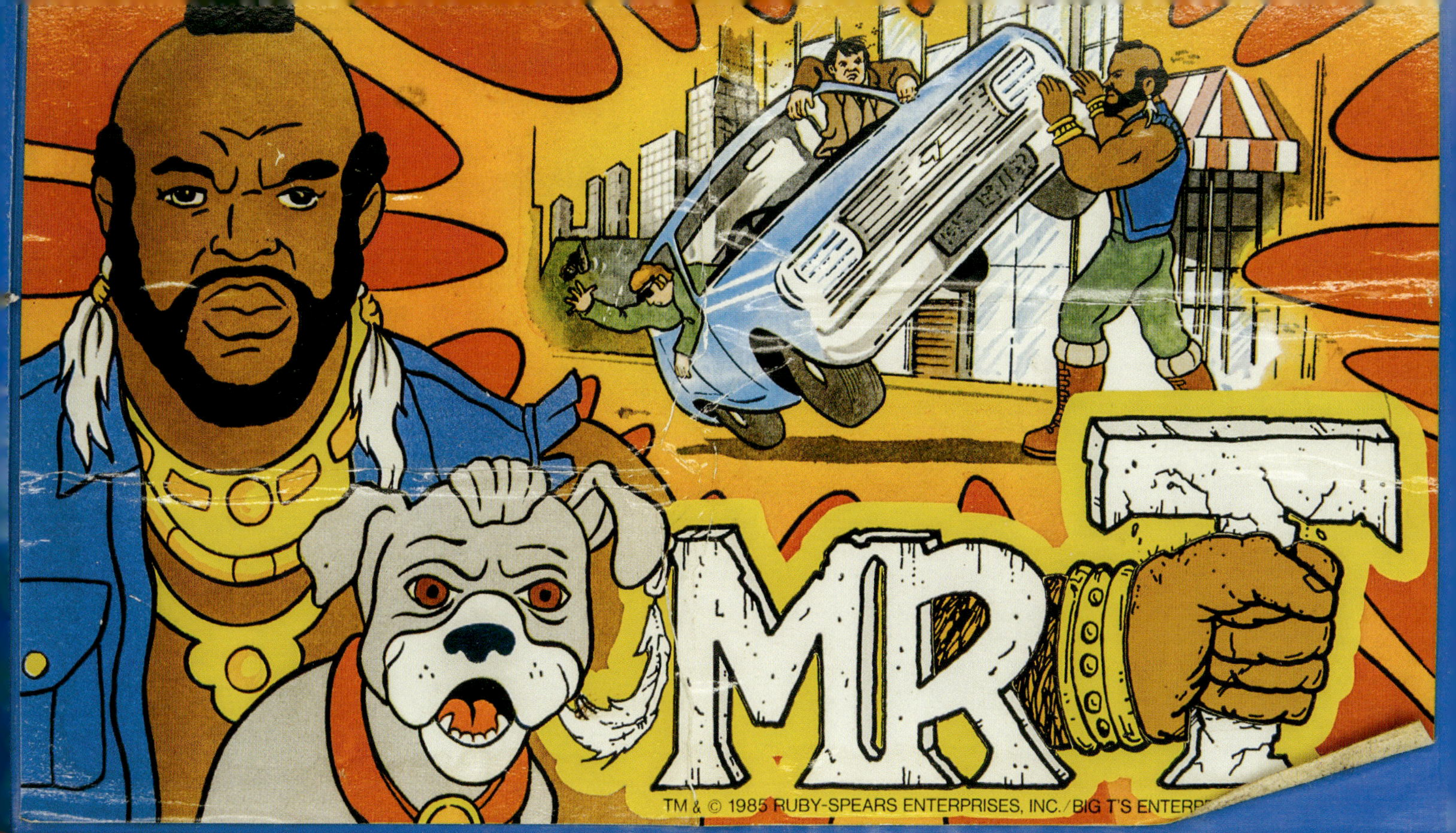
MR T
TM & © 1985 RUBY-SPEARS ENTERPRISES, INC./BIG T'S

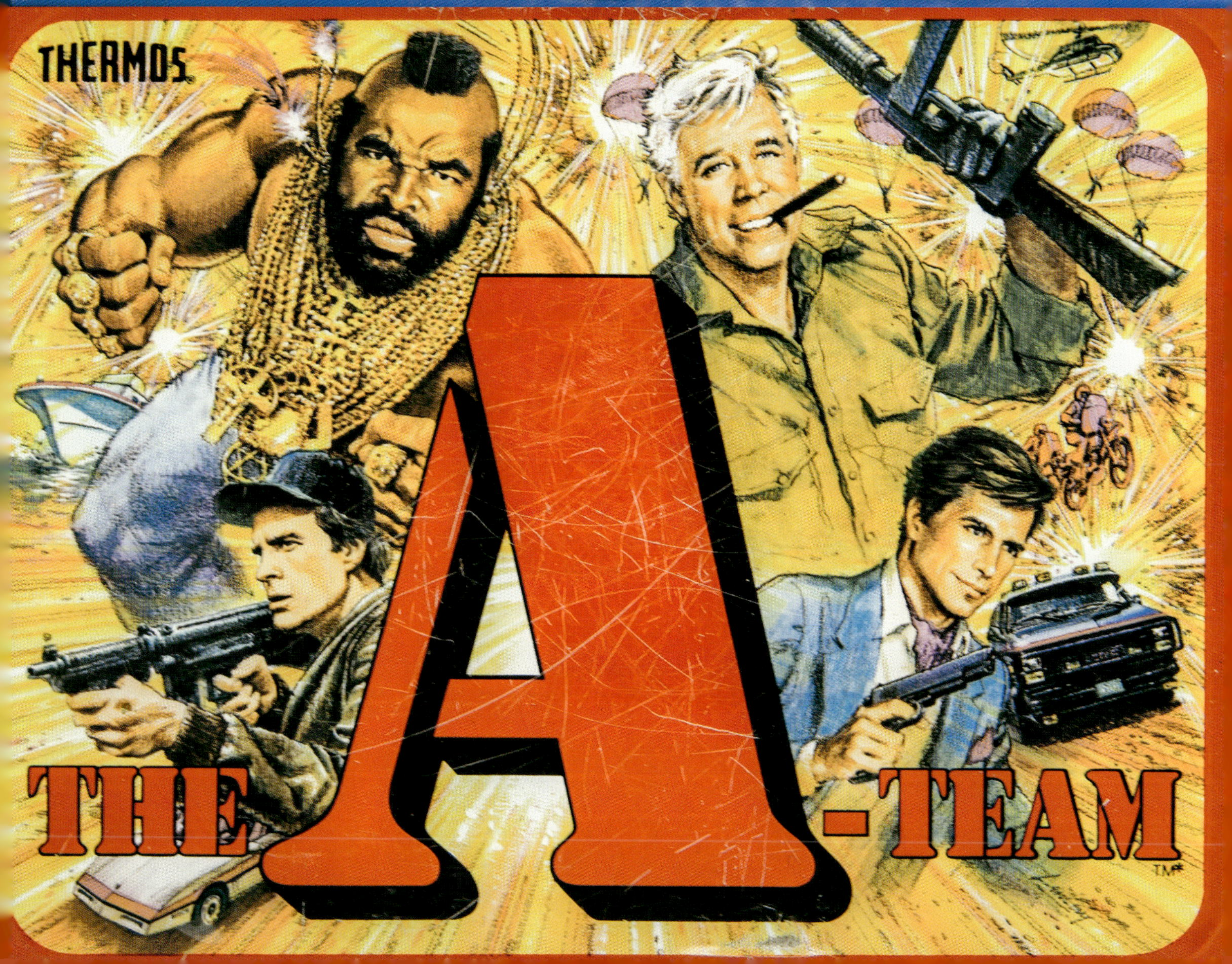
THERMOS
THE A-TEAM
TM

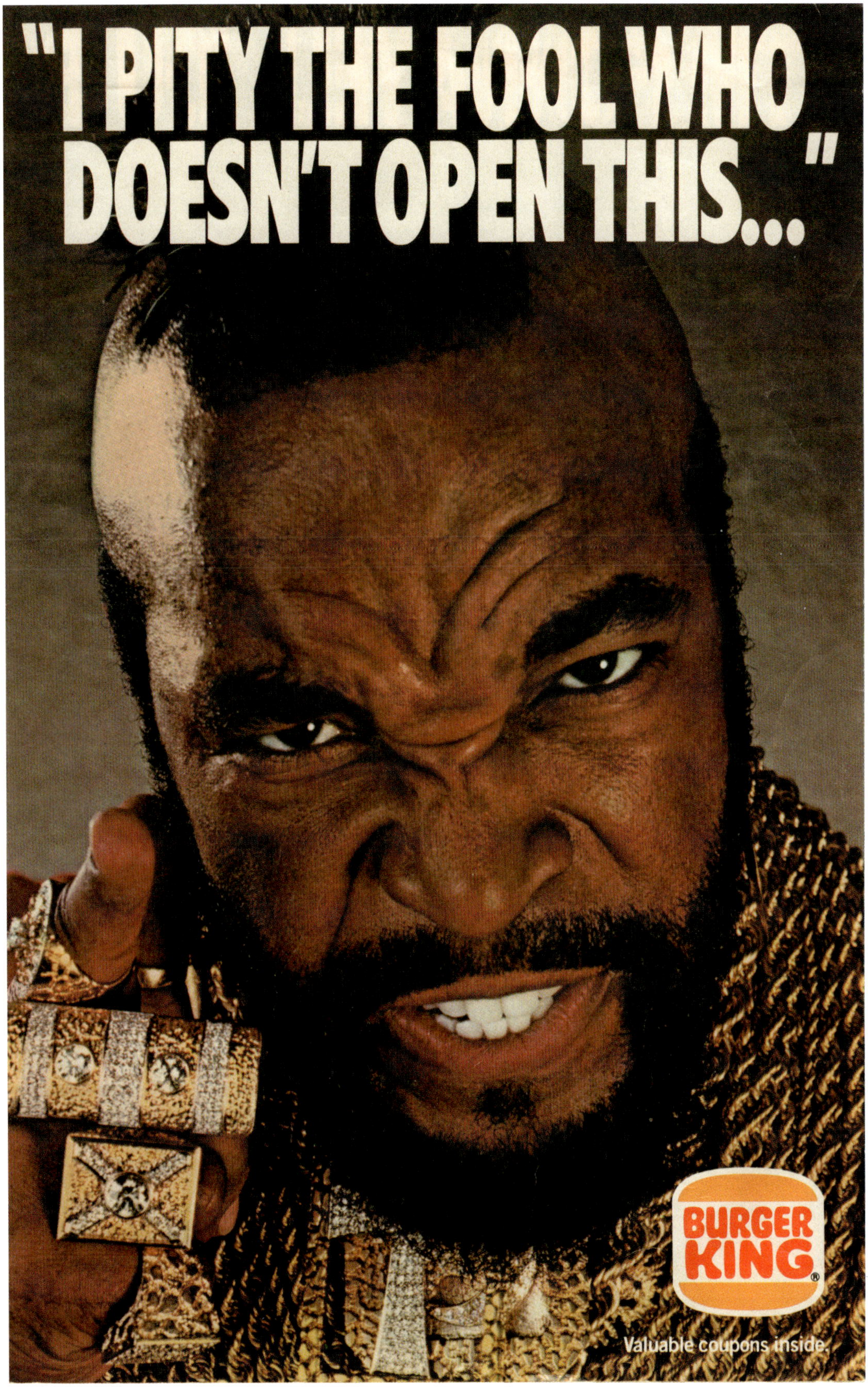
"I PITY THE FOOL WHO DOESN'T OPEN THIS..."
BURGER KING
Valuable coupons inside.

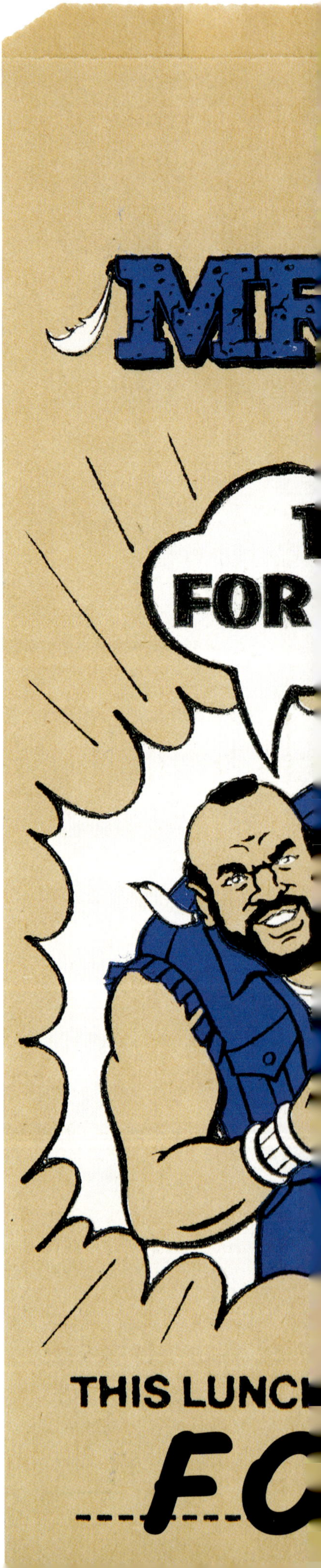
FOR
THIS

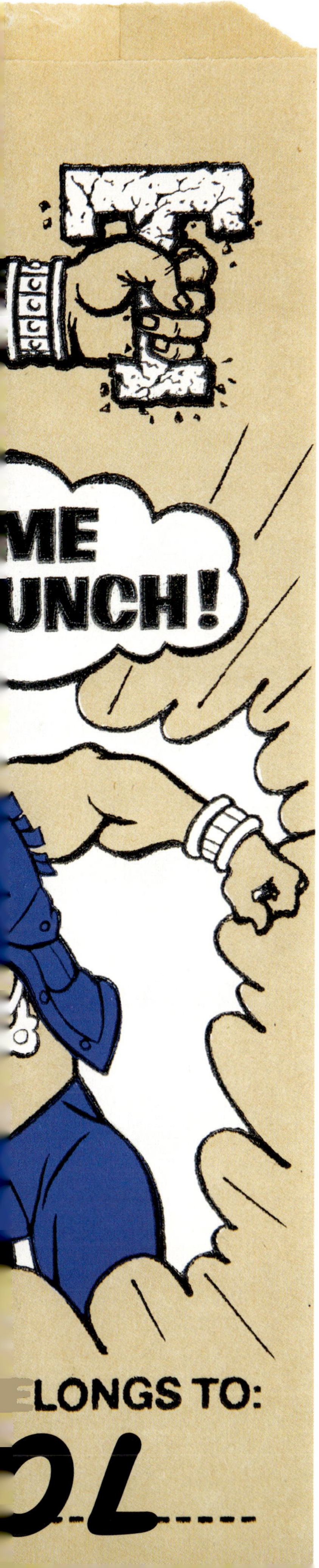
ME
UNCH!
ELONGS TO:

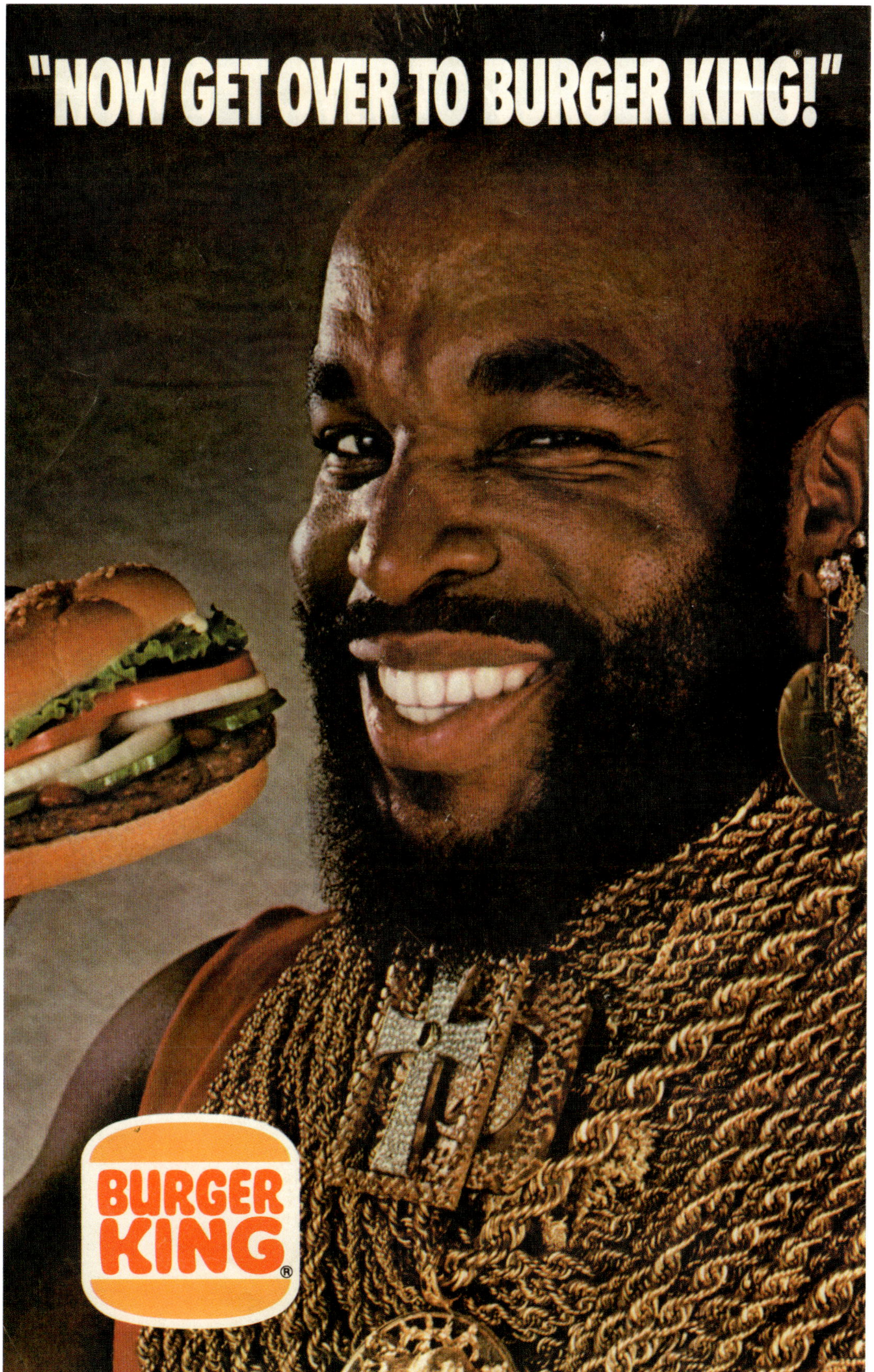
"NOW GET OVER TO BURGER KING®!"
BURGER KING®

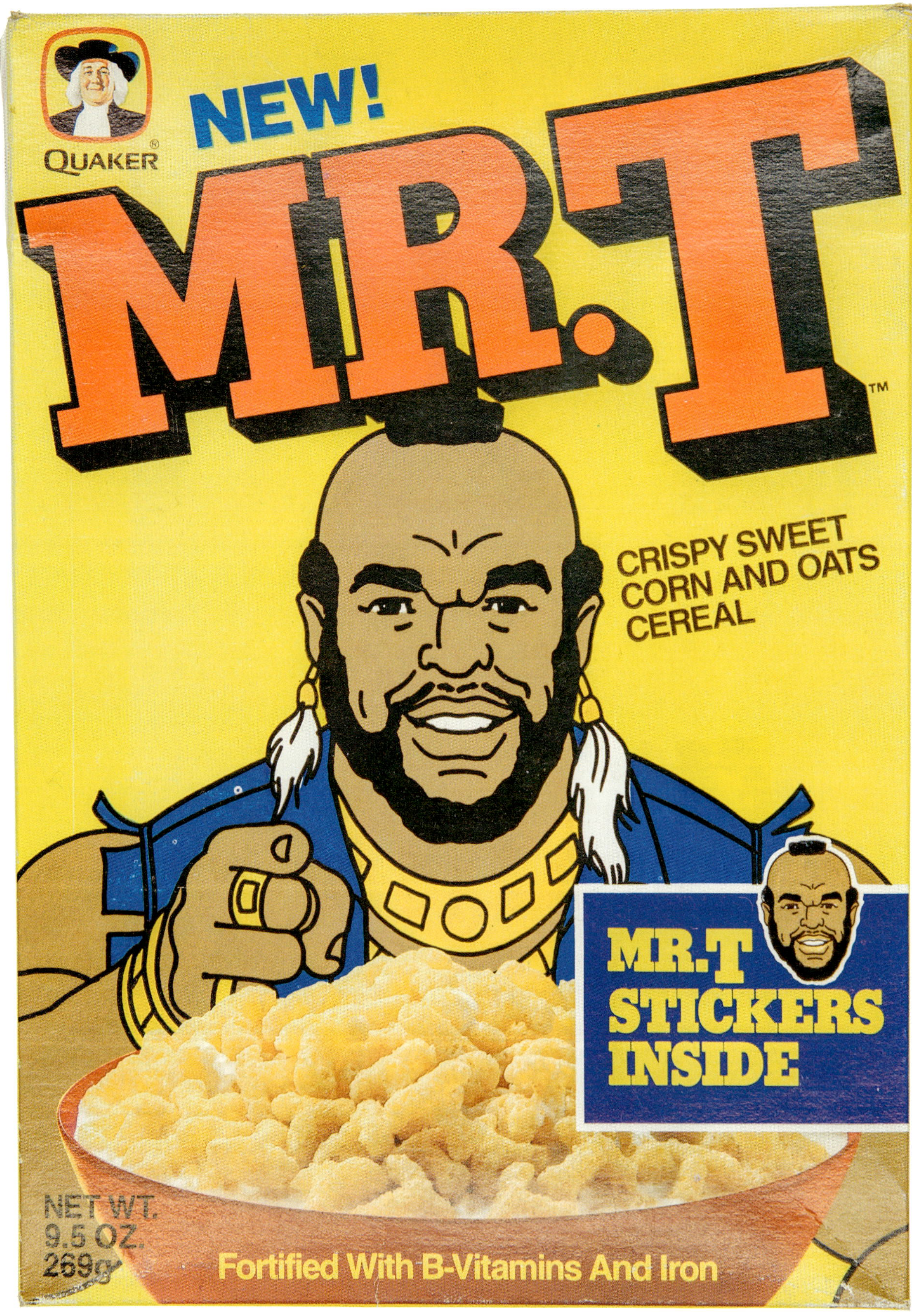
QUAKER
NEW!
MR.T
CRISPY SWEET CORN AND OATS CEREAL
MR.T STICKERS INSIDE
NET WT. 9.5 OZ. 269g
Fortified With B-Vitamins And Iron

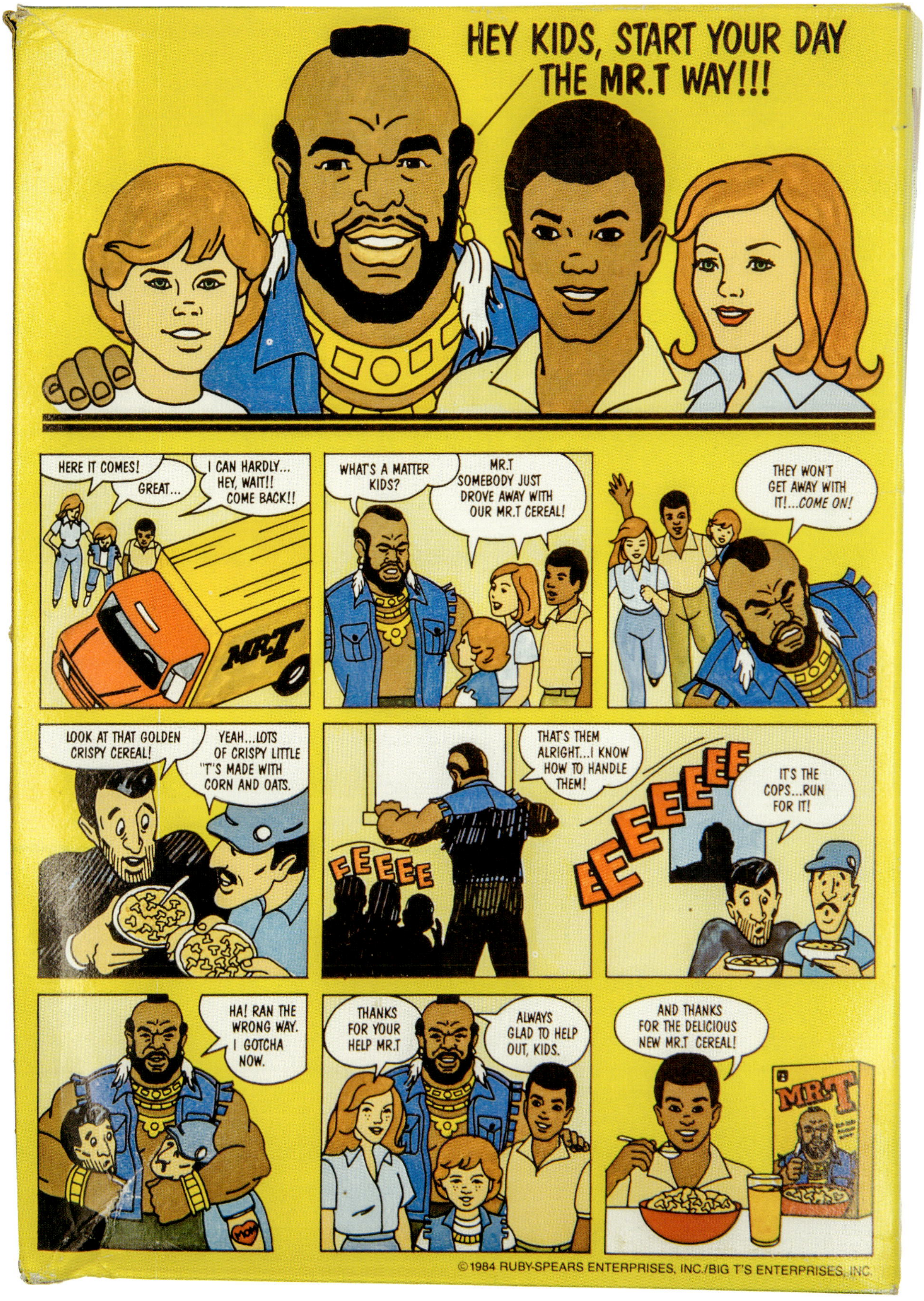
HEY KIDS, START YOUR DAY THE MR.T WAY!!!
HERE IT COMES!
GREAT...
I CAN HARDLY... HEY, WAIT!! COME BACK!!
MR.T
WHAT'S A MATTER KIDS?
MR.T SOMEBODY JUST DROVE AWAY WITH OUR MR.T CEREAL!
THEY WON'T GET AWAY WITH IT!...COME ON!
LOOK AT THAT GOLDEN CRISPY CEREAL!
YEAH...LOTS OF CRISPY LITTLE "T"S MADE WITH CORN AND OATS.
THAT'S THEM ALRIGHT...I KNOW HOW TO HANDLE THEM!
EEEEE
EEEEEEEEE
IT'S THE COPS...RUN FOR IT!
HA! RAN THE WRONG WAY. I GOTCHA NOW.
MOM
THANKS FOR YOUR HELP MR.T
ALWAYS GLAD TO HELP OUT, KIDS.
AND THANKS FOR THE DELICIOUS NEW MR.T CEREAL!
MR.T
©1984 RUBY-SPEARS ENTERPRISES, INC./BIG T'S ENTERPRISES, INC.

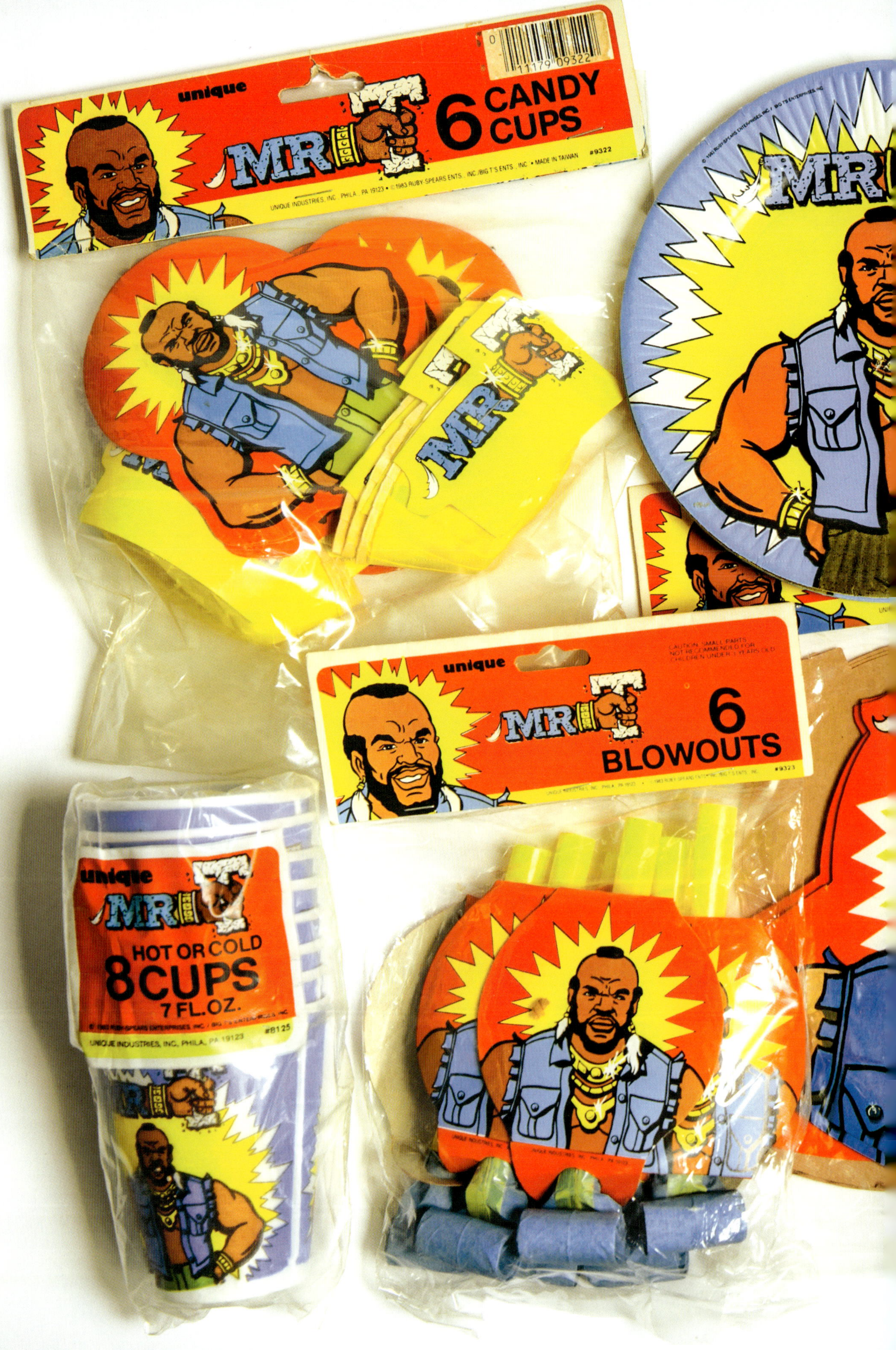
unique
MR
6 CANDY CUPS
#9322
unique
MR
6 BLOWOUTS
#9323
unique
MR
HOT OR COLD
8 CUPS
7 FL.OZ.
#8125
UNIQUE INDUSTRIES, INC. PHILA., PA 19123

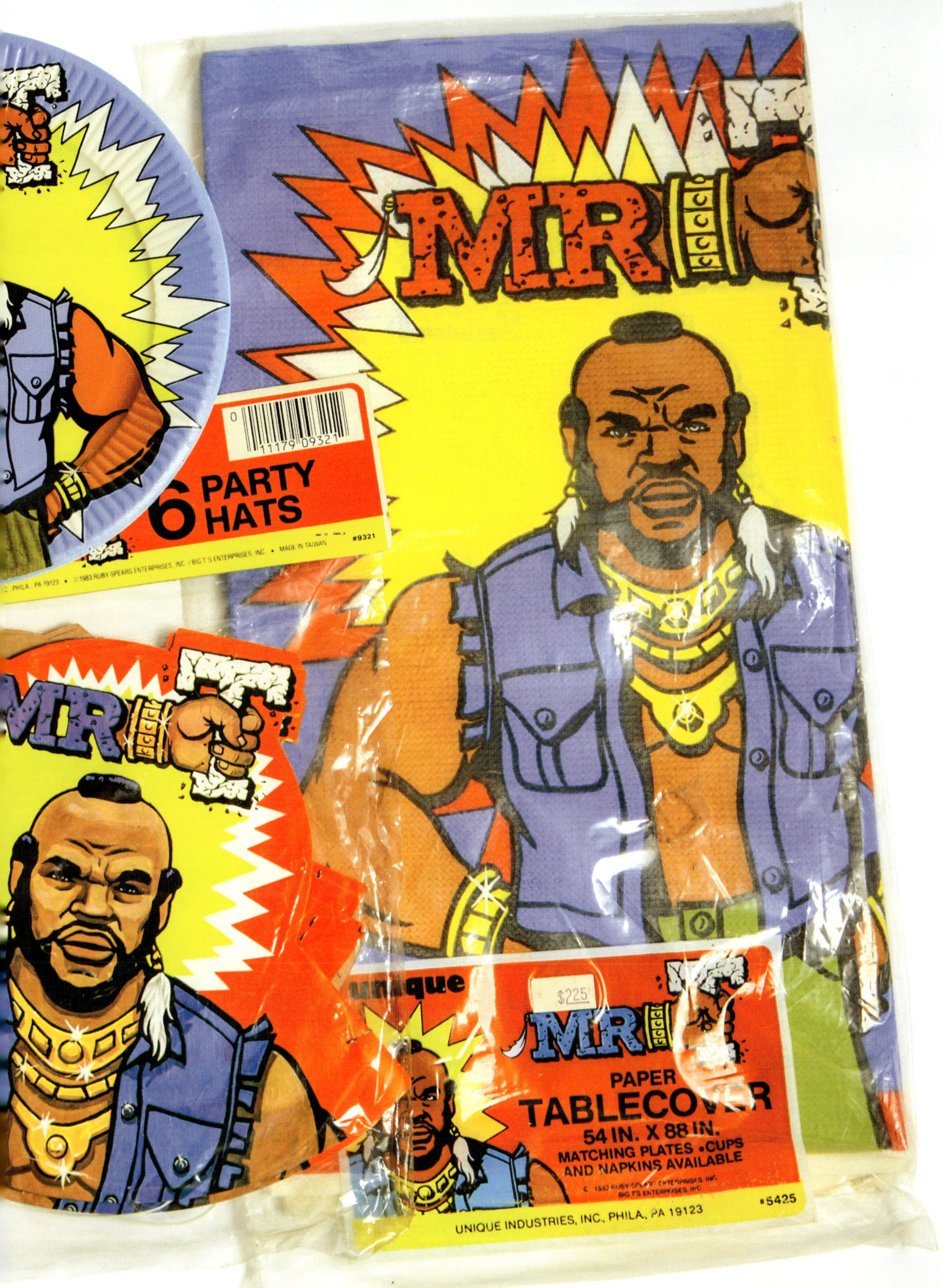

Assorted Mr. T party favors. Big T's Enterprises, 1983.

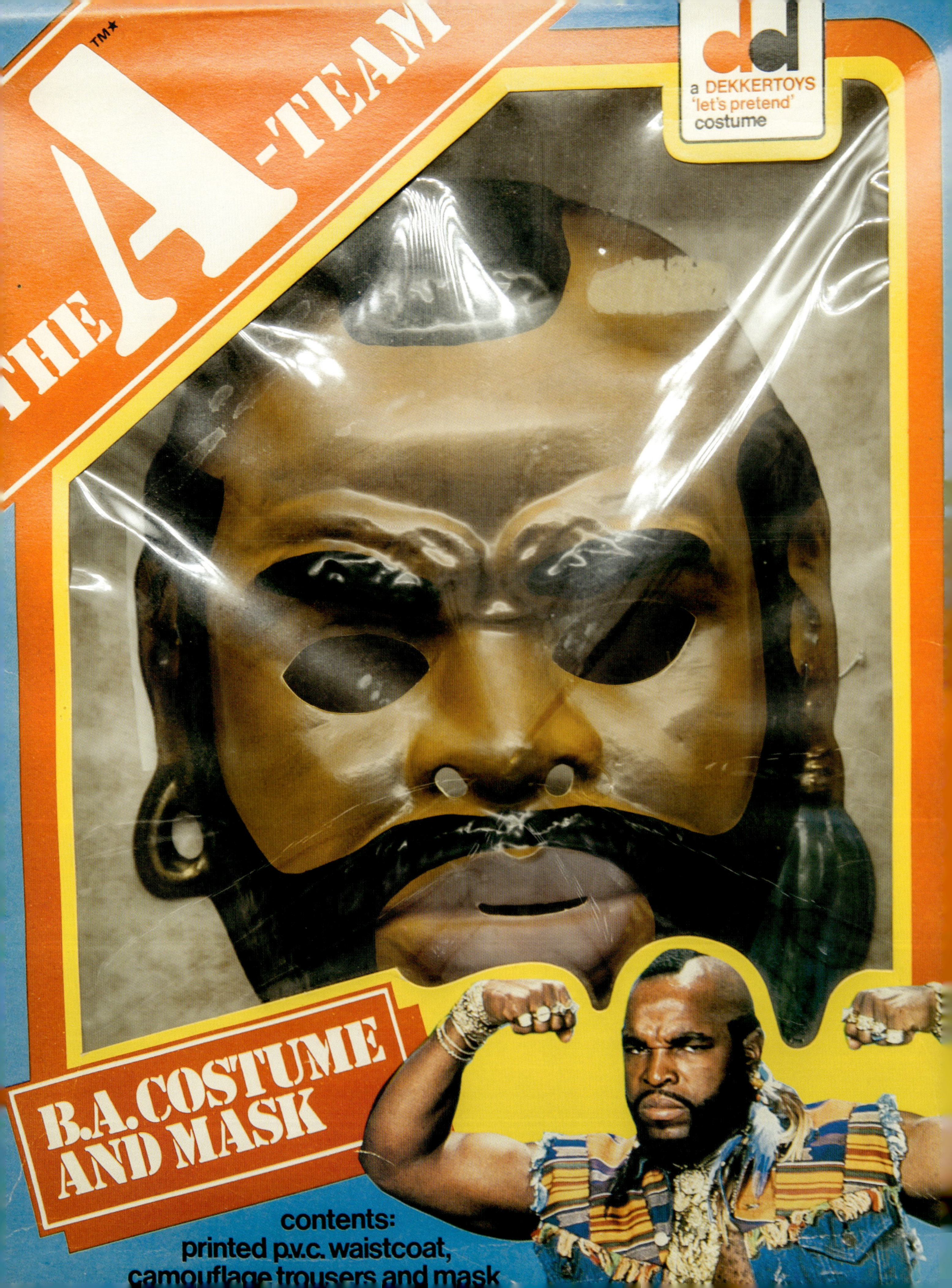
THE A-TEAM™★
a DEKKERTOYS
'let's pretend'
costume
B.A. COSTUME AND MASK
contents:
printed p.v.c. waistcoat,
camouflage trousers and mask

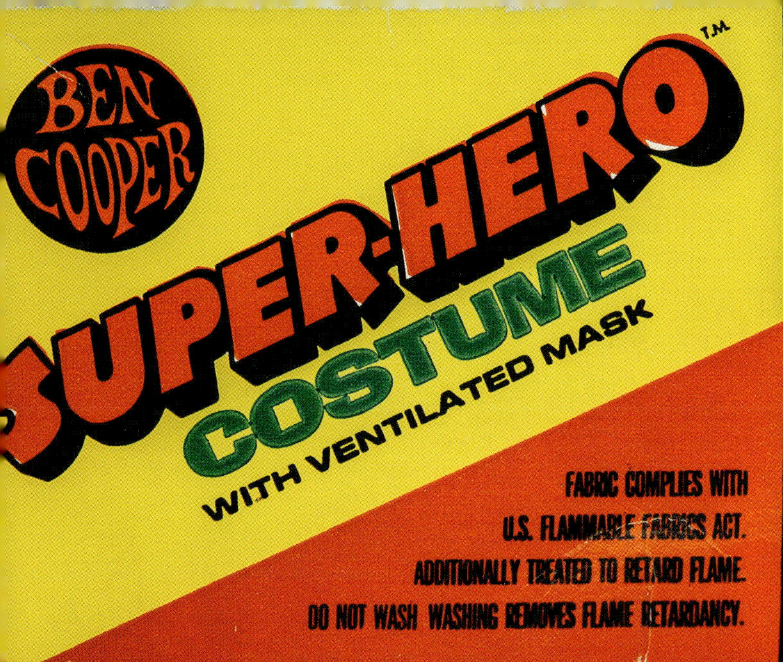

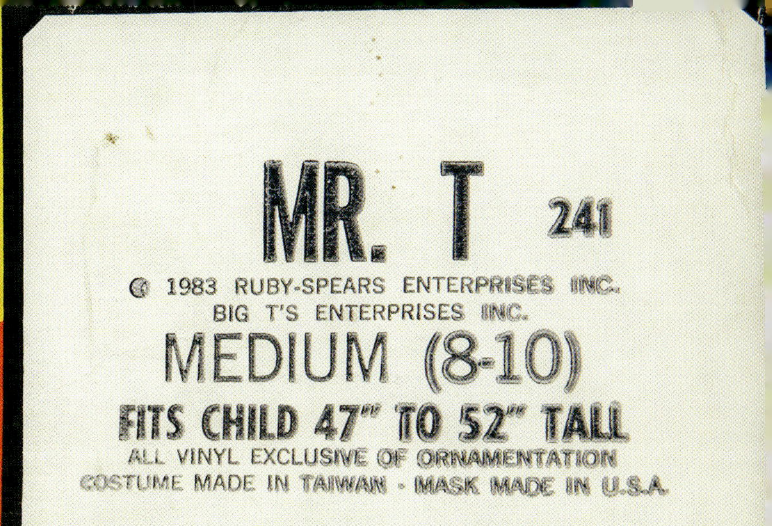

Assorted Mr. T costume packaging

LEFT *The A-Team B. A. costume and mask. Dekker Toys, 1983. UK.*

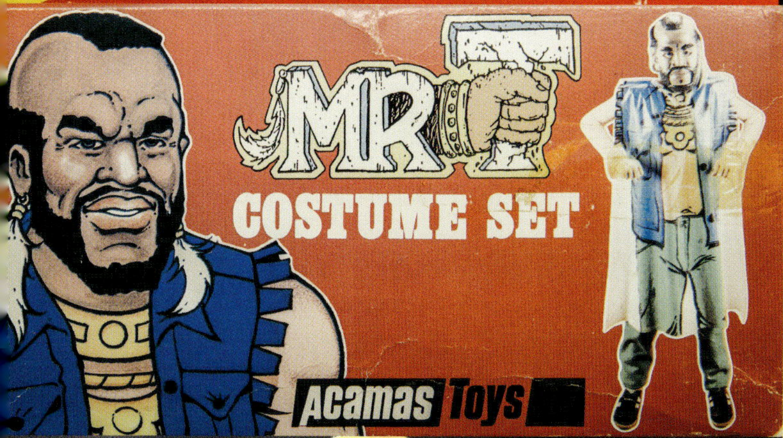

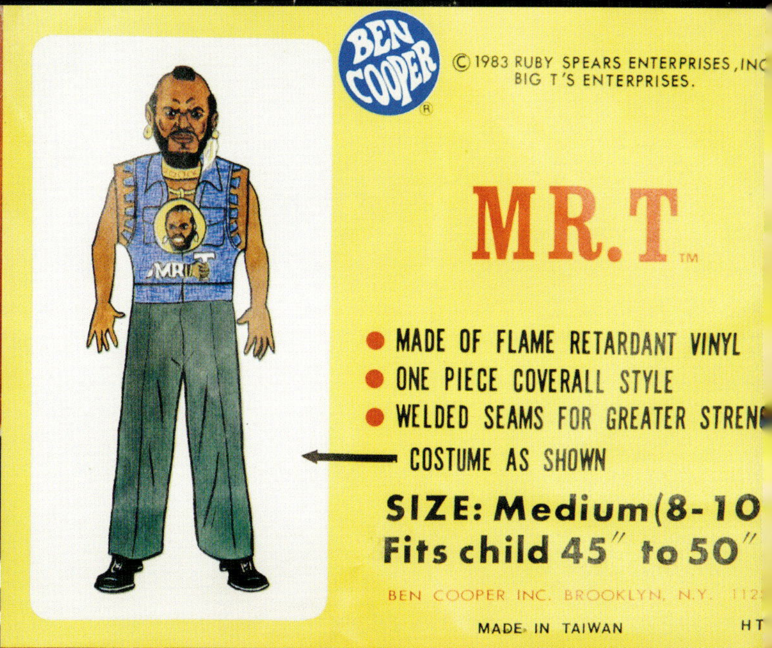

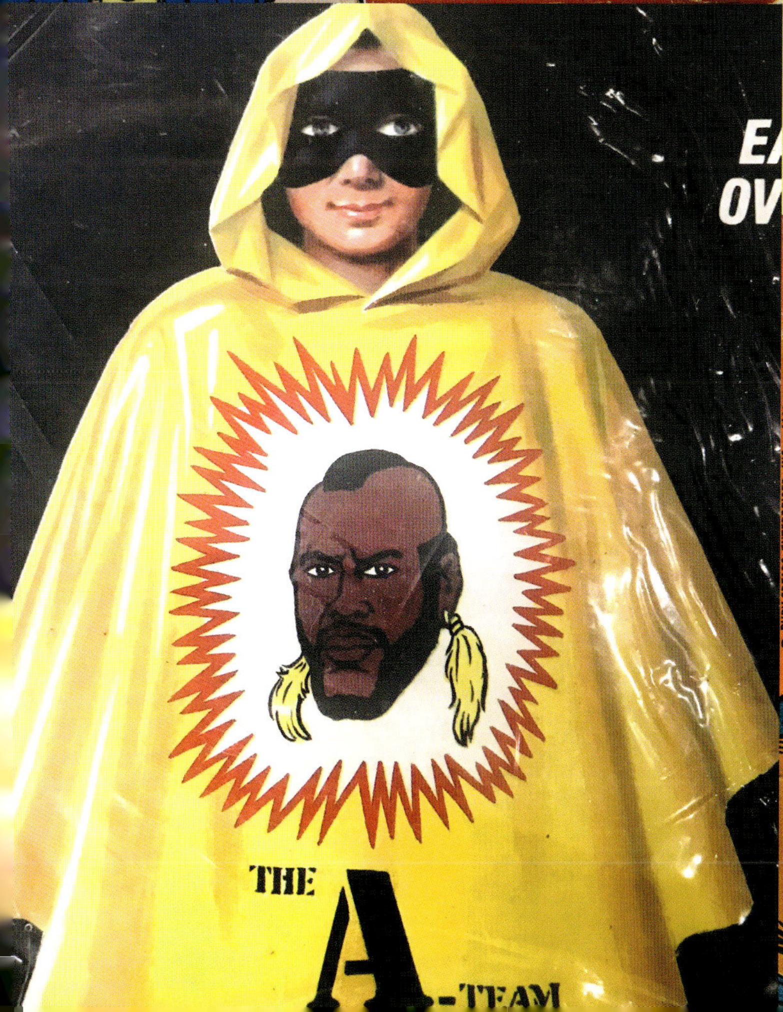

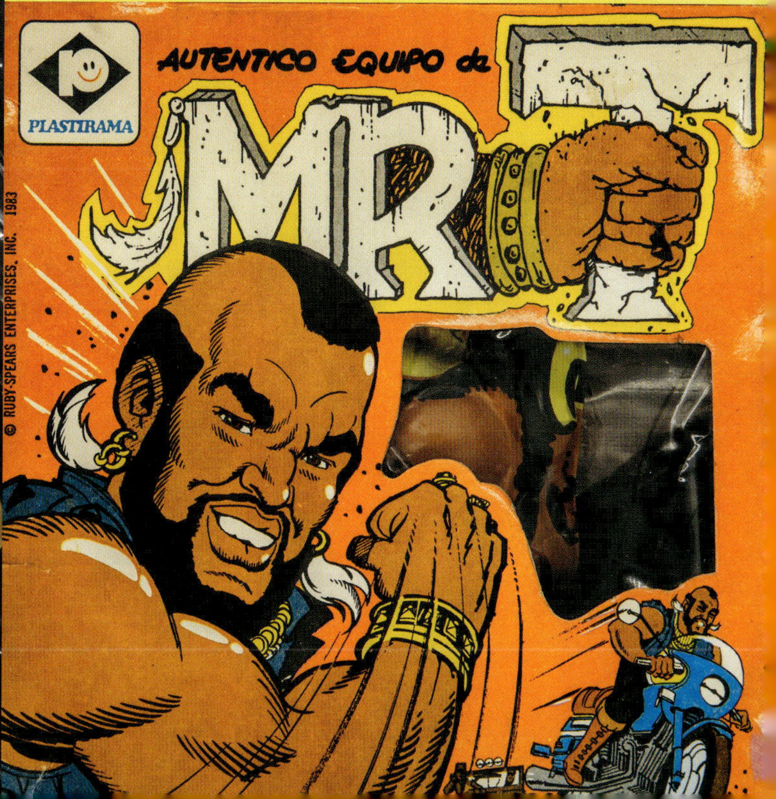

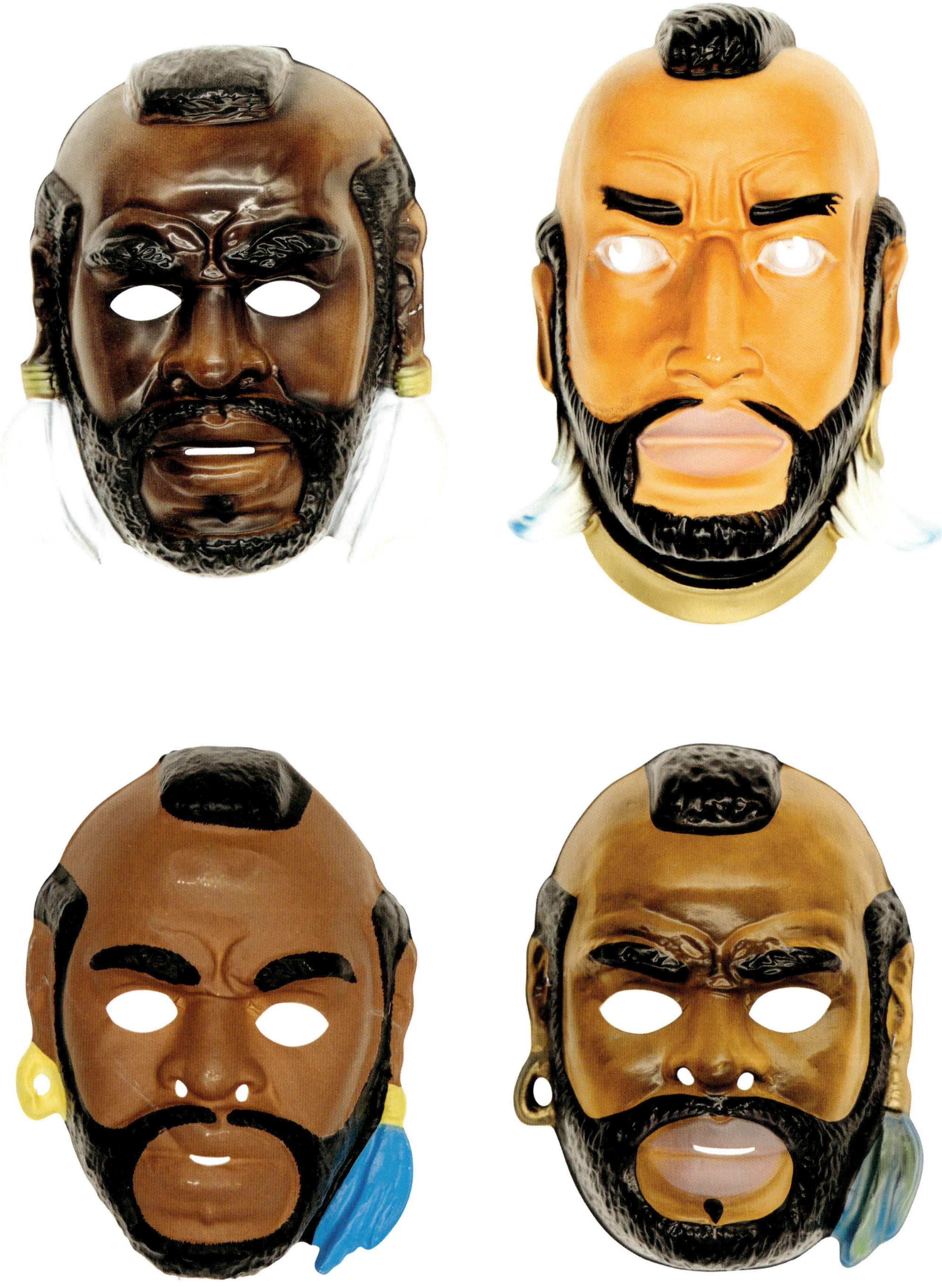

Assortment of Mr. T plastic masks.

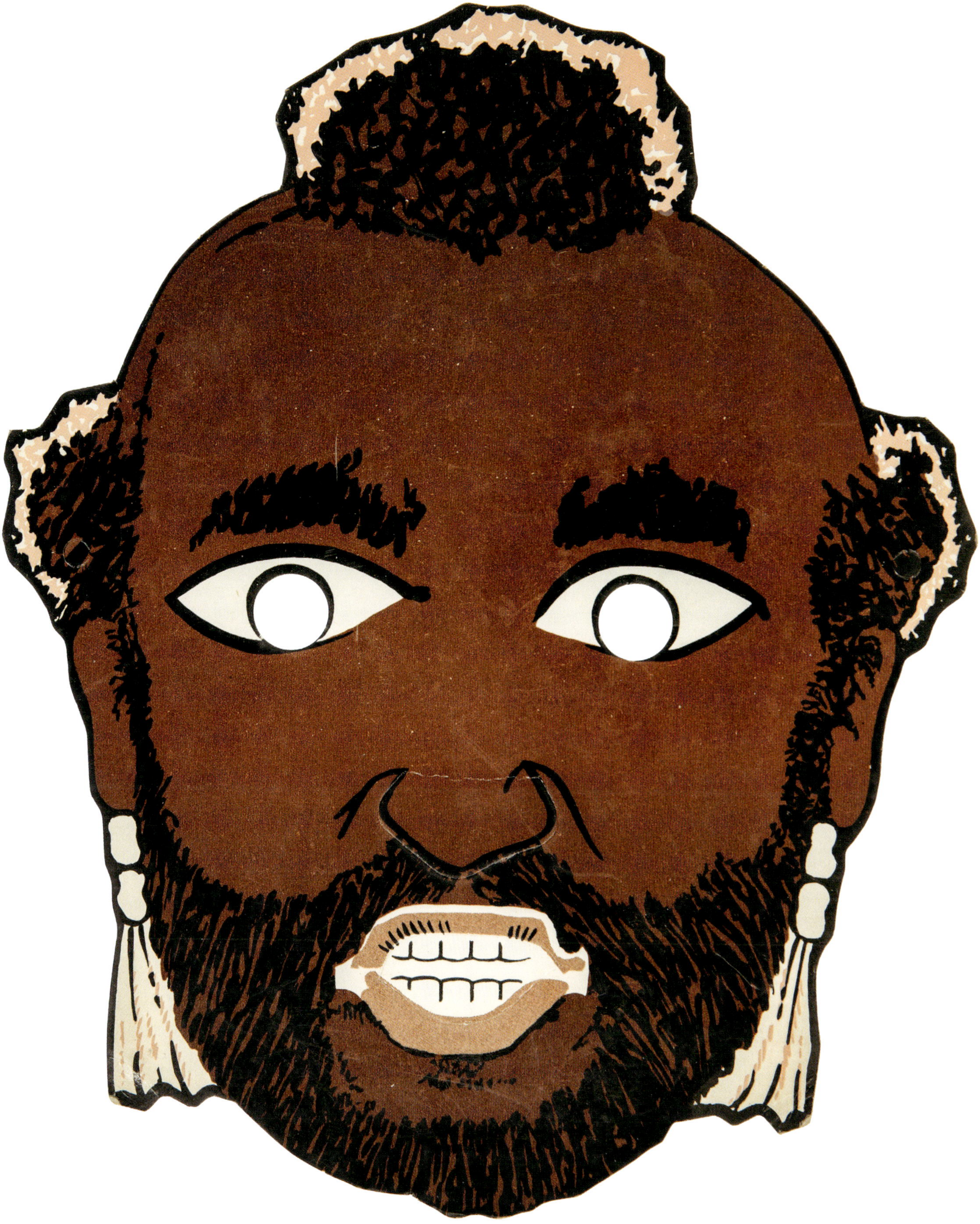

Unknown Mr. T paper mask. Argentina.

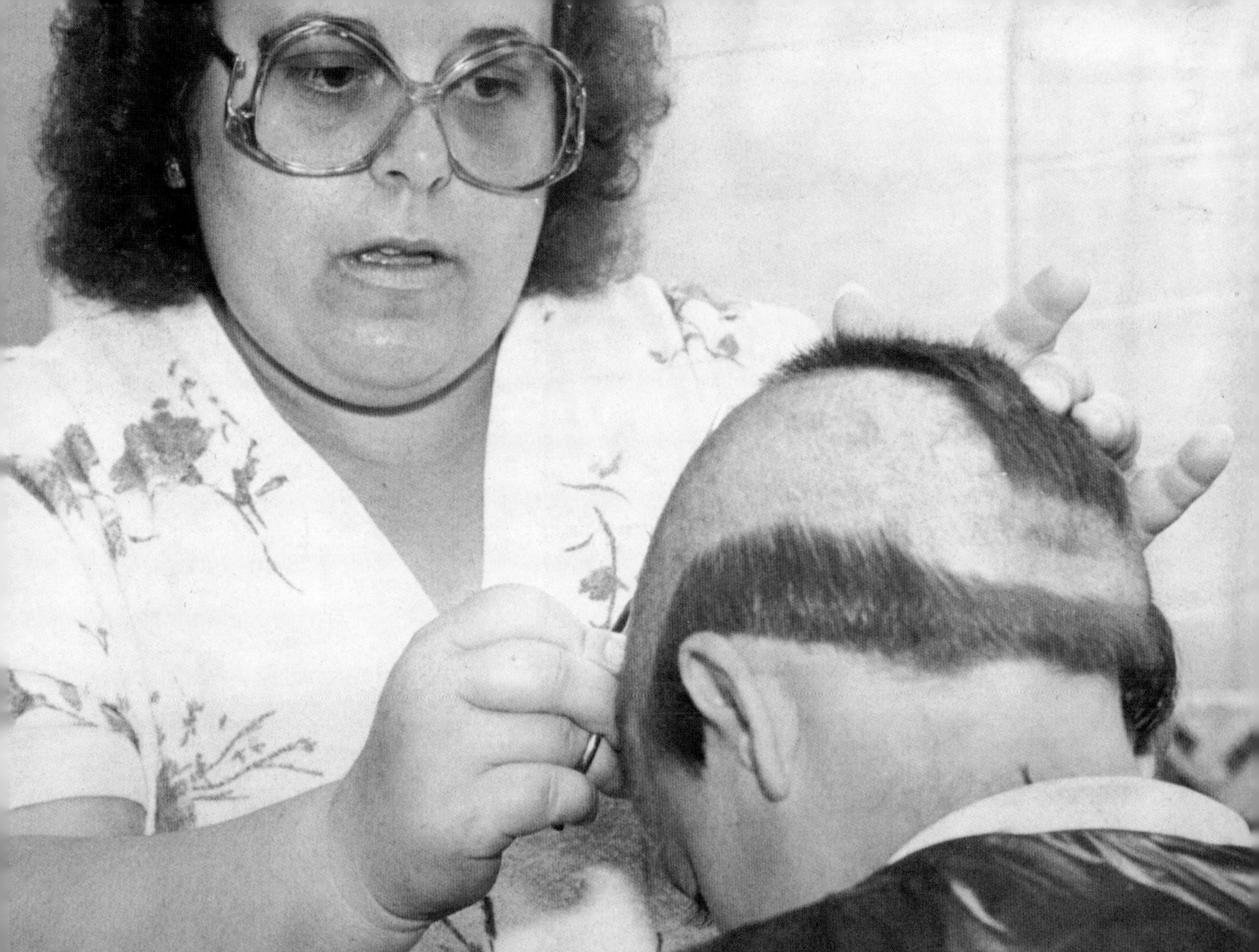
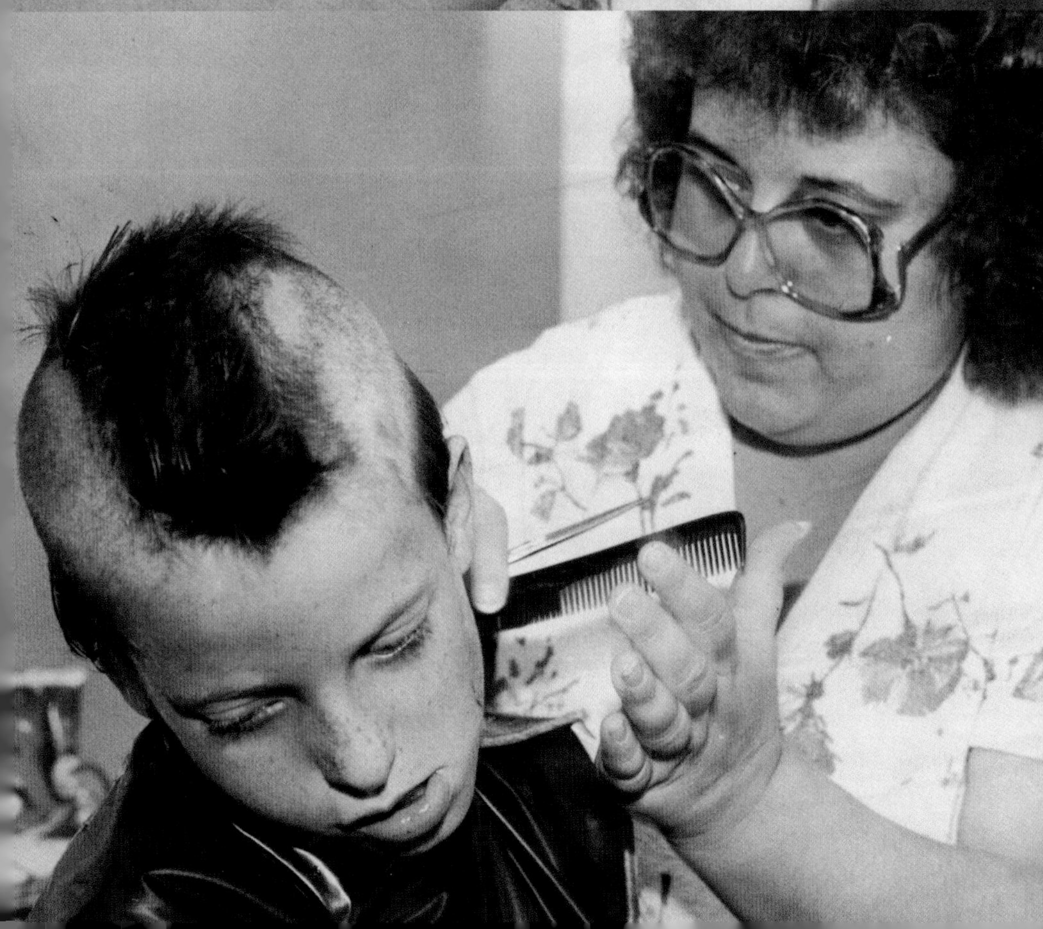
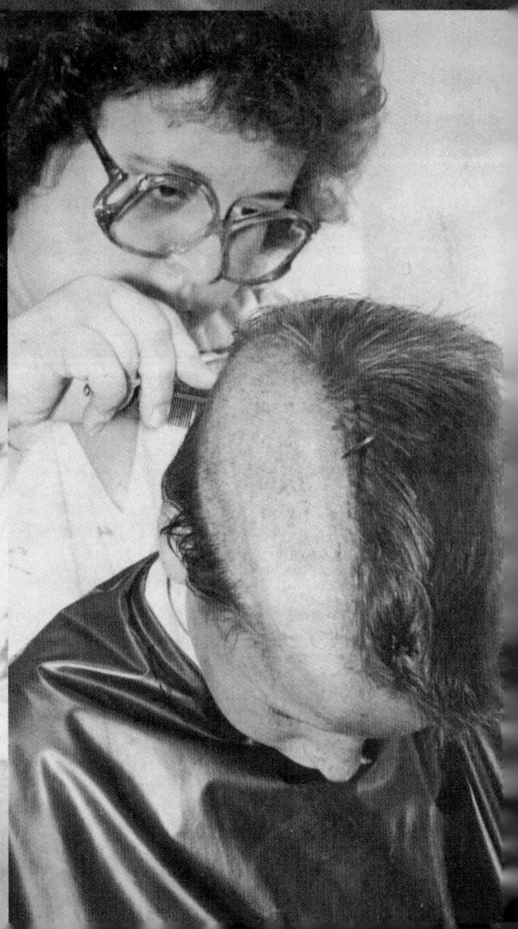

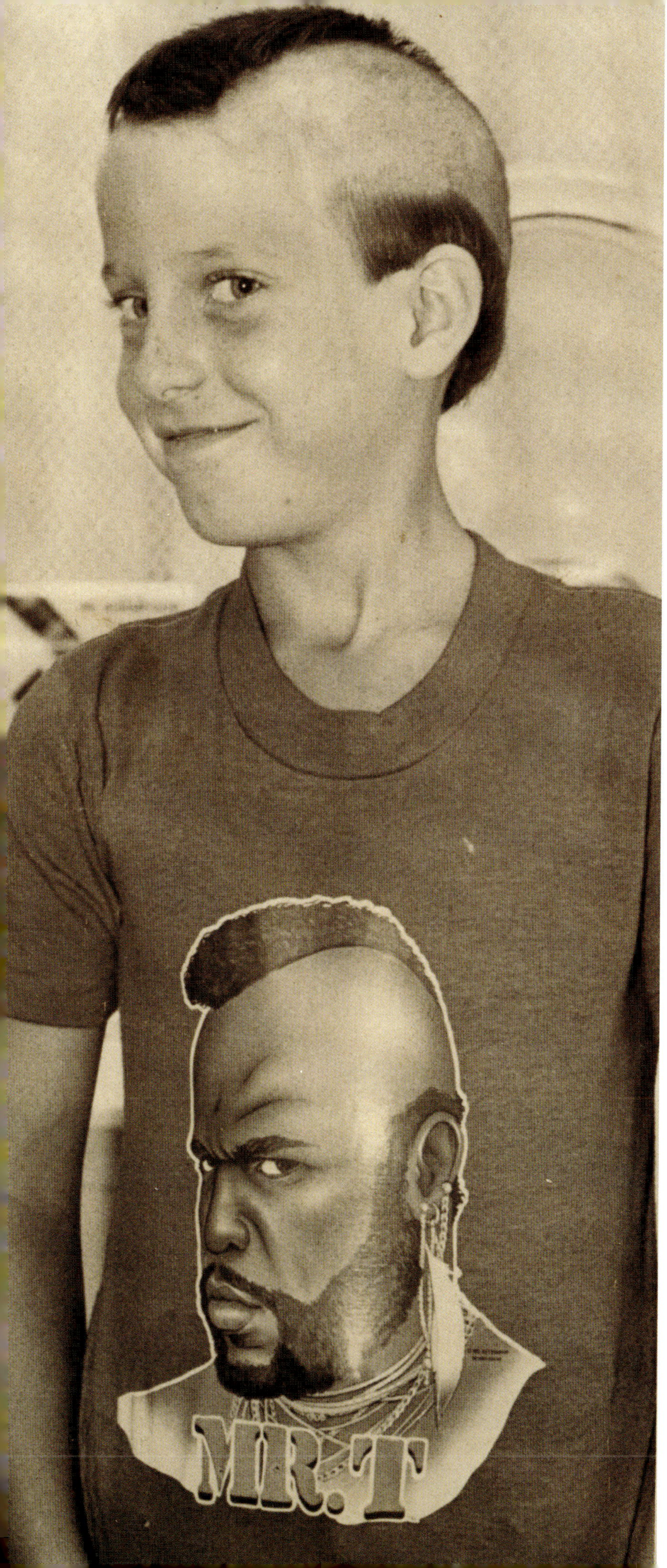

upbringing. Also like Mr. T, you don't want to piss him off and unleash his mean side. Greg and I sat down in my living room to discuss his admiration for Mr. T and his products in my living room. Originally Greg was going to use this as the basis for his own introduction, but he seemed to like the rhythm of this interview, so here it is.

Nicholas Gazin: What is your earliest memory of Mr. T?
Greg Rivera: The earliest memory I have is watching *The A-Team* with my dad. When it came on TV, on prime time. My dad liked it because nobody would ever get hurt. Any time they'd blow up a jeep or something, he would say in his thick accent, "Look, look! Not one scratch!" He loved that they could show a truck get blown up with a rocket launcher and then have a shot of the guys getting out of the truck unharmed. I also loved that Mr. T's character, B. A. Baracus, could get them out of any situation by building a tank or something.

What does B. A. stand for?
"Bad Attitude."

What was your first impression of Mr. T?
He was such a good badass and a strong character. He was funny and he was different.

How much do you know about Mr. T?
I think I know enough.

What's his real name?
Lawrence Tureaud. But I heard a story once about a guy who saw him and started chatting with him at an LA supermarket. As they were parting, he said to Mr. T, "All right, see you later, Lawrence." And Mr. T told him, "Nobody calls me that but my mama." As far as I'm concerned, his name's Mr. T, except to his mama, he's Lawrence.

That's a good story. What year was he born?
May 21, 1952. I'm not sure how many more facts I can rattle off. I was always more fascinated with collecting his stuff than enamored with the man himself. At the end of the day, he's just a person. I still to this day haven't met him.

Series of found candid snapshots of a young white boy getting a "Mr. T" mohawk by his mother. These photos really show how much Mr. T crossed the racial barrier and how everyone wanted to be like their hero!

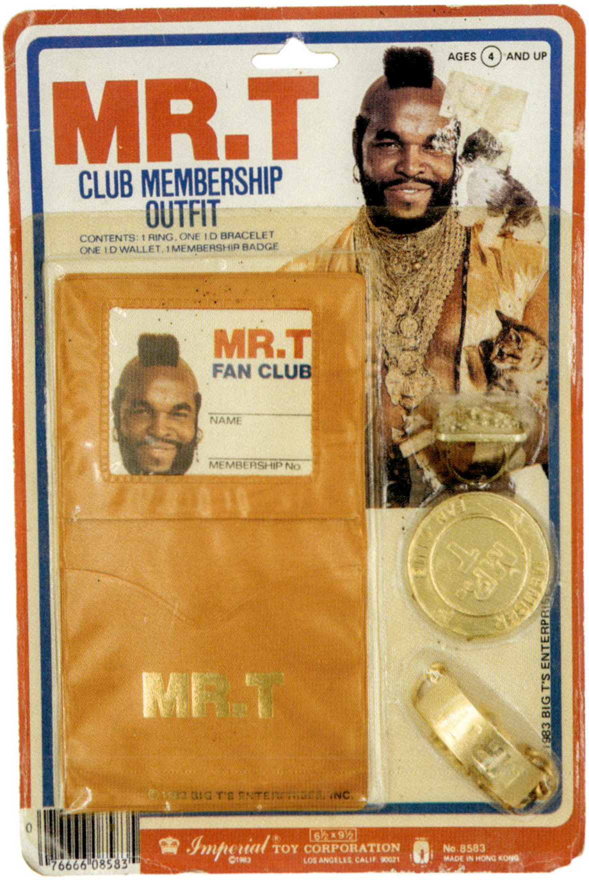

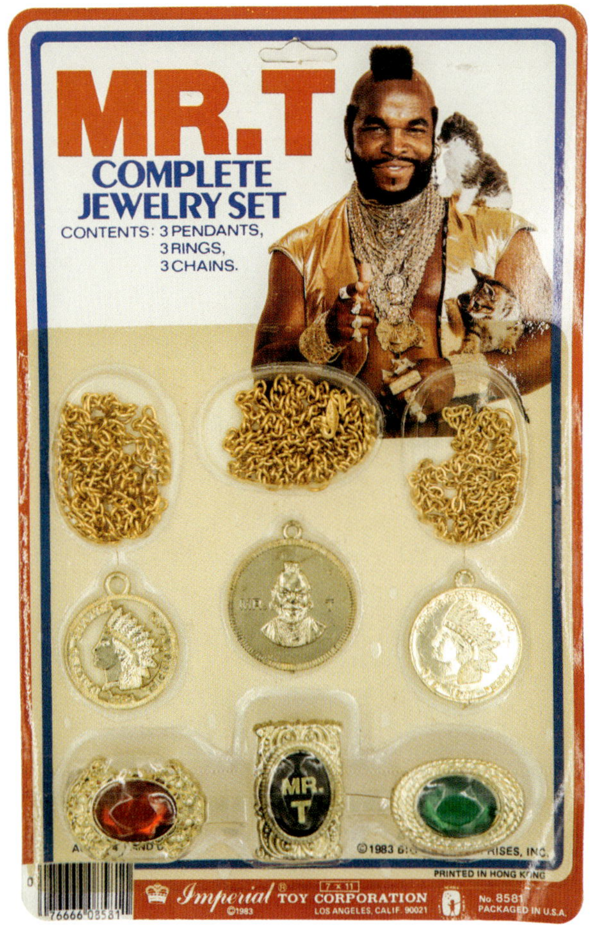

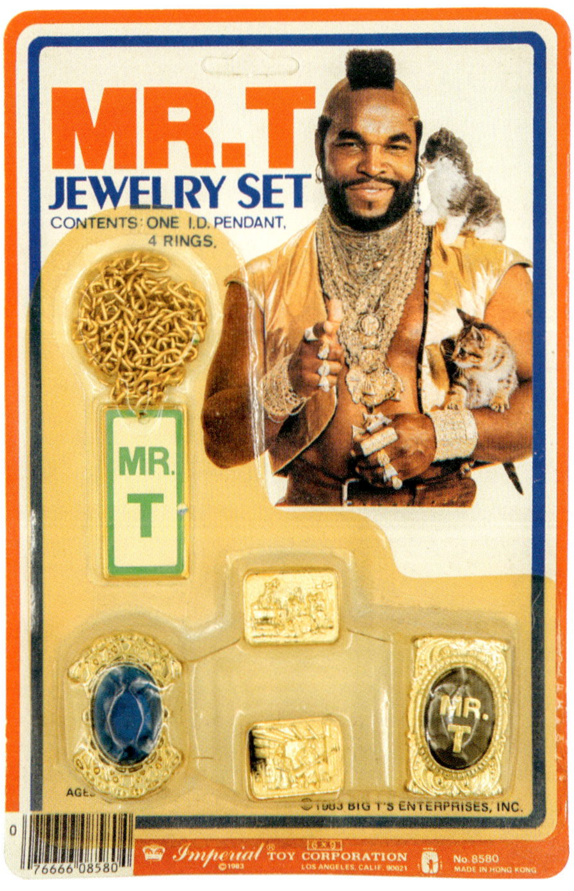

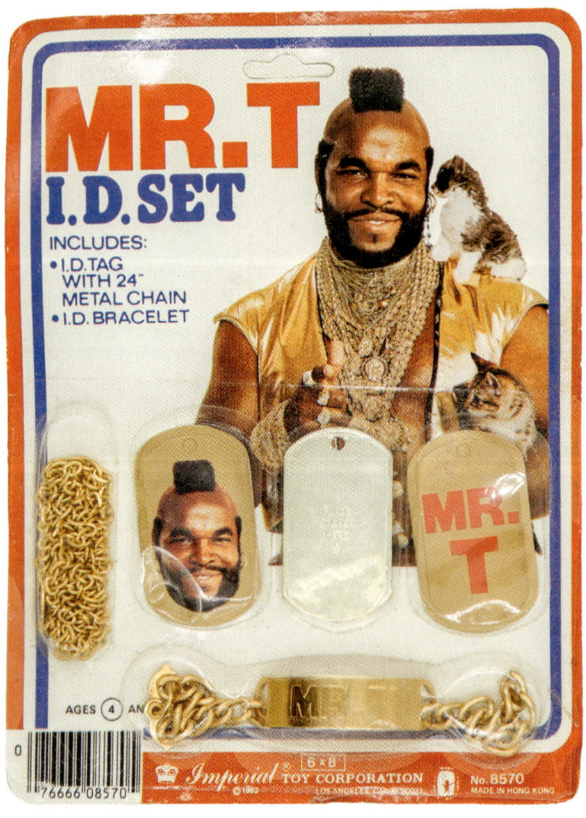

Mr. T jewelry and I.D. sets. Imperial Toy Corporation, 1983.

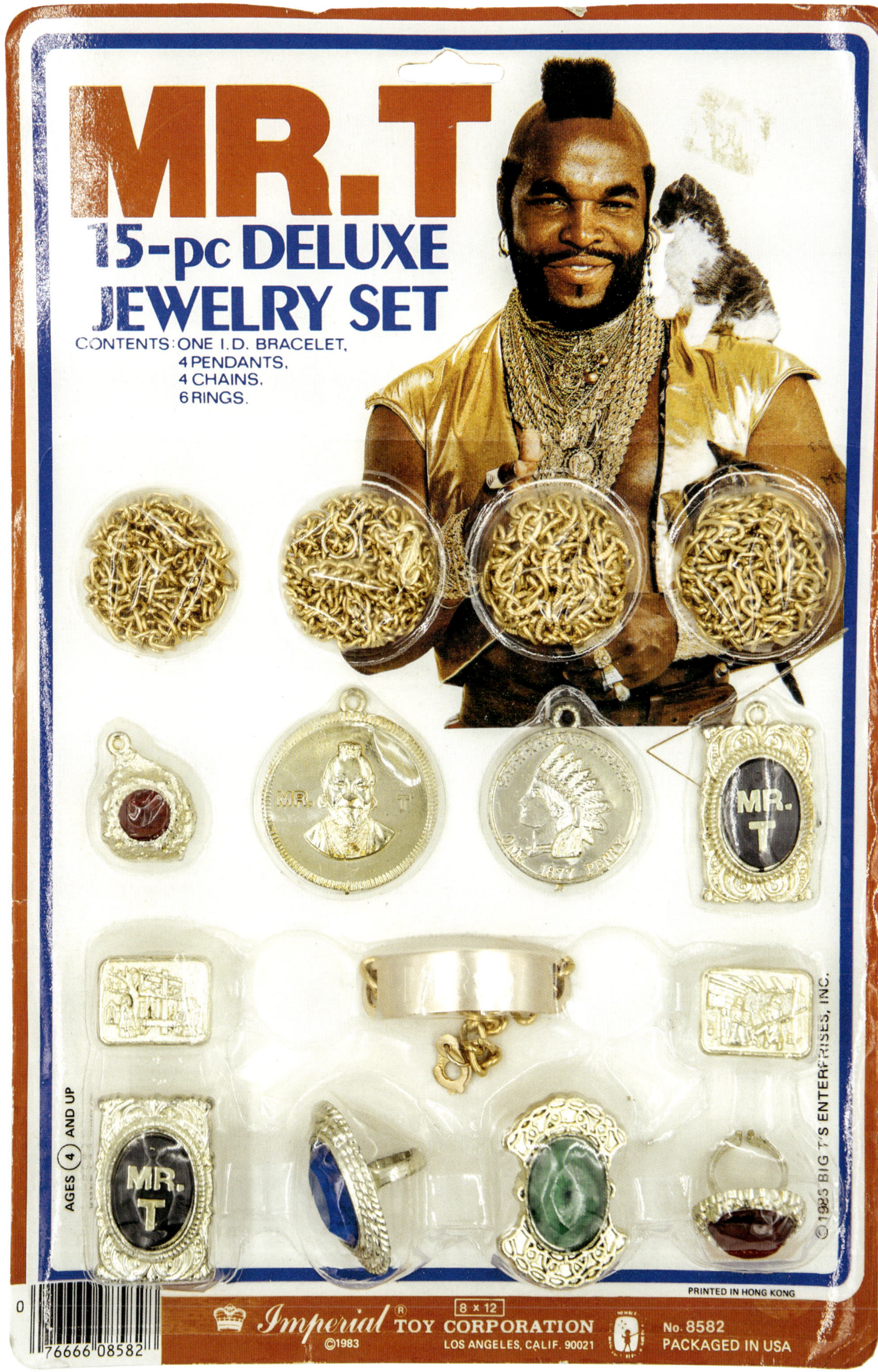
MR.T
15-pc DELUXE
JEWELRY SET
CONTENTS: ONE I.D. BRACELET,
4 PENDANTS,
4 CHAINS,
6 RINGS.
MR. T
ONE 1877 PENNY
MR. T
AGES 4 AND UP
MR. T
© 1983 BIG T'S ENTERPRISES, INC.
PRINTED IN HONG KONG
8 x 12
Imperial® TOY CORPORATION
©1983
LOS ANGELES, CALIF. 90021
No. 8582
PACKAGED IN USA
0 76666 08582

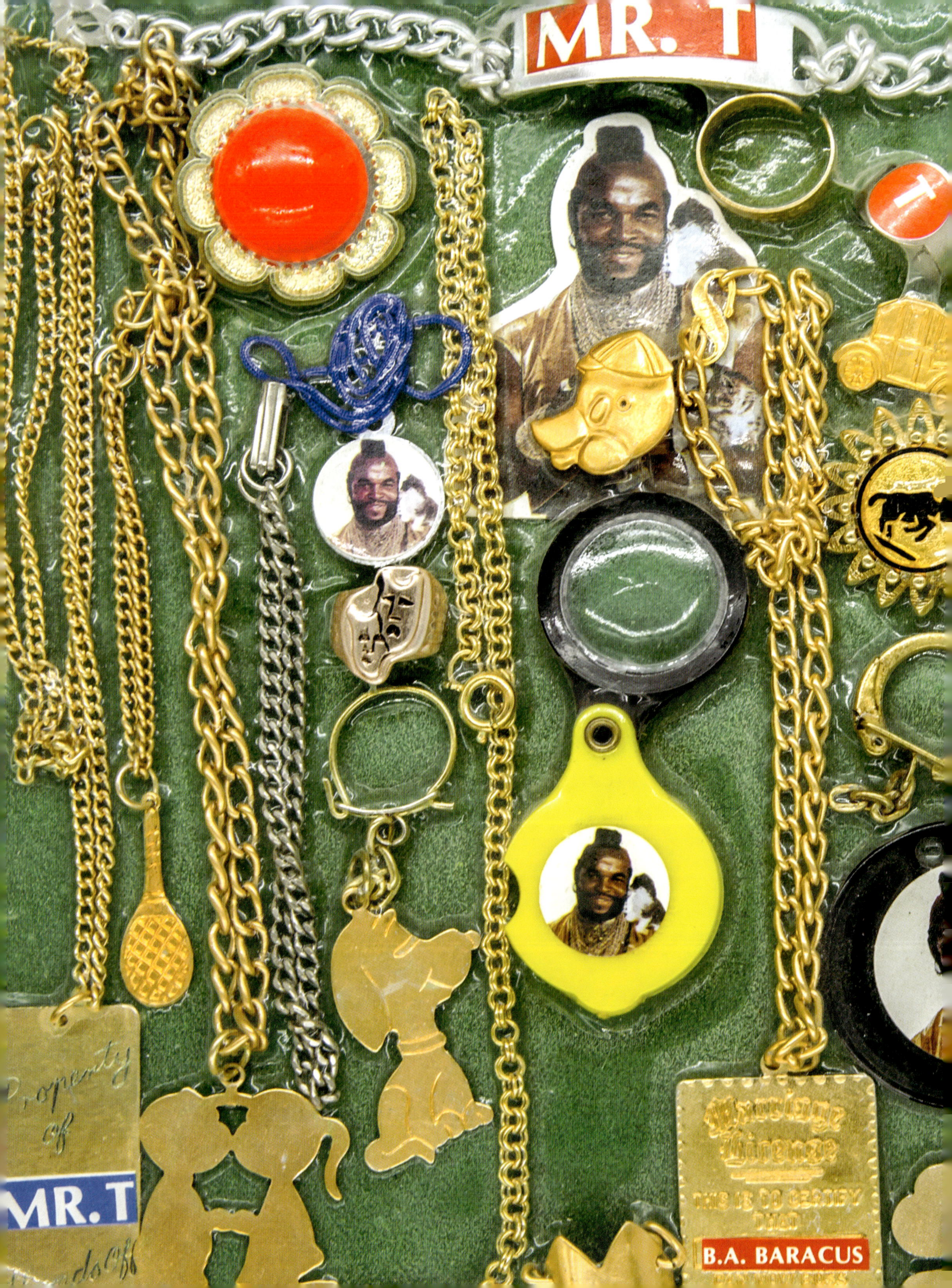

MR. T
T
Property of
MR.T
B.A. BARACUS

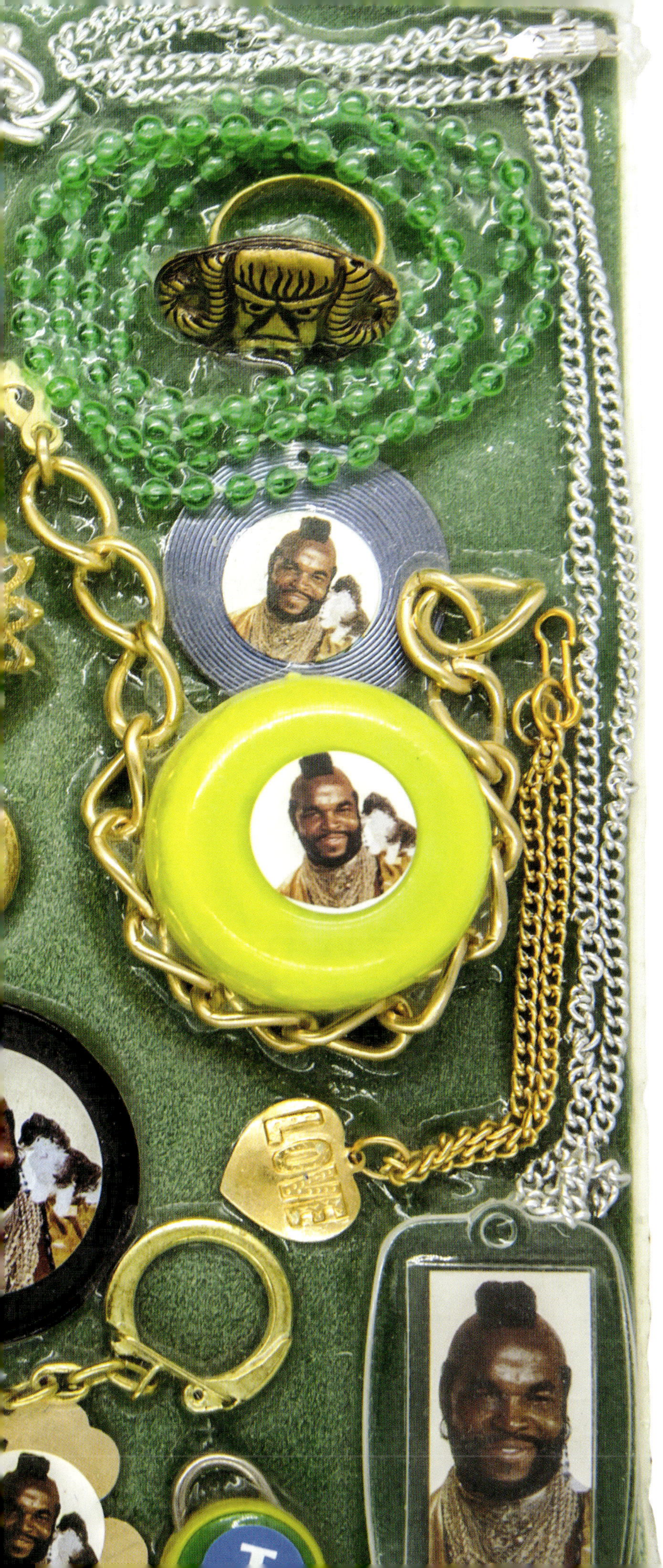

What?! You've met all kinds of people at autograph shows and you haven't met Mr. T?
Yeah. When I was younger I was really excited to meet him and tell him about my collection. I think if I met him now, I probably wouldn't mention it. I would never want to think that Mr. T would care or be excited that I collected his stuff. I'd like to meet him, but it wasn't ever a situation where I was, oh, I'm obsessed with this guy.

There's not a lot of Mr. T collectors. I only know, including myself, four. One of the guys that we know, he collects a lot of autographs and original clothing Mr. T wore in movies and stuff, and that never really interested me.

You like the image of Mr. T?
I like the image of Mr. T. I like the artwork associated with him.

Are you laughing at Mr. T?
No, I'm not laughing. I think it took me a long time to realize how much other people see Mr. T as a cartoon character, and I never saw him that way. I always saw him as a real guy who played a character. I imagined that he's probably similar to his roles, but just not as dramatic.

You mean loud and barking orders at people and not wanting to get on planes?
Not like the character of B. A. Baracus, but definitely a loud and outspoken person. I mean, watching him on Howard Stern, he really got upset when Howard talked about his mama. He also got annoyed whenever they'd start talking about any sexual matters.

Mr. T's for the kids.
Yeah, he's for the kids and he's a Christian man, and I think that's a big part of his life and who he is. He's a very outspoken Christian. One thing I always say to people is, unlike a lot of eighties celebrities, Mr. T never had any scandals.

Mr. T doesn't have any?
No.

Vending machine insert, 1980s.

How about when he cut down all the trees on his property?
Yeah, there's that, but I think the only thing you could really think of is the time he cut down the trees.

He was in this Snickers commercial where he shot Snickers bars at some guy and called him a wimp, and it seemed homophobic.
Yeah, that was the other one.

So I can think of two right off the top of my head and I'm not even a Mr. T expert, although it seems I might be a bigger one than you. You mentioned that you liked Mr. T being Christian.
Yeah. Well, I grew up Christian, so I think I also like that fact. I remember the first time I saw *Be Somebody or Be Somebody's Fool* and I took it really serious; I didn't think it was a joke.

How old were you?
I was probably in high school.

So way too old to be taking* Be Somebody or Be Somebody's Fool *seriously?
They made a full-length record as well. My favorite song on it that they made was called "Mr. T's Commandments," which was all the ways you should live your life.

"Believe it because every word is true."
Right.

"I can talk all day, but the rest is up to you."
"Honor your mother and father, the Bible makes it clear, because if you don't, God help you fool, you got Mr. T to fear."

"Mr. T's Commandments!"
You know what the funniest thing about that record is? Ice-T produced it.

That's pretty cool. Two T's; wait, are they related?
Ice-T and Mr. T? I think so.

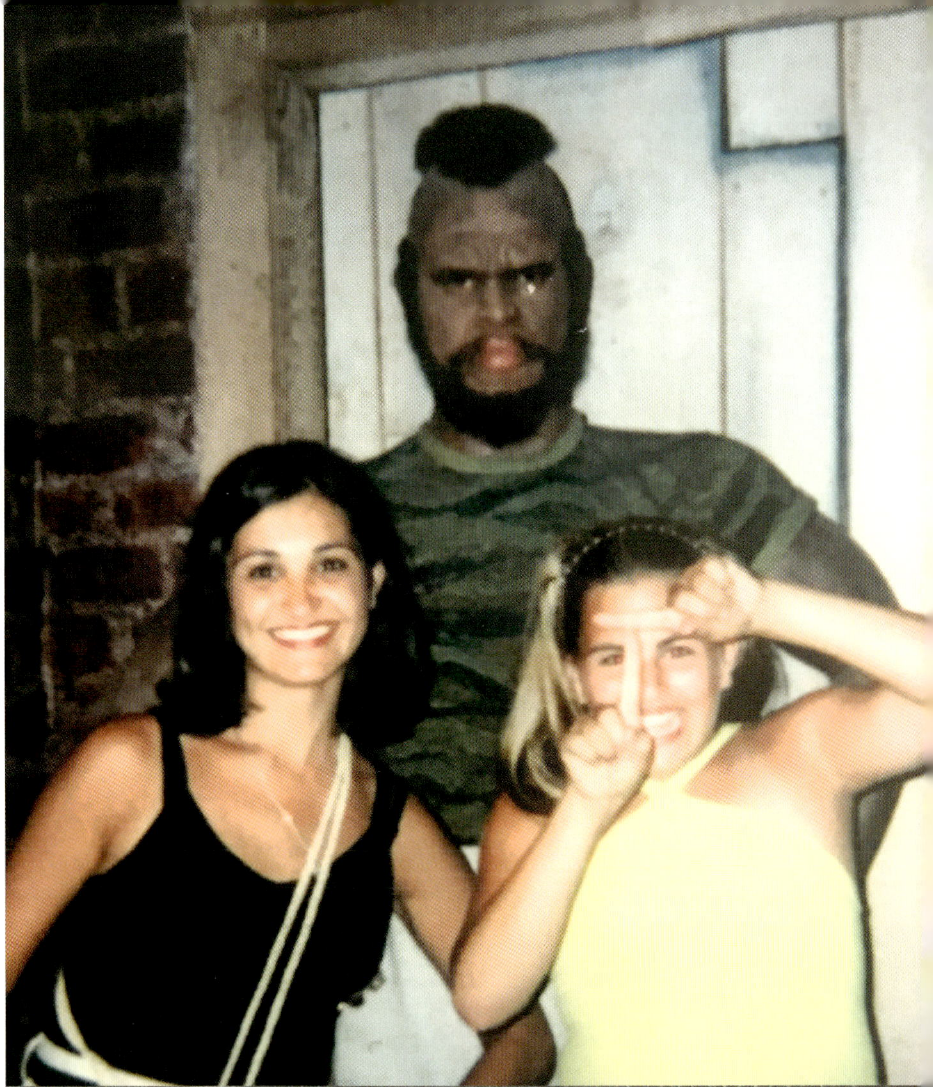

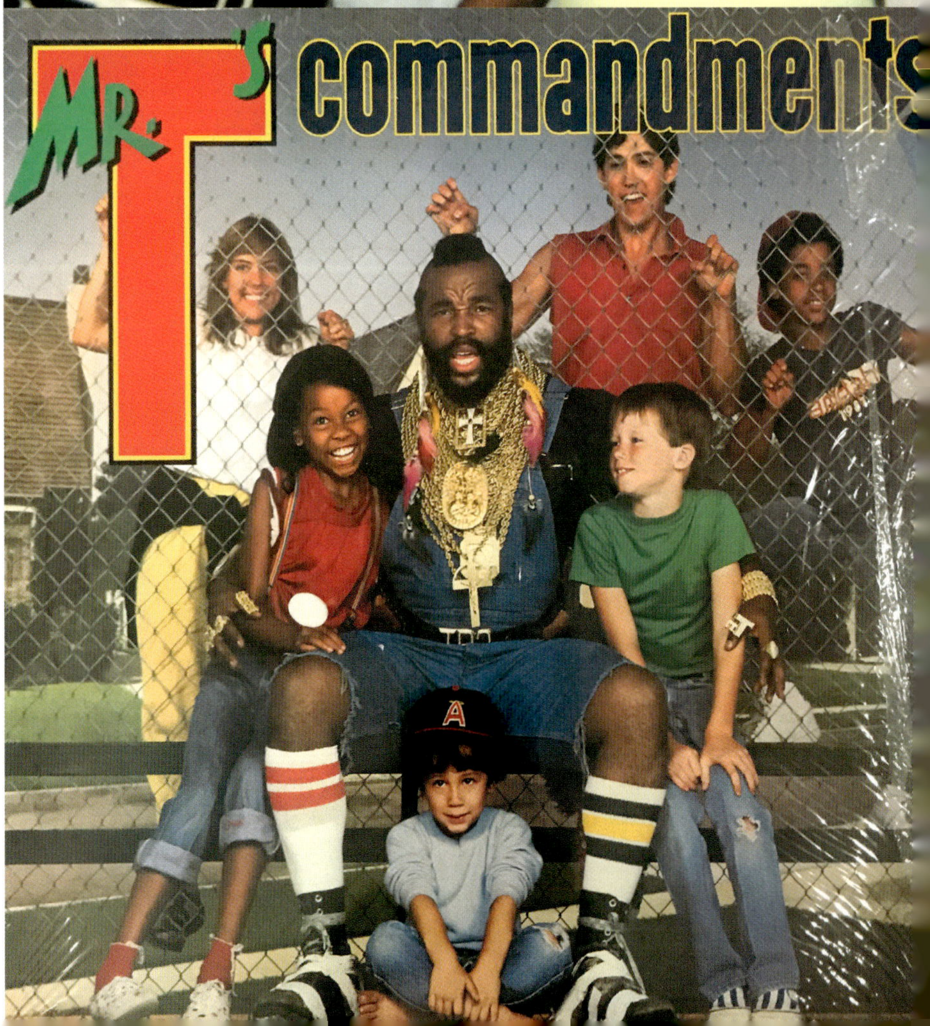

TOP LEFT *Found candid snapshot of Mr. T wax figure from unknown museum, 1980s.*

BOTTOM LEFT *Mr. T's Commandments.*

TOP RIGHT Be Somebody or Be Somebody's Fool.

BOTTOM RIGHT A-Team Feuerprüfung *VHS, Germany.*

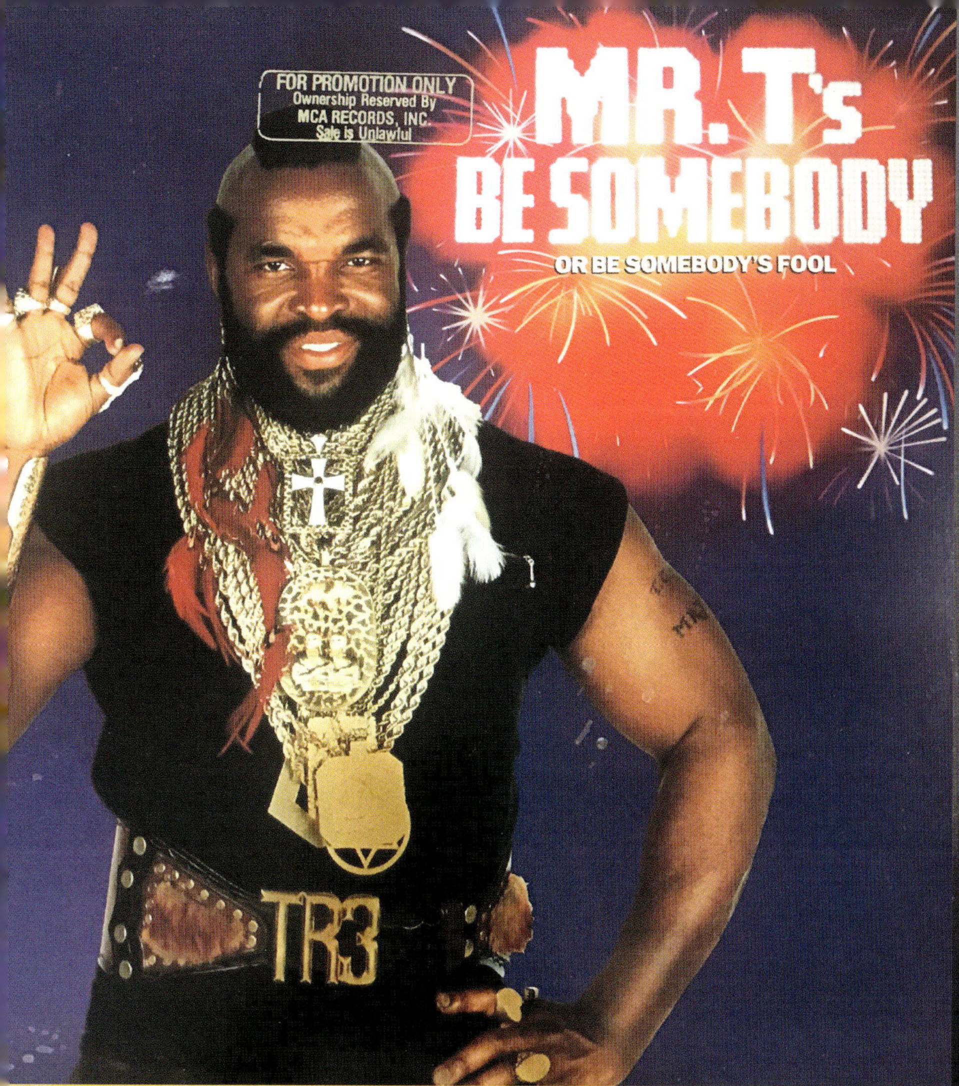

SIDE ONE

BE SOMEBODY

GREG PORÉE-MAXI ANDERSON
PRODUCED BY GREG PORÉE
Musicians: KEVIN BRANDON-Bass, GREG GRAHAM-Kroma, DX7, DAVID KRIESBURG-Kroma, DX7, MUNYUNGO-Percussion, GREG PORÉE-Guitar, OB8
Recorded at Larrabee Sound
Mixed at Conway Studio
Engineer: PETER CHAIKIN
Music Coordinator: ERNIE FIELDS JR. for Jade Sound
Associate Producer for MR. T's vocal: ICE T
Vocals: "THE DIMPLES"
Vocal Coordinator and Arranger: MAXI ANDERSON

TREAT YOUR MOTHER RIGHT

CHARLES RICHARD CASON
PRODUCED AND ARRANGED BY RICH CASON
Musicians: RICH CASON-Synthesizer
Background Vocals: JULIE SIMS
Lead Vocals: MR. T
Engineer: HANK DONIG
Recorded at Baby 'O

STYLIN'

GREG PORÉE
PRODUCED BY GREG PORÉE
Musicians: GREG GRAHAM & DAVID KREISBURG-Kroma, Dx7, Mini-moog, GREG PORÉE-OB8, Guitar, DMX, JEFF CLAYTON-Soprano Sax Solos
Recorded at Larrabee Sound
Mixed at Conway Studio
Engineer: PETER CHAIKIN
Music Coordinator: ERNIE FIELDS JR. for Jade Sound
Associate Produceet for MR. T's vocal: ICE T
Vocals: "THE DIMPLES"
Vocal Coordinator and Arranger: MAXI ANDERSON

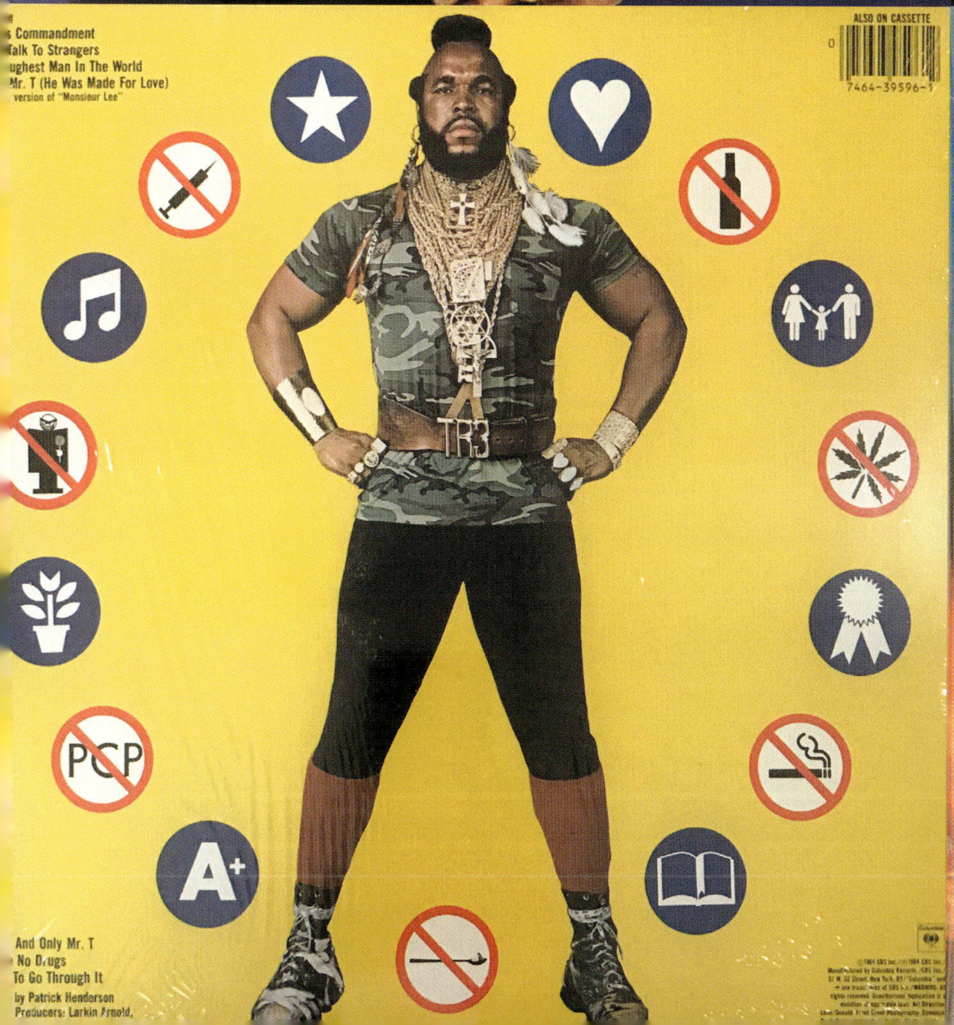

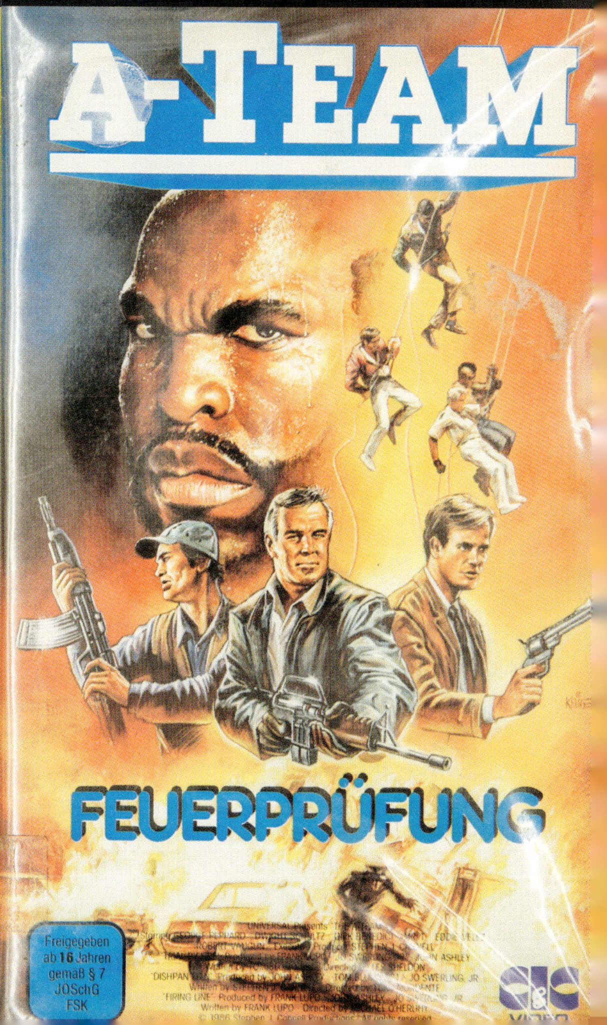

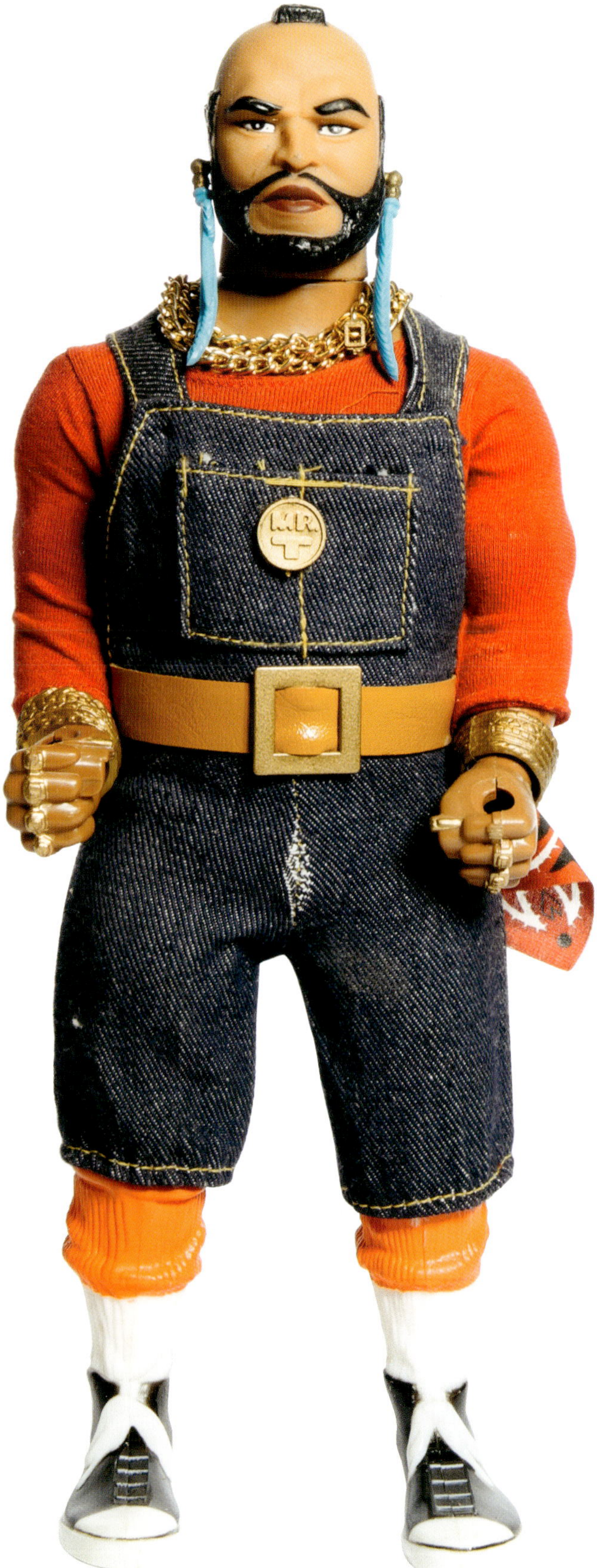

Rosenfield Goldman Inc

Release: Immediate

LEWIS GALOOB INC.

ARTICU

In May 1983, the
Galoob, Inc. signed a
Corporation of Americ
to manufacture and di
including articulated
NBC series, as well a
consist of 6" figures
Dirk Benedict and Dwi
exclusive contract wi
Mr. T doll, are also
Mr. T articulated fig
vans, helicopters and
David Galoob, pr
will make approximate
licenses. The 6" fig
the 12" Mr. T figure

9229 Sunset Boulevard,

News

Contact: Stan Rosenfield

)DUCES NEW MR. T AND "A TEAM"

) FIGURES TO MEDIA

Francisco-based toy company Lewis
:lusive contract with Merchandising
ıder the direction of Victor Temkin,
oute a number of "A TEAM" products,
.on figures of the stars of the hit
:essorized play sets. This will
Ir. T, George Peppard, Melinda Culea,
Schultz. Galoob has also signed an
·. T and, in addition to the 6"
'acturing and distributing a 12"
olus play environments featuring
ır accessories in action settings.
nt of Galoob, says his company
items under the "A TEAM" and Mr. T
will retail for under \$5.00, and
retail for under \$10.00.

continued...

ngeles, California 90069 (213) 550-7263

Was there anything from your childhood that made you really want to start collecting Mr. T memorabilia?
I remember really wanting the twelve-inch Mr. T doll as a kid. I remember my cousin had it and I was really jealous. I also remembered today when I moved from Connecticut, my mom made me sell all my toys.

Did we just discover the root of your problem?
Probably . . . I remember being in middle school and going to the flea market in Florida and finding a life-size Mr. T cereal cardboard standee display. It's actually one of the rarest pieces I own. That's the first thing I remember having and thinking this could be the start of a collection.

How much did you pay for that?
Five bucks.

How much do you think it's worth now?
A few hundred bucks.

So Mr. T stuff's not really all that valuable?
No, it's not really that valuable. That was part of the appeal when I first started buying it on eBay. It was something that was pretty easily obtainable because there was really no one else buying it.

Until you came across . . .
. . . Until I came across Mike Essl, who became my main rival in online bids for Mr. T stuff. This was around 1998, 1999.

FAR LEFT *12" Mr. T action figure. Galoob, 1983.*

LEFT *Press release announcing Galoob's A-Team and Mr. T toy line, 1983.*

Had he been collecting Mr. T stuff for longer than you?
No, I'd started getting serious about it long before meeting Mike, while I was still in college. There was this store called Populuxe. I was driving one day down the street, and I saw this sandwich board outside the store, and it had Mr. T painted on it. I turned around real quick and I went in. It was a pop culture and vintage store. Brian, who owned the store, had two or three shelves of Mr. T stuff, and I had I bought a lot of it from him. Then eBay came along and I started buying stuff there.

How big was his collection at the time?
It was nowhere near the size of mine. His was maybe one bookshelf full of stuff and mine was almost two walls filled with stuff. This was around 1998. Then we decided to make an eBay truce instead of bidding against each other.

He was like, "Look man, I can tell you're a real tough customer and you have a lot of T lust in your heart and I got some too. We'll get out of each other's way." He had a full-time job at the time so he had more money than me. I was still in college so I would also let him get more of the high-ticket items. The goal was to make sure that at least one of us won whatever Mr. T auctions appeared. It got to a point where it didn't matter who owned it because it was a mutual collection.

Eventually I moved to New York, where Mike and I became friends and the authorities, because we started a website called "Mr. T and Me." For a while it was a big part of who I was. I was this Mr. T guy that had this collection, and we were on different TV shows like *Totally Obsessed*, it was a VH1 show hosted by Fred Willard.

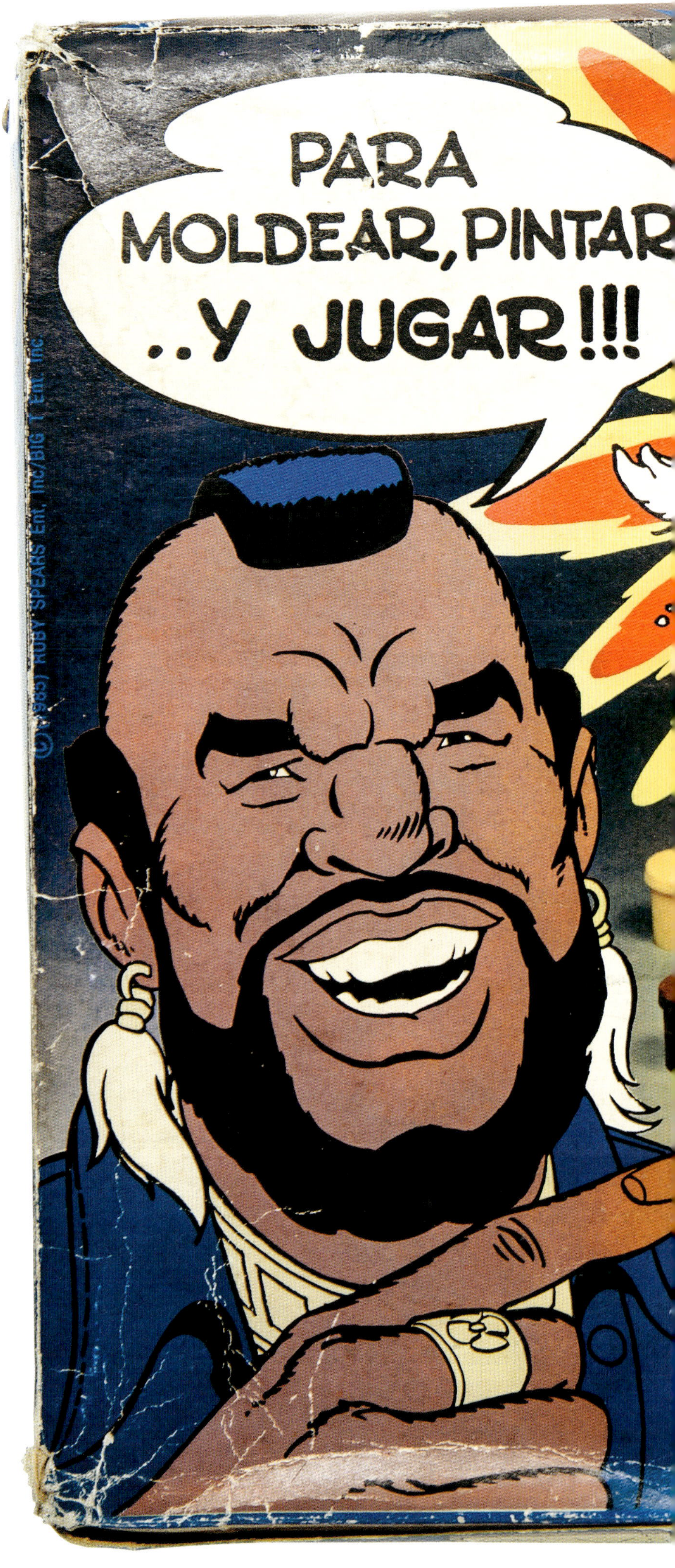

Mr. T Figure Factory. Argentina. Mr. T bubble says "To Mold, to Paint, and to Play."

NEXT SPREAD *Sealed mold for the Mr. T Figure Factory.*

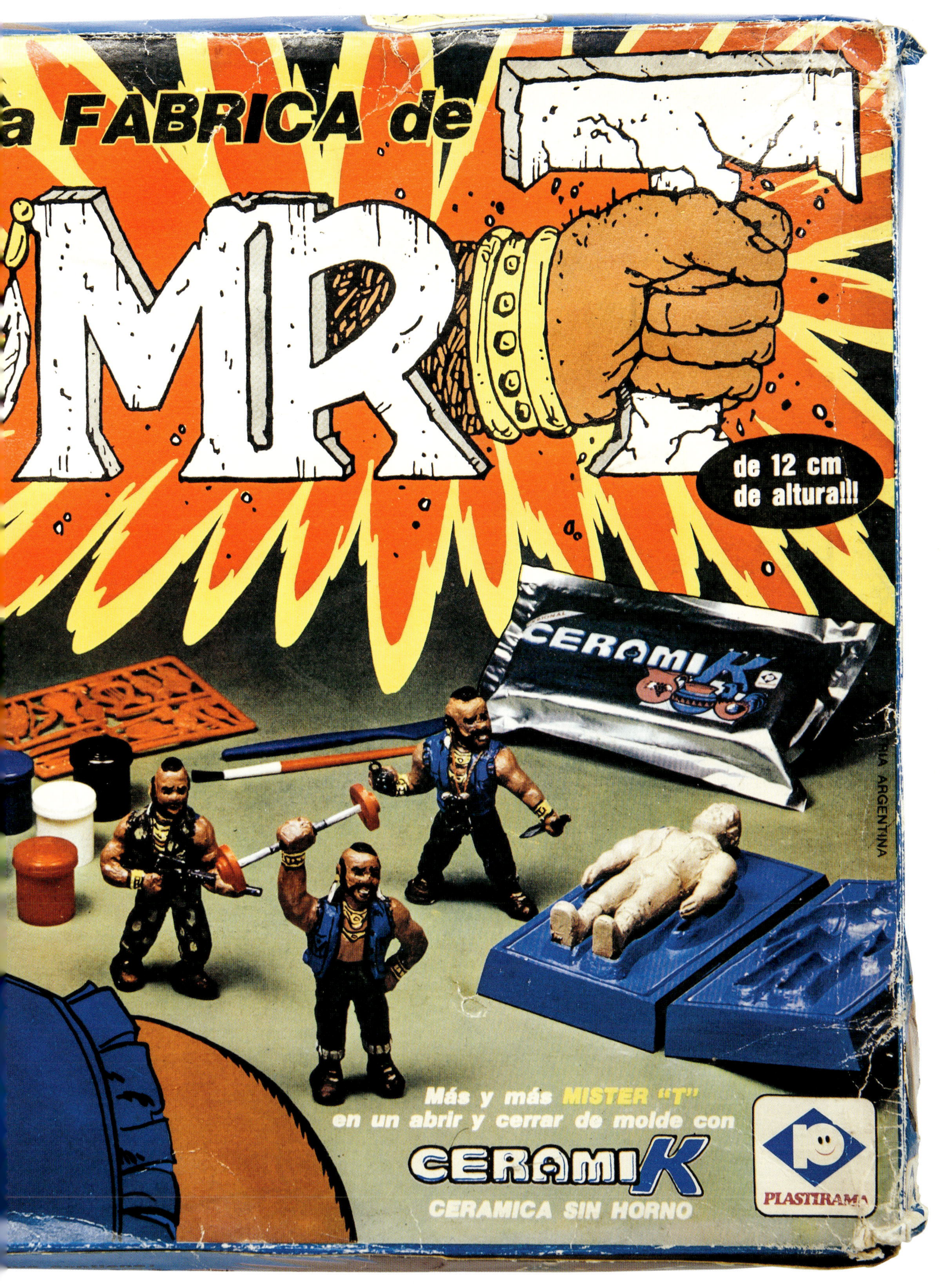
a FABRICA de
MR T
de 12 cm
de altura!!!
CERAMIK
Más y más MISTER "T"
en un abrir y cerrar de molde con
CERAMIK
CERAMICA SIN HORNO
PLASTIRAMA

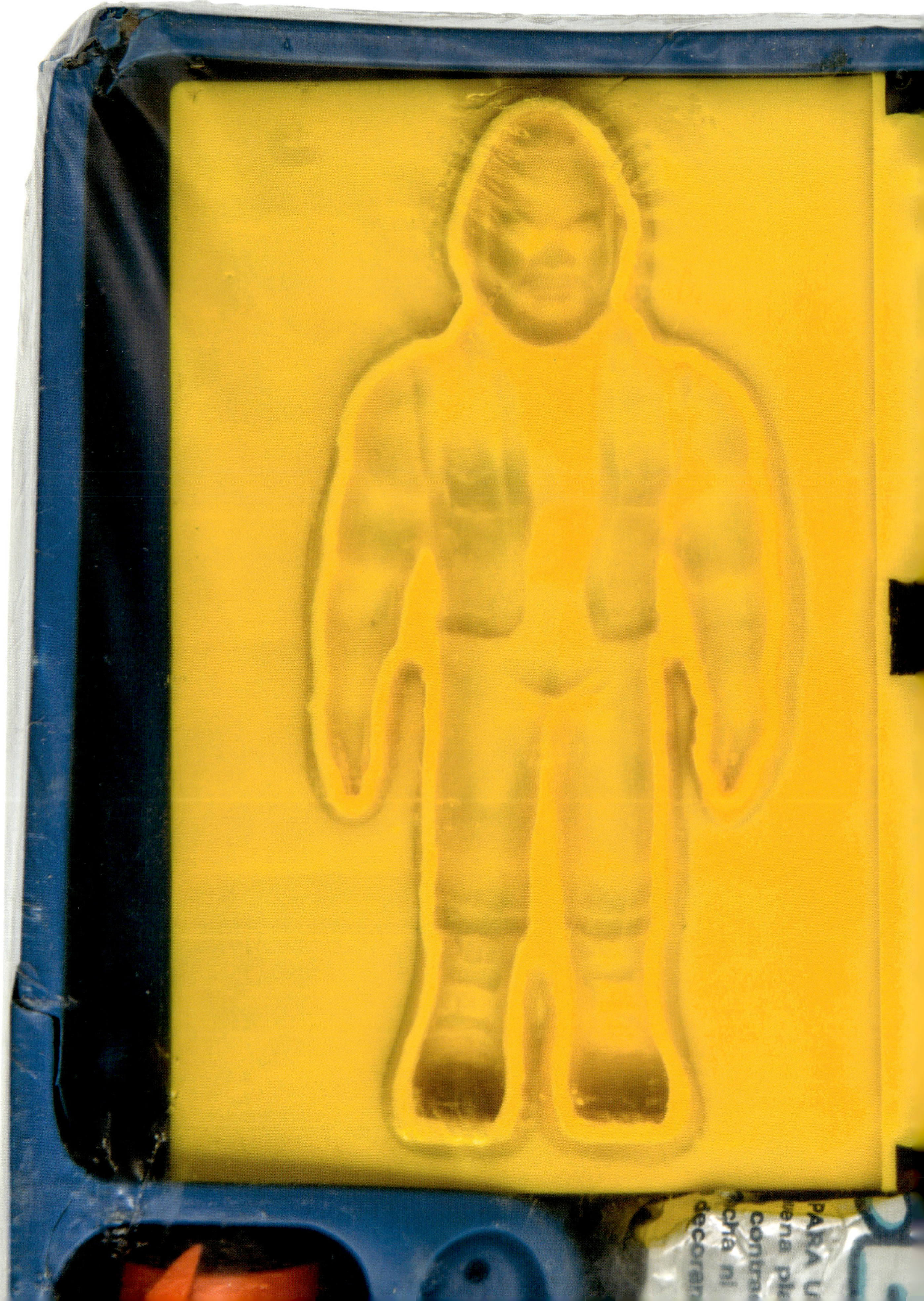

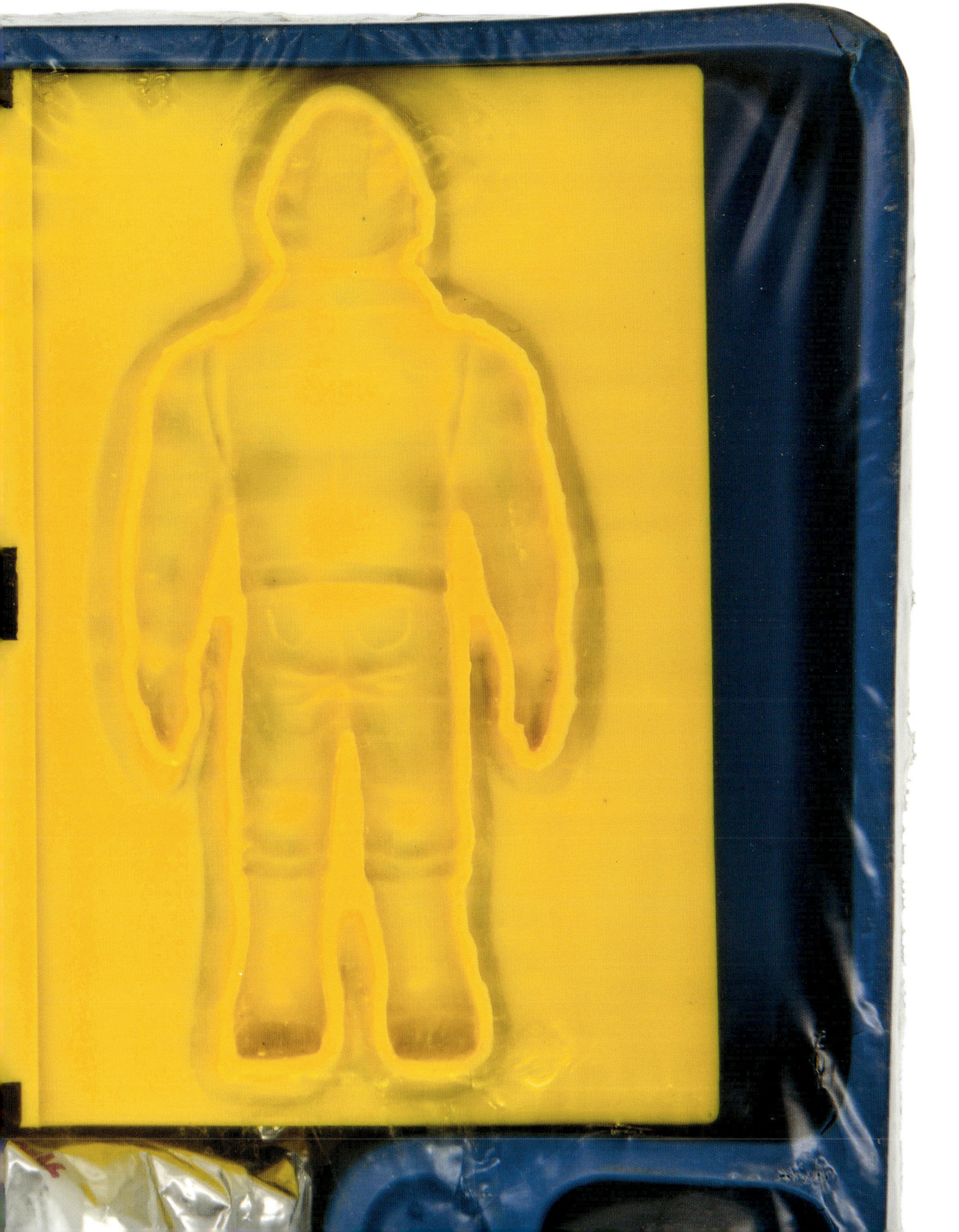

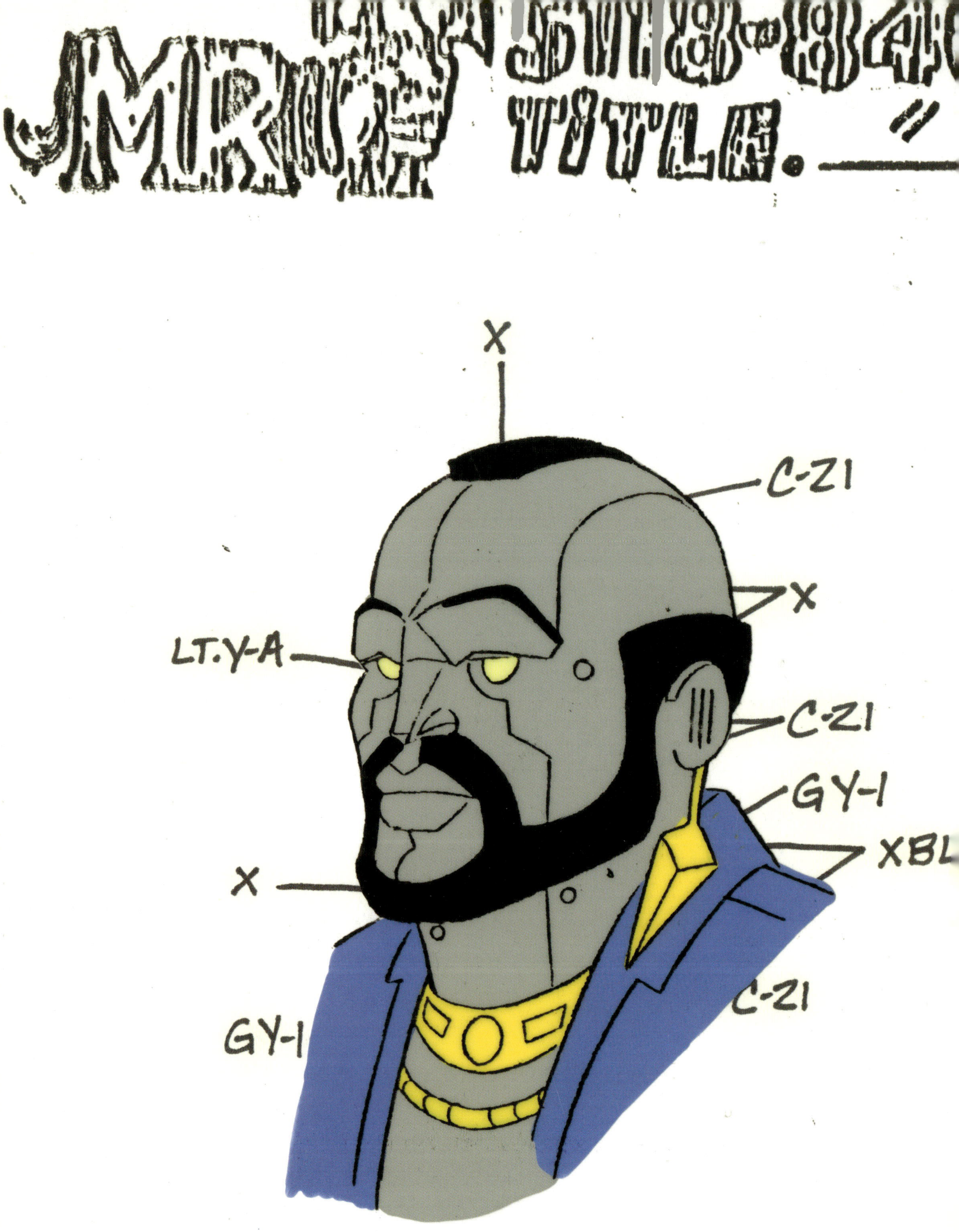
TITLE.
X
C-21
X
LT.Y-A
C-21
GY-1
XBL
X
C-21
GY-1

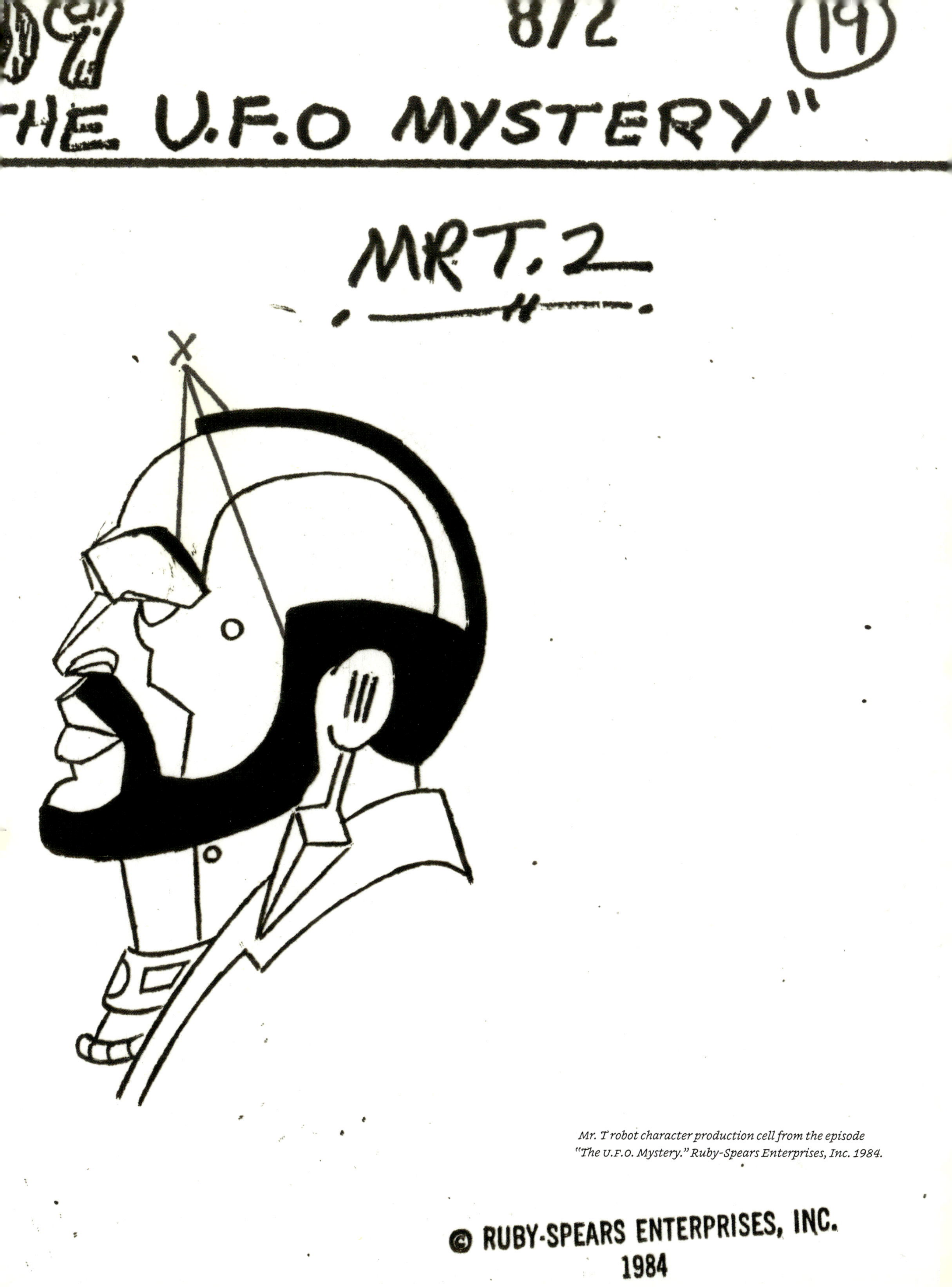

Mr. T robot character production cell from the episode "The U.F.O. Mystery." Ruby-Spears Enterprises, Inc. 1984.

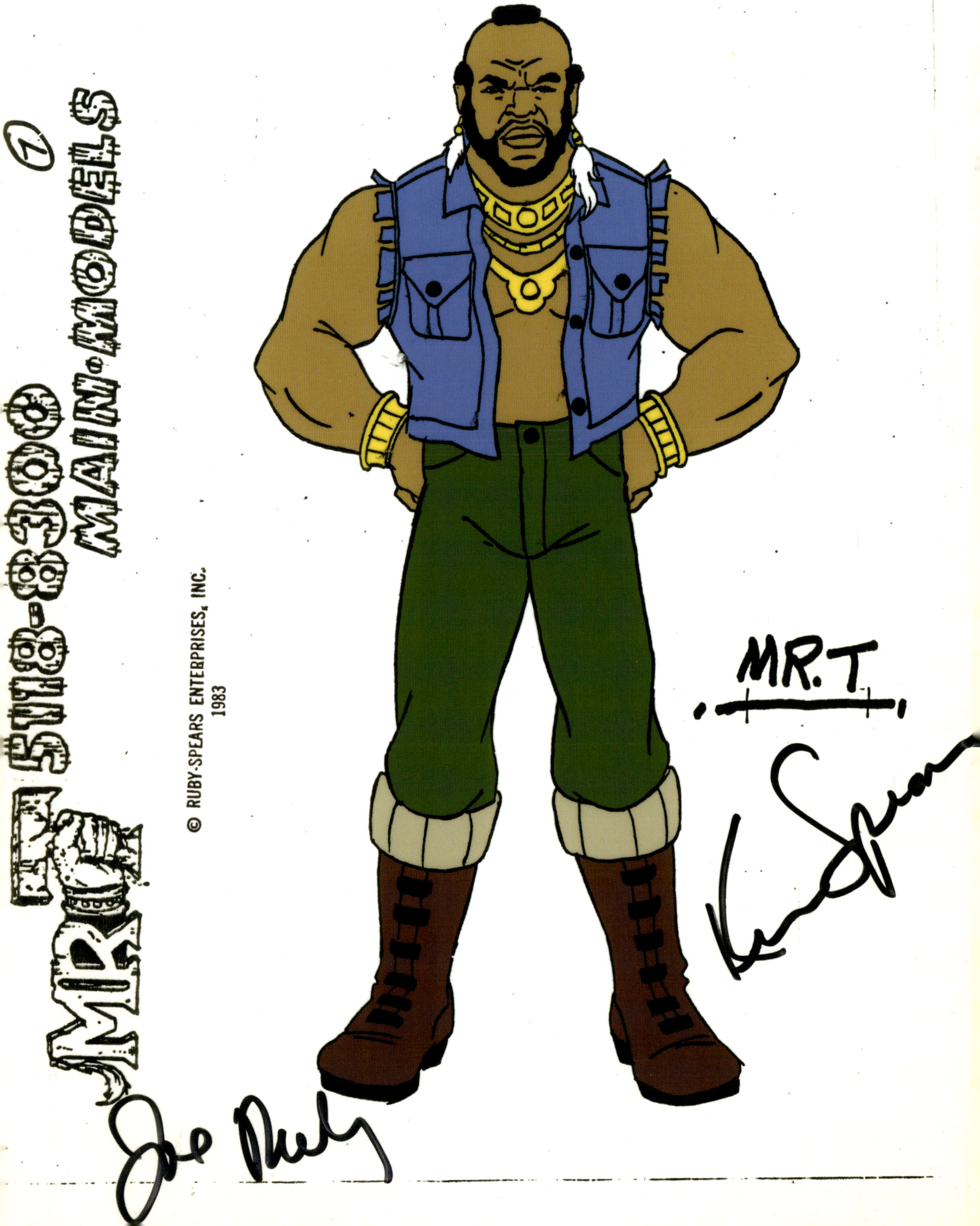
MR. T
5118-8300
MAIN MODELS
7
© RUBY-SPEARS ENTERPRISES, INC.
1983
MR. T

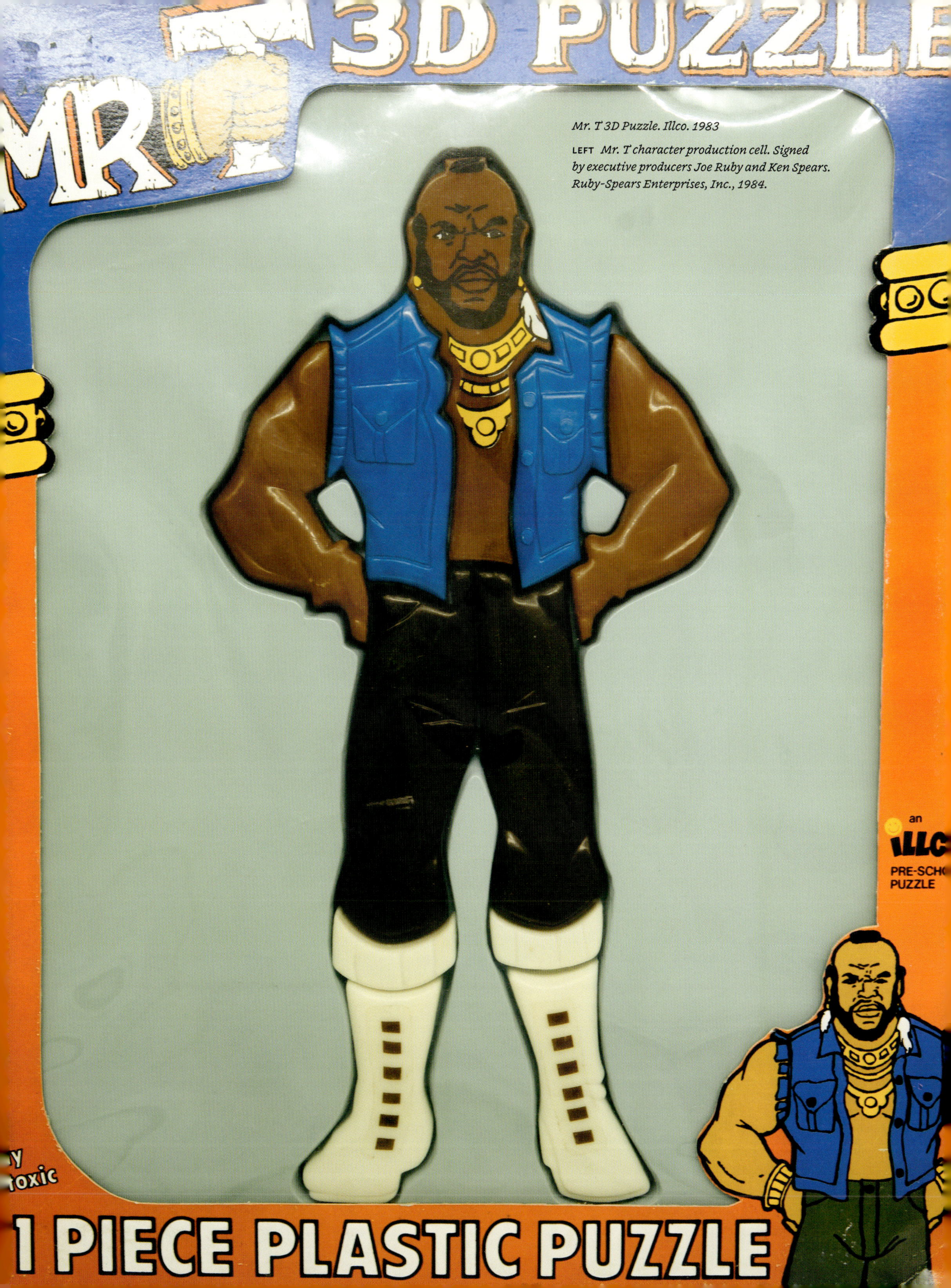

Mr. T 3D Puzzle. Illco. 1983

LEFT *Mr. T character production cell. Signed by executive producers Joe Ruby and Ken Spears. Ruby-Spears Enterprises, Inc., 1984.*

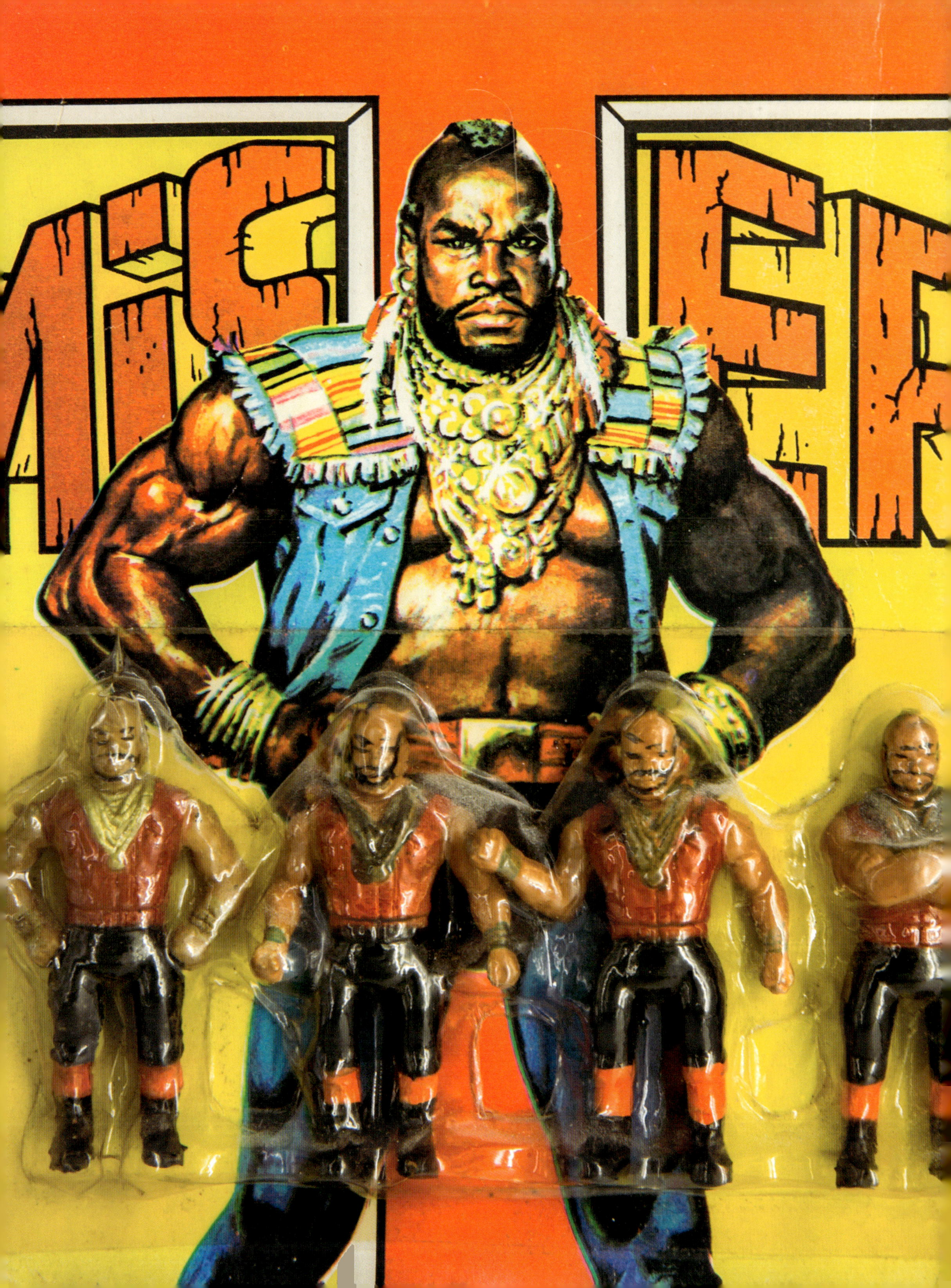

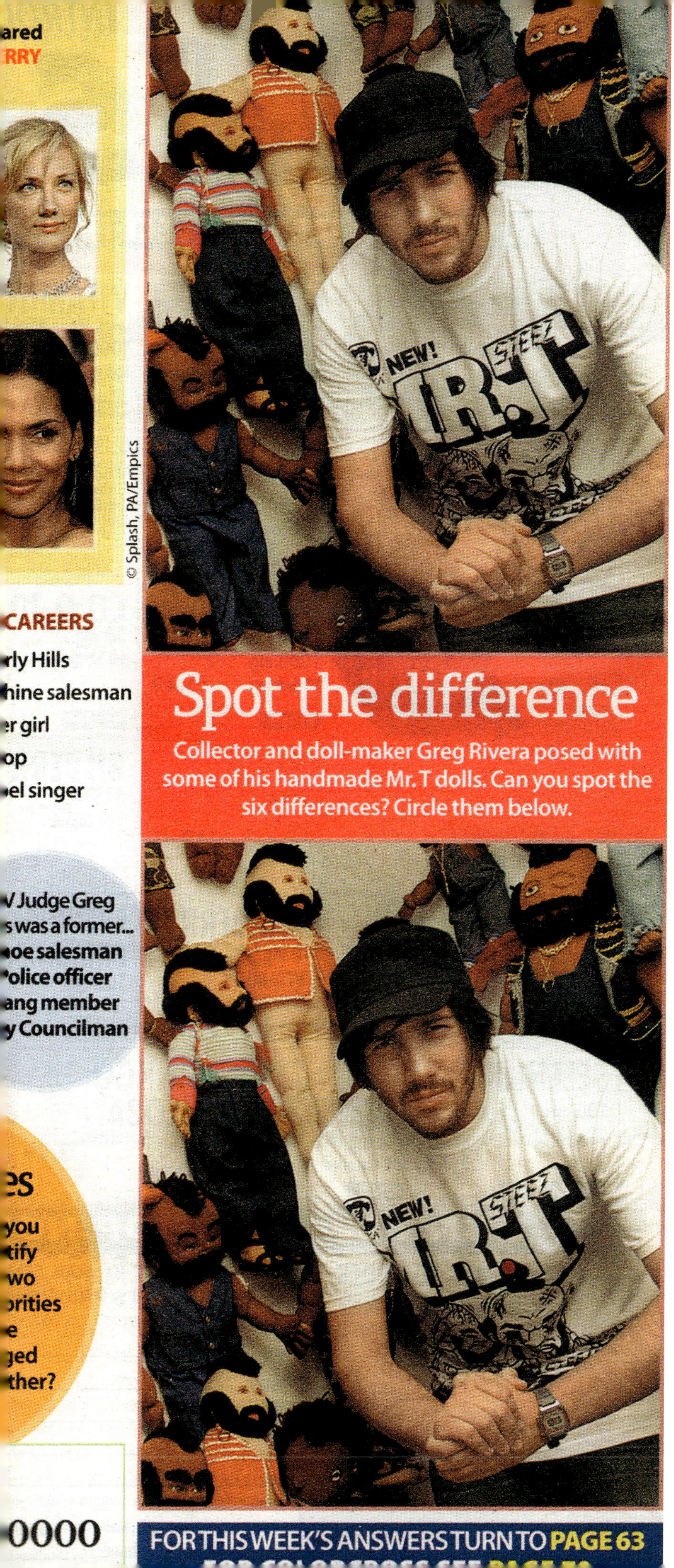
ared
RRY
© Splash, PA/Empics
CAREERS
rly Hills
hine salesman
r girl
op
el singer

Spot the difference

Collector and doll-maker Greg Rivera posed with some of his handmade Mr. T dolls. Can you spot the six differences? Circle them below.

V Judge Greg
s was a former...
oe salesman
olice officer
ang member
y Councilman

es
you
tify
wo
rities
e
ged
ther?

0000

FOR THIS WEEK'S ANSWERS TURN TO PAGE 63

What was it like appearing on TV to talk about your Mr. T collection?

I really liked it. I think Mike was a little embarrassed to appear on TV talking about our collection. I was just some dumb punk kid and more of a ham. We had to send a video into VH1 of why we wanted to be on the show, which I think is still online.

Since we're talking about press, let's fast-forward to my favorite press I received. I had this exhibition of my homemade Mr. T doll collection in 2005, at the Orchard Street Art Gallery. We got a lot of press, and one day this woman came in and said, "I'm an independent journalist and I pitch stuff to *People* magazine, the *National Enquirer*, lots of periodicals." I let her photograph me, and didn't really think much about it. One day I get a text message from somebody telling me that I was in the *National Enquirer*. I picked up the latest issue, I was flipping through the whole thing, and when I get to the last page I saw they had made a "spot the errors" game with two photos of me and my dolls.

They called me a doll maker, but I just took it for what it was. I never made any of the dolls.

That's the press for you, screwing everything up all the time. Why don't you make your own Mr. T doll?

I don't think I'm that crafty. I did think about it once; I guess I could, I just never tried to. Actually, the fabric they suggest to use is really hard to find nowadays. When I put the show together I had different artists make their own Mr. T dolls and they were struggling to find the right fabric.

Clipping from the National Enquirer.

FAR LEFT *Mister T pencil toppers. Unlicensed.*

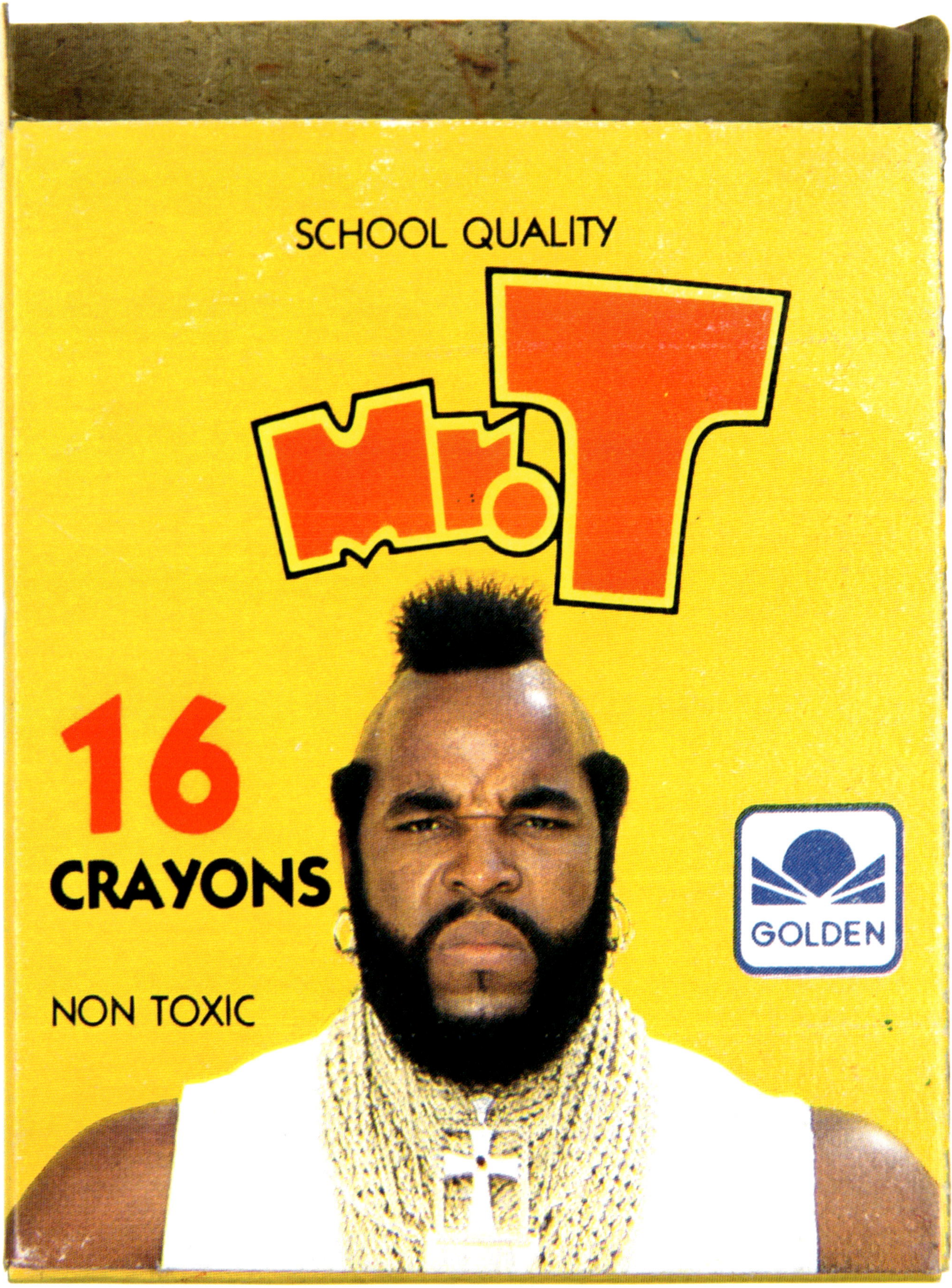
SCHOOL QUALITY
Mr. T
16
CRAYONS
NON TOXIC
GOLDEN

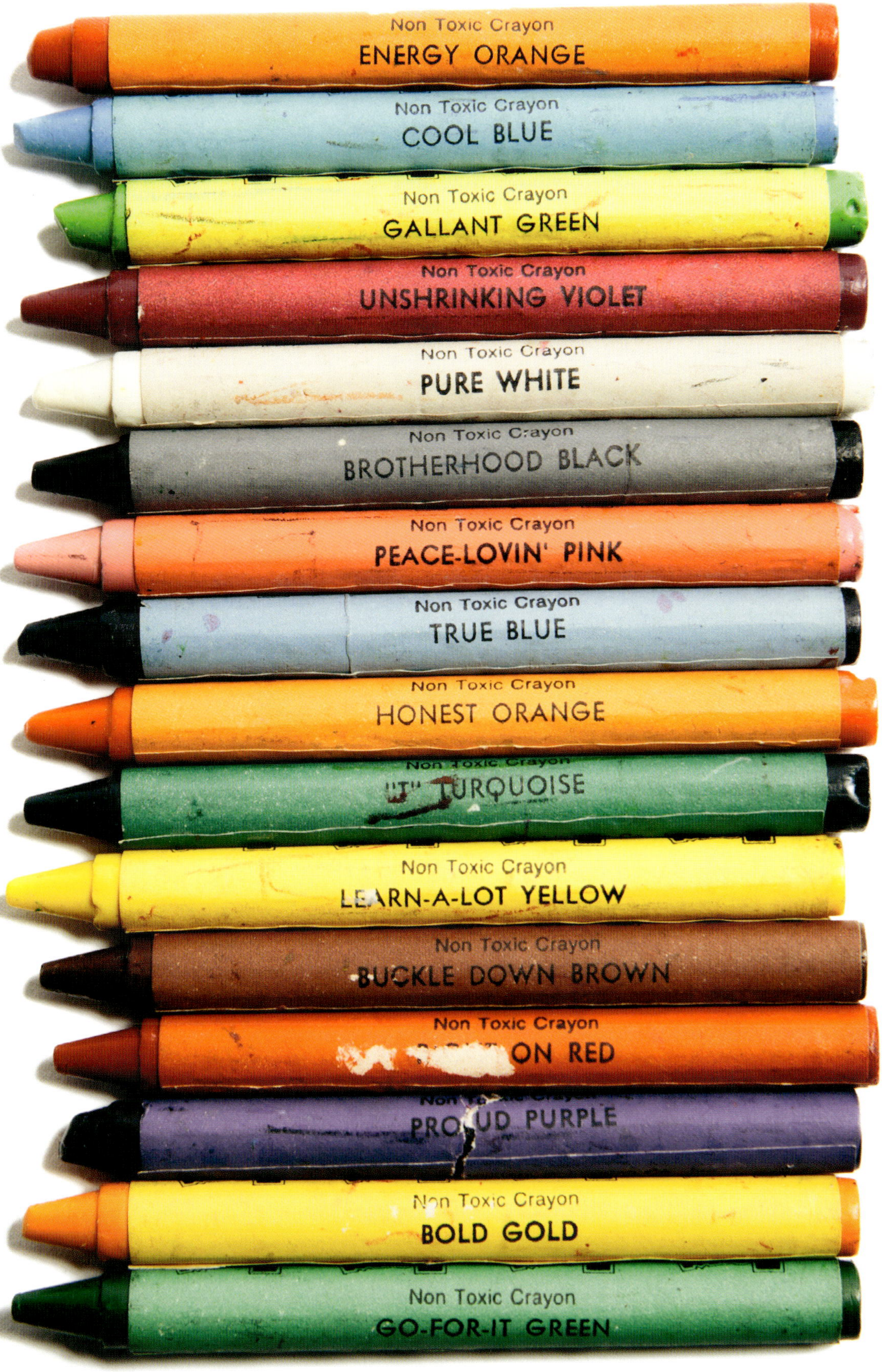

Mr. T crayons. Color names include Brotherhood Black, Honest Orange, and Right On Red.

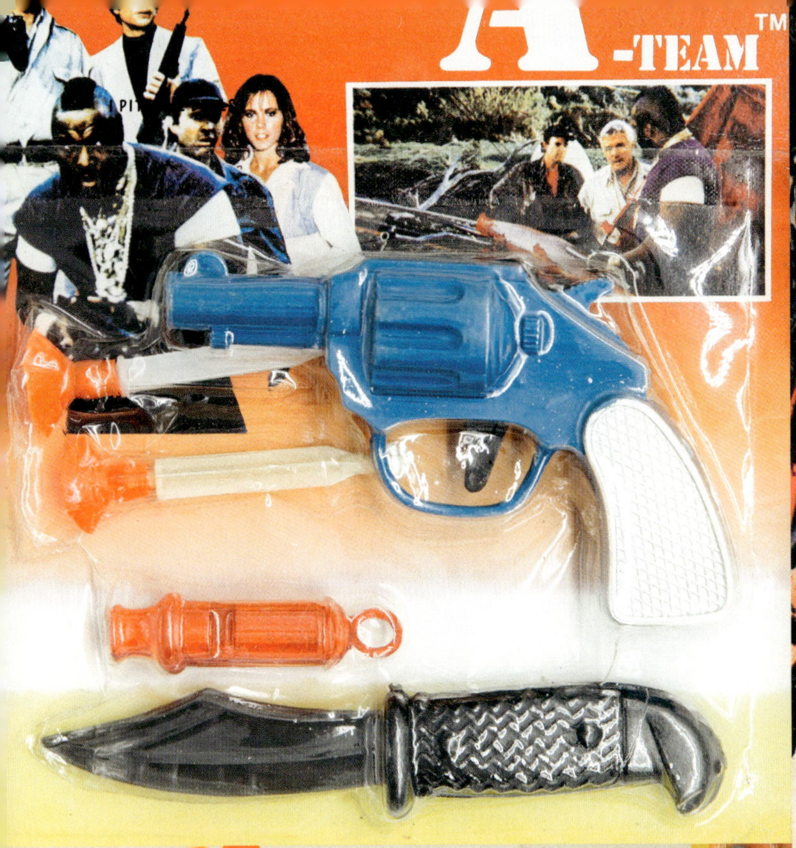
A-TEAM™

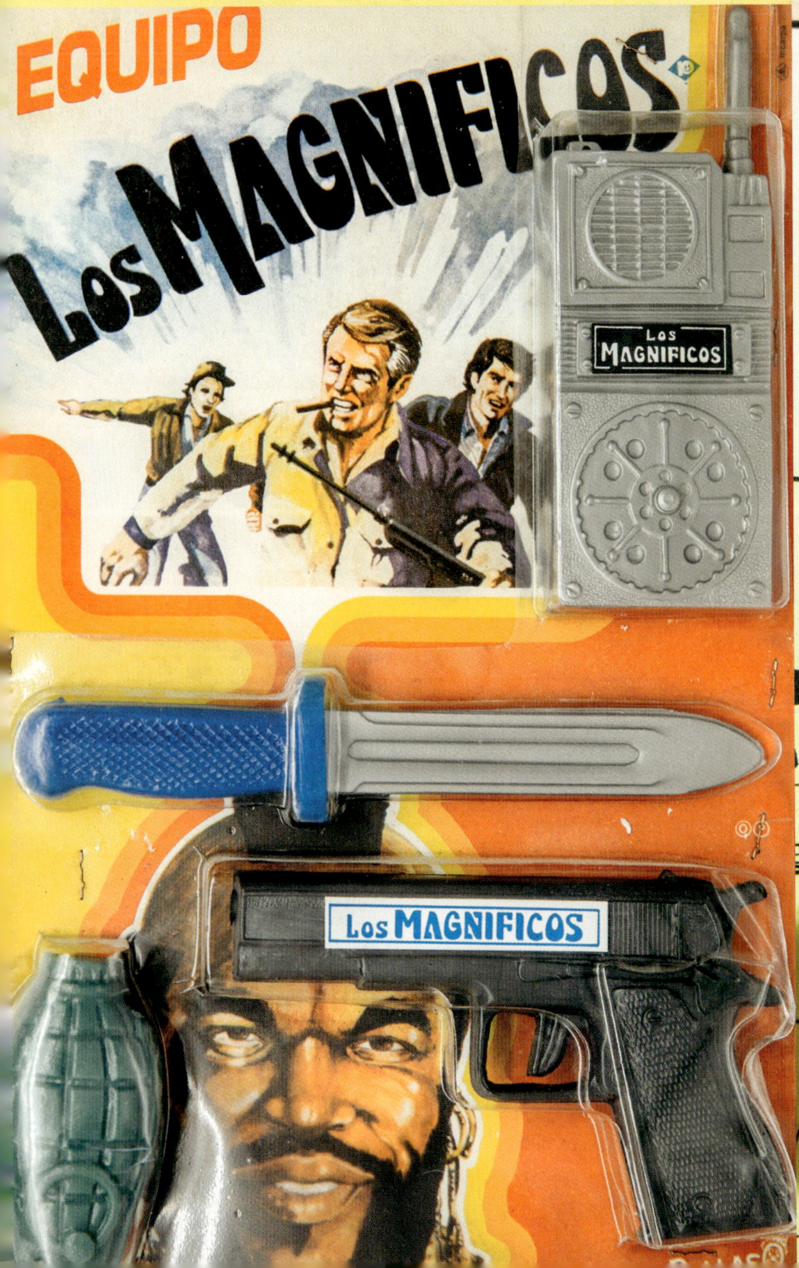
EQUIPO
Los MAGNIFICOS
LOS MAGNIFICOS
Los MAGNIFICOS

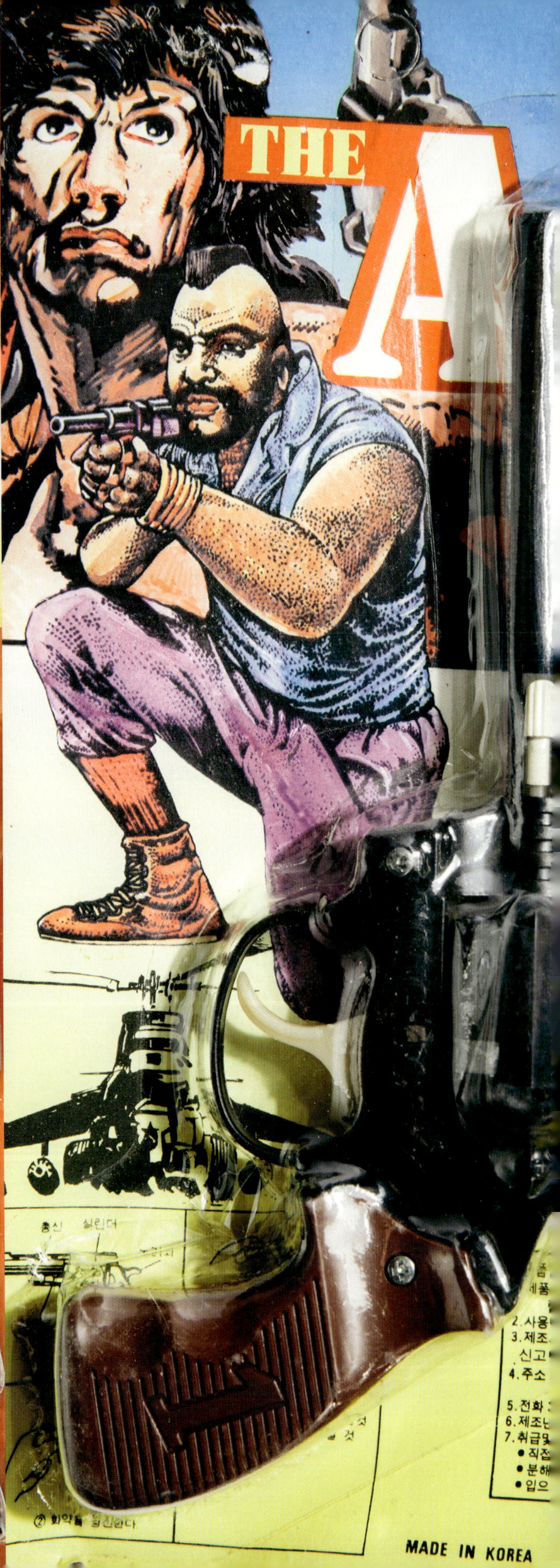
THE A
MADE IN KOREA

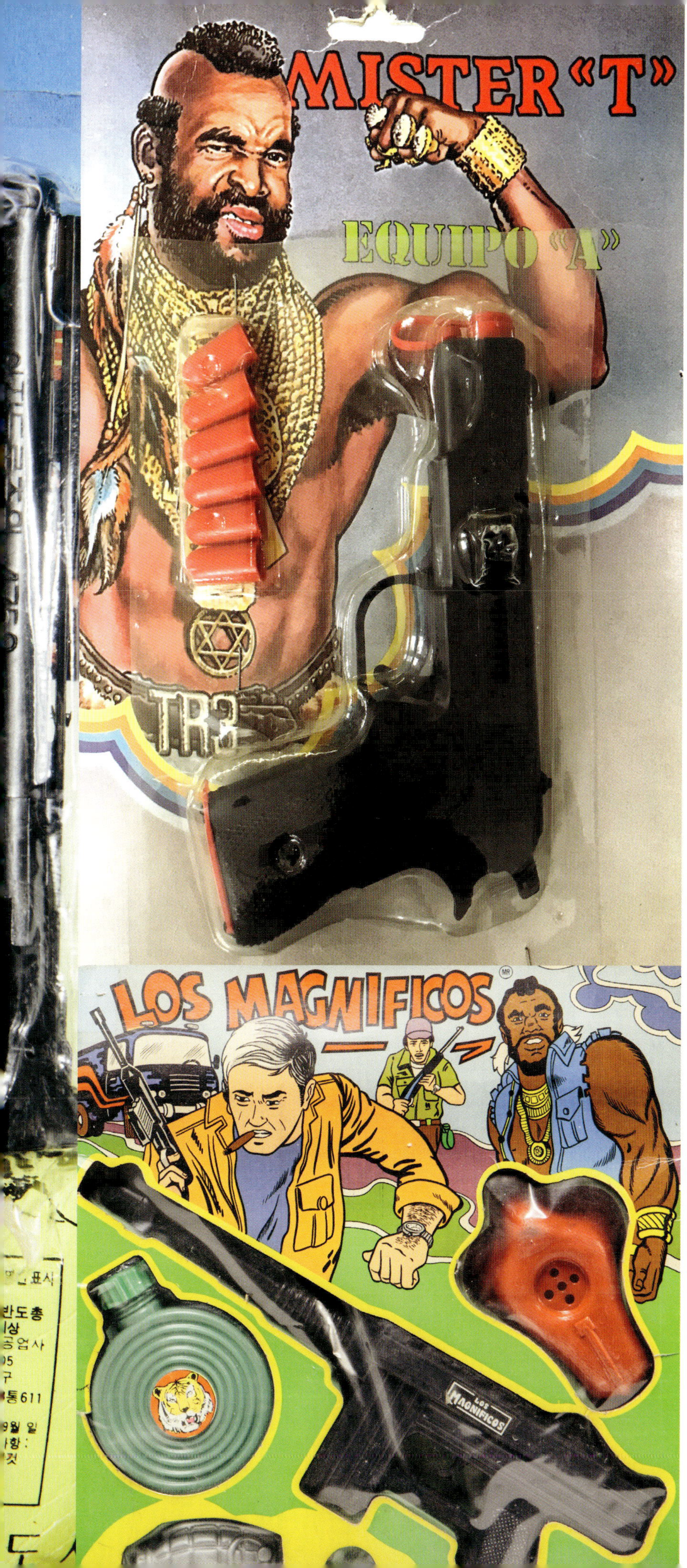

When was the first time you saw one of the handmade Mr. T dolls?
Brian, who owned Populuxe, eventually sold me his entire collection. I had ended up working there, and in lieu of getting paid I got Mr. T stuff. The one thing he wouldn't sell me was his handmade Mr. T doll that looked like a bootleg Cabbage Patch Kid. He also introduced me to eBay, and as soon as he did I literally started buying any and all custom Mr. T dolls that I saw.

How common were they at the time?
A couple would pop up every month, and I'd always win the auctions for between ten and twenty bucks.

They're all handmade and I appreciated how different each one was. Each one was a labor of love and each one represented the level of craftsmanship of each person who made them.

I loved that some adhered to the pattern, potentially made by a professional dollmaker. Then there were some that were just made for their kids as best they could manage.

When I was buying them on eBay, a lot of the descriptions would mention how the seller had made the doll for their son and that he hated it and left it in the closet. Now he was off to college and his parent was just trying to get rid of it.

Why did so many people think, "I know what my kid needs, a really soft cuddly Mr. T doll." It's not something that would obviously interest little girls, because it's not an infant like a Cabbage Patch doll. It seems too soft and cuddly to appeal to most little boys.
It's a grown-man doll that looks like George Jefferson.

CENTER *Unlicensed "Mister T" gun set. Uruguay.*

BOTTOM LEFT *Los Magnificos gun and grenade set.*

TOP LEFT *Licensed A-Team gun and knife set. Stephen J. Cannel Productions, 1983.*

BOTTOM RIGHT *Los Magnificos weapon set. Argentina.*

TOP RIGHT *Unlicensed gun set with Rambo. South Korea.*

Everybody wanted a Cabbage Patch Kid doll and couldn't get them. All these companies were making their own doll patterns. Then Martha Holcombe came up with the idea of making a Mr. T version. Cabbage Patch was popular and Mr. T was popular, so she combined them.

It's actually really hard to make the doll exactly the way the pattern book instructs you to. I think that's why they look so unique. Some people couldn't get the exact fabric. Some people painted the eyes; some people embroidered the eyes; some people got the transfer eyes. Some people handmade the clothes; other people just went and bought baby clothes, which didn't fit right.

Thousands of parents investing all this time to hand-make dolls that looked like Mr. T is very odd to me.

I think that's what probably attracted me to it. I was talking to Martha Holcombe the other day, and she mentioned that at one time Walmart was one of her biggest customers, and she was selling them thousands of doll patterns a month.

Which of the dolls are your favorites?

There's a few that we've kind of given names to. There's Sinbad. He looks like Sinbad, Gary Coleman, John Belushi, and Eric Wareheim.

There's one that looks like a Bollywood star. He's got orange skin and he's got this really flashy outfit on. There's another guy who has bushy eyebrows. We call him Evil T. There's also a lot of Baby Ts. There's the ones that have the beard but no mustache; I call them the Amish Ts. Then there's a few that are anatomically correct.

How many have dicks? And how many of them also have dicks and balls?

I think all the ones that have dicks also have balls. There's not just a dick coming out of it.

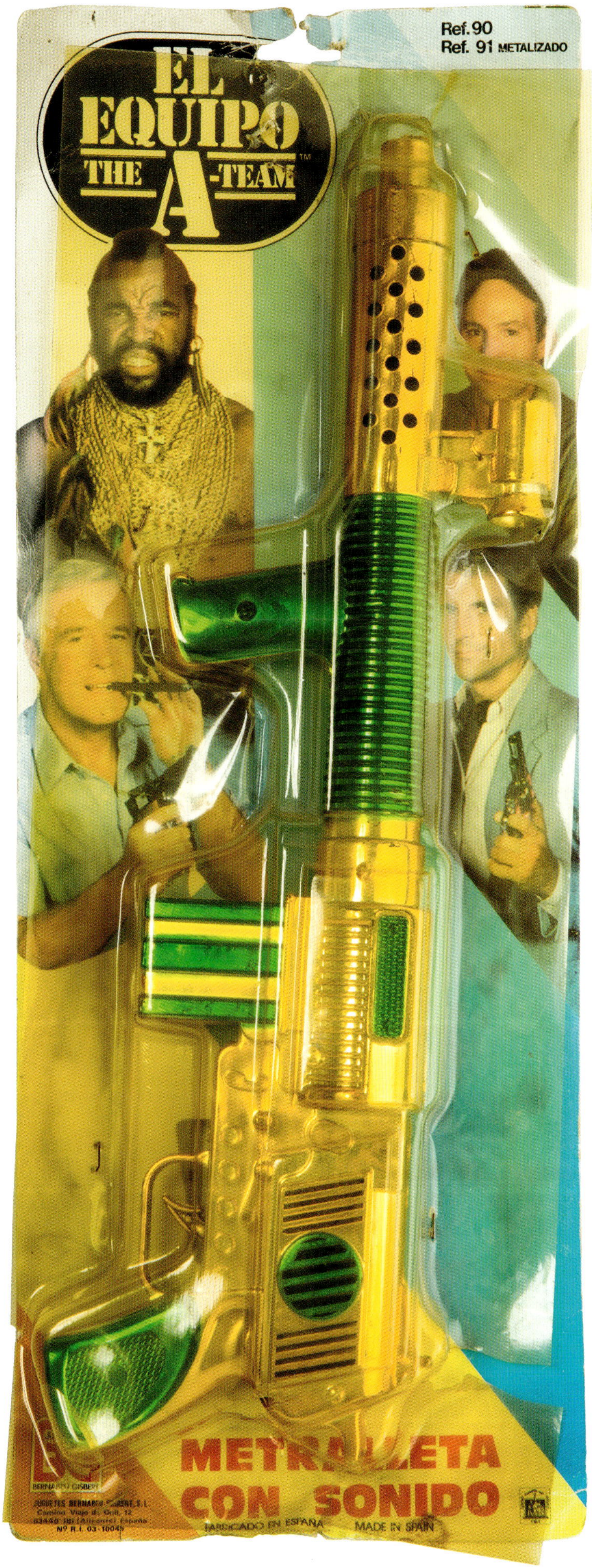

El Equipo submachine gun with sound. Spain.

RIGHT *Licensed guns: AK-47, B. A. Blaster, and M-16. Notice: no orange tip. Very realistic!*

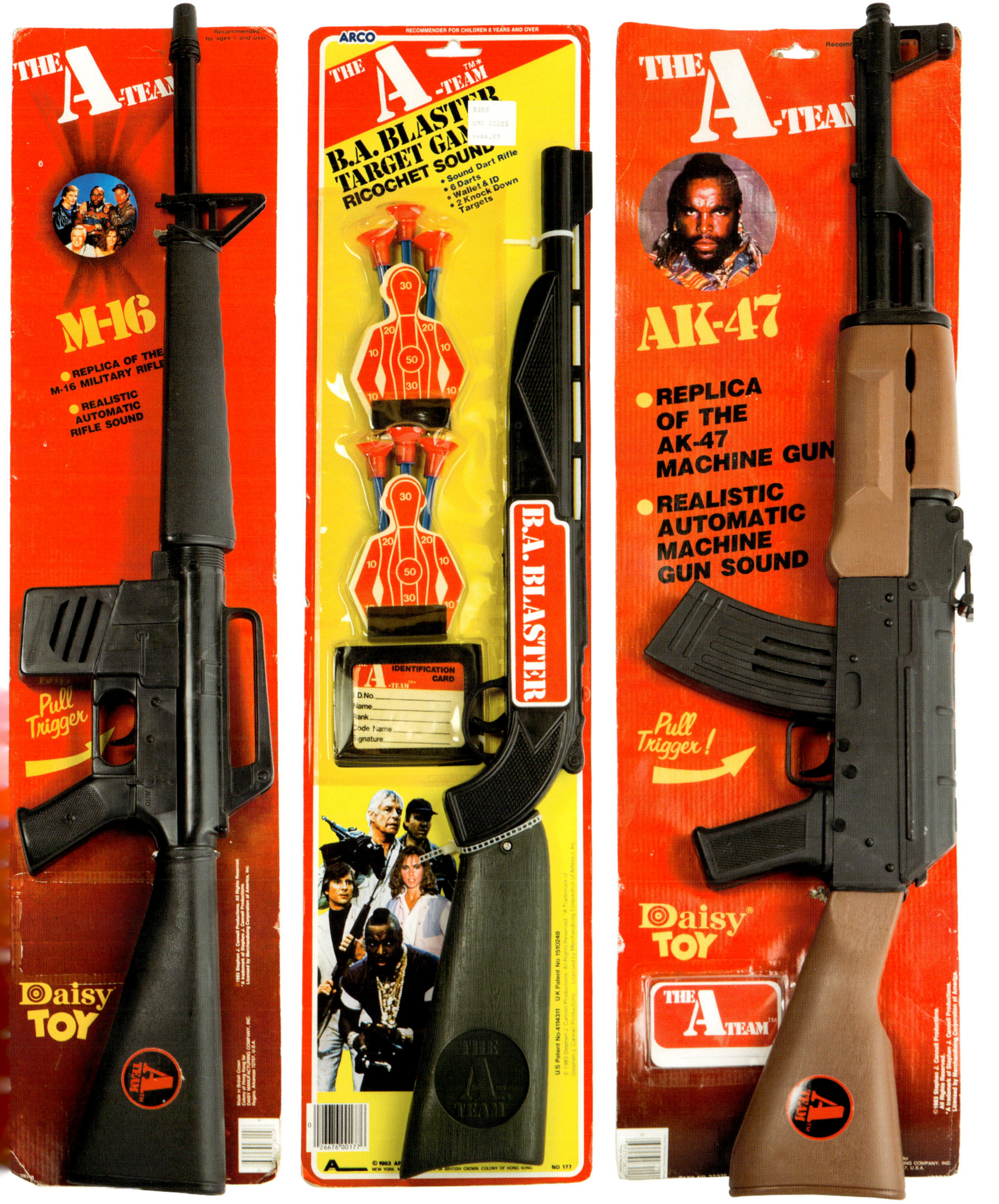
THE A-TEAM
M-16
REPLICA OF THE M-16 MILITARY RIFLE
REALISTIC AUTOMATIC RIFLE SOUND
Pull Trigger
Daisy TOY
ARCO
THE A-TEAM
B.A. BLASTER
TARGET GAM
RICOCHET SOUND
Sound Dart Rifle
6 Darts
Wallet & ID
2 Knock Down Targets
IDENTIFICATION CARD
B.A. BLASTER
NO 177
THE A-TEAM
AK-47
REPLICA OF THE AK-47 MACHINE GUN
REALISTIC AUTOMATIC MACHINE GUN SOUND
Pull Trigger!
Daisy TOY
THE A TEAM

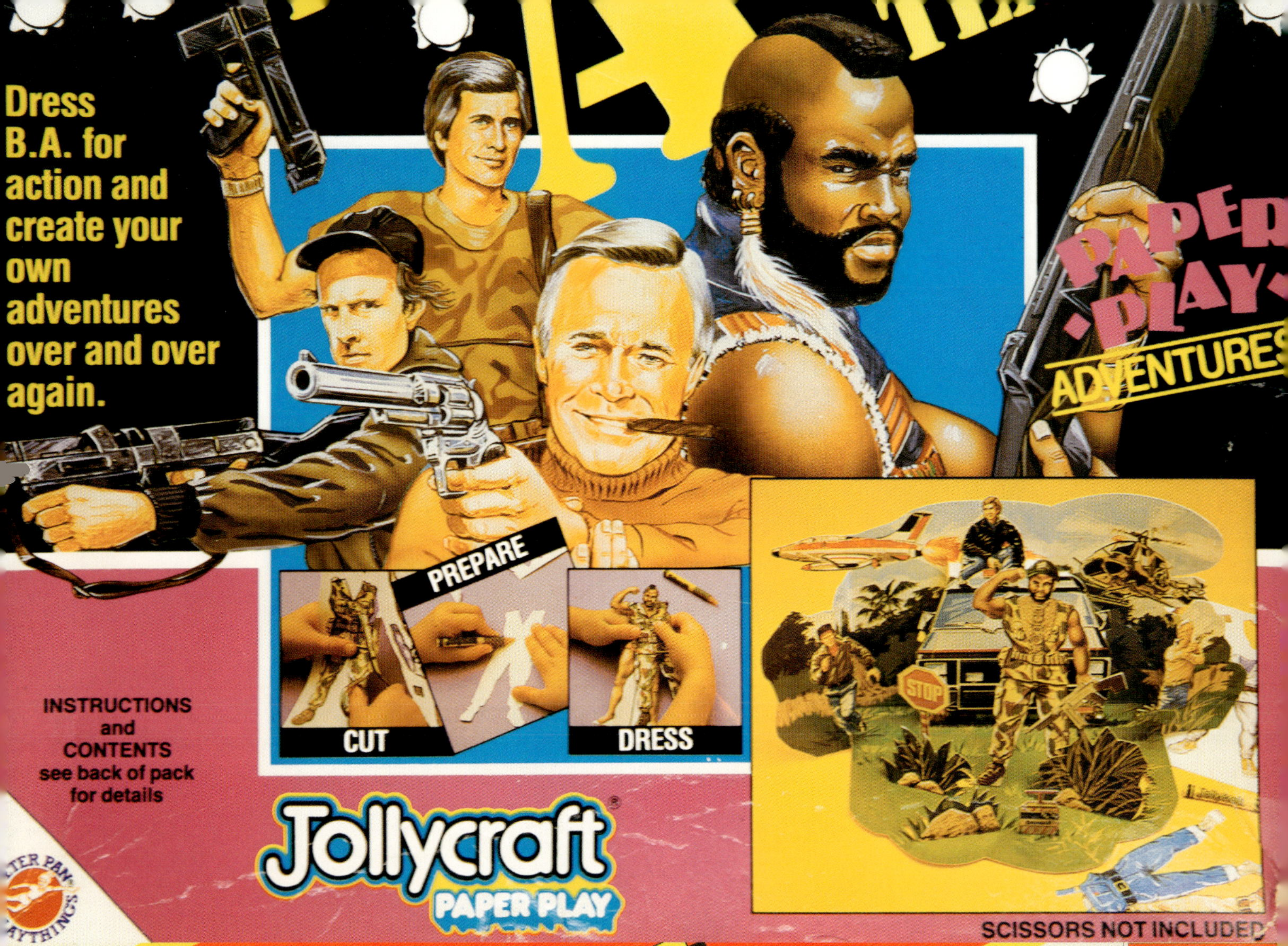
Dress B.A. for action and create your own adventures over and over again.
PAPER PLAY ADVENTURES
PREPARE
CUT
DRESS
STOP
INSTRUCTIONS and CONTENTS see back of pack for details
Jollycraft
PAPER PLAY
SCISSORS NOT INCLUDED

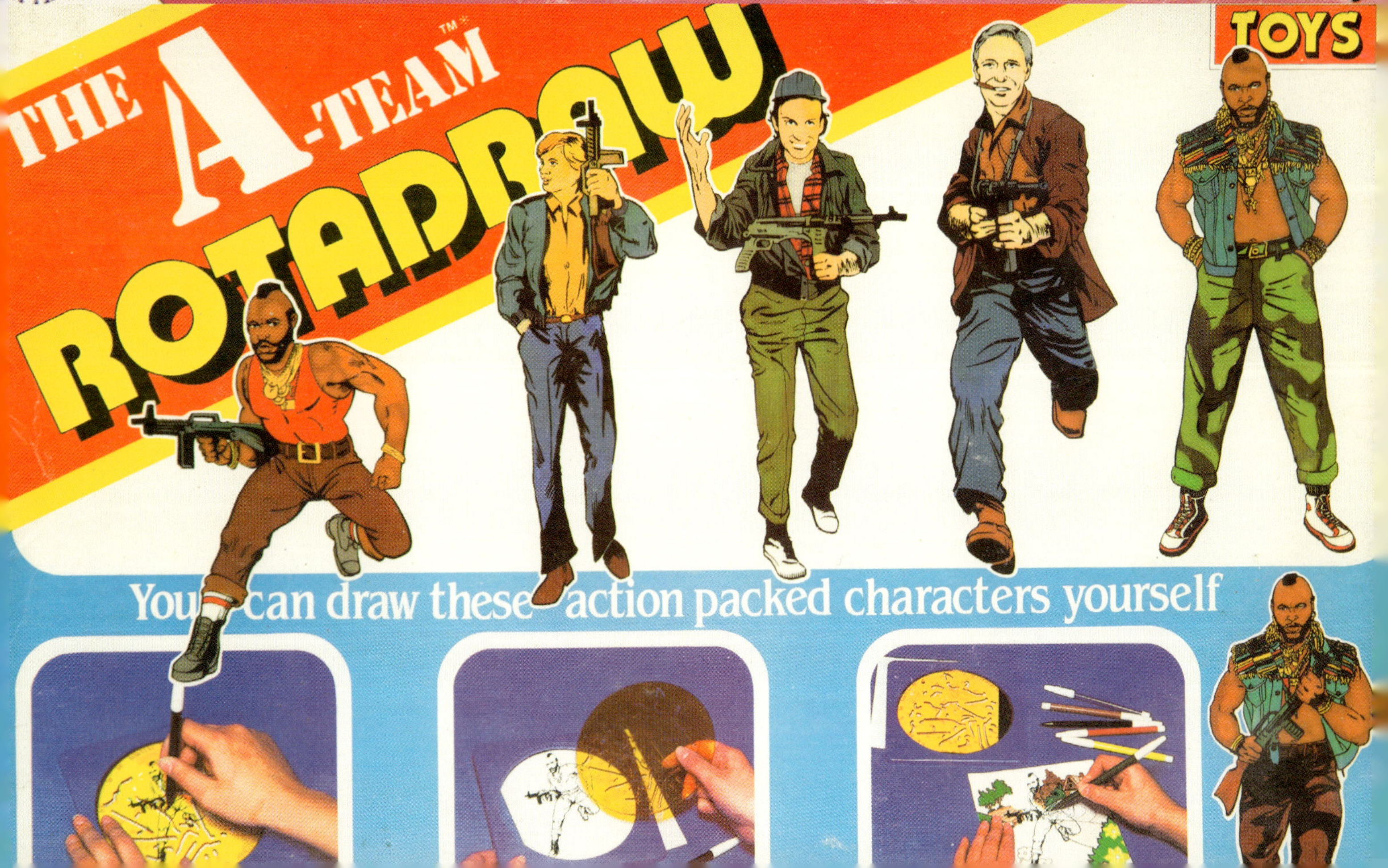
THE A-TEAM
ROTADRAW
TOYS
You can draw these action packed characters yourself

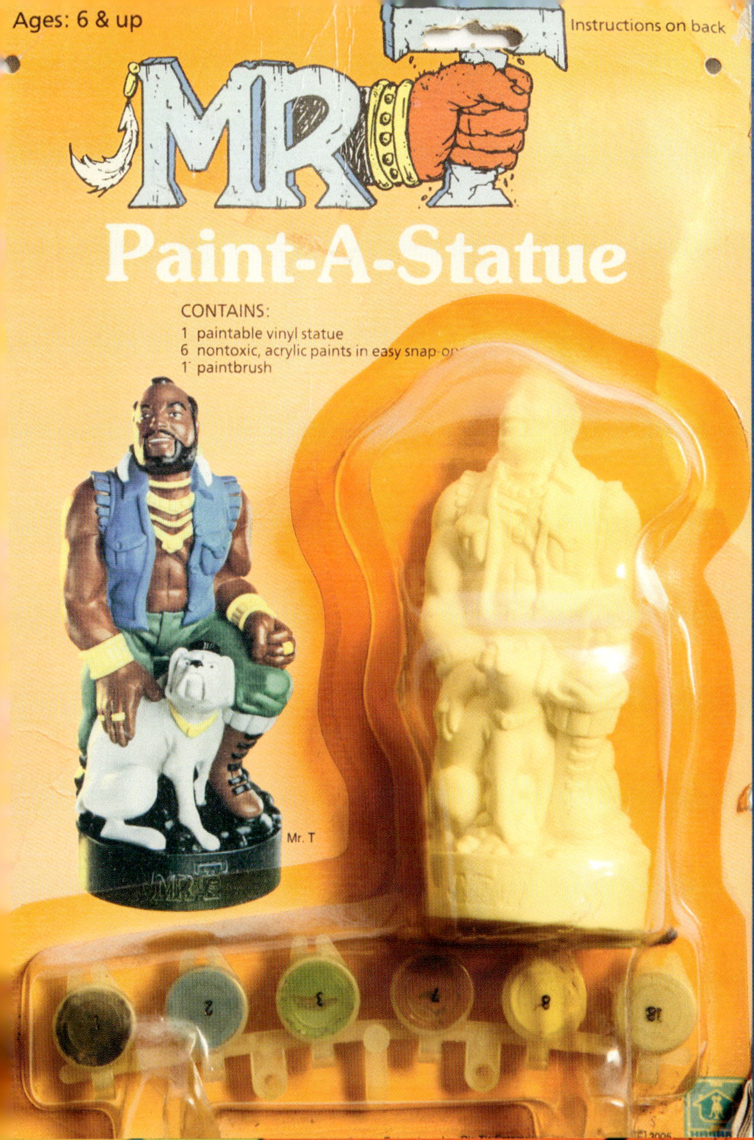
Ages: 6 & up
Instructions on back
MR T
Paint-A-Statue
CONTAINS:
1 paintable vinyl statue
6 nontoxic, acrylic paints in easy snap-on
1 paintbrush
Mr. T

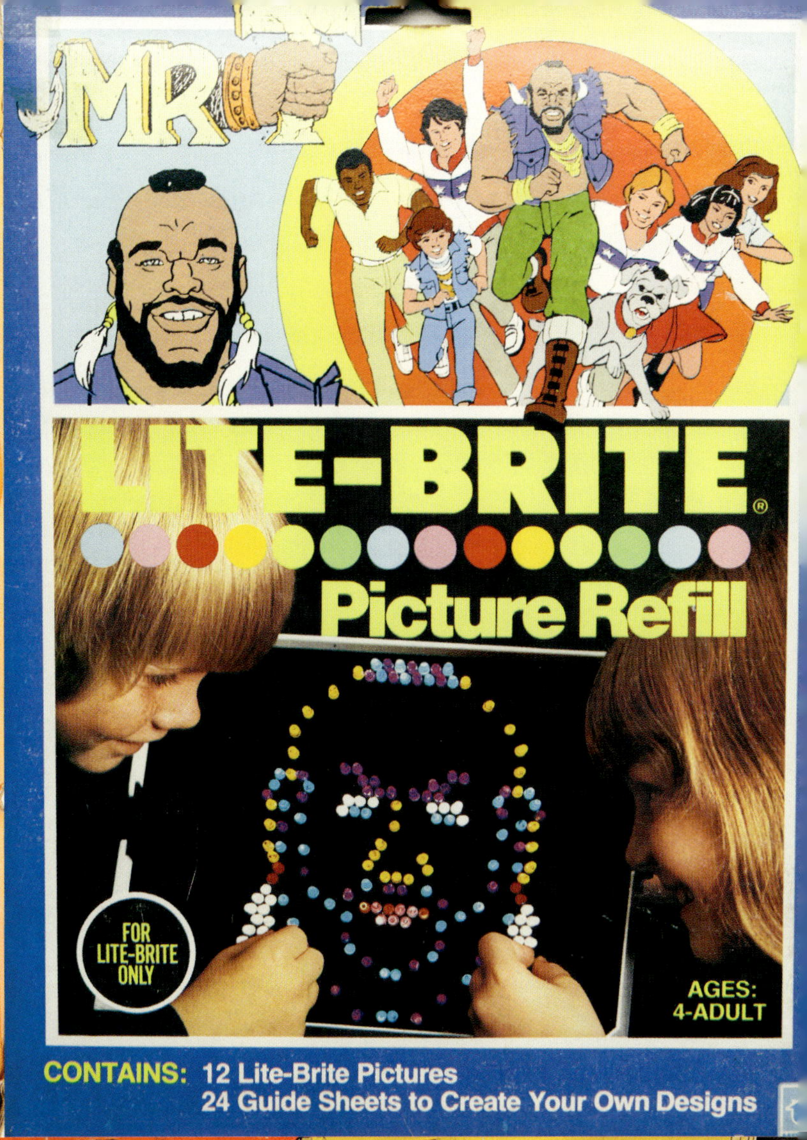
MR T
LITE-BRITE®
Picture Refill
FOR LITE-BRITE ONLY
AGES: 4-ADULT
CONTAINS: 12 Lite-Brite Pictures
24 Guide Sheets to Create Your Own Designs

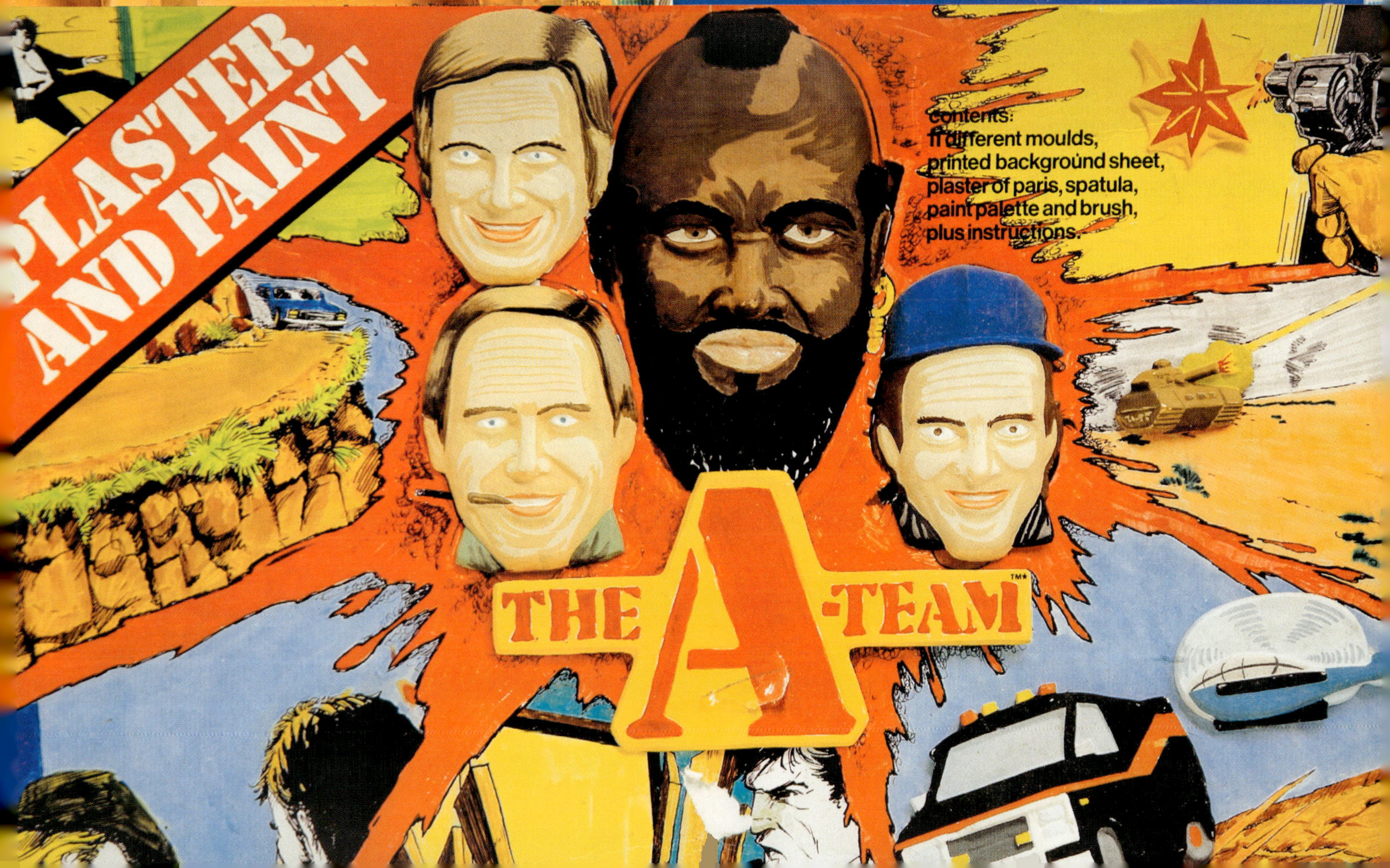
PLASTER AND PAINT
contents:
11 different moulds,
printed background sheet,
plaster of paris, spatula,
paint palette and brush,
plus instructions.
THE A-TEAM™

That wasn't in the original pattern, was it?
No, somebody decided to do that and I'm still trying to figure out why. Martha thinks there was a point where people were making the dolls for adults. But I wanted to think that it was more like hippie sex positivity.

Do you collect the dolls even if they don't have a complete outfit?
I like to leave the dolls as they are. Occasionally over the years when I've seen toddler Nikes or little boots at a thrift store, I've bought them for the dolls. But, generally, all the dolls that I have are as I found them. A lot of times people ask, "Why is this doll naked?" or "Why doesn't this doll have pants?" At some point the pants were lost and this is just how it is.

How many of those Mr. T dolls have you got?
I think about two hundred.

Do you still buy them?
I've been trying not to buy any more because I feel it's kind of pointless. There was a time where I thought I was going to collect them all, but I've collected enough of them and who knows how many were made? If you just had one, people would be amazed, and then if you had fifty, people would be even more blown away. Having two hundred, people respond with "Wow, this is kind of crazy."

I wouldn't describe you as* kind of *crazy, Greg. Do you think you have a disease called T-mania perhaps?
I do.

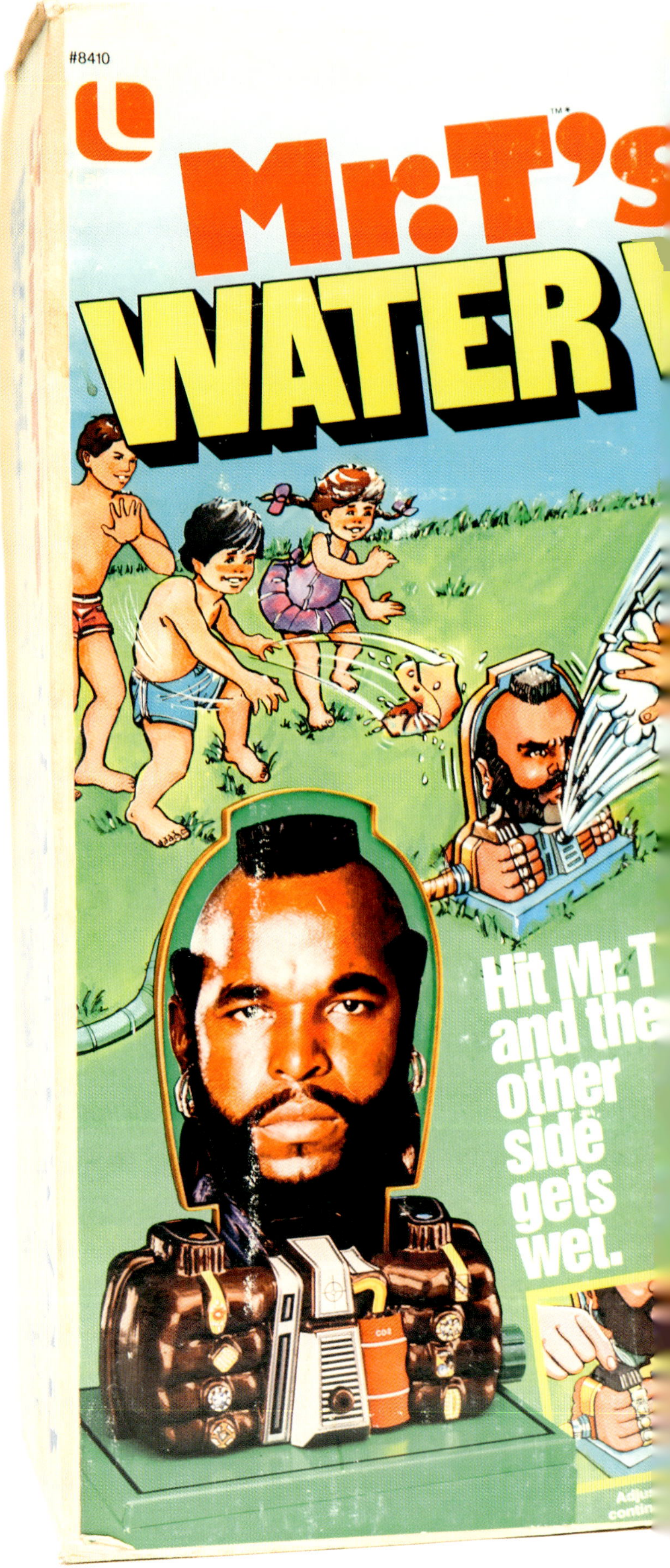

Mr. T's Water War. One of the most bizarre items made with the Big T license. Be the first to throw a wet sponge at Mr.T's head and water sprays from his rings! Leisure Dynamics Inc., 1983.

PREVIOUS SPREAD *The A-Team Paper Play Adventures. Jolycraft, 1980s. Mr. T Paint-A-Statue. Hasbro, 1980s. Lite-Brite picture refill. Hasbro, 1980s. The A-Team Plaster and Paint, UK. The A-Team Rotodraw. Salters Toys, 1980s.*

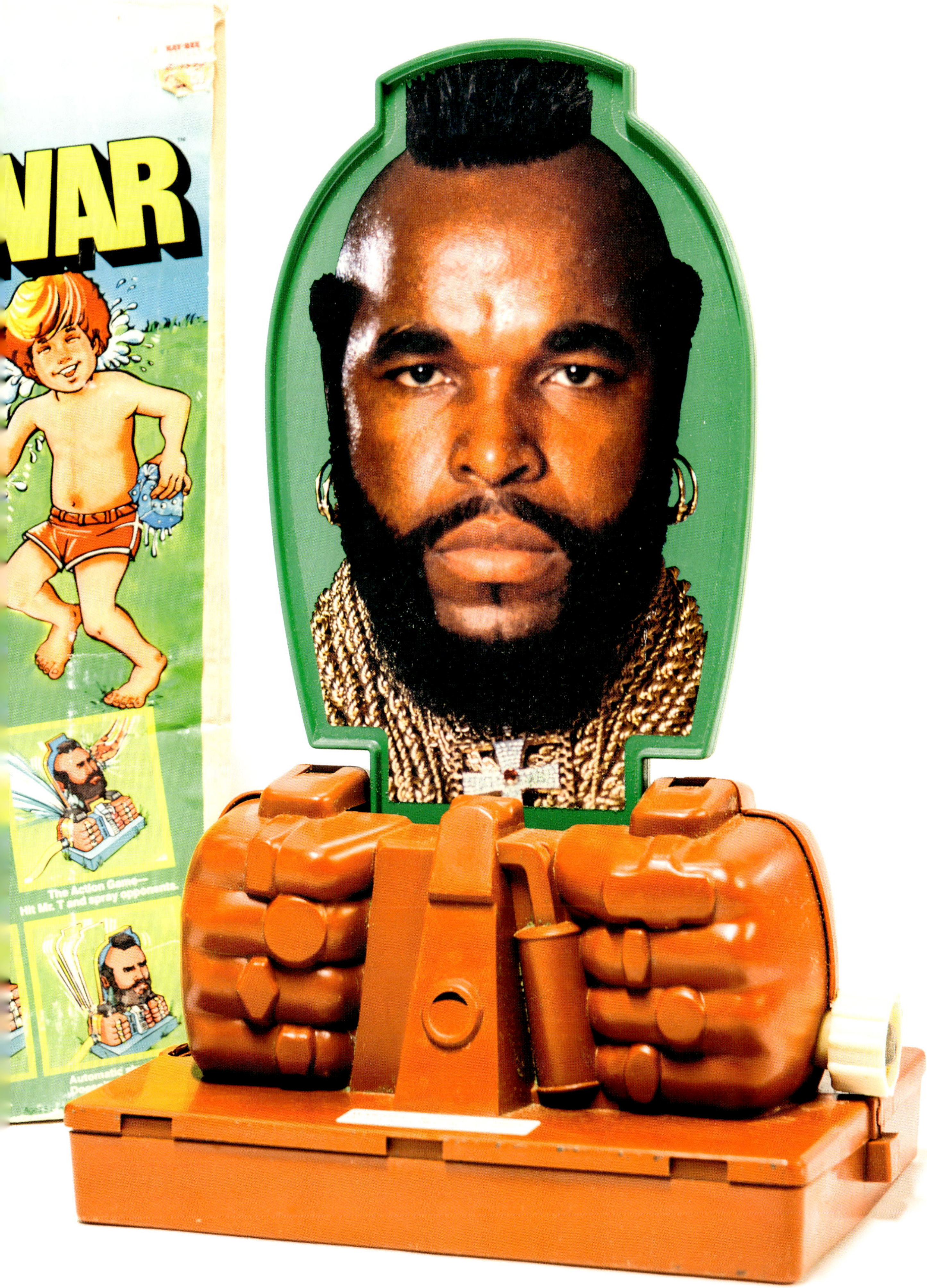
WAR
The Action Game—
Hit Mr. T and spray opponents.

FAR RIGHT *Licensed Mr. T plastic bank. This bank was used to make countless unlicensed knock-offs, including on the far right, which was from a pop-culture shop in Boston, as well as the cookie jar by an unknown maker in the back. The salt and pepper shakers as well as the small ceramic bank are from the UK. The back plaster figure is an unlicensed but seemingly available sculpt from the 1980s.*

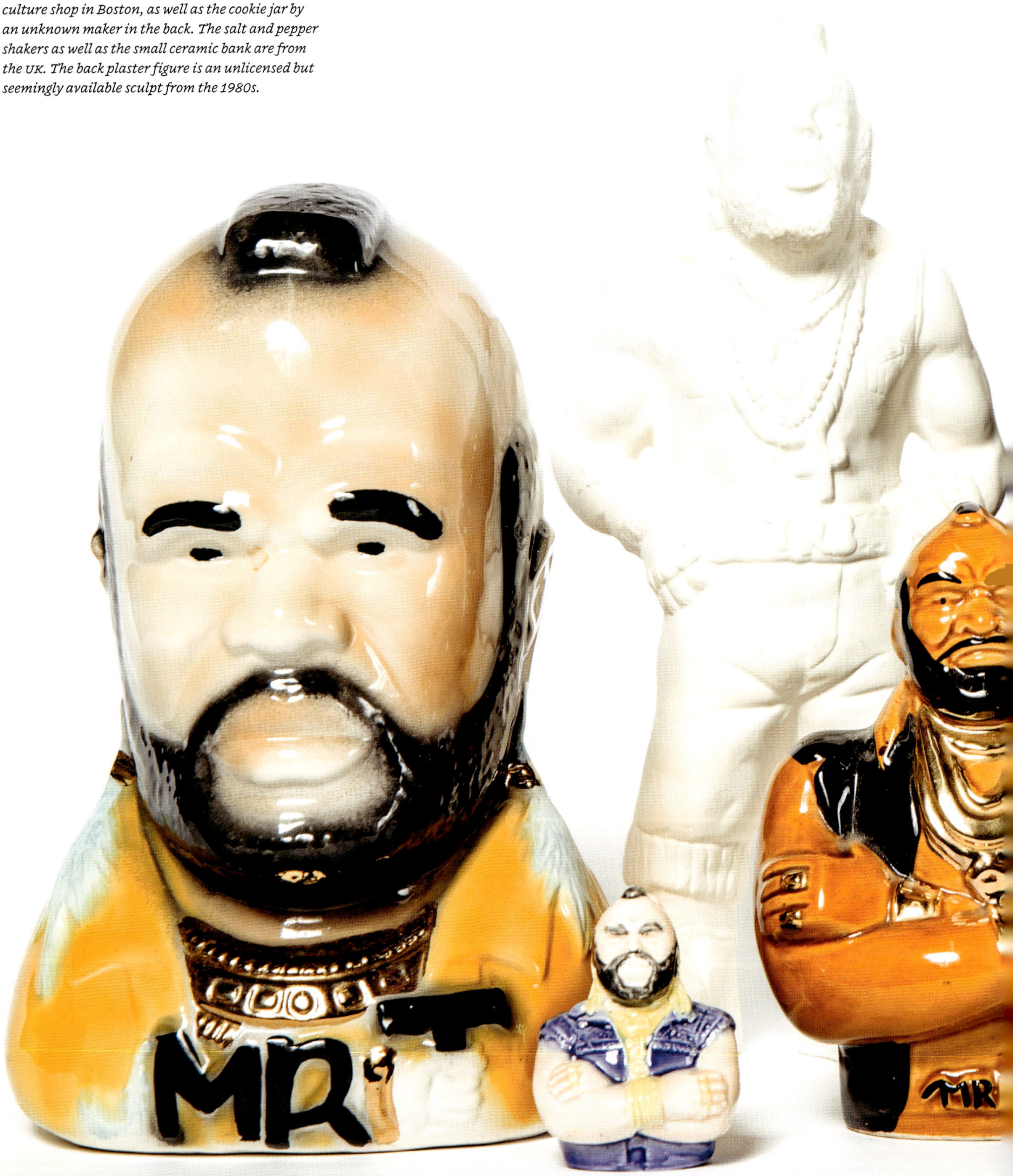

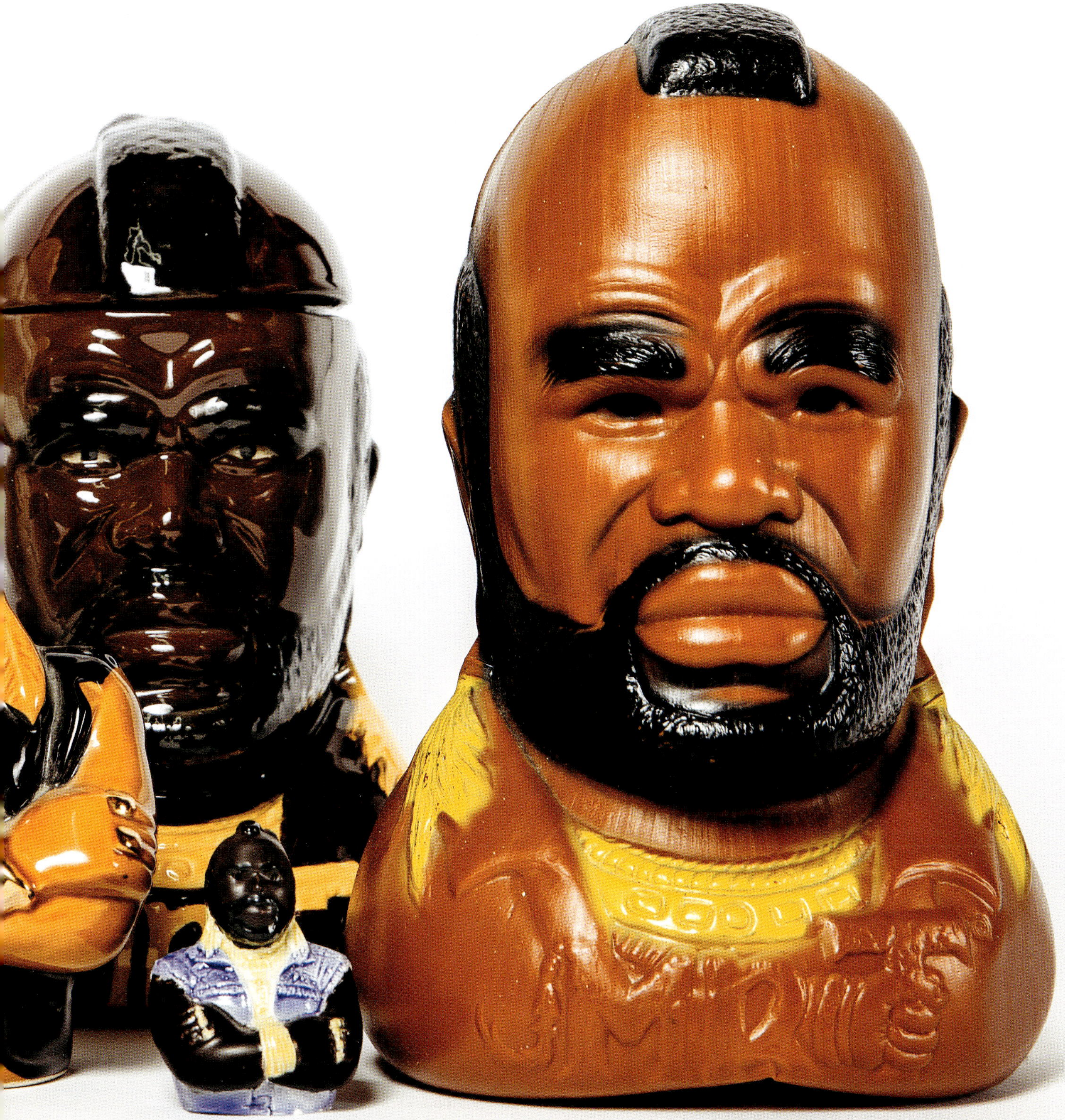

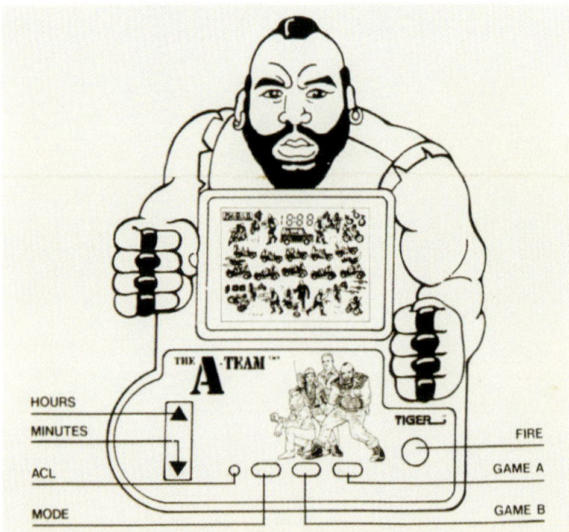
THE A-TEAM
TIGER
HOURS
MINUTES
ACL
MODE
FIRE
GAME A
GAME B

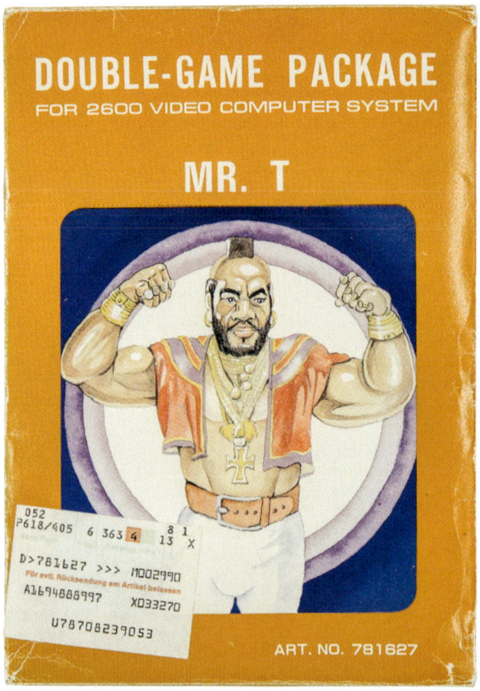
DOUBLE-GAME PACKAGE
FOR 2600 VIDEO COMPUTER SYSTEM
MR. T
ART. NO. 781627

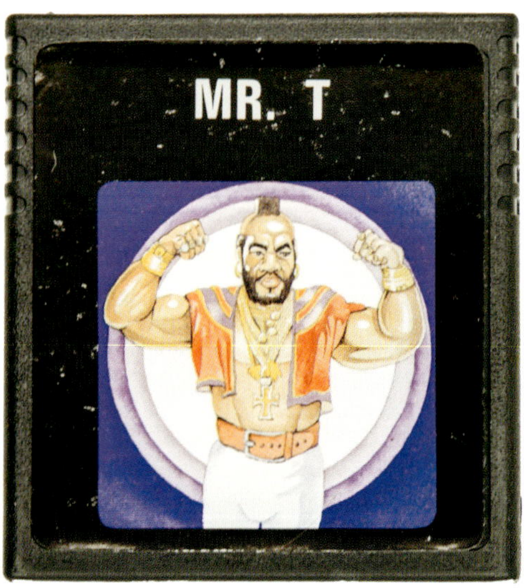
MR. T

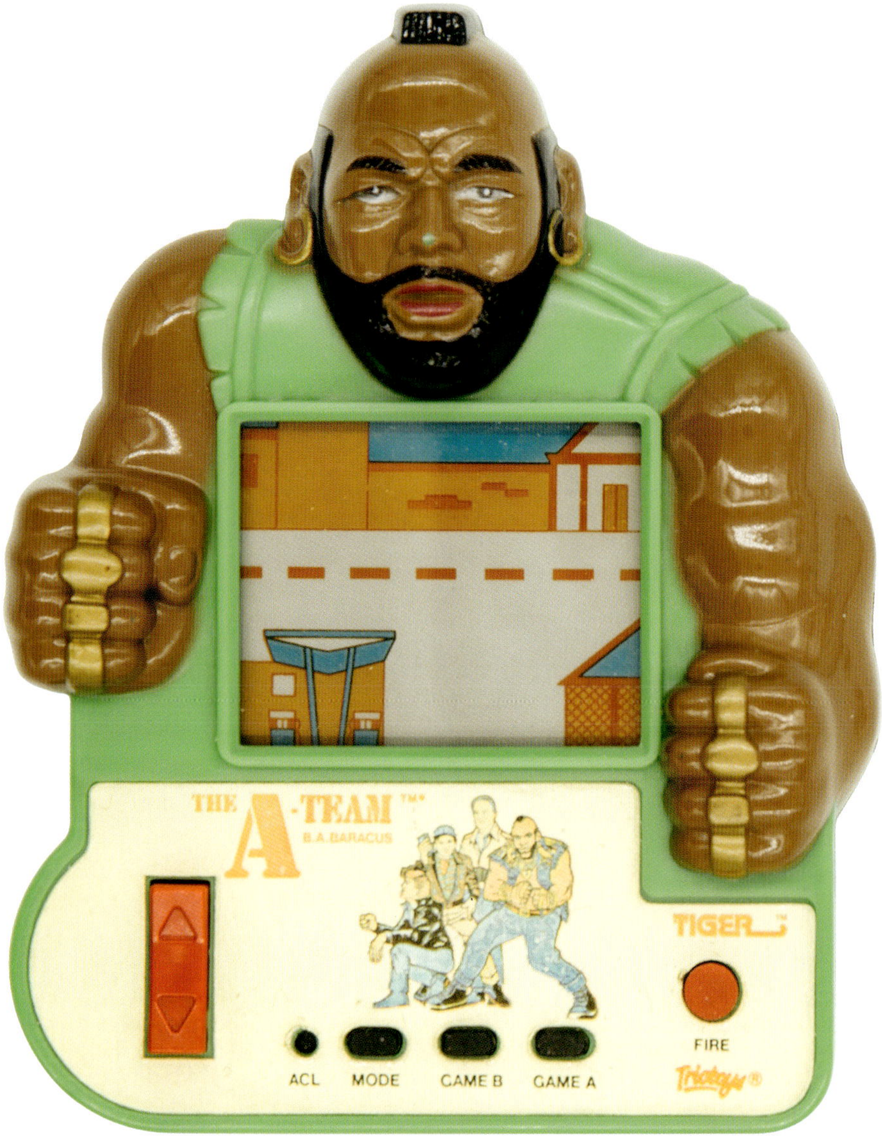
THE A-TEAM
B.A. BARACUS
TIGER
FIRE
ACL
MODE
GAME B
GAME A

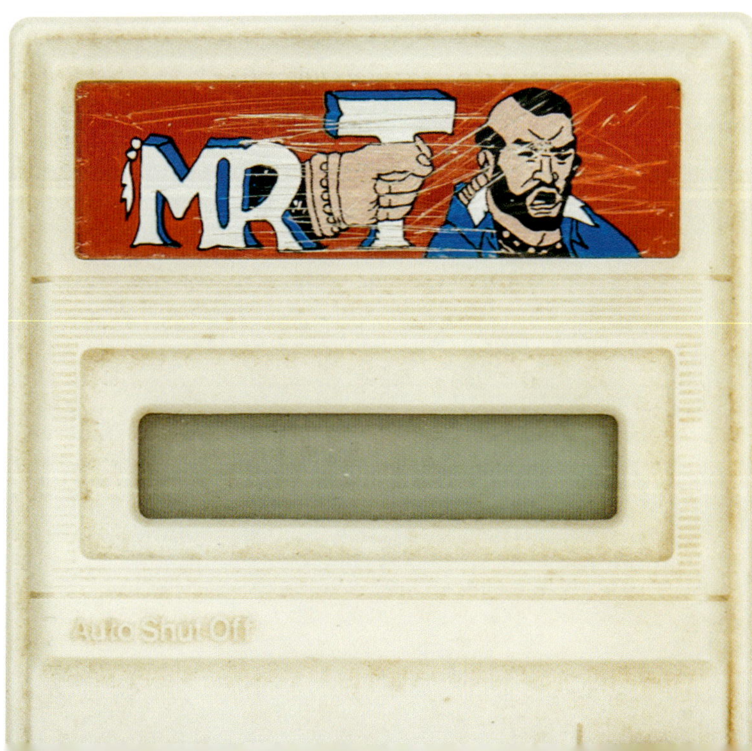
MR T
Auto Shut Off

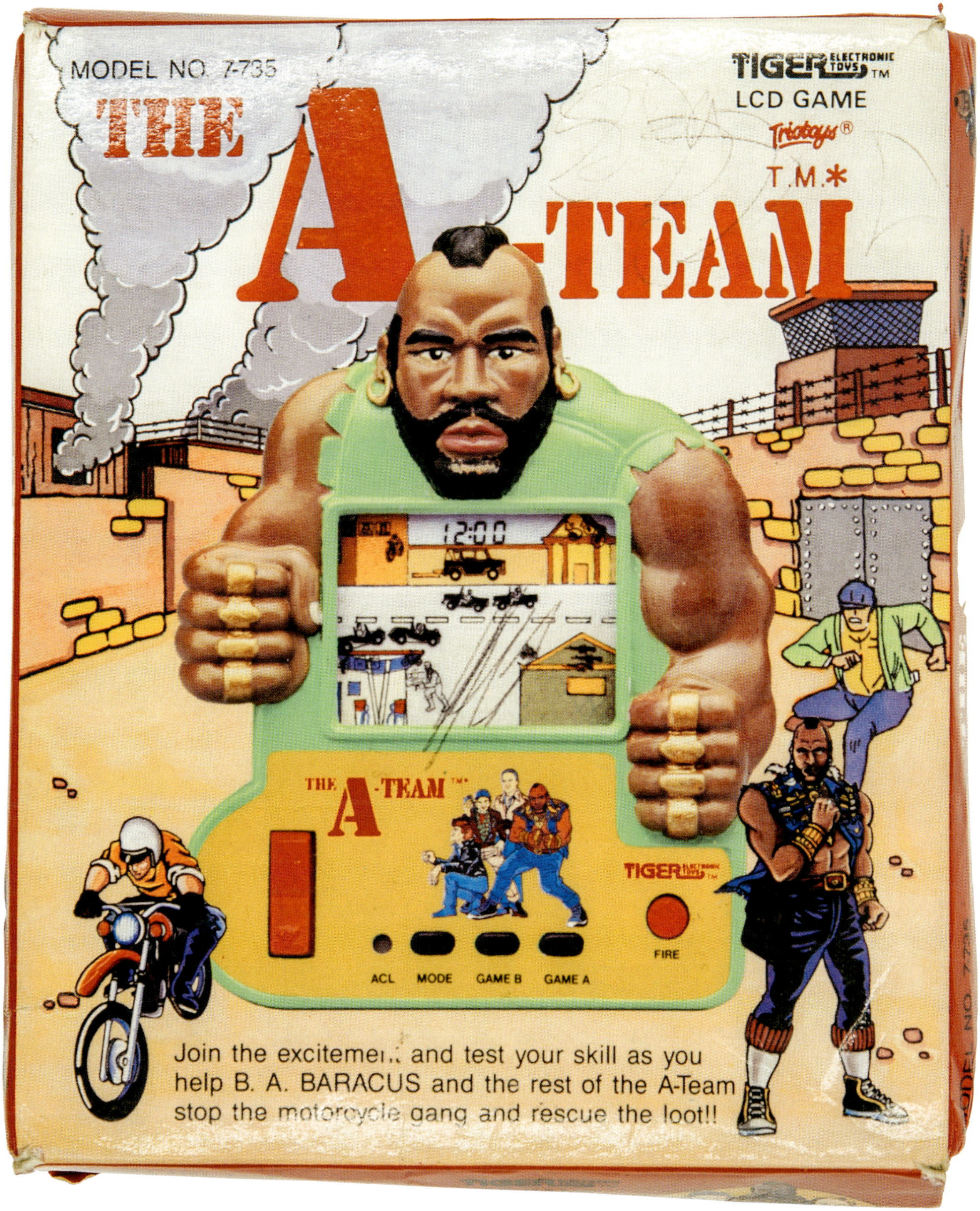

A-Team video games and a Mr. T calculator.

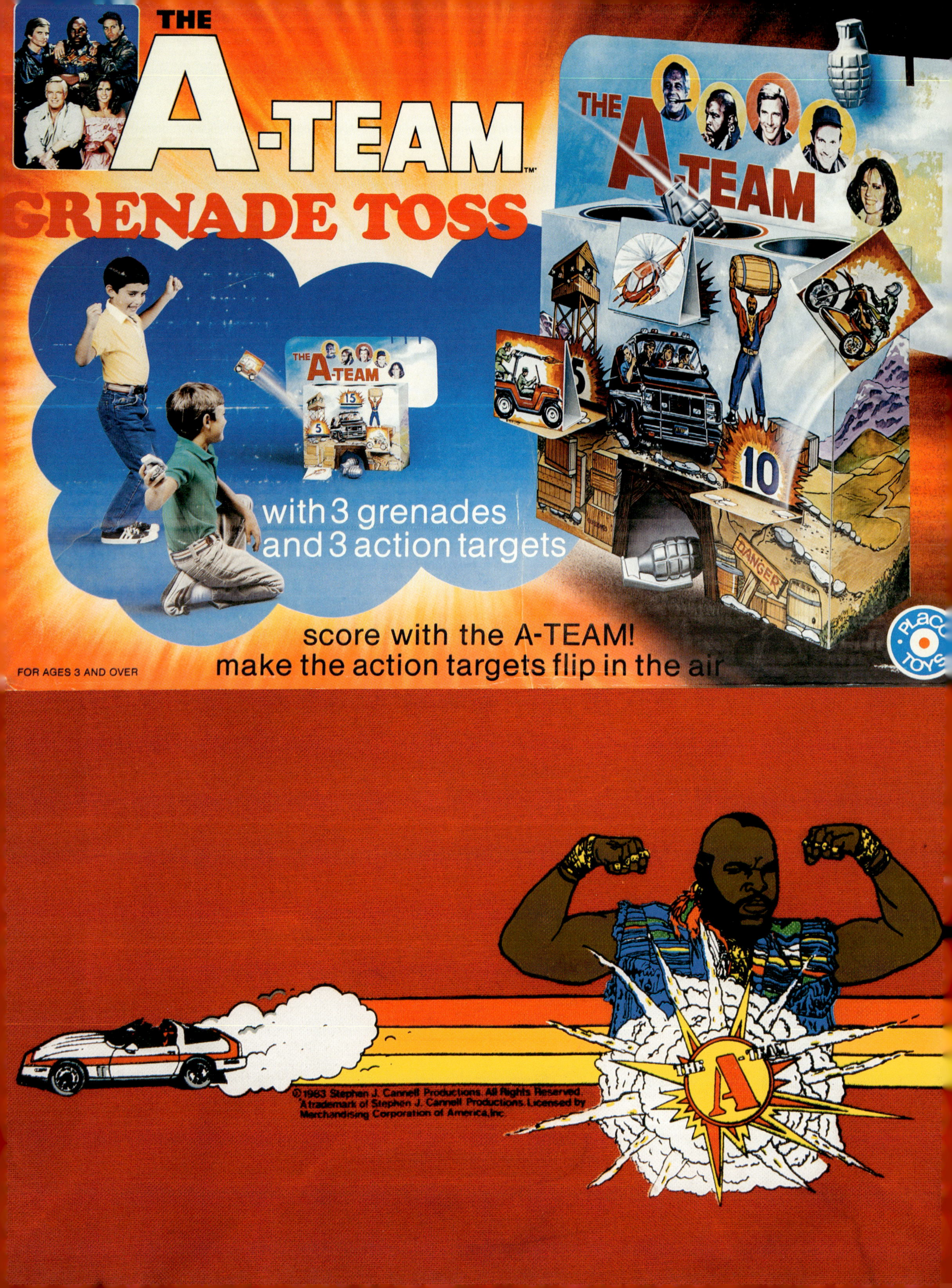
THE A-TEAM™
GRENADE TOSS
with 3 grenades
and 3 action targets
score with the A-TEAM!
make the action targets flip in the air
FOR AGES 3 AND OVER
DANGER
© 1983 Stephen J. Cannell Productions. All Rights Reserved.
*A trademark of Stephen J. Cannell Productions. Licensed by Merchandising Corporation of America, Inc.

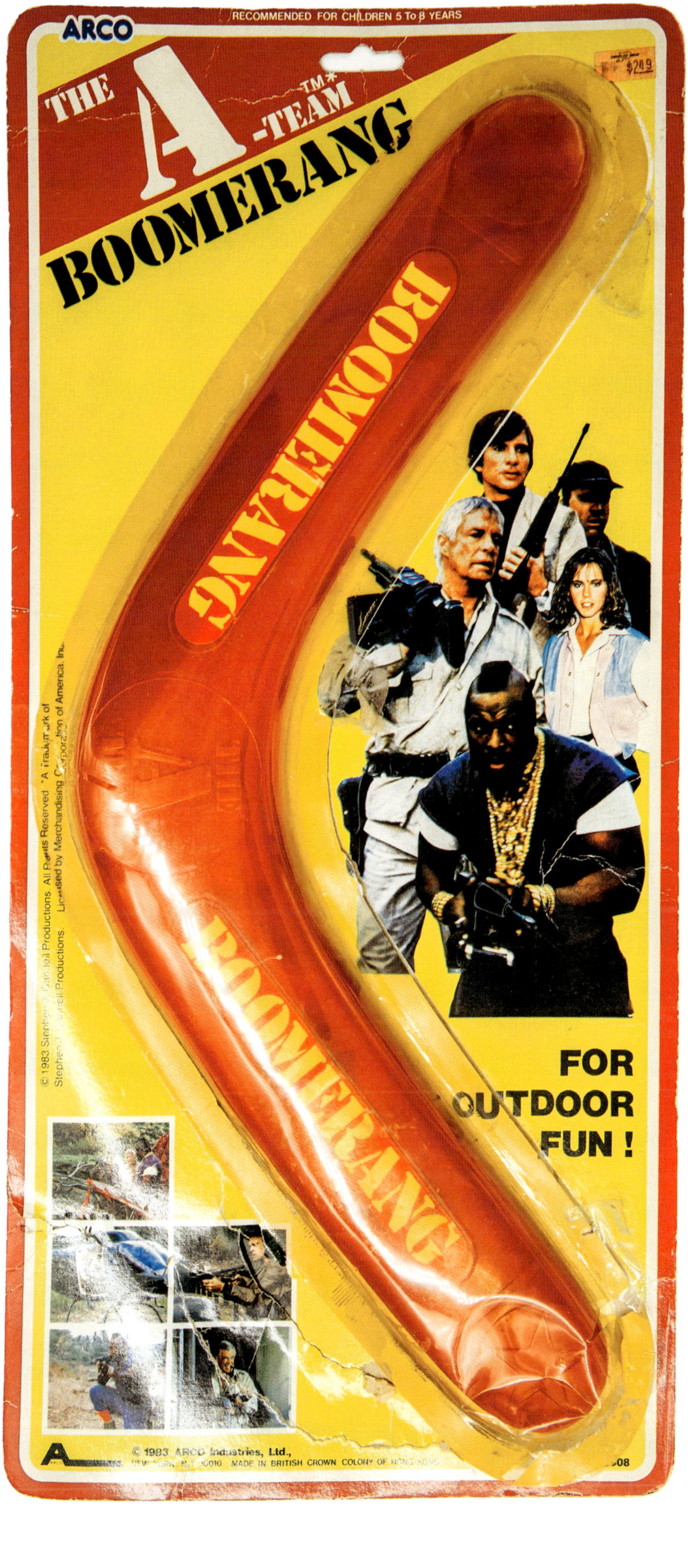

Do you think of these Mr. T dolls as folk art?
I do. The *American Folk Art* magazine interviewed me about them ten years ago. In the issue I'm in, there's a weather vane and a really oddly shaped girl with her dog painted, and then there's me and my dolls. My collection was recognized by the American Folk Art Museum as modern-day folk art. I would love for my dolls to be in the American Folk Art Museum's permanent collection, but we'll see what happens.

Where do you want all your stuff to go when you die?
Actually I've thought about getting rid of stuff before I died, especially the mass-produced stuff. I don't have a big enough home to display it in, and I don't even know that I'd want to if I did, unless I lived in some giant mansion that had more rooms than I knew what to do with. I could make a Mr. T room. I don't have that much desire to do that. I mean what my goal is, after we put out the book, is to have at least one, but probably multiple art shows where I sell off the collection.

I always thought it'd be cool for all of the dolls to go to one place. I was in the *Ripley's Believe it or Not* book last year, and I had called the Ripley's Museum in LA to suggest my donating the dolls to them.

And what did they say?
They said no.

The A-Boomerang because Mr. T never ever had one.

FAR LEFT TOP *The A-Team Grenade Toss. Placo Toys. (Not suitable for todays generation)*

FAR LEFT BOTTOM *The A-Team cloth totebag. Stephen J. Cannel Productions, 1983.*

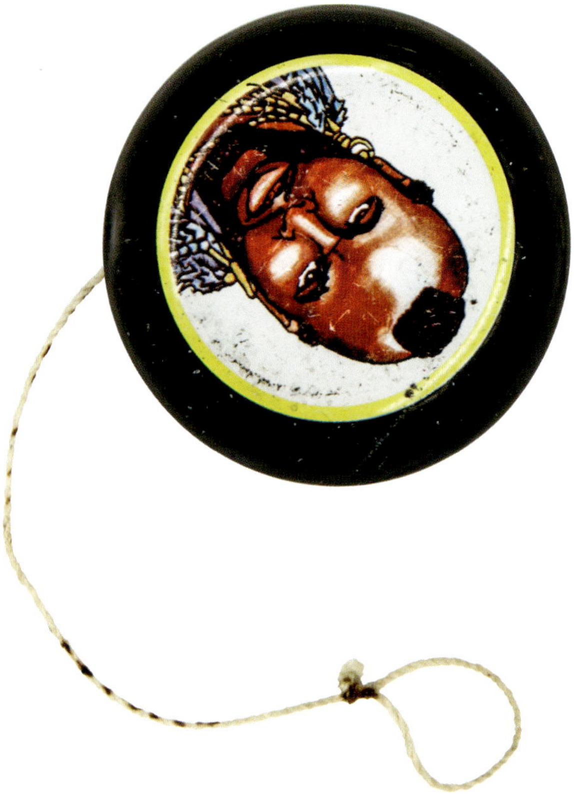

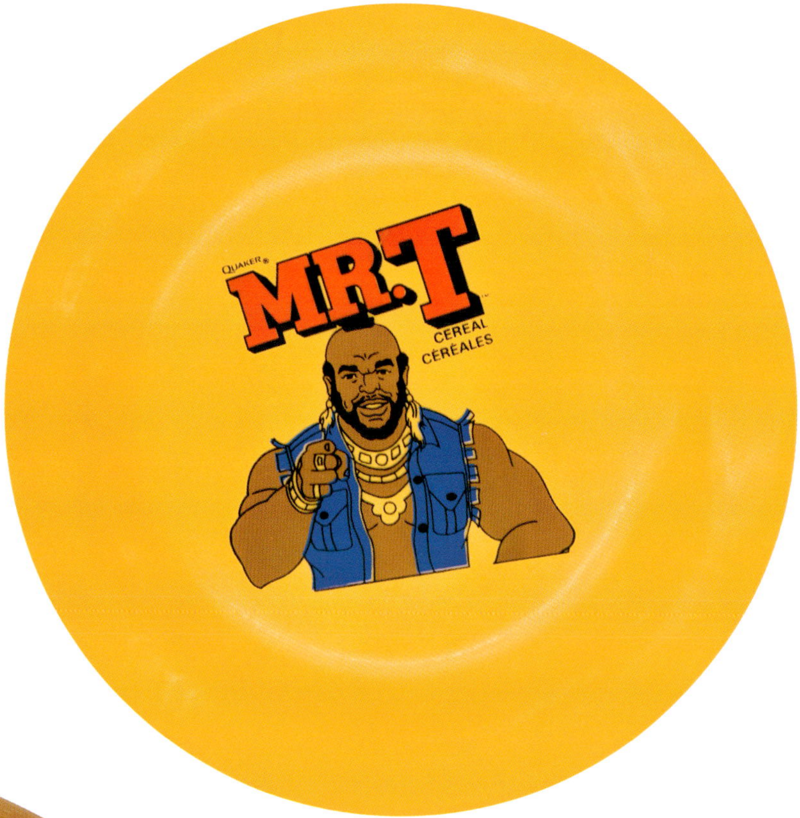

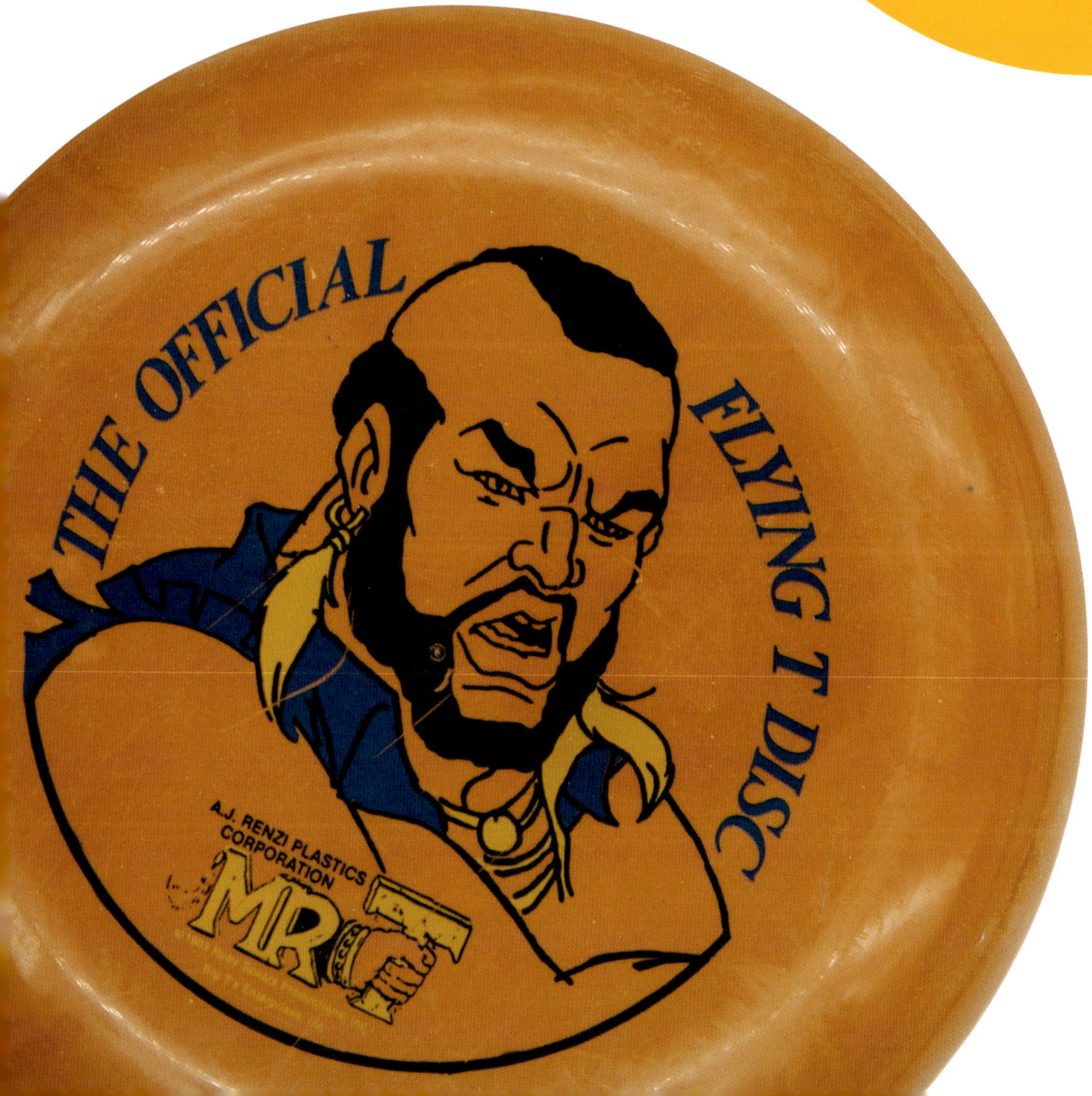

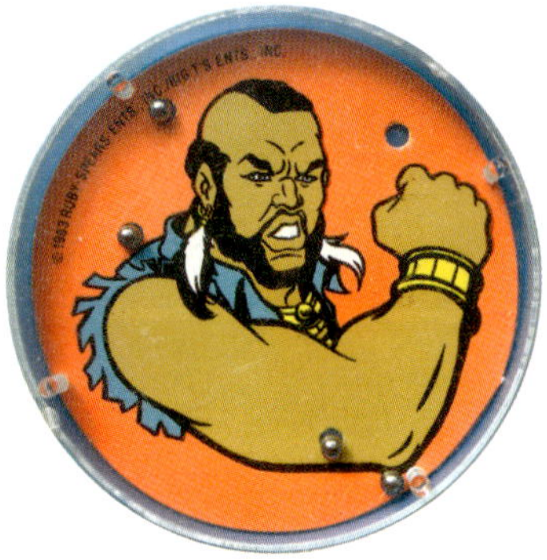

Mr. T gets around.

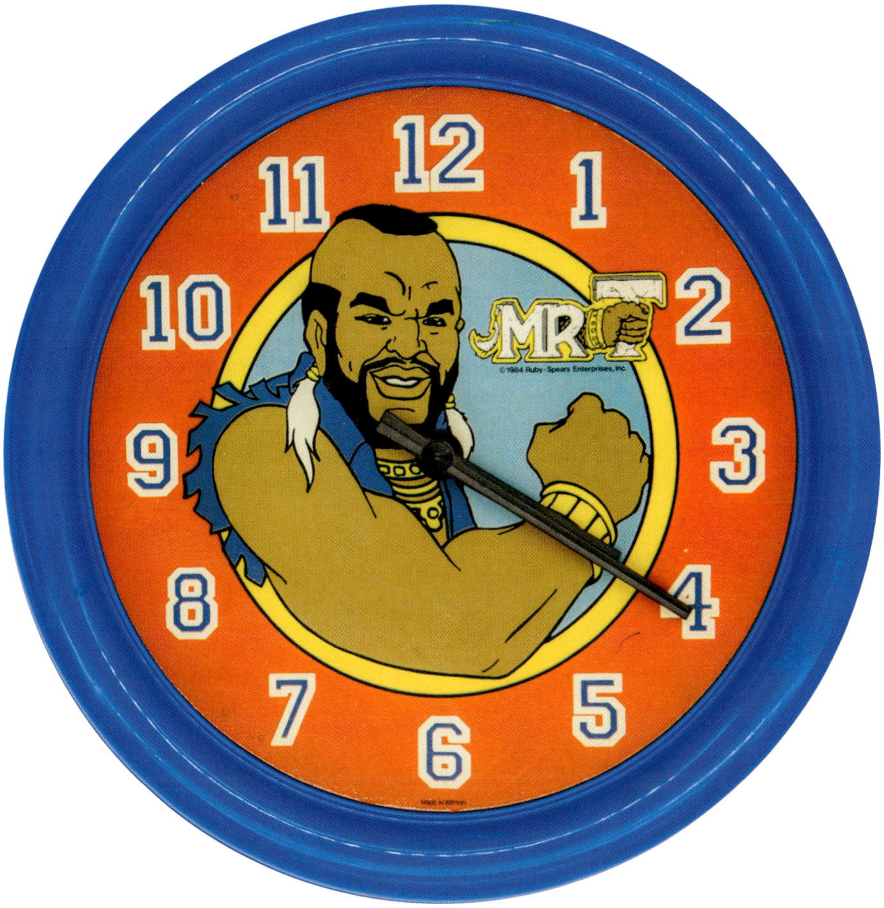
MR T
©1984 Ruby-Spears Enterprises, Inc.

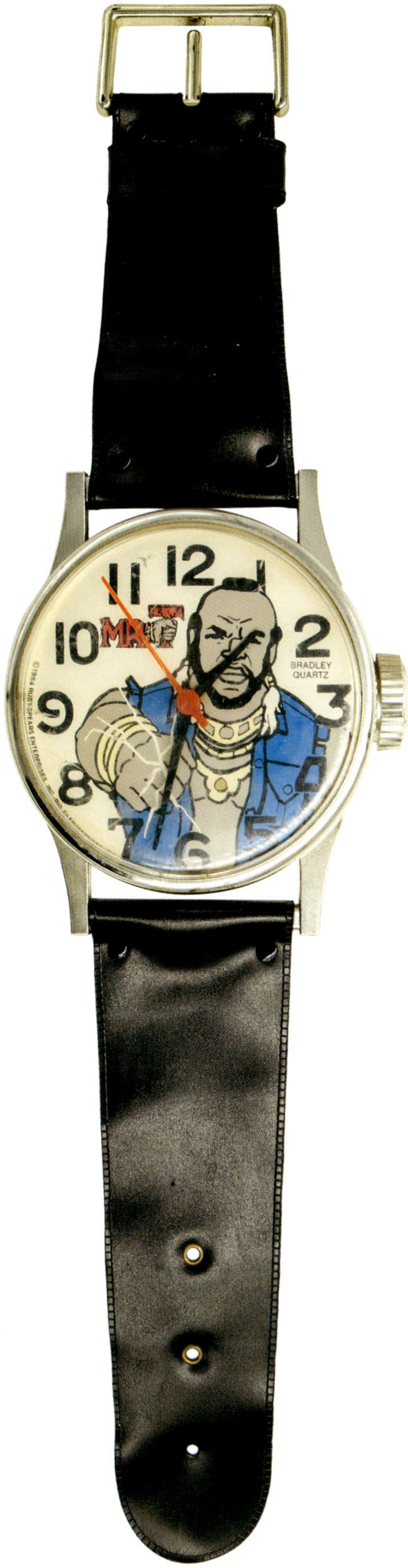
MR T
BRADLEY
QUARTZ

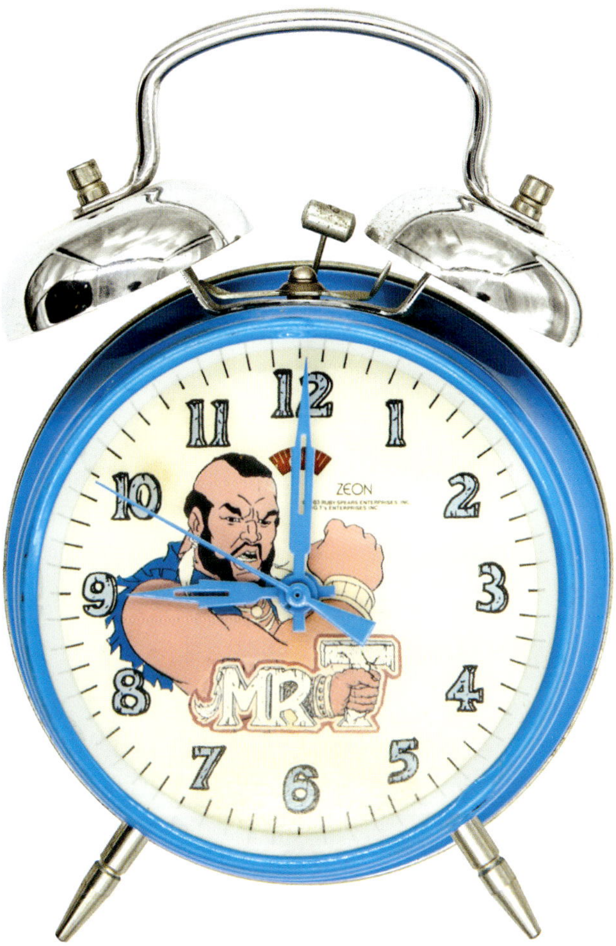
ZEON
MR T

Have you considered just burning them?
No. I don't see there's any point in that.

So where are all the dolls now; your house??
They are actually at Quang Le's house in Santa Ana. They take up an entire room while he's photographing them all for the book.

Now that the dolls are out of storage, are they going to come back and live with you and your wife, Lesa, in your home?
No, I think Lesa would kill me if I brought all that stuff back now! I have to remember Mr. T's words. "Don't be possessed by your possessions!"

Nicholas Gazin is an artist, a writer, and the art editor of *Vice Magazine*. He lives in Brooklyn with his cat, Banjo.

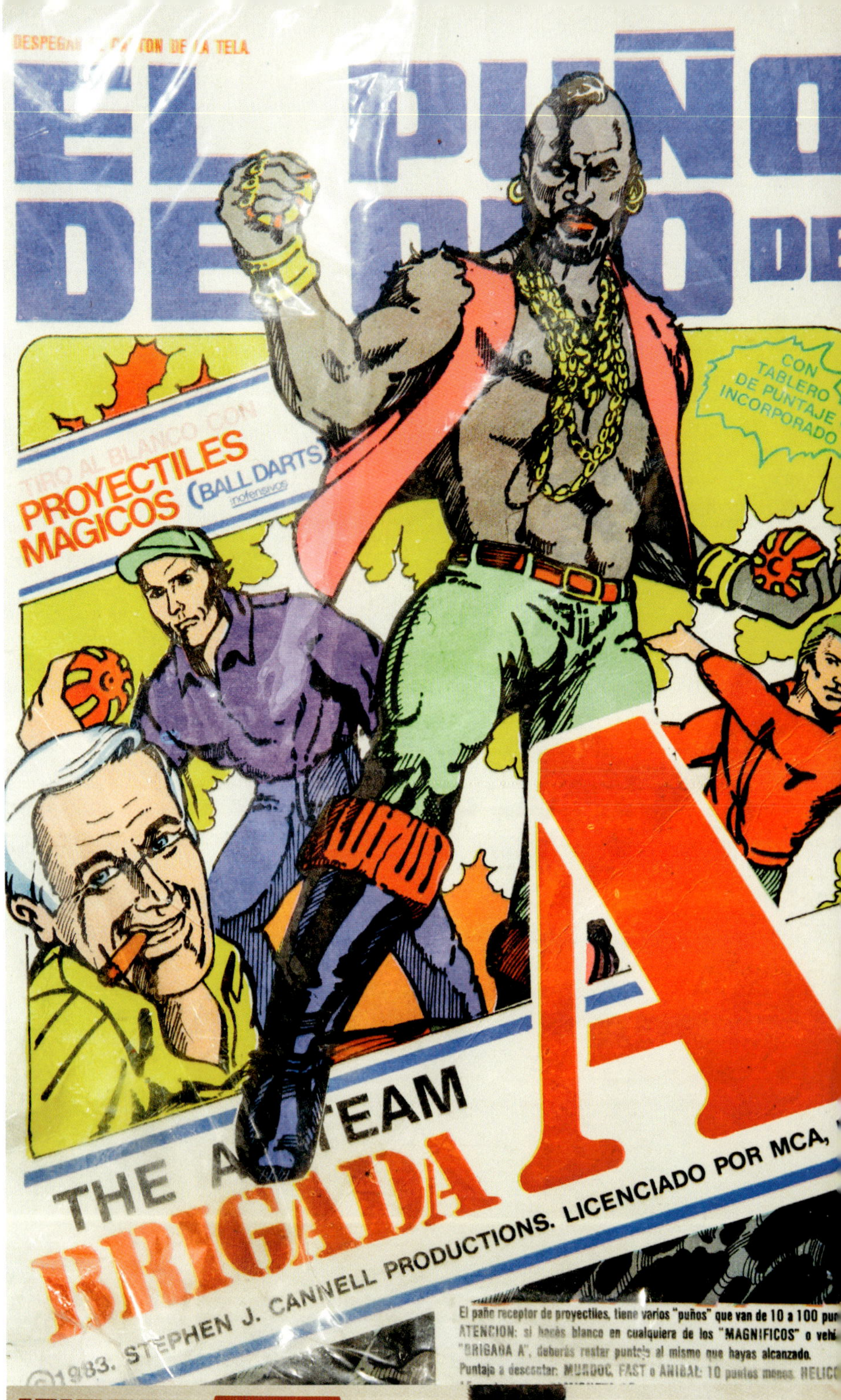

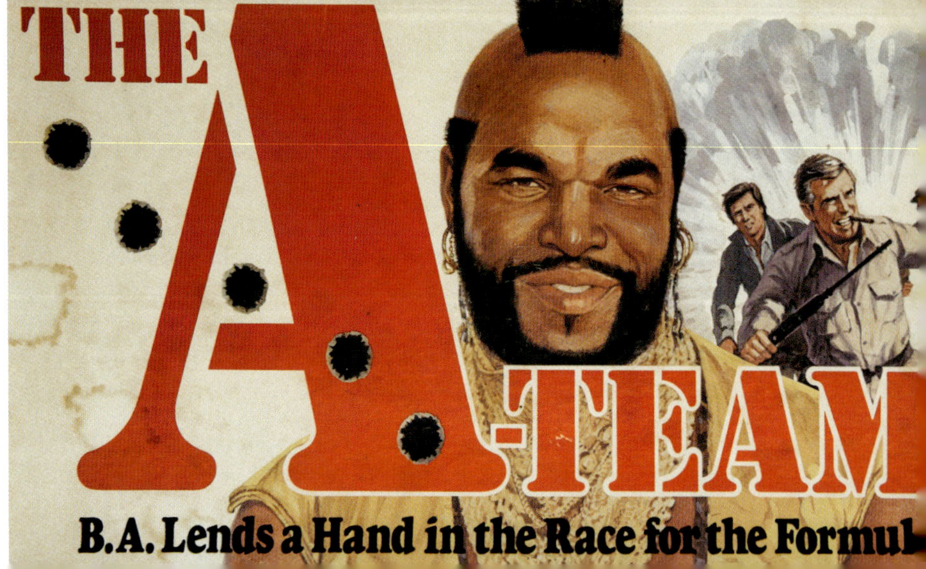

TOP AND RIGHT *The A-Team ball-dart games. 1983.*

BOTTOM *The A-Team board game. 1983.*

NEXT SPREAD *Mr. T was the spokesperson for TR-3 automotive resin glaze. In a TR-3 commercial Mr. T says: "TR-3 goes on easy, stays on hard. Makes your car beautiful, like me." Air freshener, pin, Christmas card. TR-3 Products. 1983.*

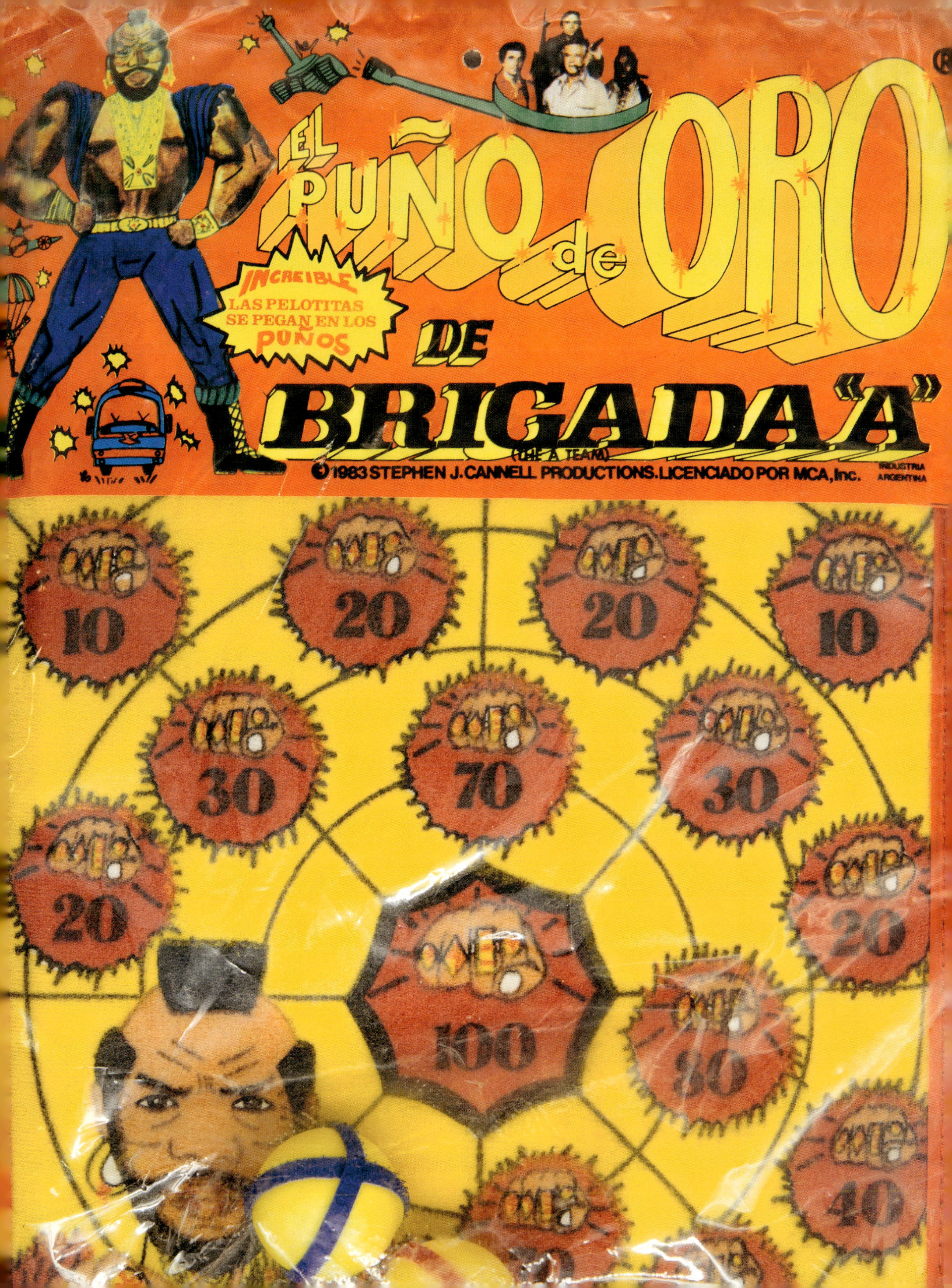

EL PUÑO de ORO®
INCREIBLE
LAS PELOTITAS
SE PEGAN EN LOS
PUÑOS
DE
BRIGADA "A"
(THE A TEAM)
© 1983 STEPHEN J. CANNELL PRODUCTIONS. LICENCIADO POR MCA, Inc.
INDUSTRIA ARGENTINA
10
20
20
10
30
70
30
20
20
100
30
40

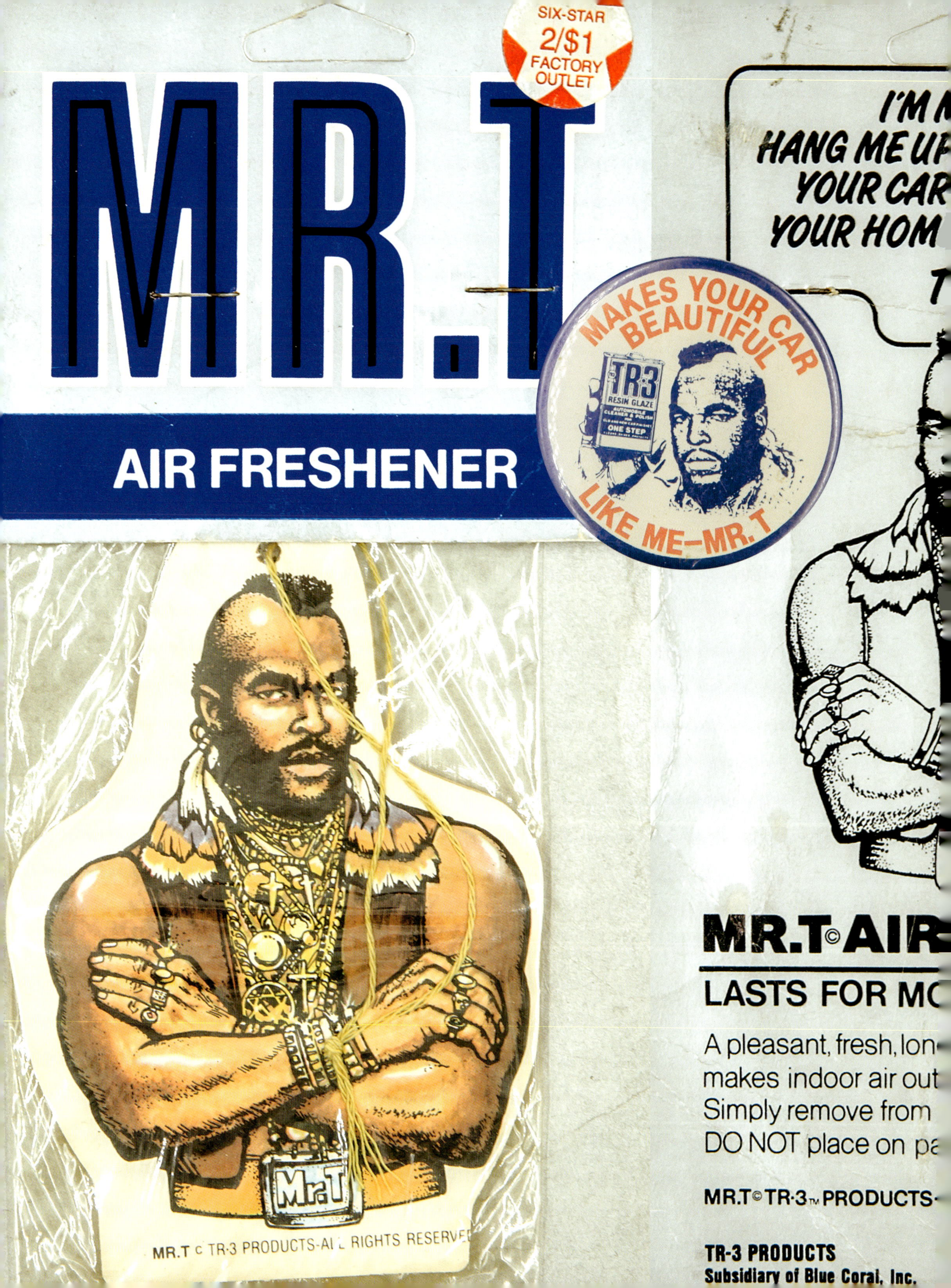
SIX-STAR
2/$1
FACTORY OUTLET
MR.T
AIR FRESHENER
MAKES YOUR CAR BEAUTIFUL
TR-3
RESIN GLAZE
ONE STEP
LIKE ME—MR.T
Mr.T
MR.T © TR-3 PRODUCTS-ALL RIGHTS RESERVE
I'M
HANG ME UP
YOUR CAR
YOUR HOM
MR.T© AIR
LASTS FOR MO
A pleasant, fresh, lon
makes indoor air out
Simply remove from
DO NOT place on pa
MR.T© TR-3™ PRODUCTS
TR-3 PRODUCTS
Subsidiary of Blue Coral, Inc.

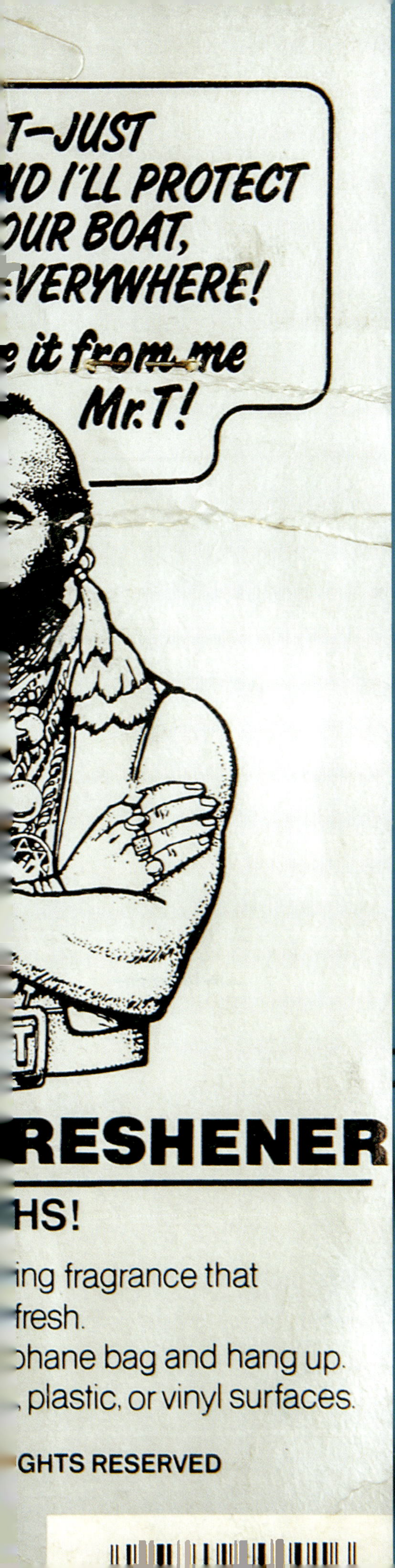
T-JUST
ND I'LL PROTECT
OUR BOAT,
EVERYWHERE!
e it from me
Mr.T!
RESHENER
HS!
ing fragrance that
fresh.
phane bag and hang up.
, plastic, or vinyl surfaces.
GHTS RESERVED

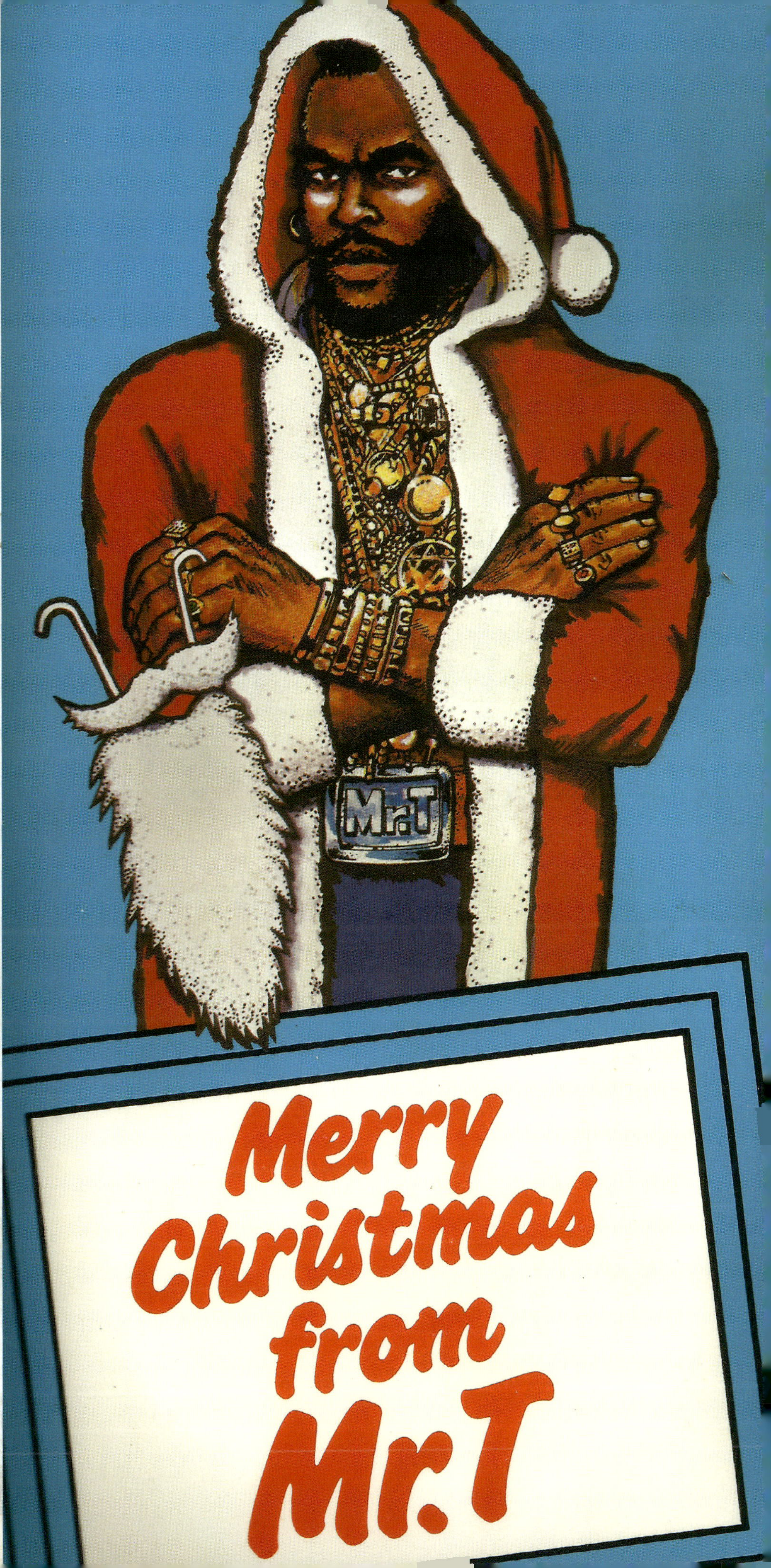
Mr.T
Merry
Christmas
from
Mr.T

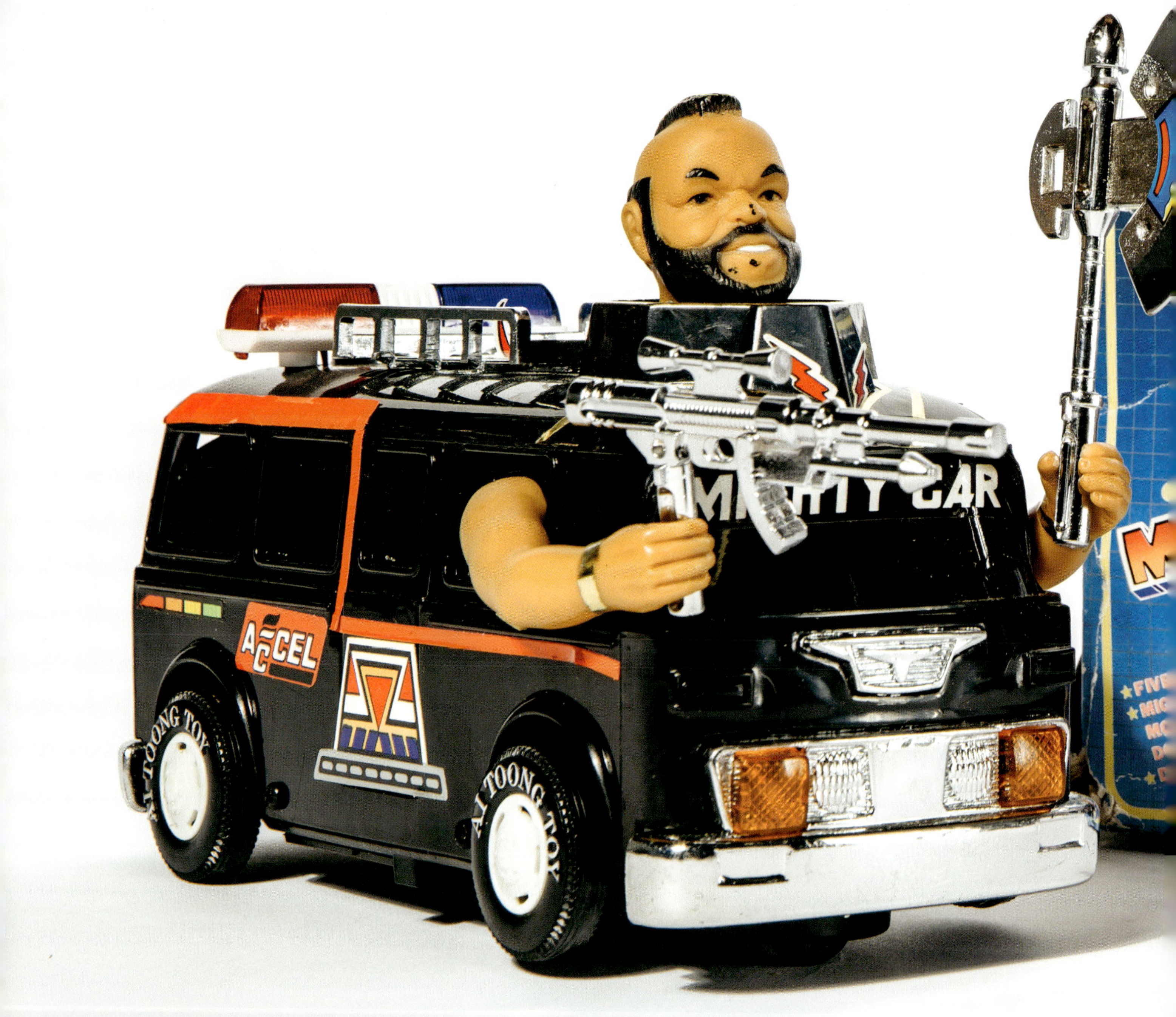
ACCEL
AI TOONG TOY

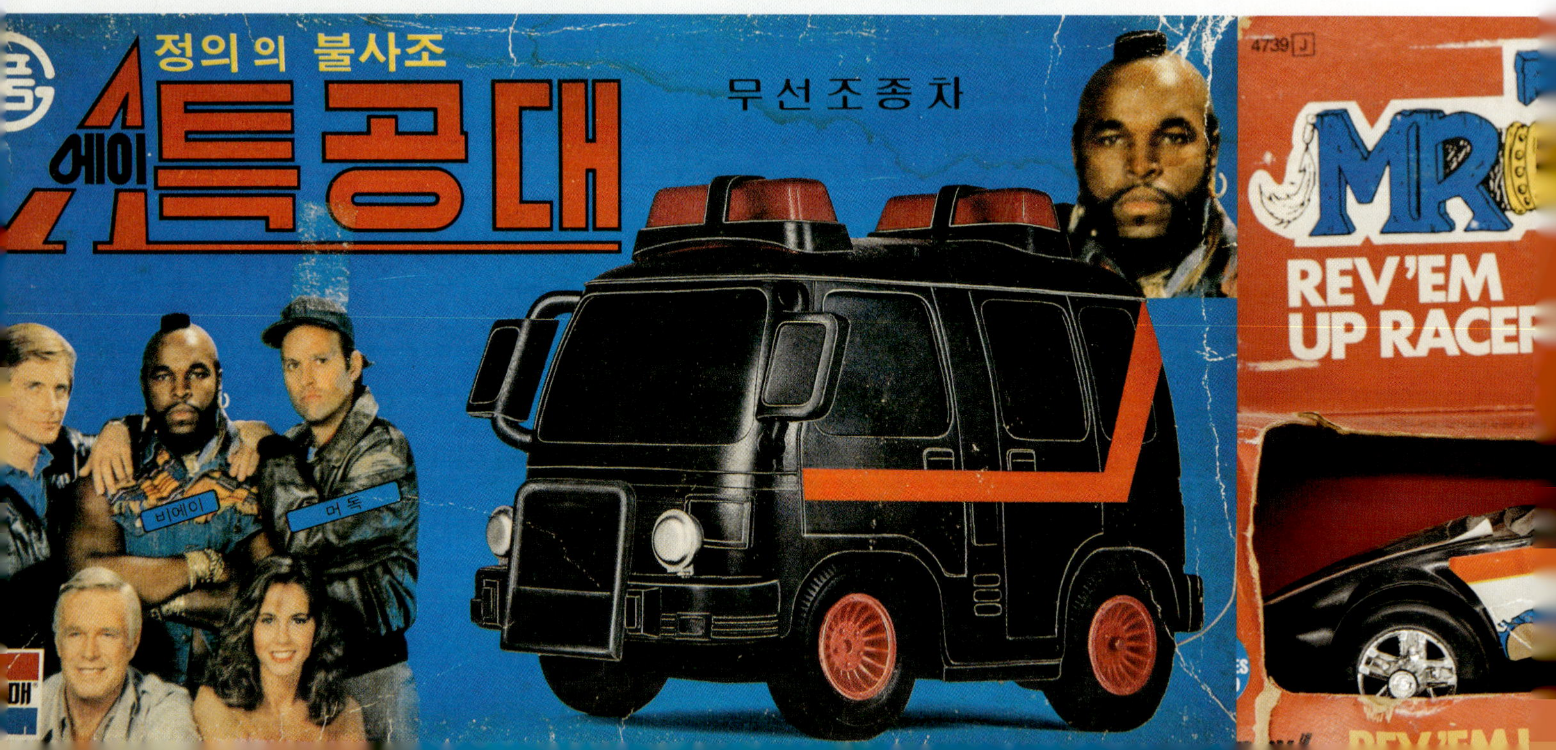
정의의 불사조
에이 특공대
무선조종차
비에이
머독
4739 J
MR
REV'EM
UP RACER

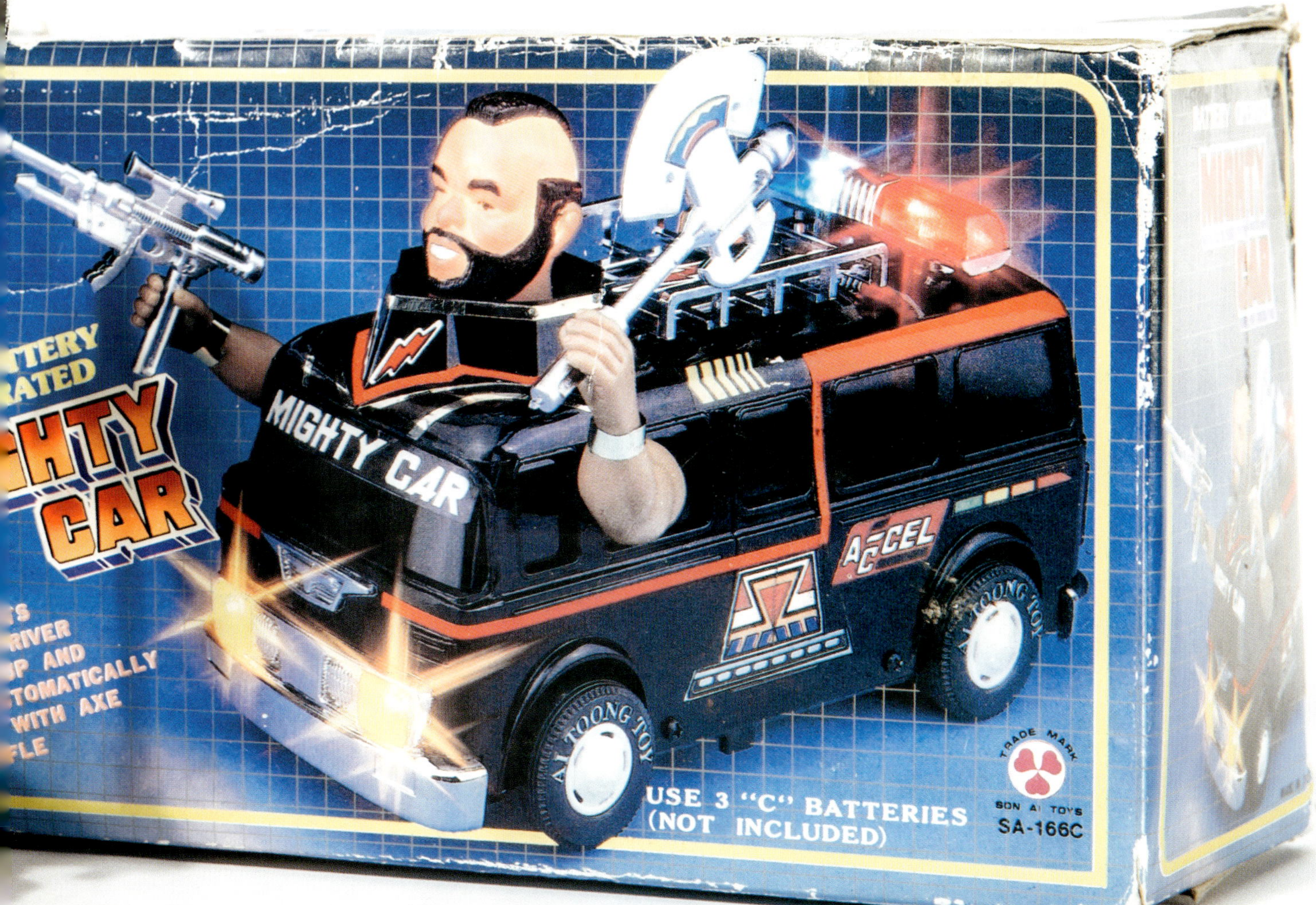
MIGHTY CAR
ACCEL
USE 3 "C" BATTERIES
(NOT INCLUDED)
TRADE MARK
SON AI TOYS
SA-166C

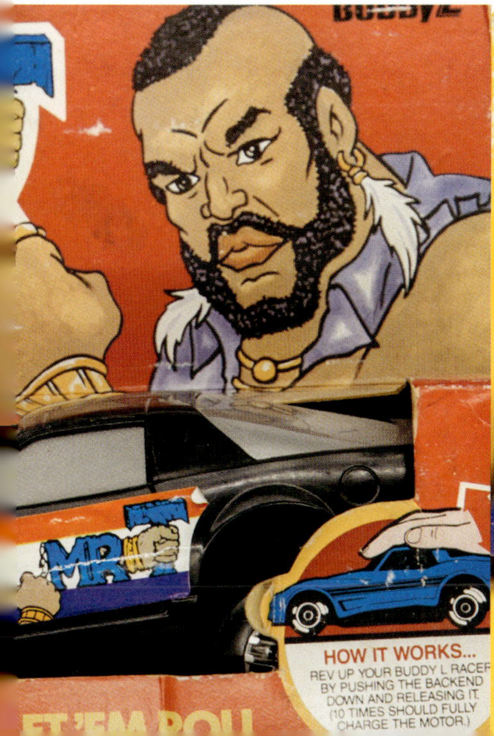
HOW IT WORKS...
REV UP YOUR BUDDY L RACER BY PUSHING THE BACKEND DOWN AND RELEASING IT. (10 TIMES SHOULD FULLY CHARGE THE MOTOR.)

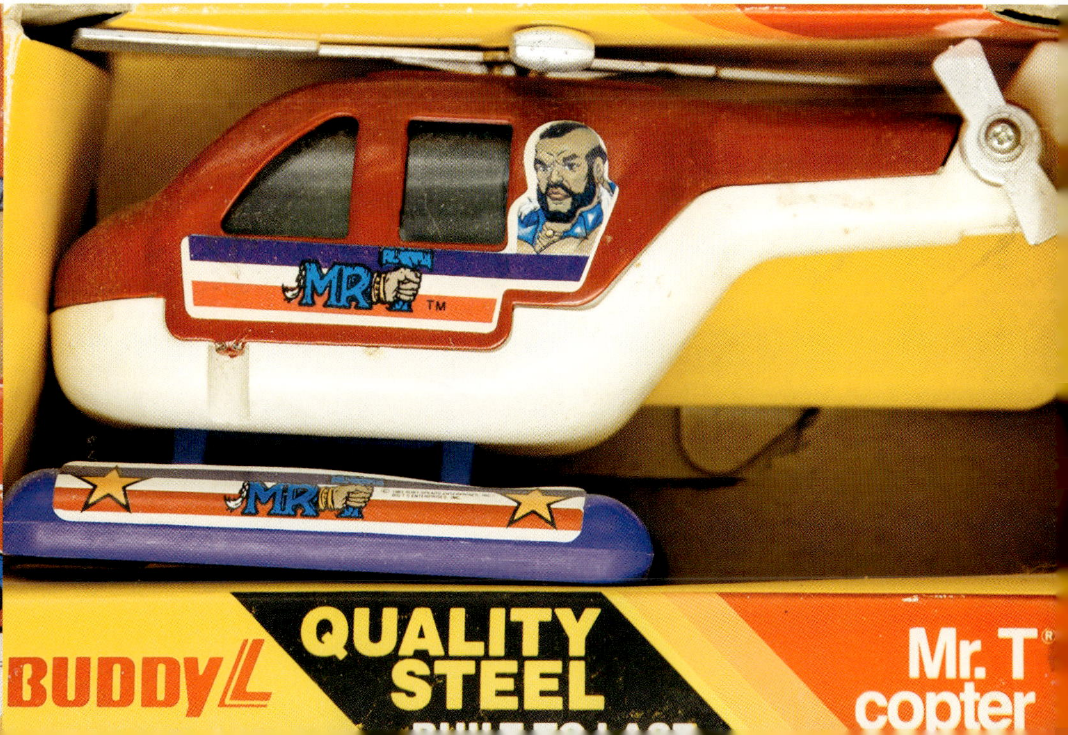
BUDDY L
QUALITY STEEL
Mr. T copter

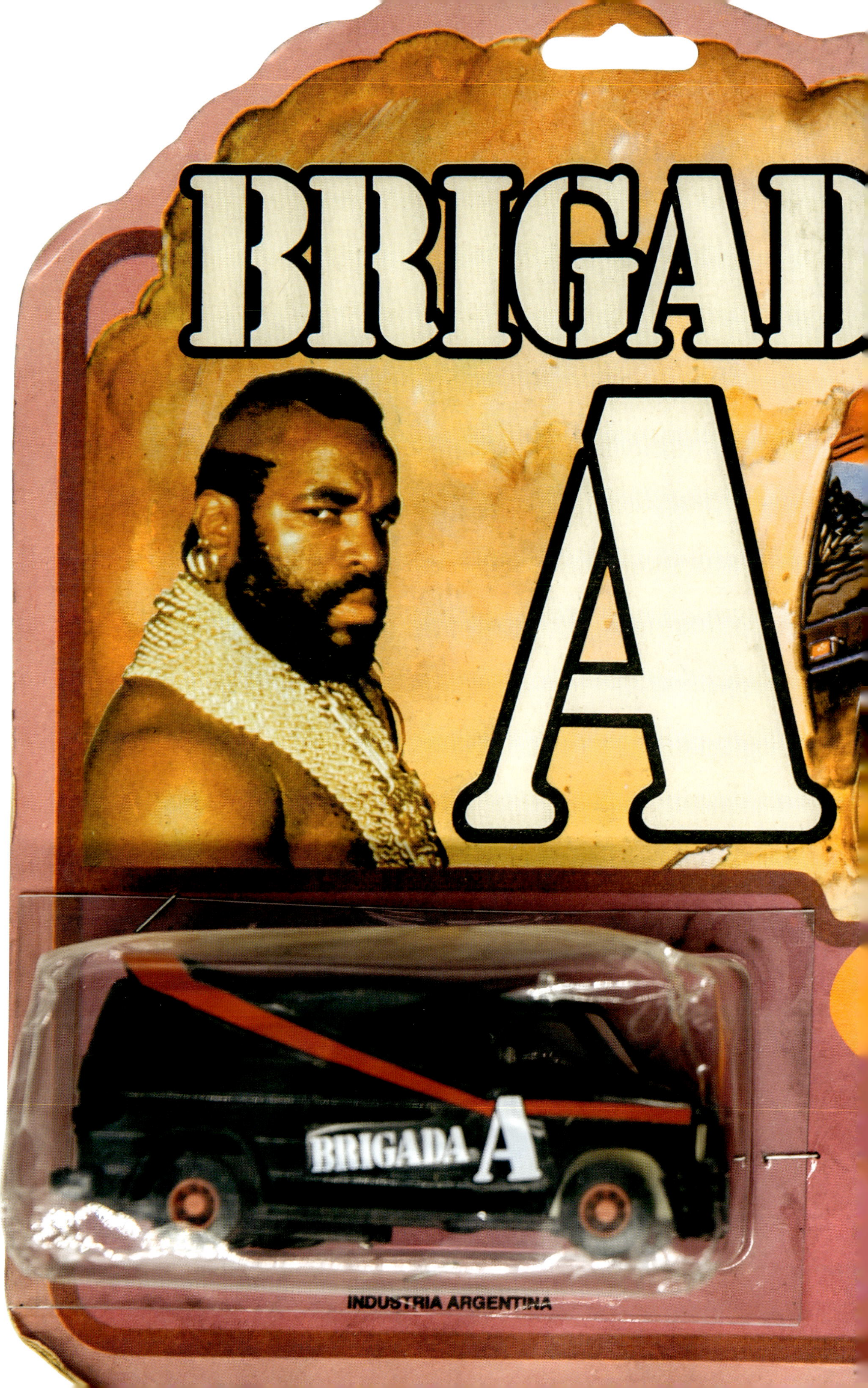
BRIGAD
A
BRIGADA A
INDUSTRIA ARGENTINA

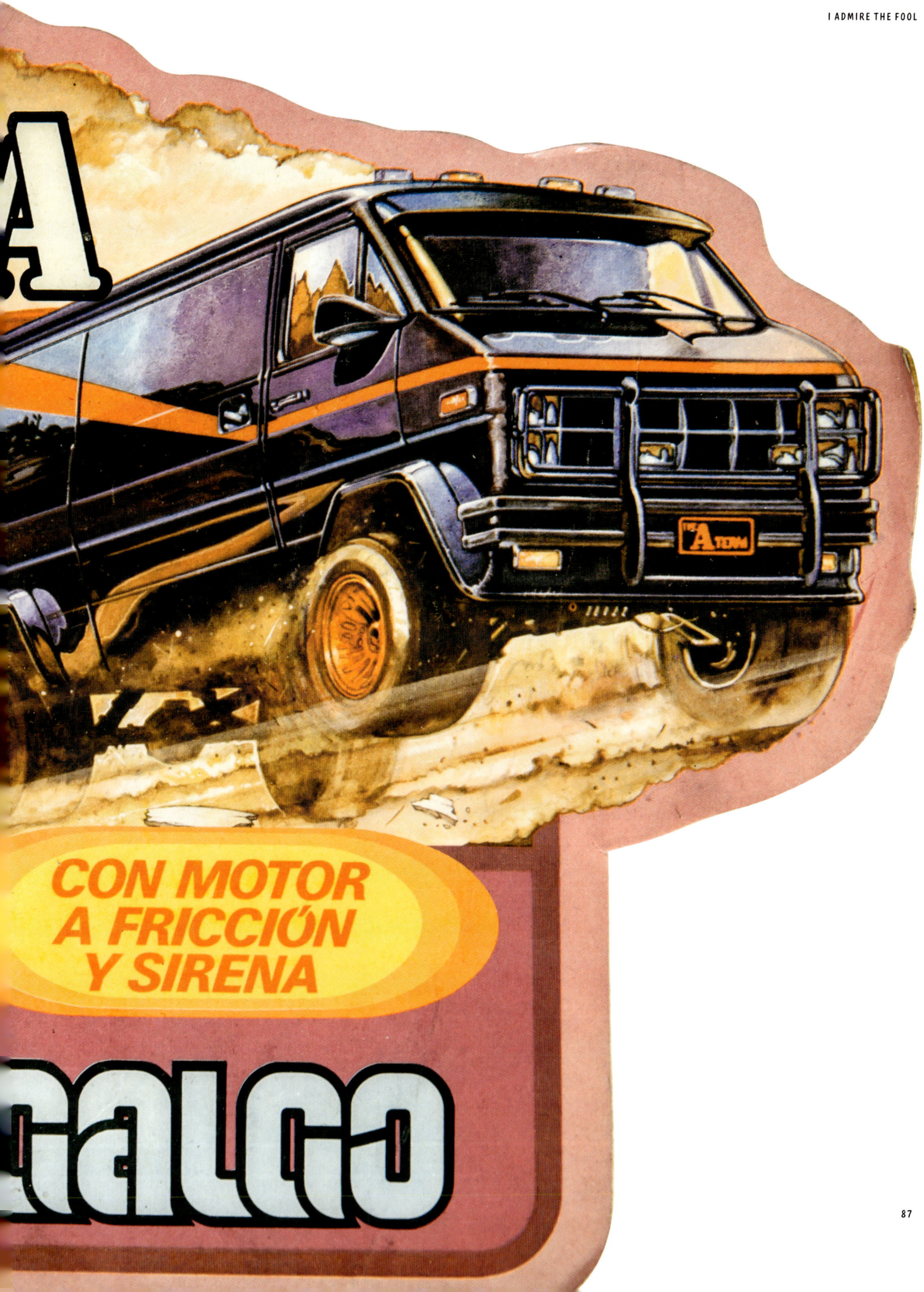
CON MOTOR
A FRICCIÓN
Y SIRENA
ealco

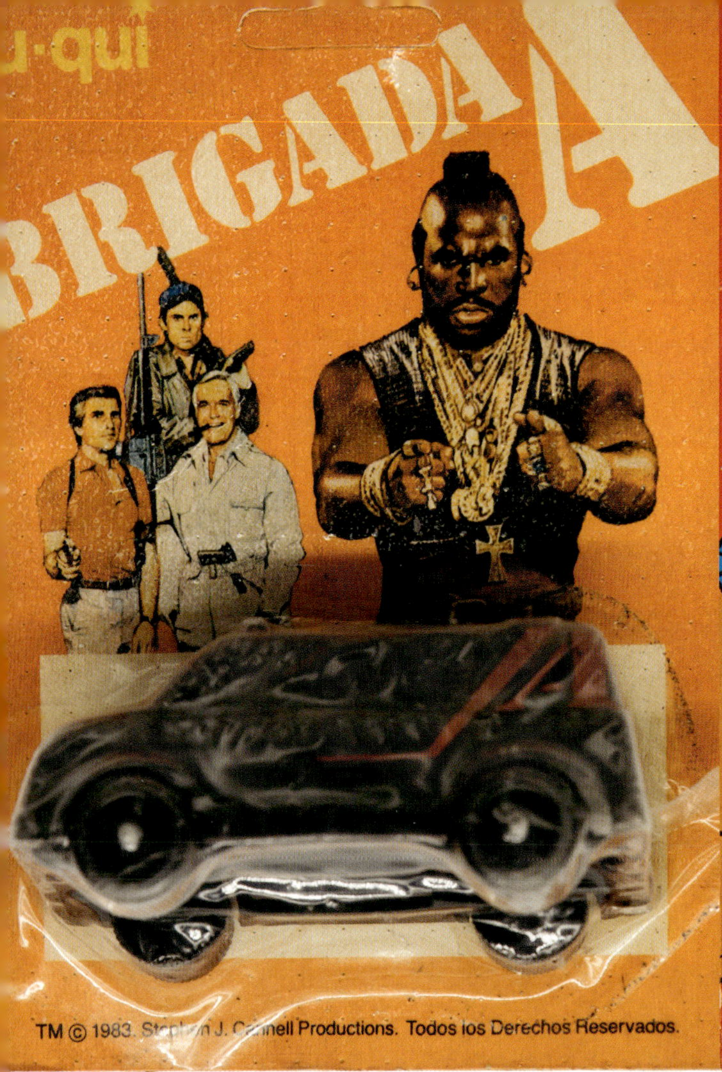
u·qui
BRIGADA A
TM © 1983.
Productions. Todos los Derechos Reservados.

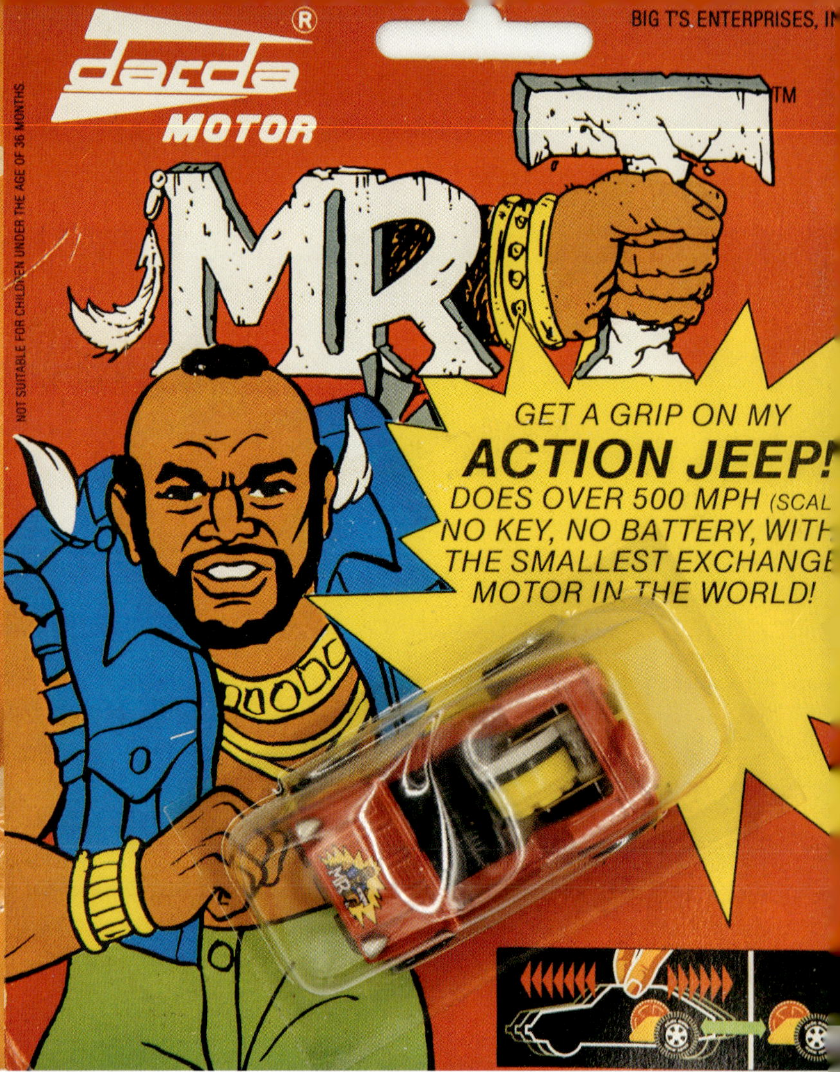
BIG T'S ENTERPRISES, IN
darda®
MOTOR
MR T
TM
NOT SUITABLE FOR CHILDREN UNDER THE AGE OF 36 MONTHS.
GET A GRIP ON MY
ACTION JEEP!
DOES OVER 500 MPH (SCAL
NO KEY, NO BATTERY, WITH
THE SMALLEST EXCHANGE
MOTOR IN THE WORLD!

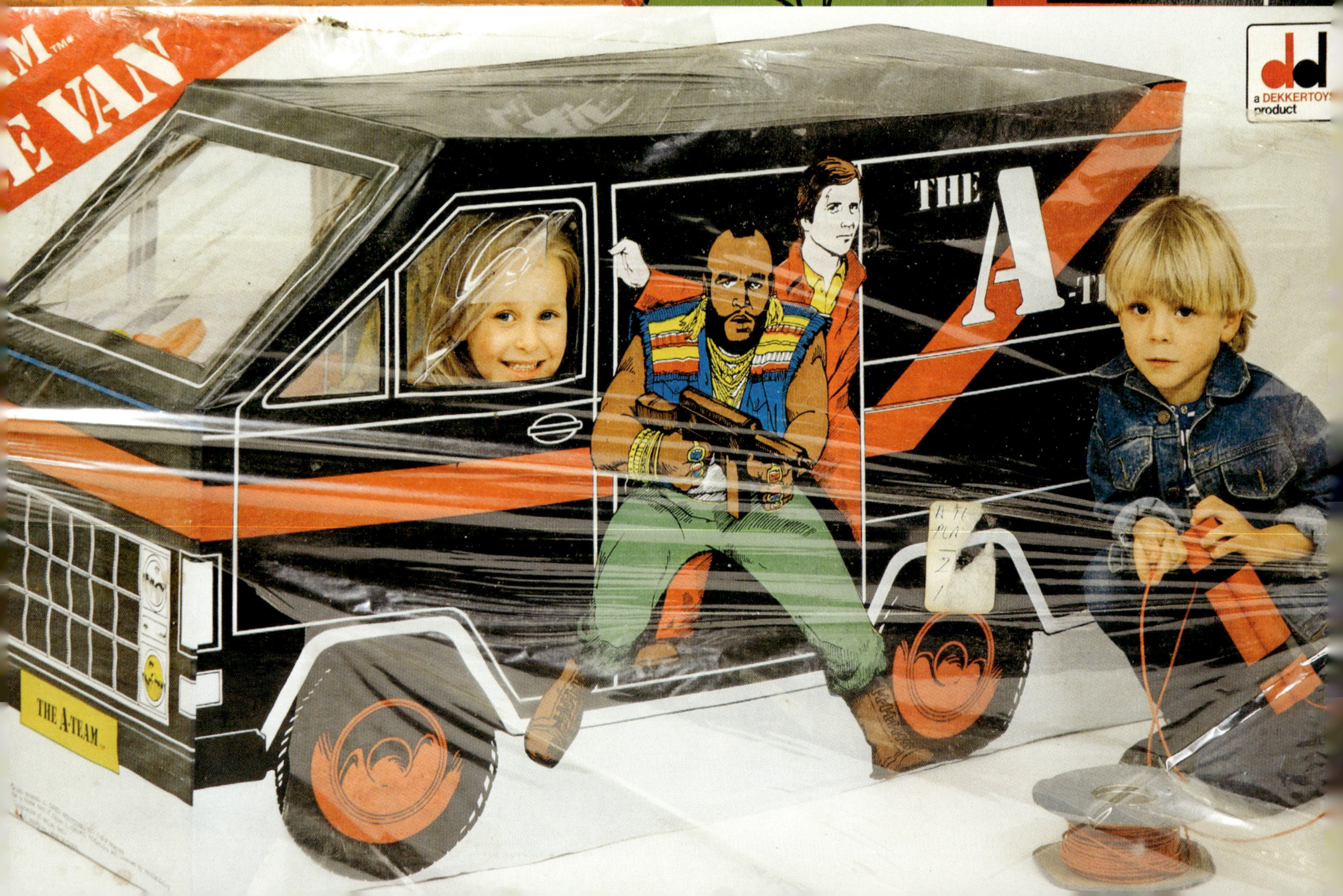
M TM
E VAN
a DEKKERTOYS product
THE A-T
THE A-TEAM

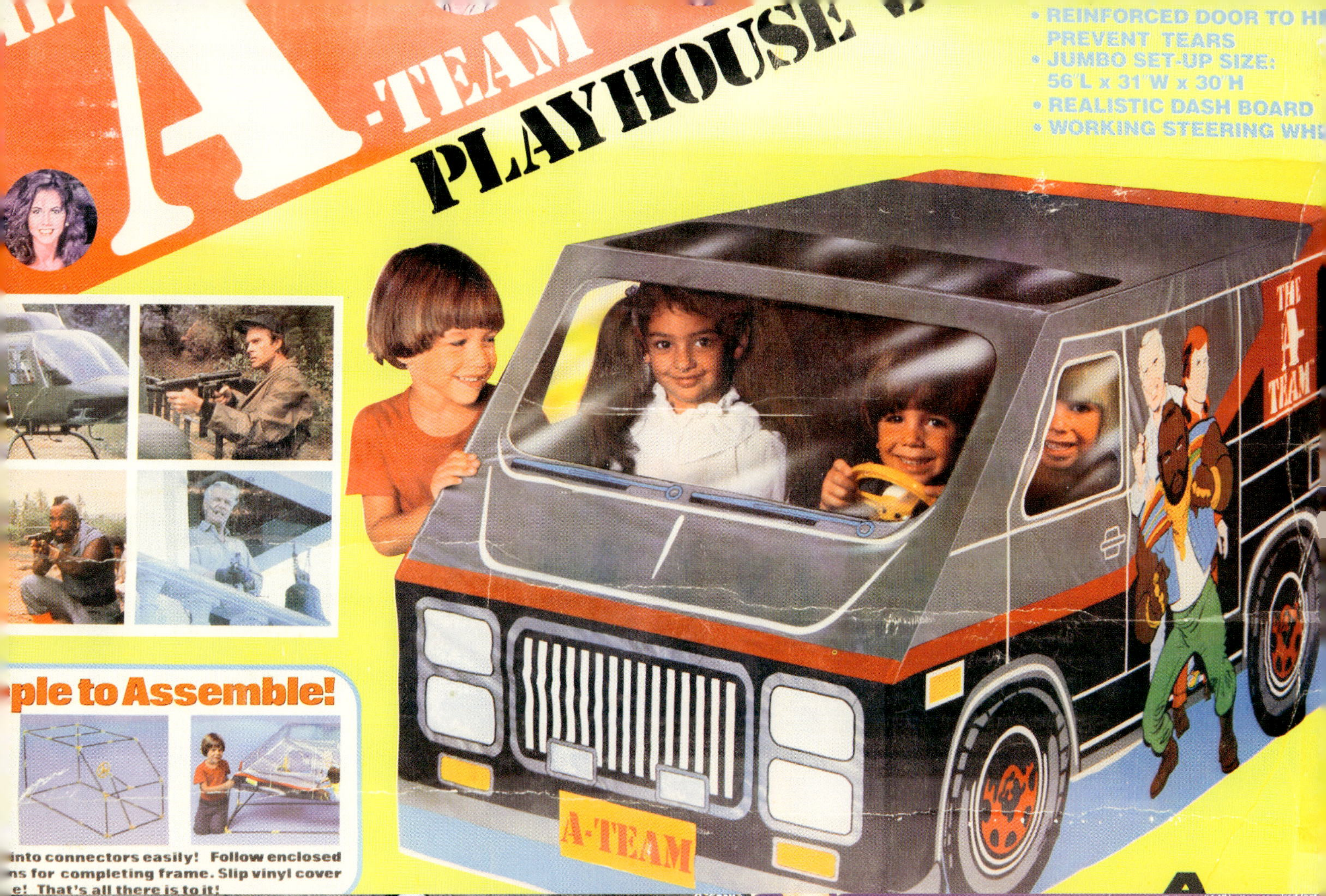
A-TEAM
PLAYHOUSE
• REINFORCED DOOR TO HE
PREVENT TEARS
• JUMBO SET-UP SIZE:
56"L x 31"W x 30"H
• REALISTIC DASH BOARD
• WORKING STEERING WHE
ple to Assemble!
into connectors easily! Follow enclosed
ns for completing frame. Slip vinyl cover
e! That's all there is to it!
A-TEAM

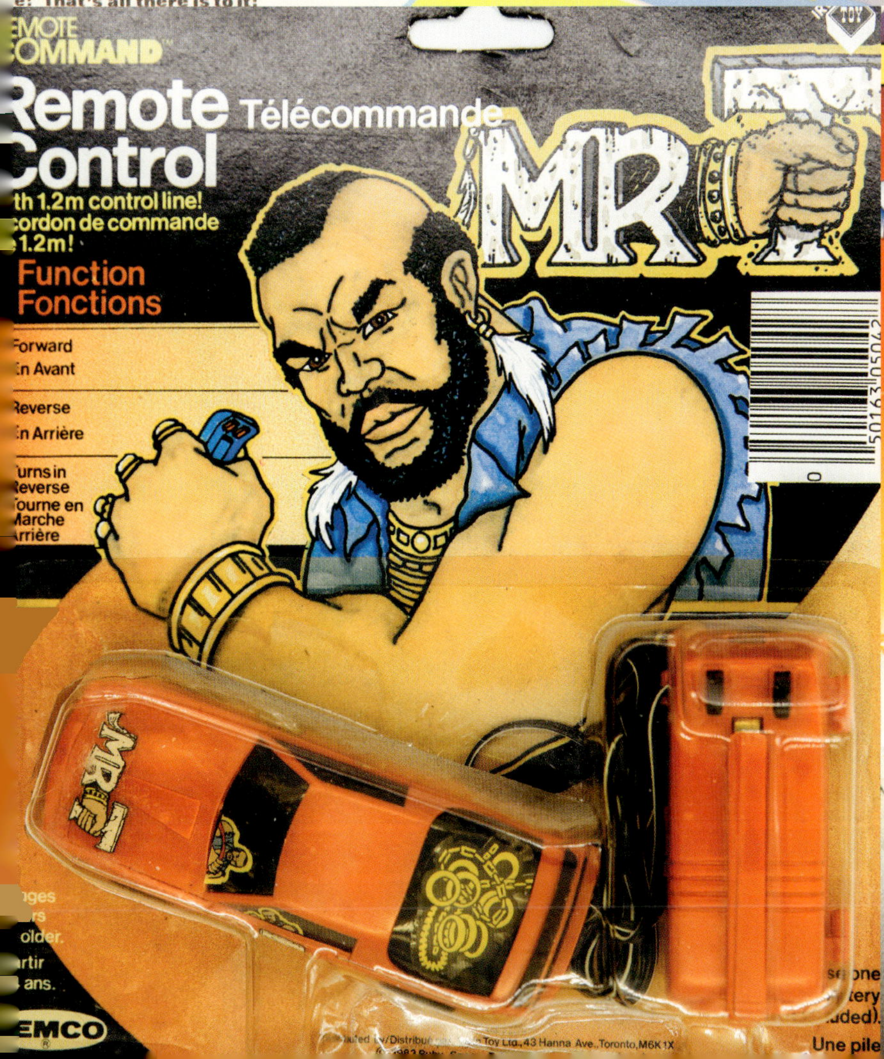
EMOTE
OMMAND
Remote Télécommande
Control
th 1.2m control line!
cordon de commande
1.2m!
Function
Fonctions
Forward
En Avant
Reverse
En Arrière
Turns in
Reverse
Tourne en
Marche
Arrière
MR
EMCO

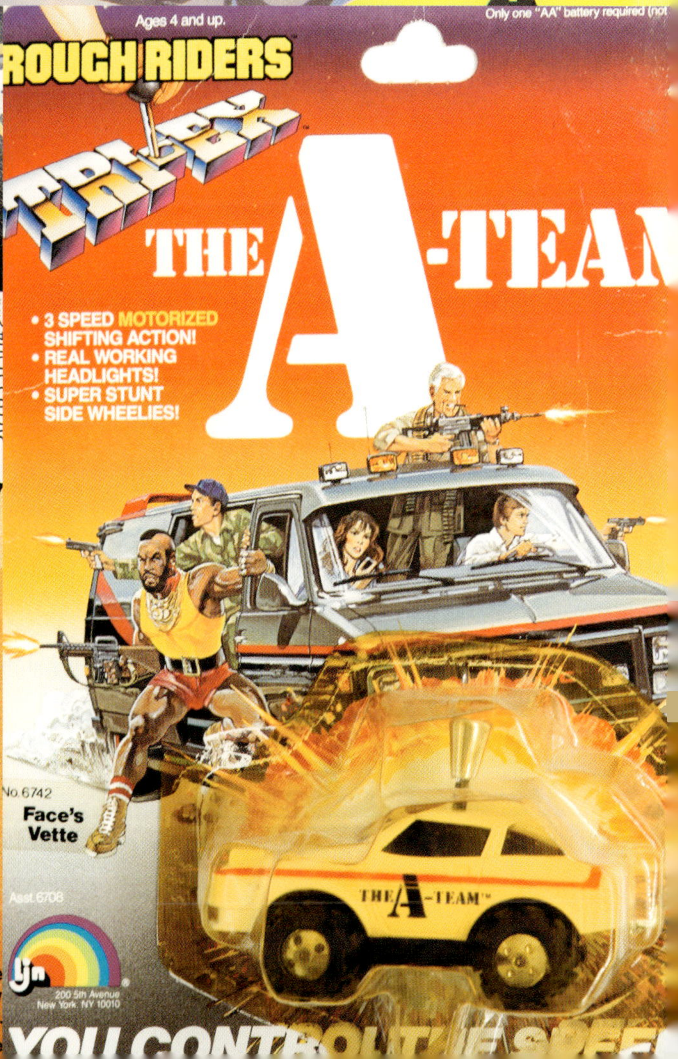
Ages 4 and up.
ROUGH RIDERS
TRI-EX
THE A-TEAM
• 3 SPEED MOTORIZED
SHIFTING ACTION!
• REAL WORKING
HEADLIGHTS!
• SUPER STUNT
SIDE WHEELIES!
No.6742
Face's
Vette
Asst 6708
THE A-TEAM
200 5th Avenue
New York NY 10010

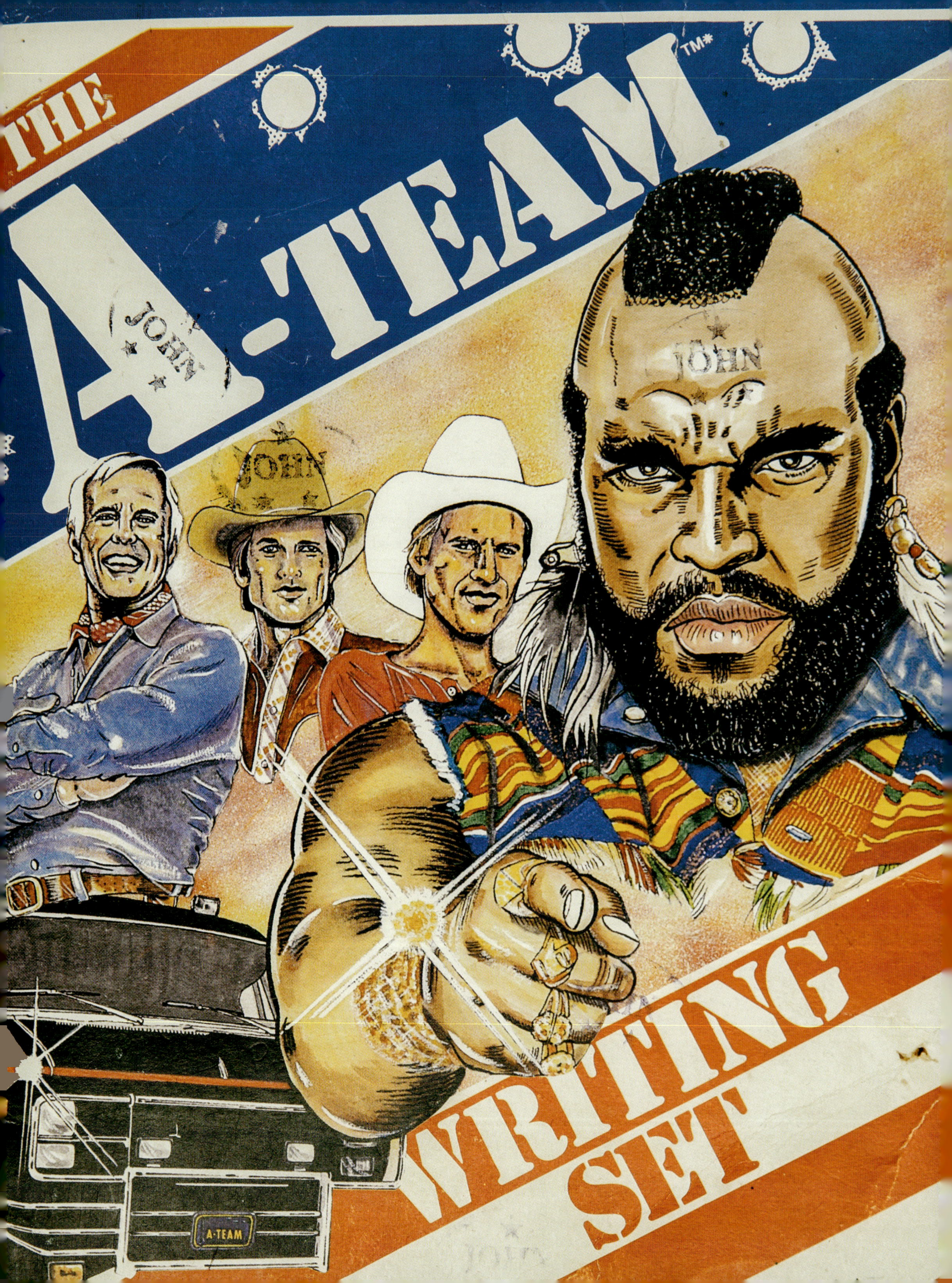
THE
A-TEAM™*
JOHN
WRITING
SET
A-TEAM

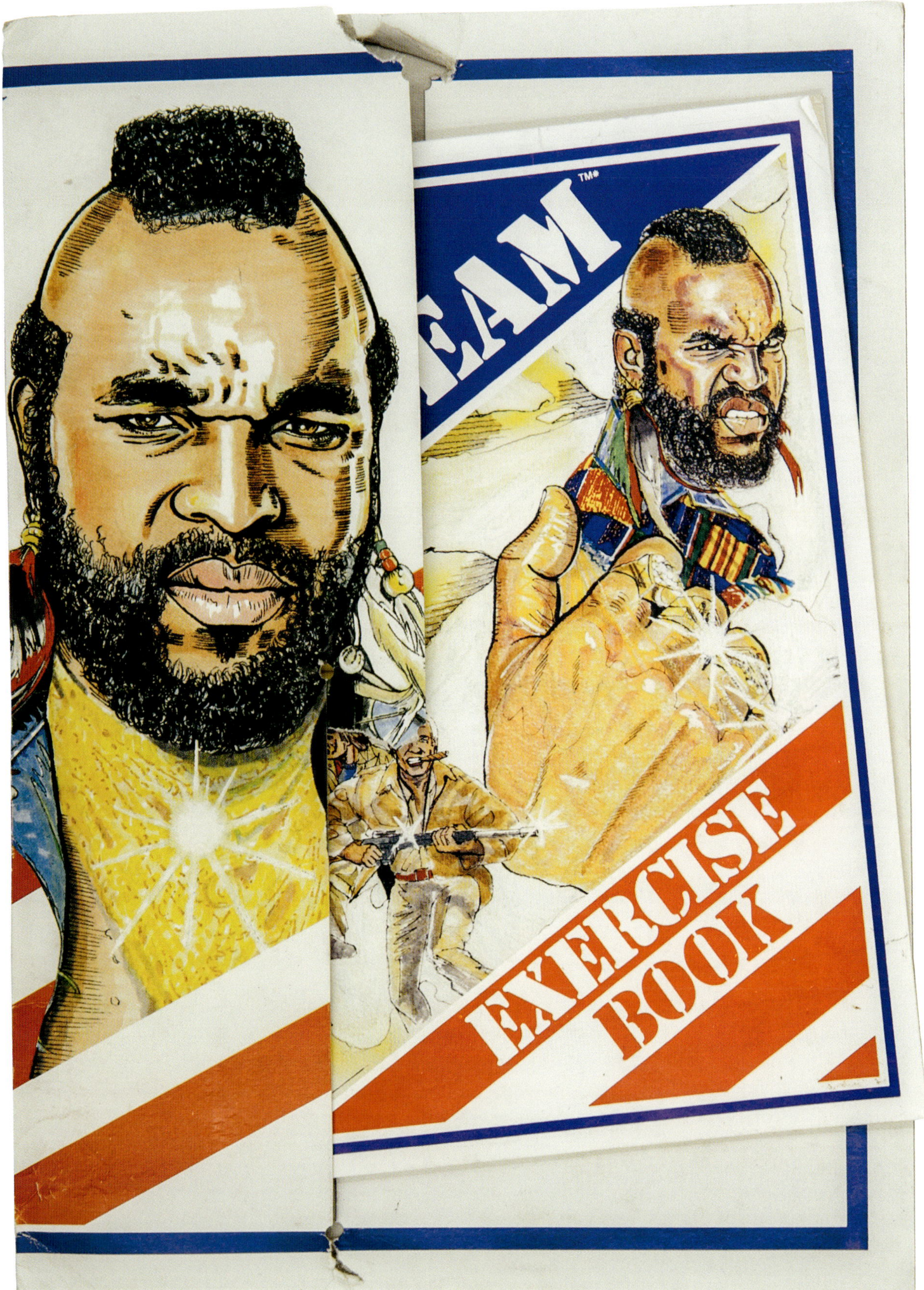
EAM™
EXERCISE
BOOK

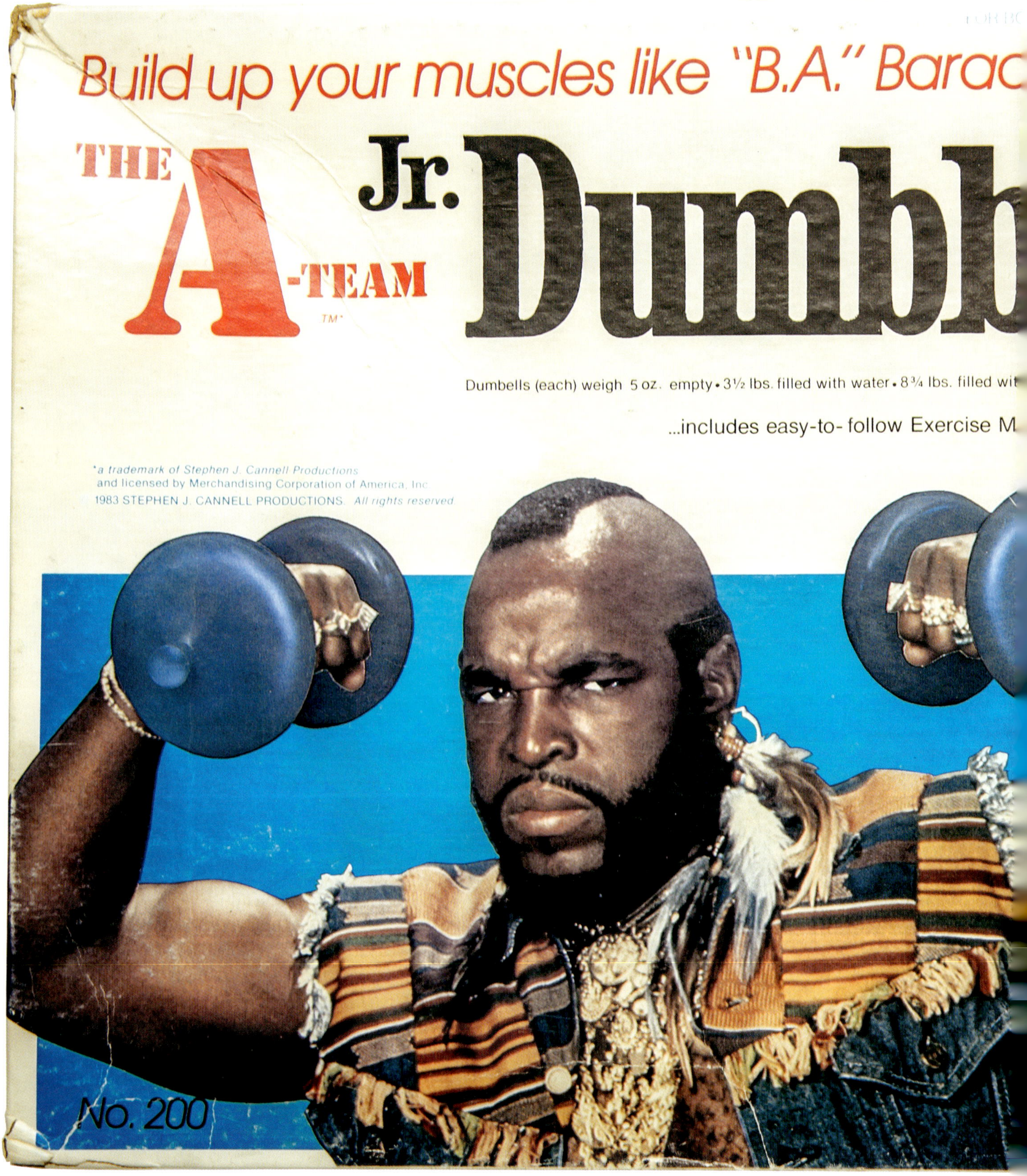
Build up your muscles like "B.A." Barac
THE A-TEAM TM*
Jr. Dumbb
Dumbells (each) weigh 5 oz. empty • 3½ lbs. filled with water • 8¾ lbs. filled wit
...includes easy-to- follow Exercise M
*a trademark of Stephen J. Cannell Productions
and licensed by Merchandising Corporation of America, Inc.
1983 STEPHEN J. CANNELL PRODUCTIONS. All rights reserved
No. 200

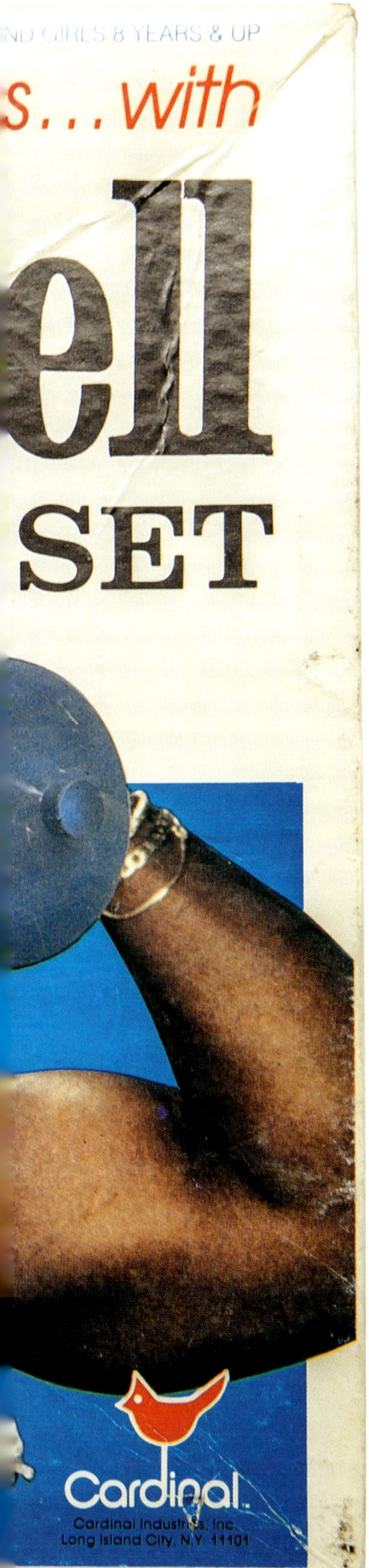
ND GIRLS 8 YEARS & UP
s . . . with
ell
SET
Cardinal
Cardinal Industries, Inc.
Long Island City, N.Y. 11101

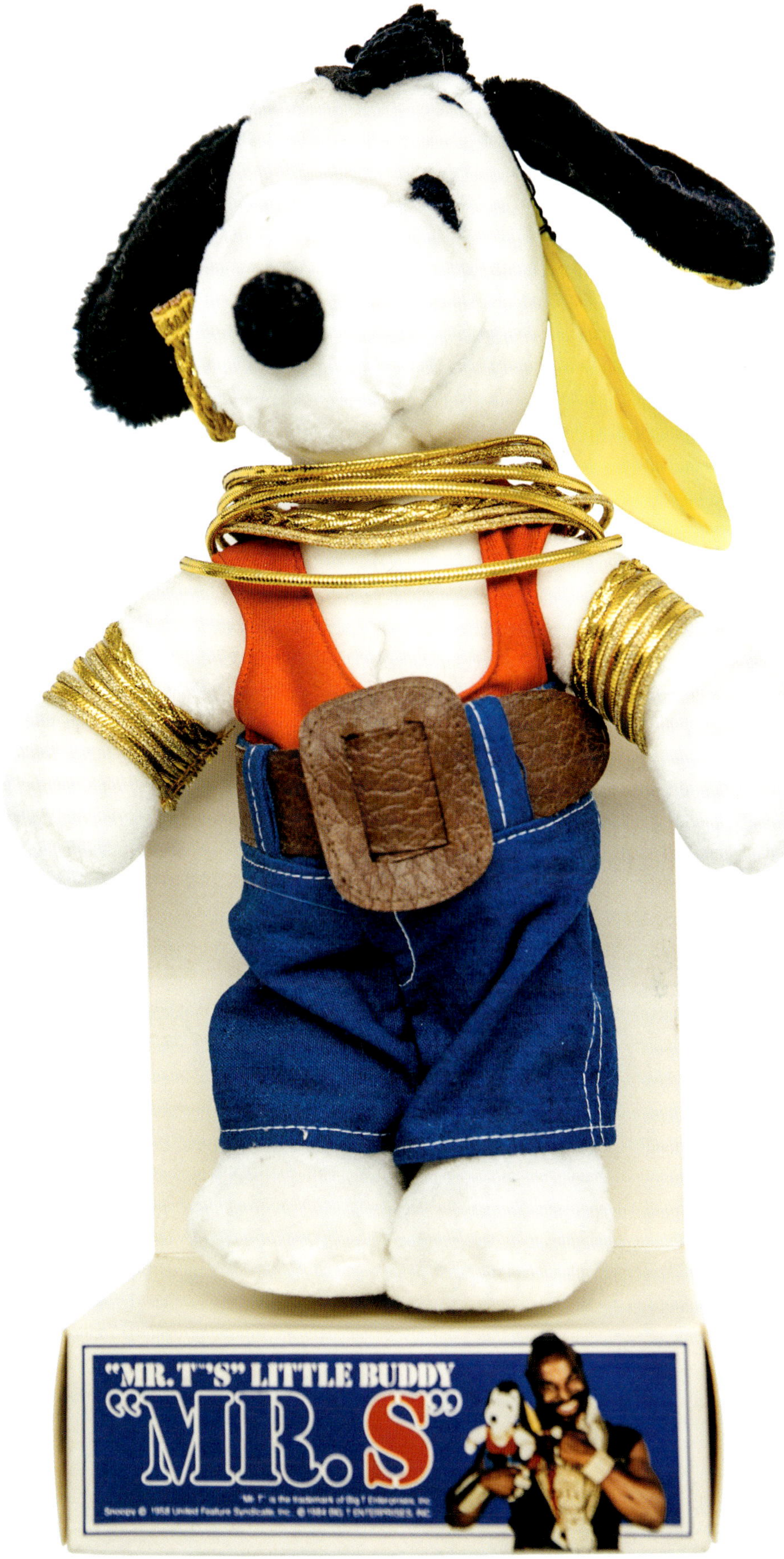
"MR. T"S" LITTLE BUDDY
"MR. S"

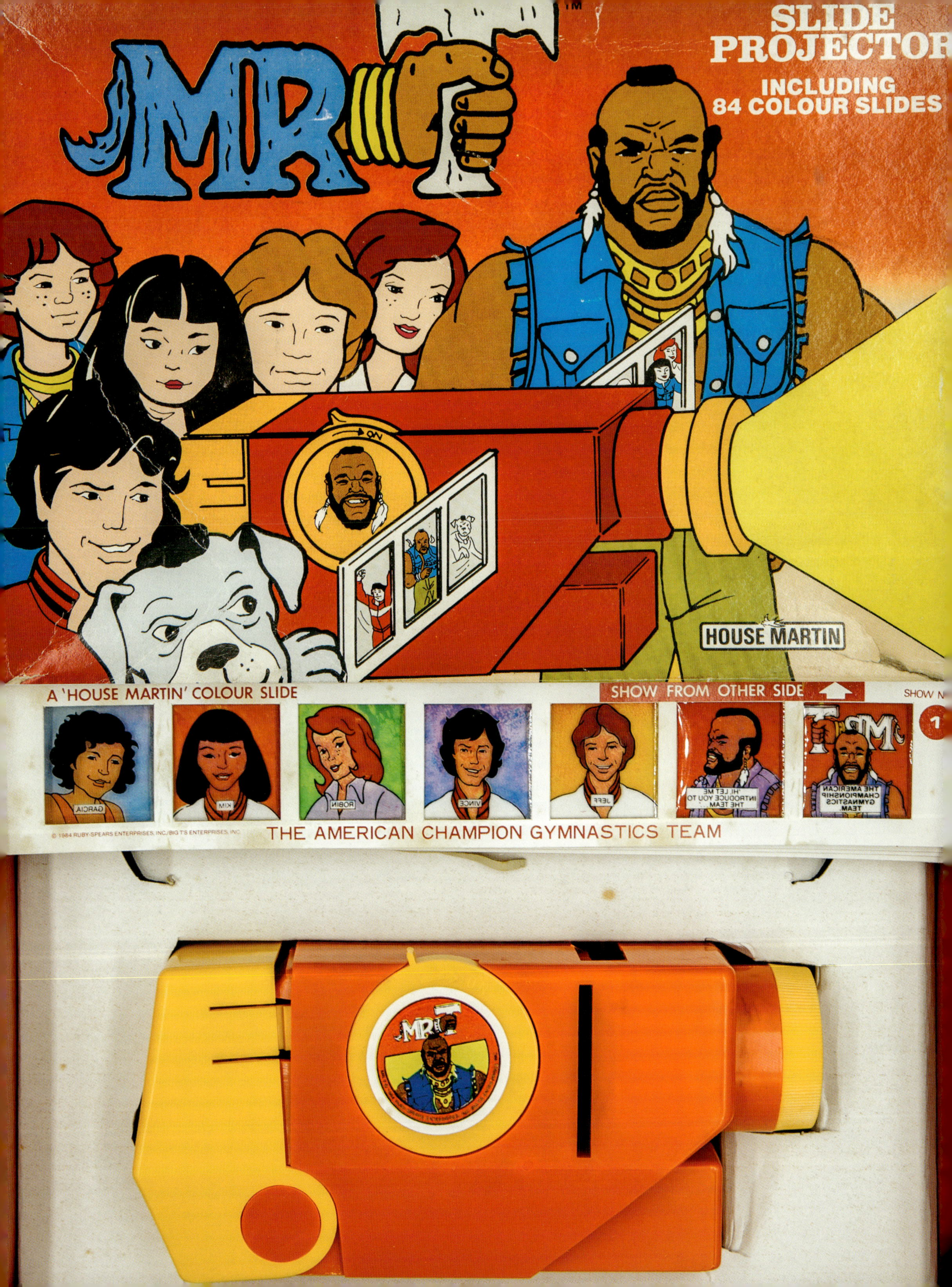
MR T
SLIDE PROJECTOR
INCLUDING 84 COLOUR SLIDES
HOUSE MARTIN
A 'HOUSE MARTIN' COLOUR SLIDE
SHOW FROM OTHER SIDE
1
© 1984 RUBY-SPEARS ENTERPRISES, INC./BIG T'S ENTERPRISES, INC.
THE AMERICAN CHAMPION GYMNASTICS TEAM

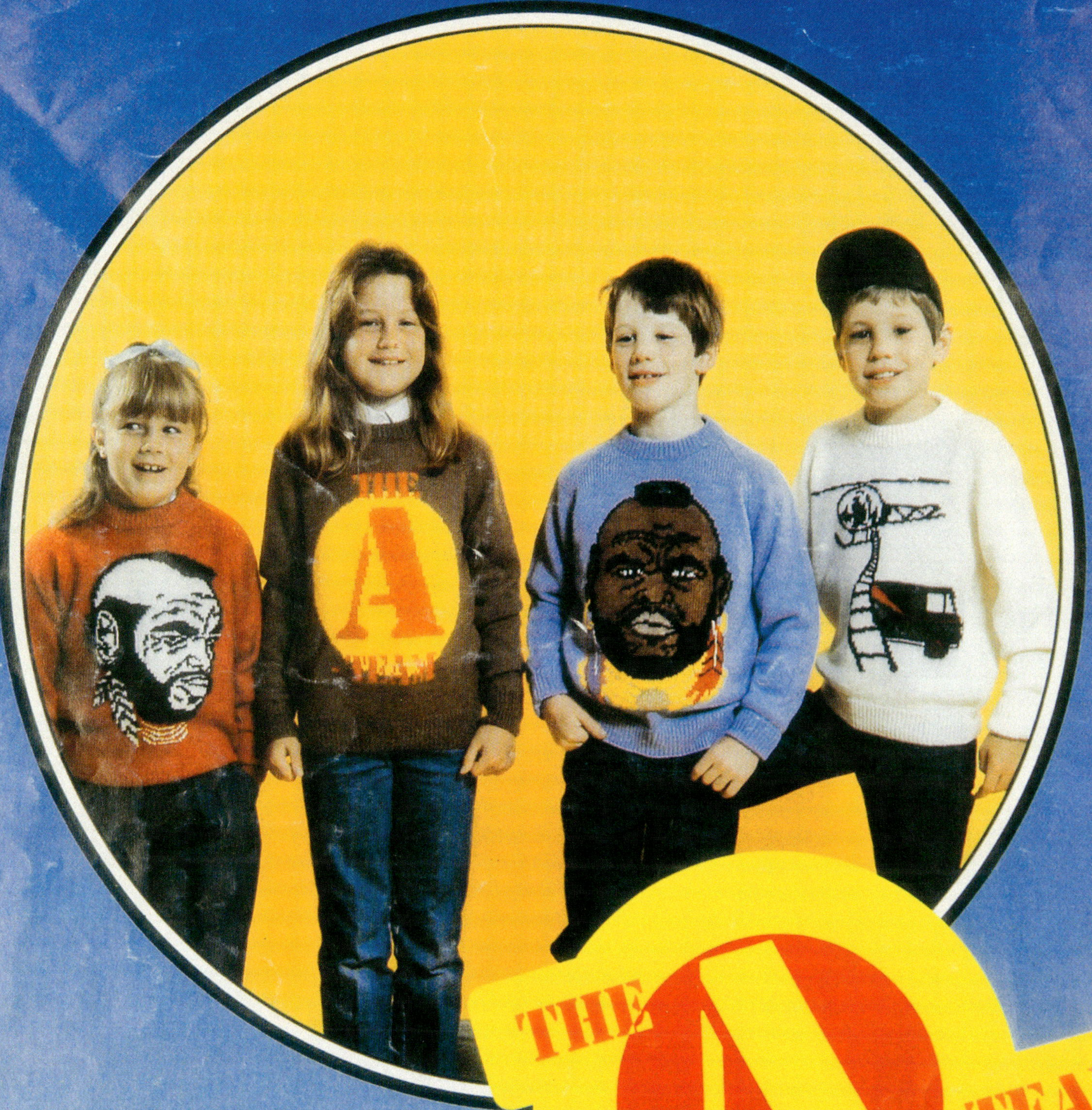

THE A-TEAM™*

Children's & Adult's SIZES: 24"- 44"

4 ply wool

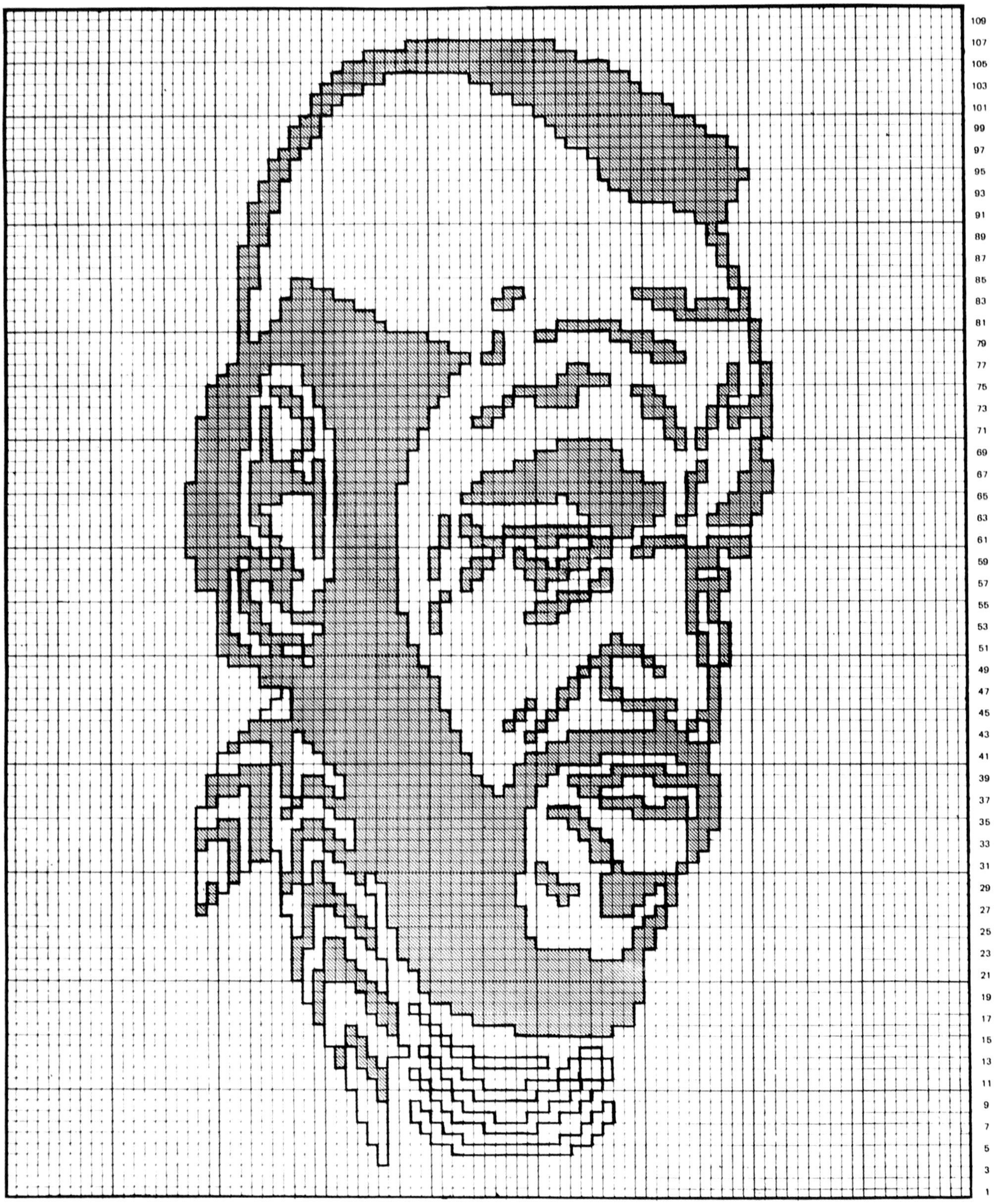

KEY — MS — White — **Black**

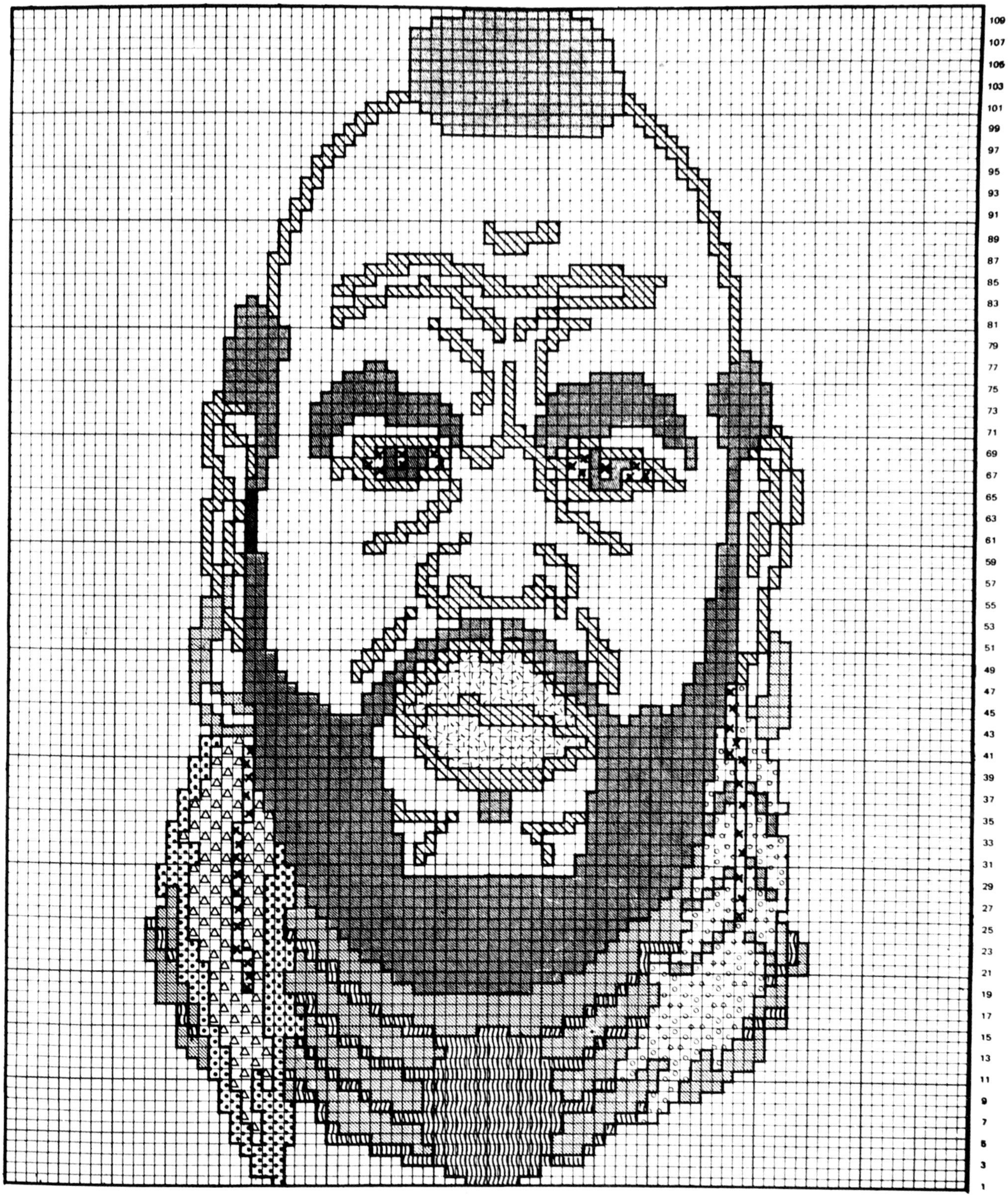

KEY

MS | Brown | D.Brown | Pink

Gold | Yellow | Black | Beige

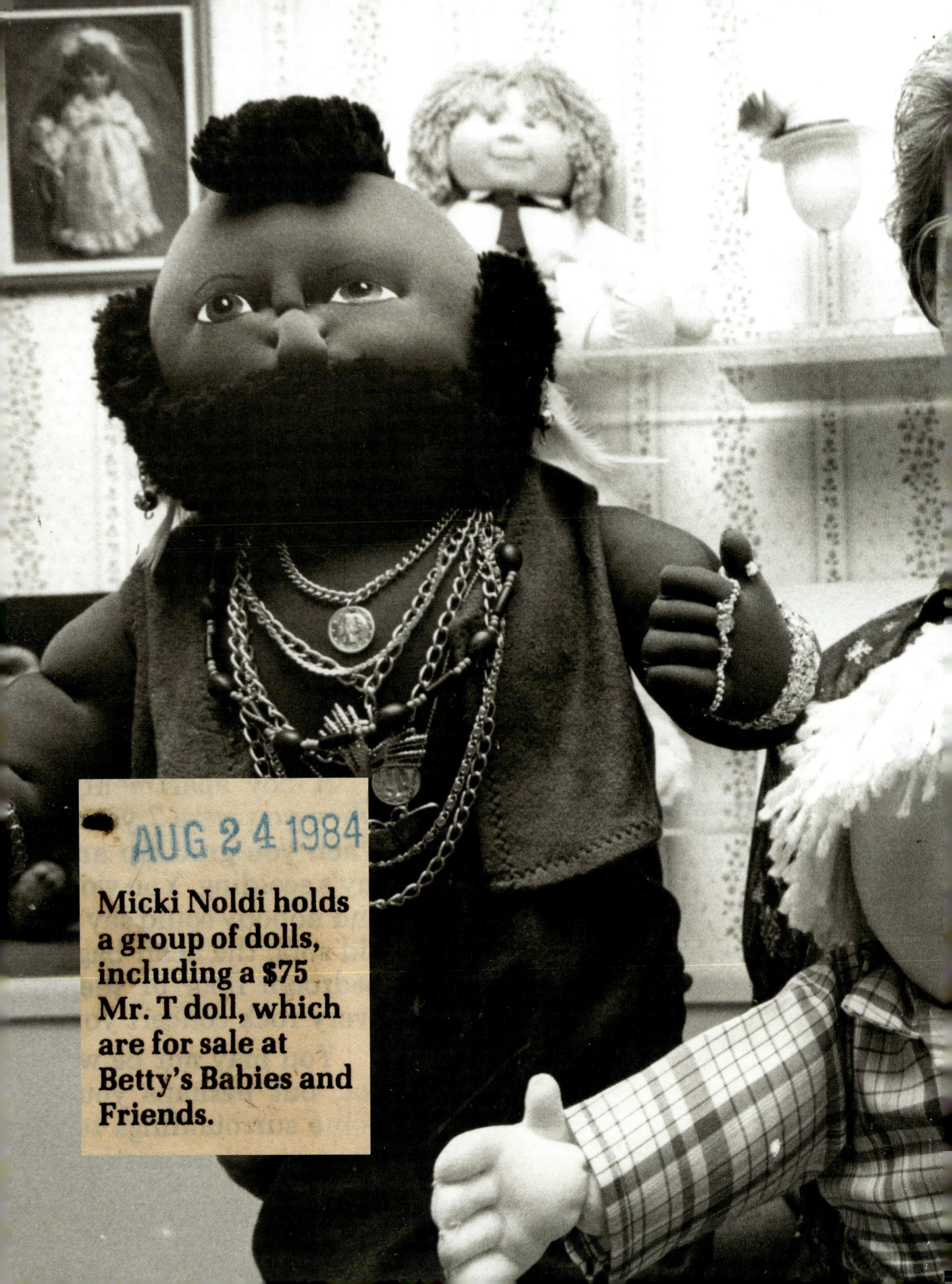

AUG 24 1984

Micki Noldi holds a group of dolls, including a $75 Mr. T doll, which are for sale at Betty's Babies and Friends.

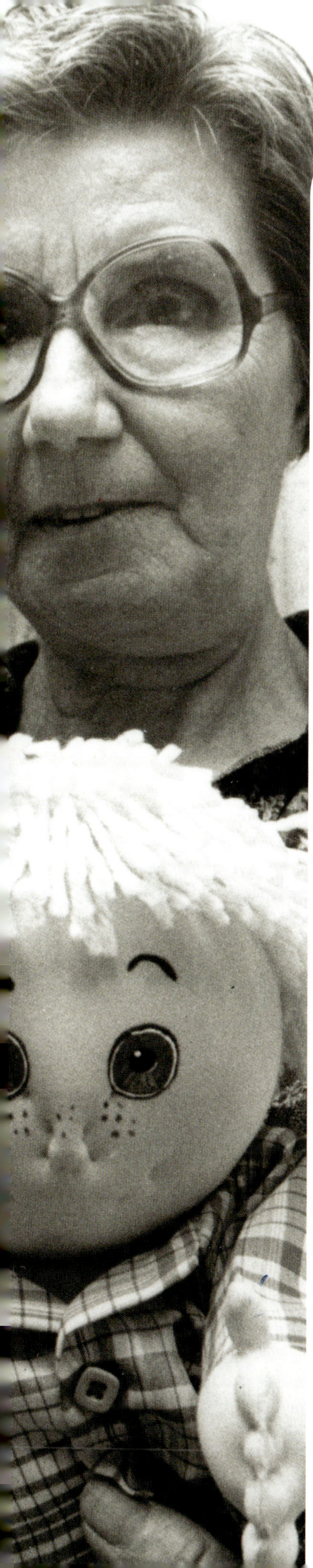

MARTHA'S DOLLS

If it wasn't clear already, Martha Holcombe, or Miss Martha as she is known by many, created the original *Mr. T Soft Sculpture Pattern Book* that all the dolls in my book are based on. It wasn't easy finding Martha since her company has been shut down for over fifteen years but I finally found her through the power of the internet. I had originally planned to travel to Gadsden, Alabama, to interview Martha in person, but after a few phone calls she decided it best to answer questions by email. It's a shame because I had the best time talking to Martha on the phone. At 70 years old, she's quick, witty, and has an amazing sense of humor. I hope you are still able to see some of that in her answers.

How did you get started making dolls?
In the summer of 1980, the church I was attending needed a new roof as well as other repairs. Our pastor asked the members to pray about making a "faith promise" to the church to raise enough to make necessary repairs. I prayed, and the amount I felt I was to give was $800, so that is what I pledged. I was a stay-at-home mom with three children and had no intention of going to work or starting a business. My education was in the mental health field, so I basically knew nothing about running a business. The Cabbage Patch craze was huge at the time, but I did not like the way the dolls looked. I was always trying new craft ideas and creating things. I was familiar with sewing since I made a lot of my clothes and clothes for my girls, so I designed a doll pattern, made a doll, and took it to church to see the response. People were very excited about the doll, so I thought I would make dolls to sell to get the $800. Shortly after that, I was looking through the magazine *Decorating & Craft Ideas*. I noticed the ads in the back for all types of crafts. It was like a light bulb going off in my head; "sell the patterns." I took out a ⅛-page ad in the above mentioned magazine for a soft-sculpture doll pattern that I did not yet have ready to sell. It took me three months working long hours every day to get the pattern and the instructions finished. A couple of days after the ad came out, I received twenty orders in the mail for $4.50 each. I was overjoyed. Every day more and more orders

Press photo for a story about doll maker Micki Noldi, including a Mr. T doll she made from the Miss Martha pattern. This photo is very indicative of the type of people who were making the dolls back in the 1980s!

#P444

Miss Martha Originals Inc.

INTRODUCES

MR. T

SOFT SCULPTURE DOLL PATTERN

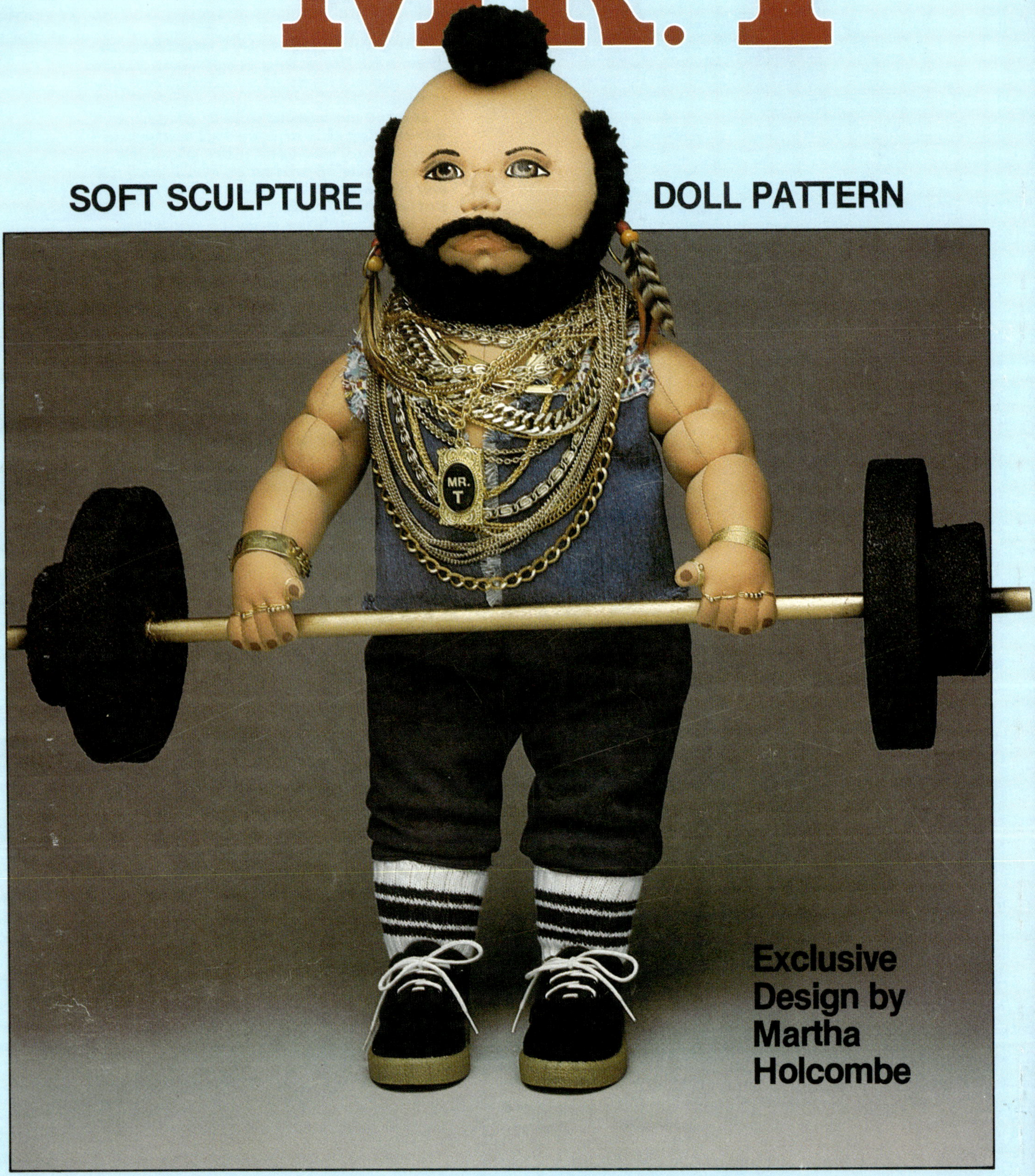

Licensed by Big T's Enterprises, Inc.

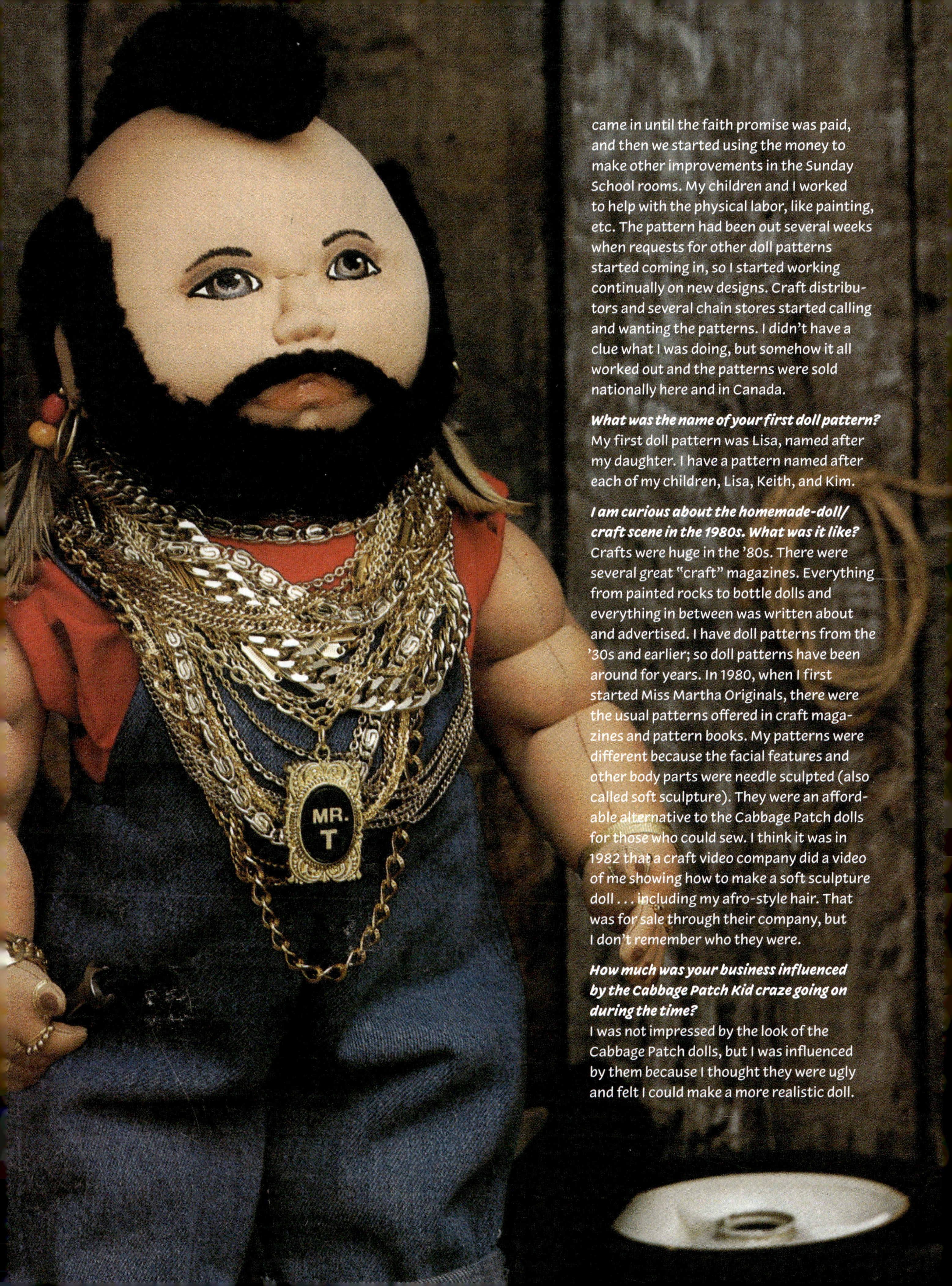

came in until the faith promise was paid, and then we started using the money to make other improvements in the Sunday School rooms. My children and I worked to help with the physical labor, like painting, etc. The pattern had been out several weeks when requests for other doll patterns started coming in, so I started working continually on new designs. Craft distributors and several chain stores started calling and wanting the patterns. I didn't have a clue what I was doing, but somehow it all worked out and the patterns were sold nationally here and in Canada.

What was the name of your first doll pattern?
My first doll pattern was Lisa, named after my daughter. I have a pattern named after each of my children, Lisa, Keith, and Kim.

I am curious about the homemade-doll/ craft scene in the 1980s. What was it like?
Crafts were huge in the '80s. There were several great "craft" magazines. Everything from painted rocks to bottle dolls and everything in between was written about and advertised. I have doll patterns from the '30s and earlier; so doll patterns have been around for years. In 1980, when I first started Miss Martha Originals, there were the usual patterns offered in craft magazines and pattern books. My patterns were different because the facial features and other body parts were needle sculpted (also called soft sculpture). They were an affordable alternative to the Cabbage Patch dolls for those who could sew. I think it was in 1982 that a craft video company did a video of me showing how to make a soft sculpture doll . . . including my afro-style hair. That was for sale through their company, but I don't remember who they were.

How much was your business influenced by the Cabbage Patch Kid craze going on during the time?
I was not impressed by the look of the Cabbage Patch dolls, but I was influenced by them because I thought they were ugly and felt I could make a more realistic doll.

Who came up with the idea of doing a Mr. T doll, and why Mr. T?
Since I designed the patterns for the dolls, it was my idea of doing a Mr. T doll. Mr. T was a role model for kids and a very likable character. I thought the people buying my patterns would enjoy making their own unique version of him.

What do you think made Mr. T so likable? What made him a good role model for children? Do you remember the first time you heard him or saw him and said he would be a really good doll?
Mr. T was likable and a good role model for children, especially black children. He was the good guy trying to catch the bad guy like a superhero in a comic book. Many black children didn't have a father in the home, and Mr. T was someone they could look up to.

Did you actually ever get to talk to or communicate in some way with Mr. T? He obviously saw the finished doll. Did the agency express to you his reaction to it?
Carolyn Snead, the manager of MMO, contacted the licensing agent. We had to send a sample of the pattern to get it approved by Mr. T. Neither Carolyn nor I spoke with Mr. T. The agency was friendly and helpful. Unfortunately, we were not told of his reaction to the doll.

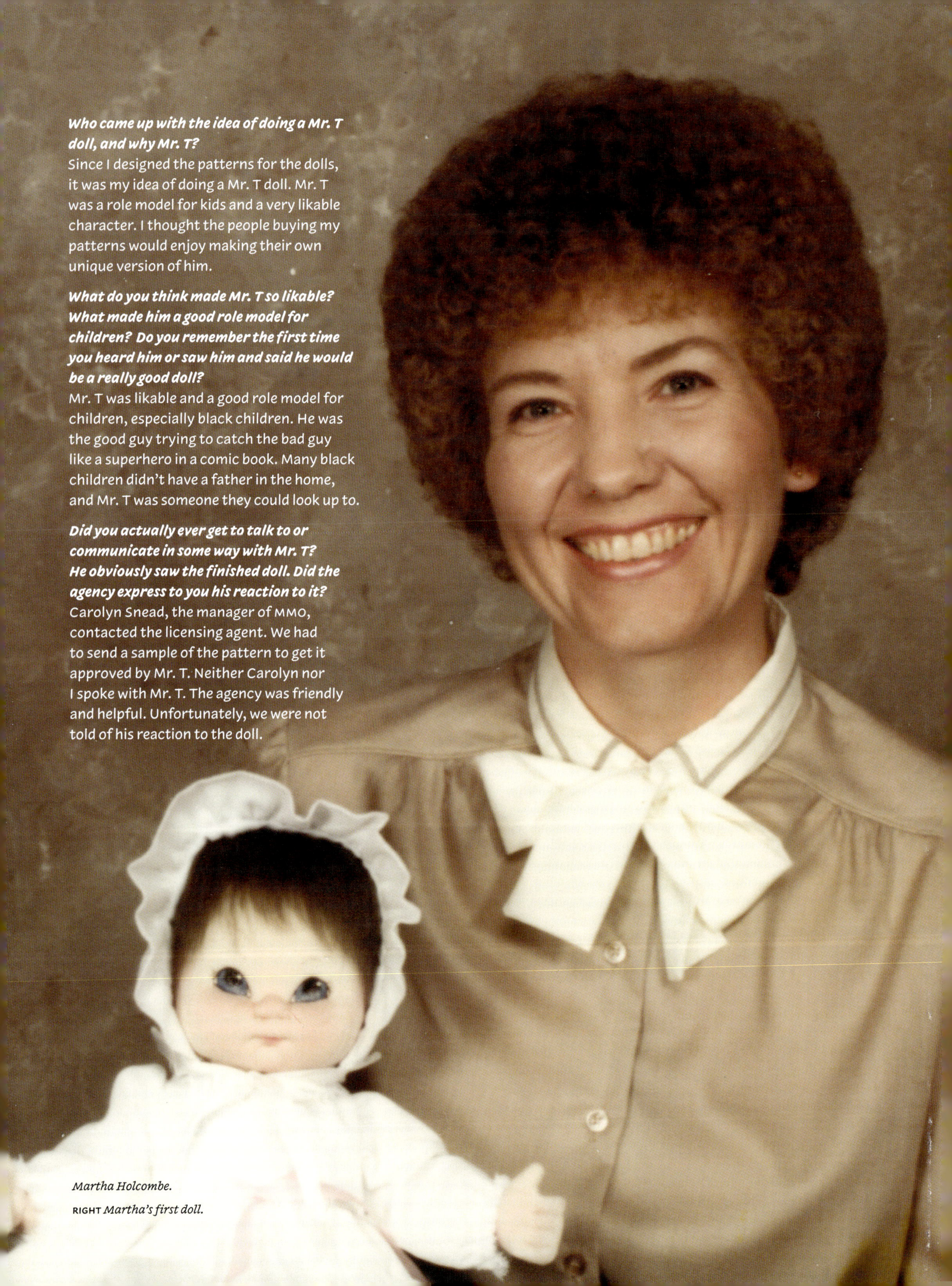

Martha Holcombe.

RIGHT *Martha's first doll.*

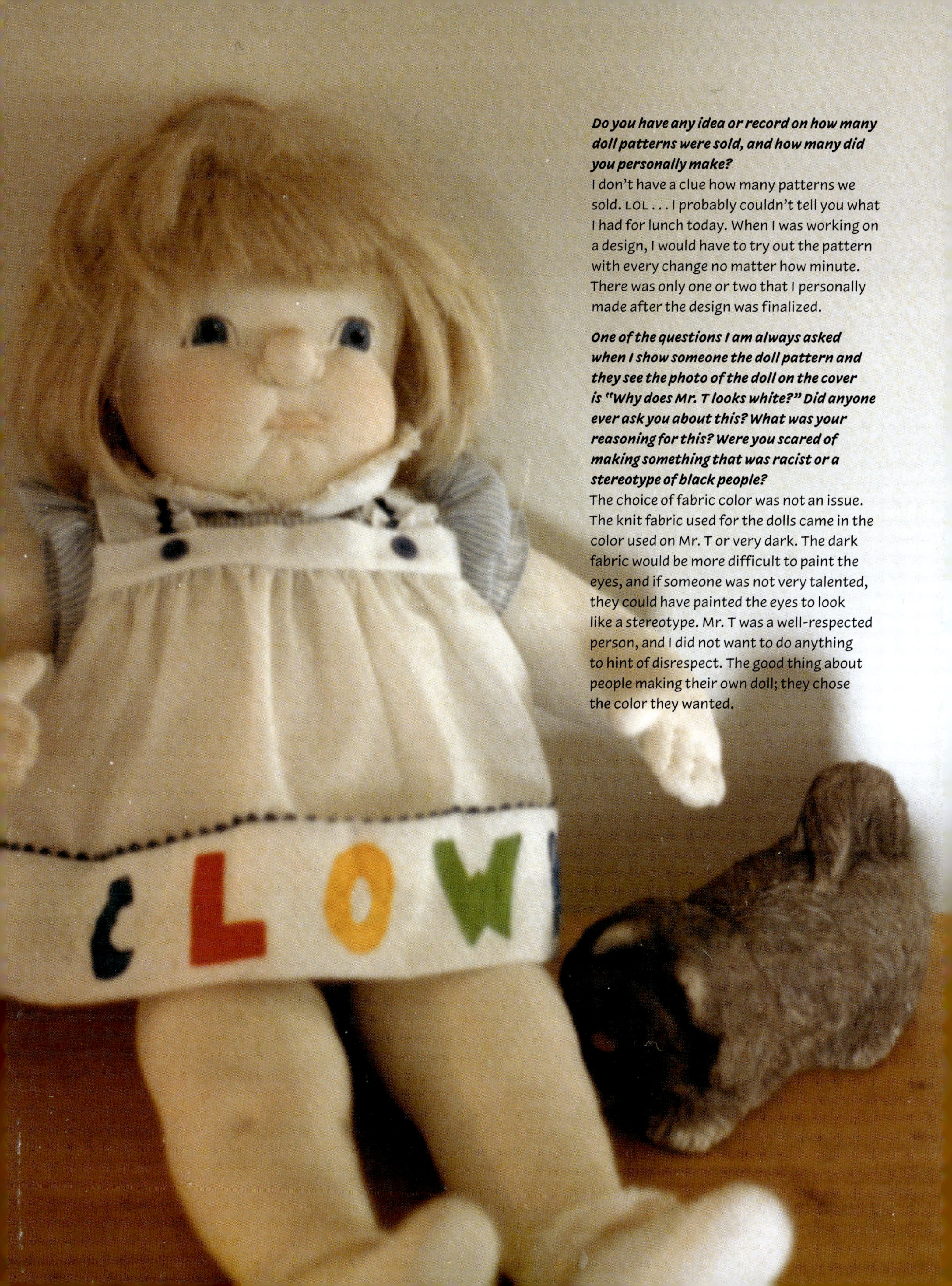

Do you have any idea or record on how many doll patterns were sold, and how many did you personally make?

I don't have a clue how many patterns we sold. LOL . . . I probably couldn't tell you what I had for lunch today. When I was working on a design, I would have to try out the pattern with every change no matter how minute. There was only one or two that I personally made after the design was finalized.

One of the questions I am always asked when I show someone the doll pattern and they see the photo of the doll on the cover is "Why does Mr. T looks white?" Did anyone ever ask you about this? What was your reasoning for this? Were you scared of making something that was racist or a stereotype of black people?

The choice of fabric color was not an issue. The knit fabric used for the dolls came in the color used on Mr. T or very dark. The dark fabric would be more difficult to paint the eyes, and if someone was not very talented, they could have painted the eyes to look like a stereotype. Mr. T was a well-respected person, and I did not want to do anything to hint of disrespect. The good thing about people making their own doll; they chose the color they wanted.

I know when we talked on the phone you told me something along the lines of "People don't want to admit it, but racism does exist." I know you said you didn't want to disrespect him, but were you ever scared of racism in general impeding the sale of the doll pattern? Or did you think Mr. T crossed that racial barrier and despite any racial tension it didn't matter because he was such an exceptional role model?

Mr. T crossed the racial barrier, so there wasn't a problem selling his pattern.

What was the response like? Fan mail? Photos? Letters?

The response was good, and yes, we got fan mail, photos, and letters, but that was so long ago that there is nothing still around. We sold to distributors all over the country, Walmart and several chain stores, so it was widely distributed.

Eventually though, your company shut down. Why did you shut down? What happened to the industry?

With the patterns, we grew from a corner in my living room to our garage, then to a rented storefront, then another building, until finally we built our own building in the Industrial Park in Gadsden, Alabama in 1984. I forgot to mention that our sales went through the roof, which got the attention of every knock-off artist. It took about six to nine months after we became successful that my patterns were showing up everywhere under different names with slight changes in the patterns . . . just enough to get by copyright infringement. Nobody was dumb enough to knock off Mr. T because it

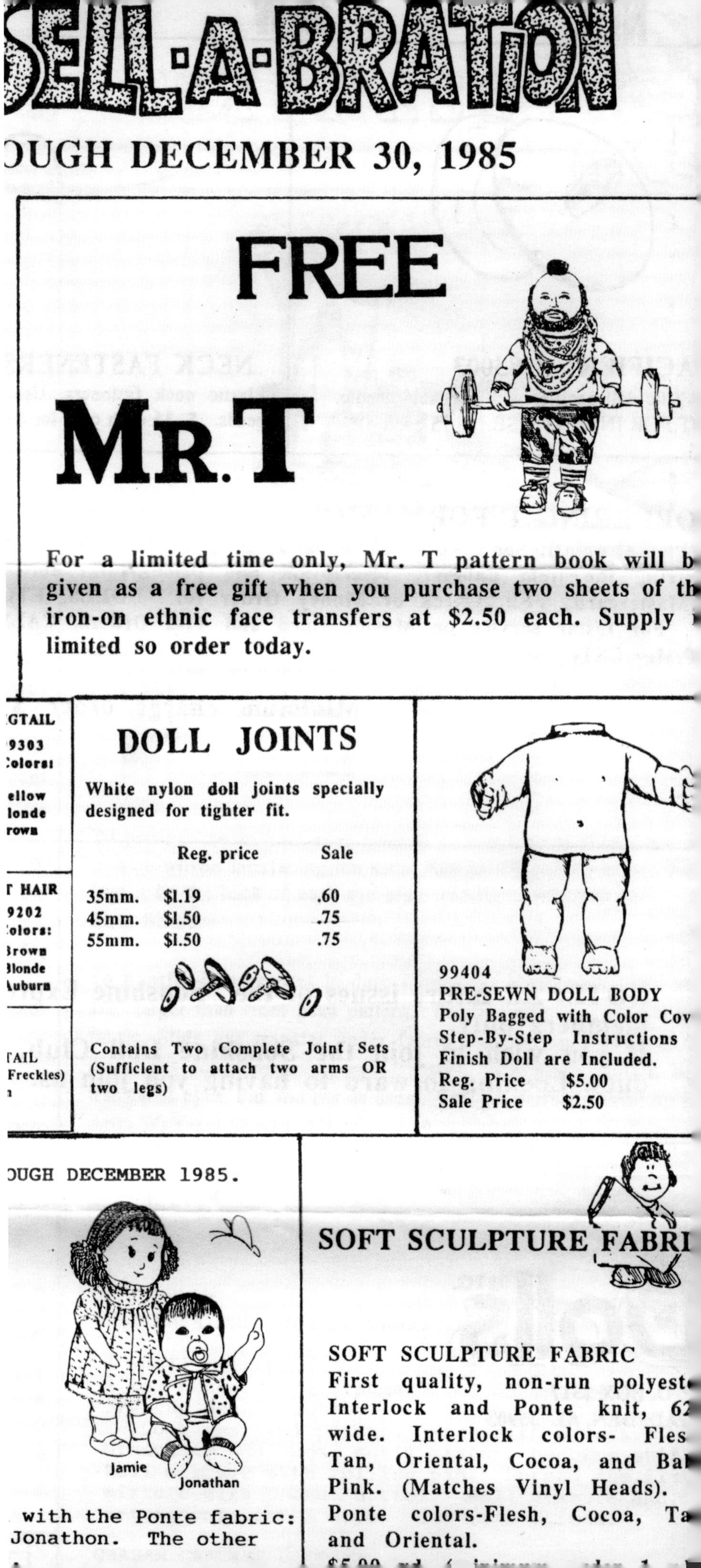

was a licensed pattern. What goes up, must come down. And that is what happened to us. We had just put up a new building when the bottom completely fell out of the pattern business. We didn't even have the money to make our building payments. All I had to work with was my hands and talent, so I sculpted nine little black figurines and called them All God's Children (AGC). They were made from resin and crushed pecan shell flour. I sculpted black figurines because that is what I loved doing. I did not enjoy sculpting white ones. I told our banker that if he would work with us, in one year's time I would have the #1 black line in the USA.

That is exactly what happened. Our first trade show with AGC was in Dallas, Texas, and we were so successful that the dealers had people waiting in line for the UPS to make a delivery of AGC. The secondary market went shockingly high, and business was great up until 1995. Sales had gotten to be about 12,000,000 per year, but I was the only artist. Everything depended on my ability to create. My mom, sister, grandmother, and stepdad all became terminally ill, and I could not be creative. Everything started slowing down at a fast rate. By 2001, I had lost those I just mentioned. I had lost the desire to create, so even when I sculpted it did not have the right look. I forgot to mention in 1993, we purchased a beautiful 36,000-square-foot building and built our own park for our collectors to come once a year to a family reunion. I should have sent you some of our magazines from the good old days. eBay killed the secondary market on our line and also on most of the other top lines.

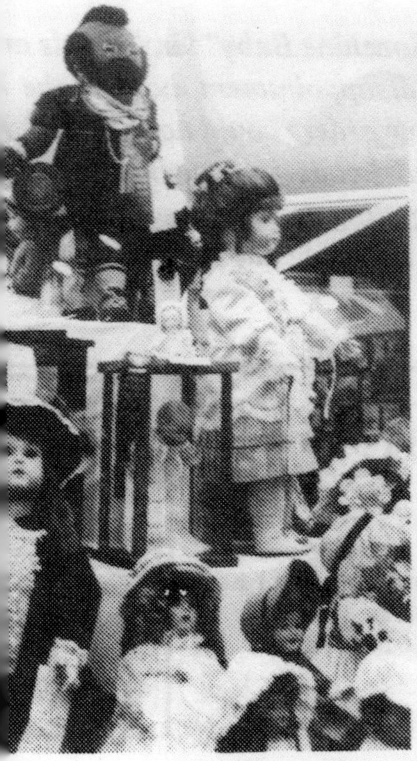

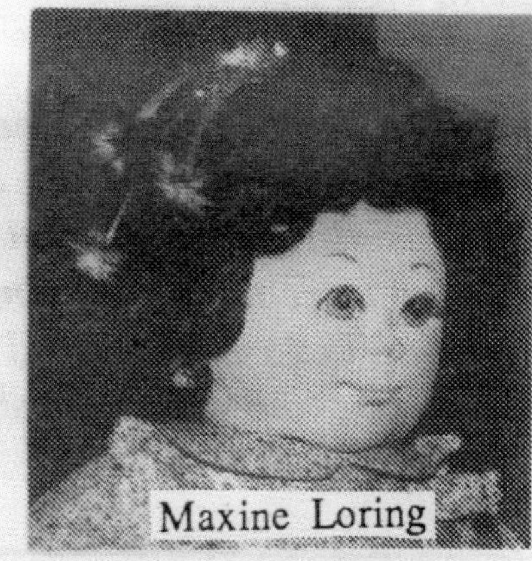

Texas State Fair
All the judges went wild. They thought he was just it. One judge said she wouldn't have a cloth doll until she saw Mr. T.
My friends nearly had to make me enter the fair.
Dot Chick, Abilene, TX

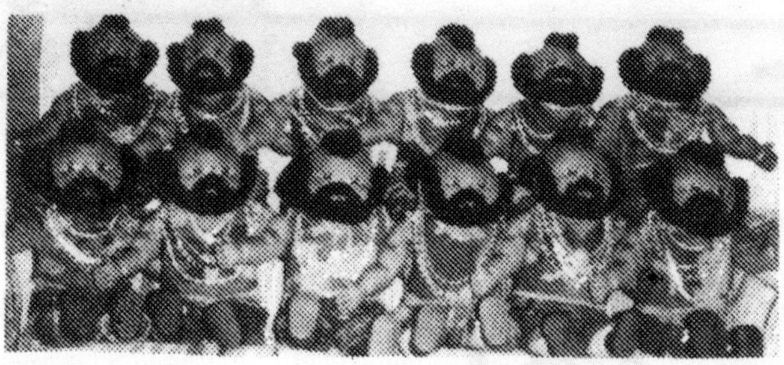

Dear Miss Martha,

I think the Sonshine Doll Club with newsletters is a wonderful idea.

My membership fee was sent after I first received the news.

I am contributing a picture of my recent project. My ten grandsons all received a Mr. T from me and they are delighted. I told each of them to add more "gold" themsleves. Thank goodness, my other six grandchildren are girls. I gave them "pretty" dolls. I kept one Mr. T for my shop and sold the extra one for $75.00.

I have all your doll patterns and love them. I've tried some different ones (brands) but always come back to yours. Thanks loads!

Virginia Johnson
Medina, Texas

Dear Martha,

I want you to know that my Mr. T won first prize in our Augusta Exchange Club fair, in the soft sculpture and first in the entire show! Two (2) ribbons! Thanks !

I have made your "Sonshine and Roses" and I just love her!

I have made many, many rag dolls but I love yours the best! I also gave some at Ronald McDonald House!

P.S. I have sent in my dues for your Sonshine Doll Club.

Henrietta Avrett
Augusta, G A

Pages from Miss Martha's newsletter, Sonshine Express*, 1985.*

The TV show *How it's Made* featured AGC in one of their shows. Enesco Corp. and Hallmark were licensed to do some of my figurines that I sculpted for them. Enesco had the "Miss Martha Collection" and Hallmark had three ornaments before I canceled my contract with them. Enesco made a video showing the making of the Miss Martha Collection. It was very well done. It is a known fact in the collectibles industry that the life of a line is about twelve years. We pushed it past the limit to about twenty-eight years but paid the price. We finally shut down because I was tired of the stress. The collectible industry took a tremendous hit when the Beanie Baby craze happened. That was the "in" collectible. People were actually using their kids' college money to invest in those little things. When the creator said he was shutting down production, that flattened collectibles.

You went from making dolls named after your kids, to a doll of Mr. T, then to exclusively black kids and other lesser-known black figures in history. Why did you like sculpting black people more? Was it an educational thing? Did it have to do with where you grew up? From an outsider it seems like a place like Alabama must have had a lot of racism growing up. Was this a reaction to that?

That's where my heart was. It was just something I enjoyed doing. I used it as an educational thing with the historical figurines. It had nothing to do with where I grew up. All of the South had a lot of racism, but many other areas of the country did as well; they just managed to hide it better. My work was not a reaction to racism, but God did use my work to bring unity to the races. There were several thousand collectors who attended our family reunions, and they made lasting friendships. Their response was "Martin Luther King would be so proud if he could see this." Everything was very segregated until the mid-sixties. My family was dysfunctional, so I struggled to survive. Racism was not something I ever thought about.

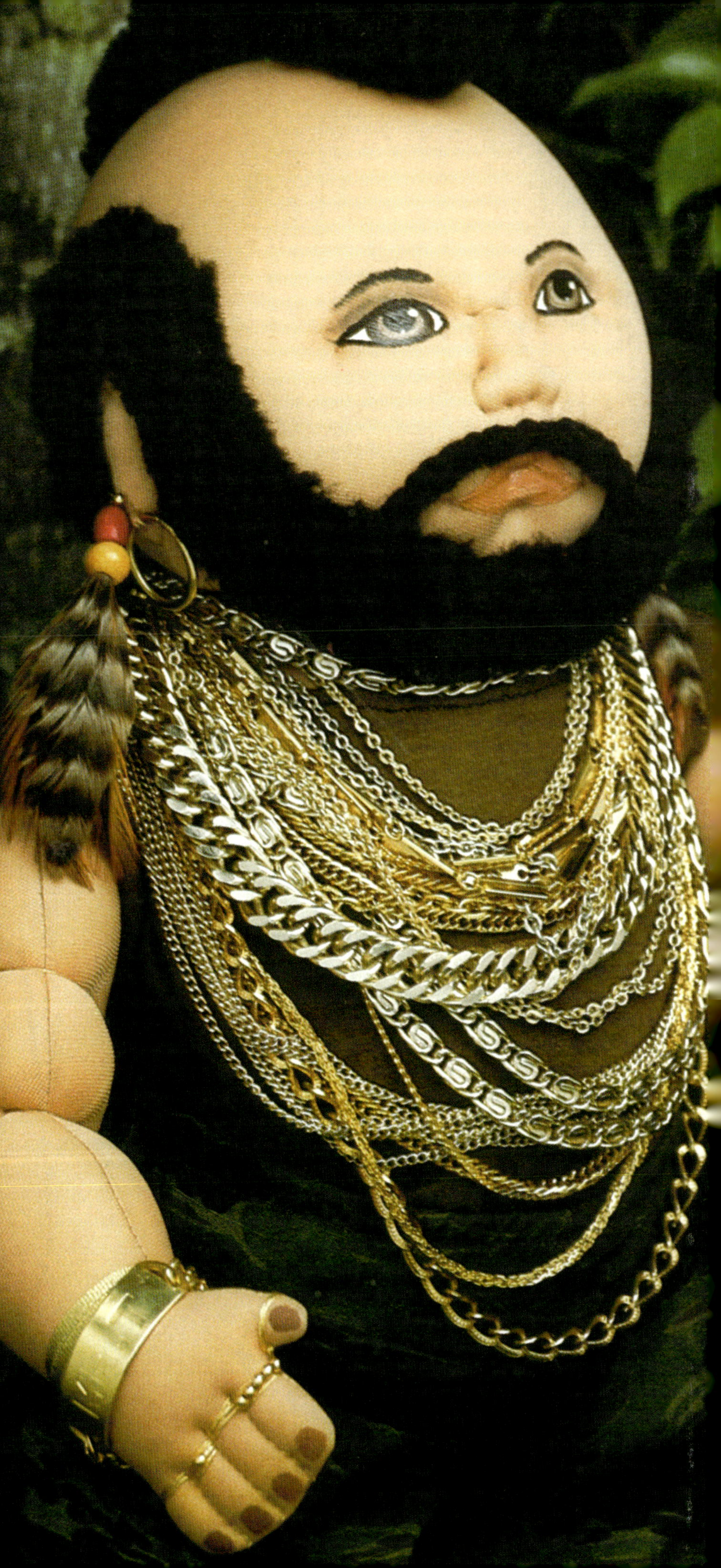

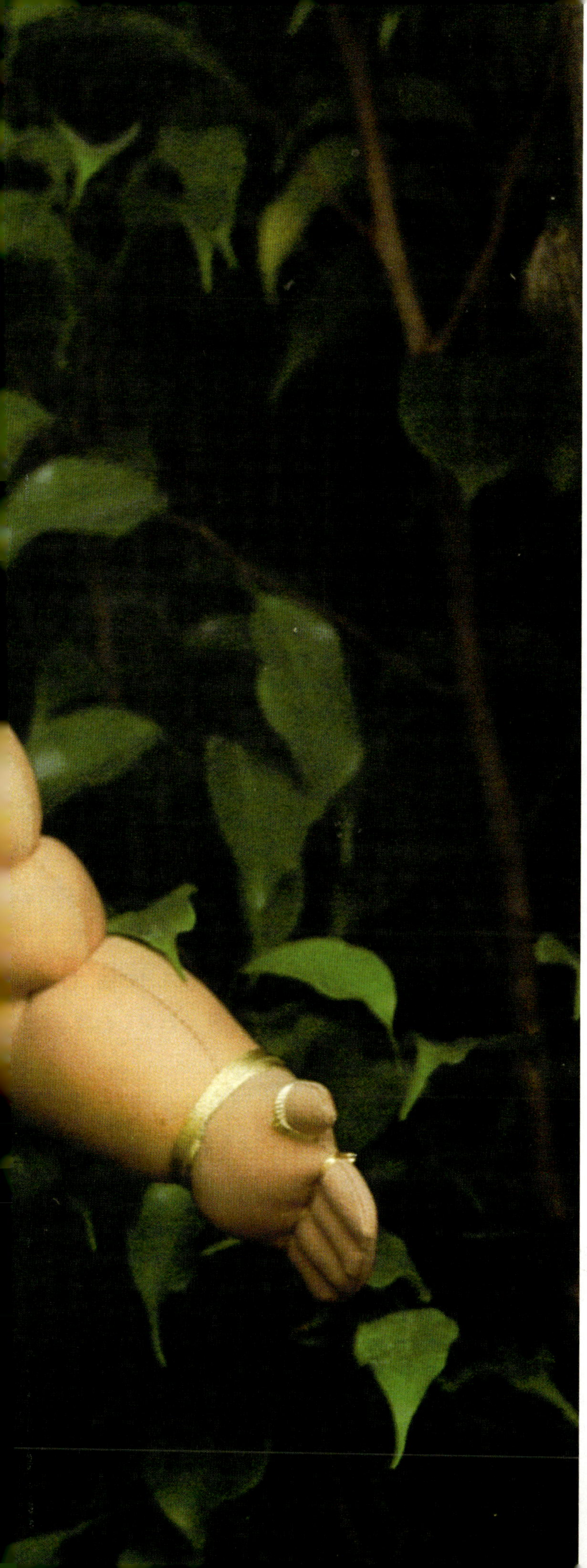

desired. Take a small stitch, pull tight enough to indent fabric.

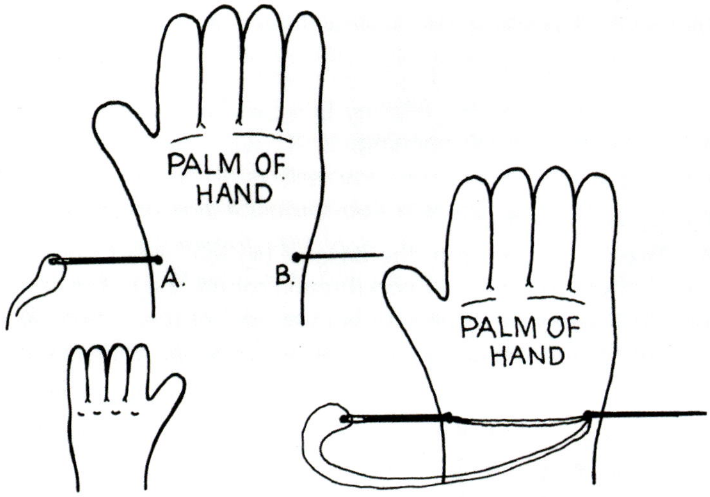

E. Top of foot - (optional) Insert needle through ankle and back twice. Loop thread around on the top of the foot and insert needle in the ankle dot on the other side of foot, pulling thread tightly. Repeat once.

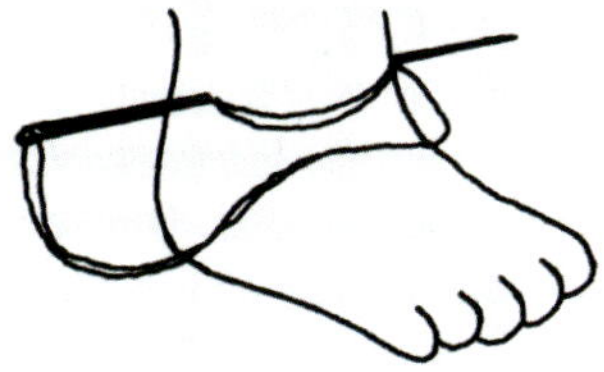

F. Arms and Elbows - Insert needle at A, exit on inside of arm at B. With thread on **OUTSIDE** of fabric, insert needle at A, exit at B, pulling thread tightly. With thread on **OUTSIDE** of fabric, insert needle at A, exit at D inside arm, pulling thread tightly. With thread on **OUTSIDE** of fabric, insert needle at C, exit at D pulling thread tightly. With thread on **OUTSIDE** of fabric, insert needle at C, exit at elbow dot X pulling thread tightly. Insert needle at X digging deep into filling, exit at lower elbow dot Y. Insert needle at Y, exit at X pulling thread tightly to shape elbow. Insert needle at X, bring out at seamline and tack.

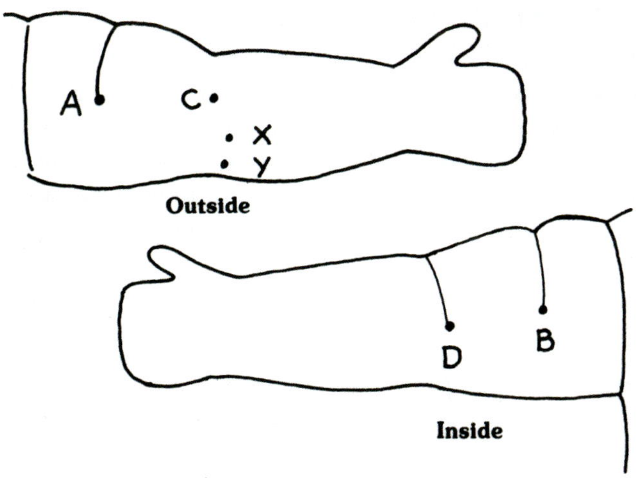

Step 12.

Hair, Beard and Mustache: This is made by wrapping yarn around strips of paper using the measurements given below. Wrap the yarn evenly around each strip until completely covered. Do not allow yarn to bunch up. To make stitching easier, place a thin piece of paper under each wrapped strip and stitch down the center twice. Carefully tear away paper.

Attach strips of yarn where indicated using a backstitch. After all yarn is attached, clip loops and comb with a large toothed comb. Clip yarn evenly.

A. Mustache - One strip 4"x 1/2". Place center of strip under nose.

B. Beard - Two strips 9"x 1 1/2". Place first strip starting at top of ear and going under chin to top of other ear. Stitch other strip 1/4" from first one.

One strip 4"x 1". Stitch under bottom lip.

C. Hair - Cut three 8 1/2"x 2" strips for the top of head. Stitch first strip along the center head seam beginning 1/2" in front of seam. Stitch the other two strips (one on each side) beside center strip. One 13"x 1 1/4" strip. Stitch from top of ear down around neckline to top of the other ear.

A.

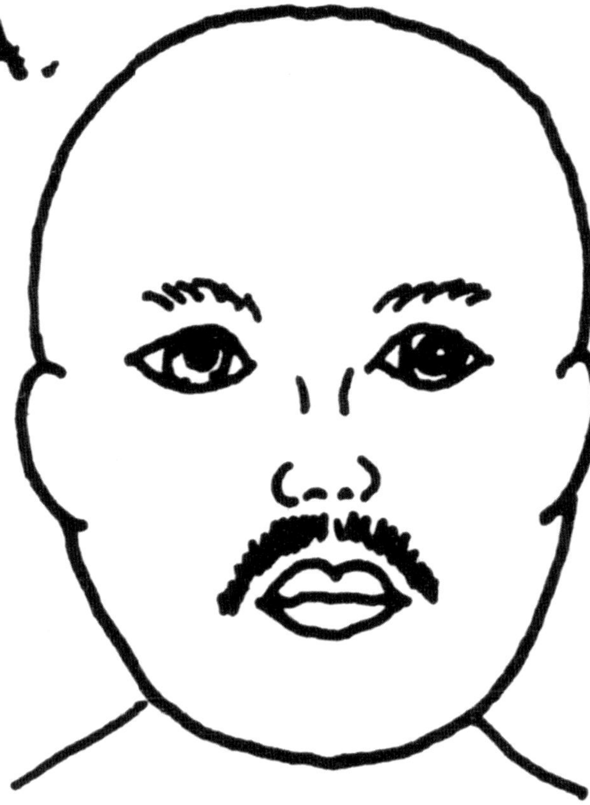

B.

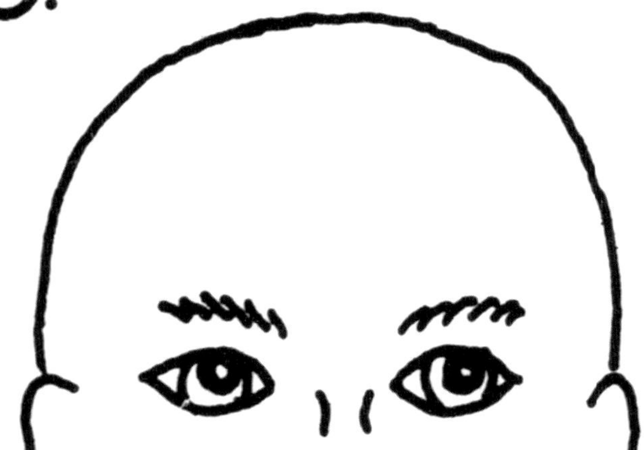

C.

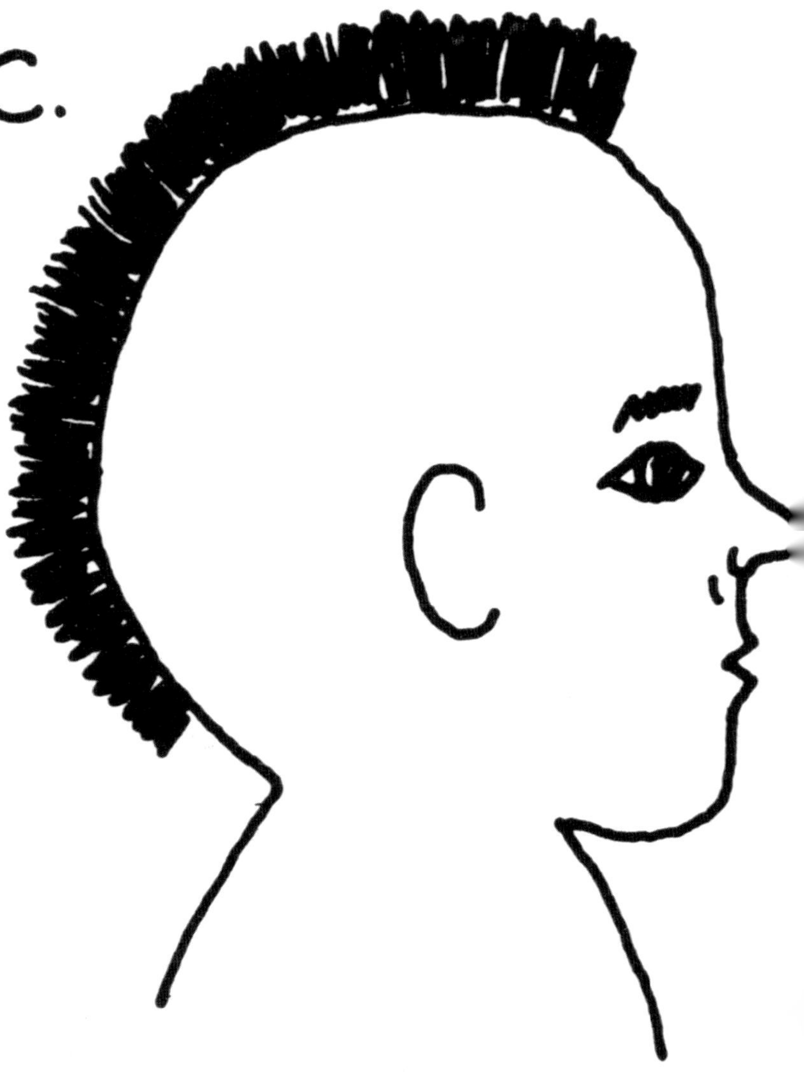

B.

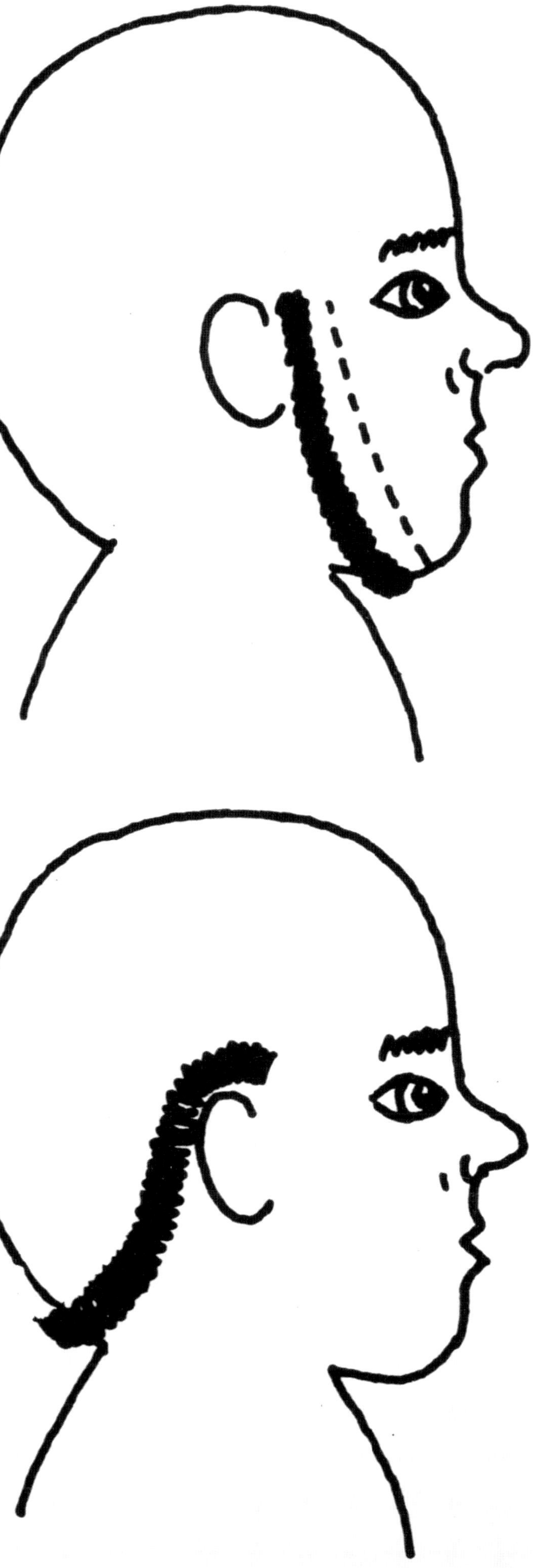

Did you ever consider these dolls folk art? Do you consider yourself a folk artist?
I am a southern memory folk artist.

Have you heard of anyone else collecting the Mr. T Dolls like I had?
Haha, I have never heard of anyone collecting the dolls as you have.

Some of my dolls are anatomically correct. Why do you think that is?
There were dolls being sold anatomically correct, so creative people just like to be creative. You never know what is in someone's mind when they choose to do something unique.

What is life like these days, and are you surprised you are talking about this thirty years later?
Nothing surprises me anymore . . . well, almost nothing. My husband was sick for five years, and I was his caregiver. That has taken a toll on my health but I am still kicking, just not stirring up much dust. I have been working off and on (mostly off) for about six years on a unique doll pattern but just have not finished it. Maybe it will be finished by fall . . . maybe not. I serve in deliverance ministry and teach others about healing and deliverance. I am just now moving slowly back into that since my husband's death on September 29, 2017. My goal for this year is several ministry trips, an art retreat, and just enjoying life for a while. I would love to see at least twelve people come to know Christ as their Savior this year. Actually I would like to see thousands, but I will settle for twelve to start with.

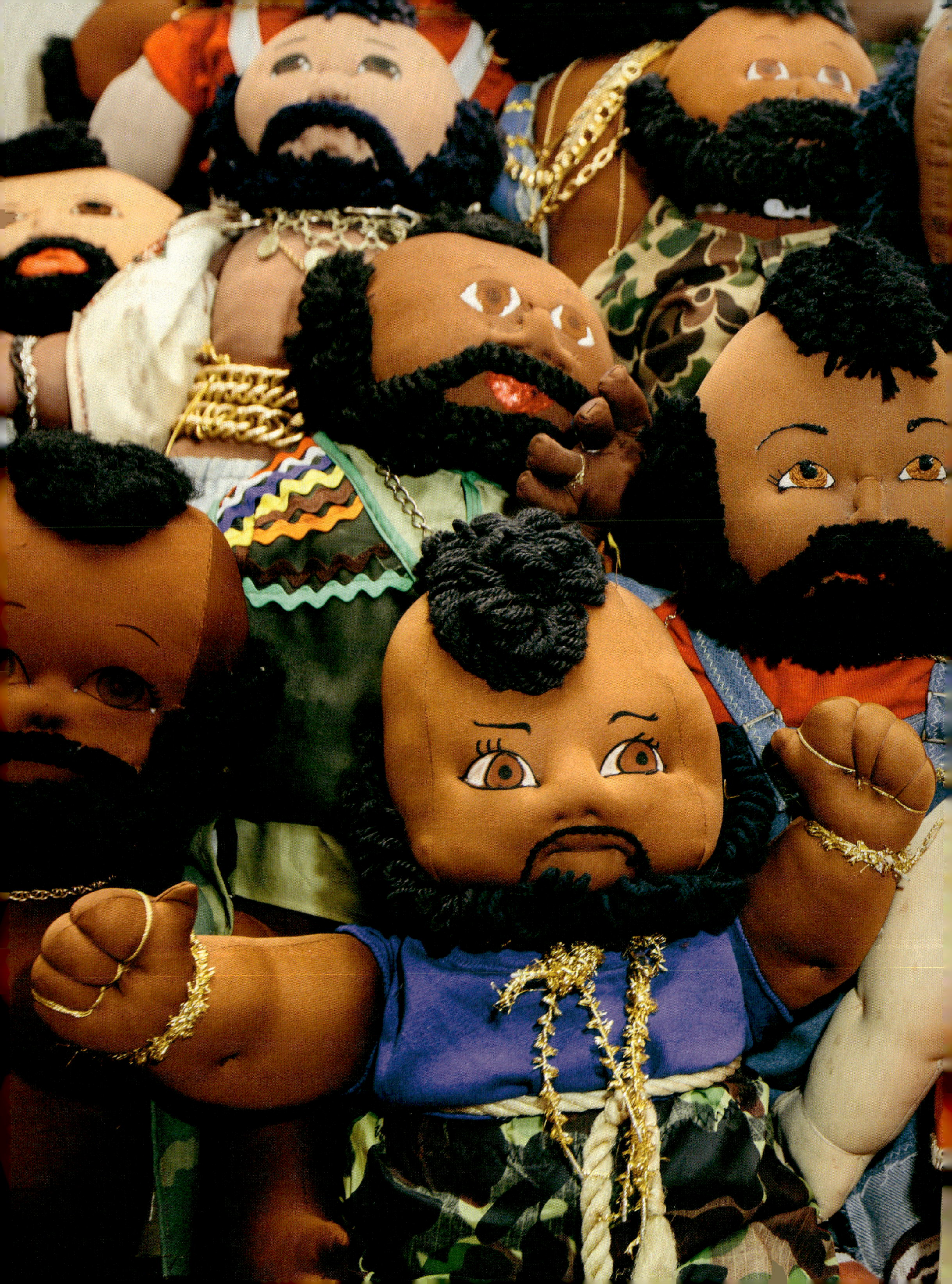

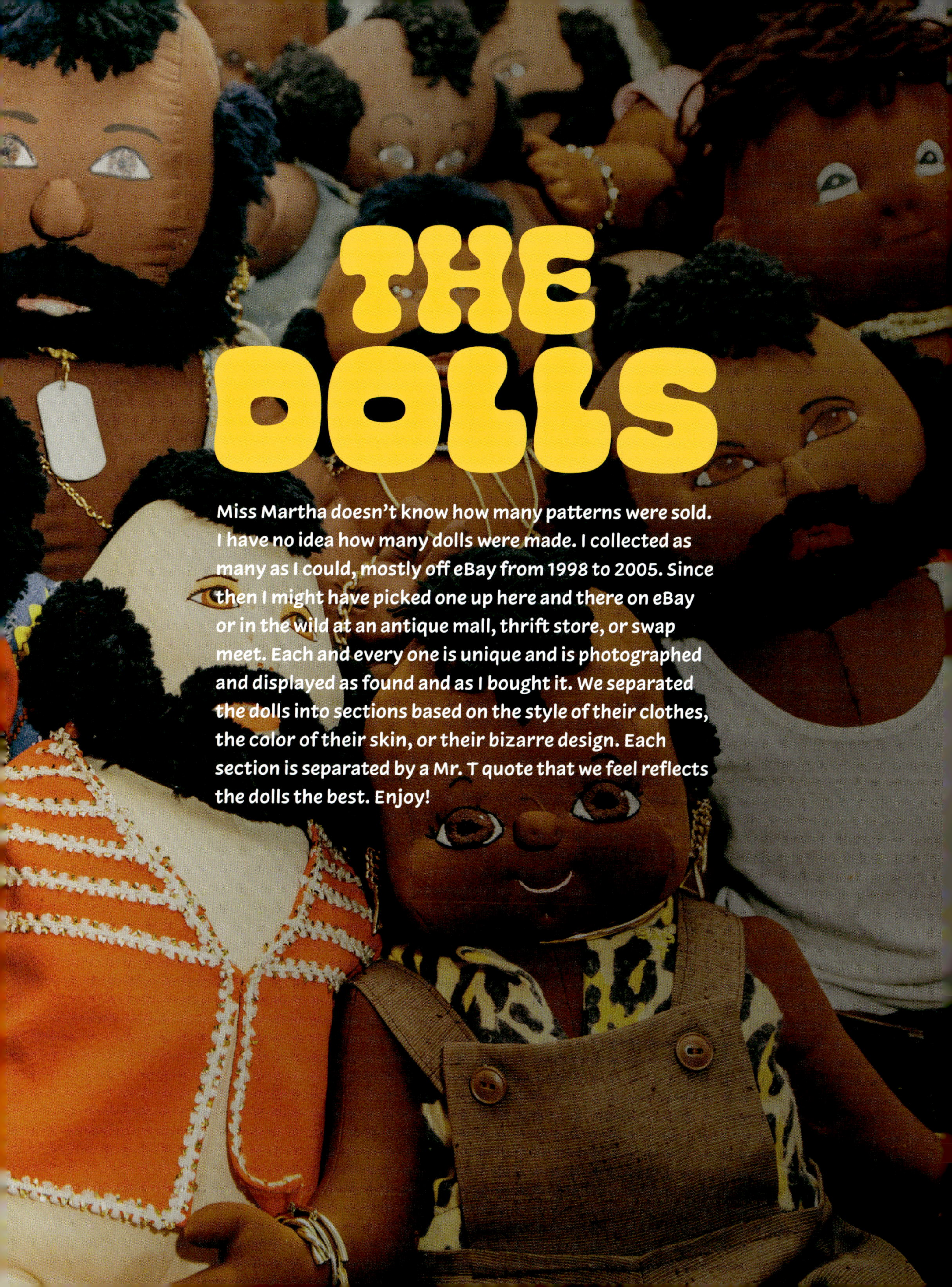

THE DOLLS

Miss Martha doesn't know how many patterns were sold. I have no idea how many dolls were made. I collected as many as I could, mostly off eBay from 1998 to 2005. Since then I might have picked one up here and there on eBay or in the wild at an antique mall, thrift store, or swap meet. Each and every one is unique and is photographed and displayed as found and as I bought it. We separated the dolls into sections based on the style of their clothes, the color of their skin, or their bizarre design. Each section is separated by a Mr. T quote that we feel reflects the dolls the best. Enjoy!

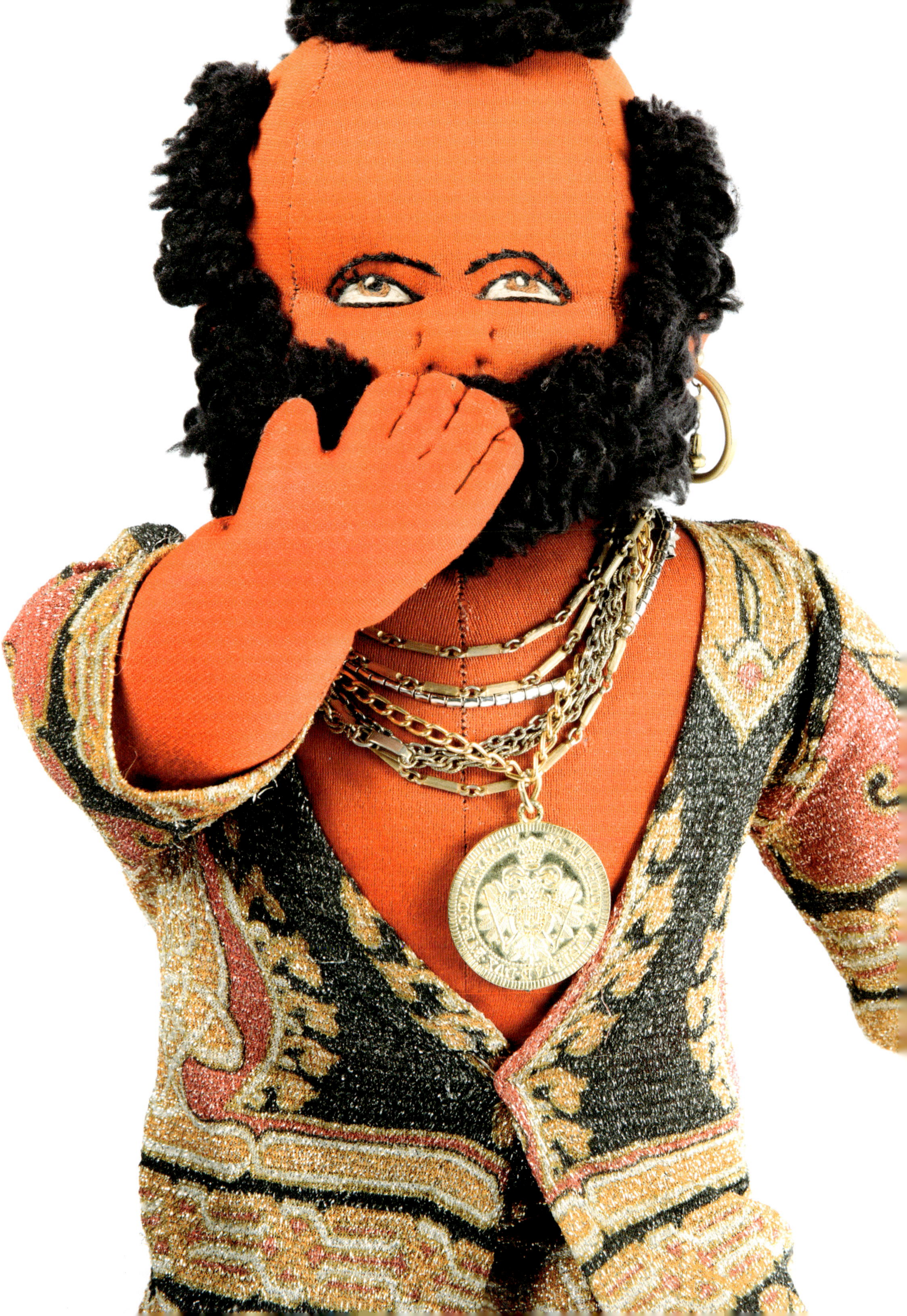

I BELIEVE IN THE GOLDEN RULE THE MAN WITH THE GOLD RULES

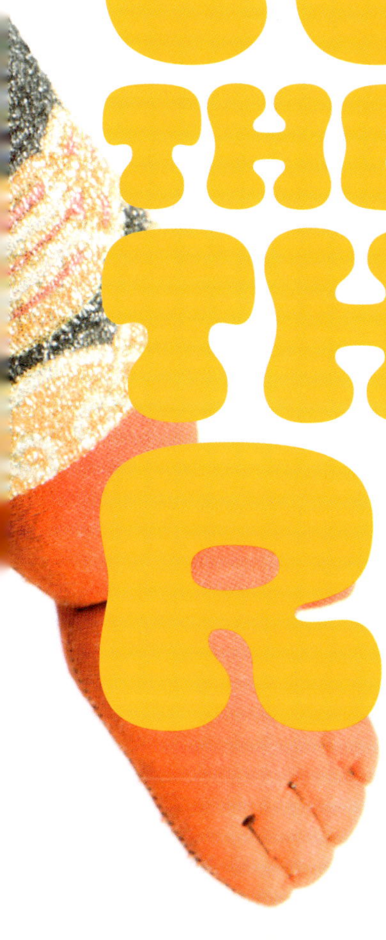

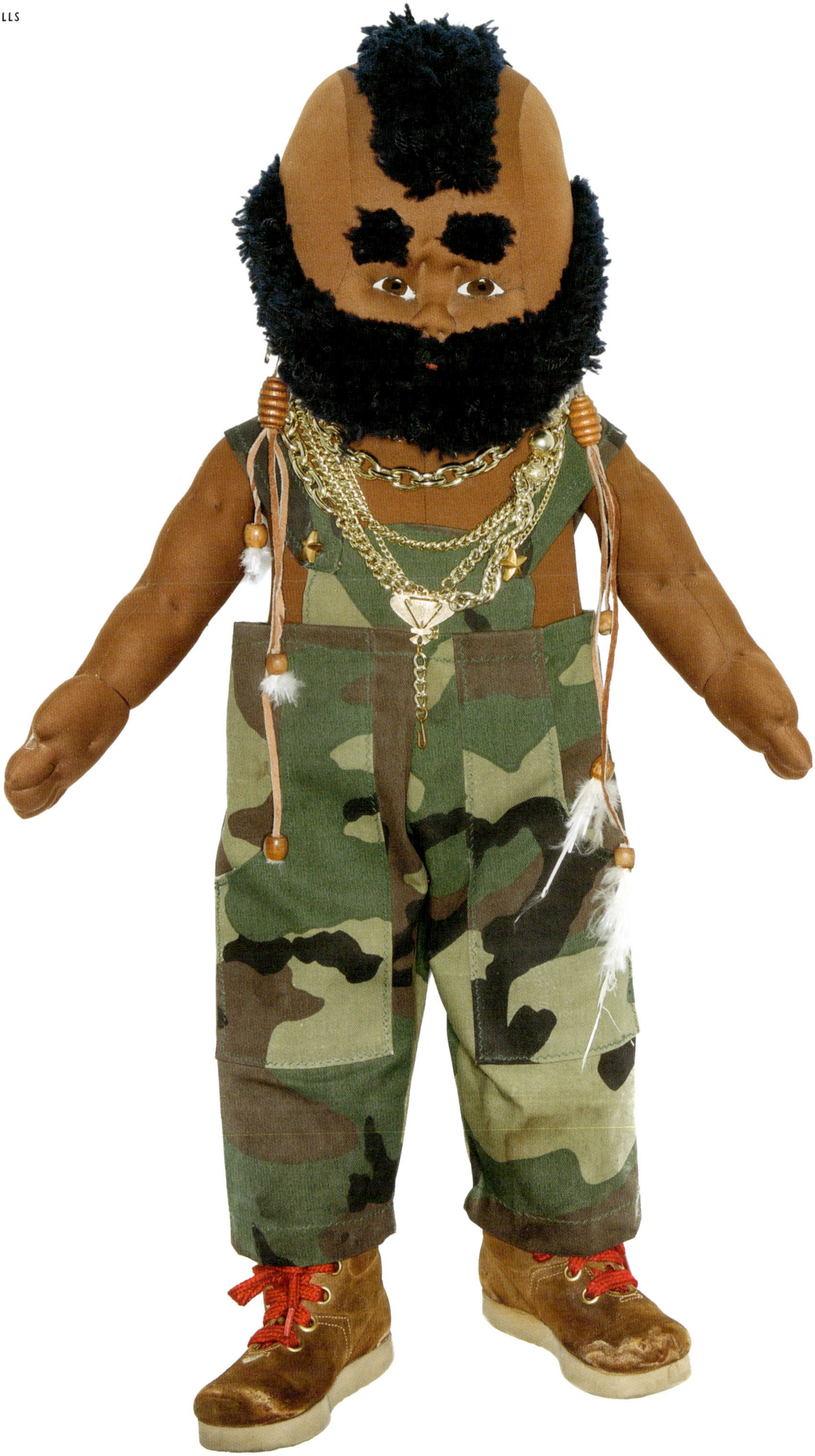

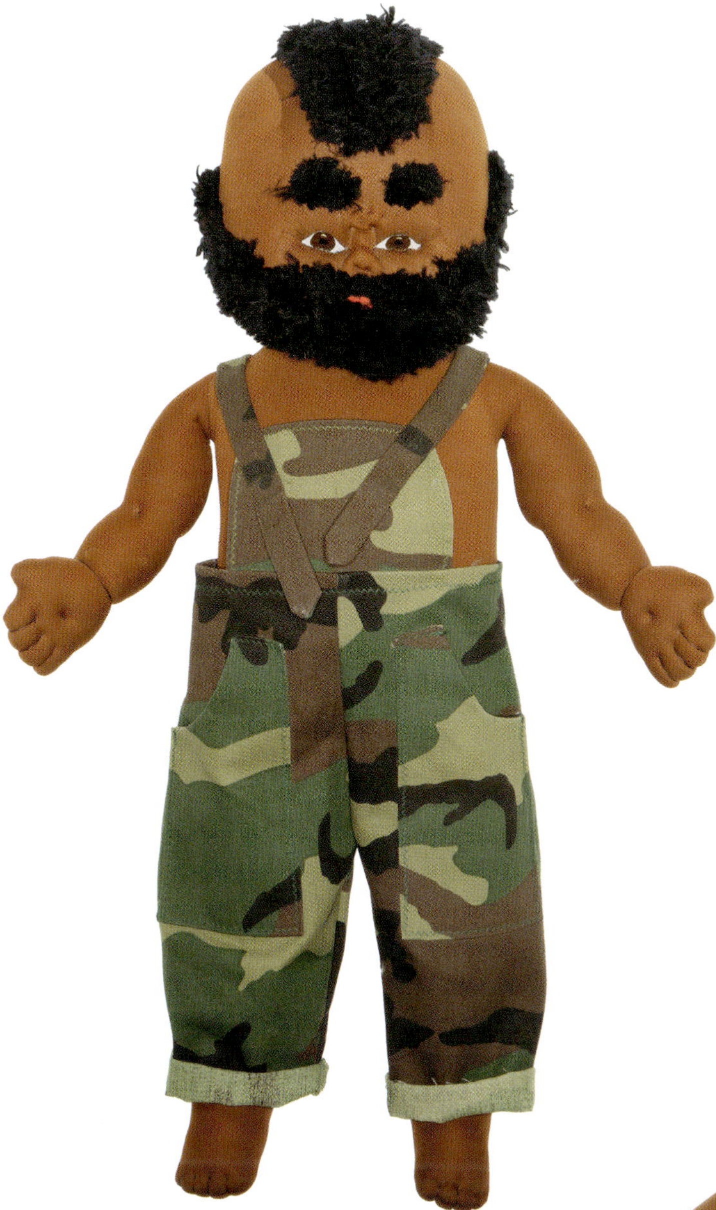

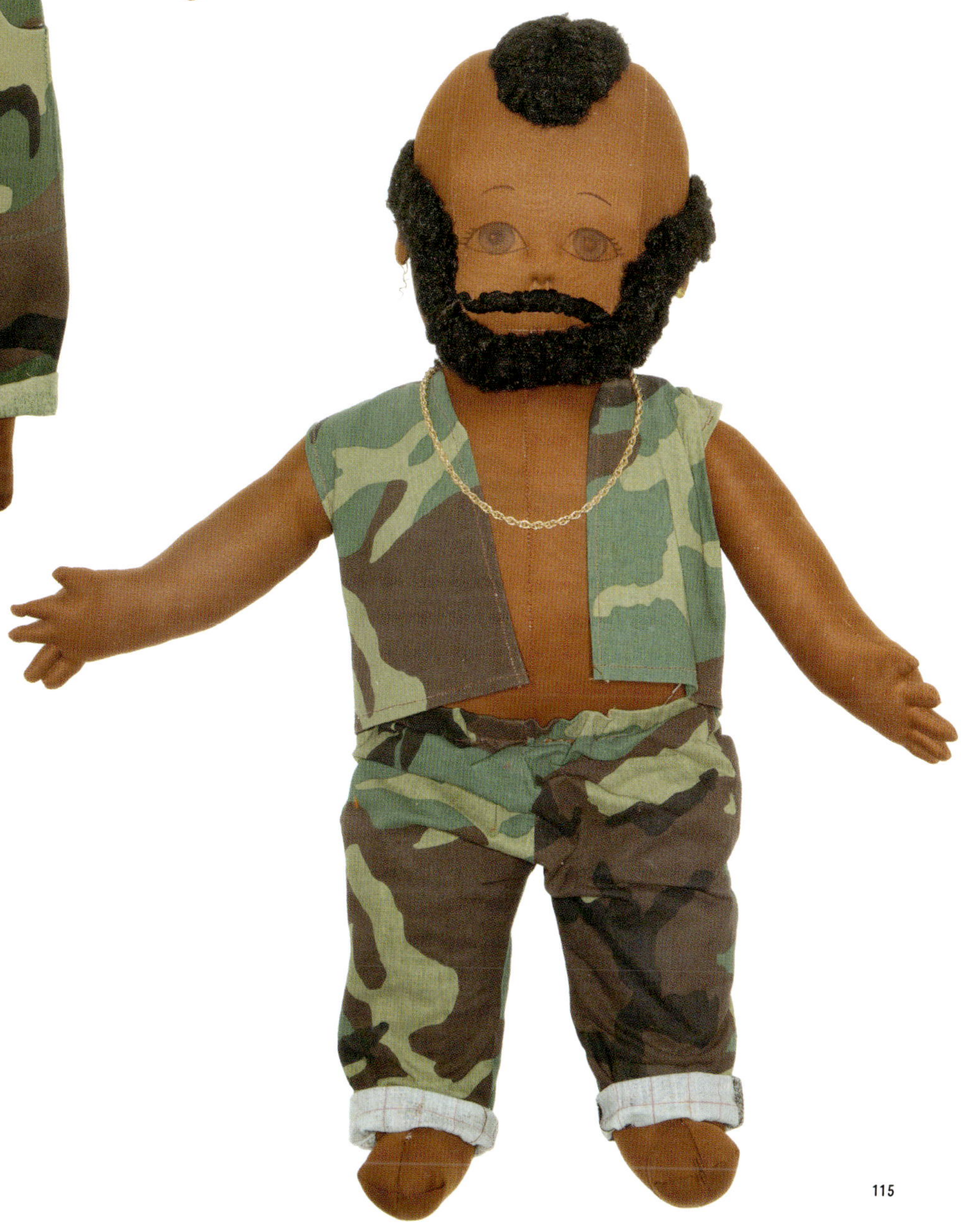

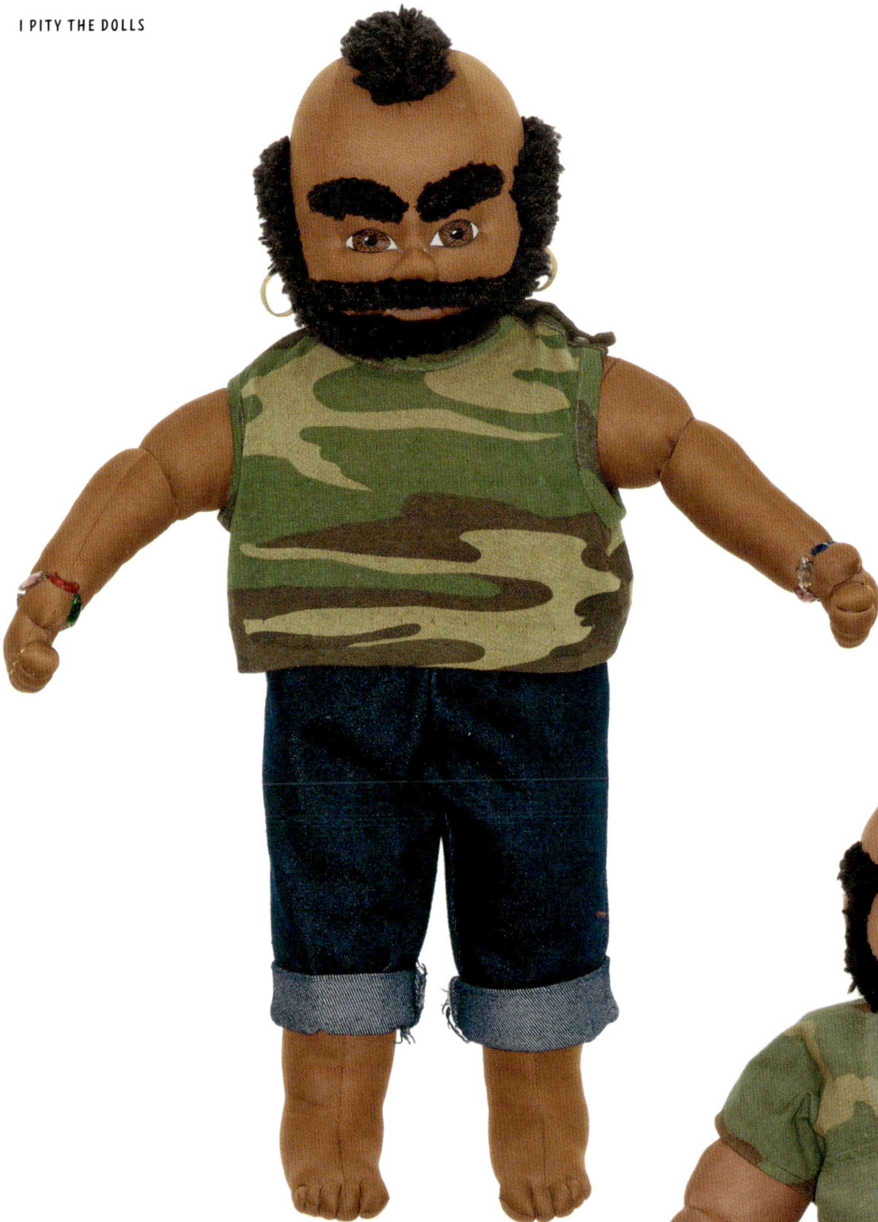

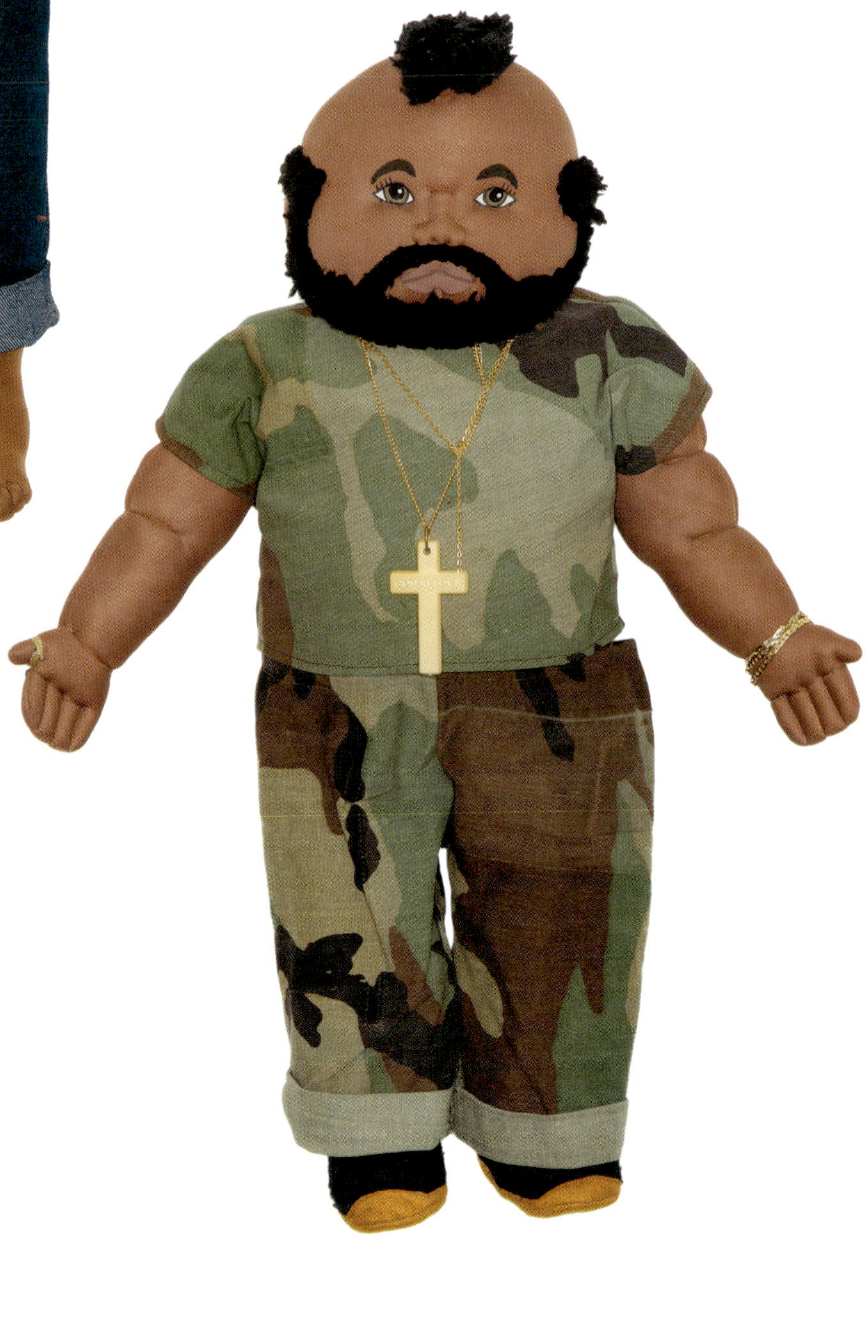

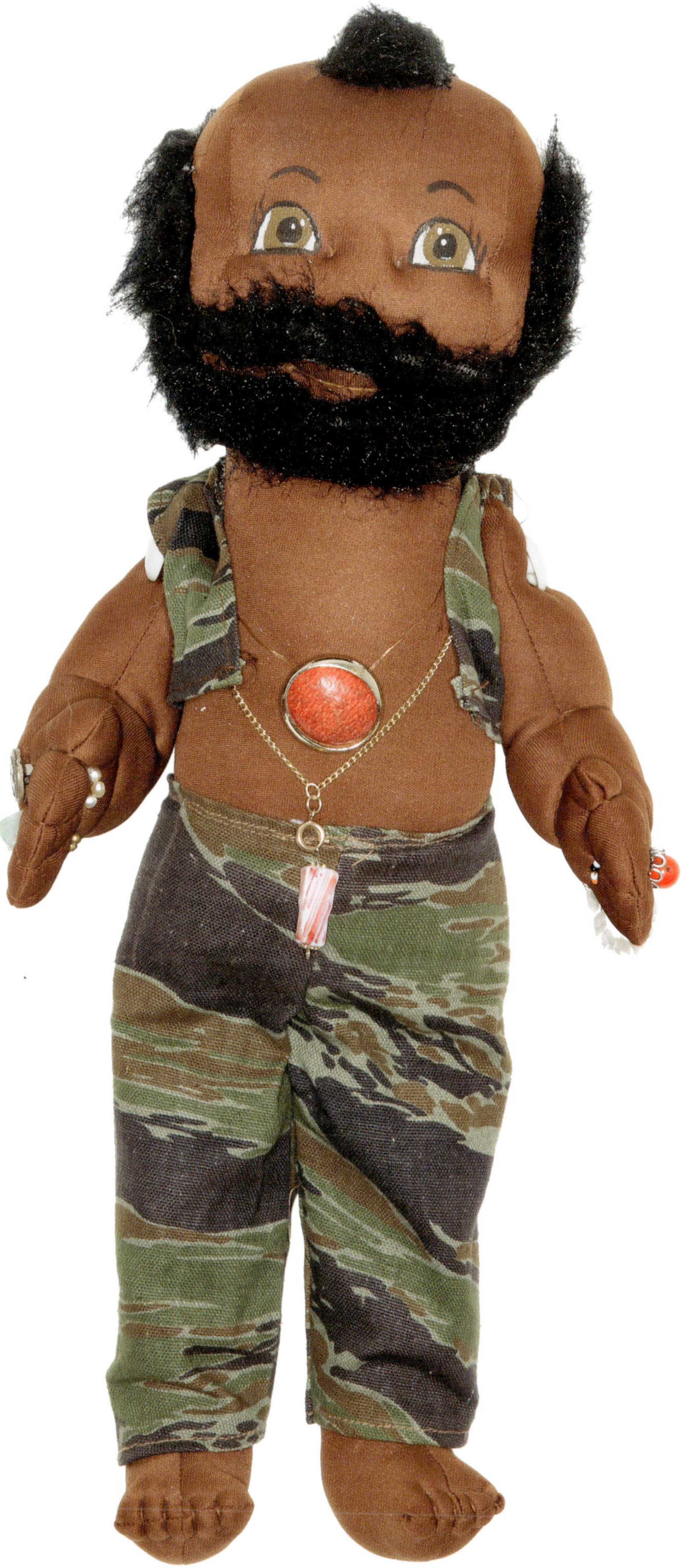

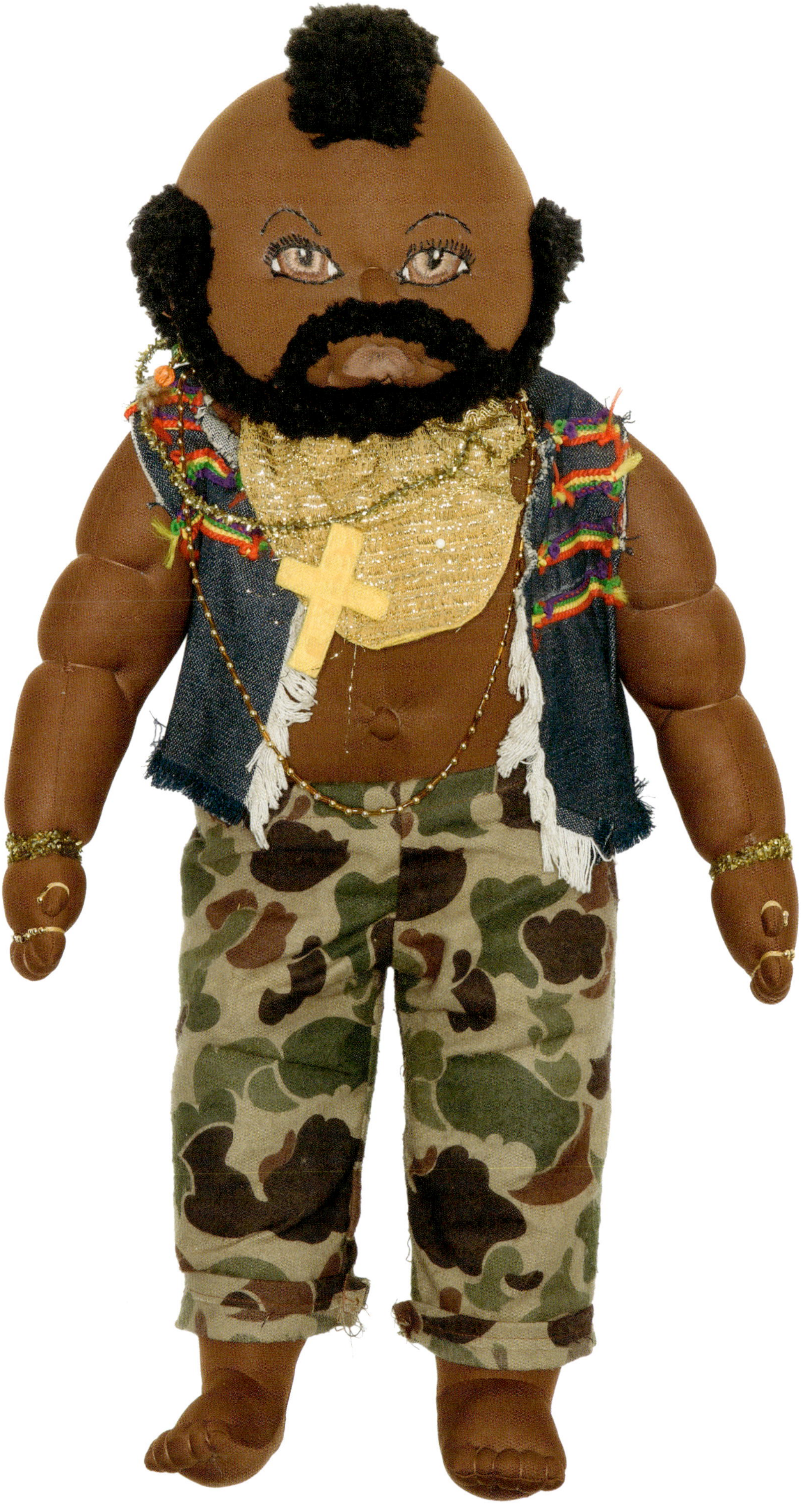

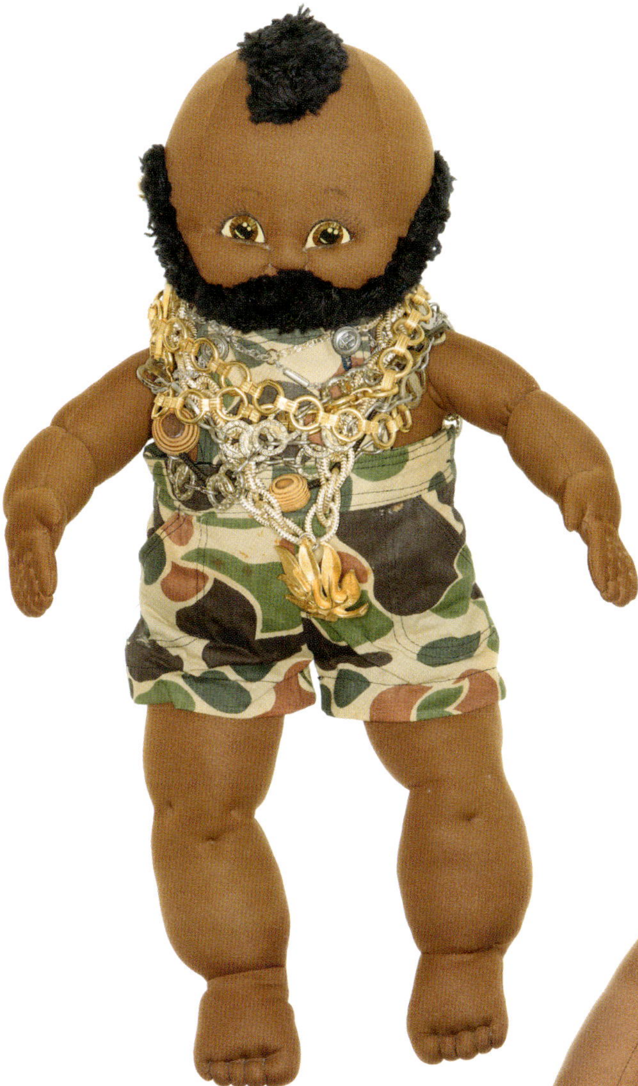

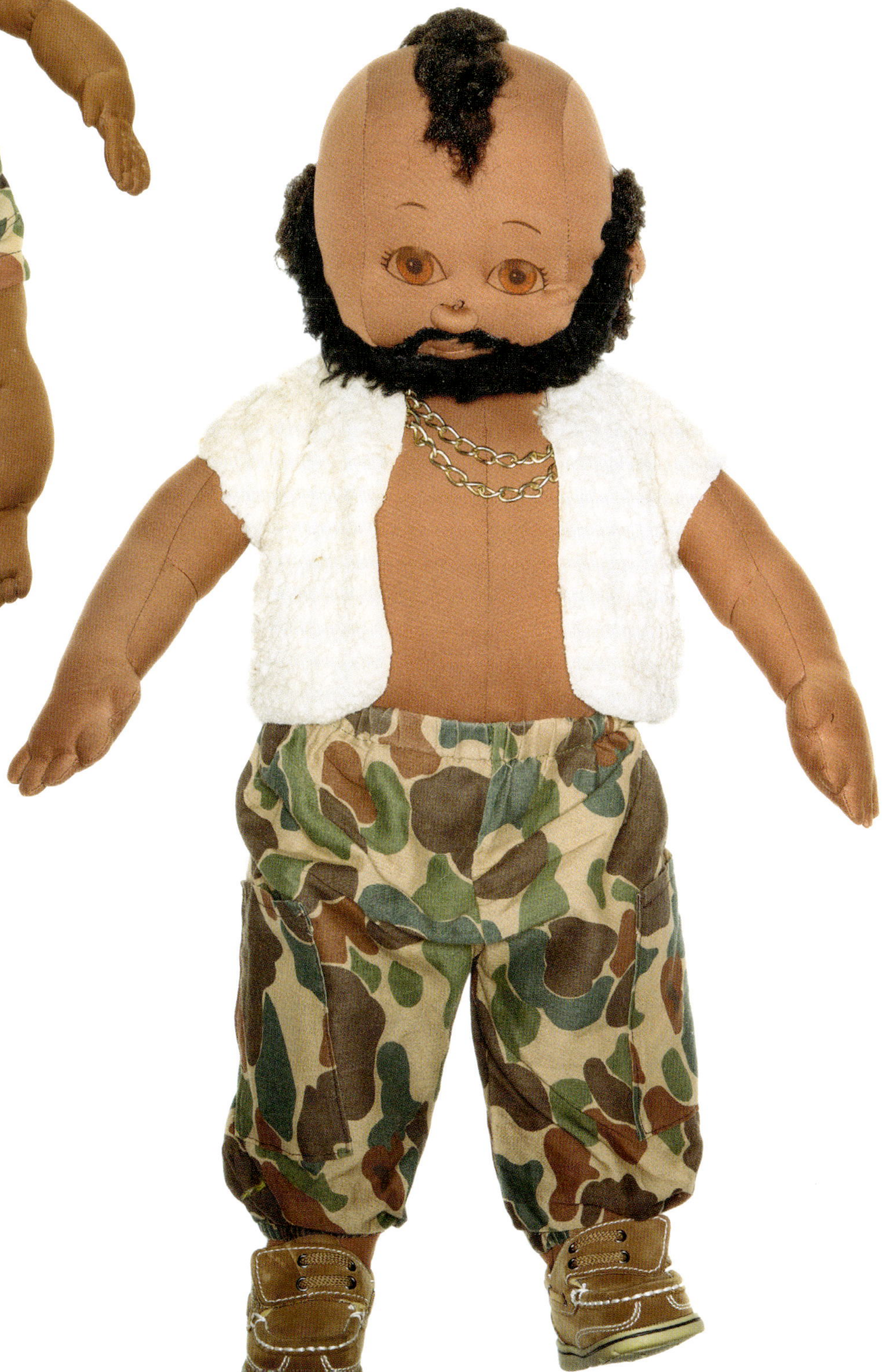

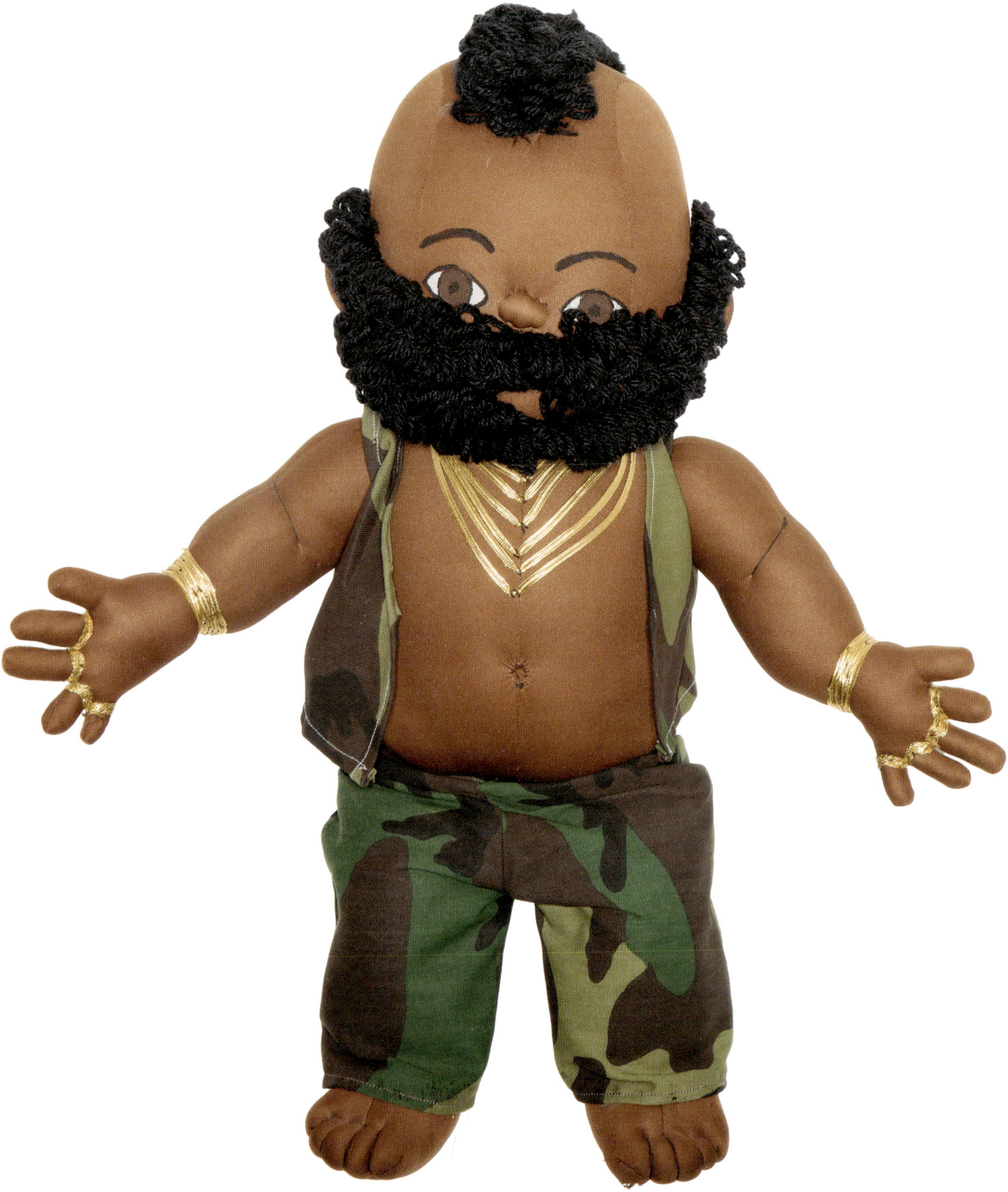

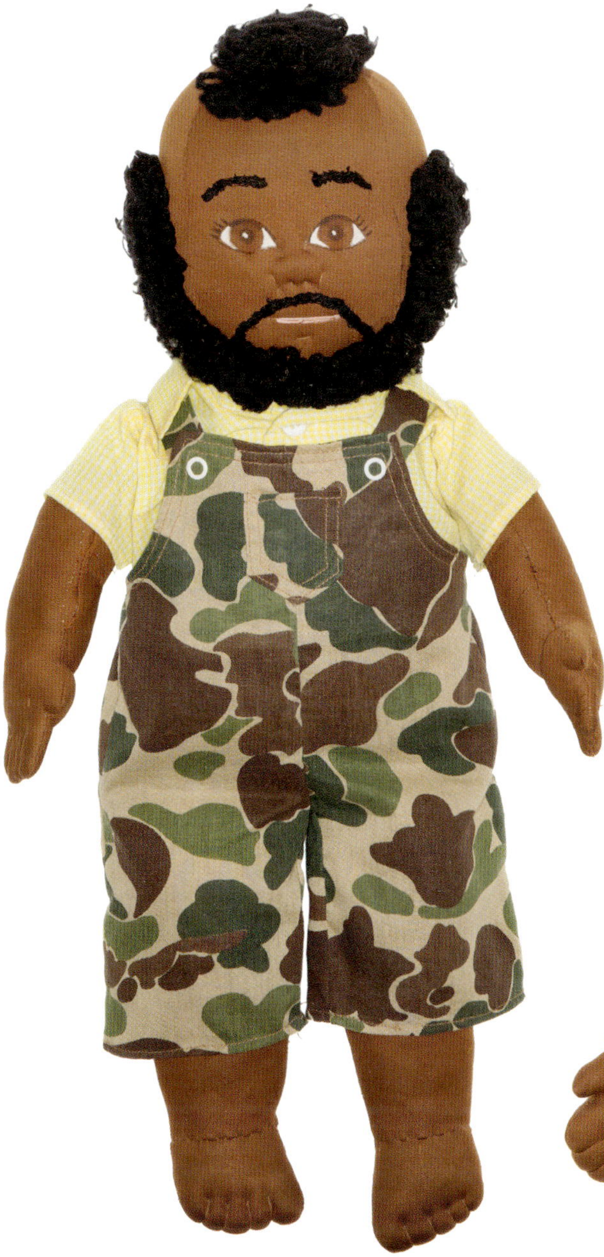

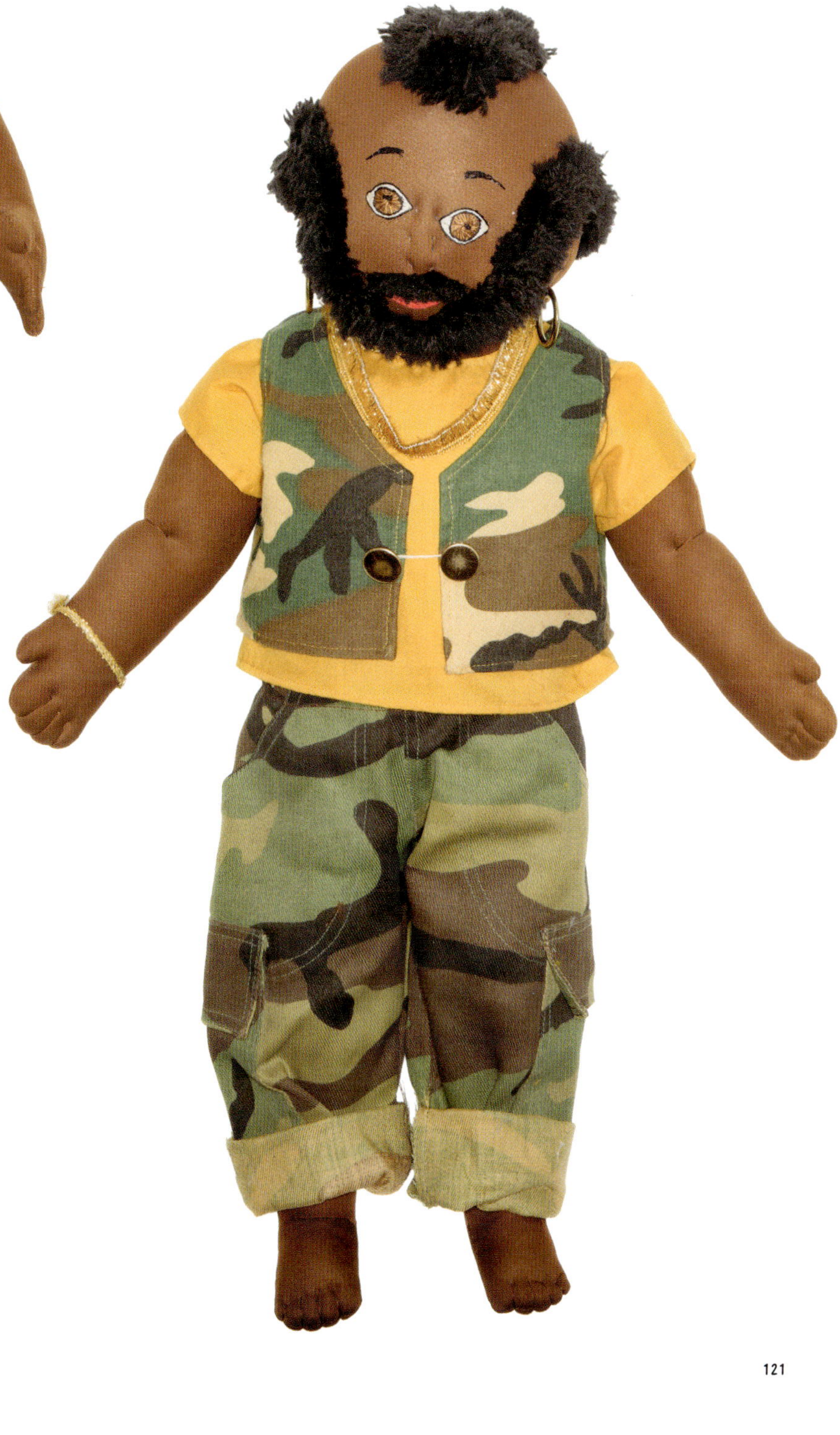

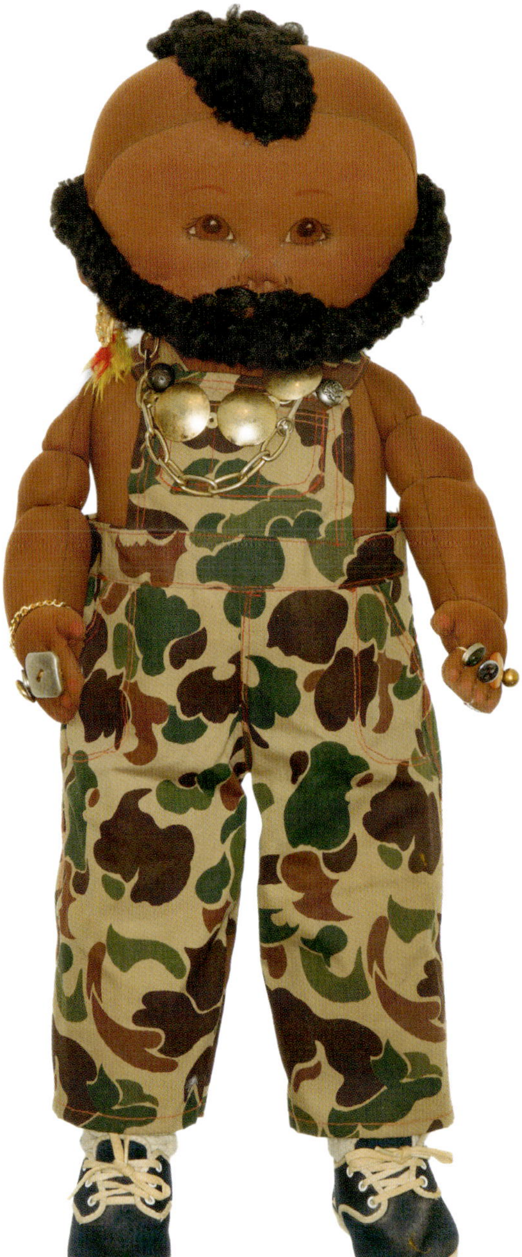

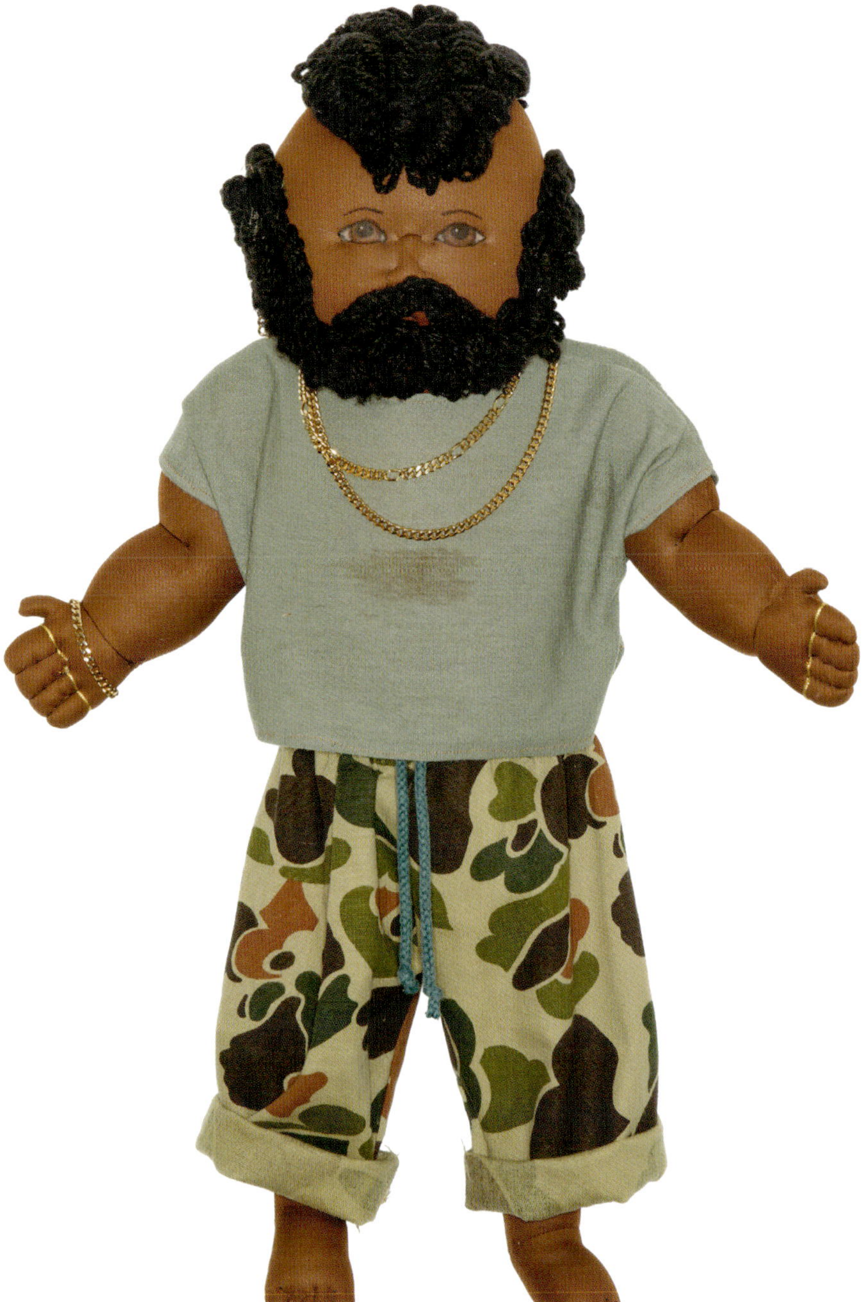

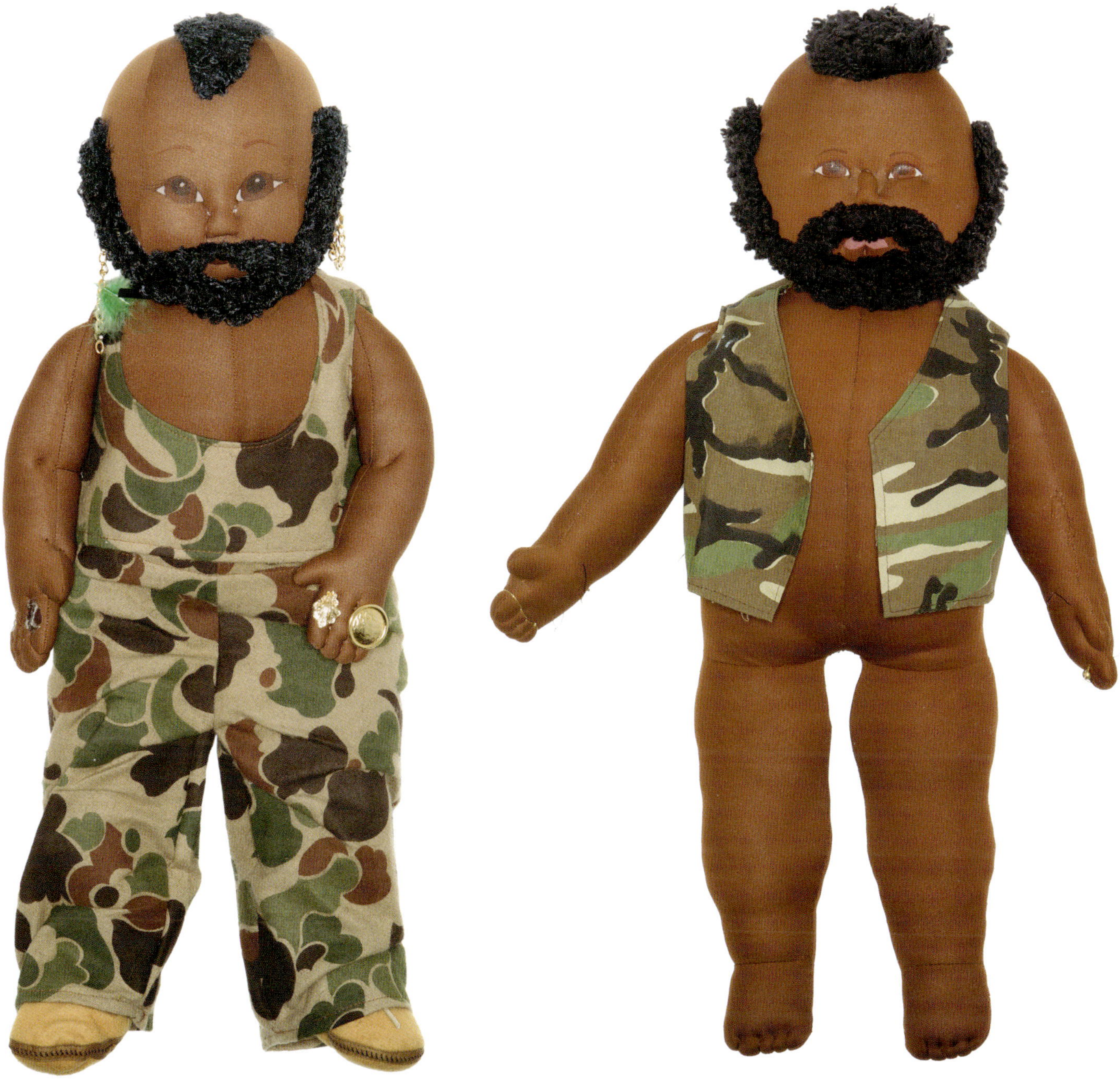

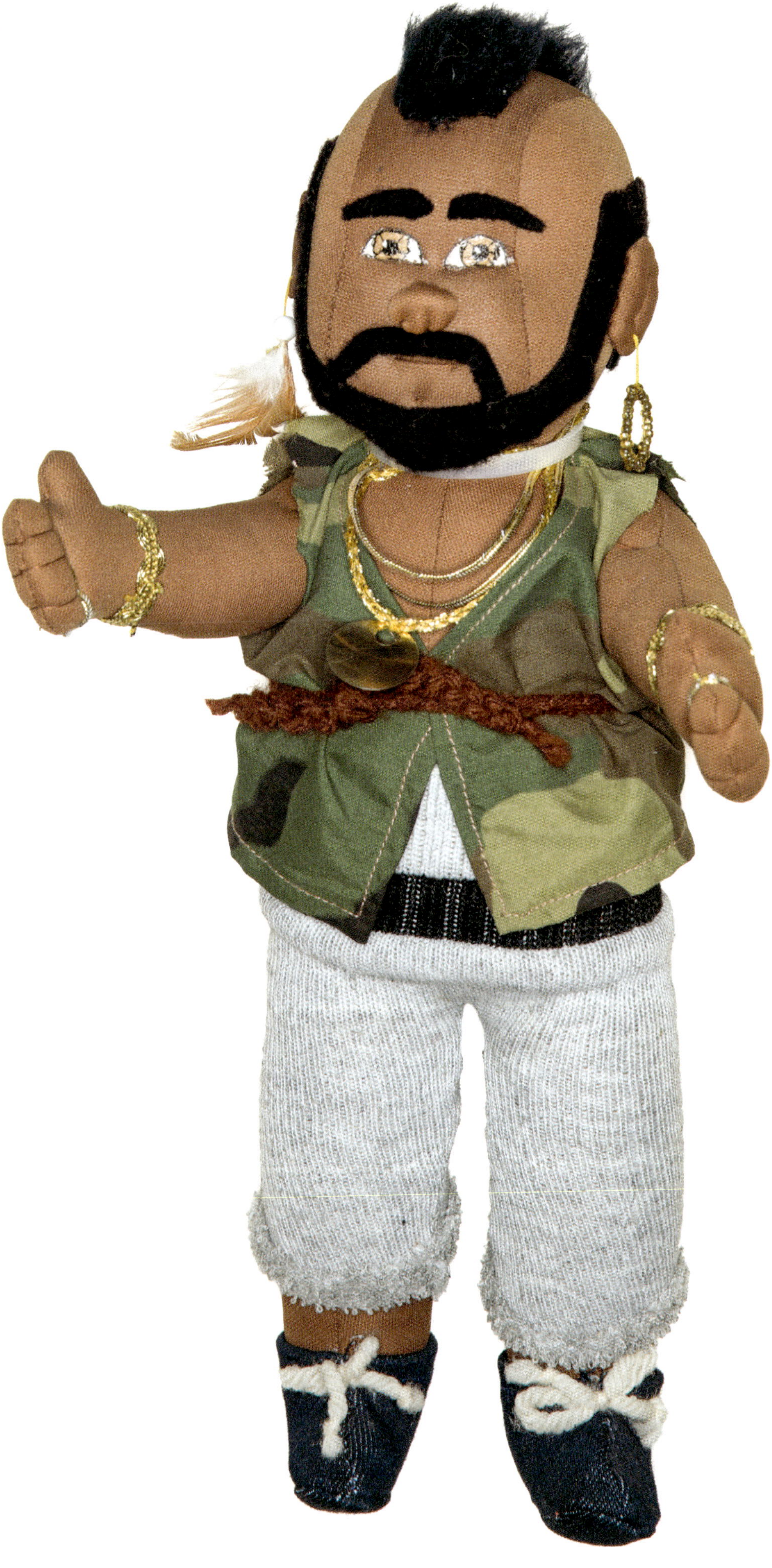

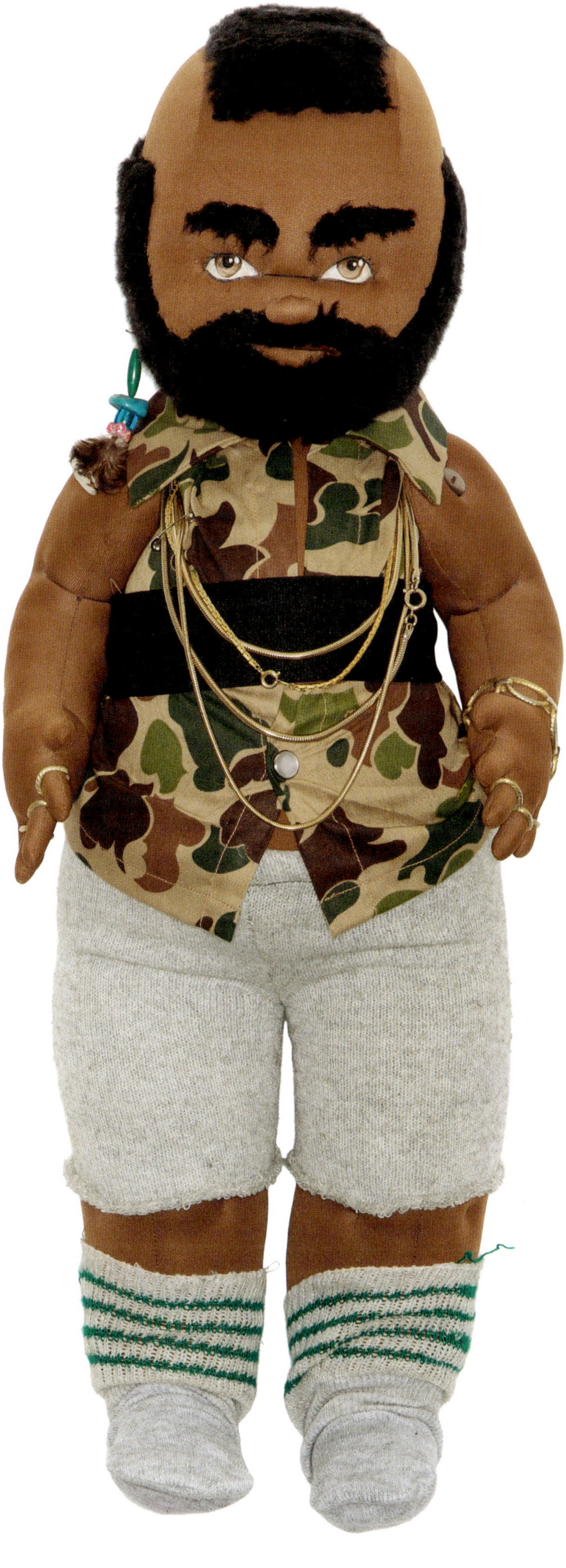

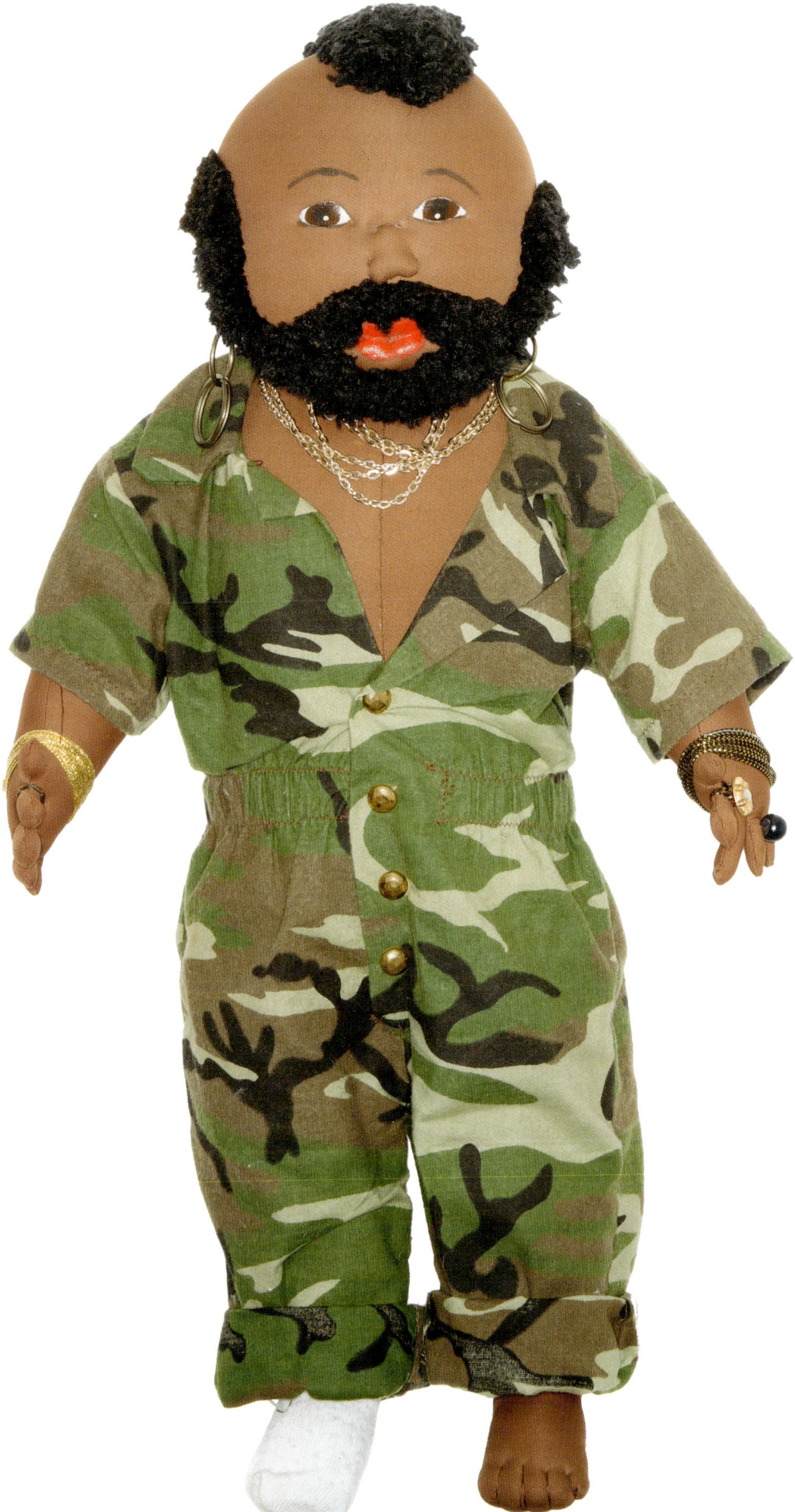

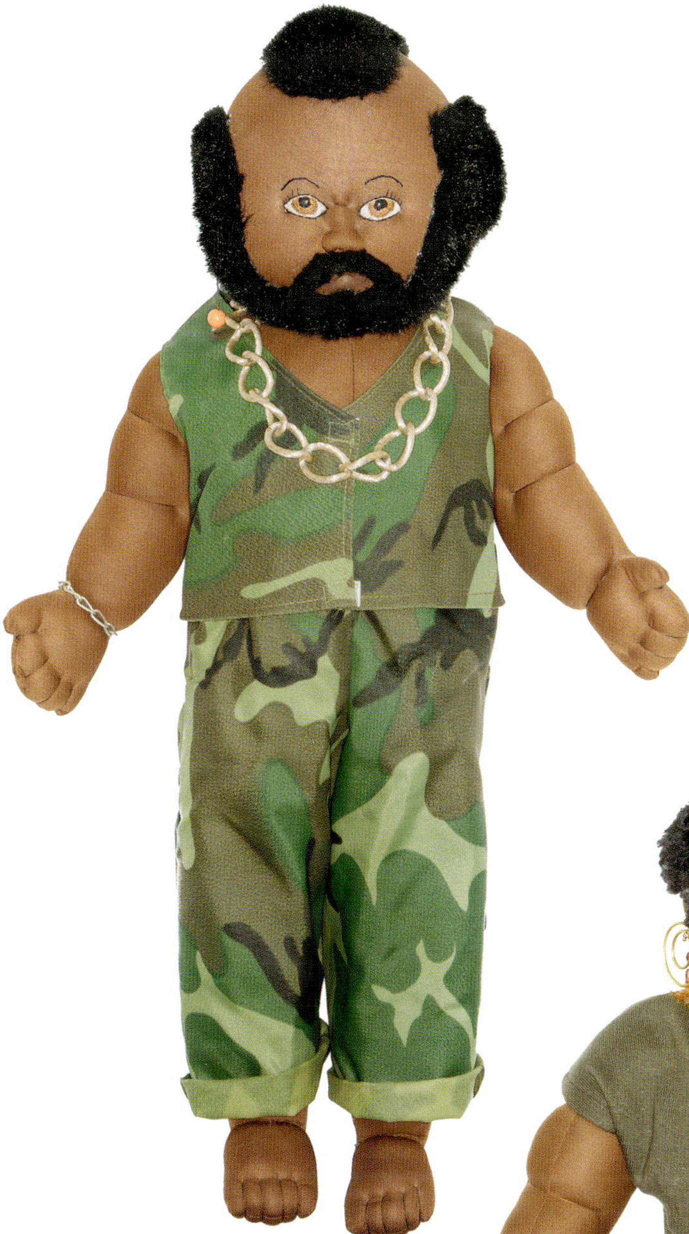

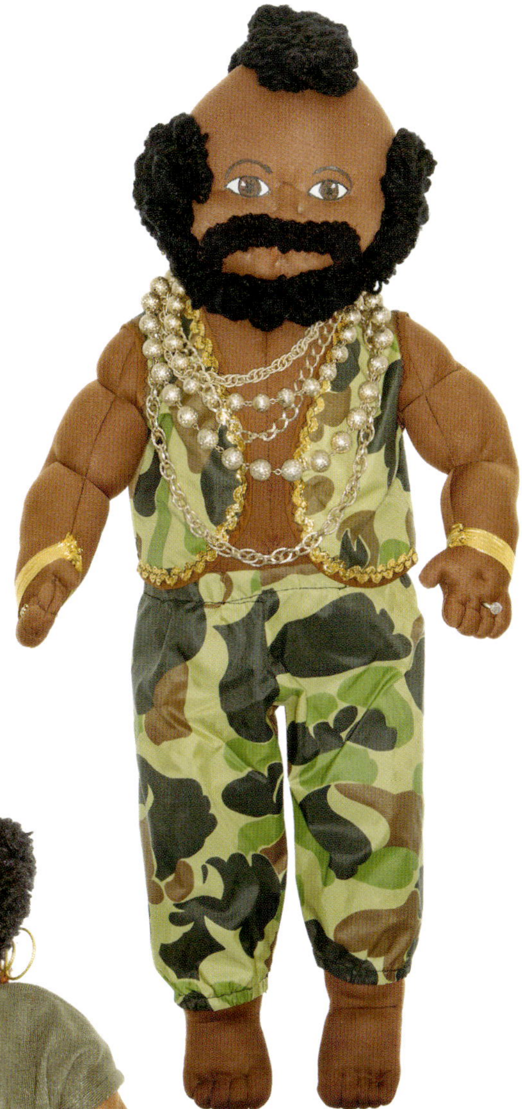

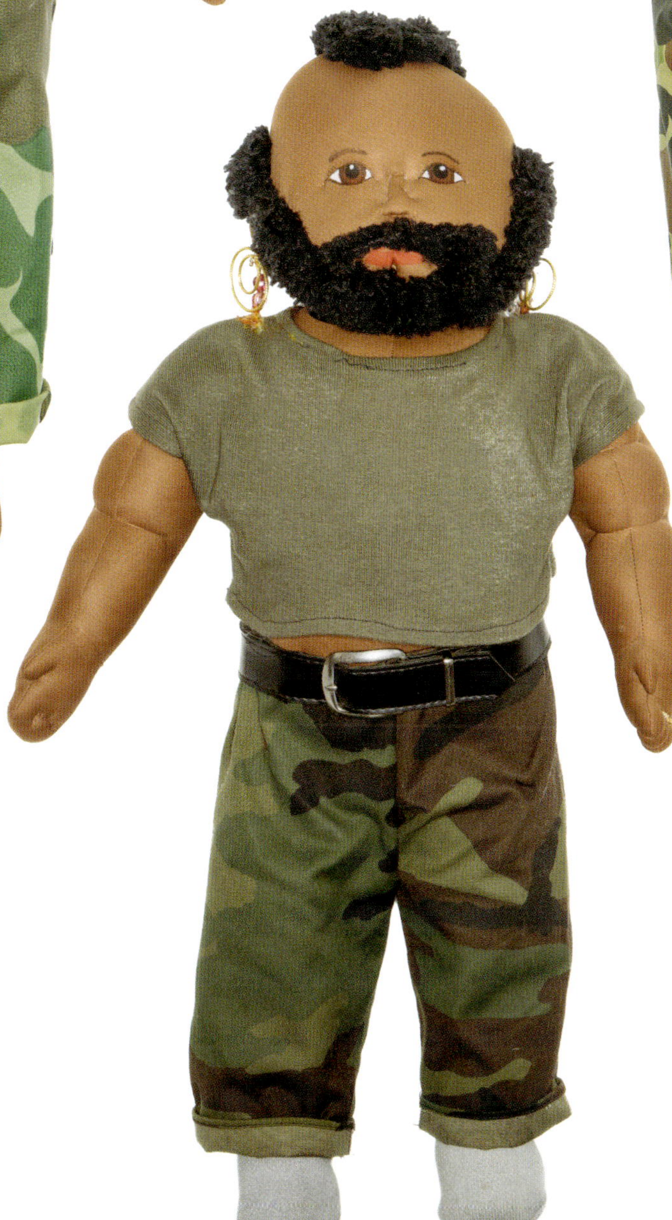

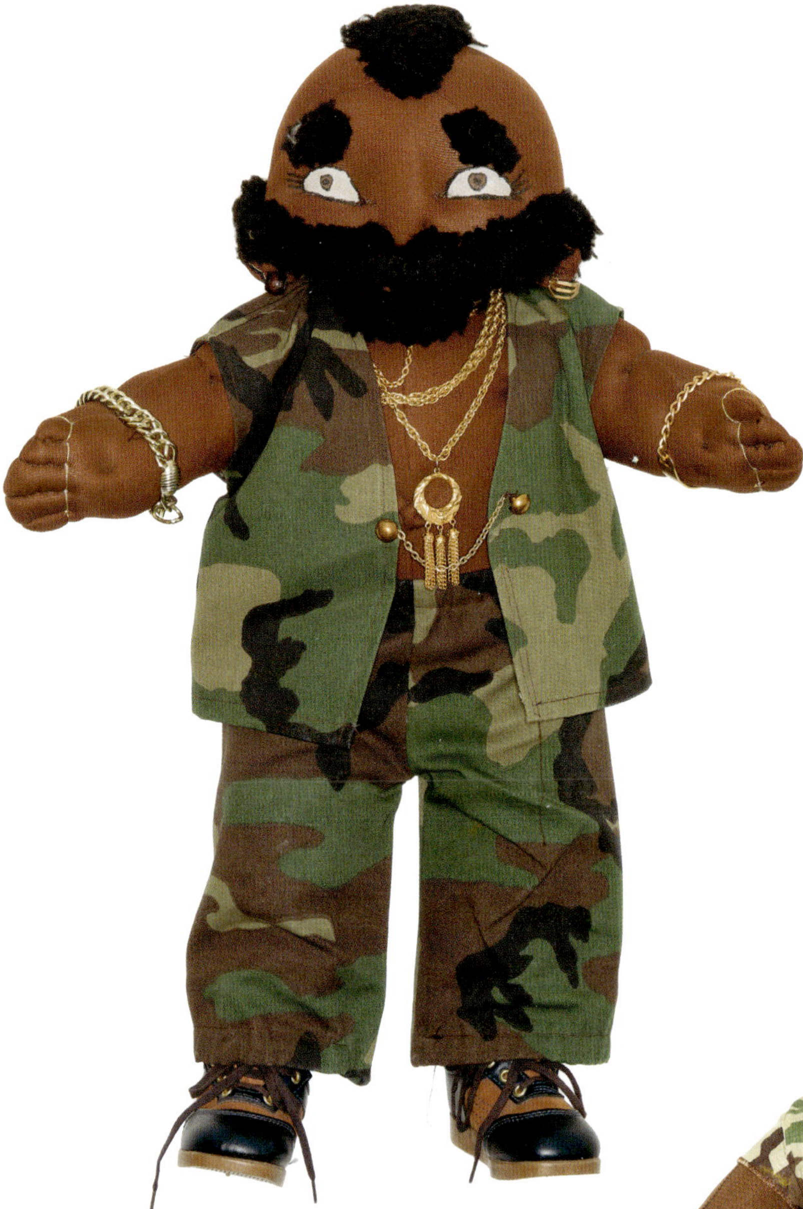

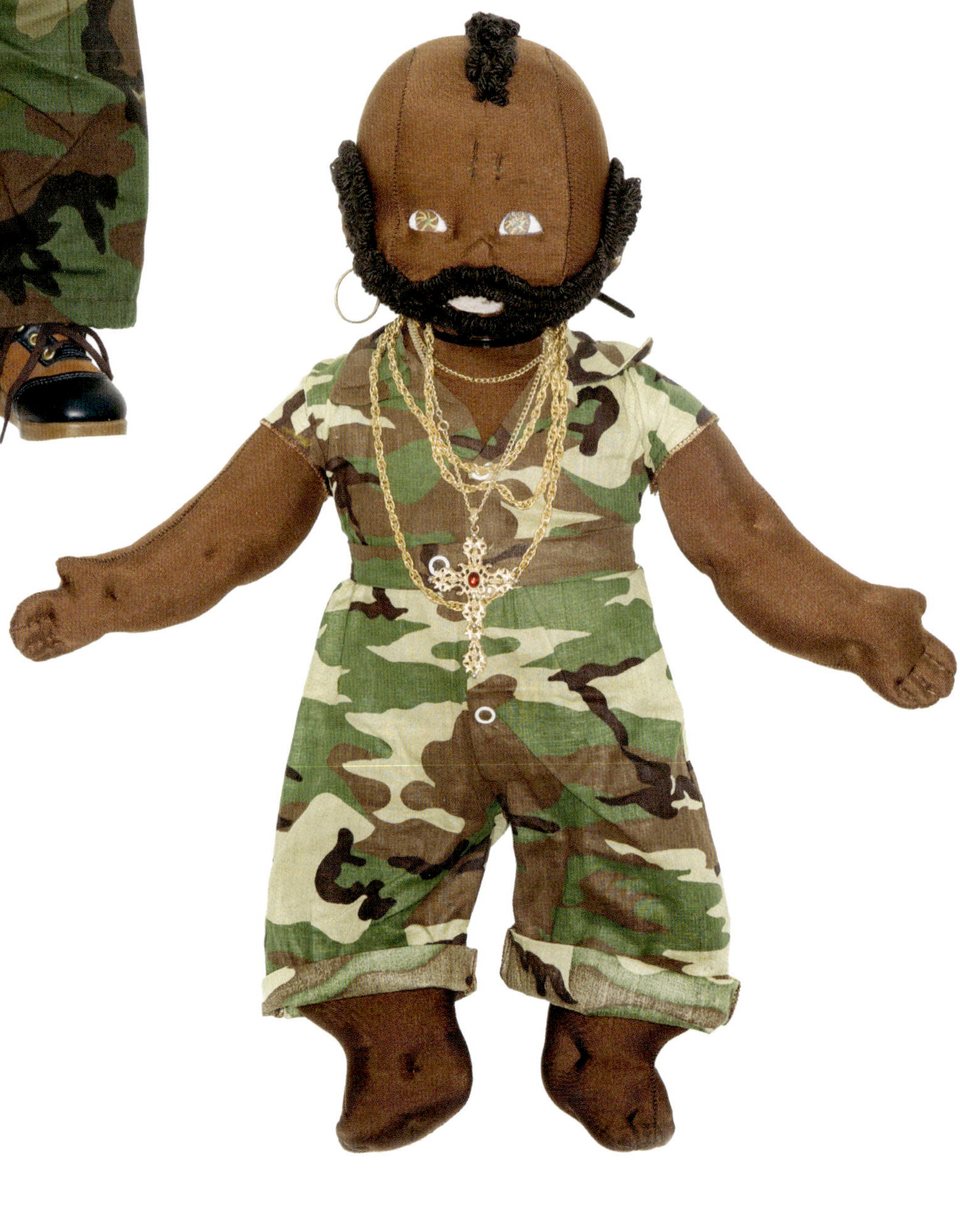

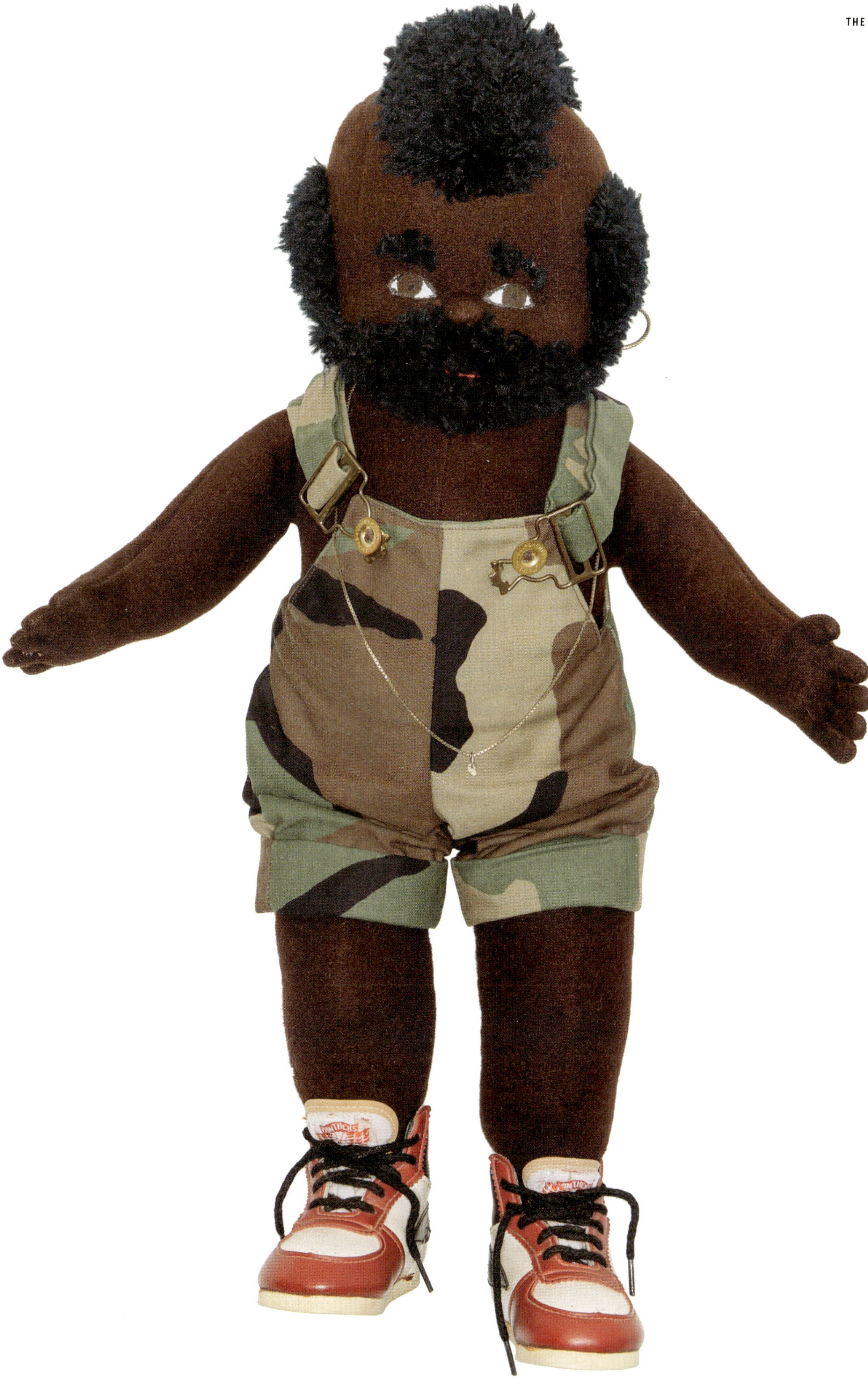

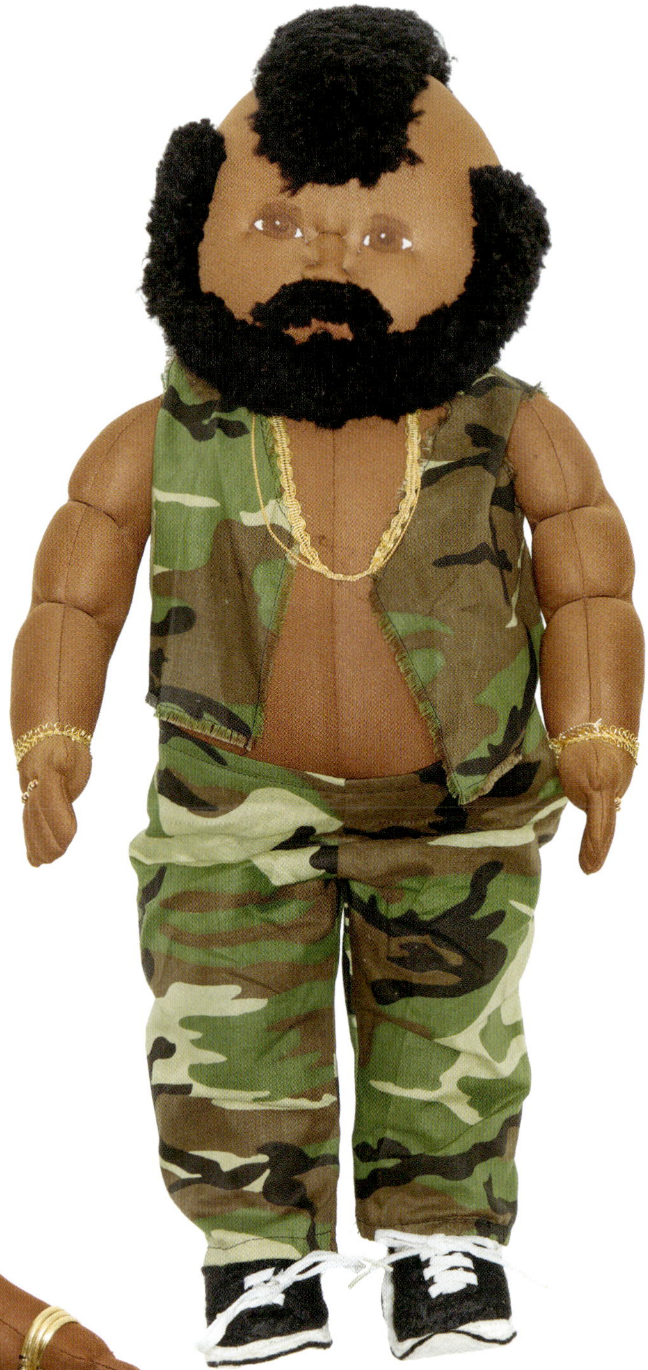

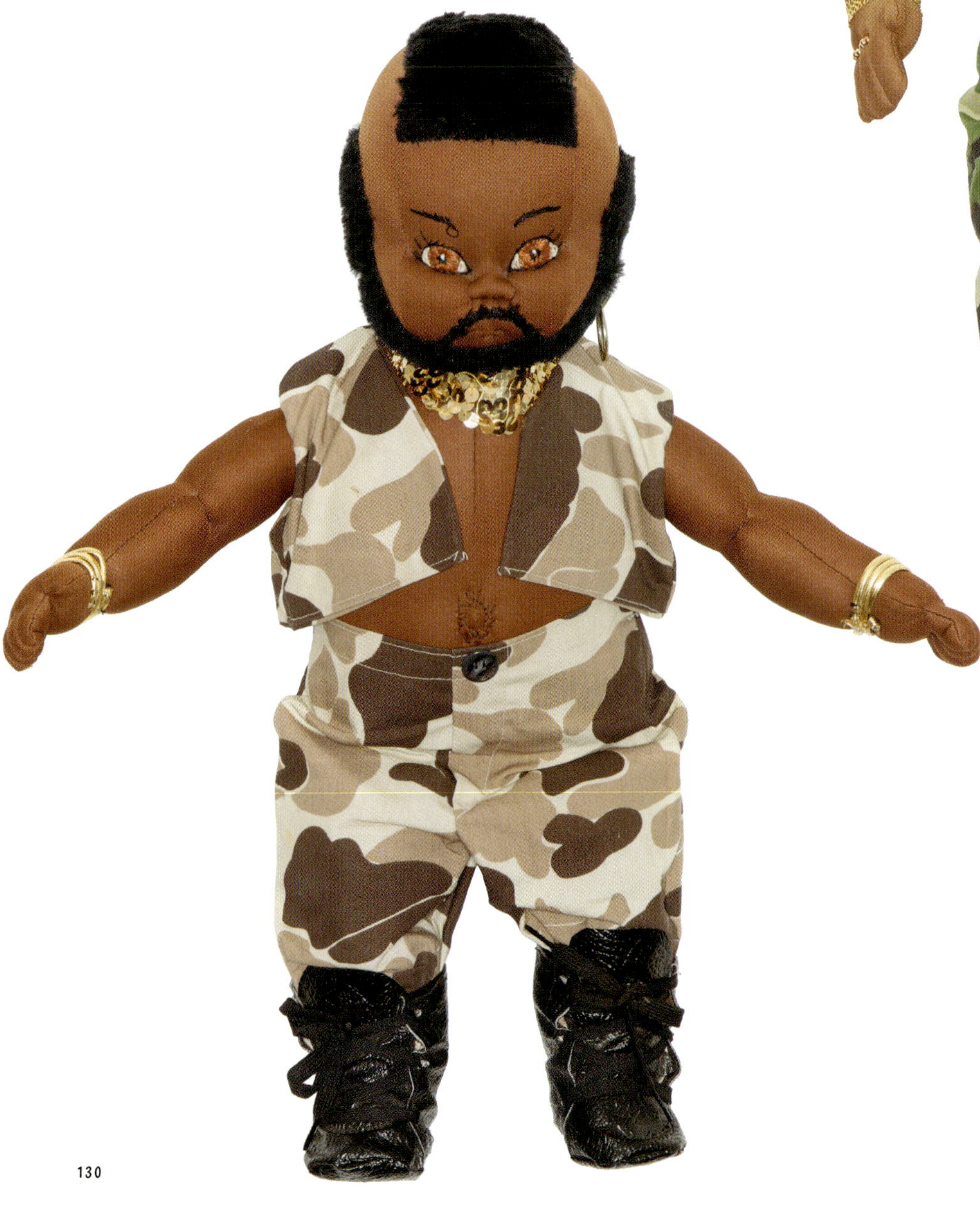

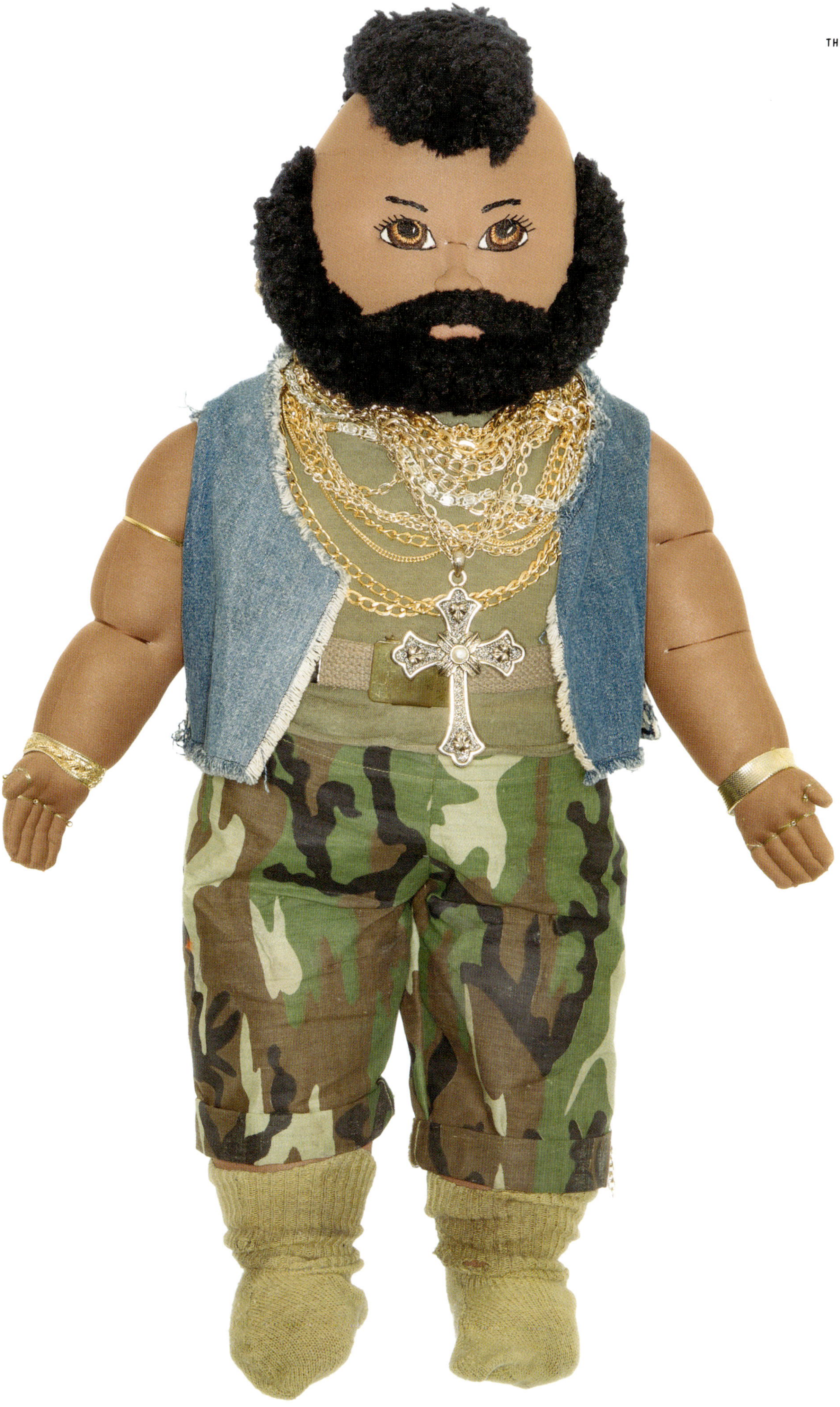

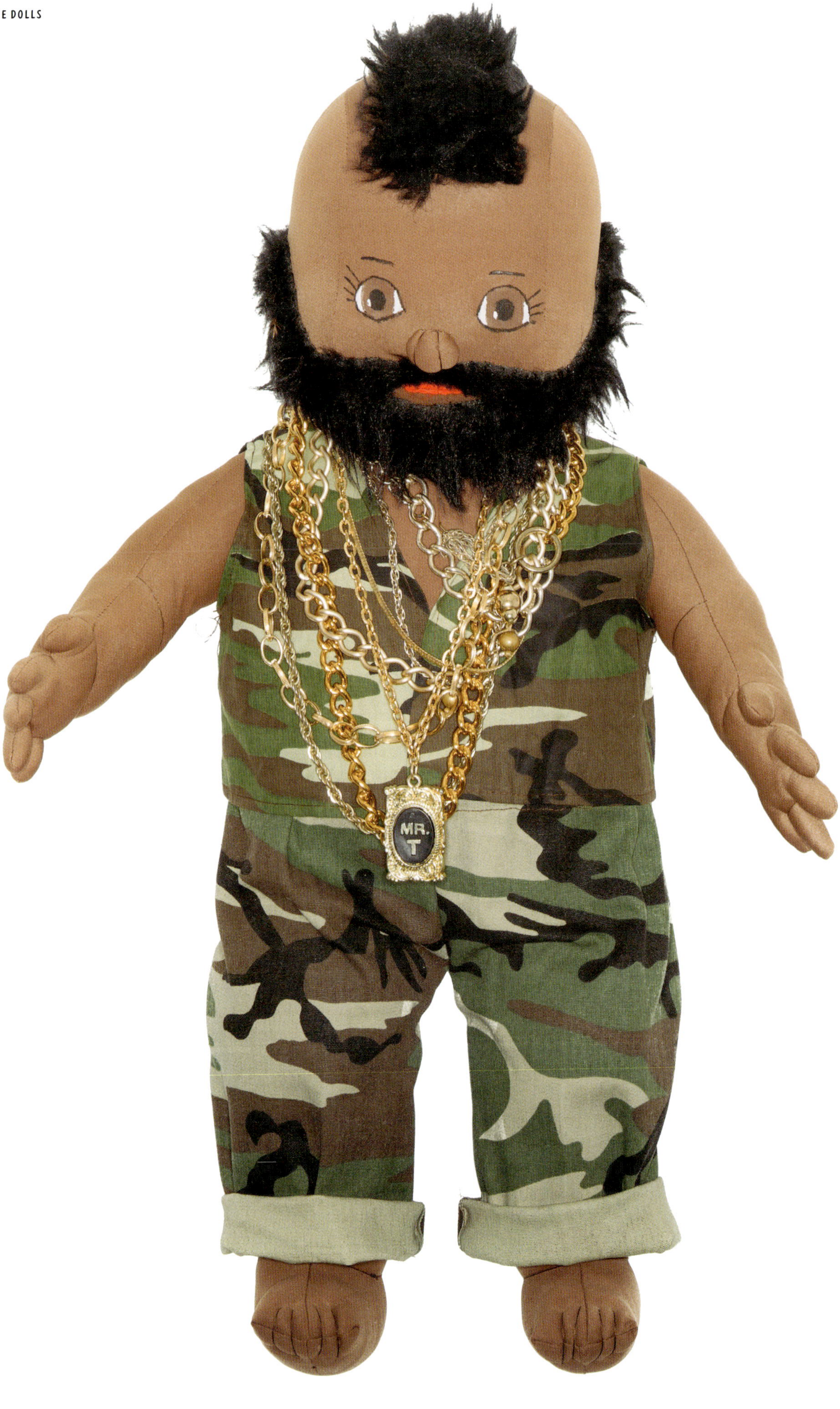
MR.
T

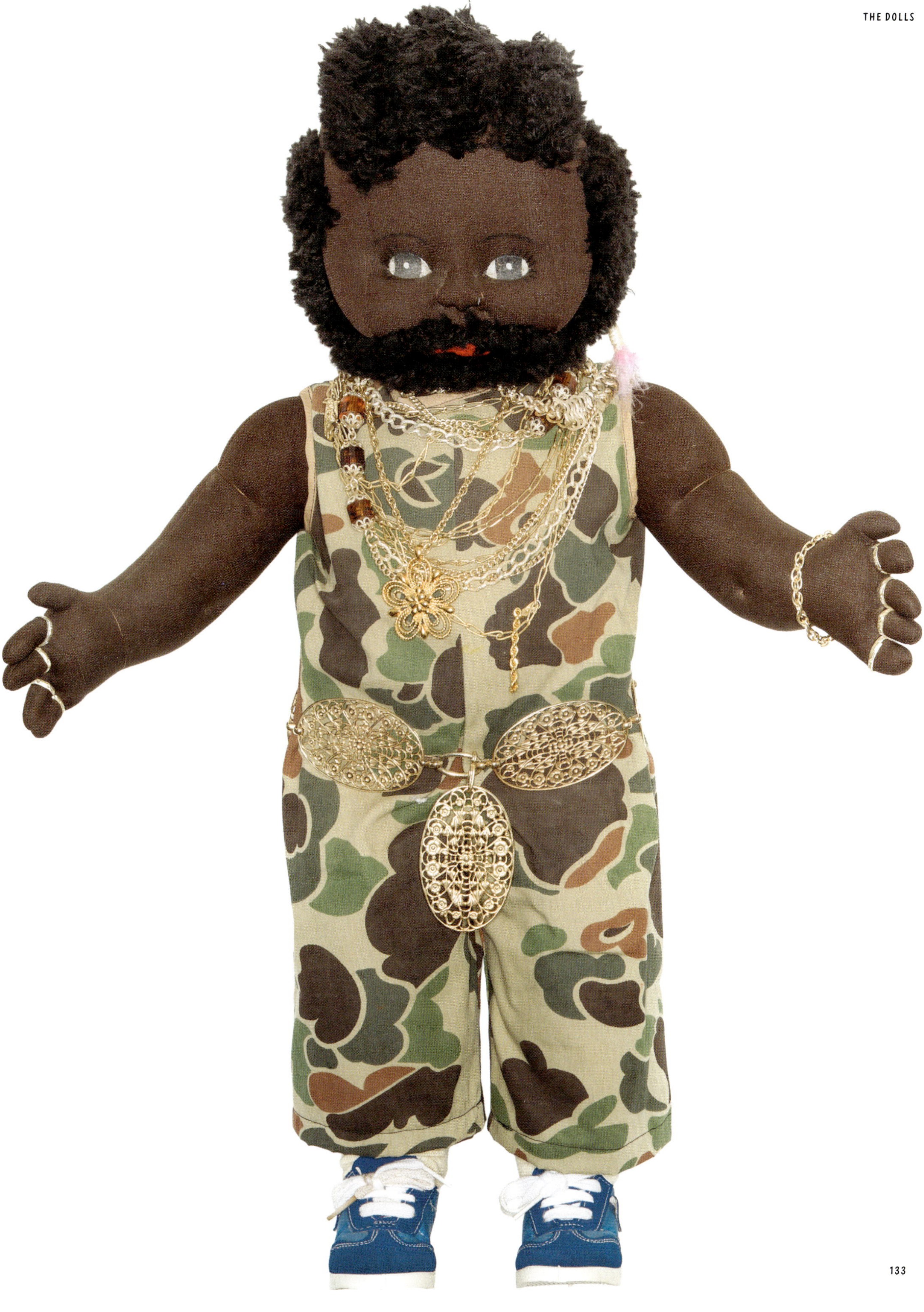

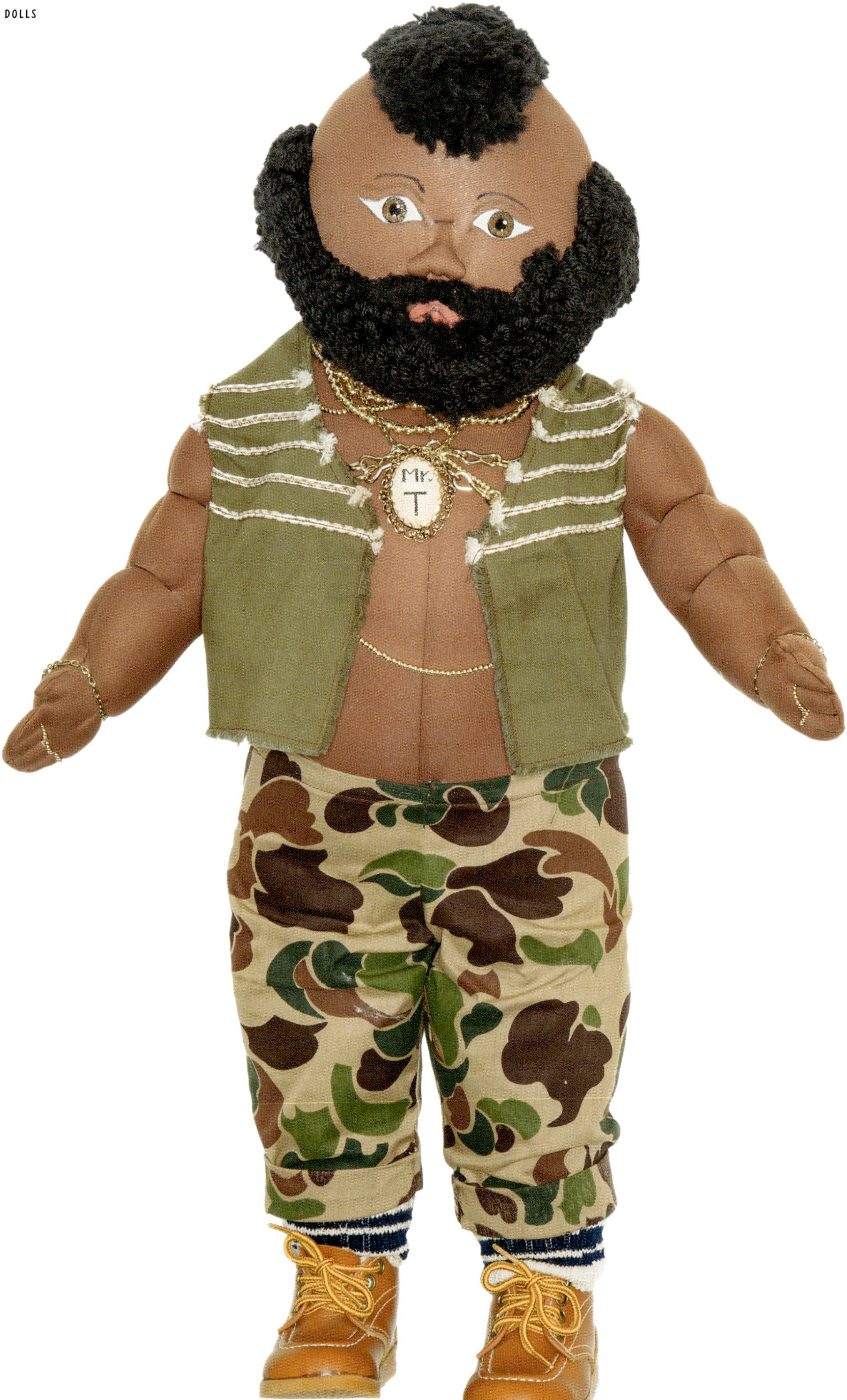
Mr.
T

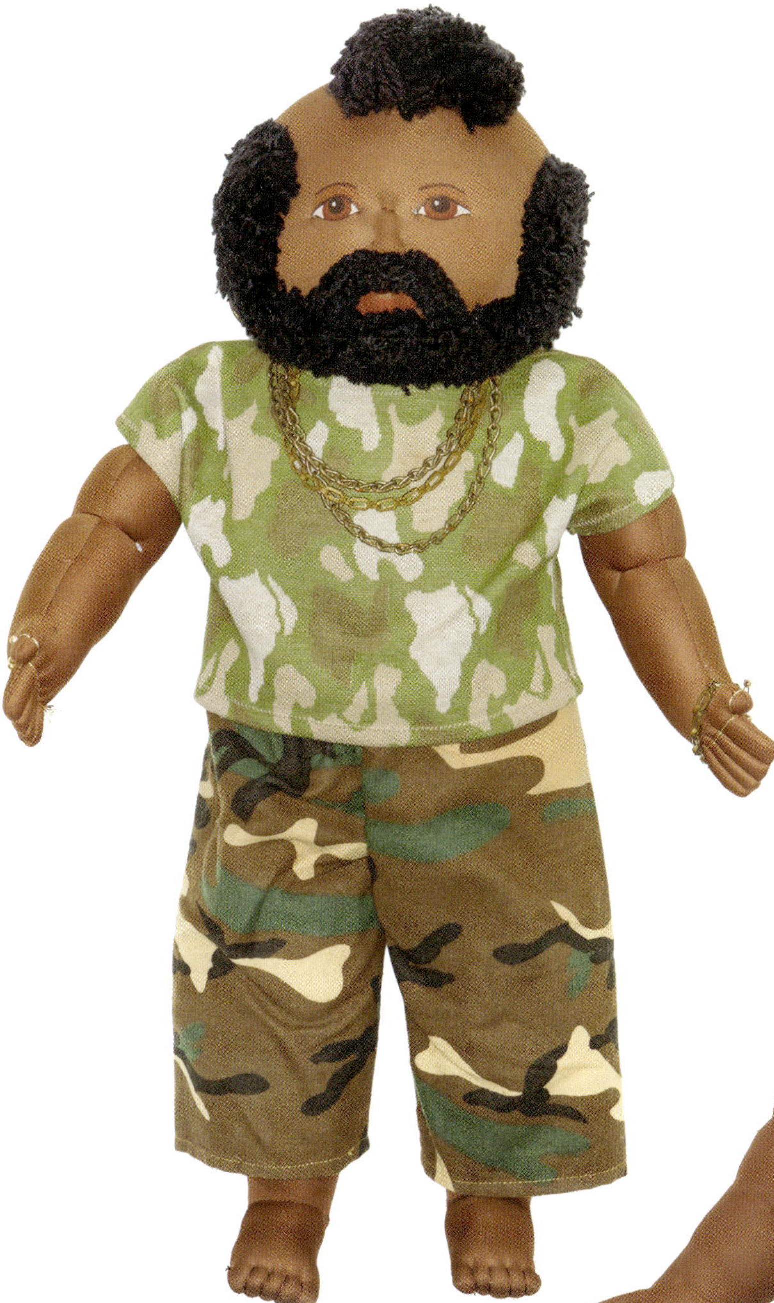

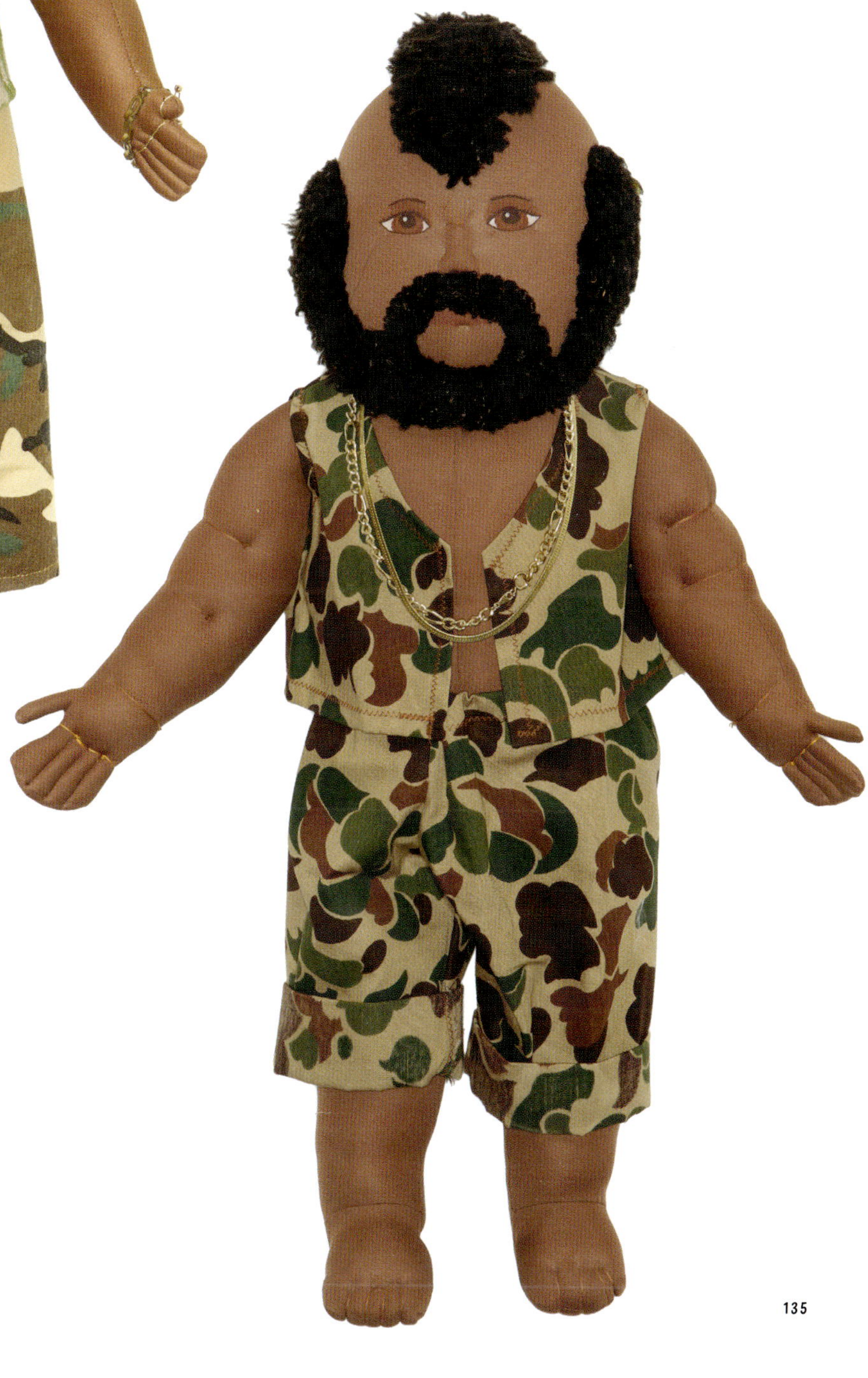

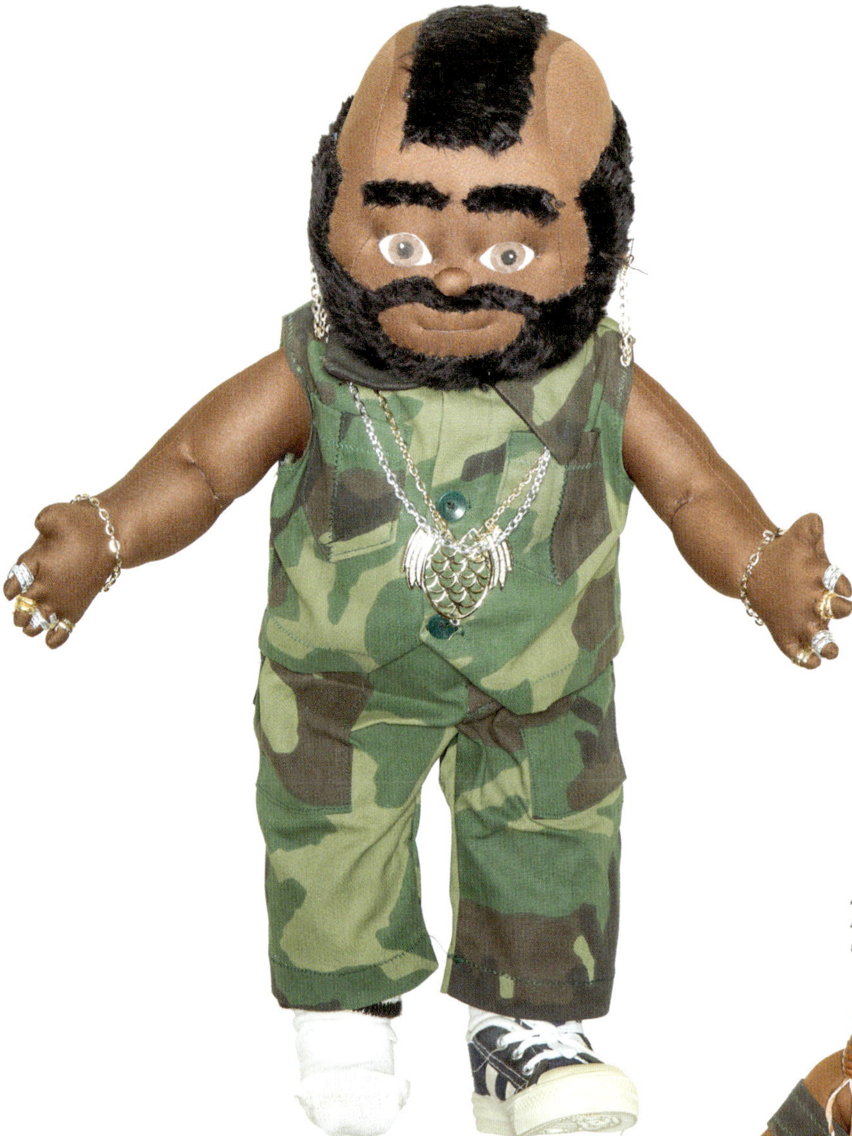

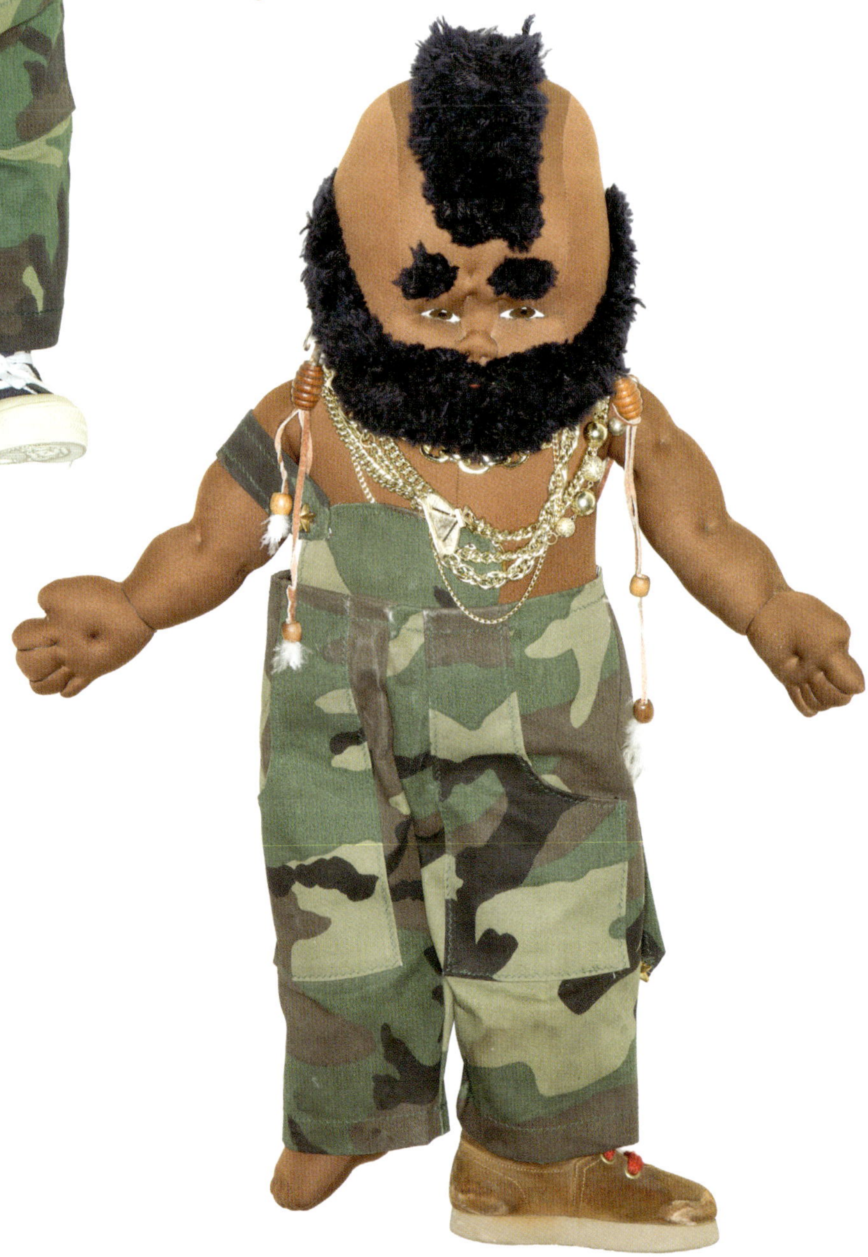

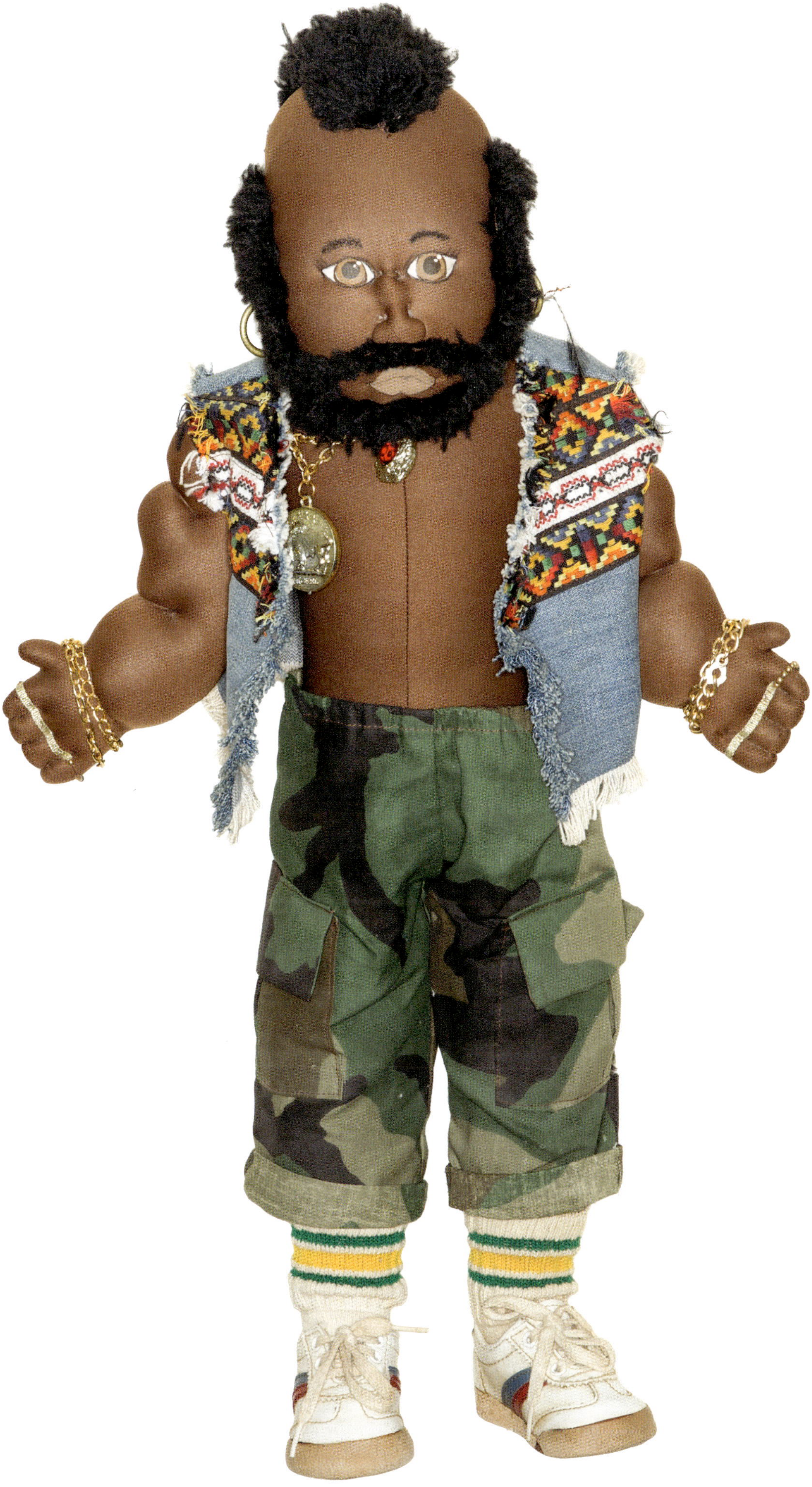

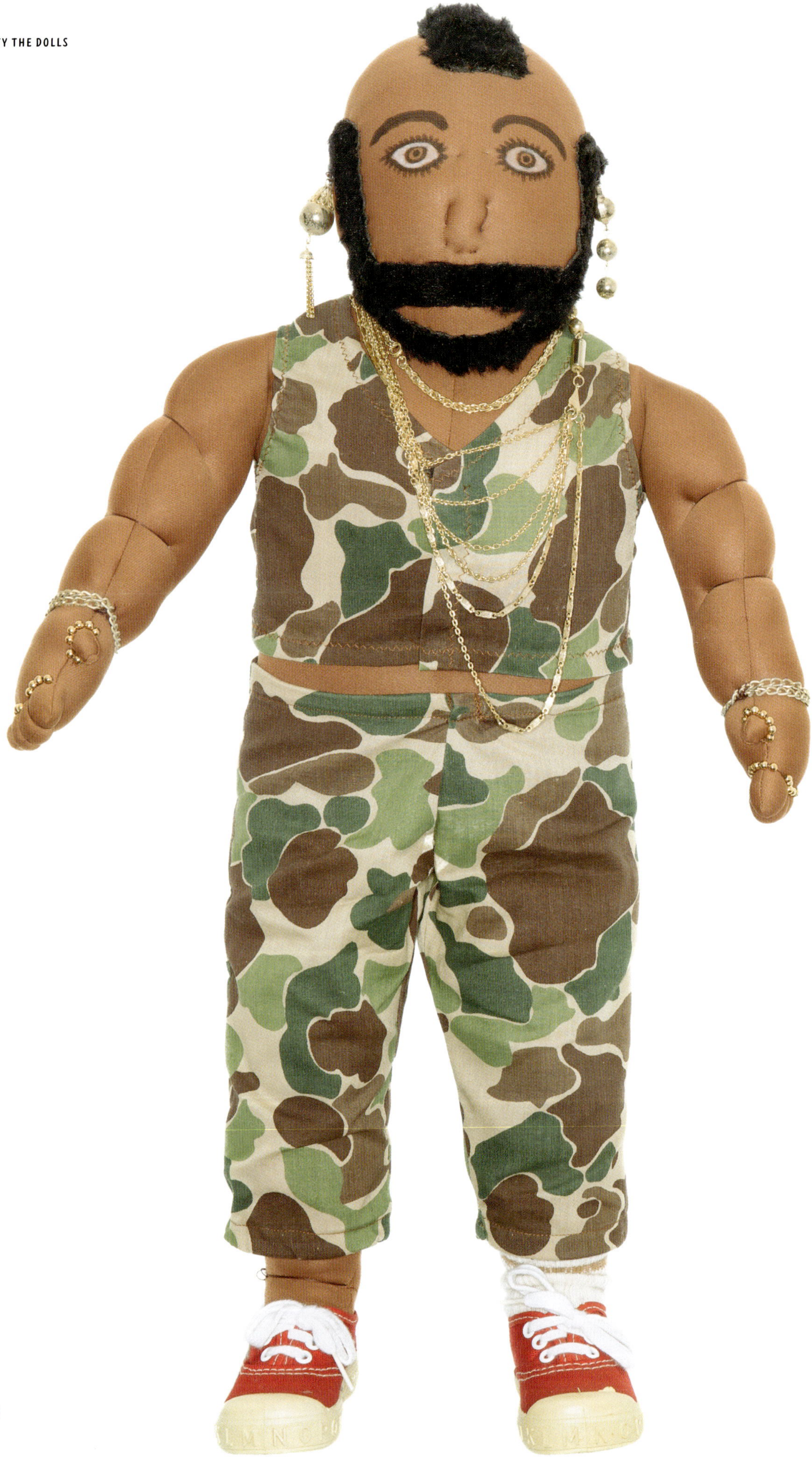

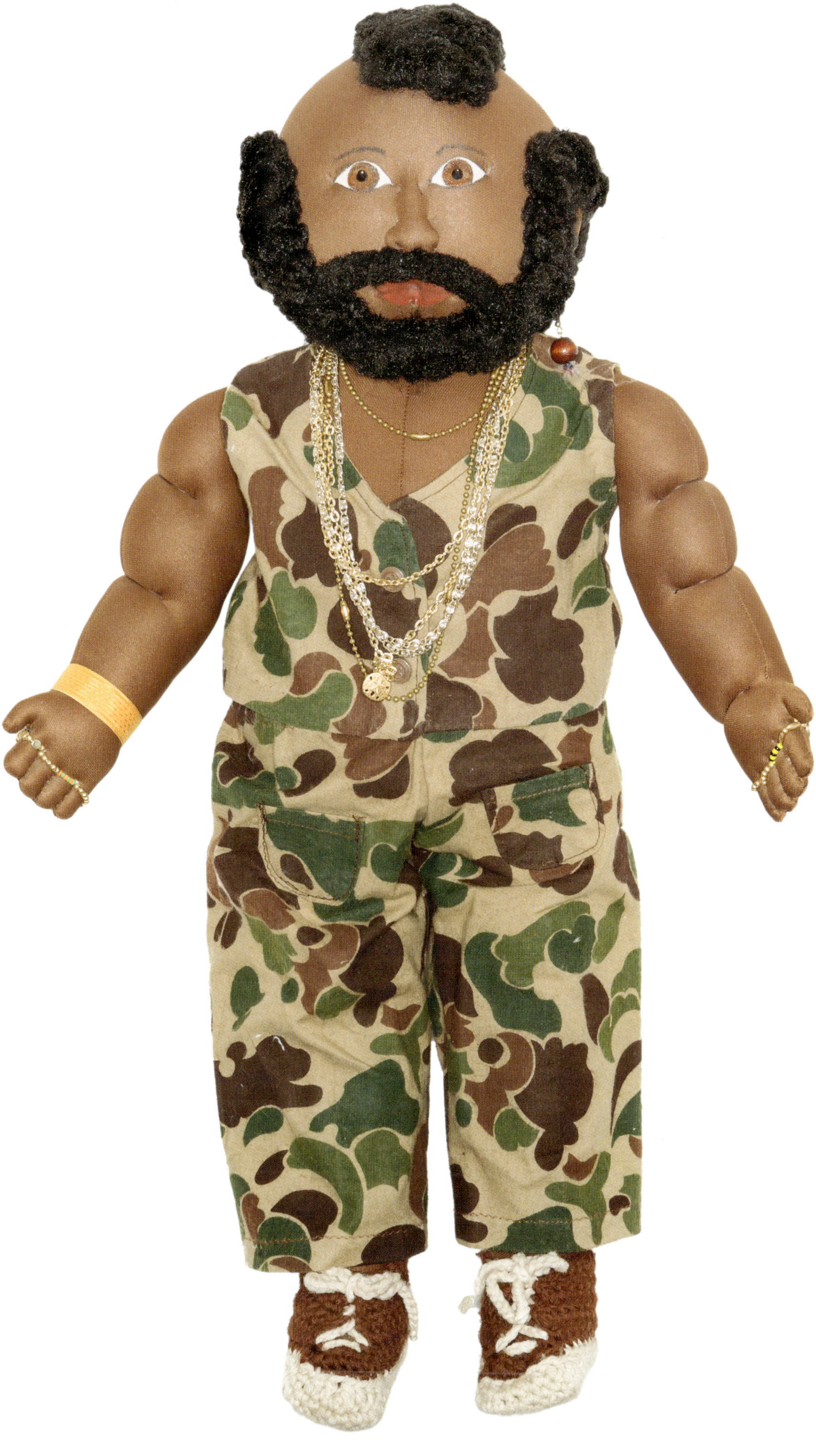

THE NAME IS
MR. T
FIRST NAME
MISTER
MIDDLE NAME
PERIOD
LAST NAME
"T"

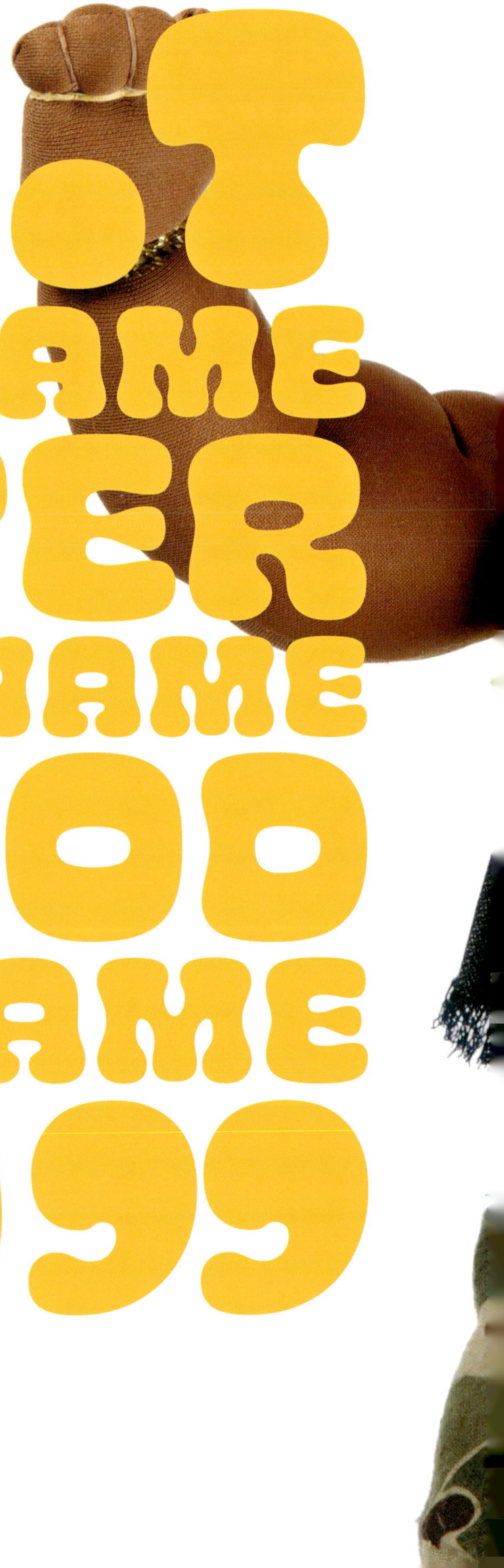

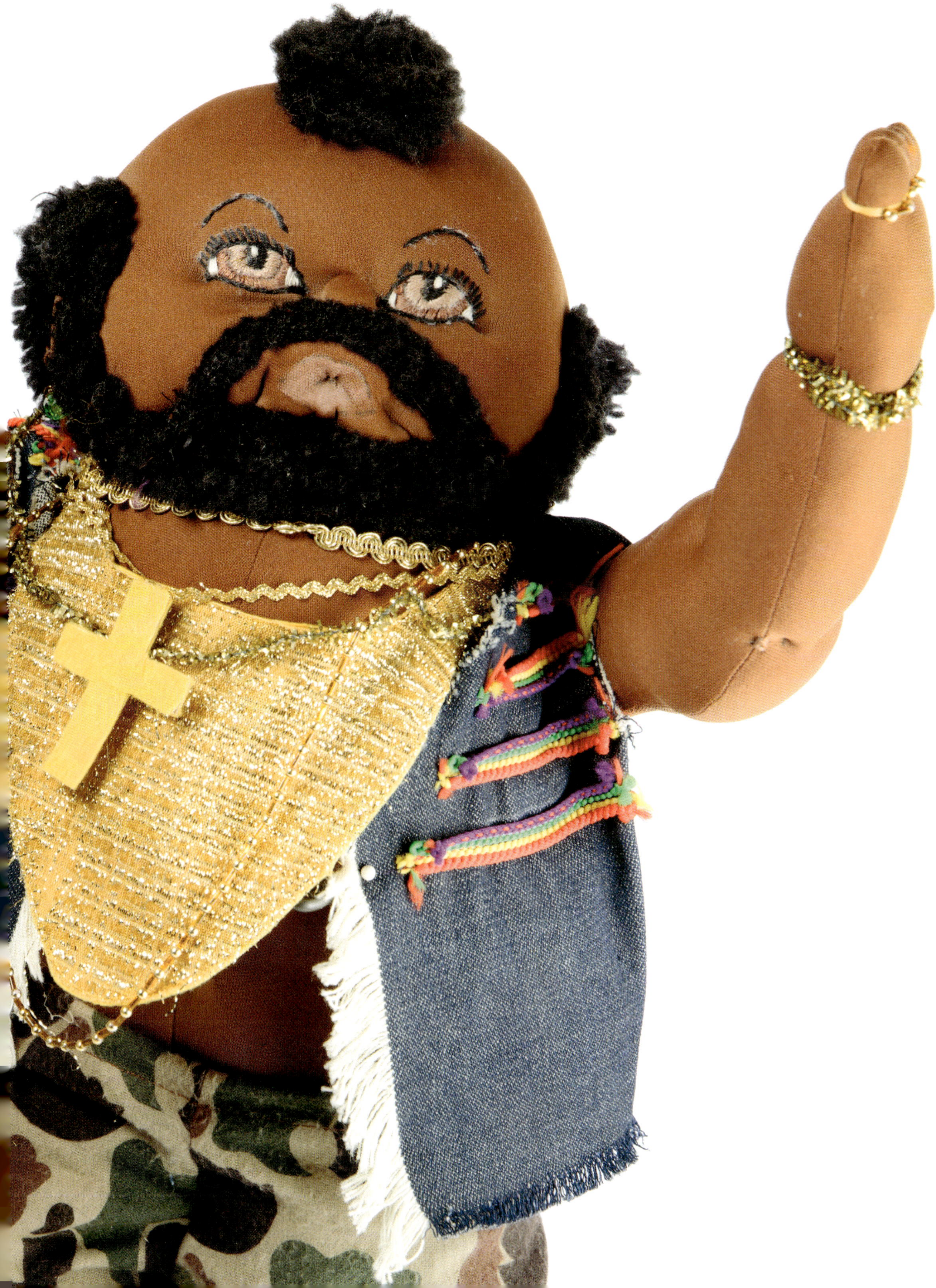

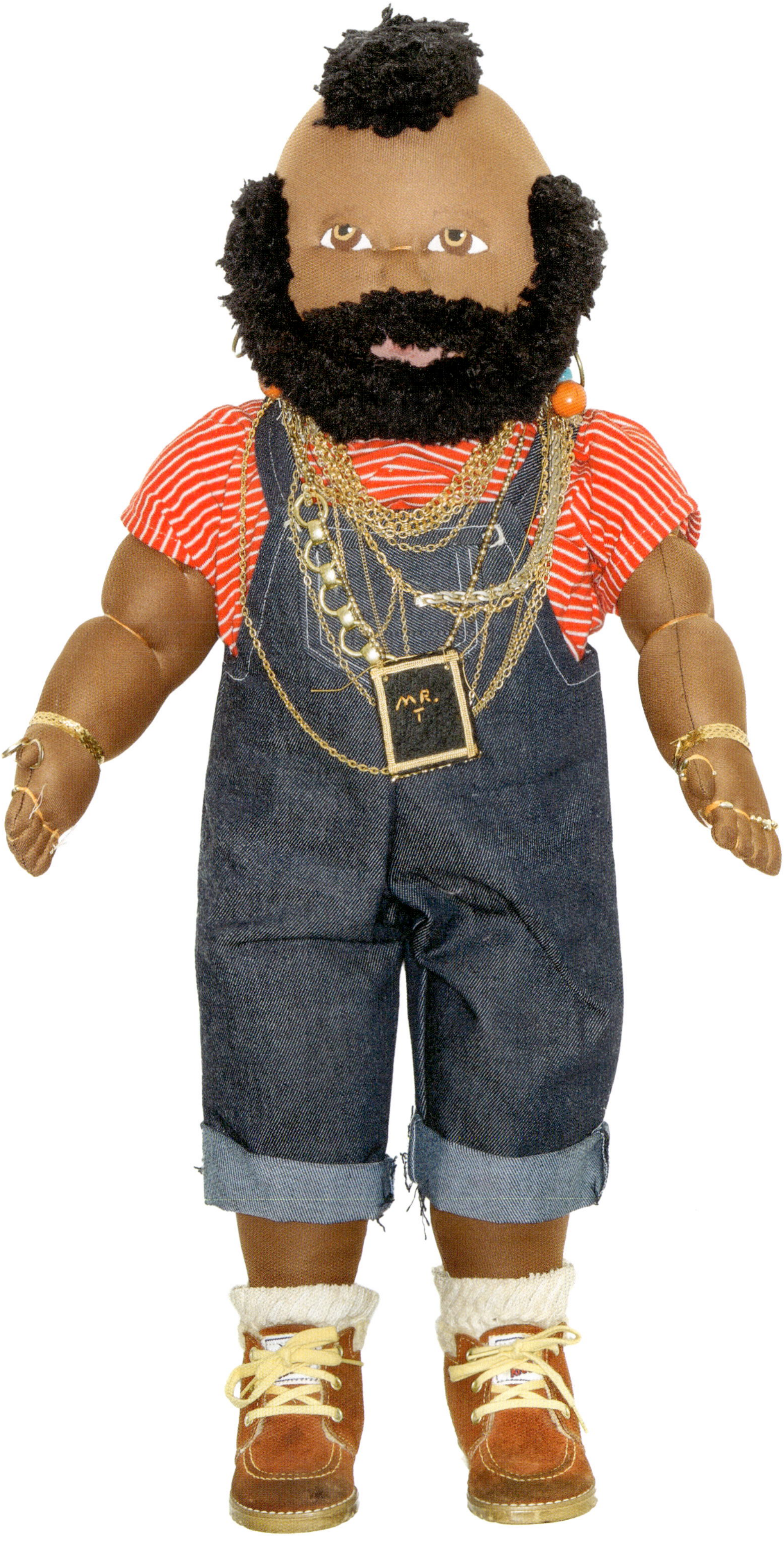
MR.
T

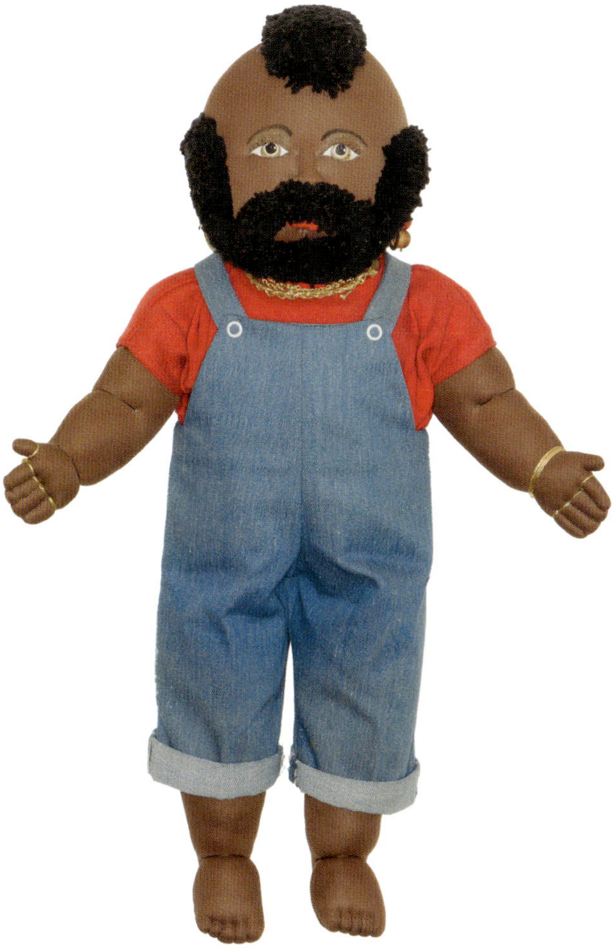
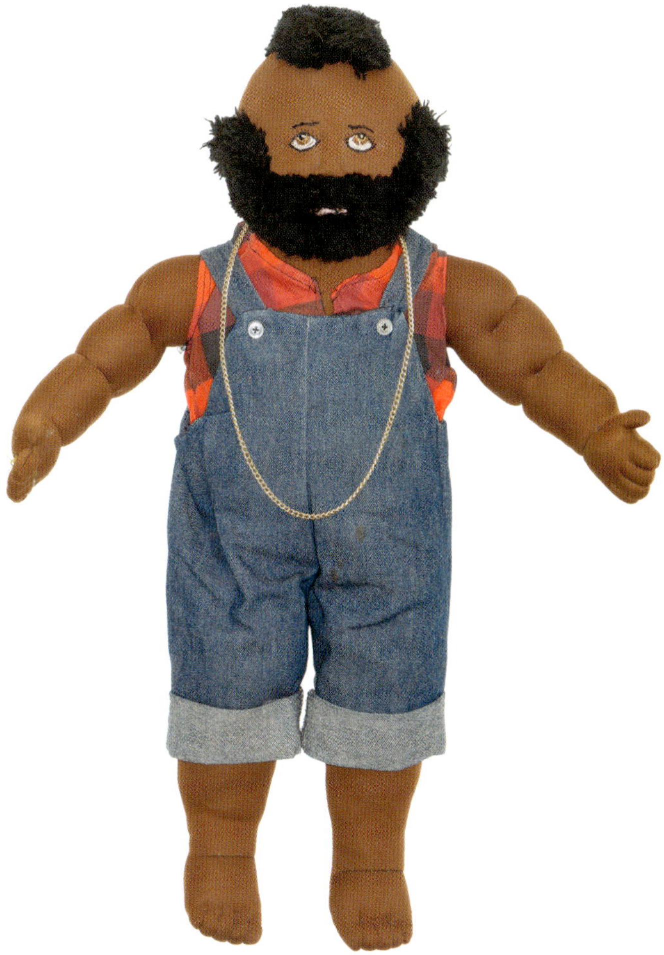
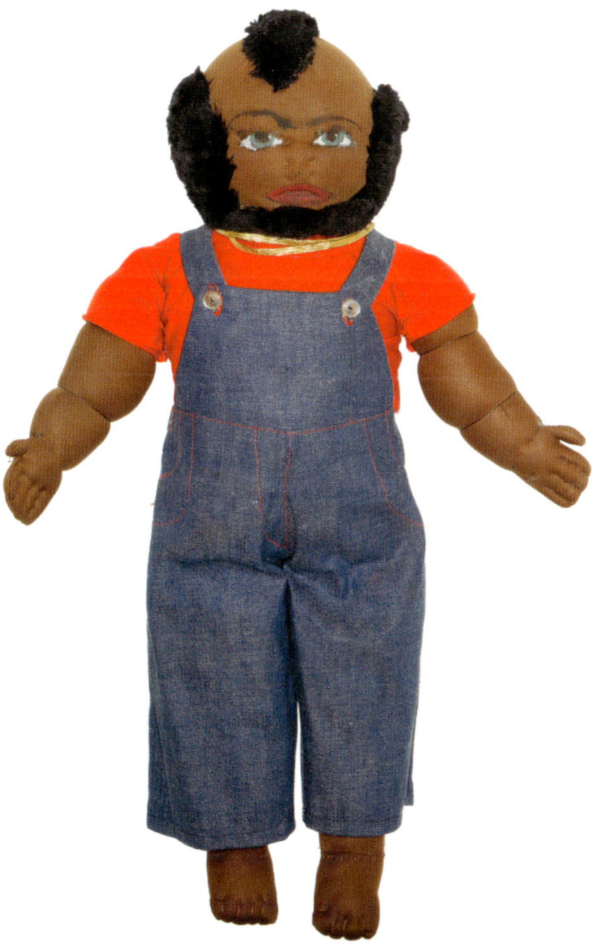
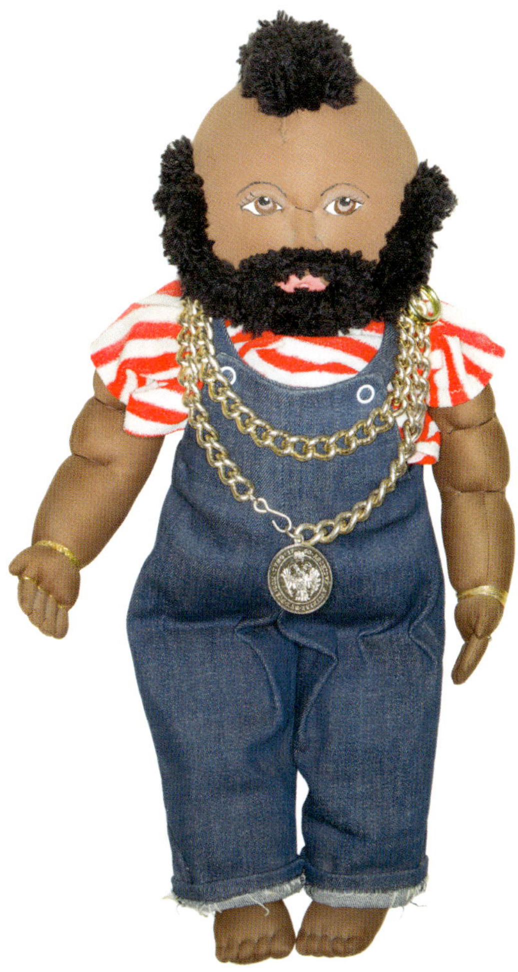

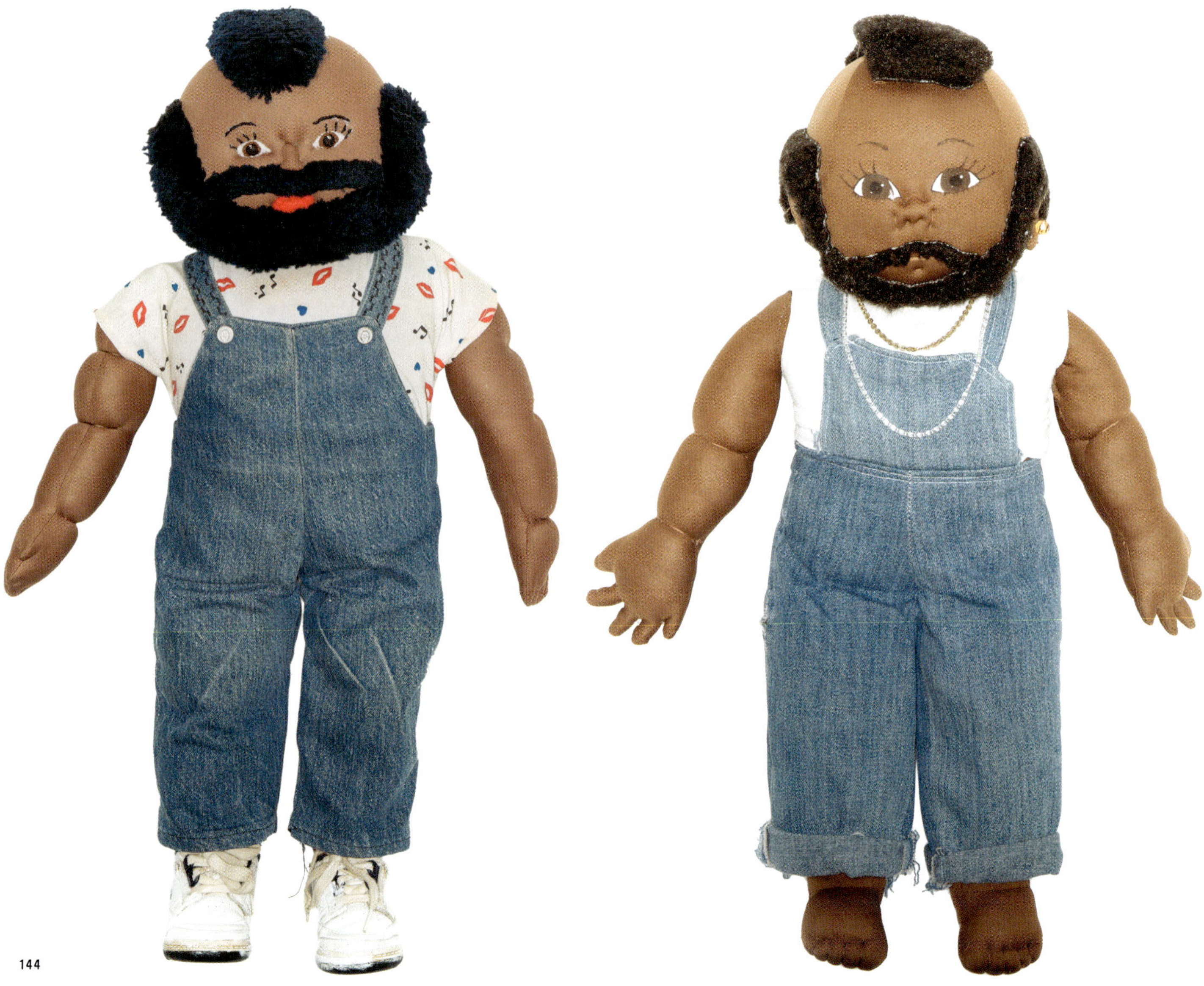

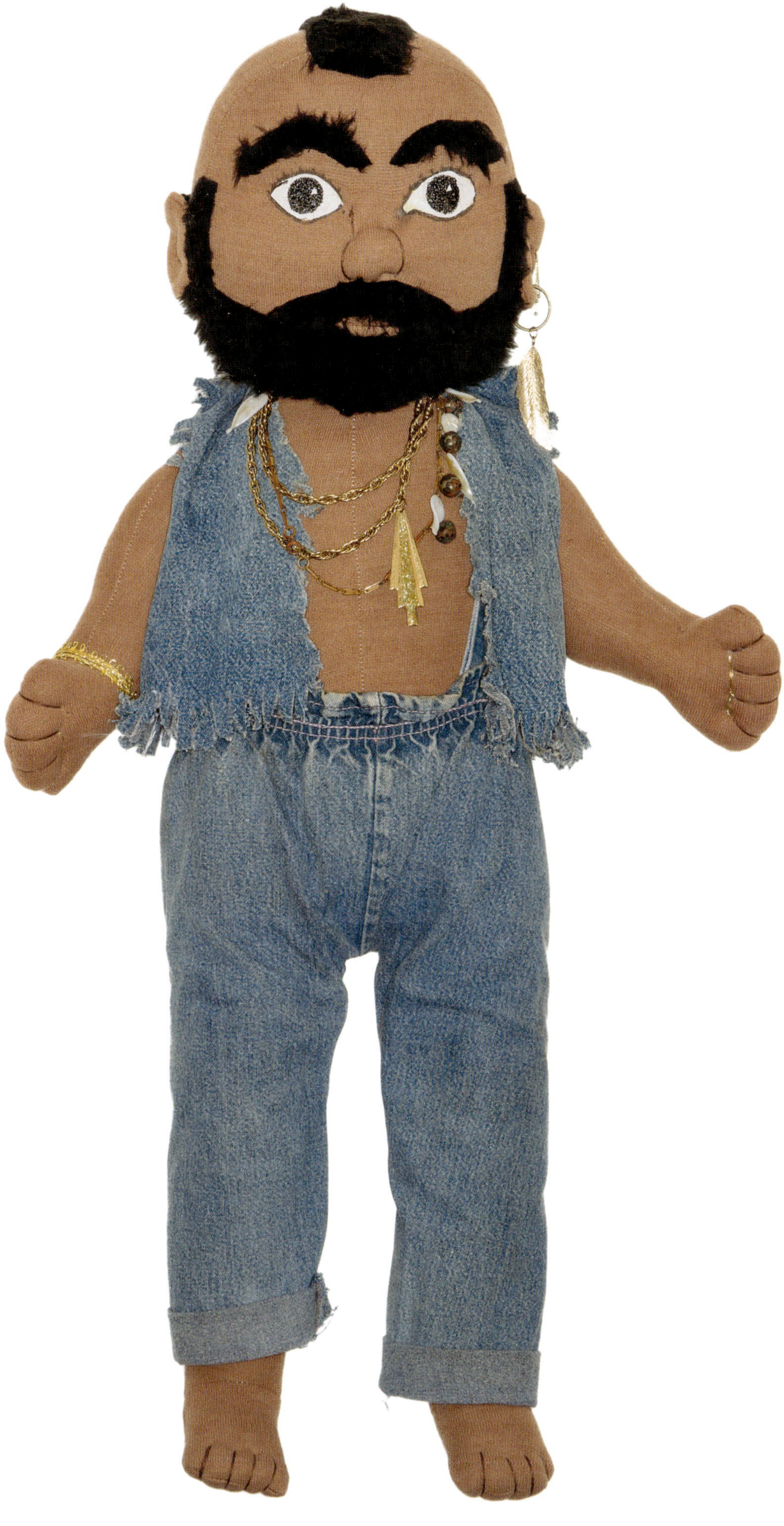

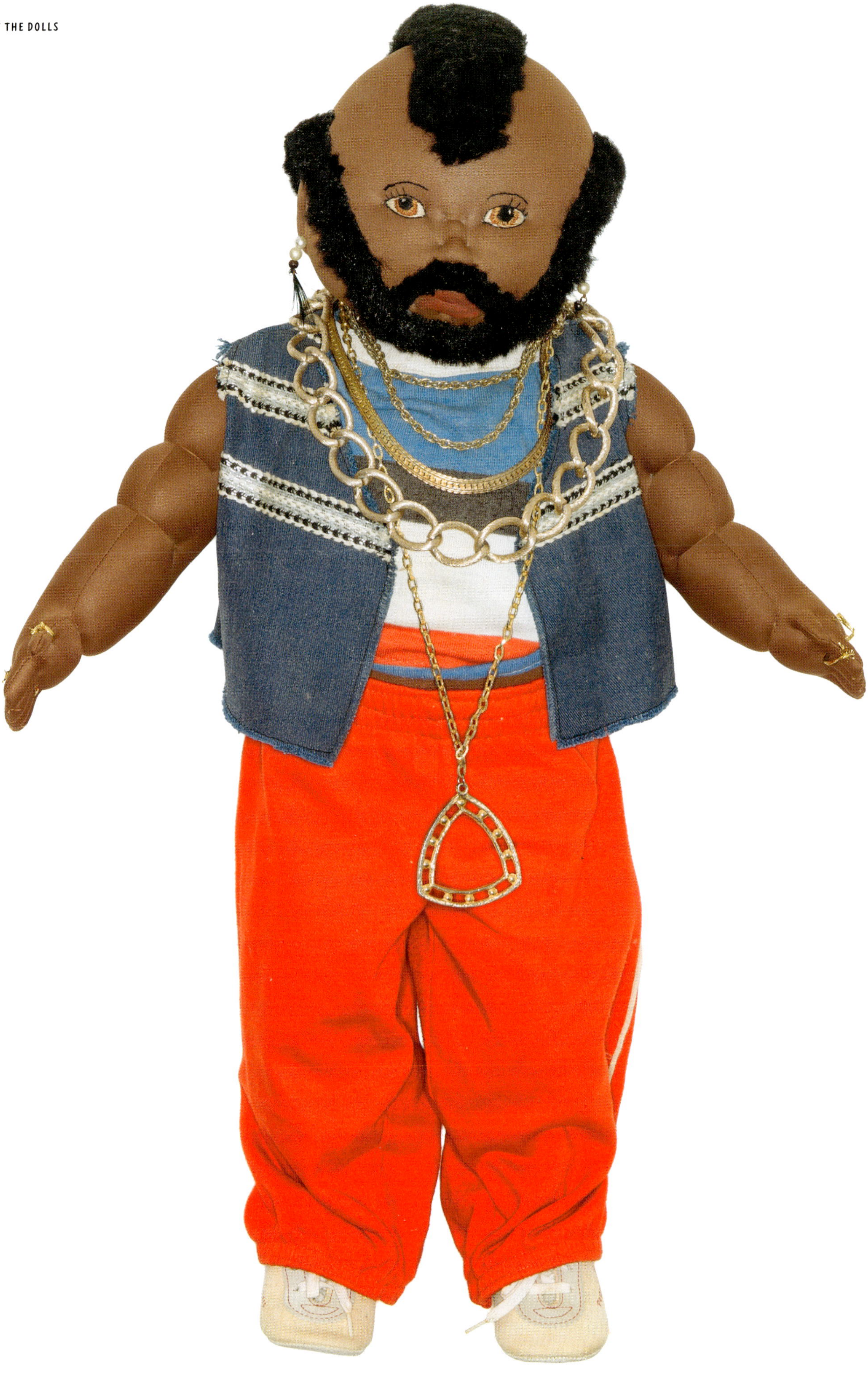

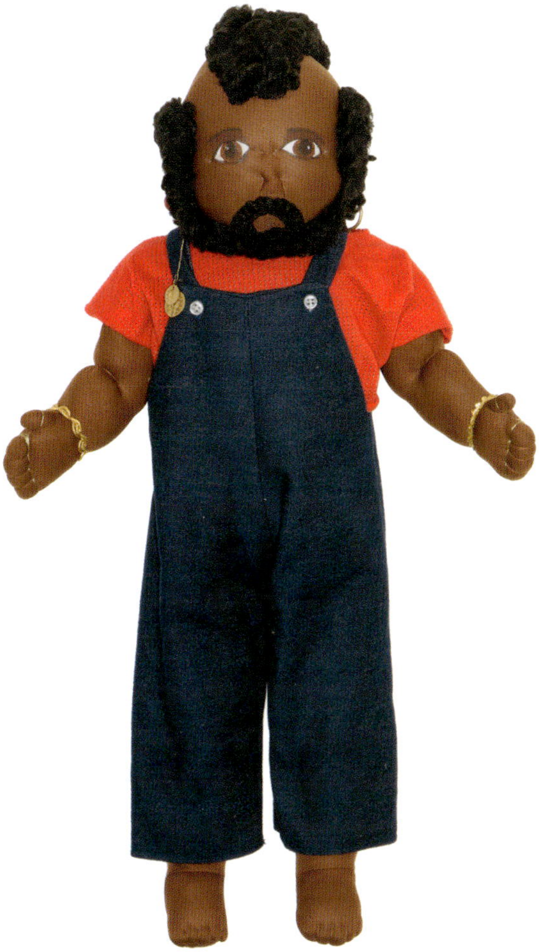
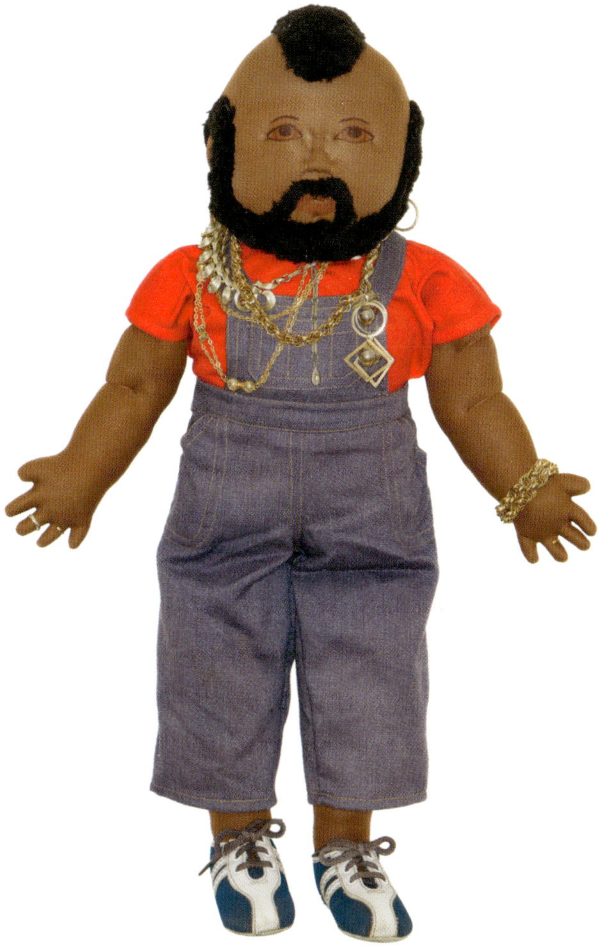
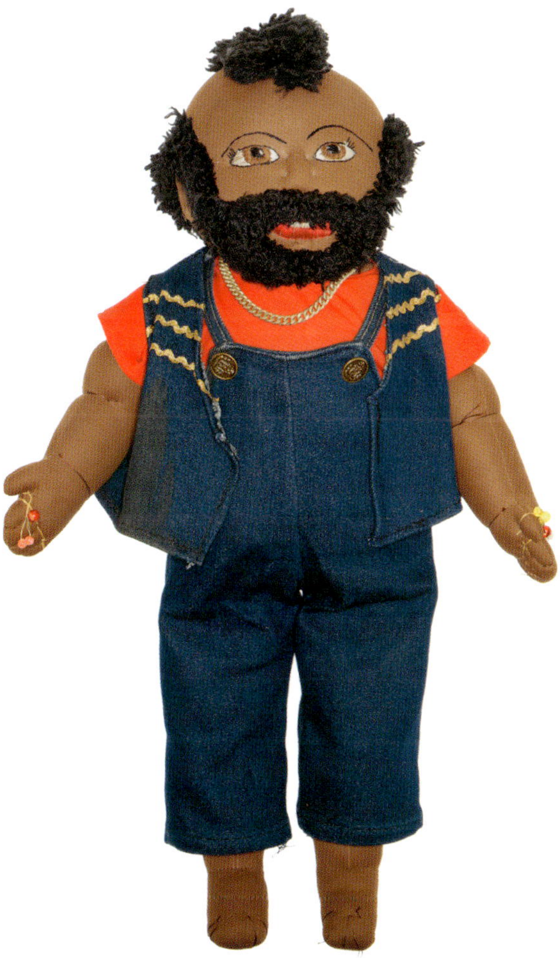
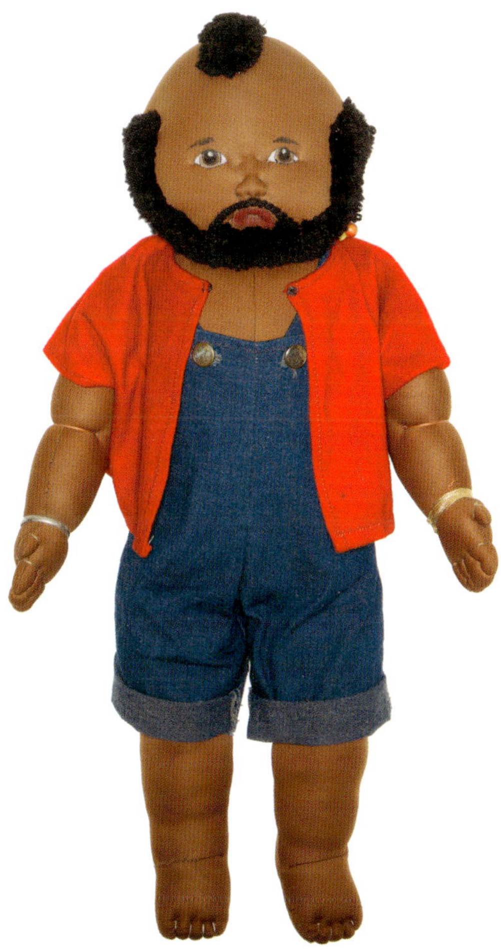

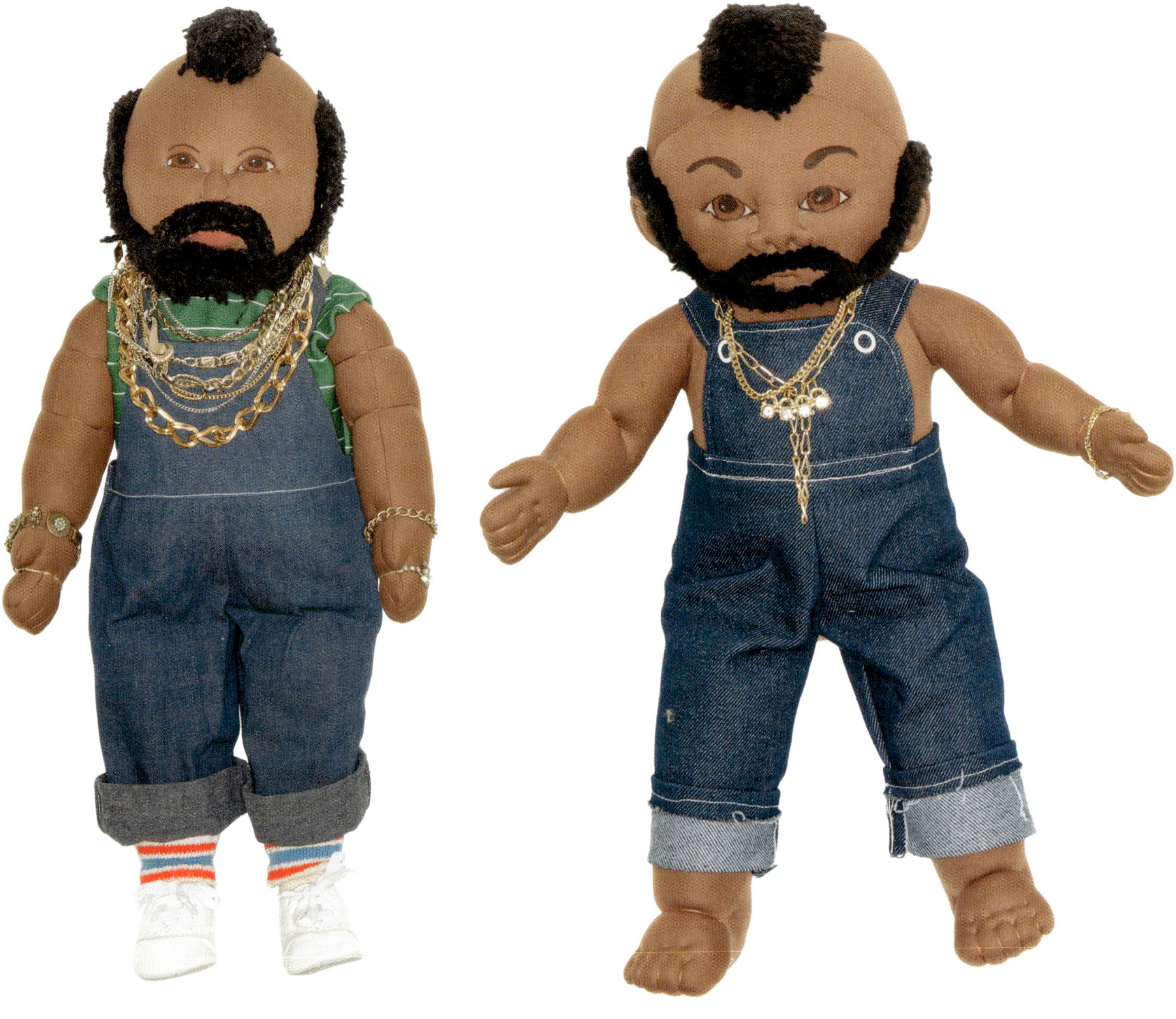

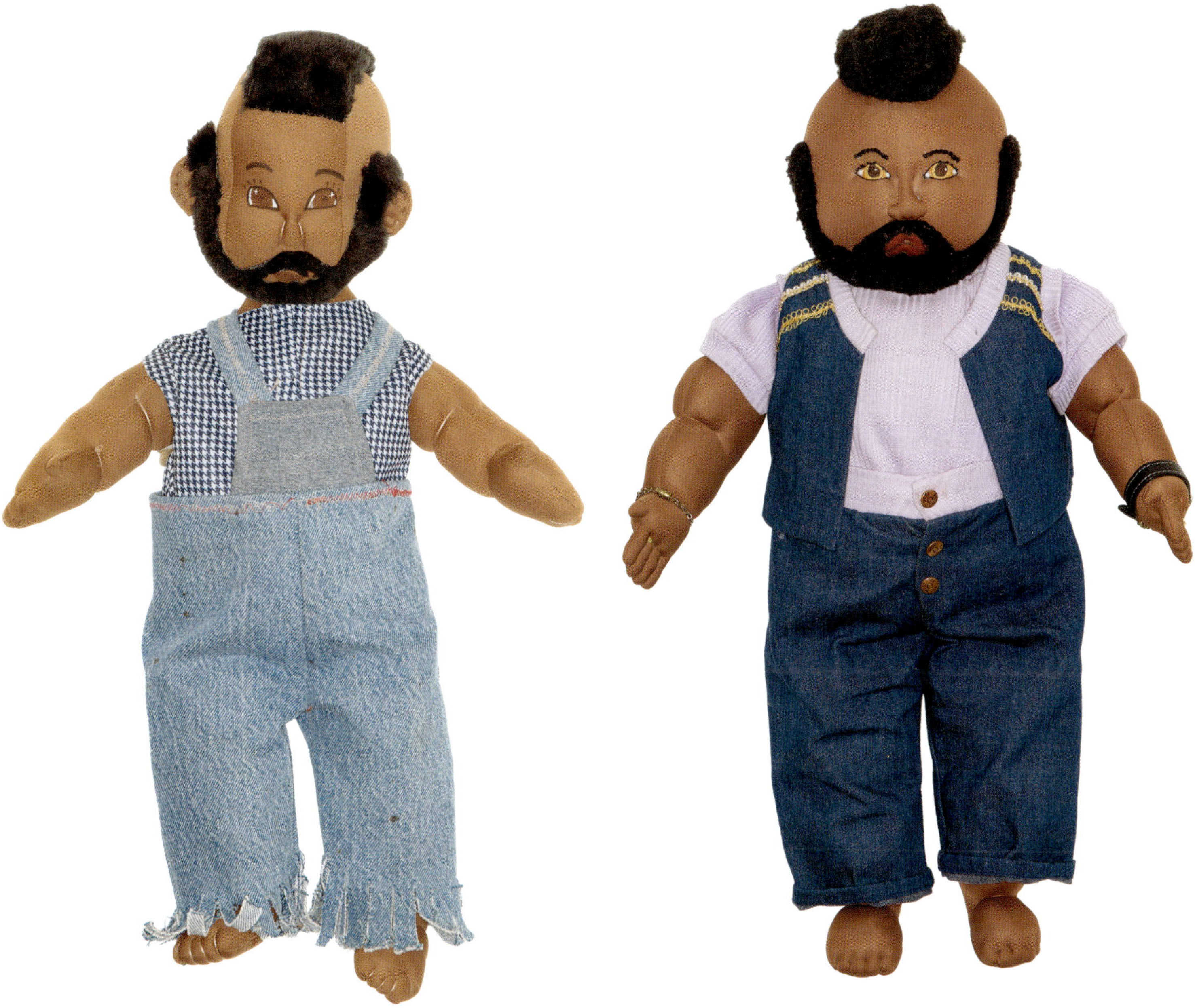

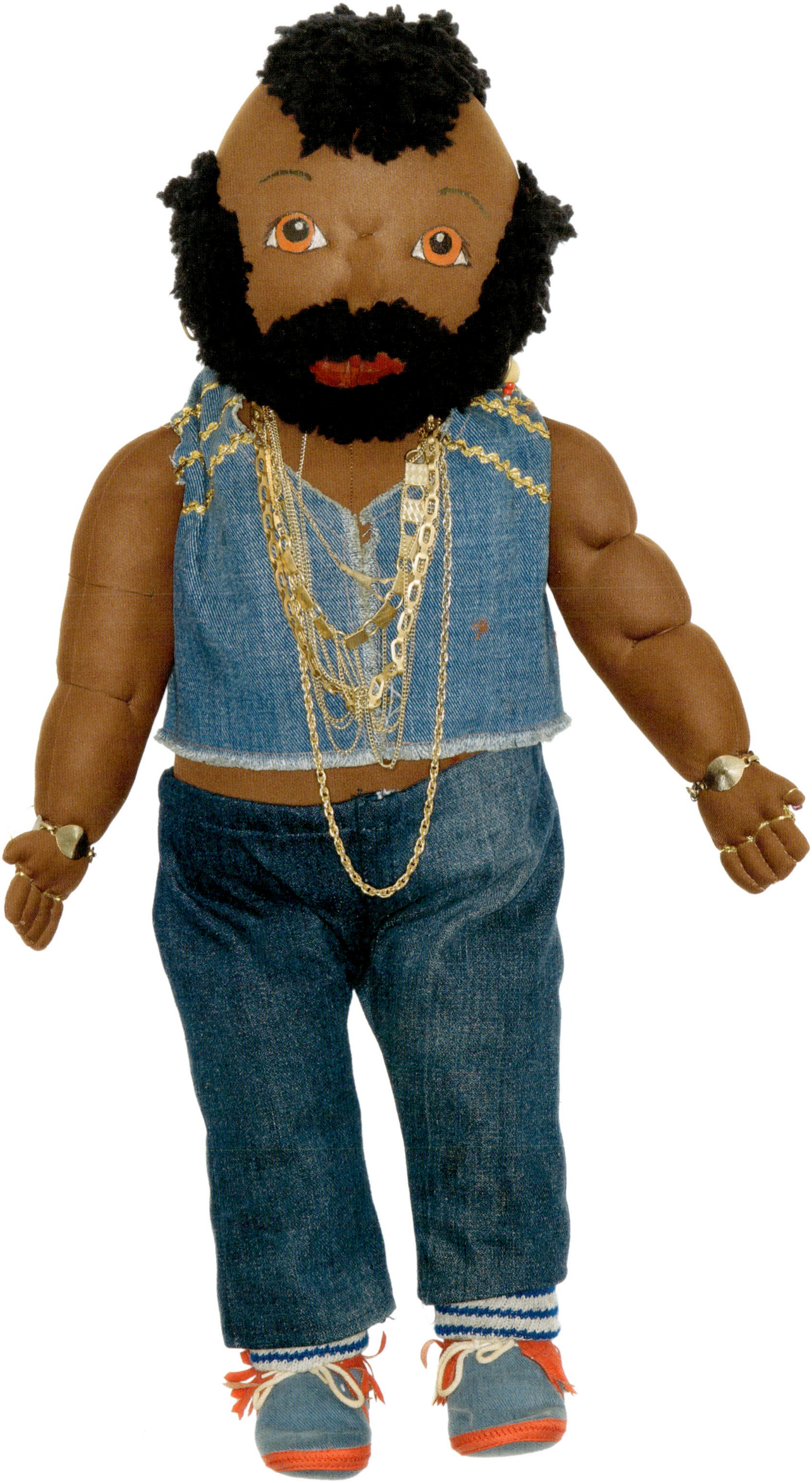

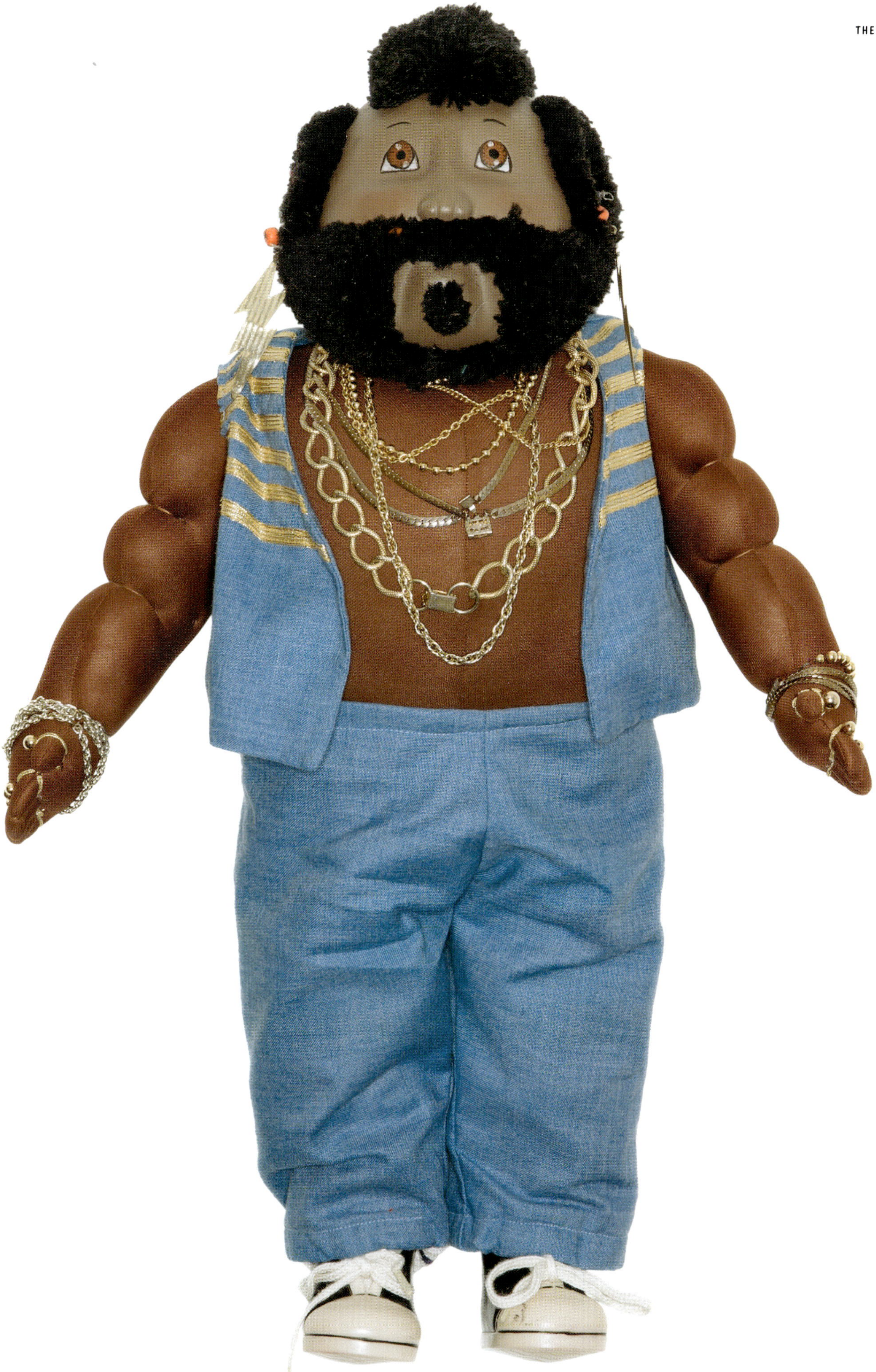

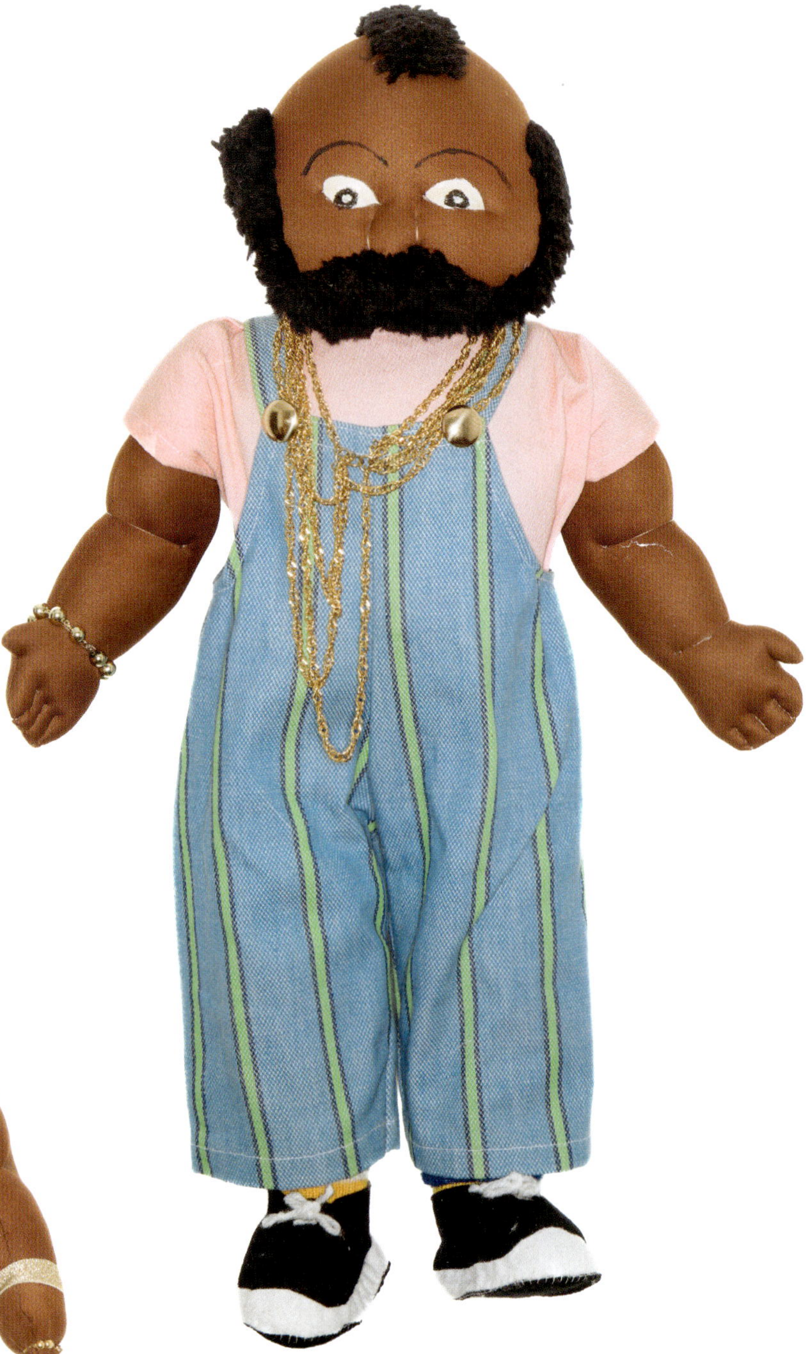

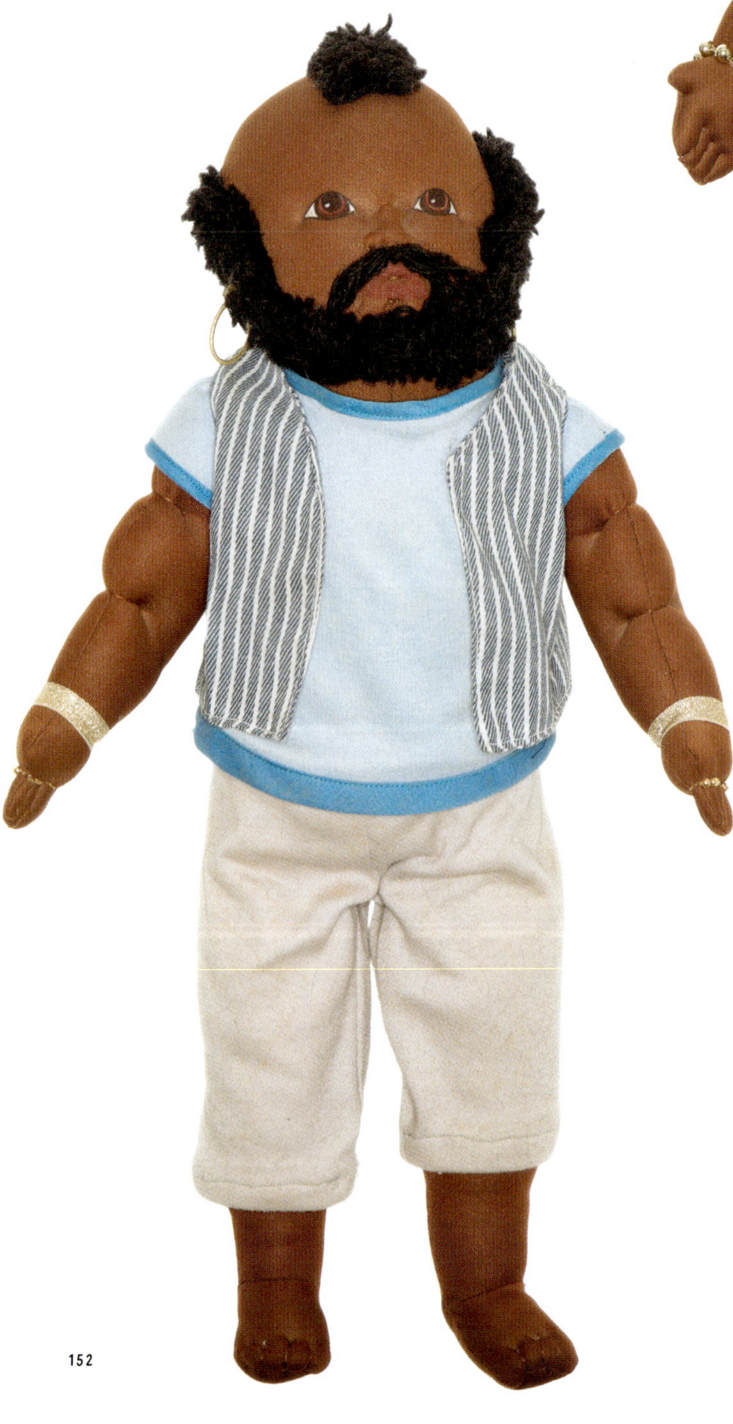

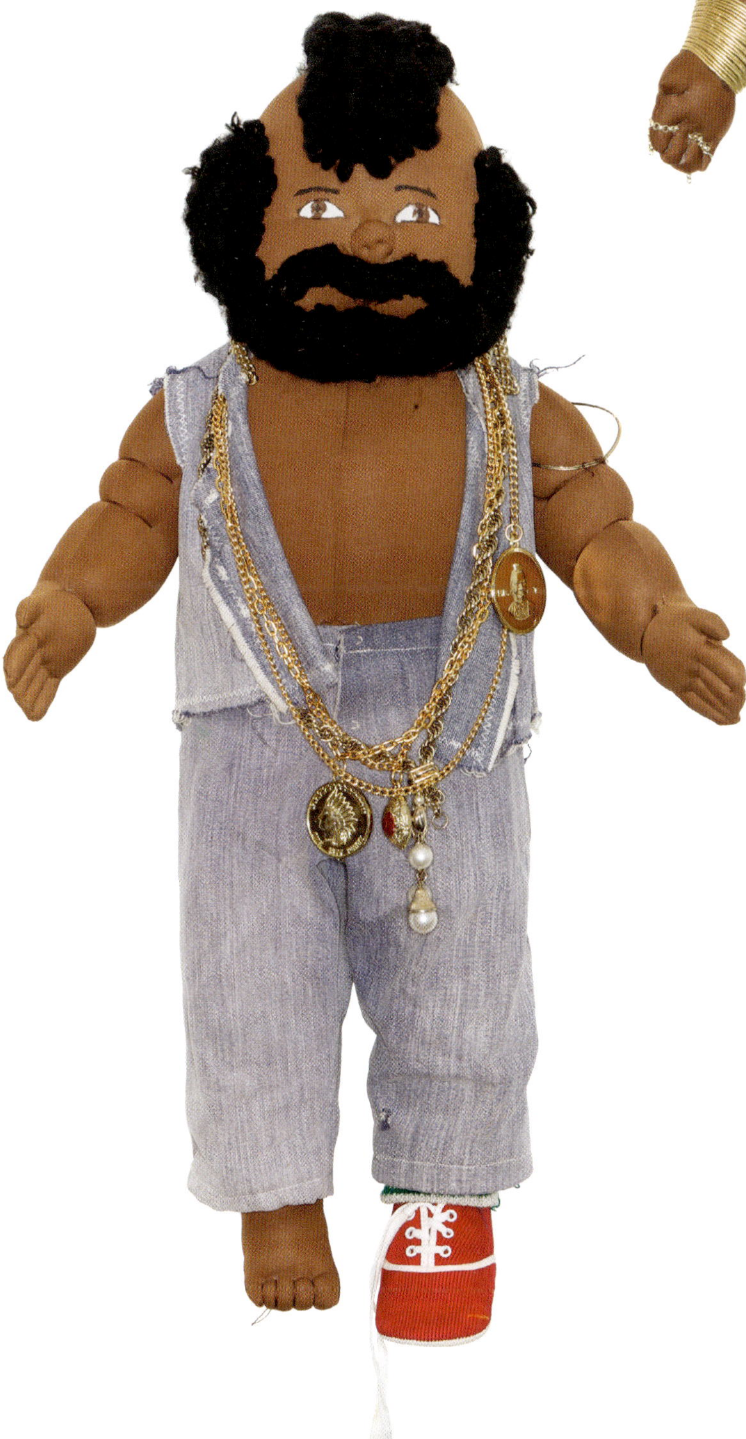

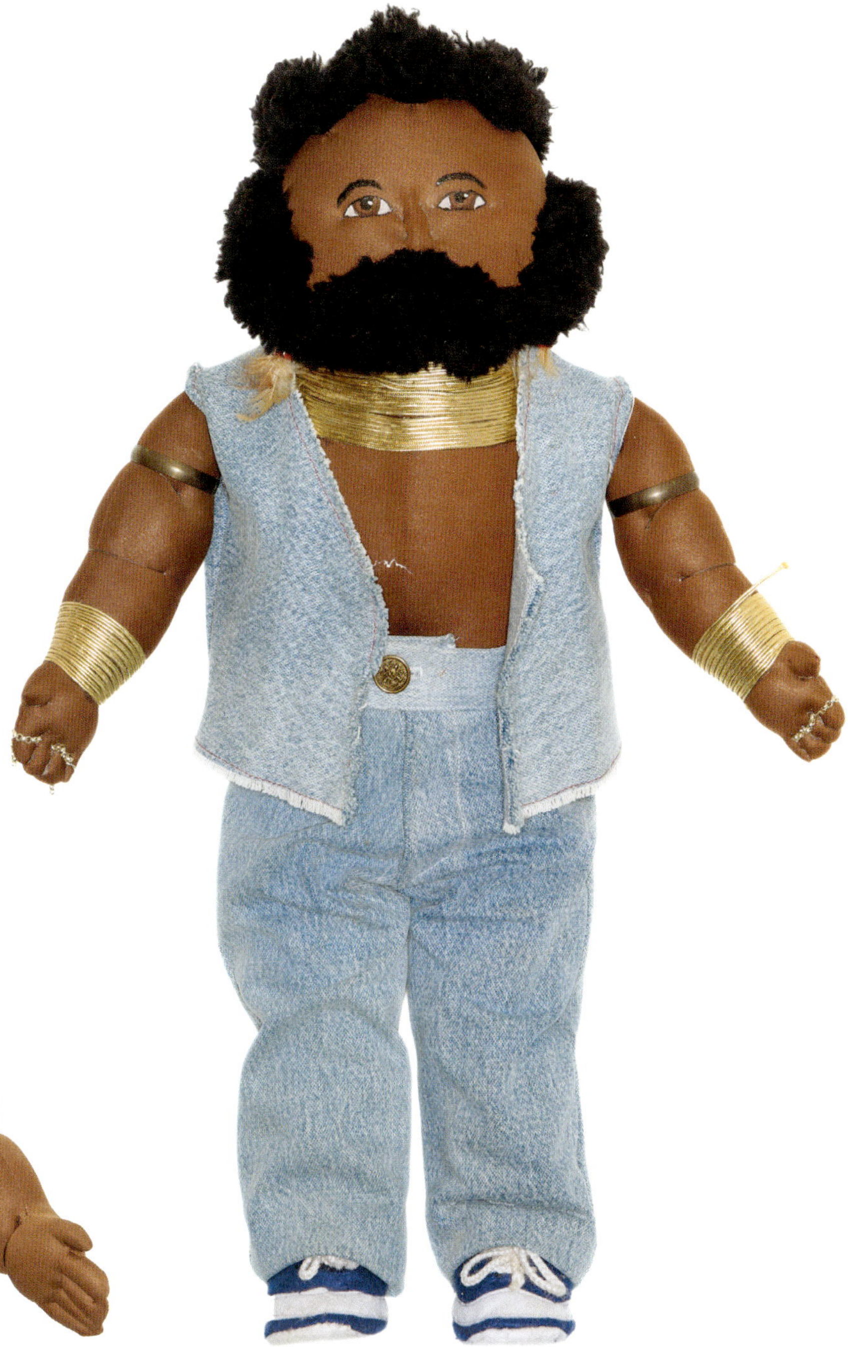

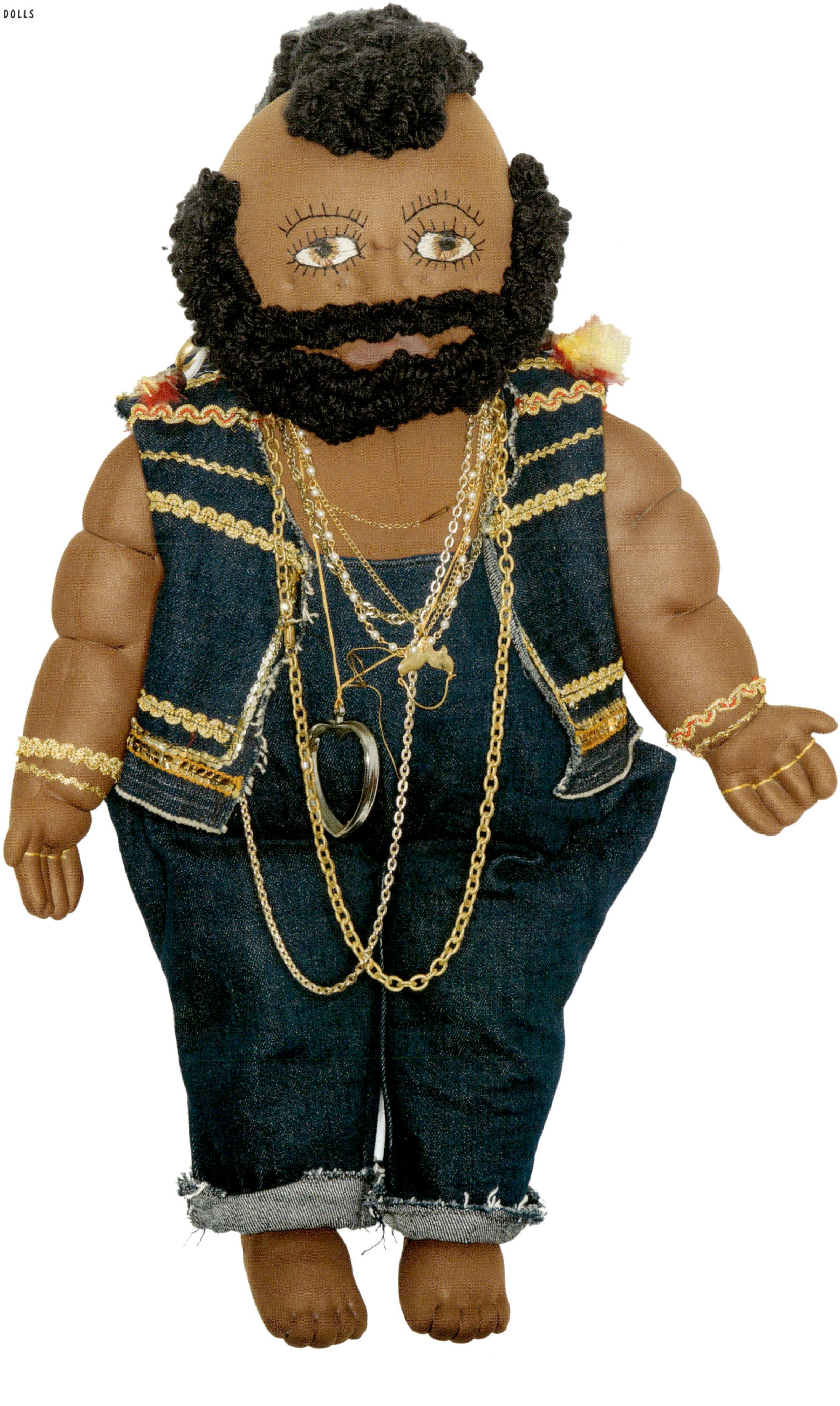

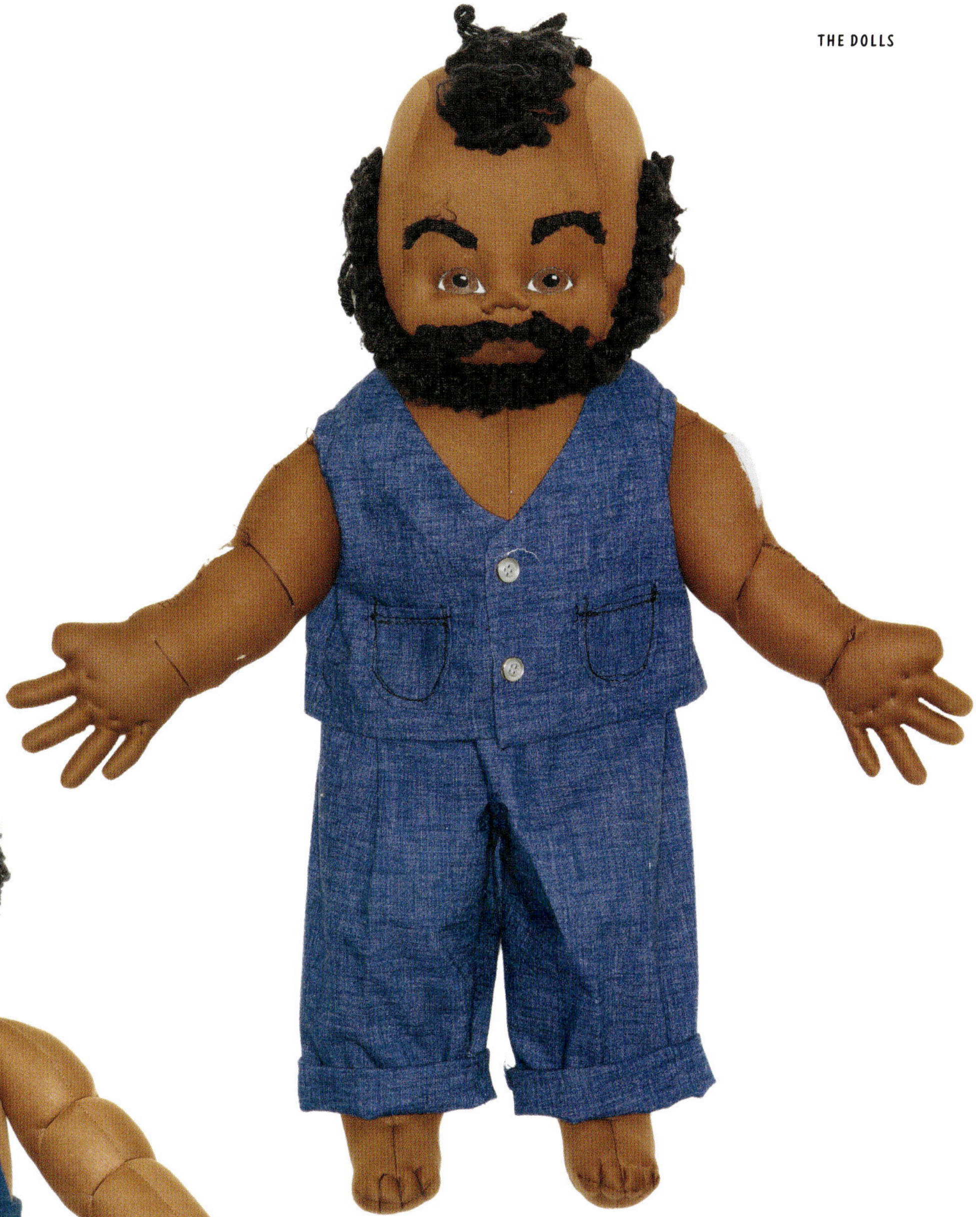

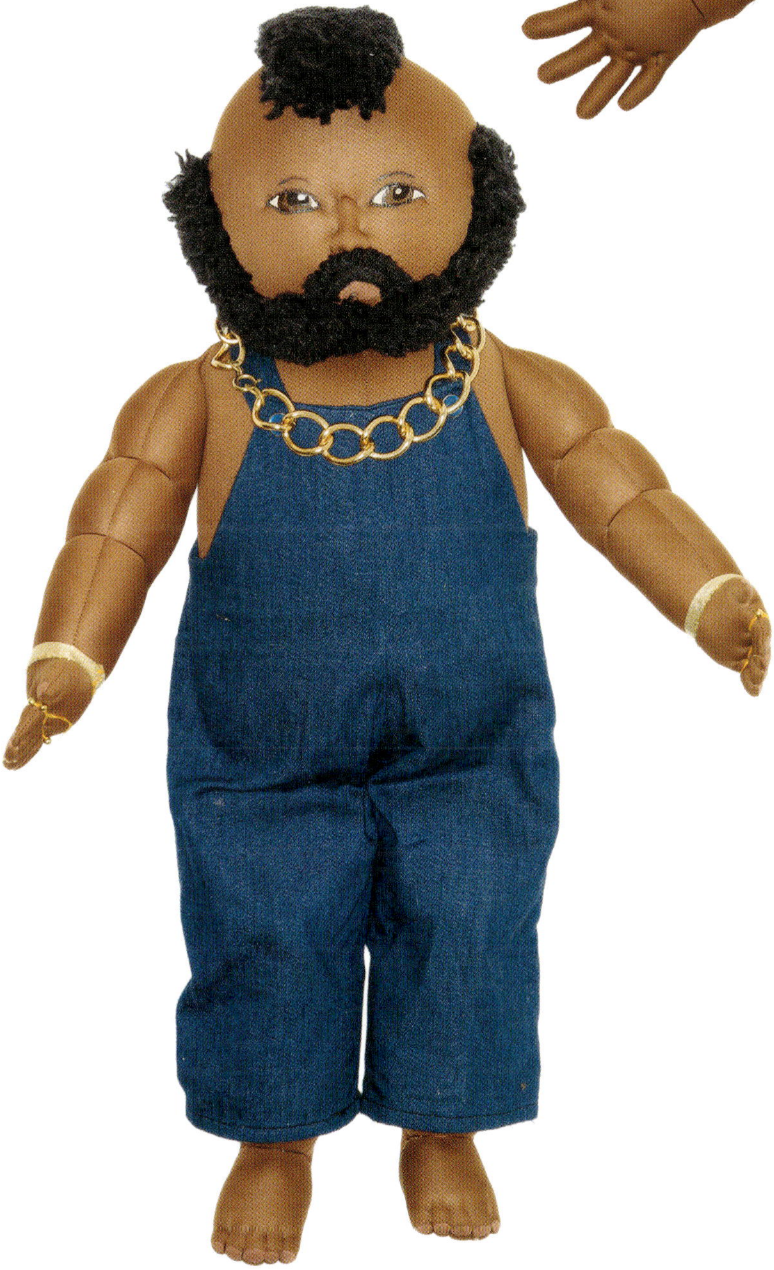

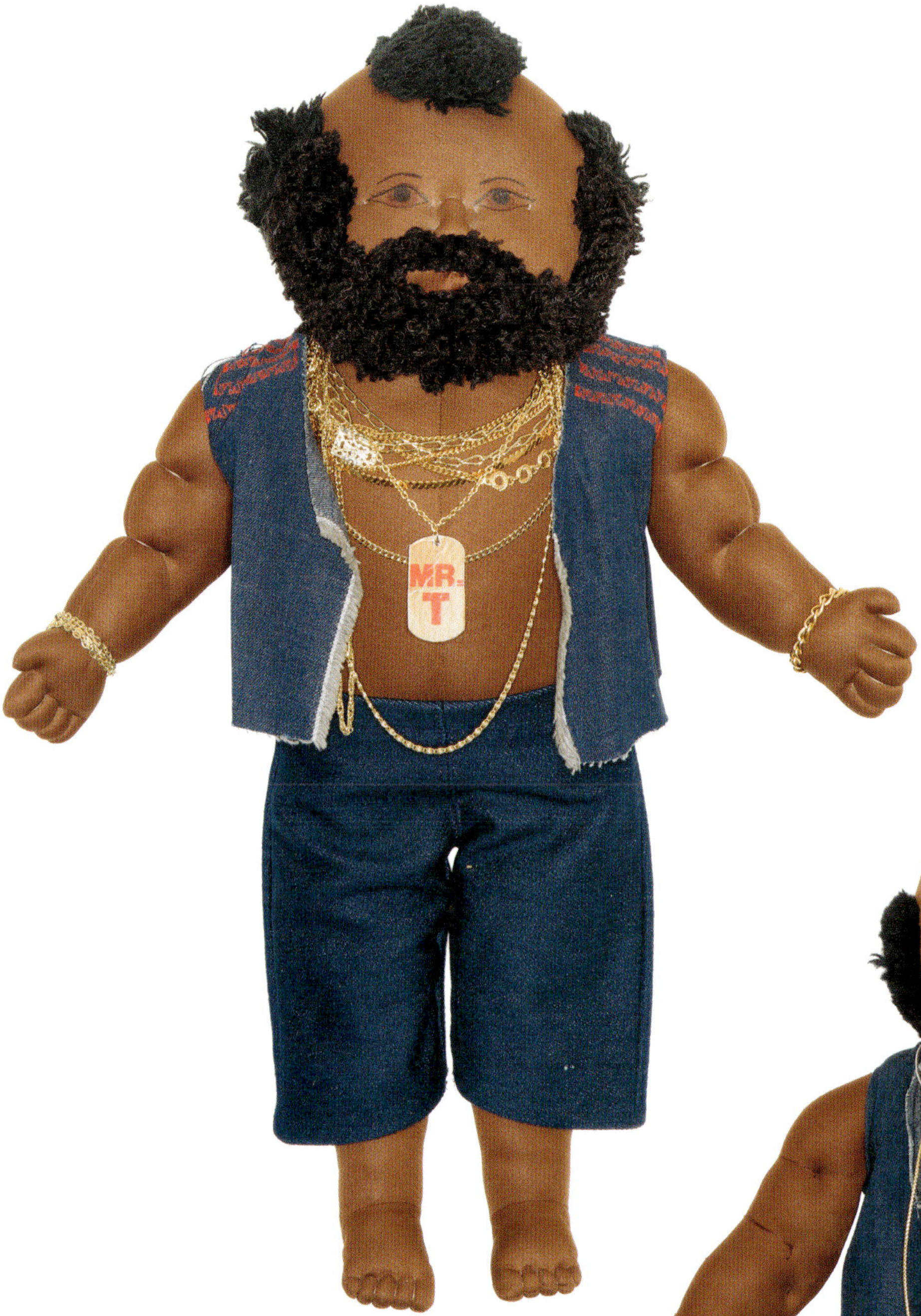
MR.
T

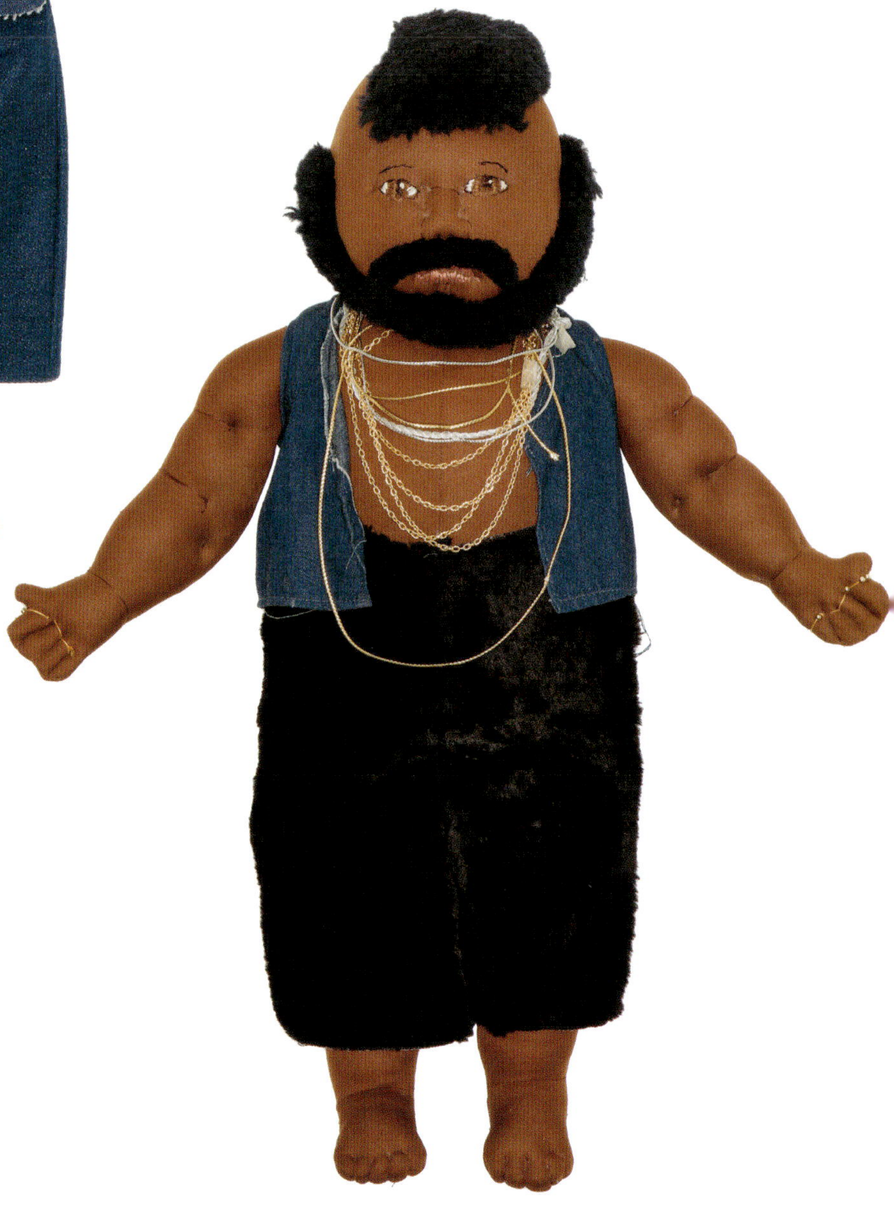

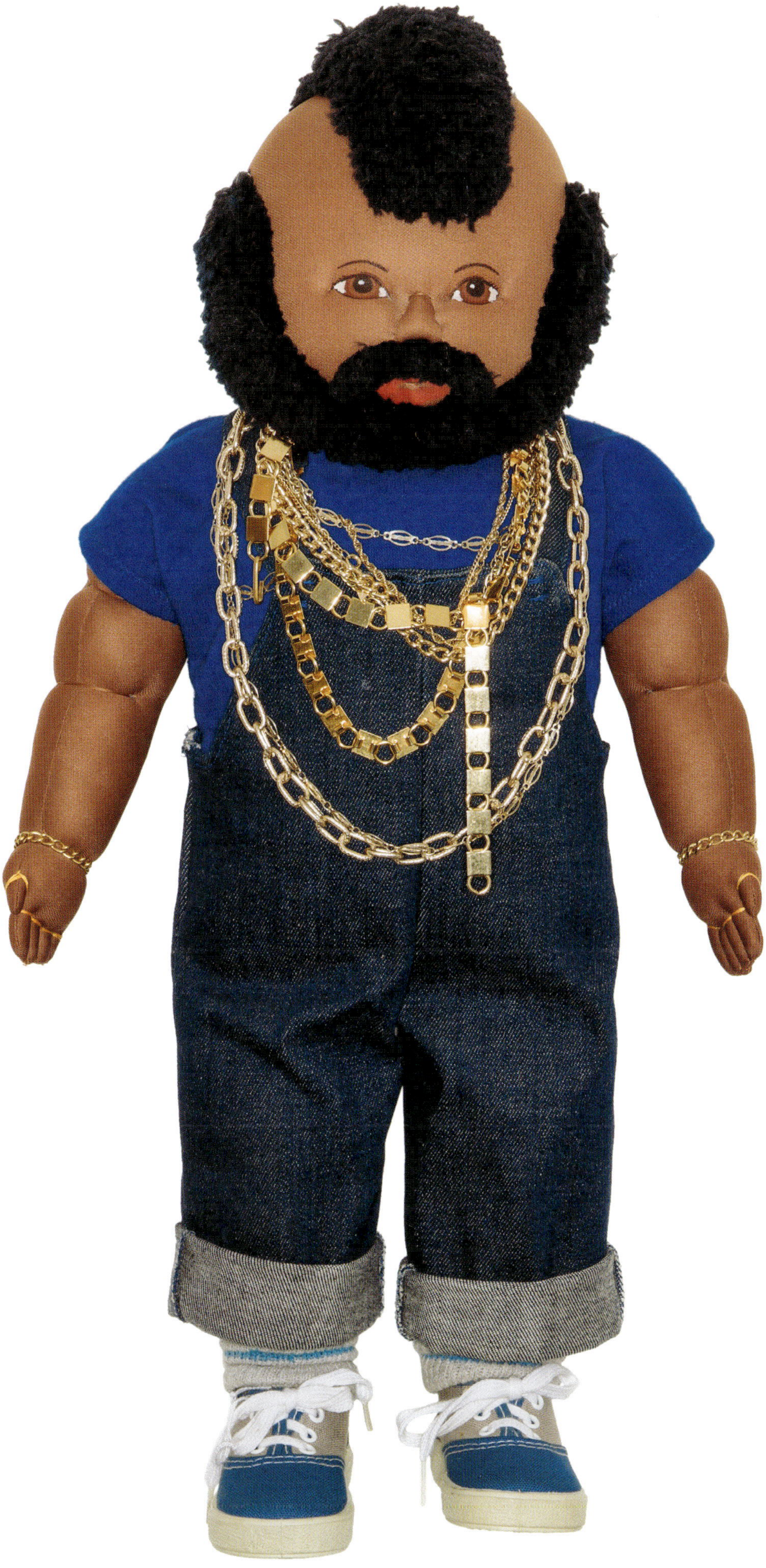

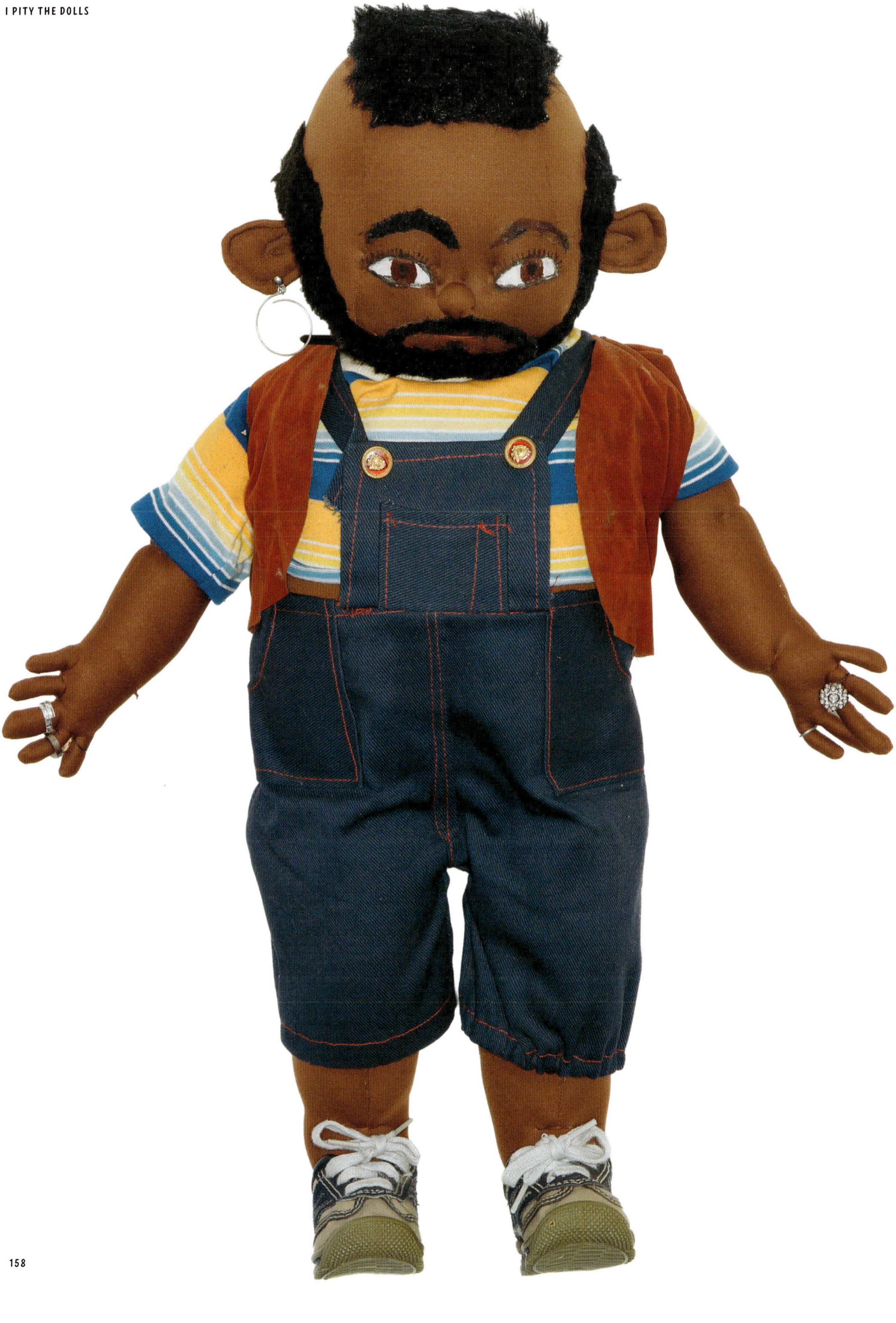

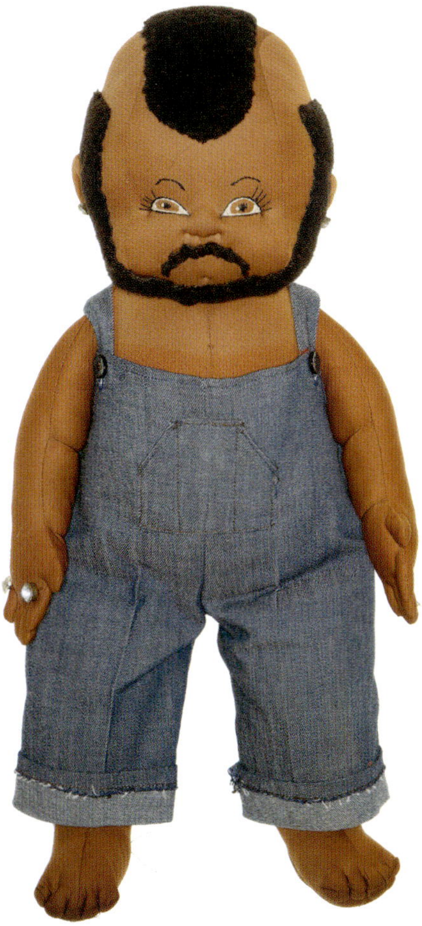

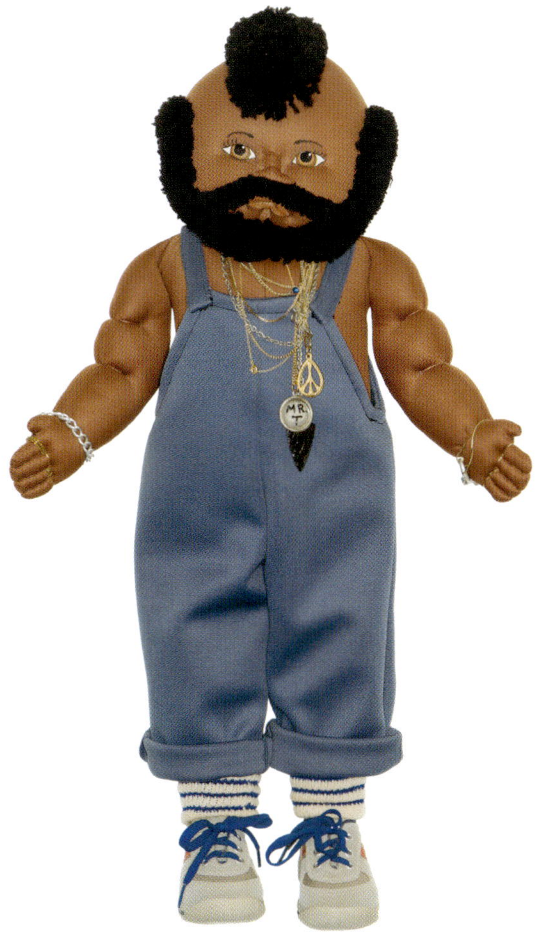

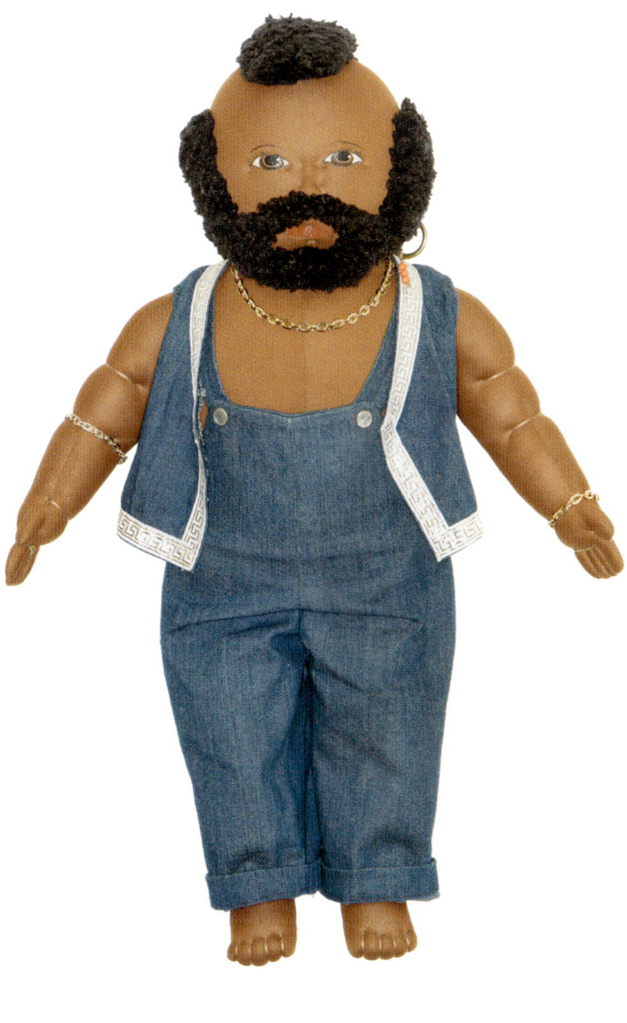

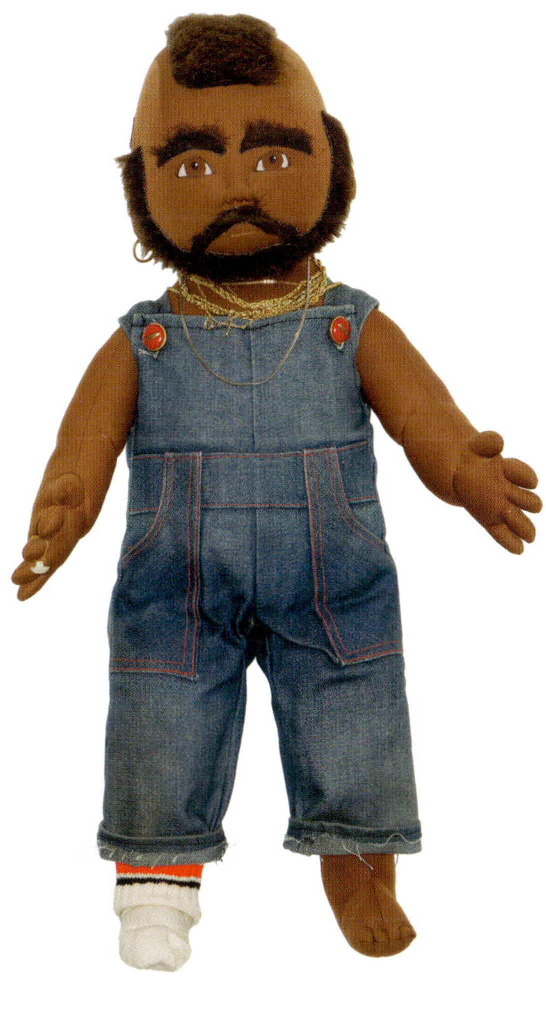

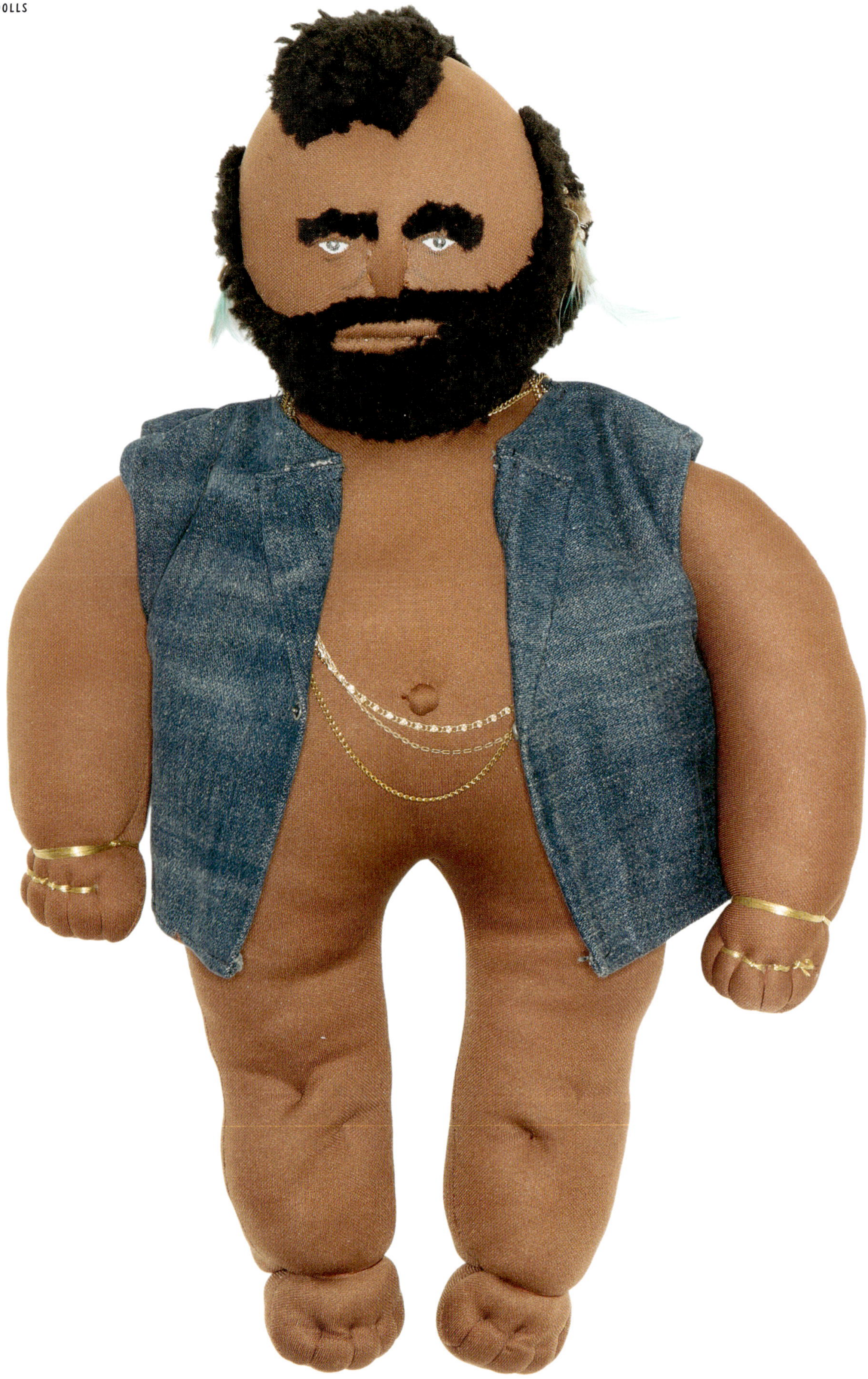

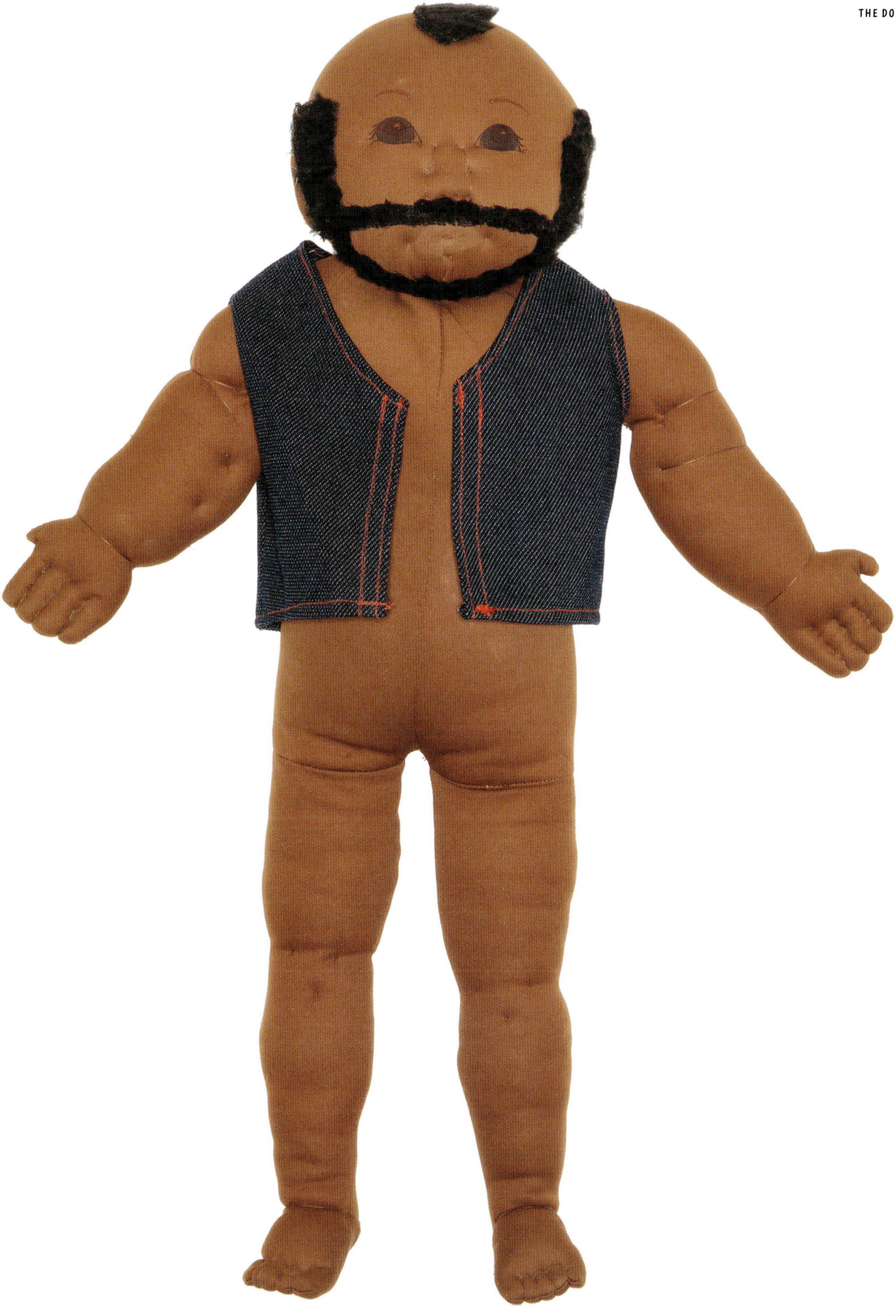

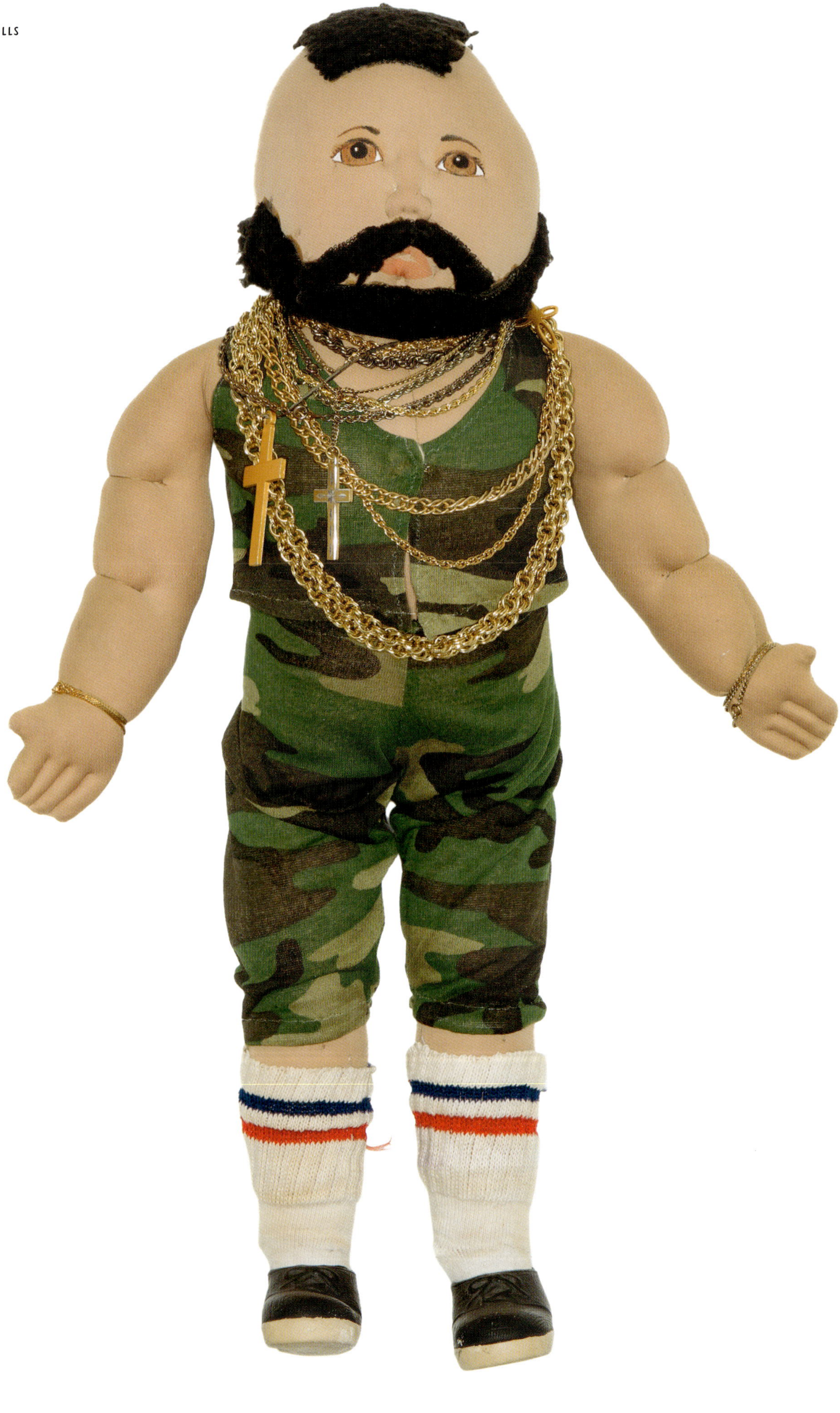

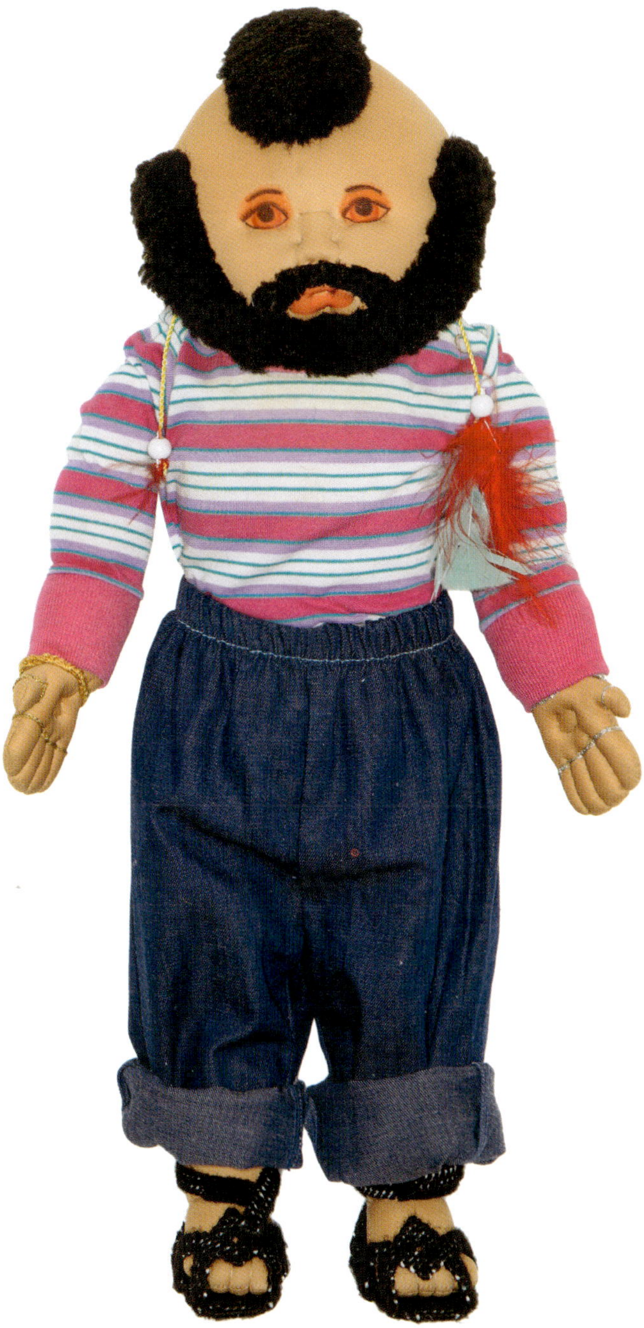

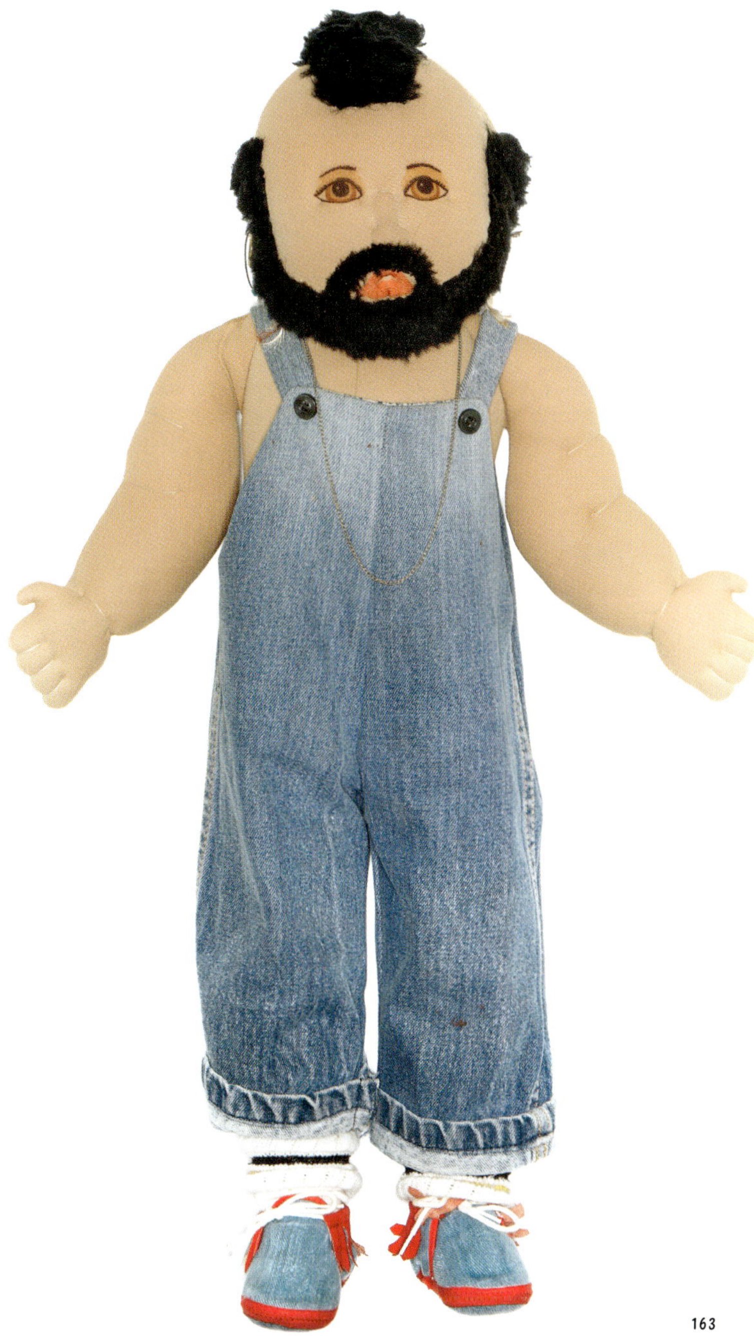

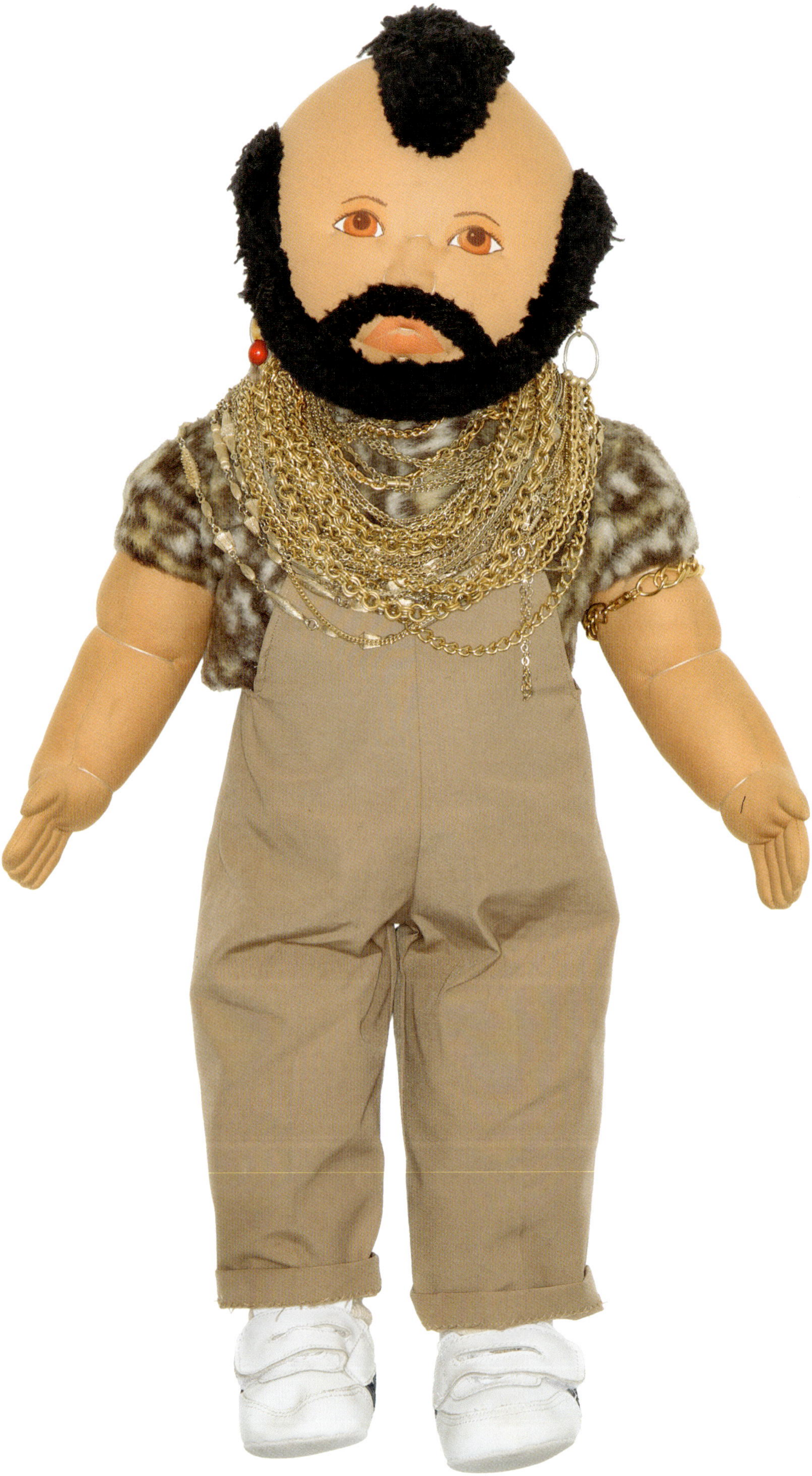

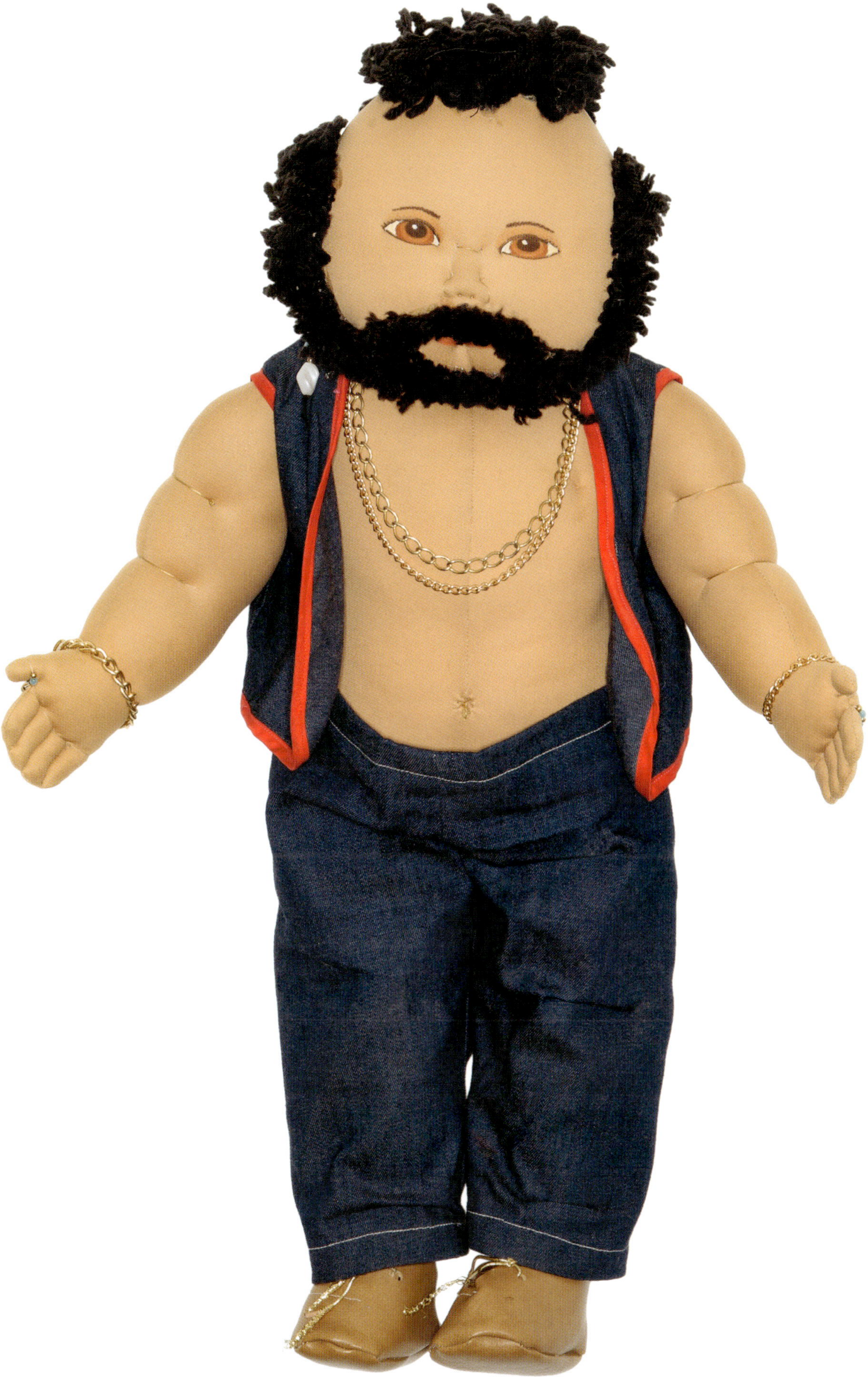

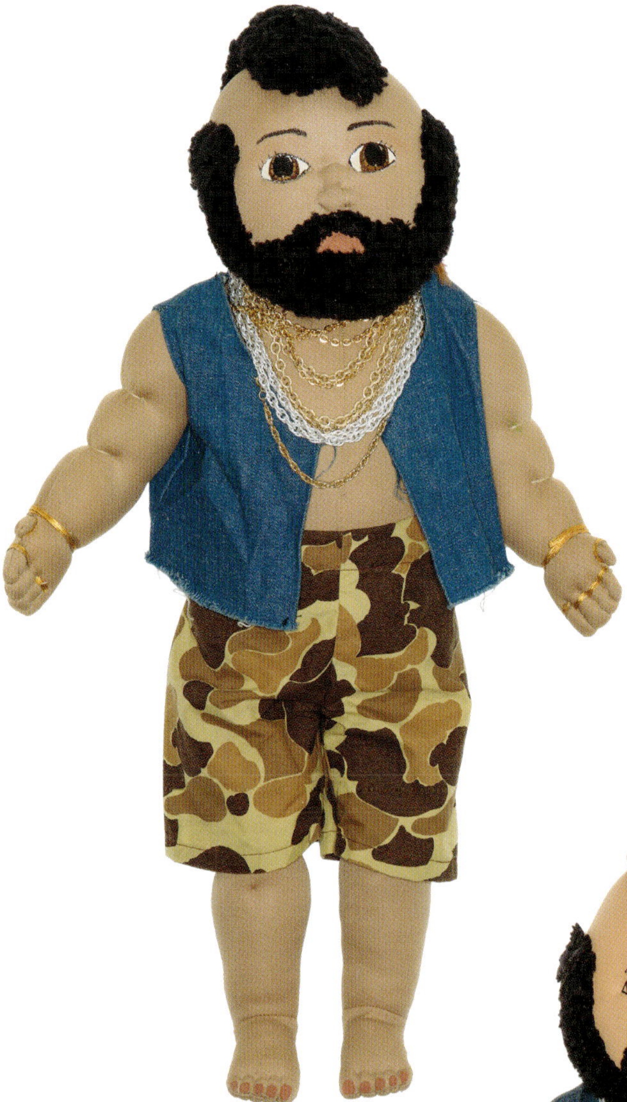

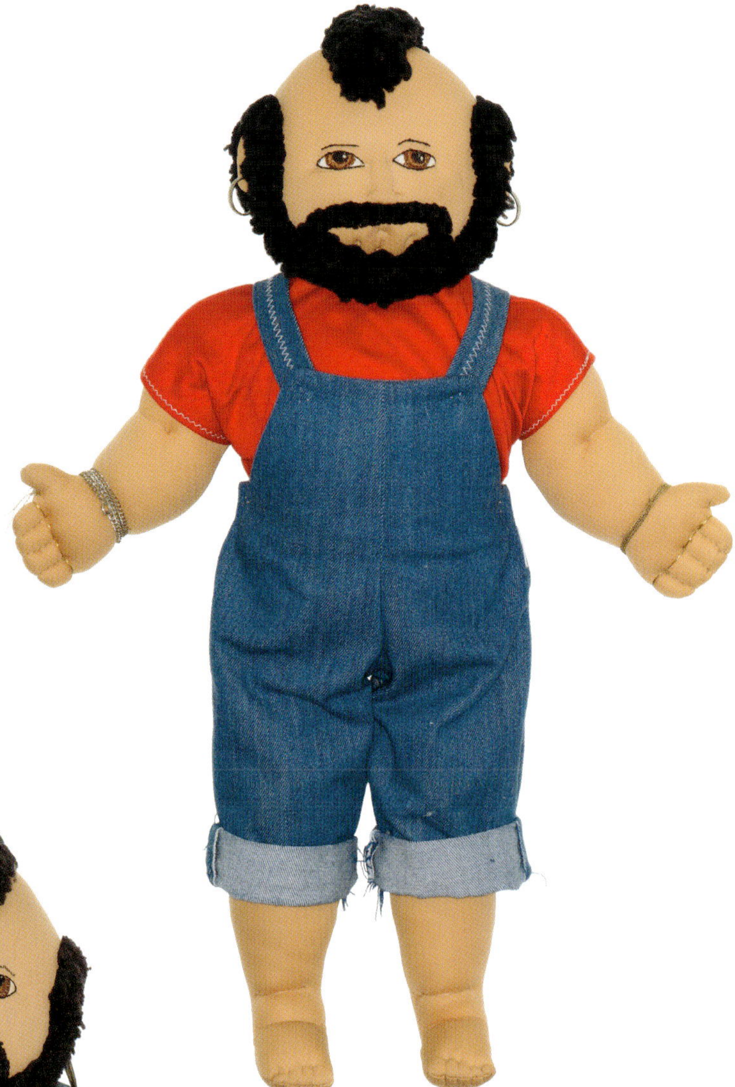

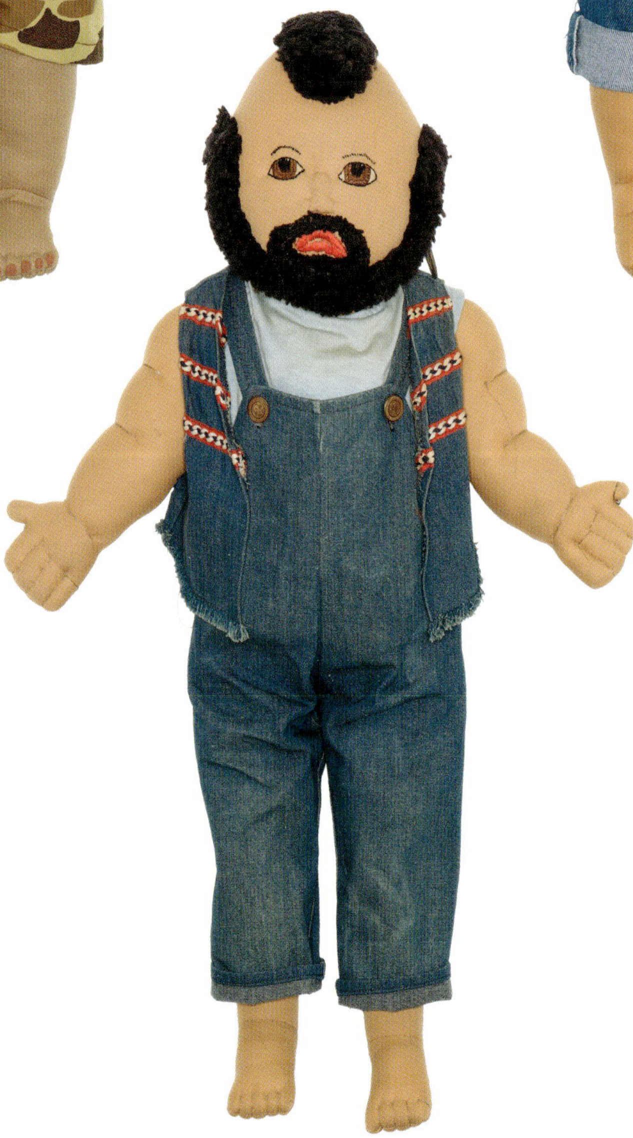

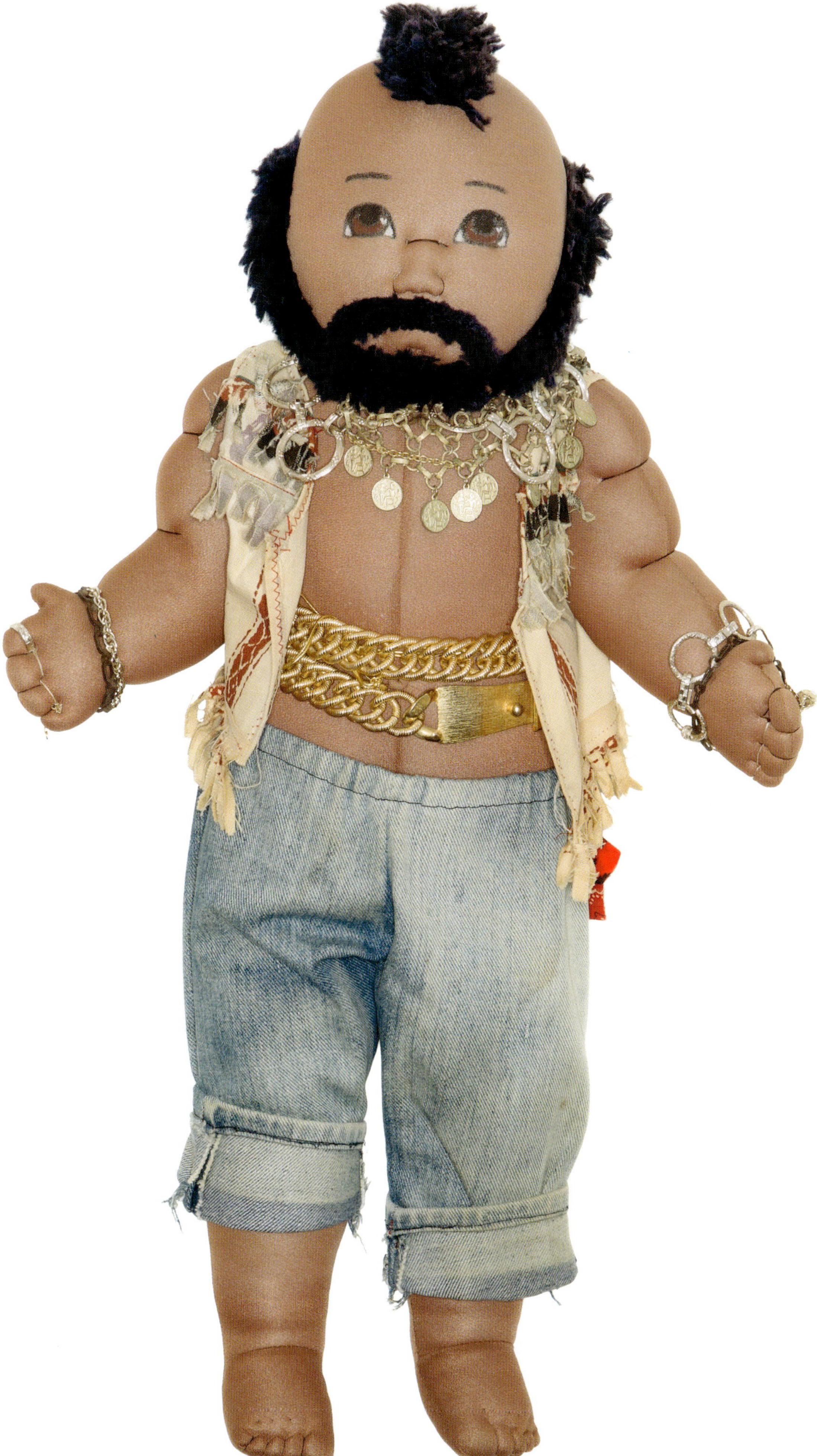

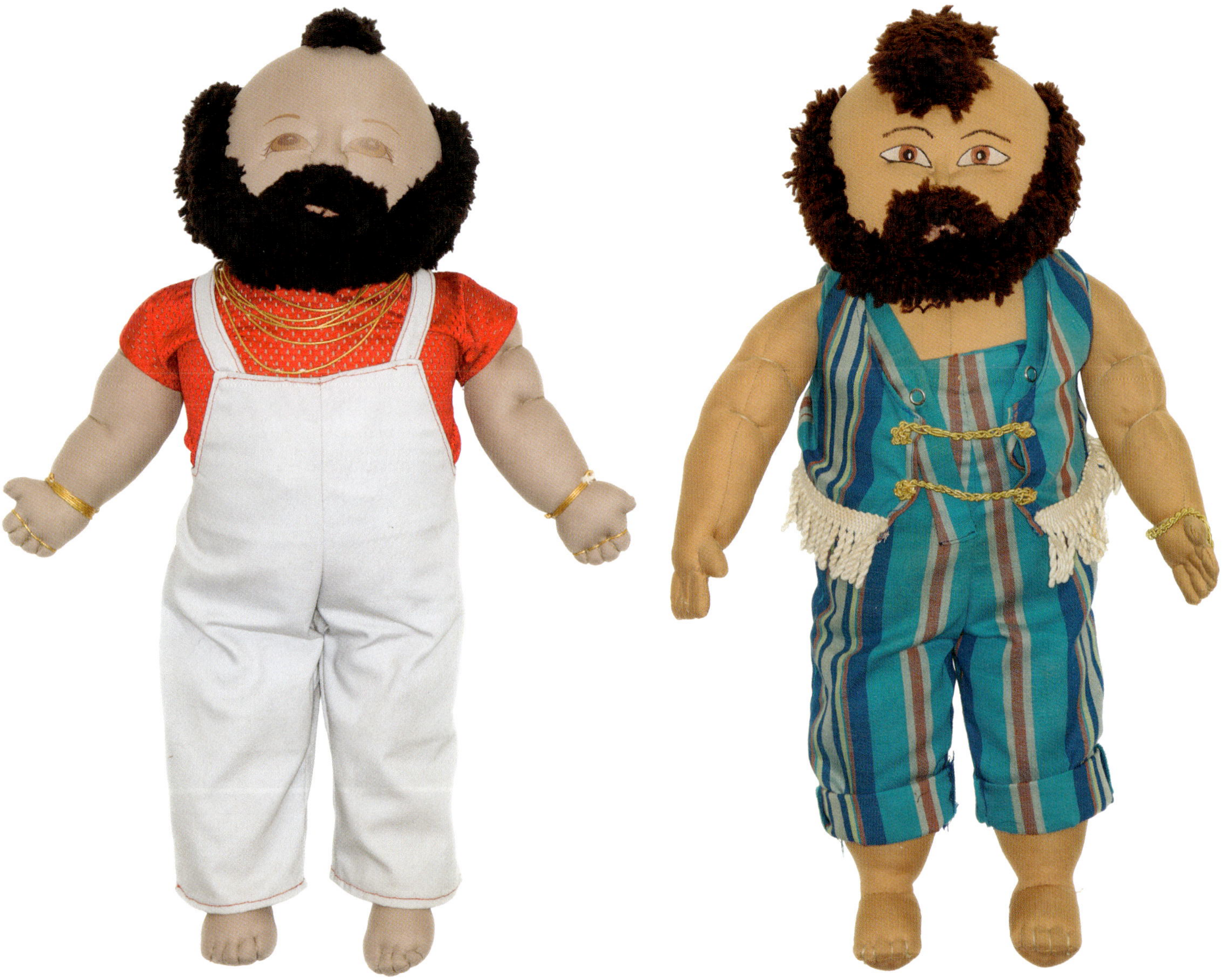

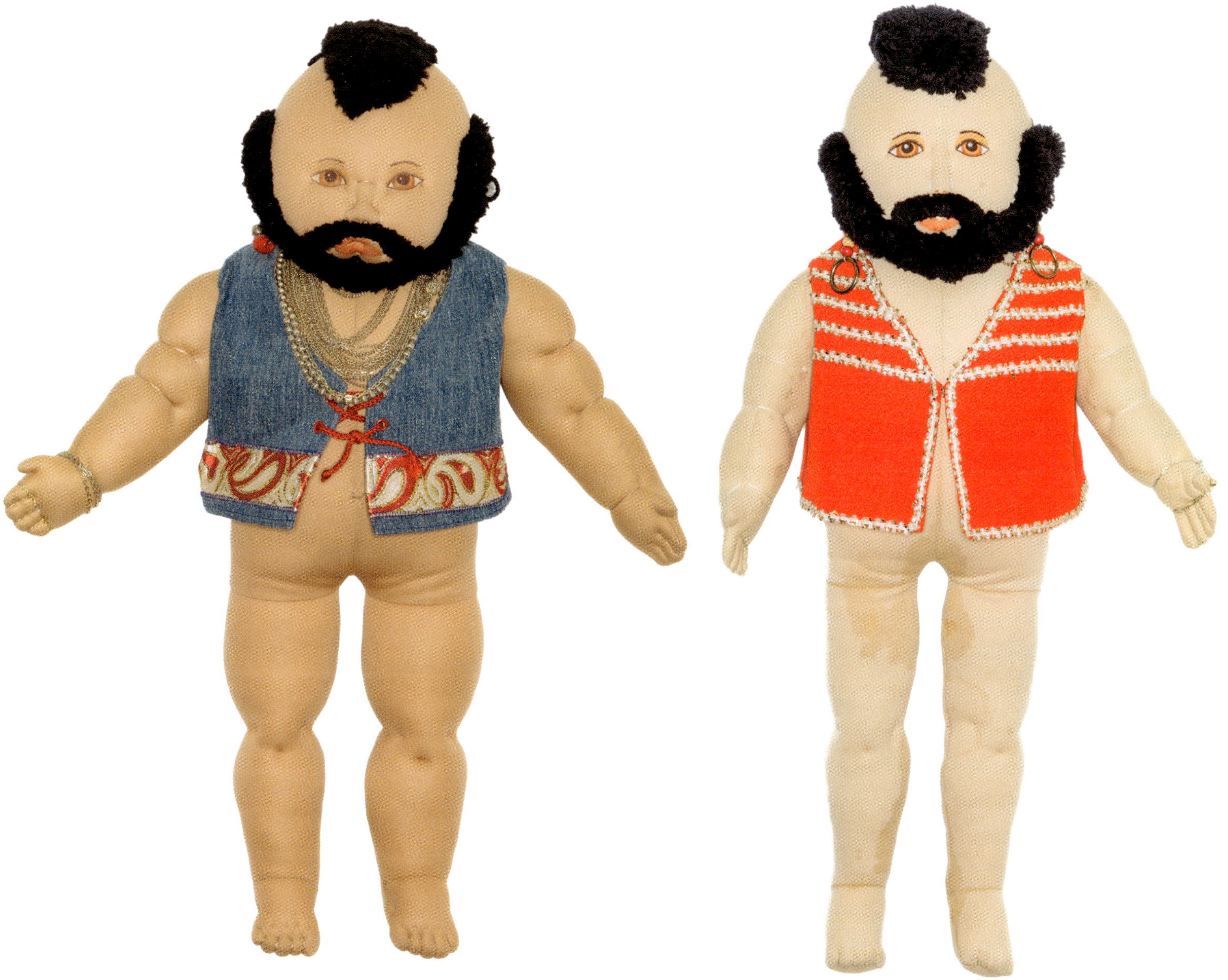

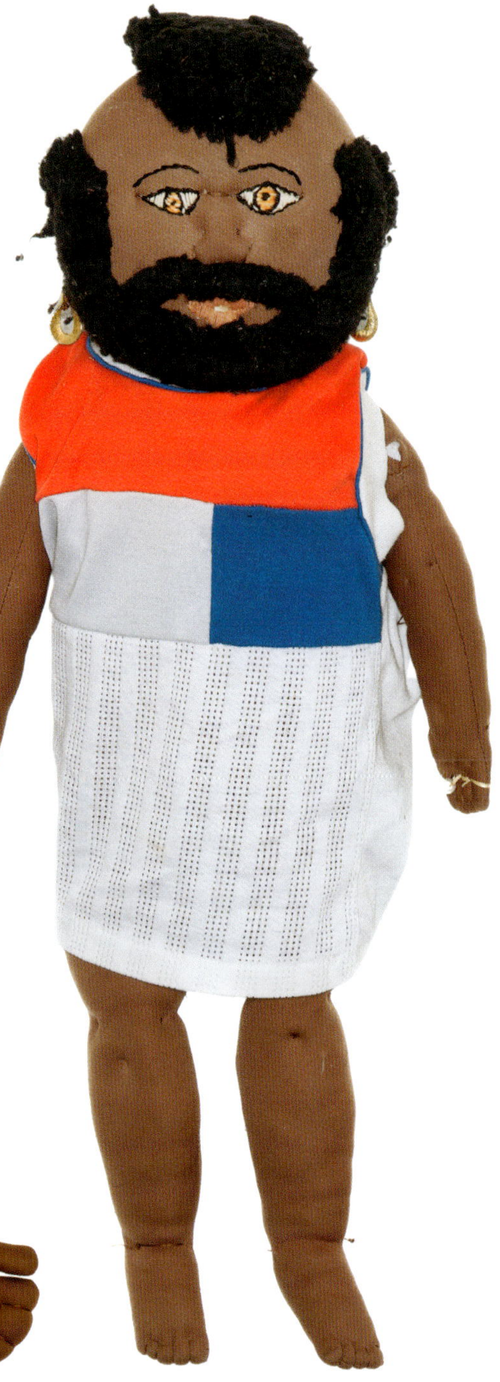

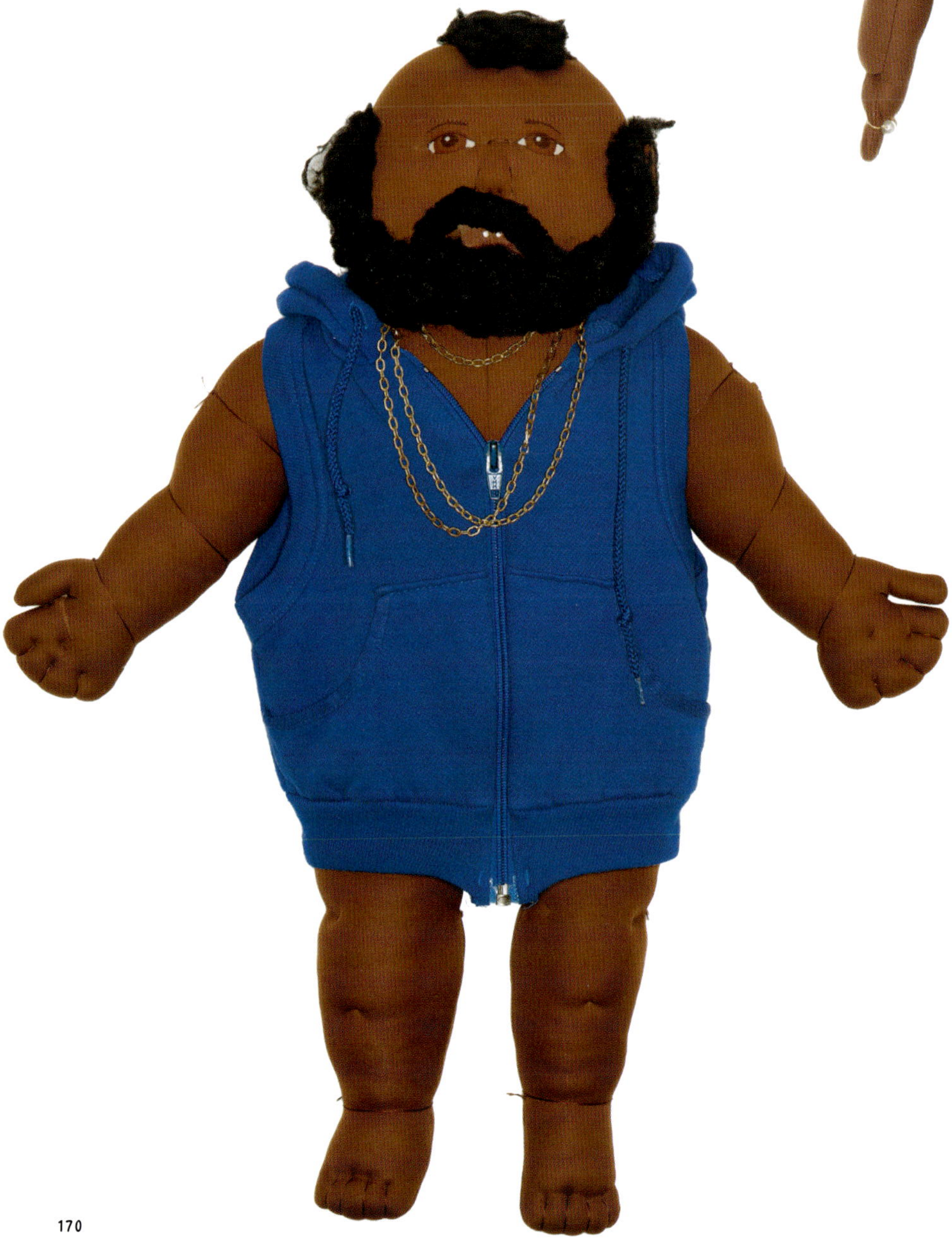

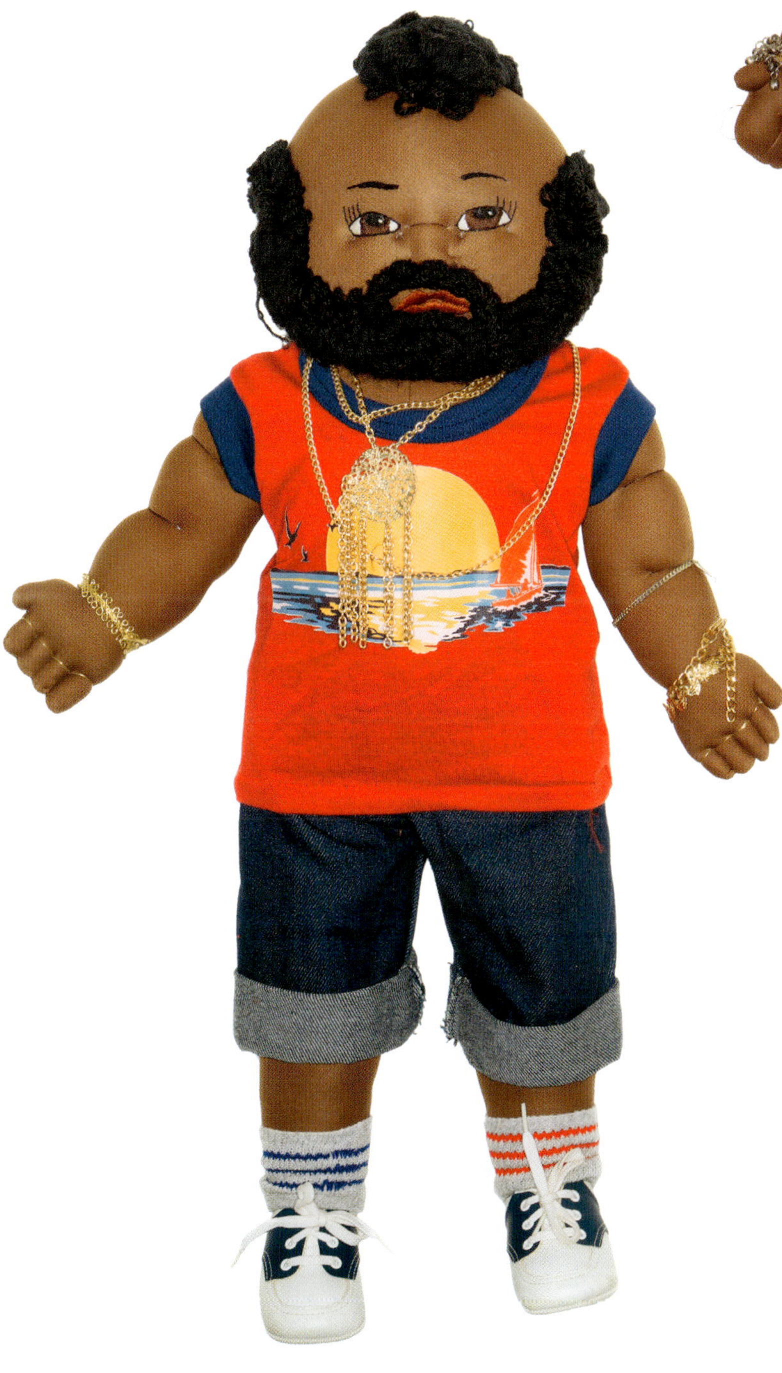

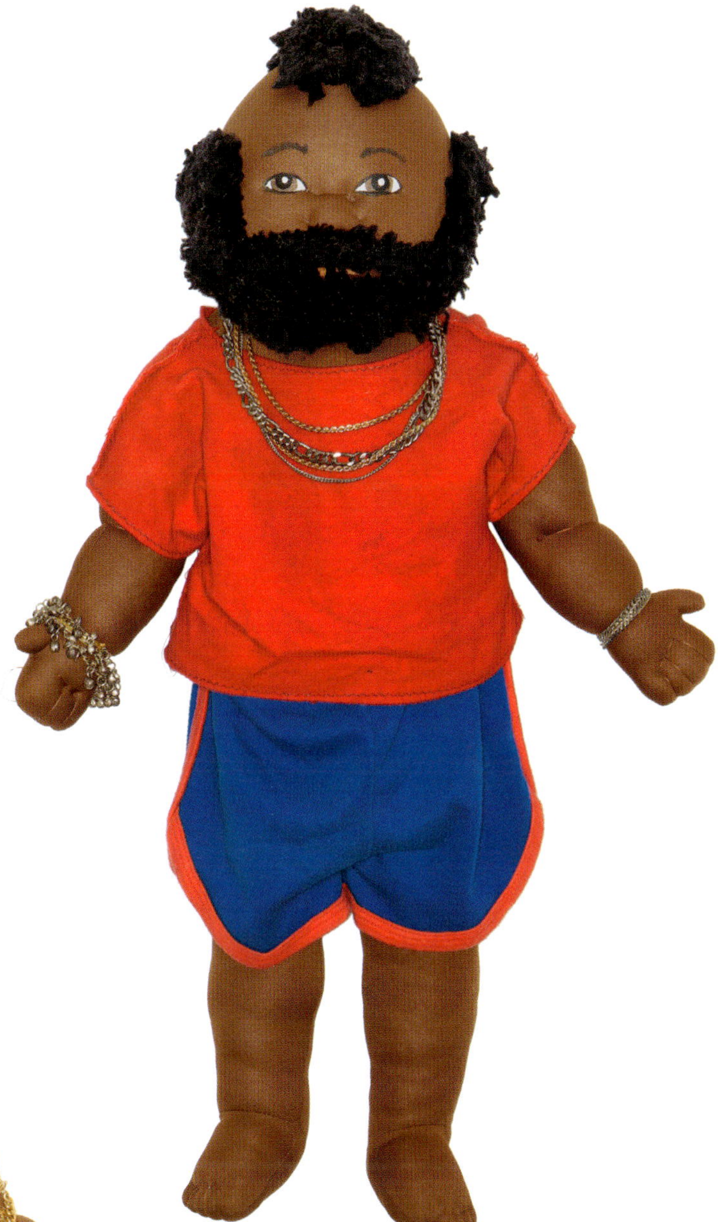

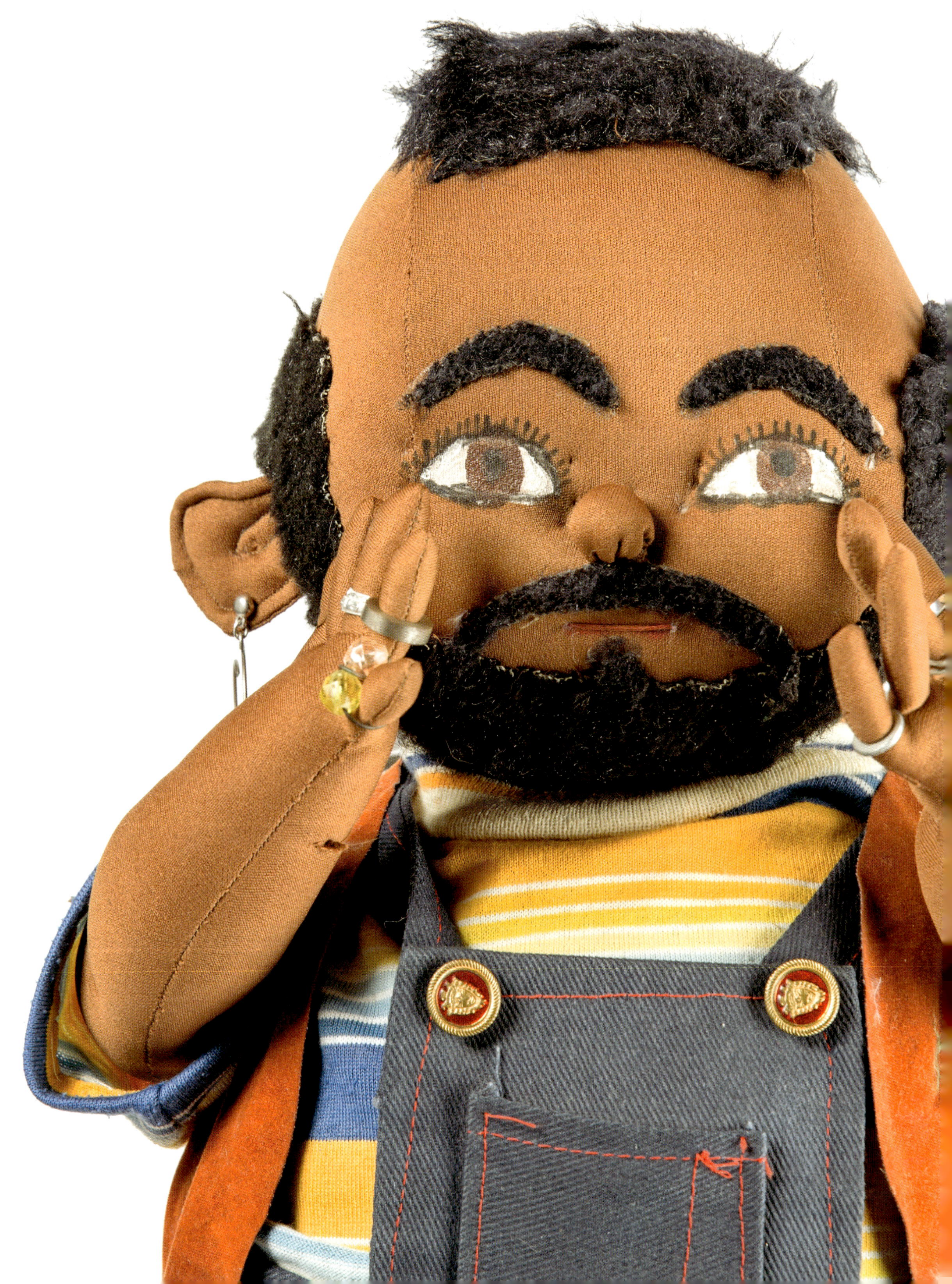

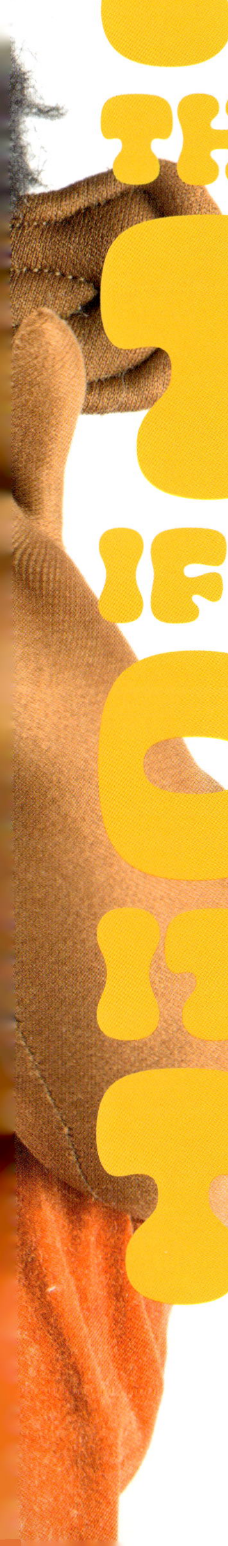

IF YOU'RE A MAN THE "T" STANDS FOR TOUGH IF YOU'RE A WOMAN OR CHILD IT STANDS FOR TENDER!

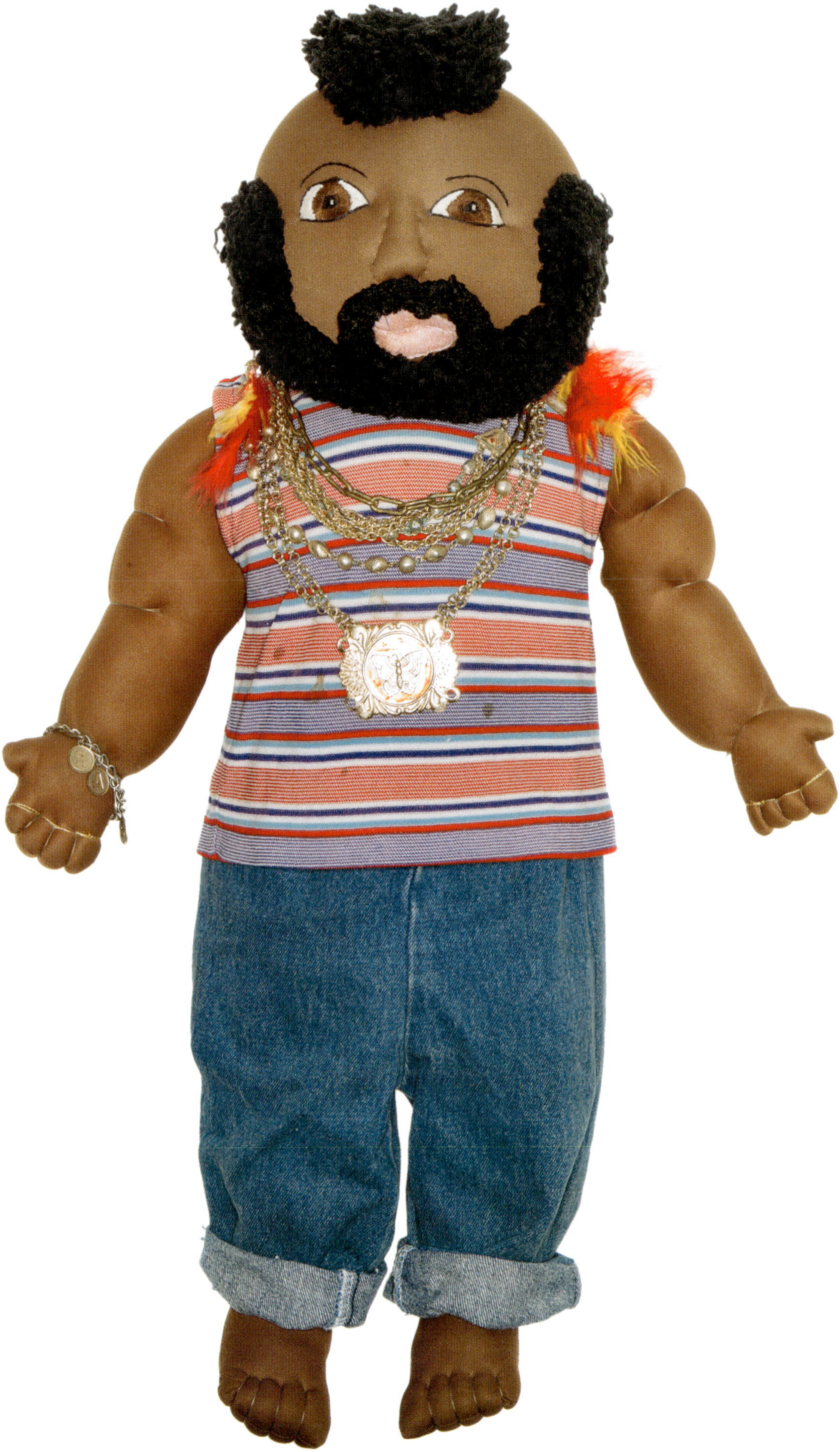

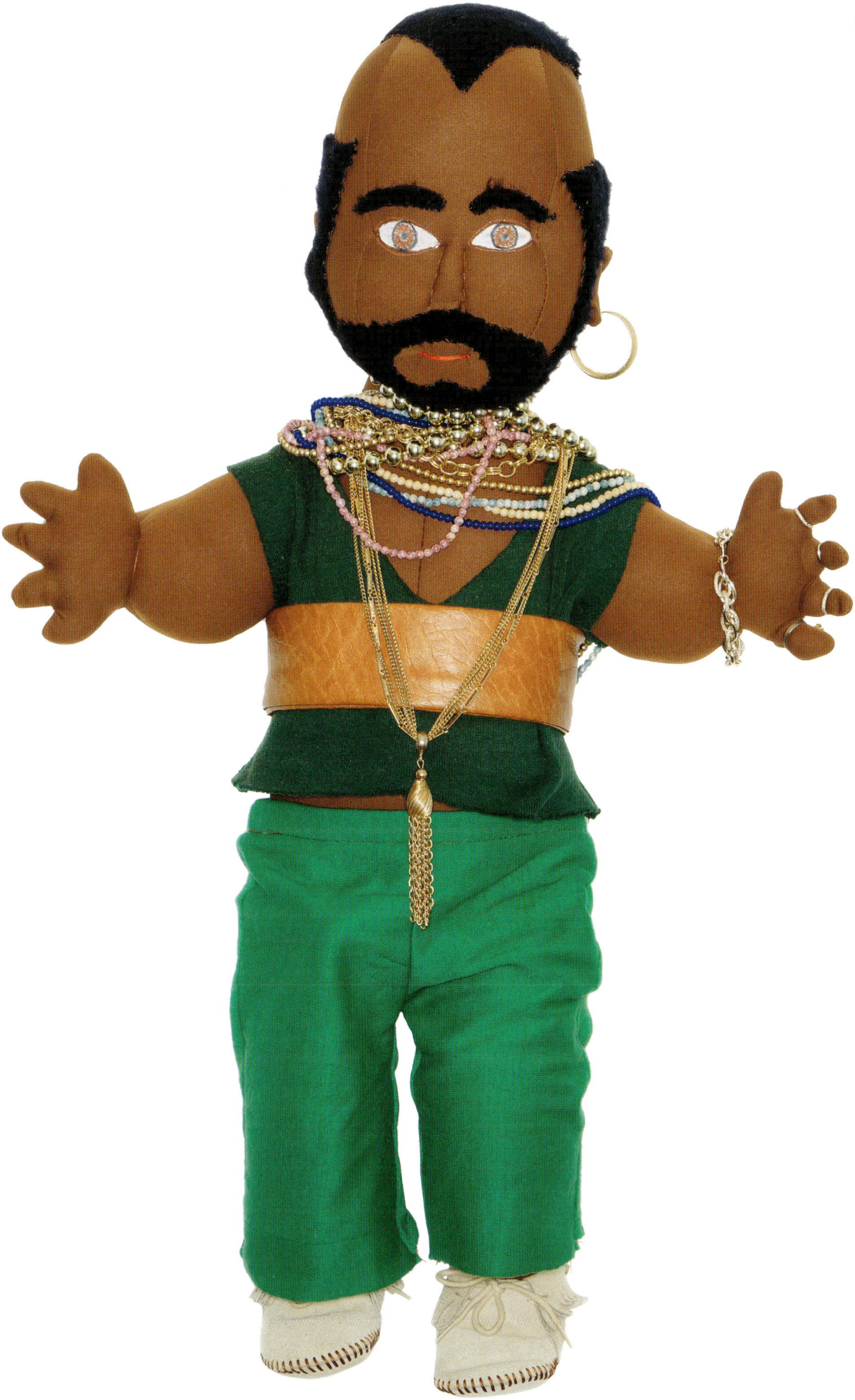

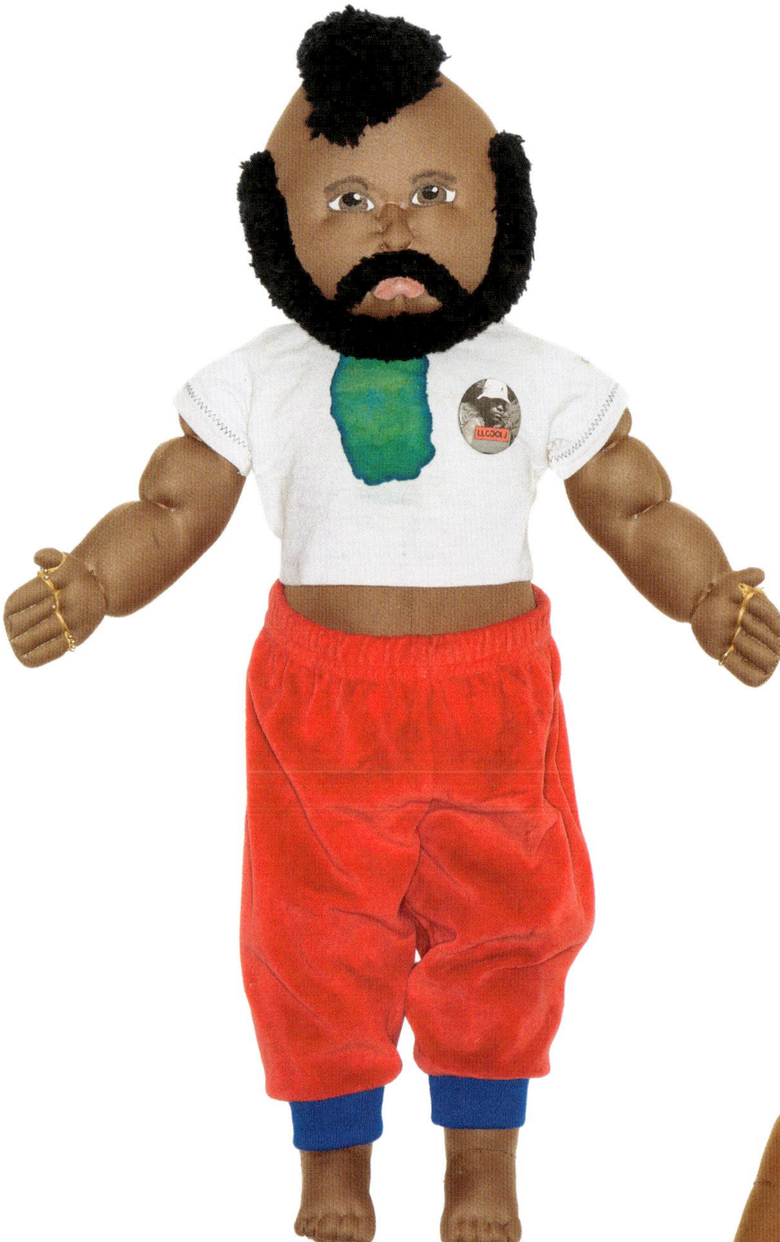

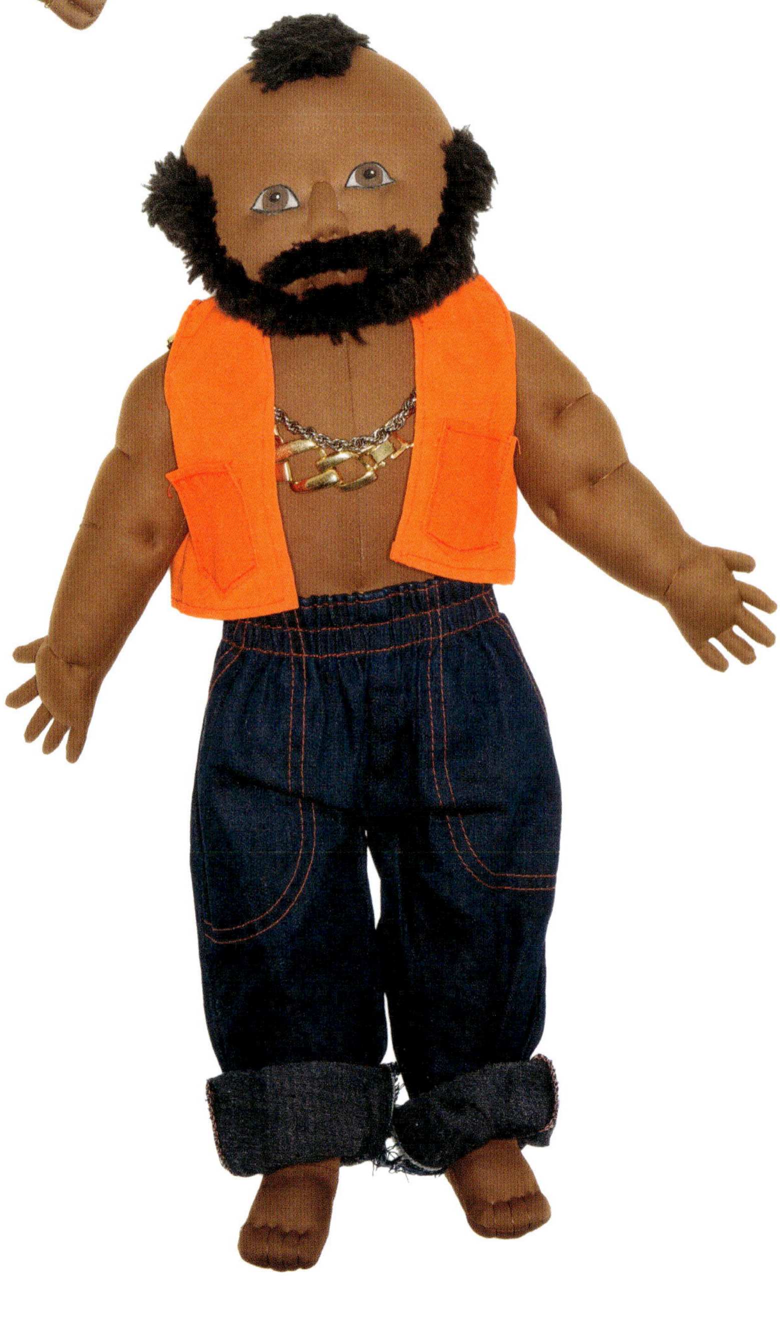

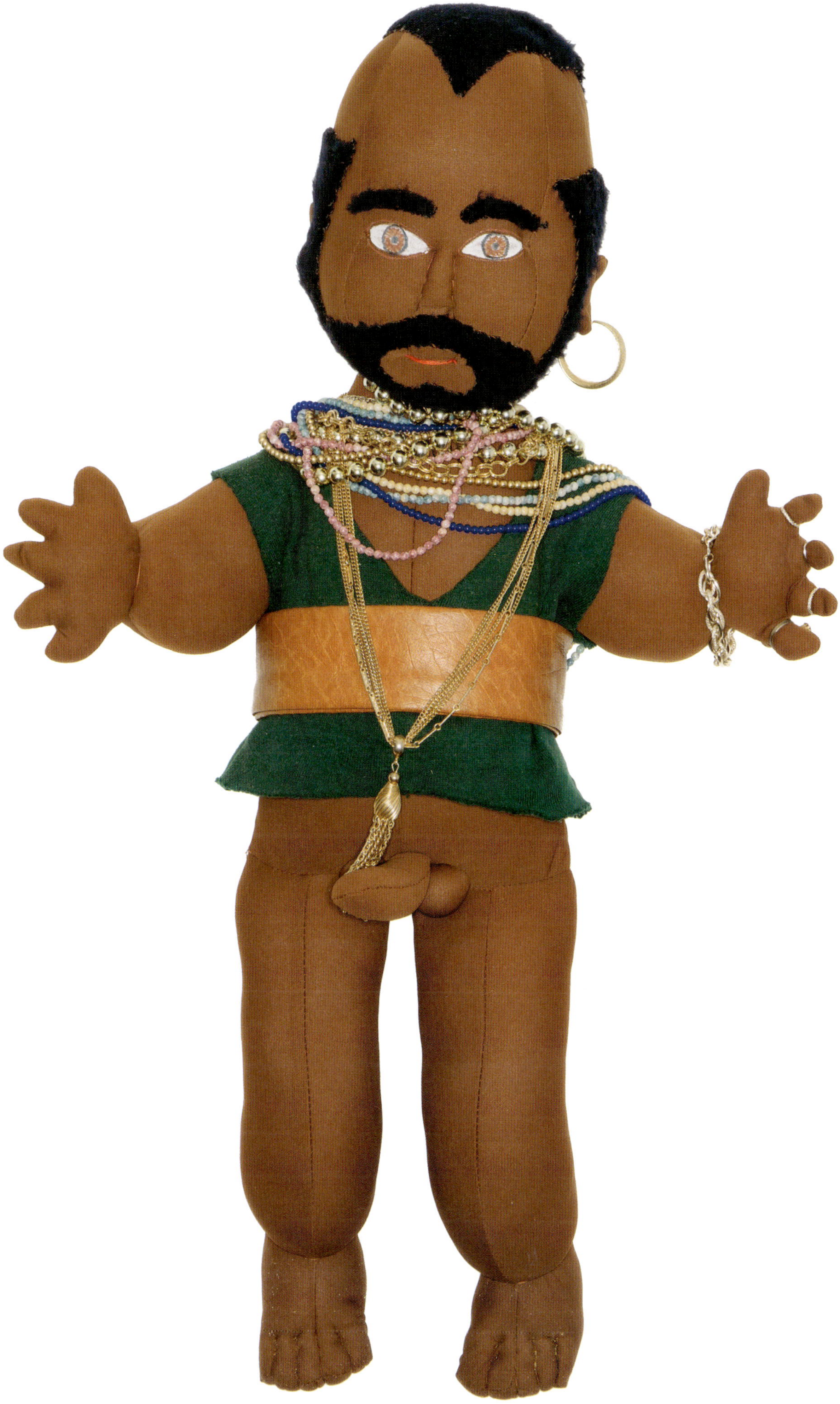

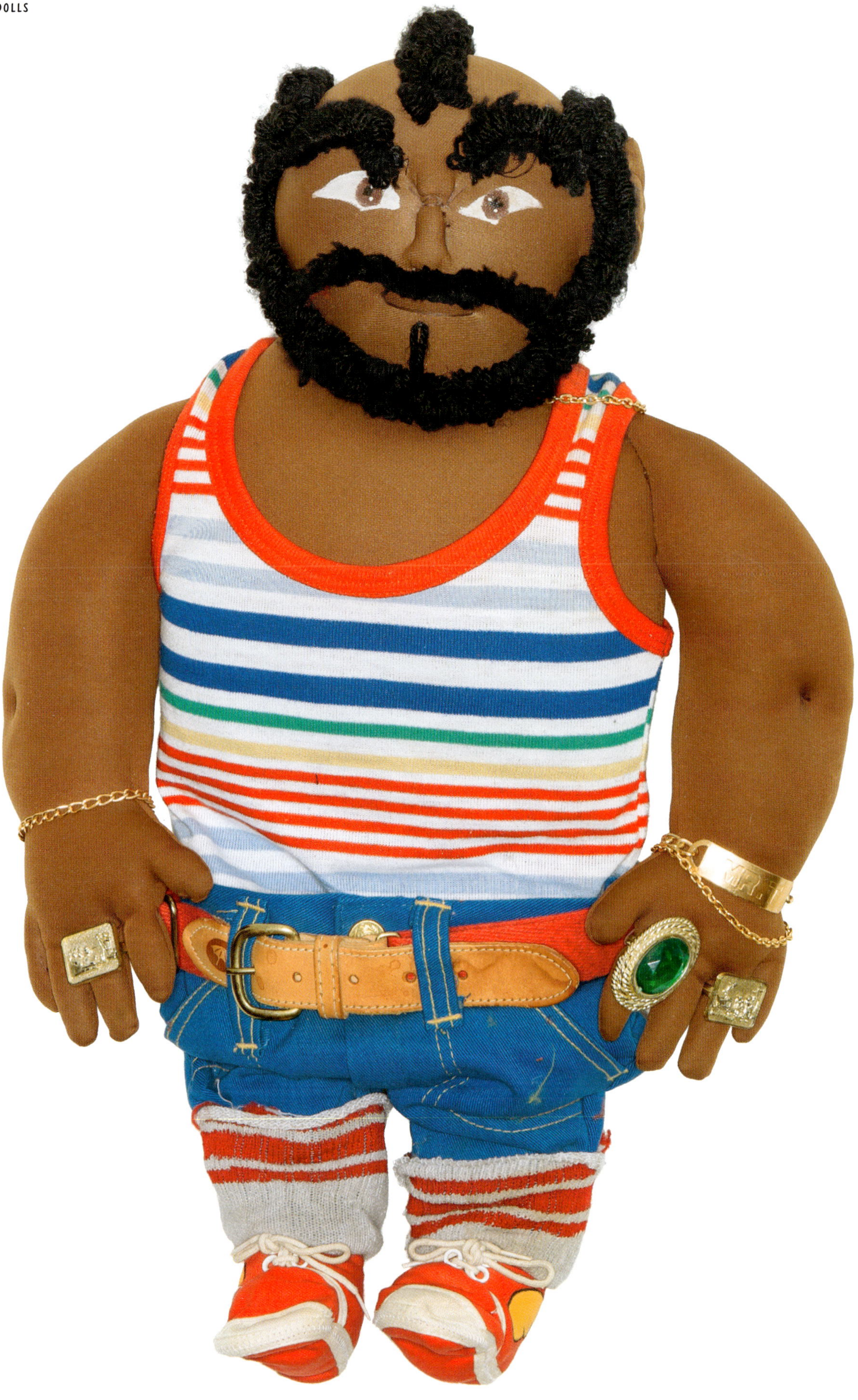

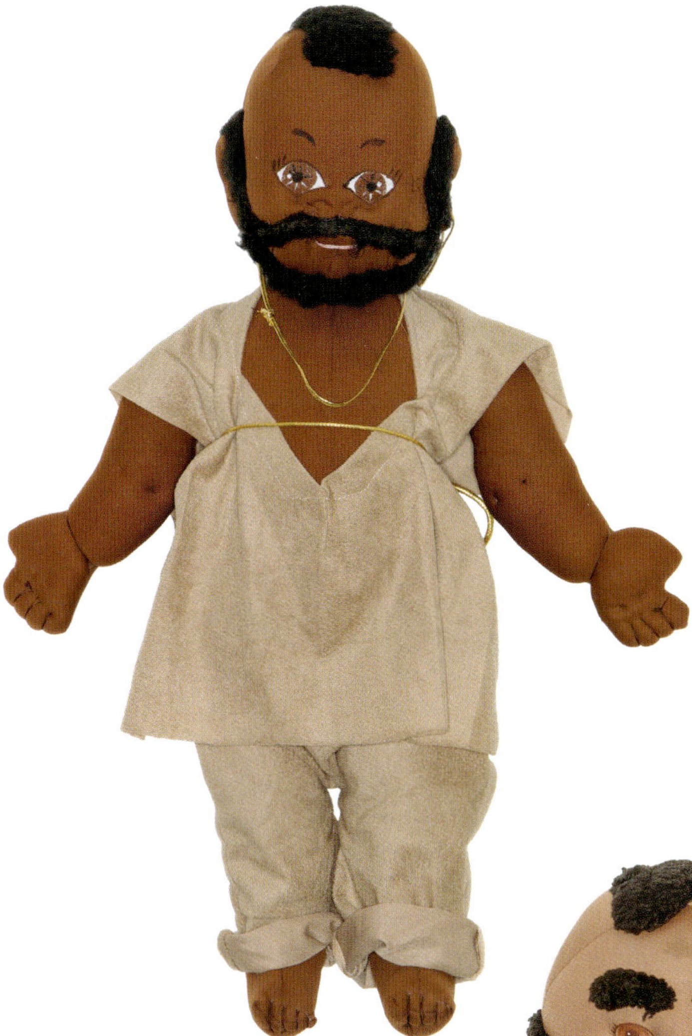

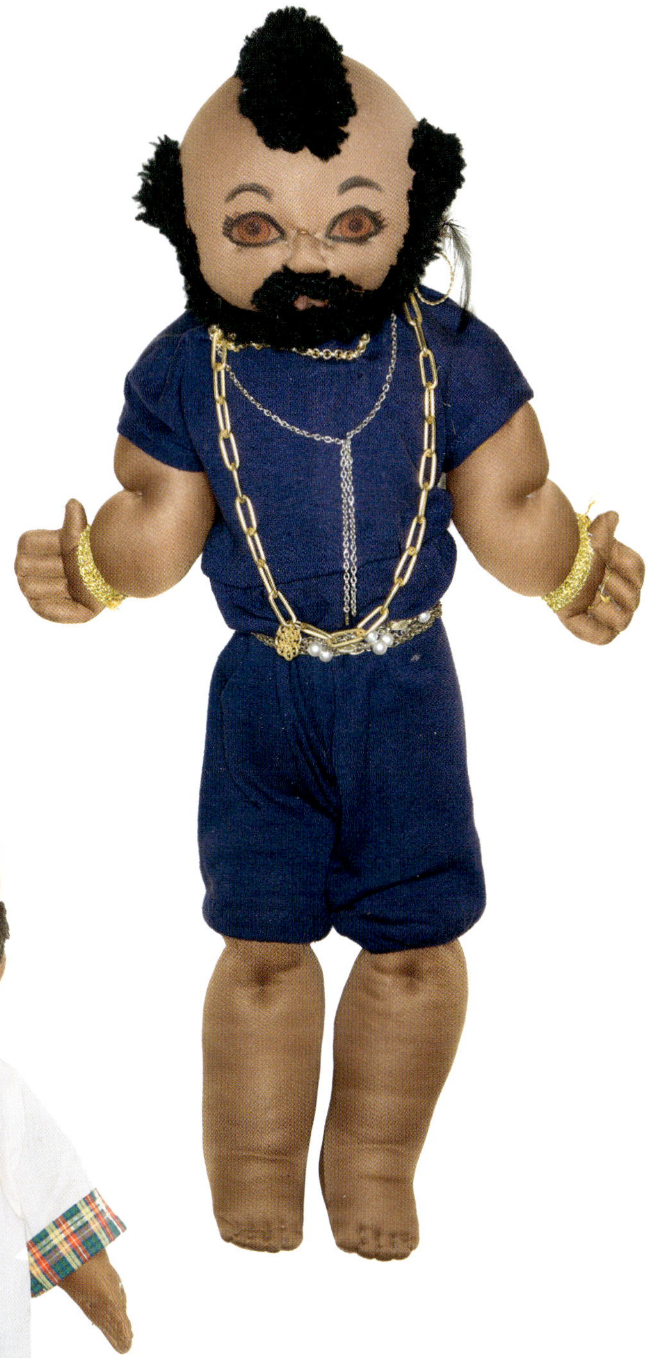

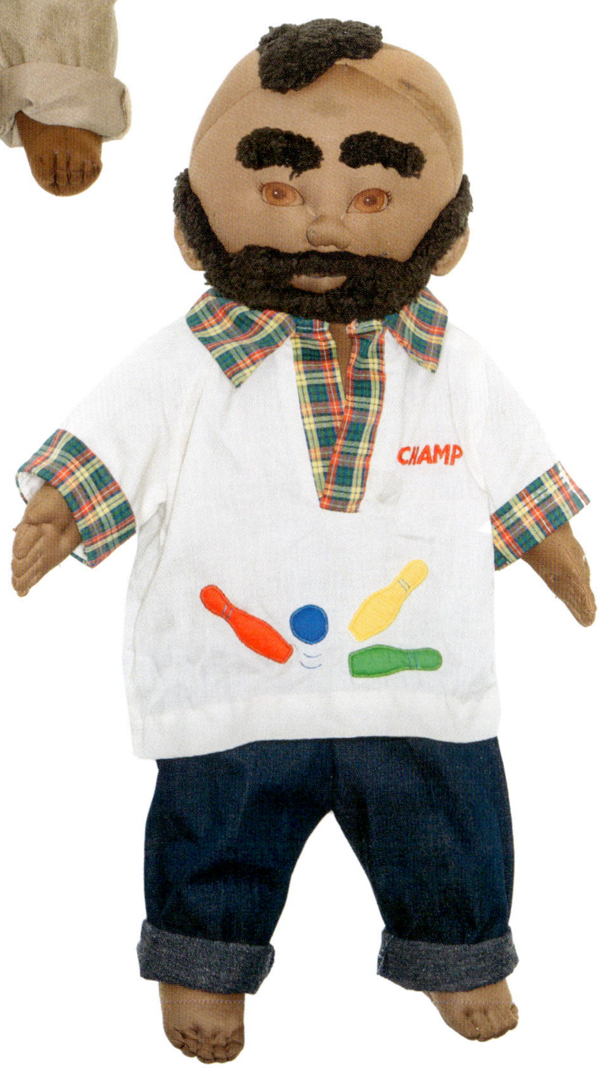
CHAMP

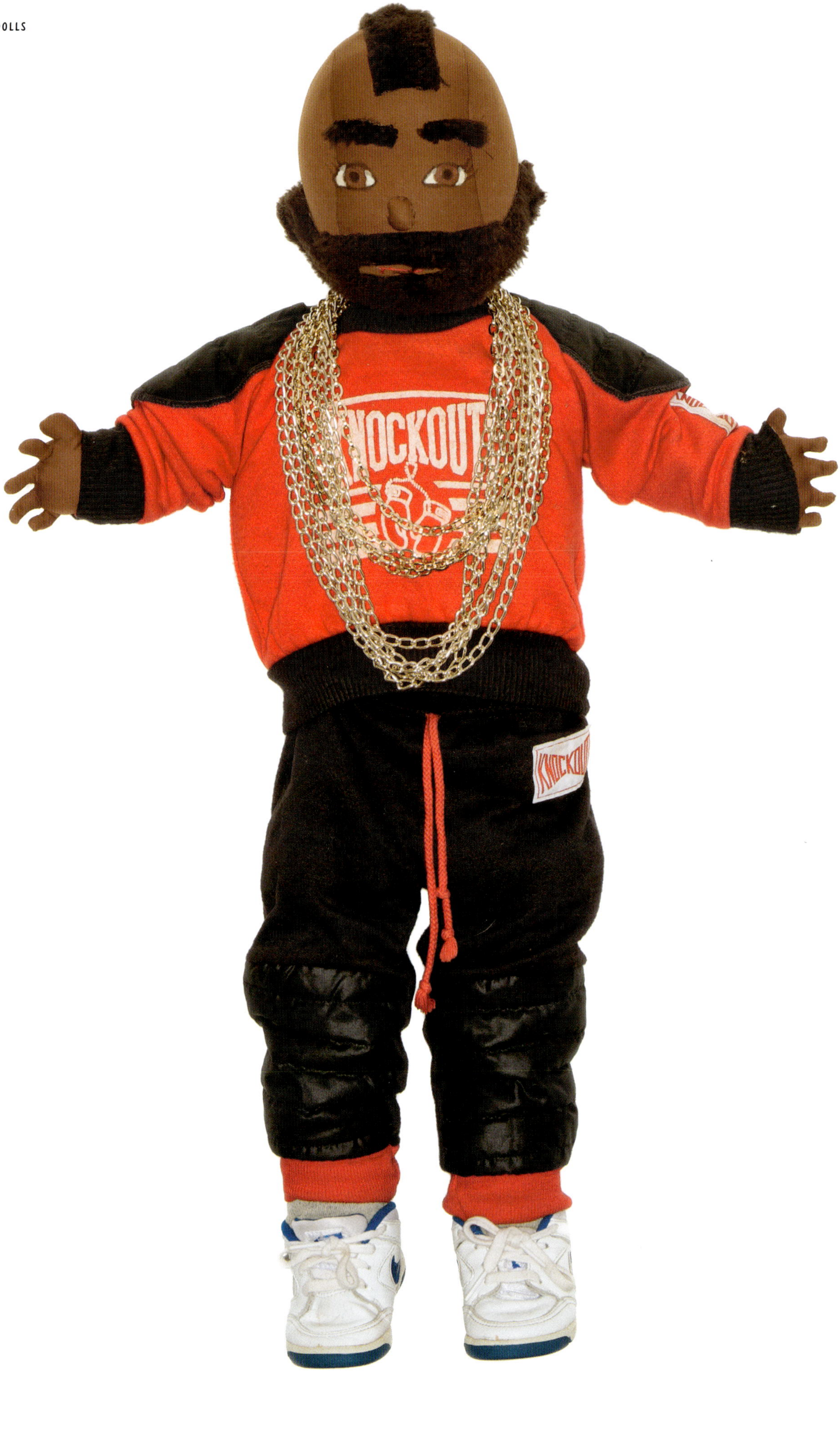
KNOCKOUT
KNOCKOUT

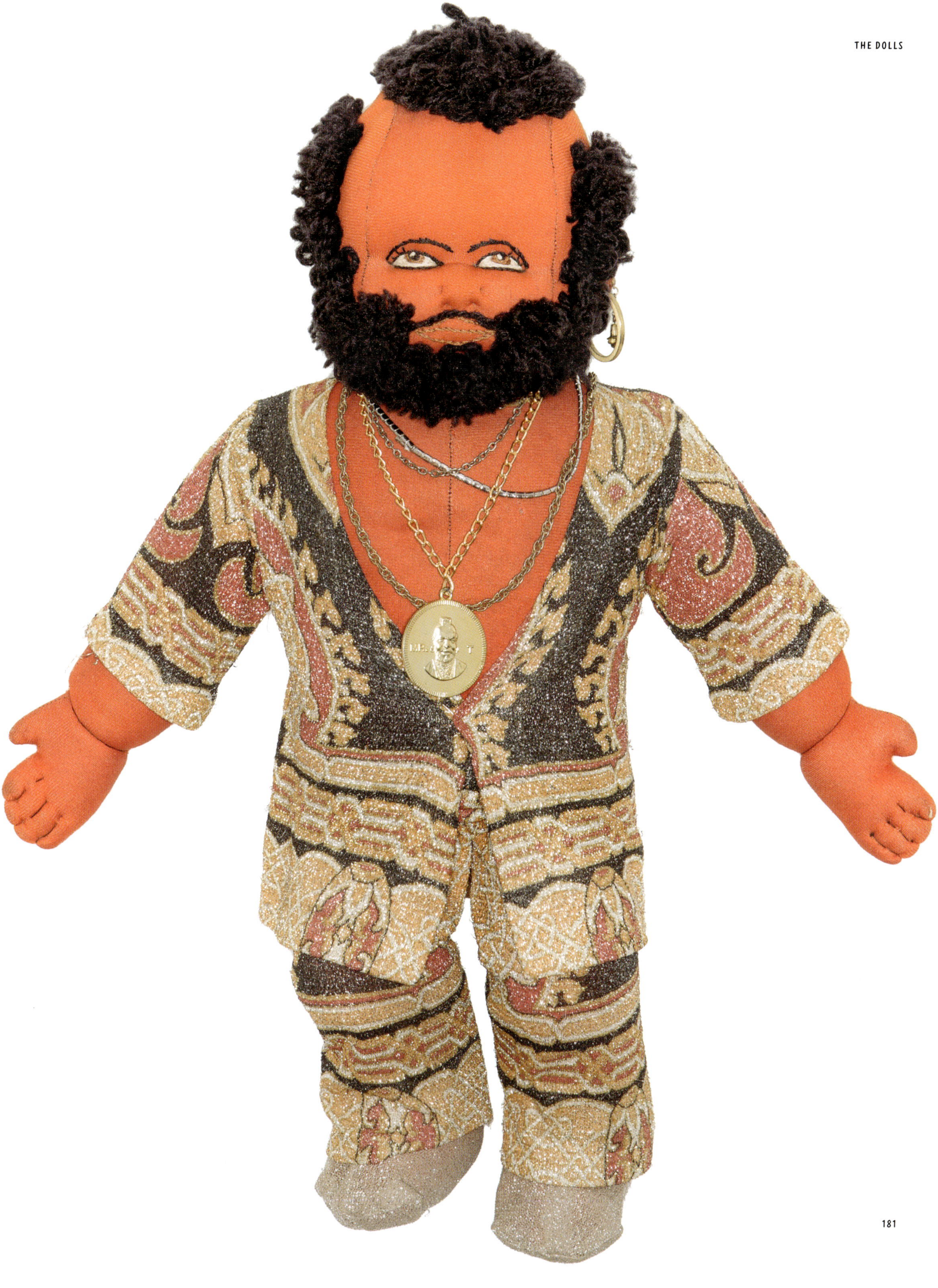

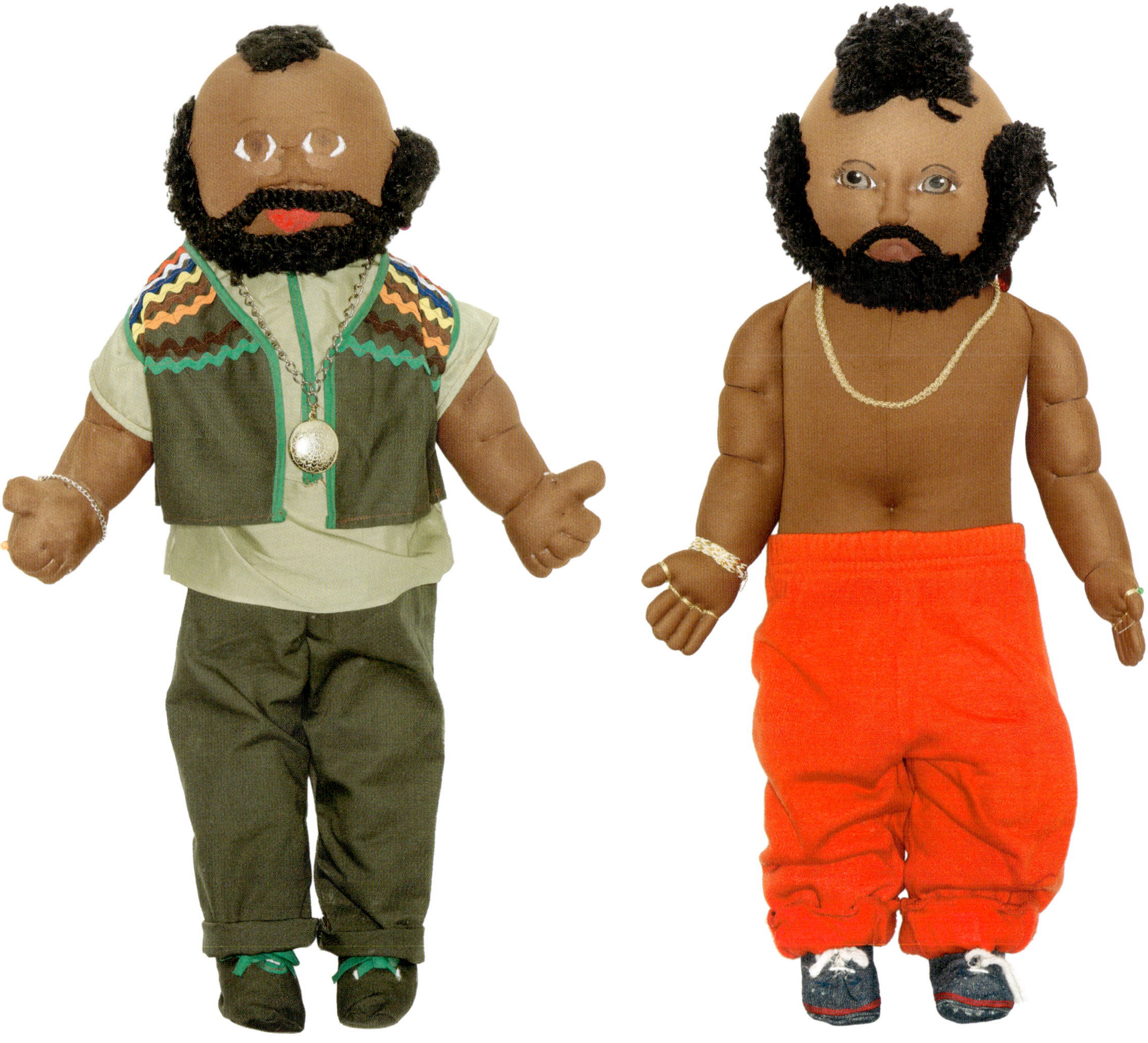

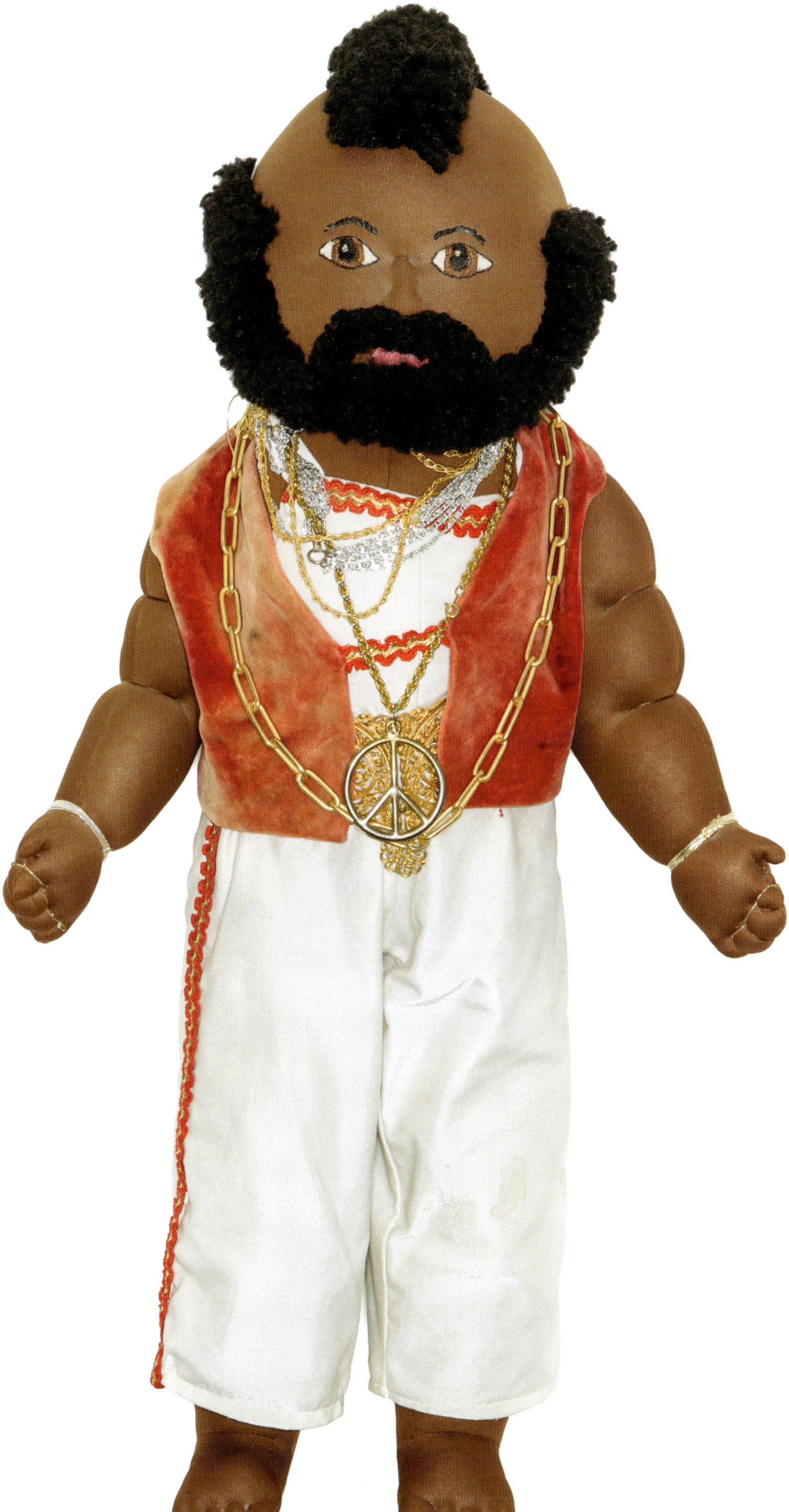

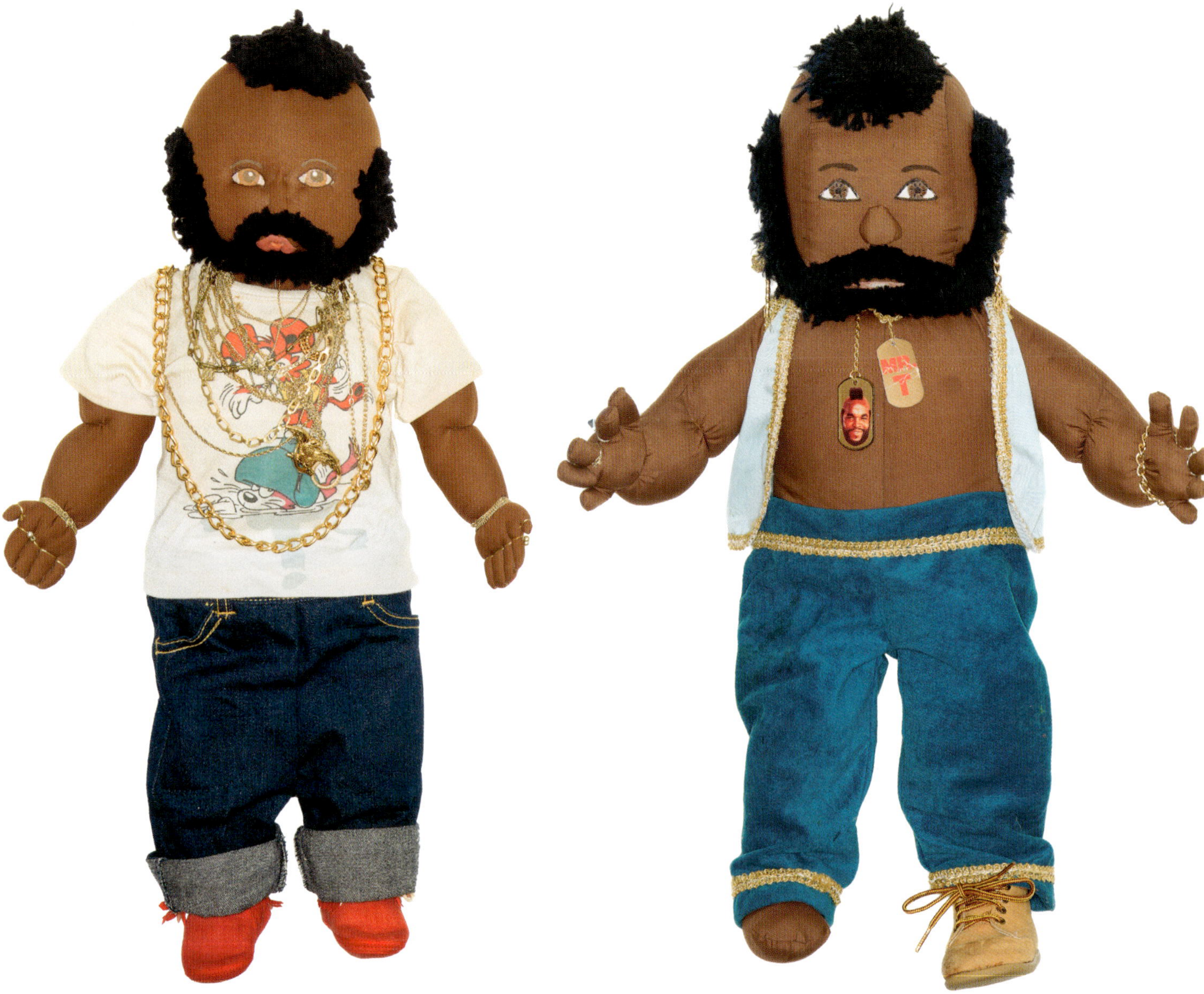
MR.
T

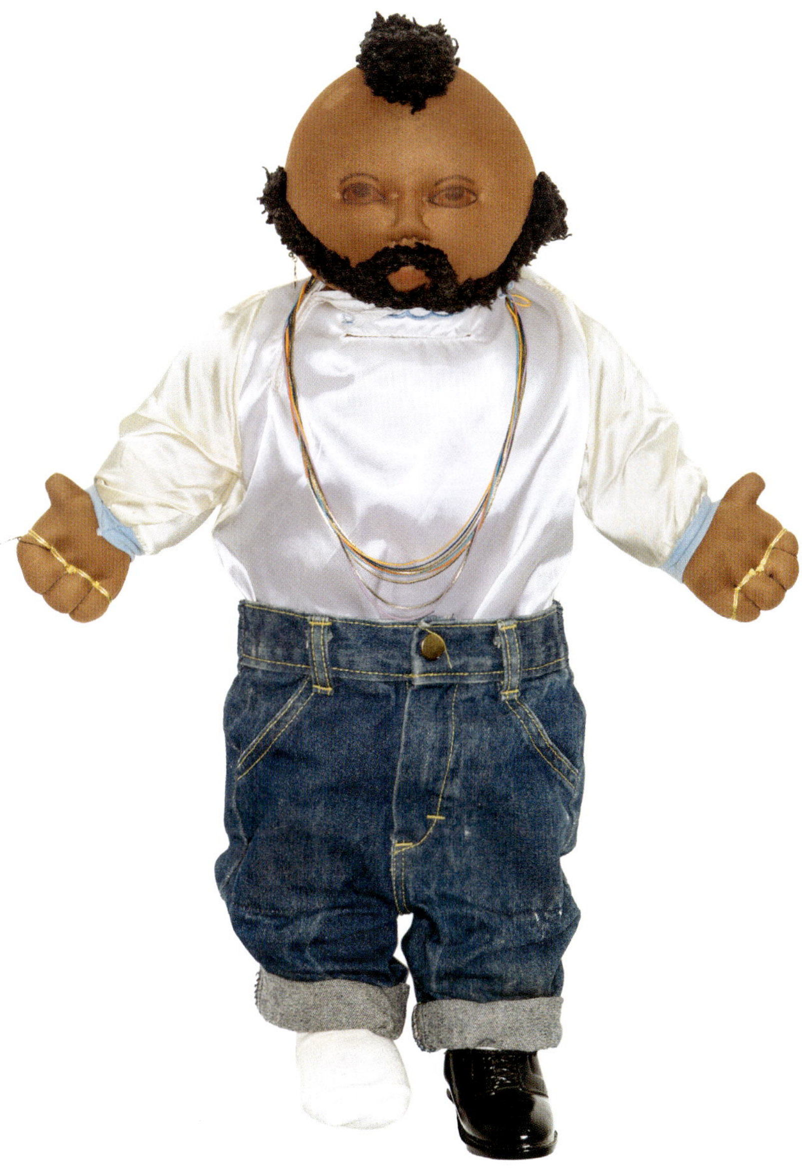

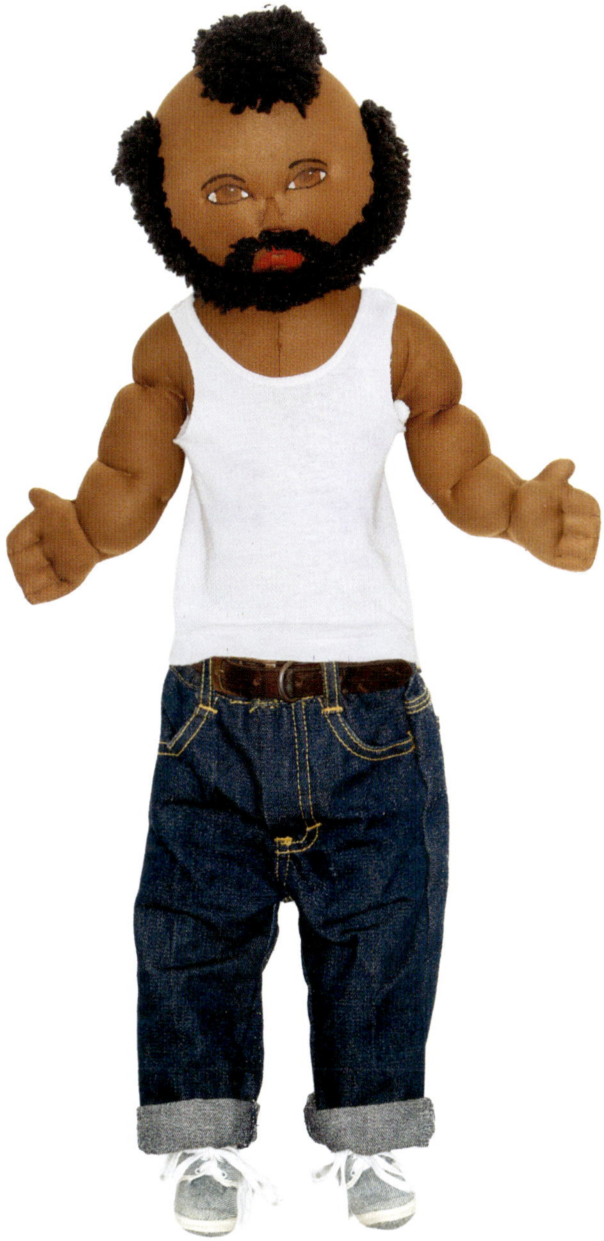

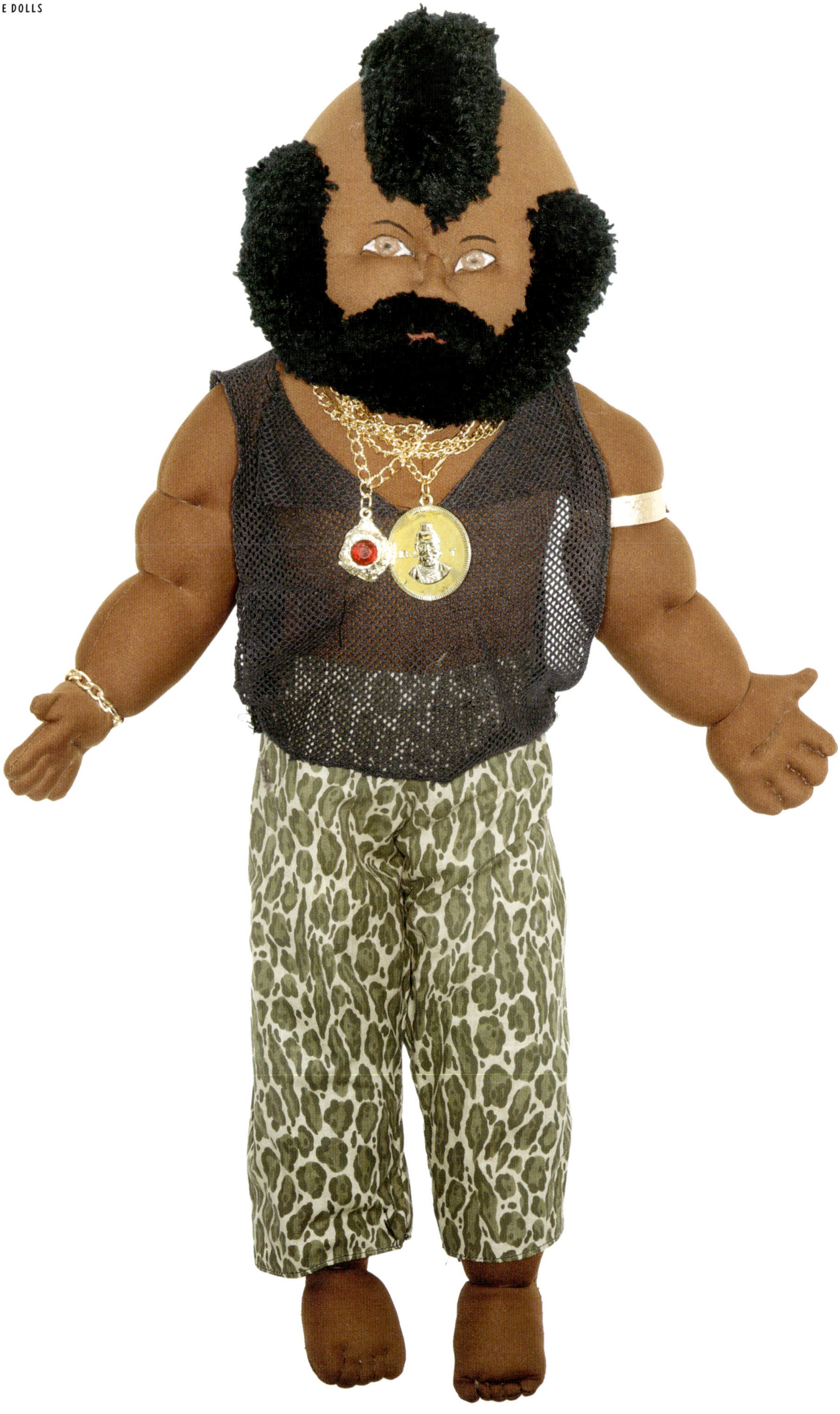

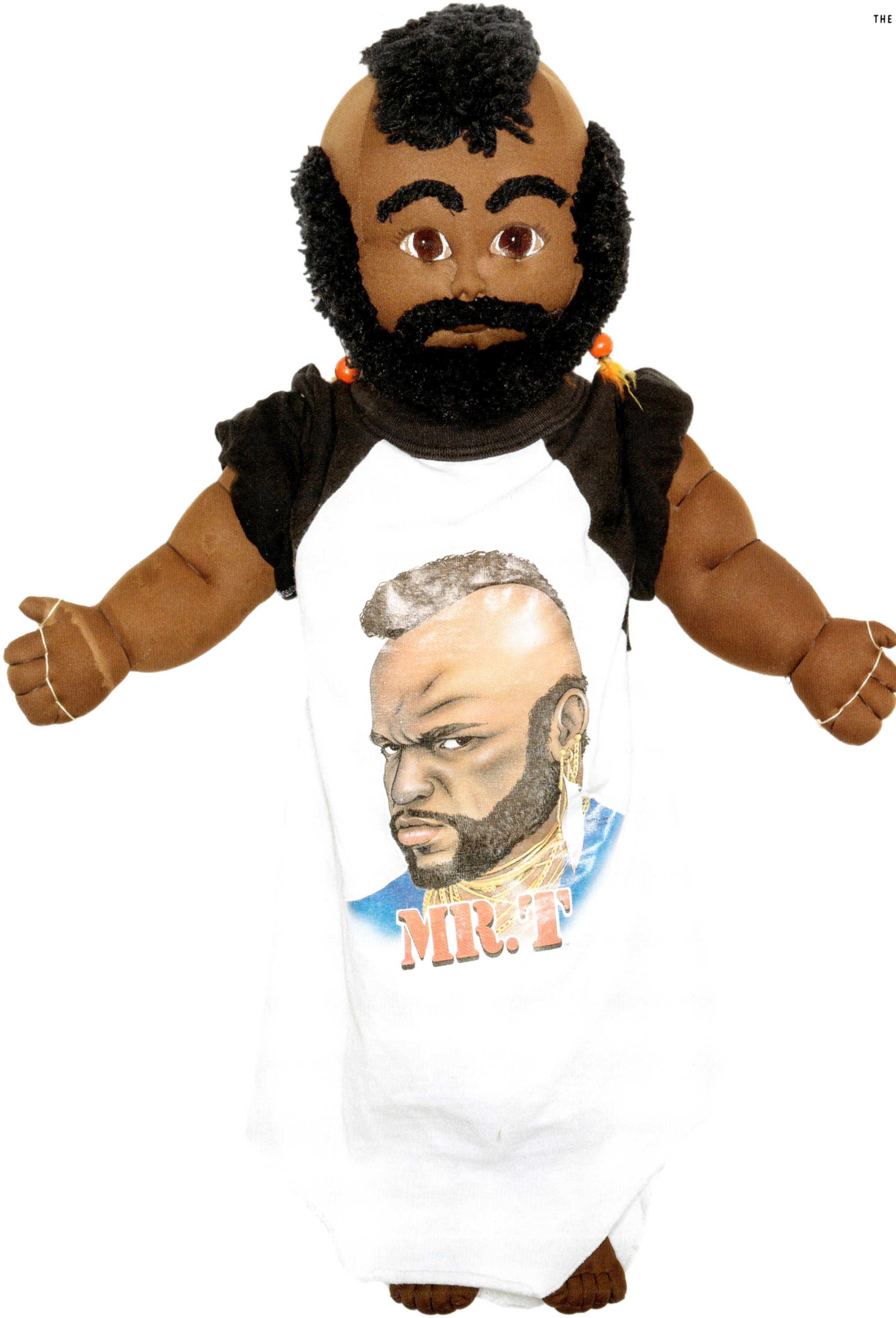
MR.T

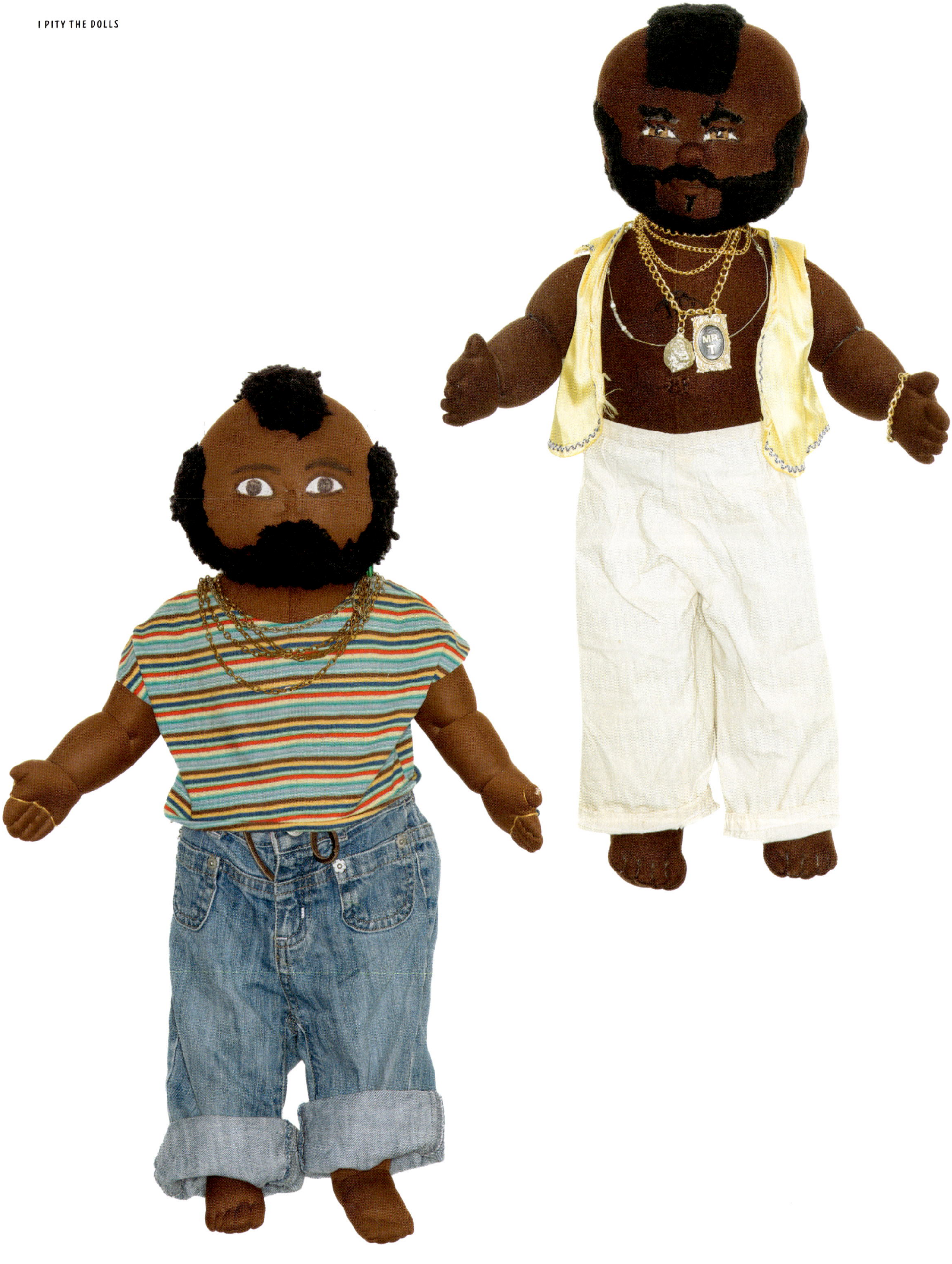
MR. T

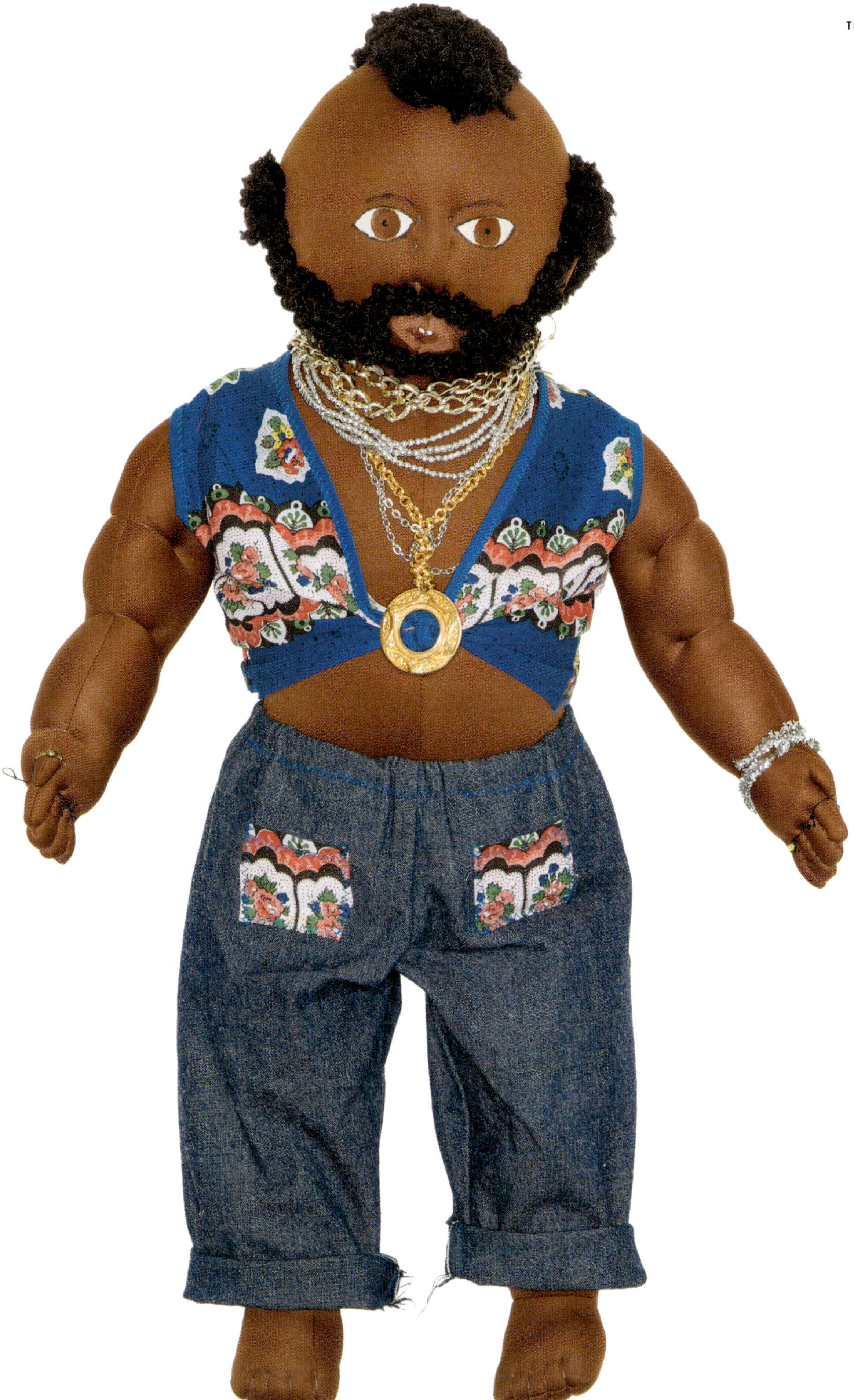

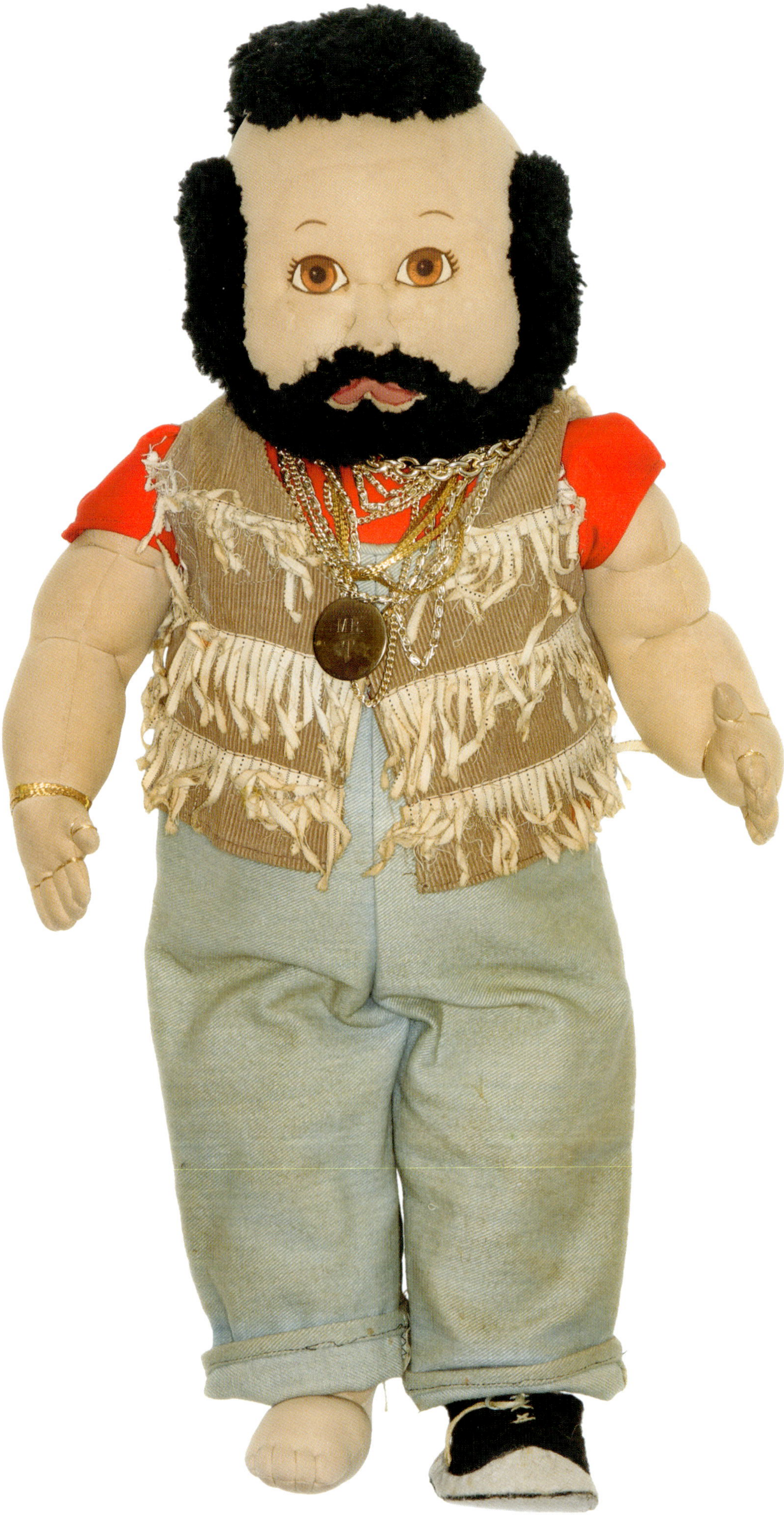

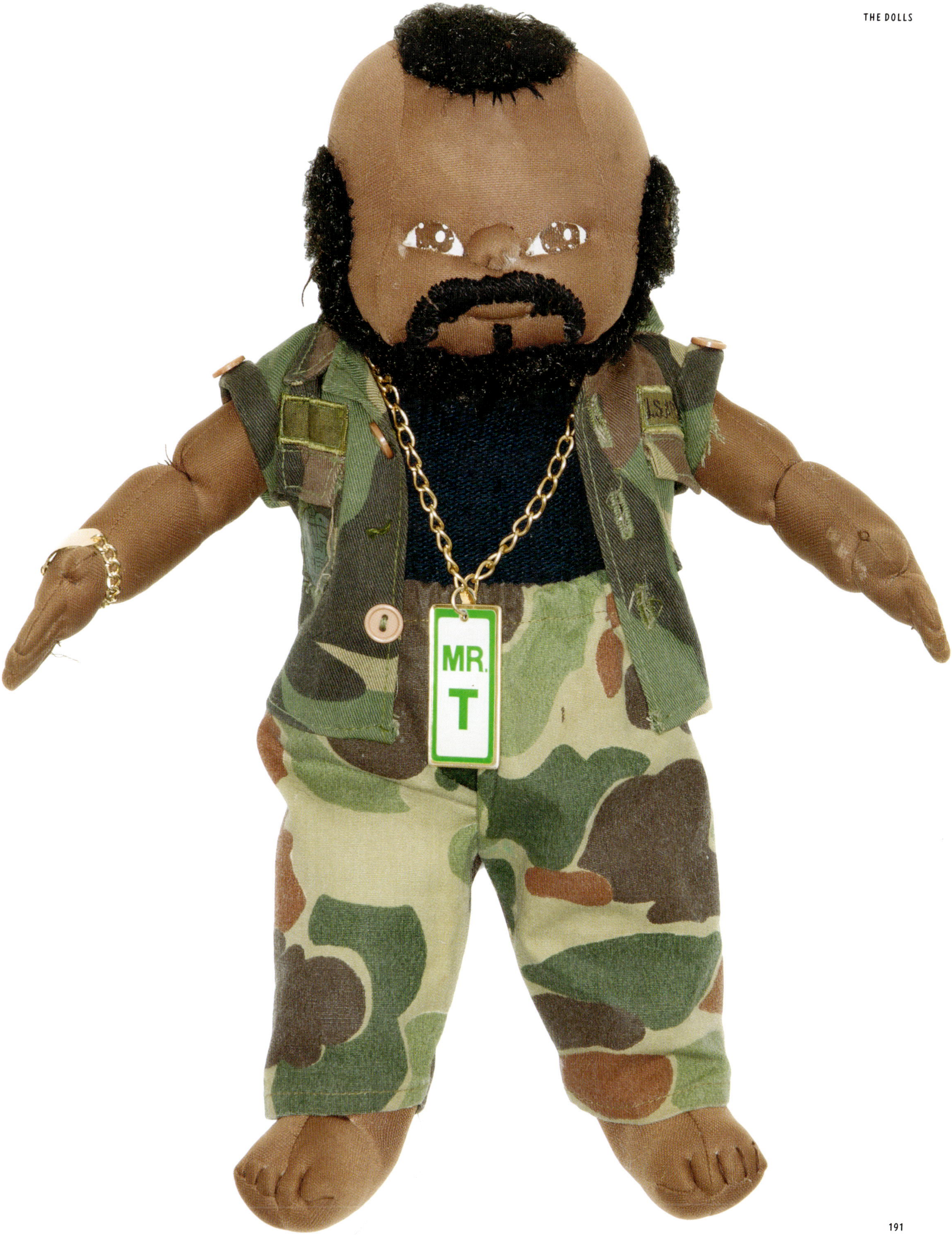
MR.
T

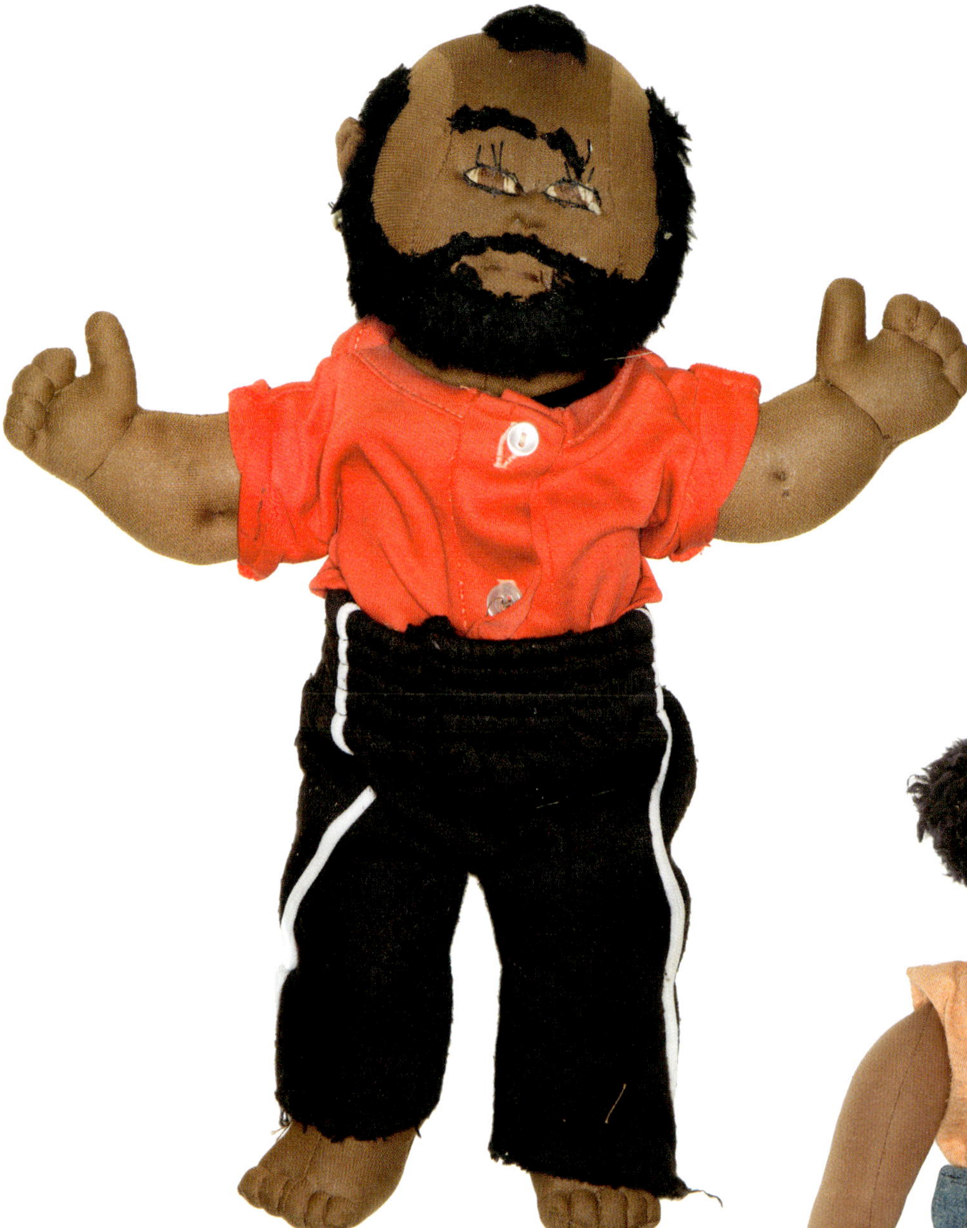

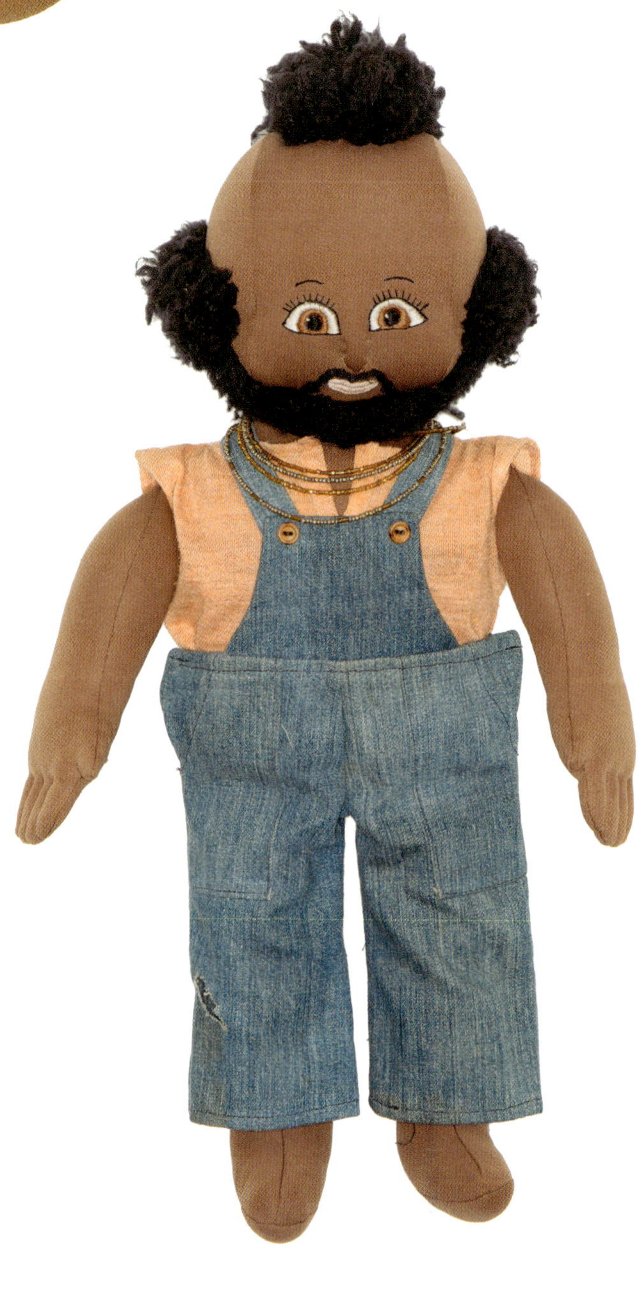

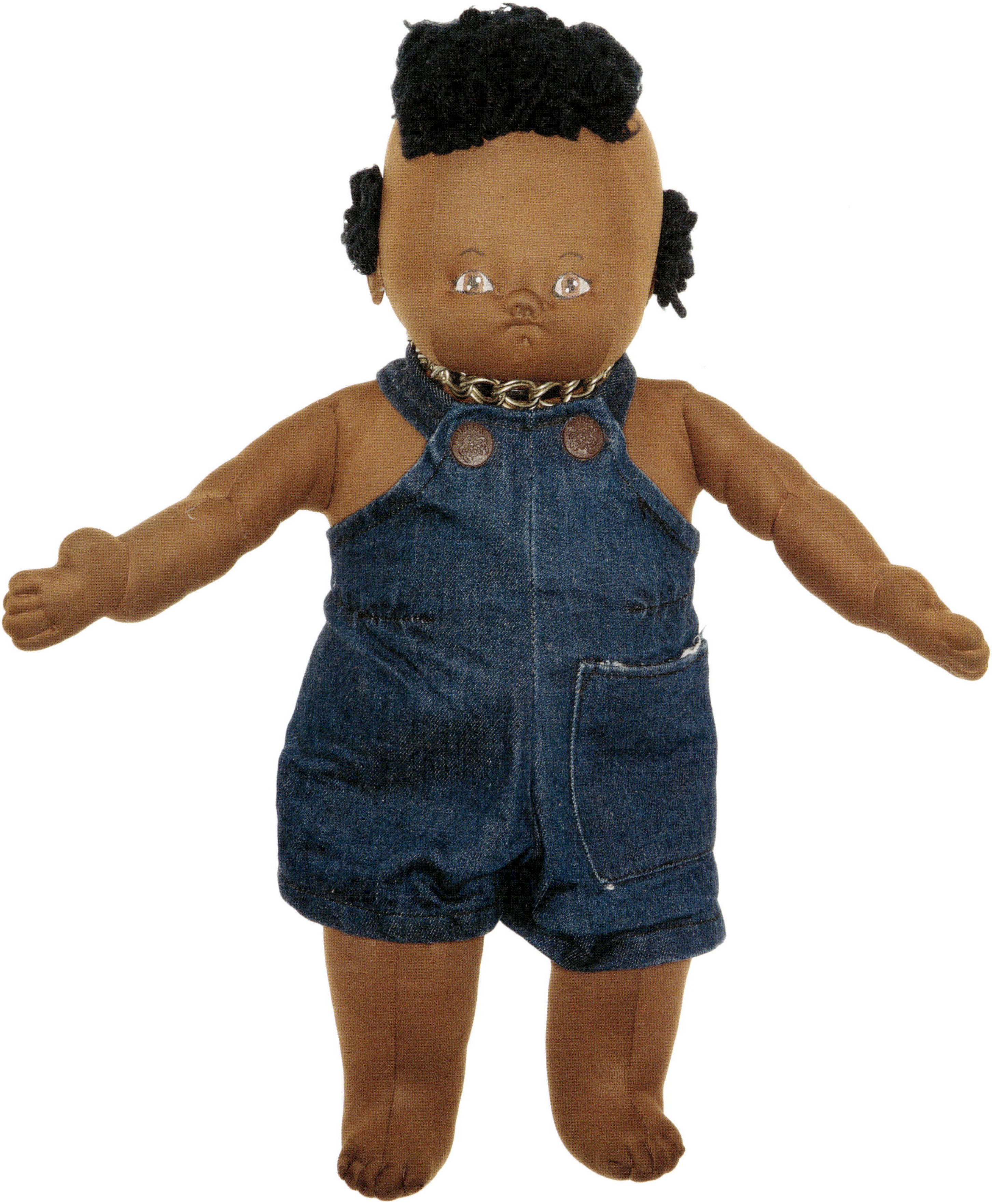

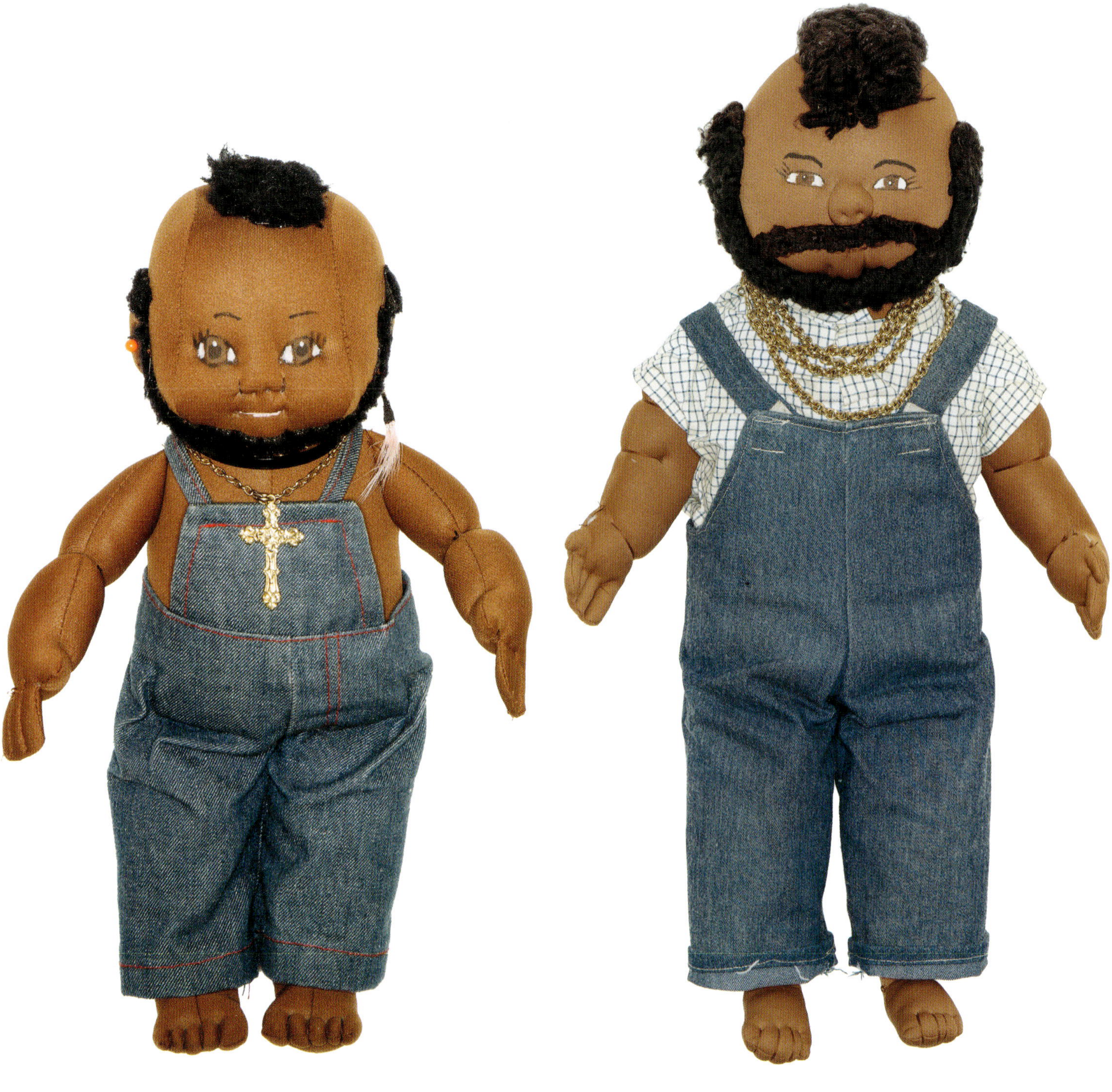

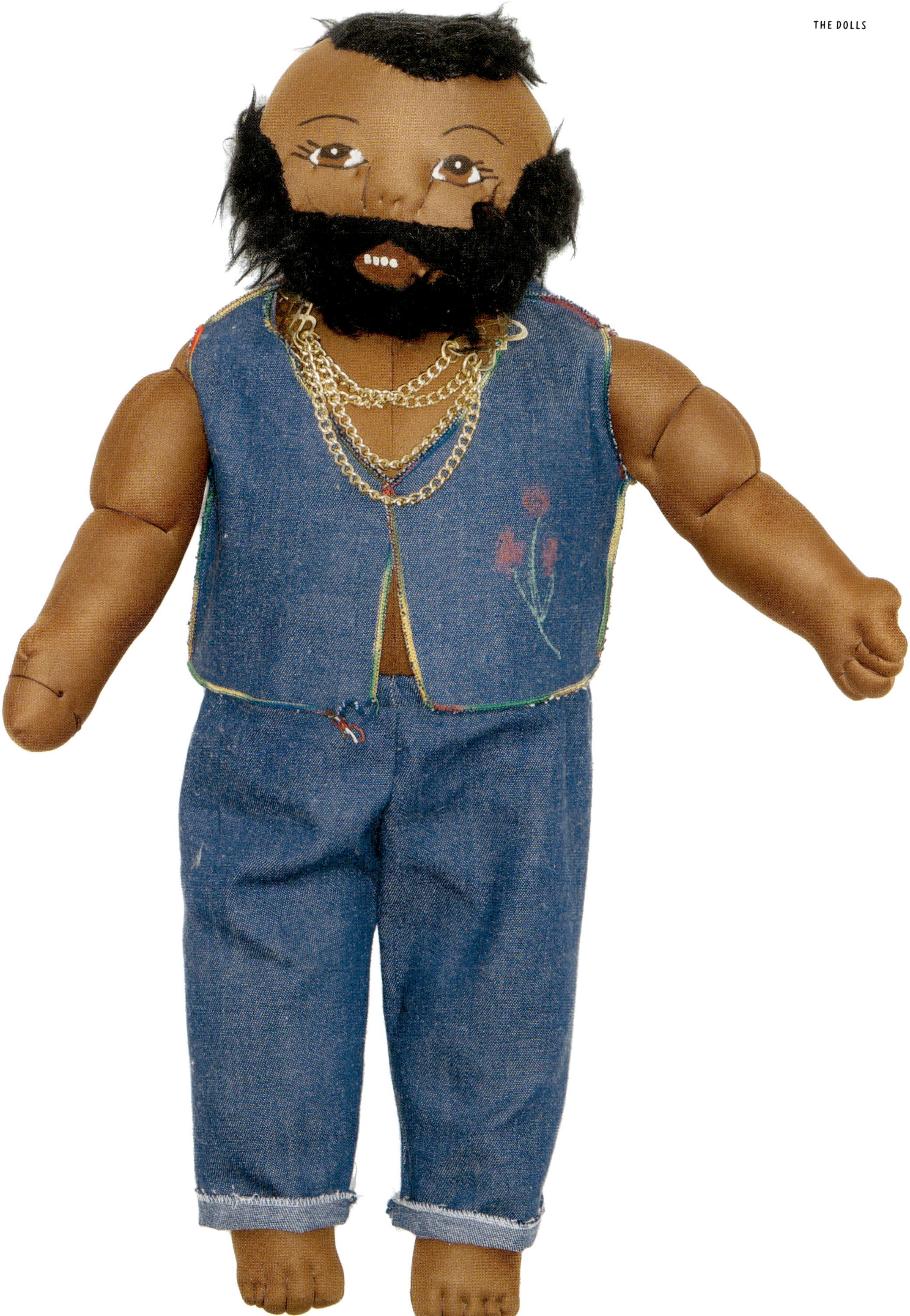

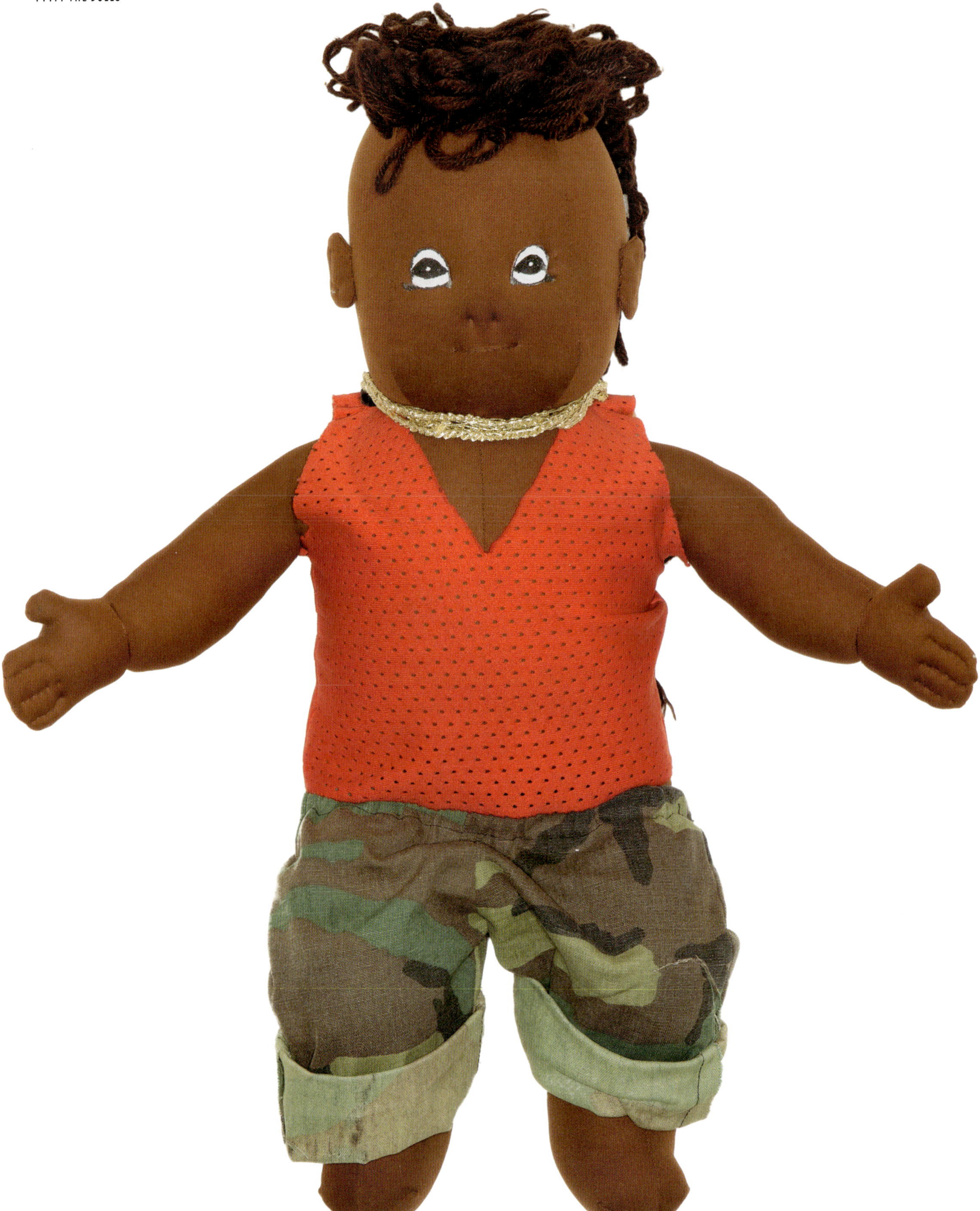

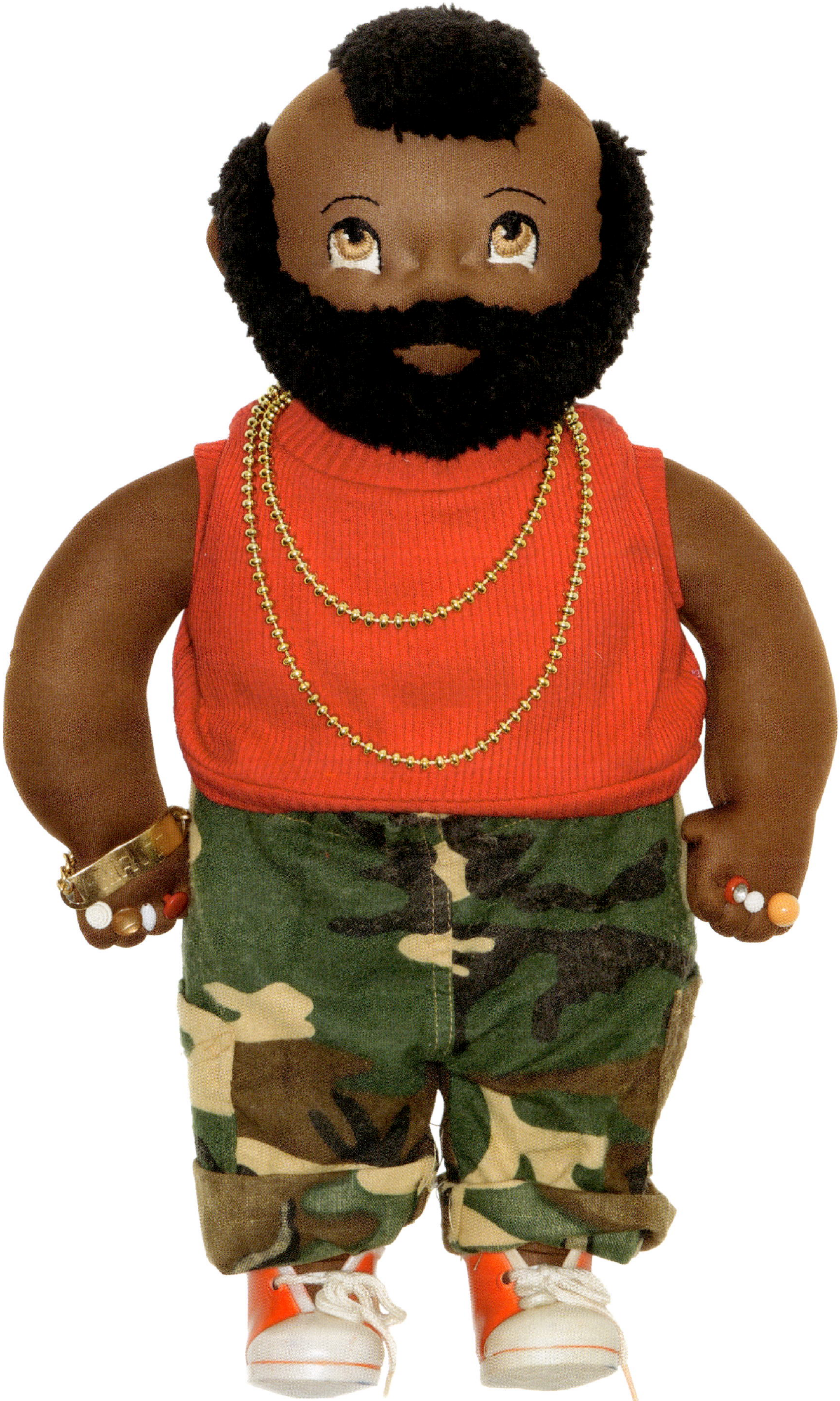

HEY EVERYBODY GOTTA WEAR CLOTHES IF YOU DON'T YOU GET ARRESTED

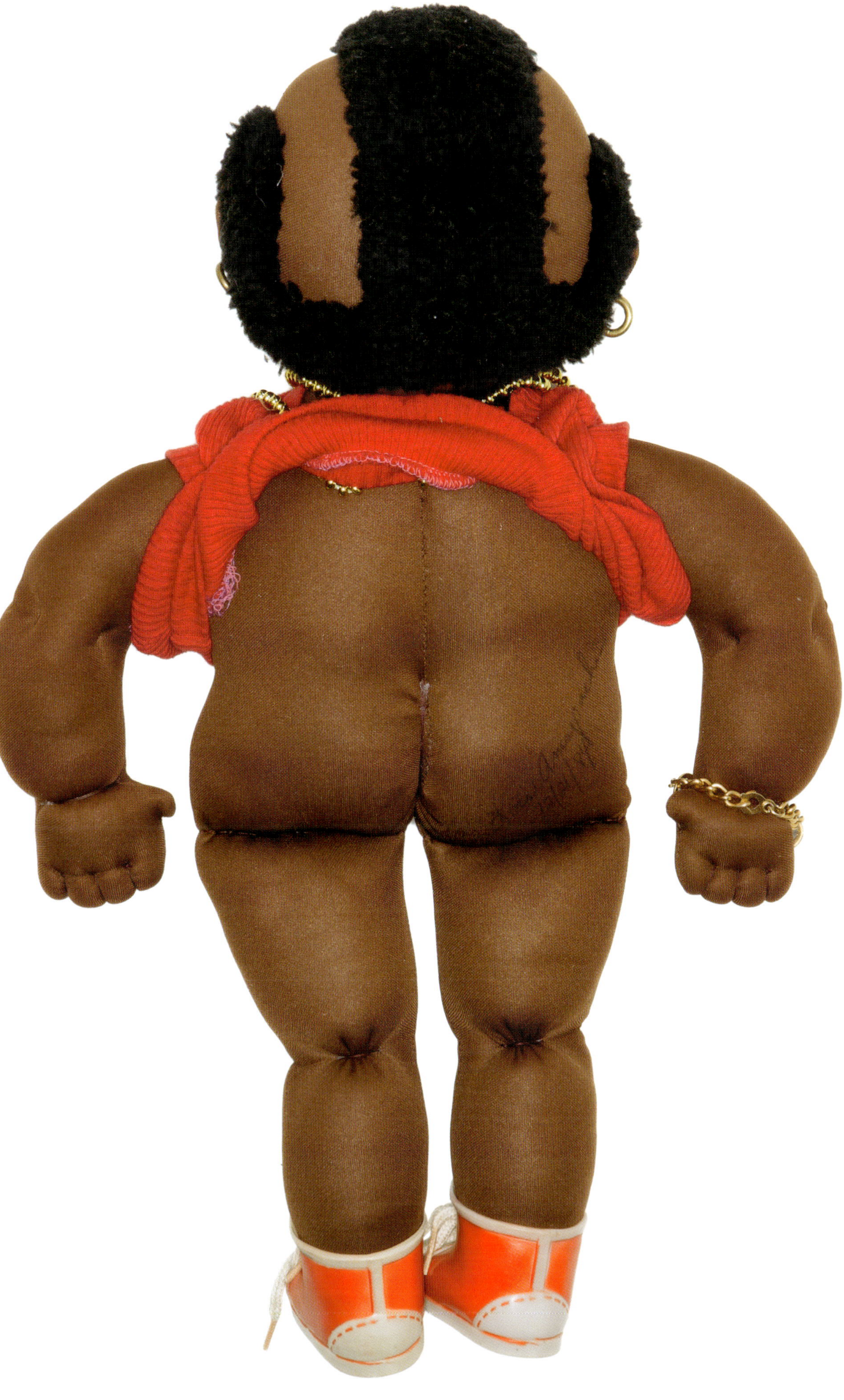

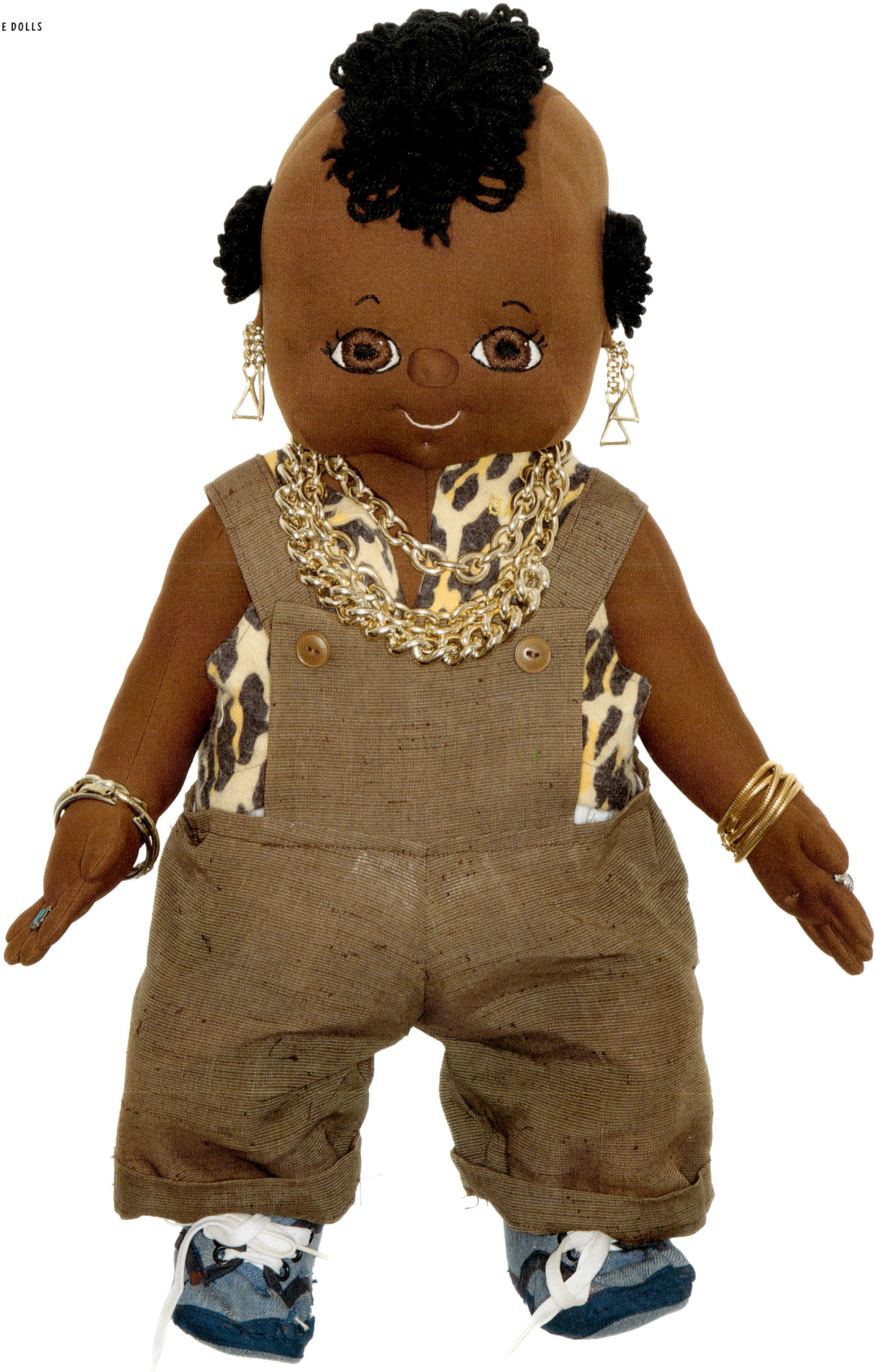

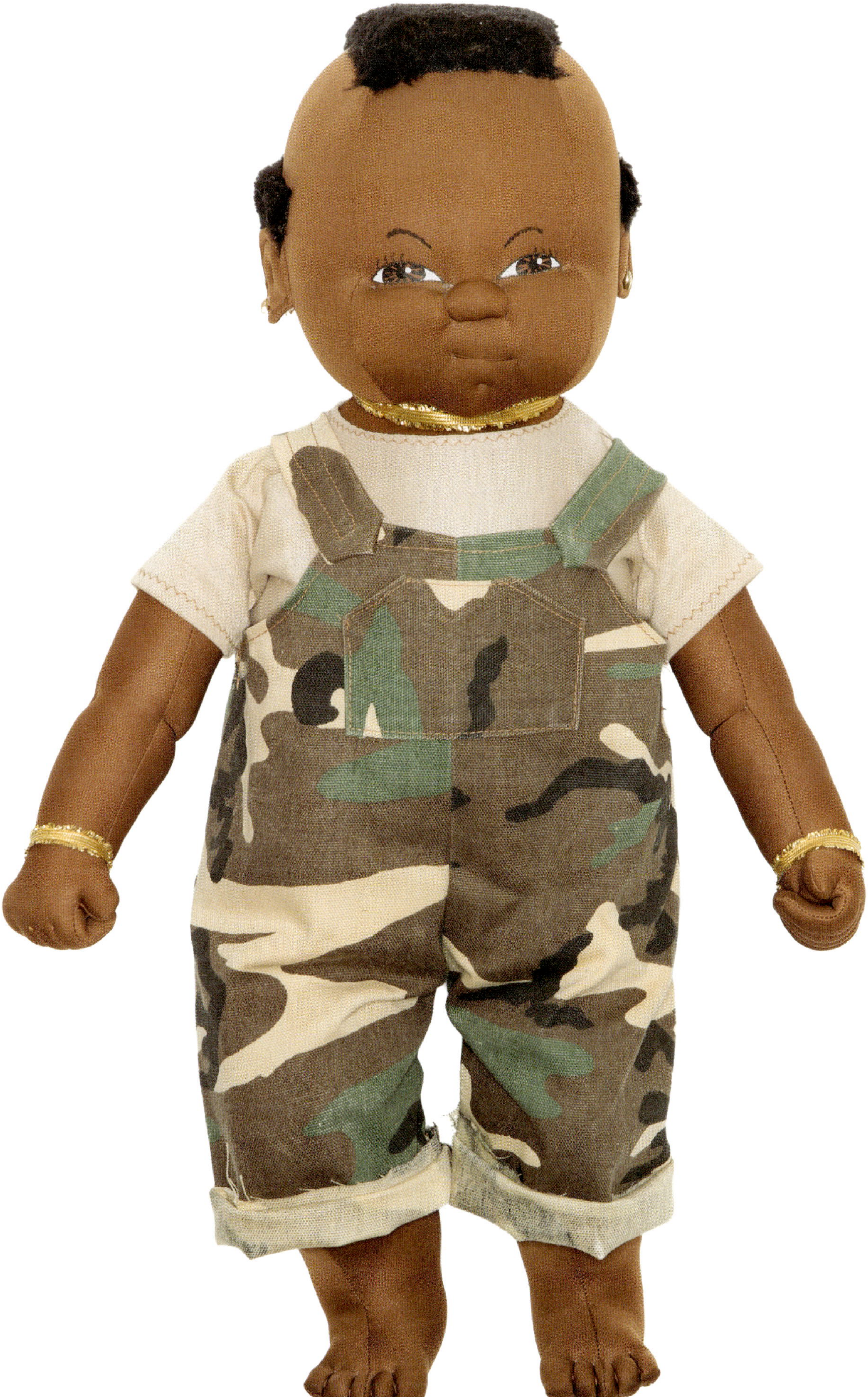

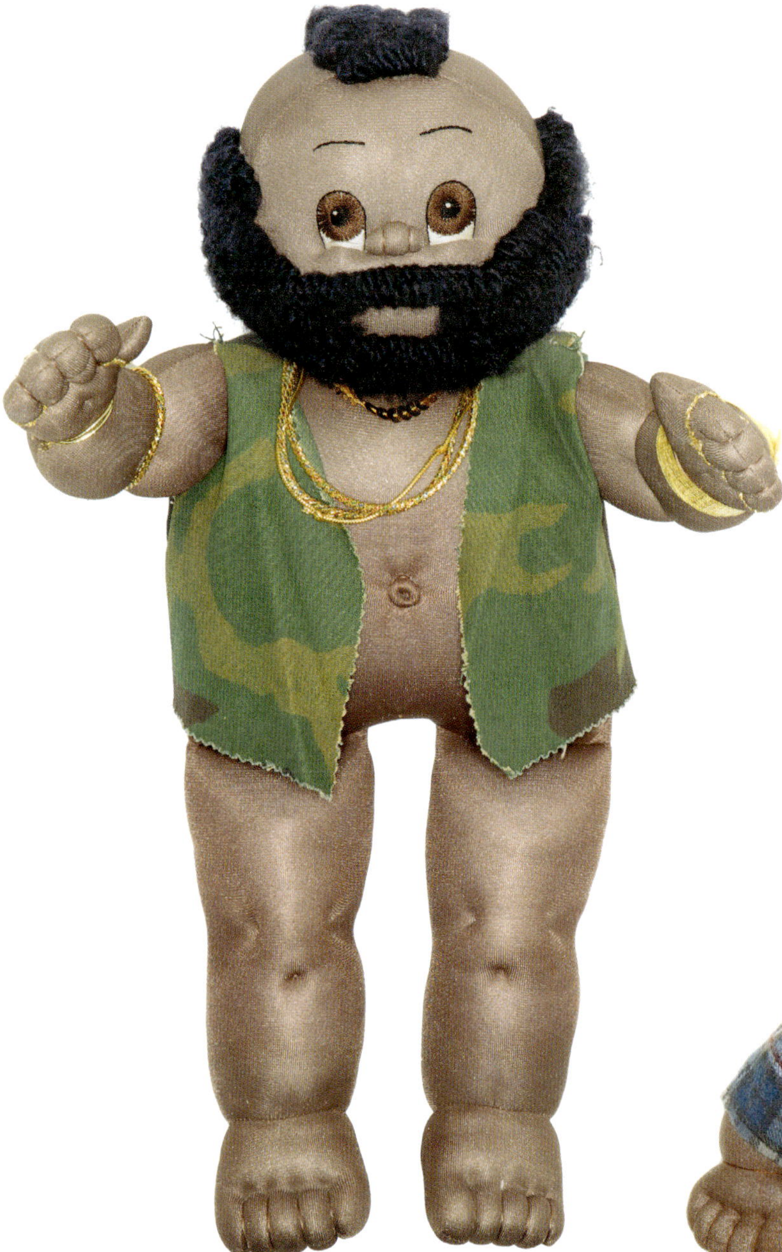

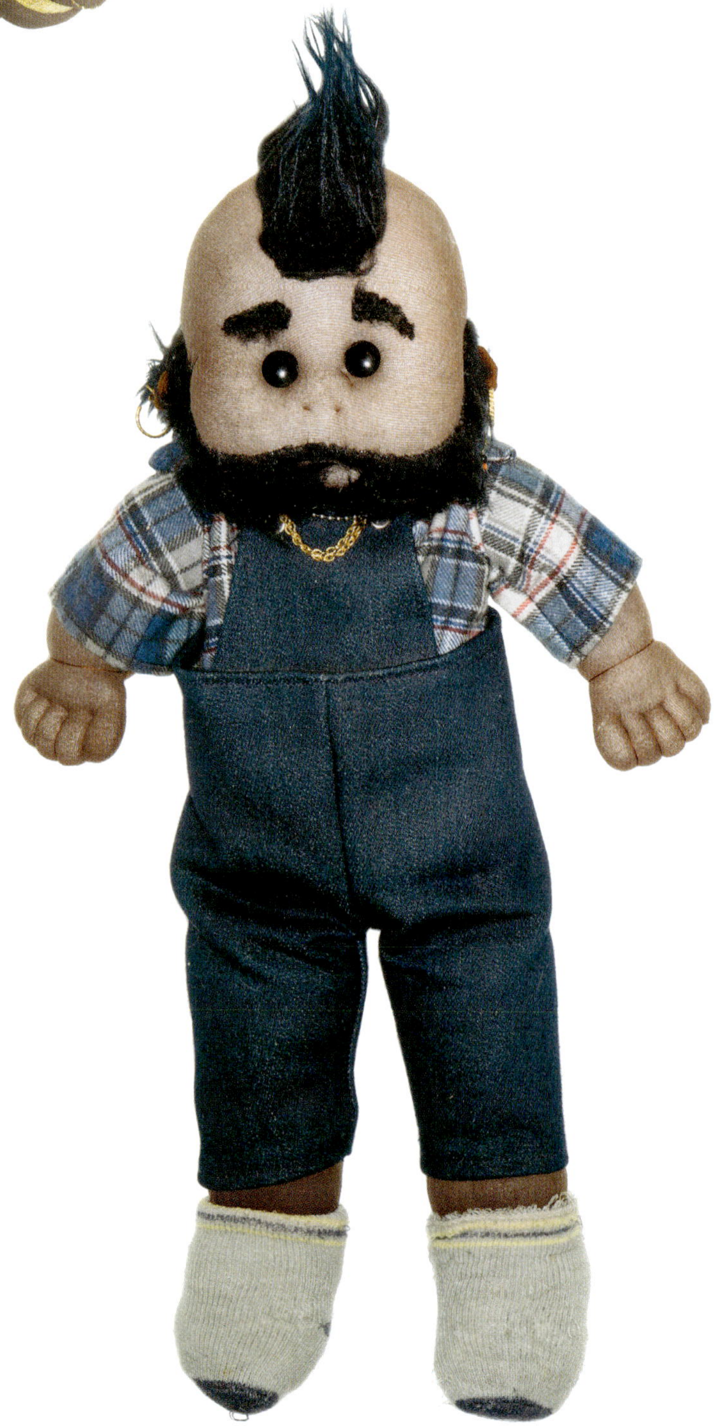

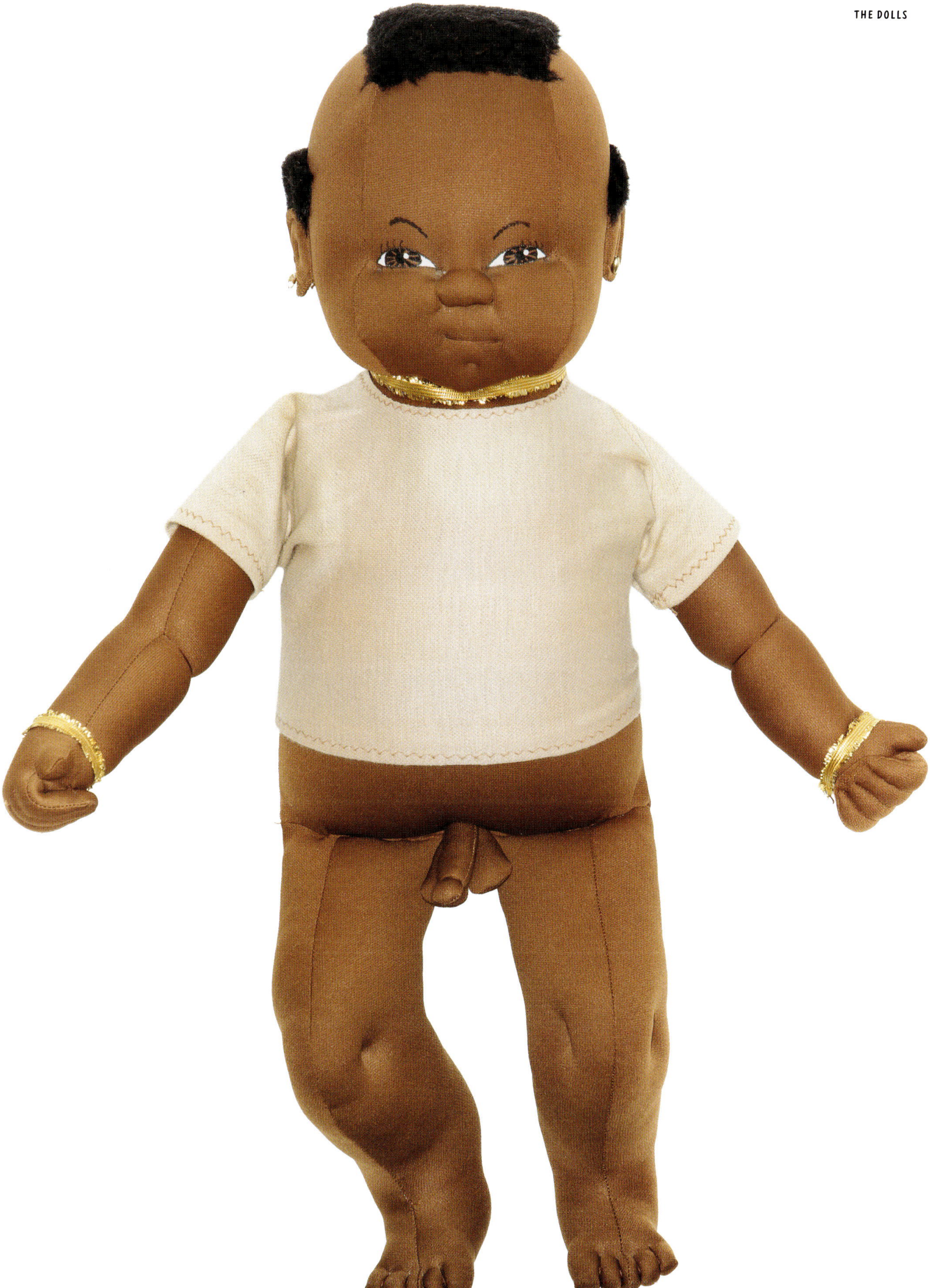

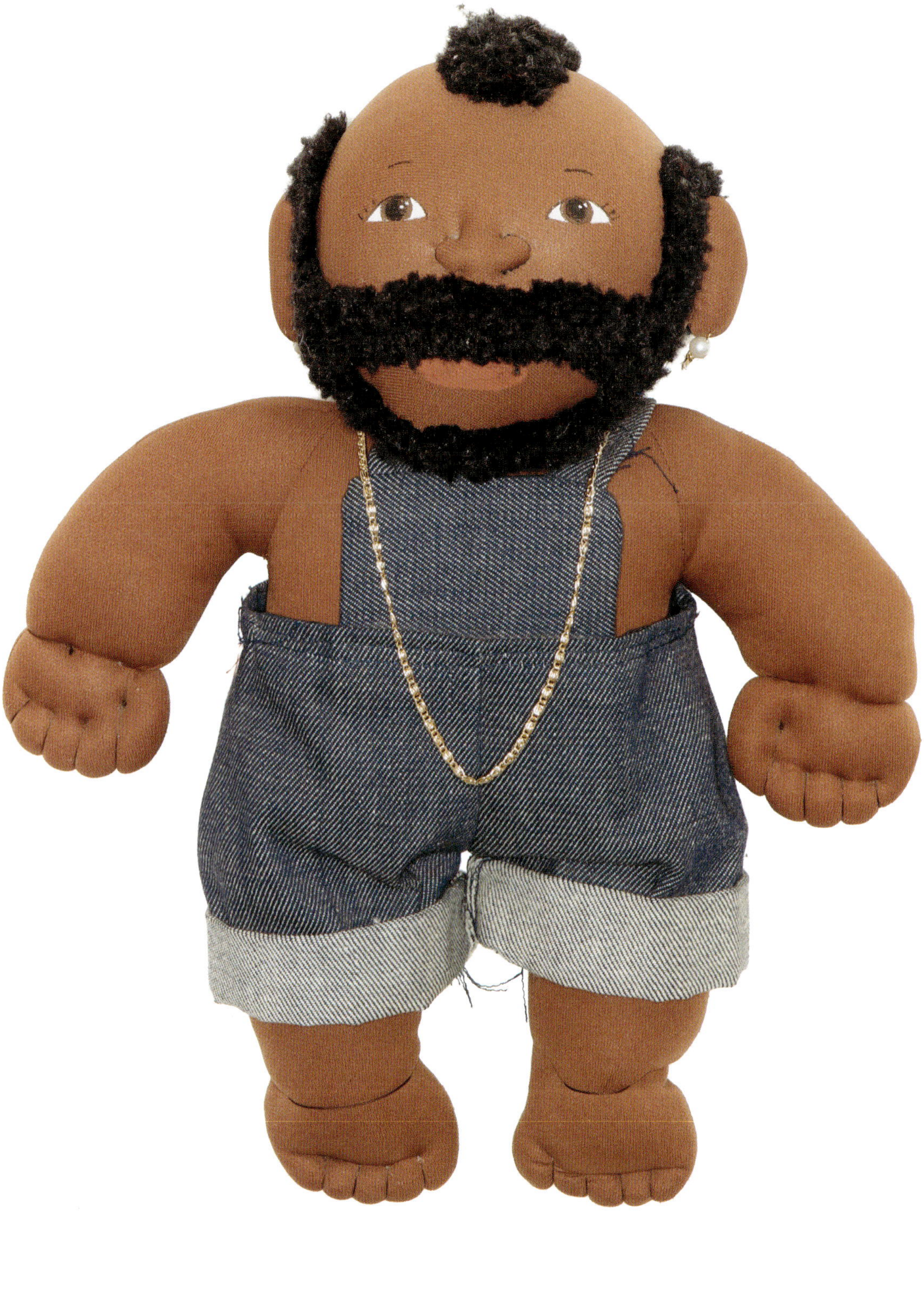

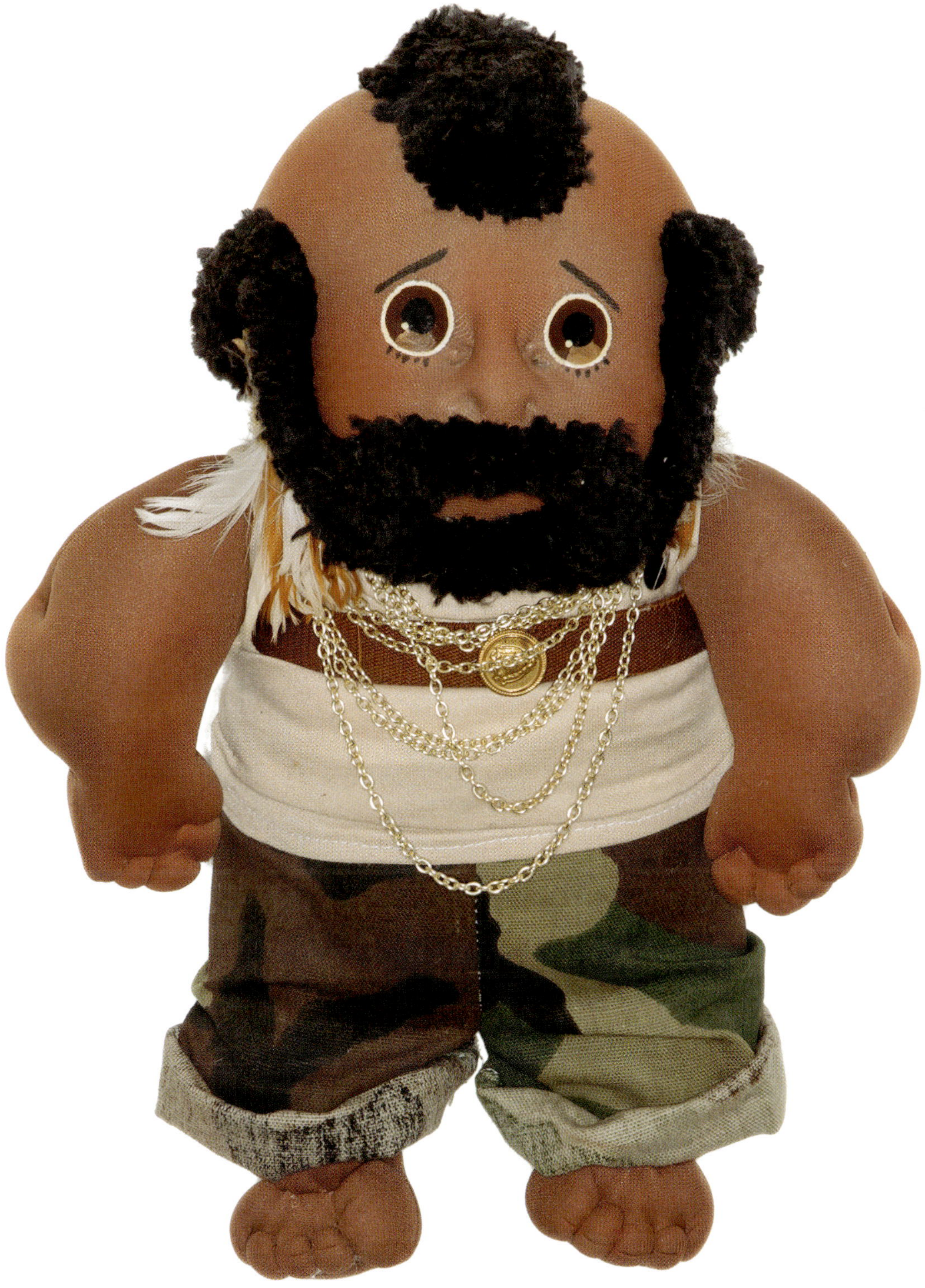

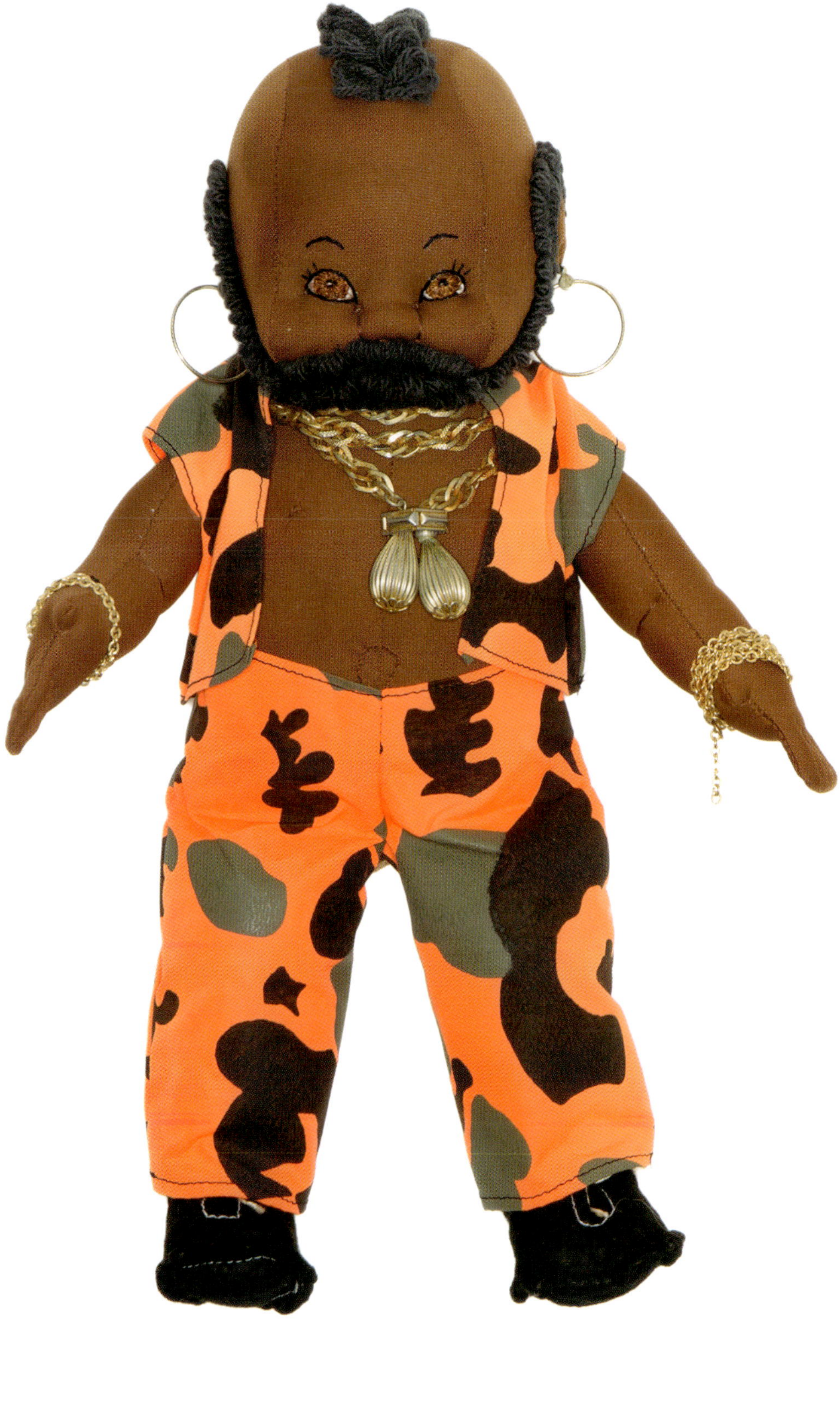

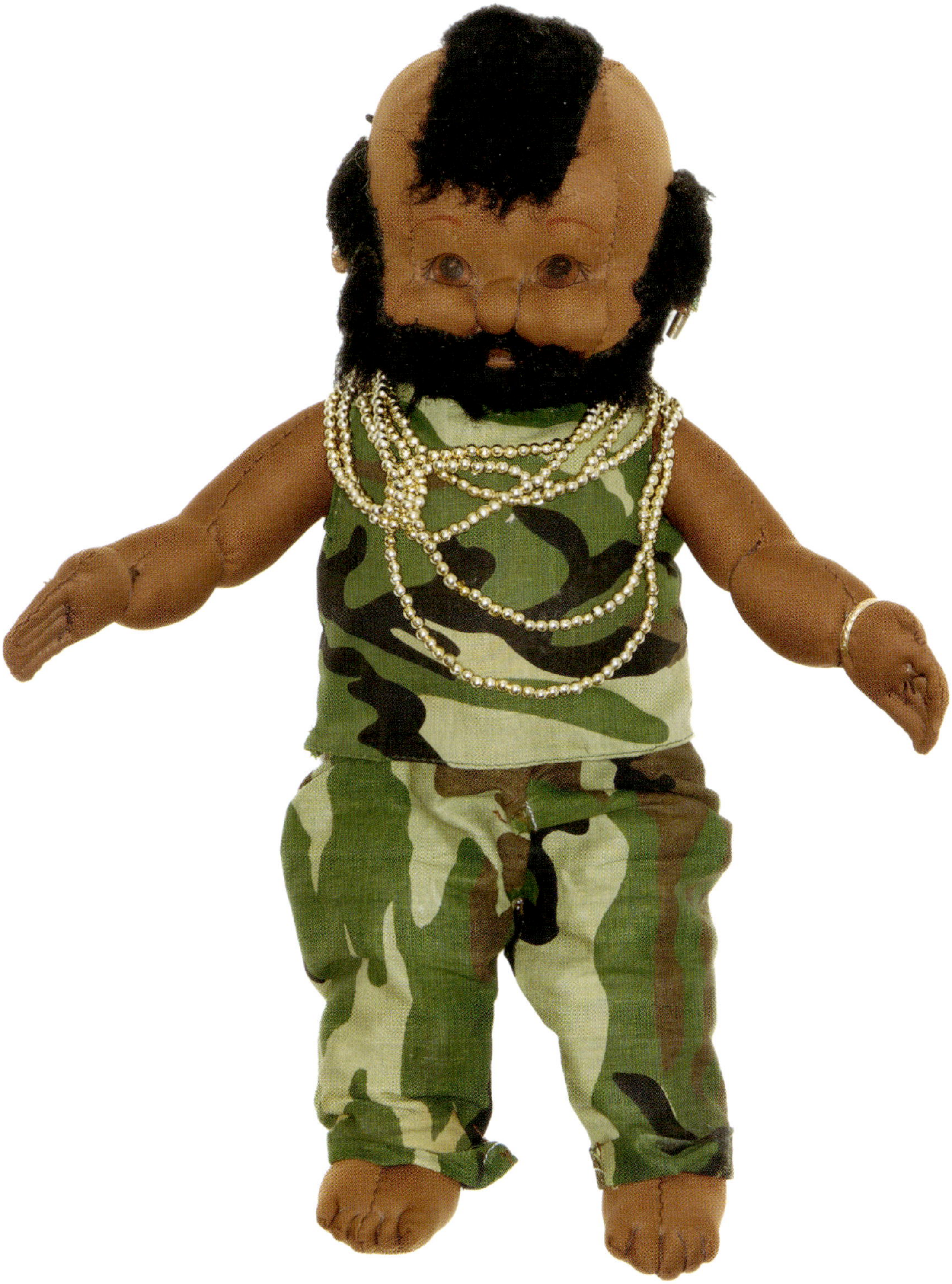

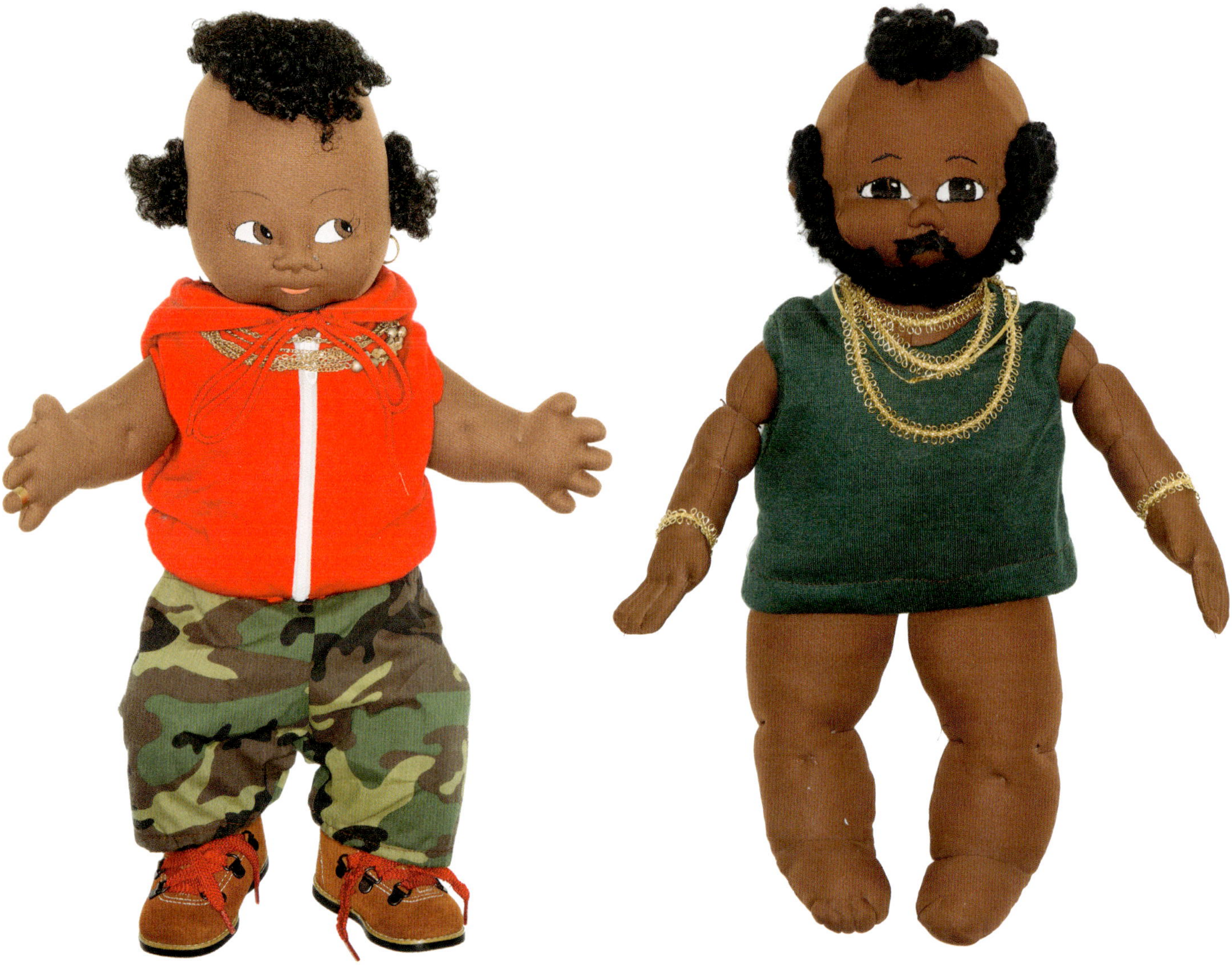

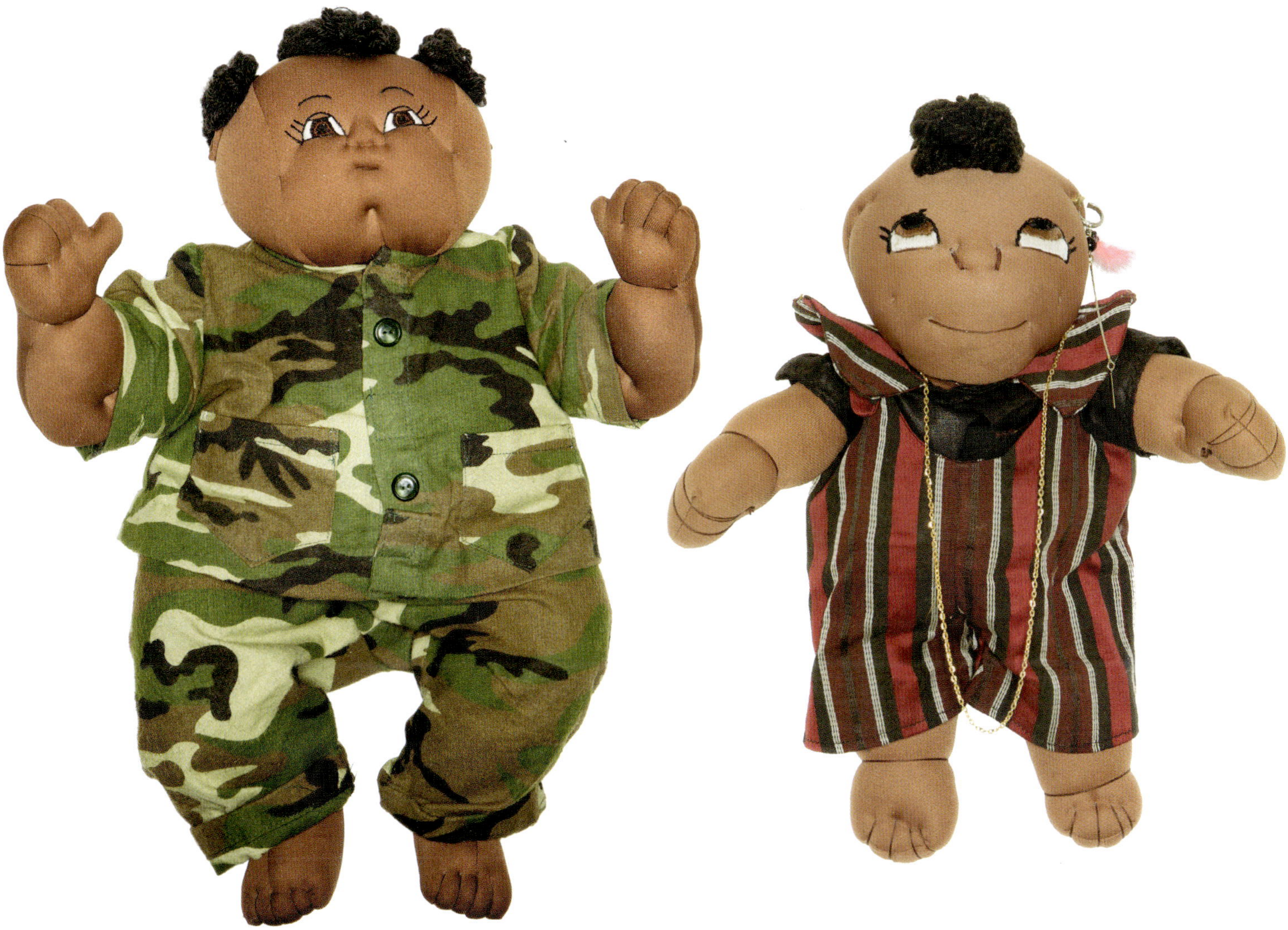

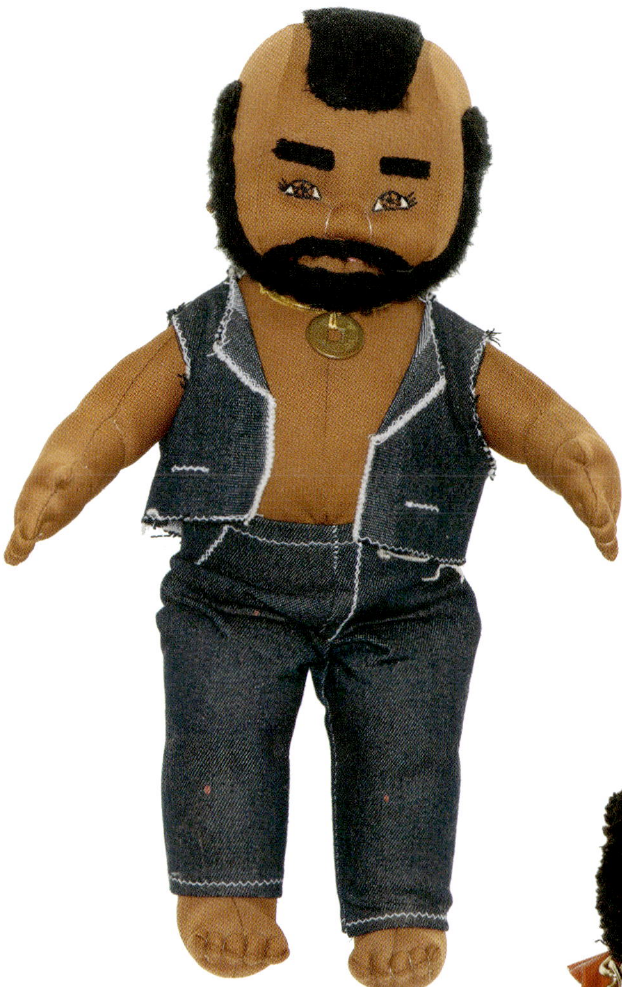

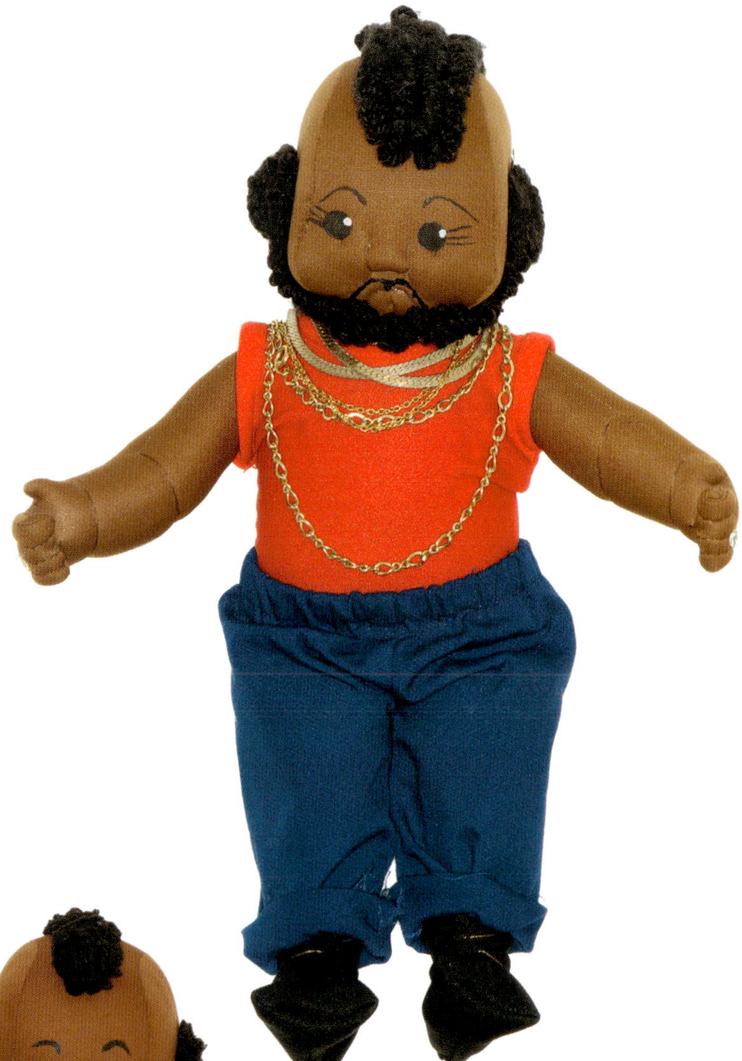

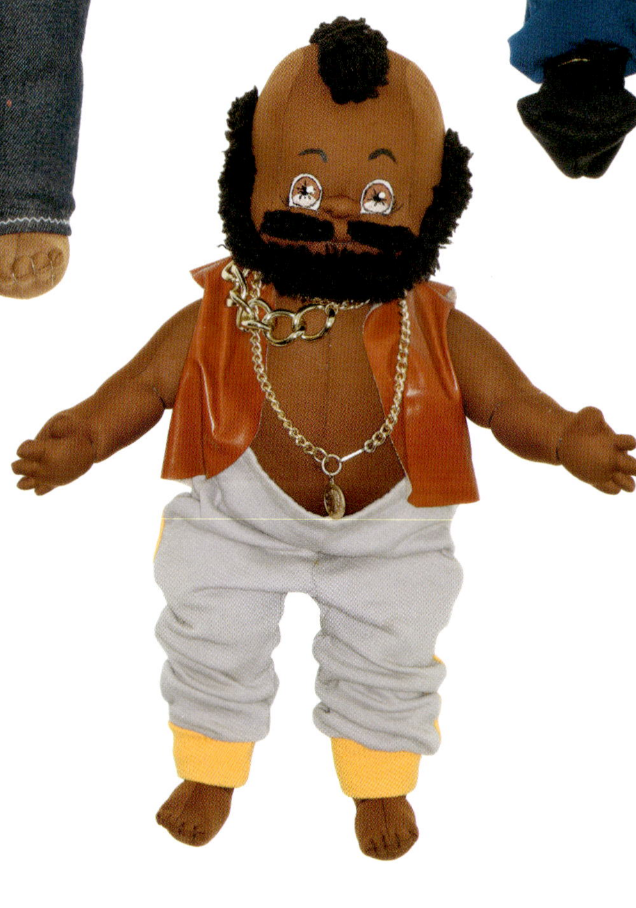

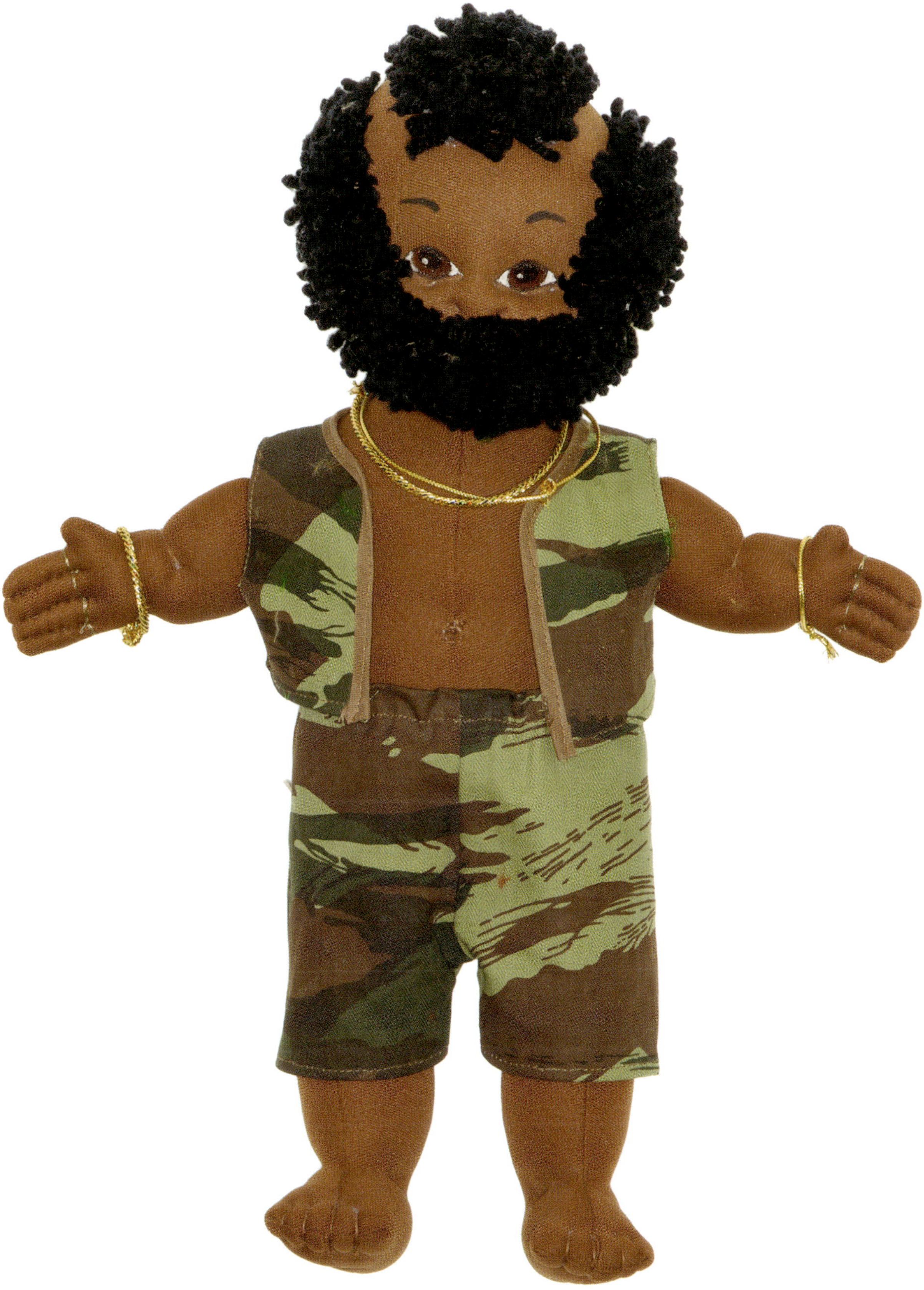

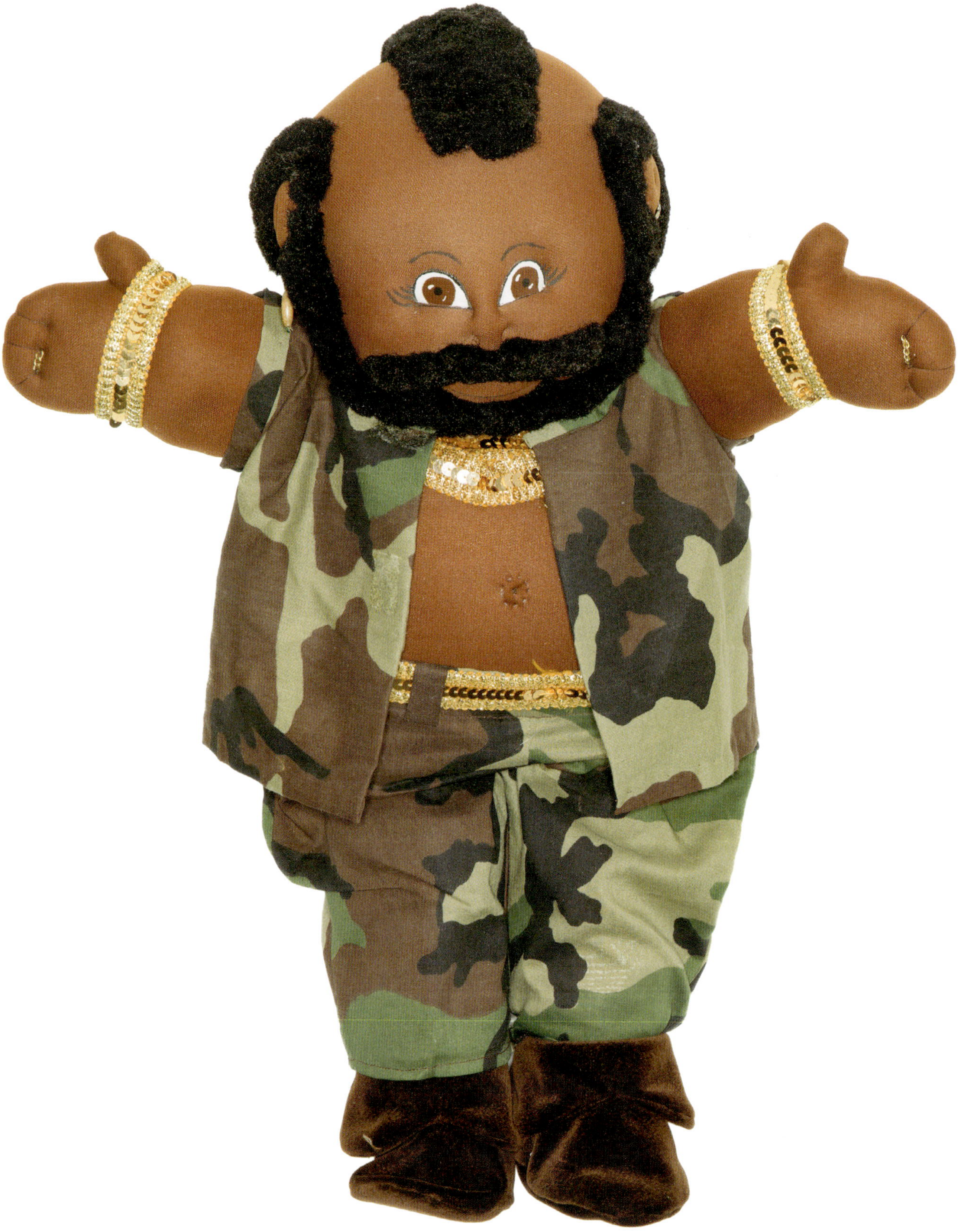

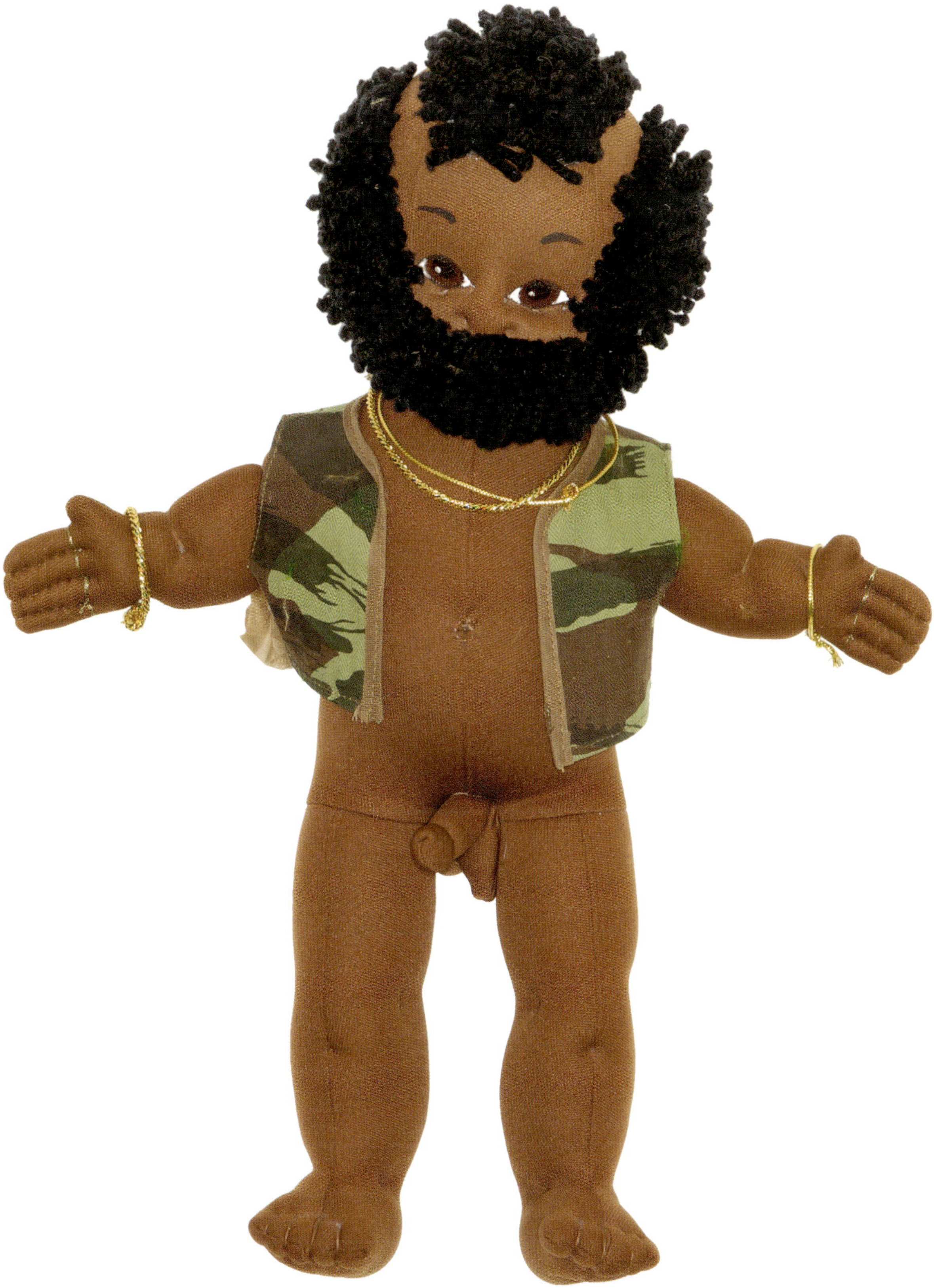

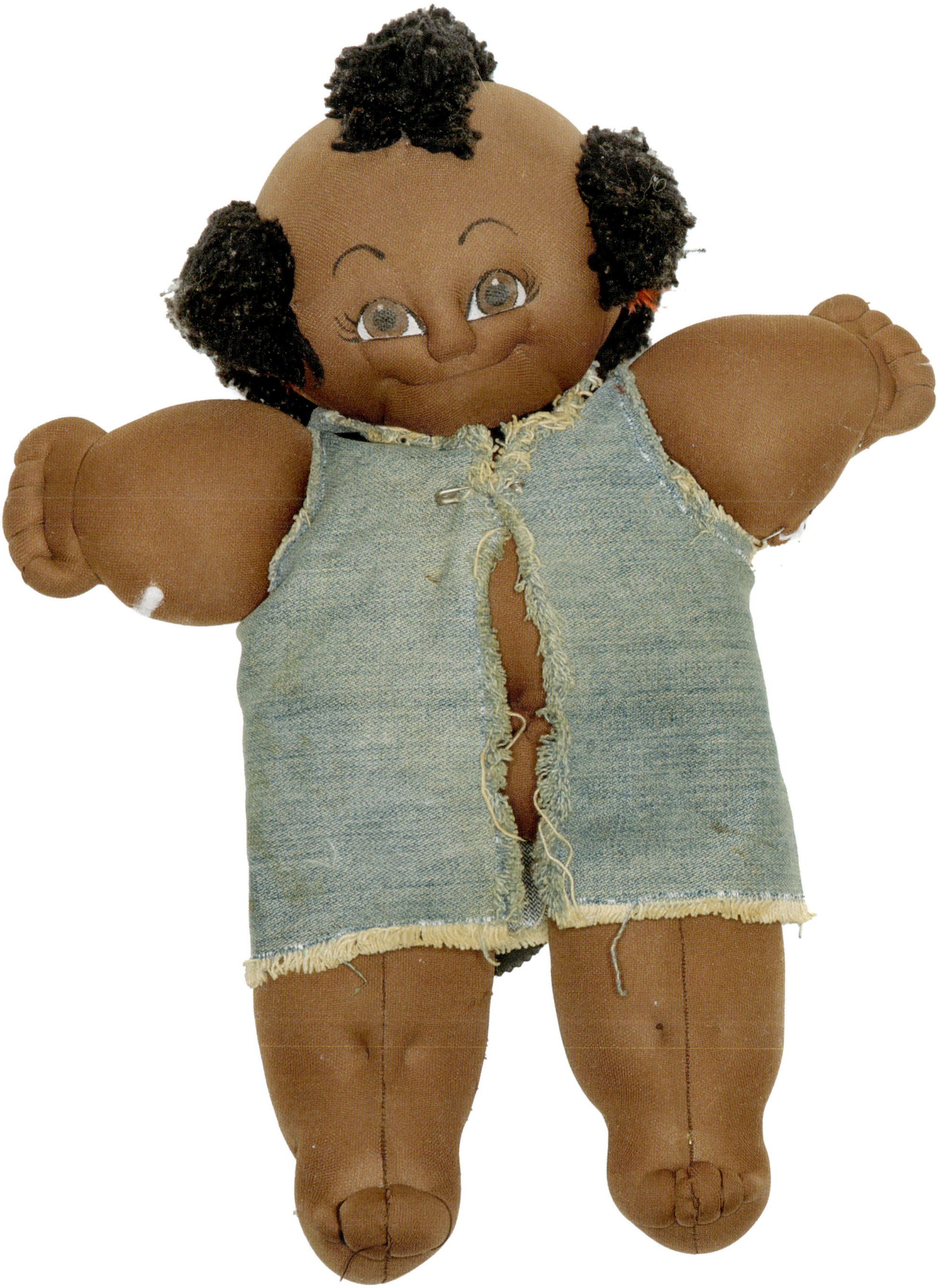

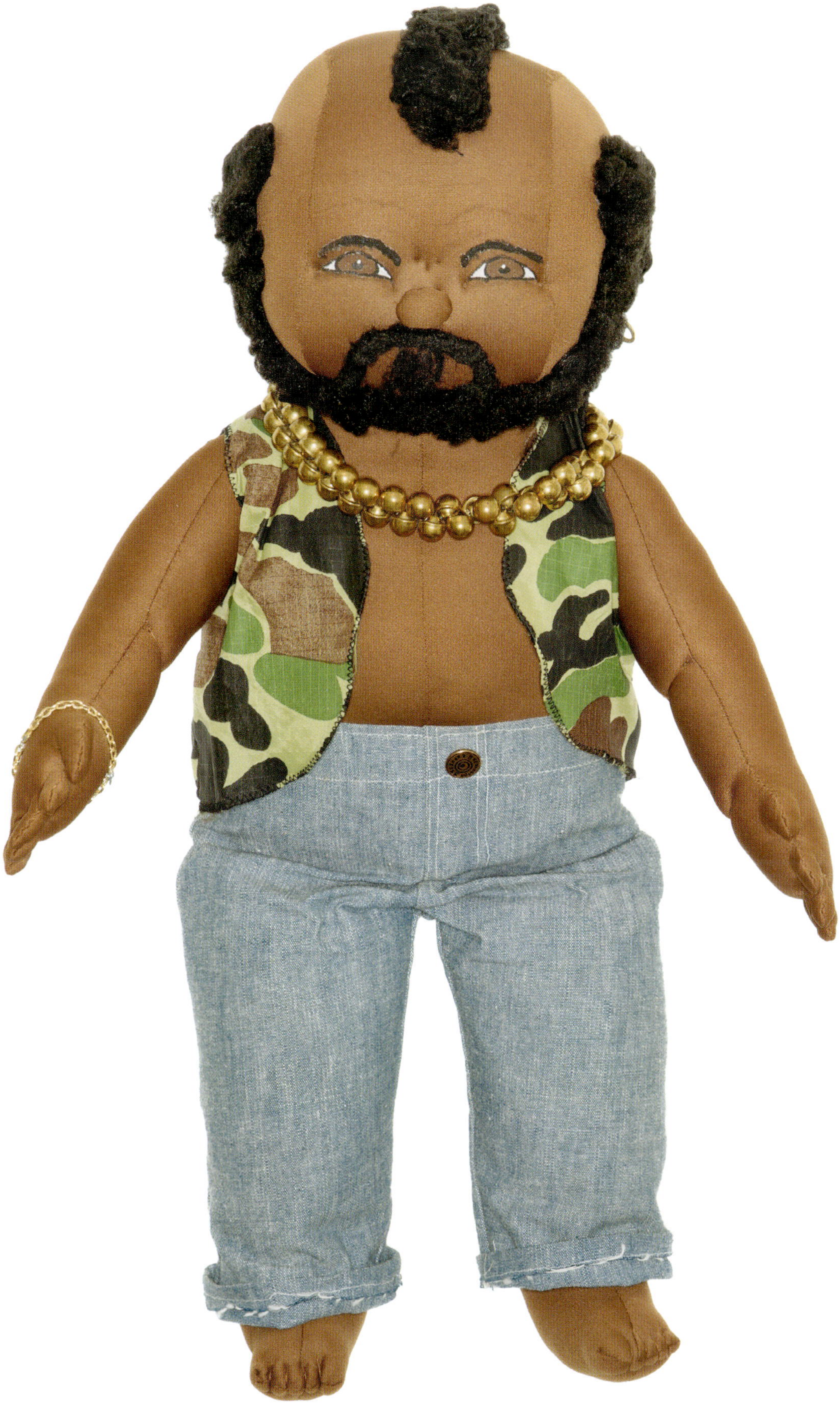

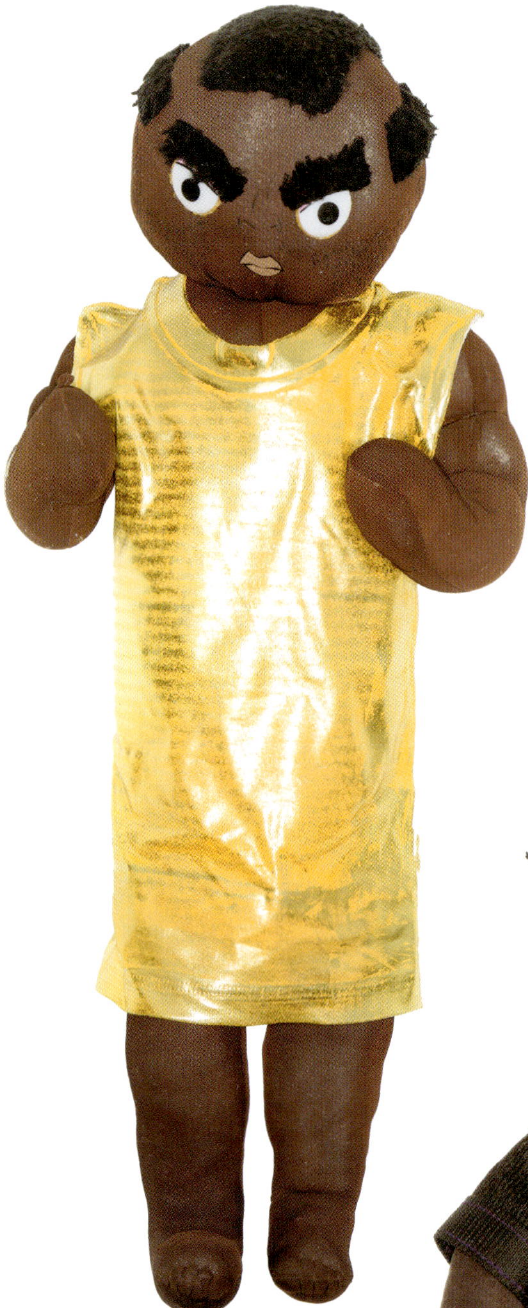
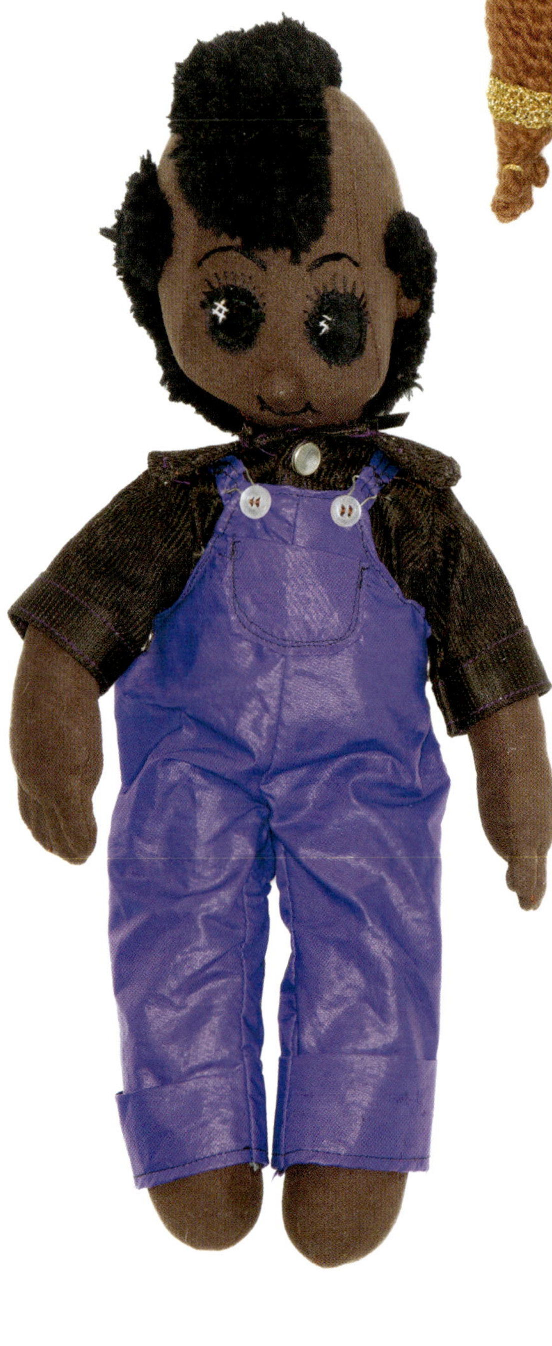
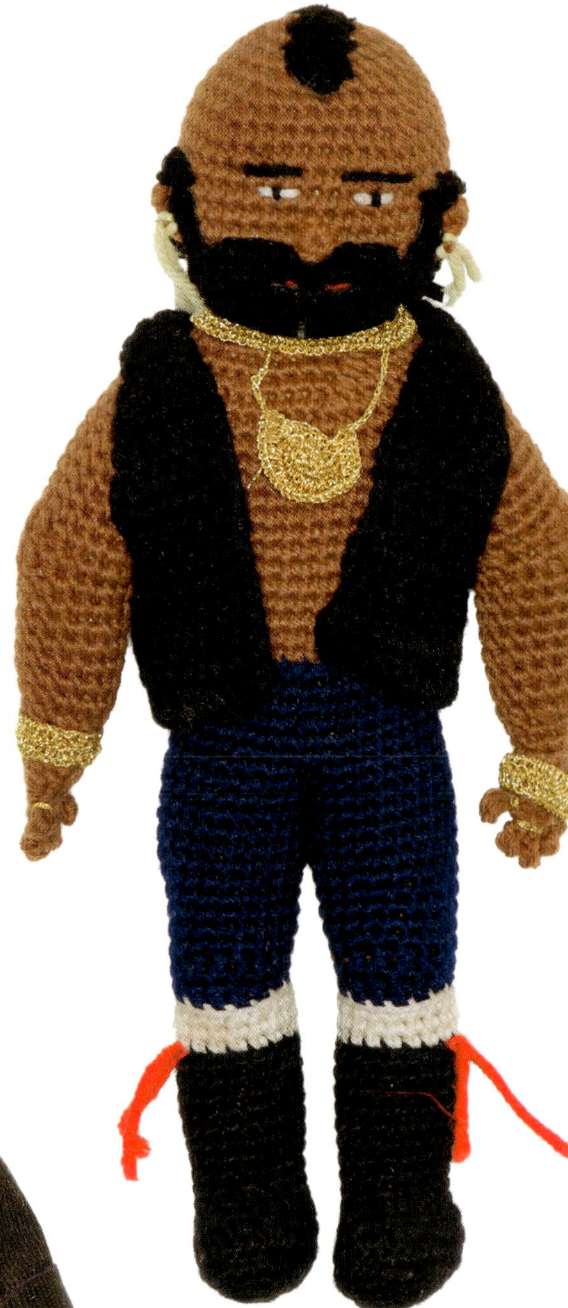

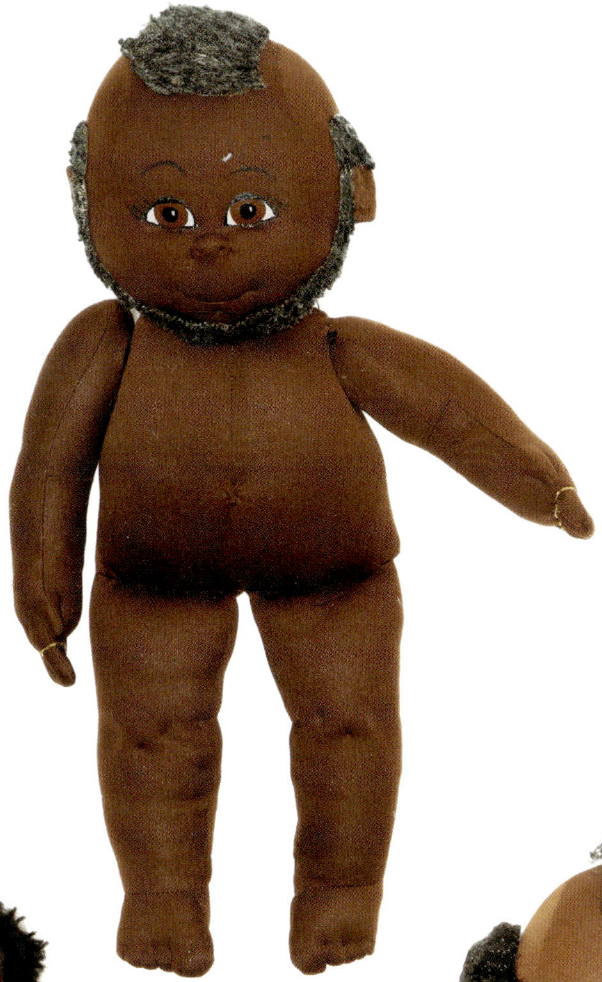

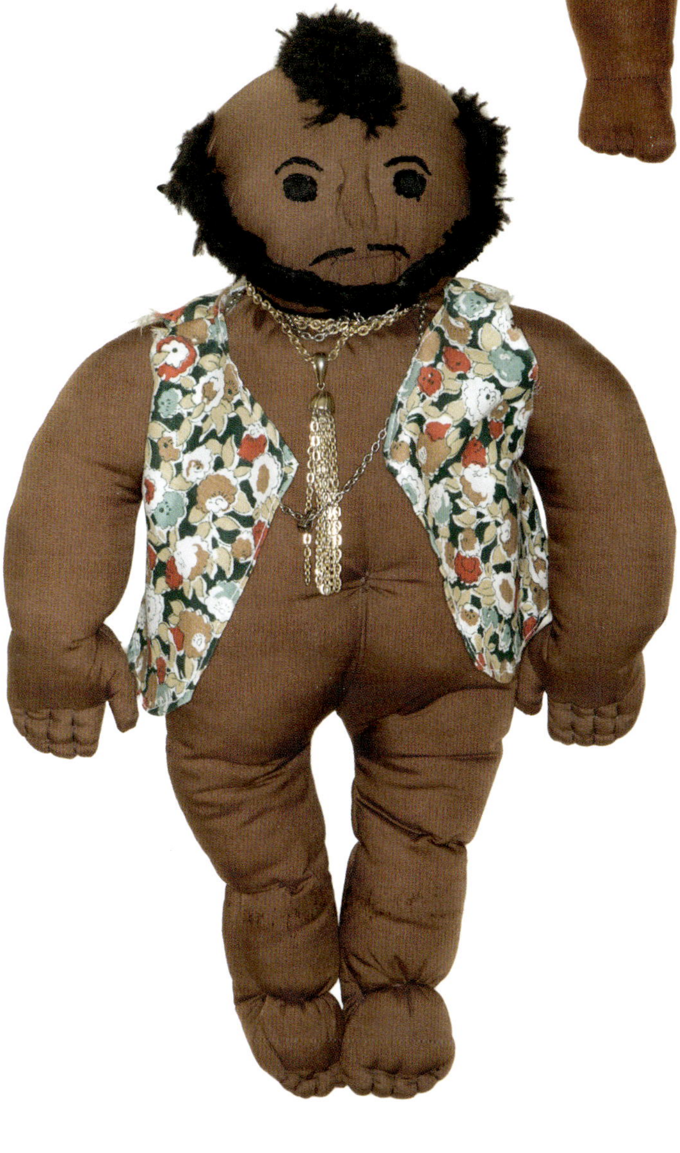

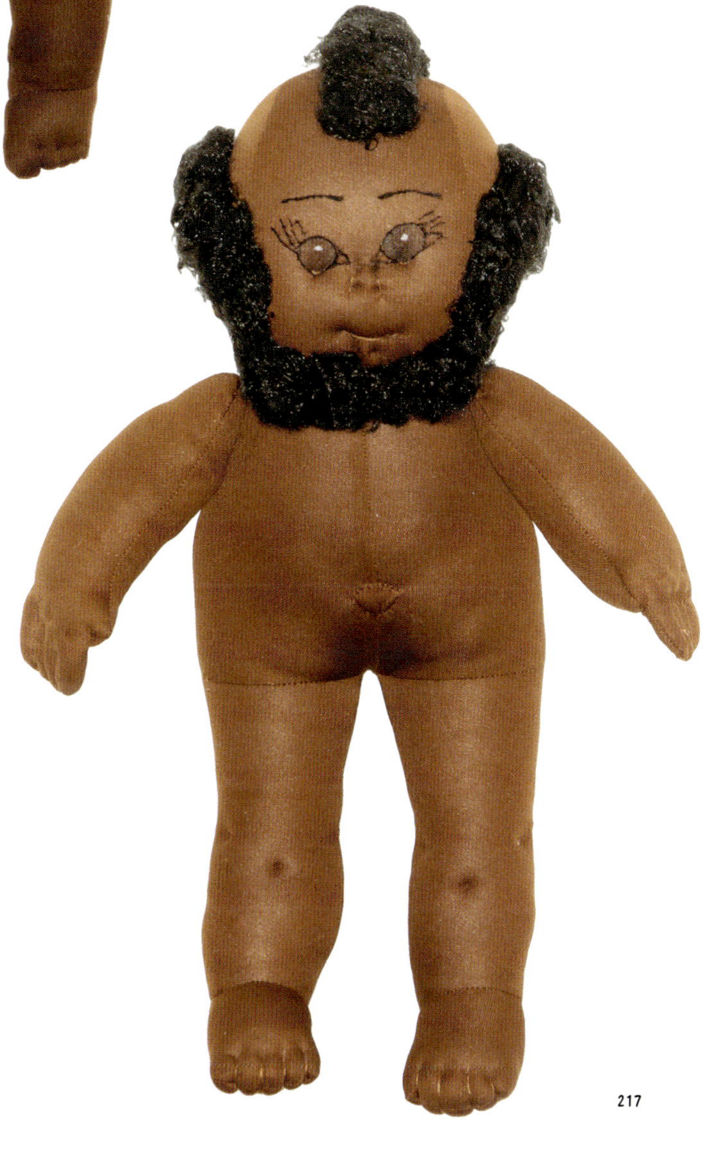

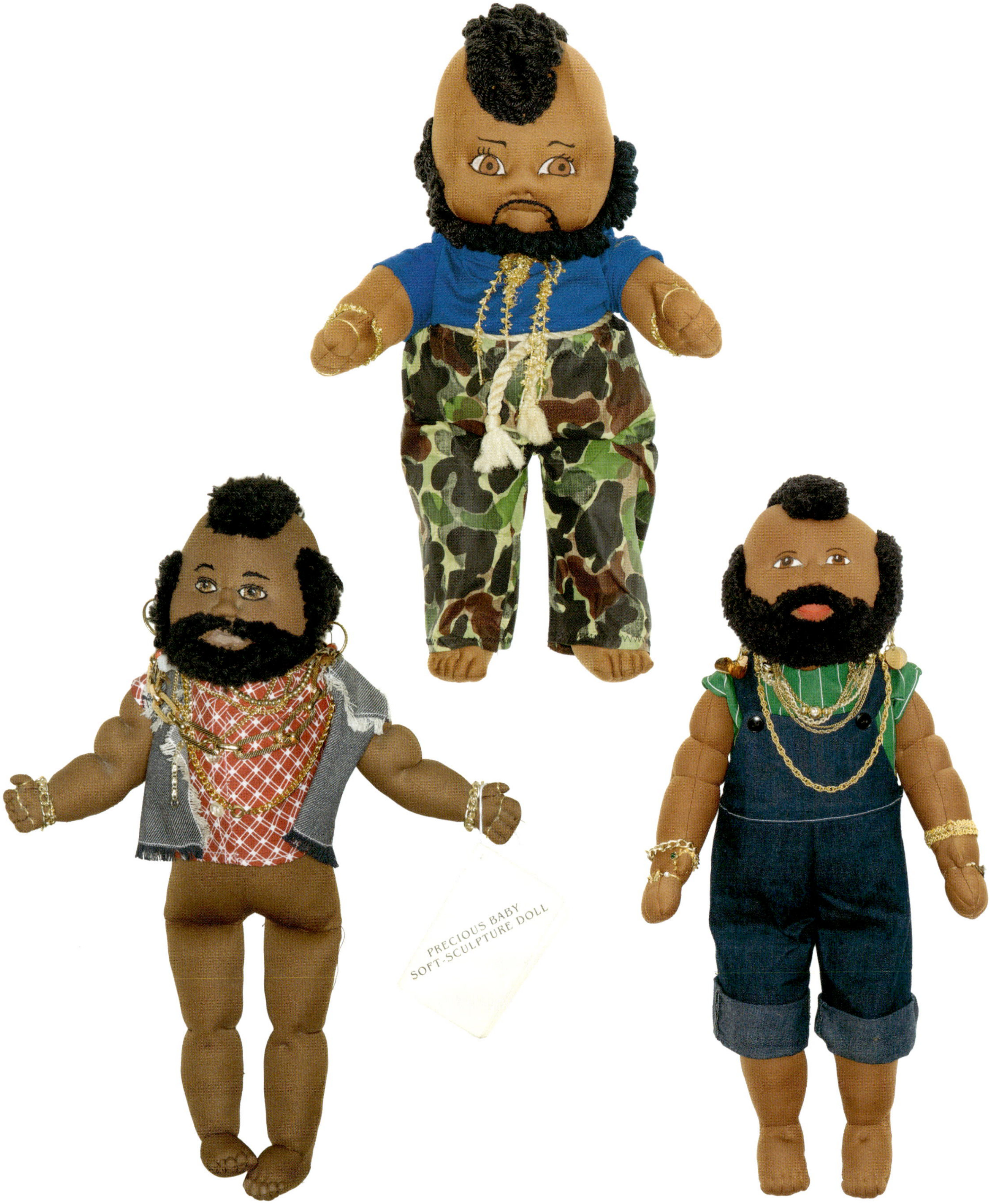
PRECIOUS BABY
SOFT-SCULPTURE DOLL

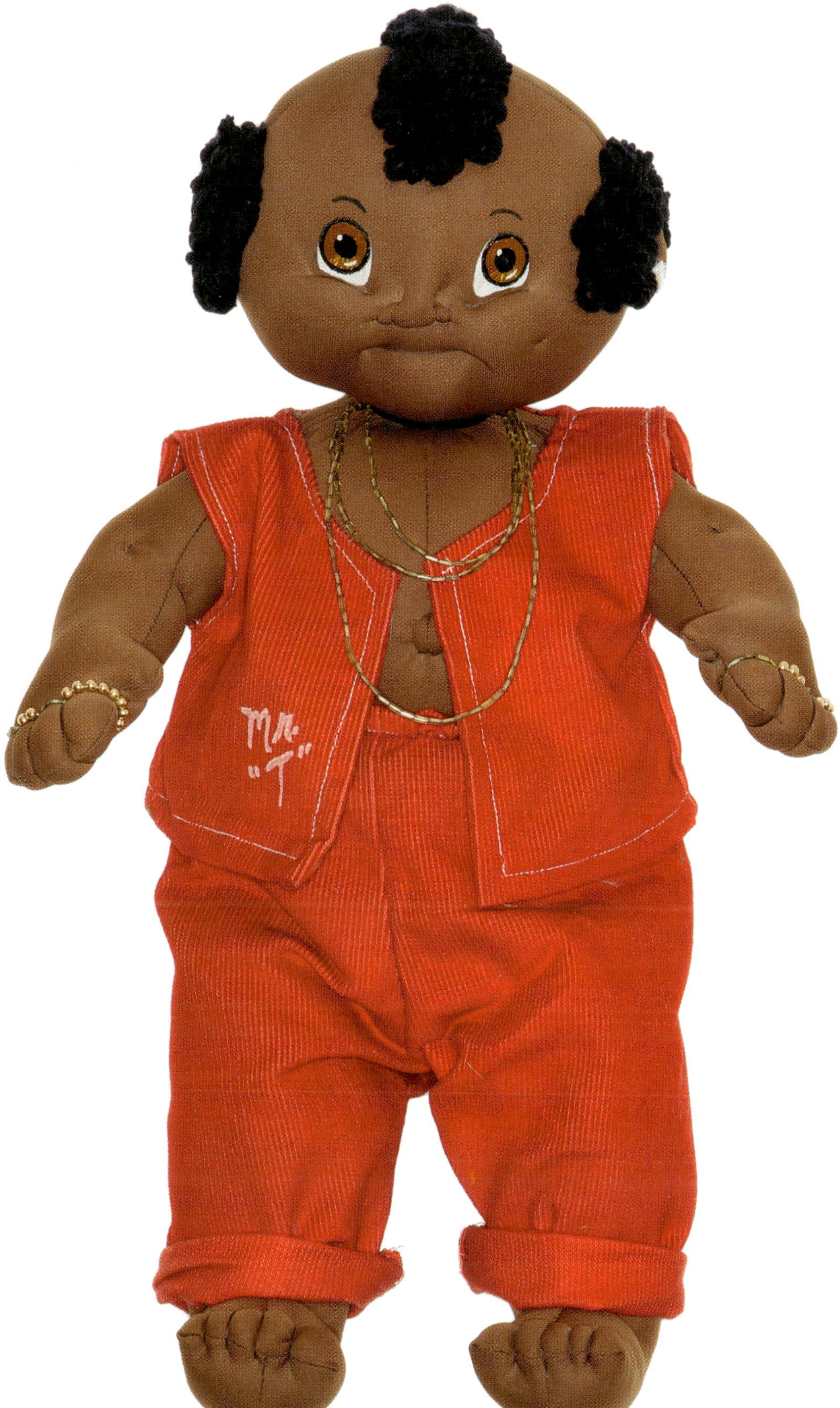
Mr. "T"

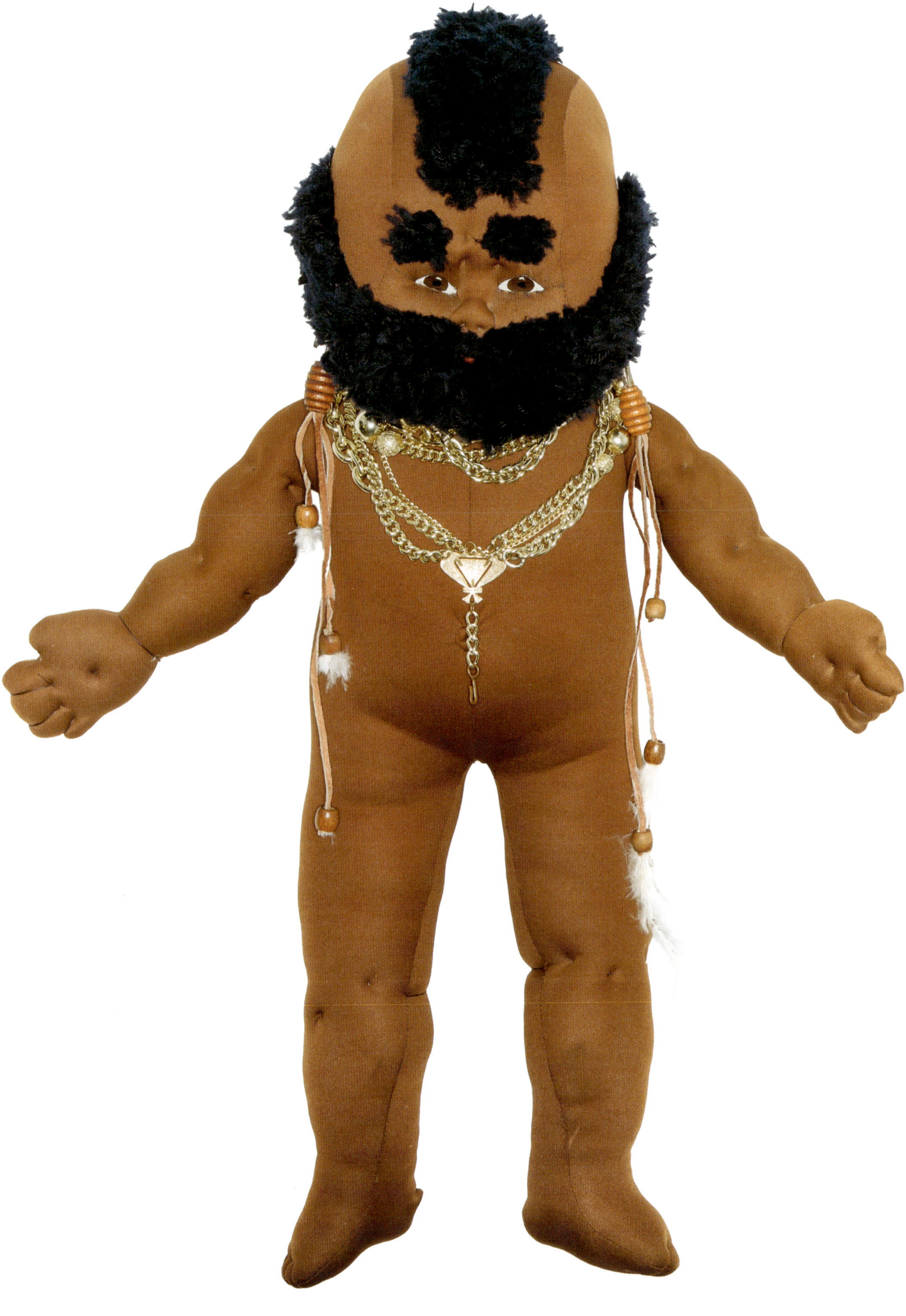

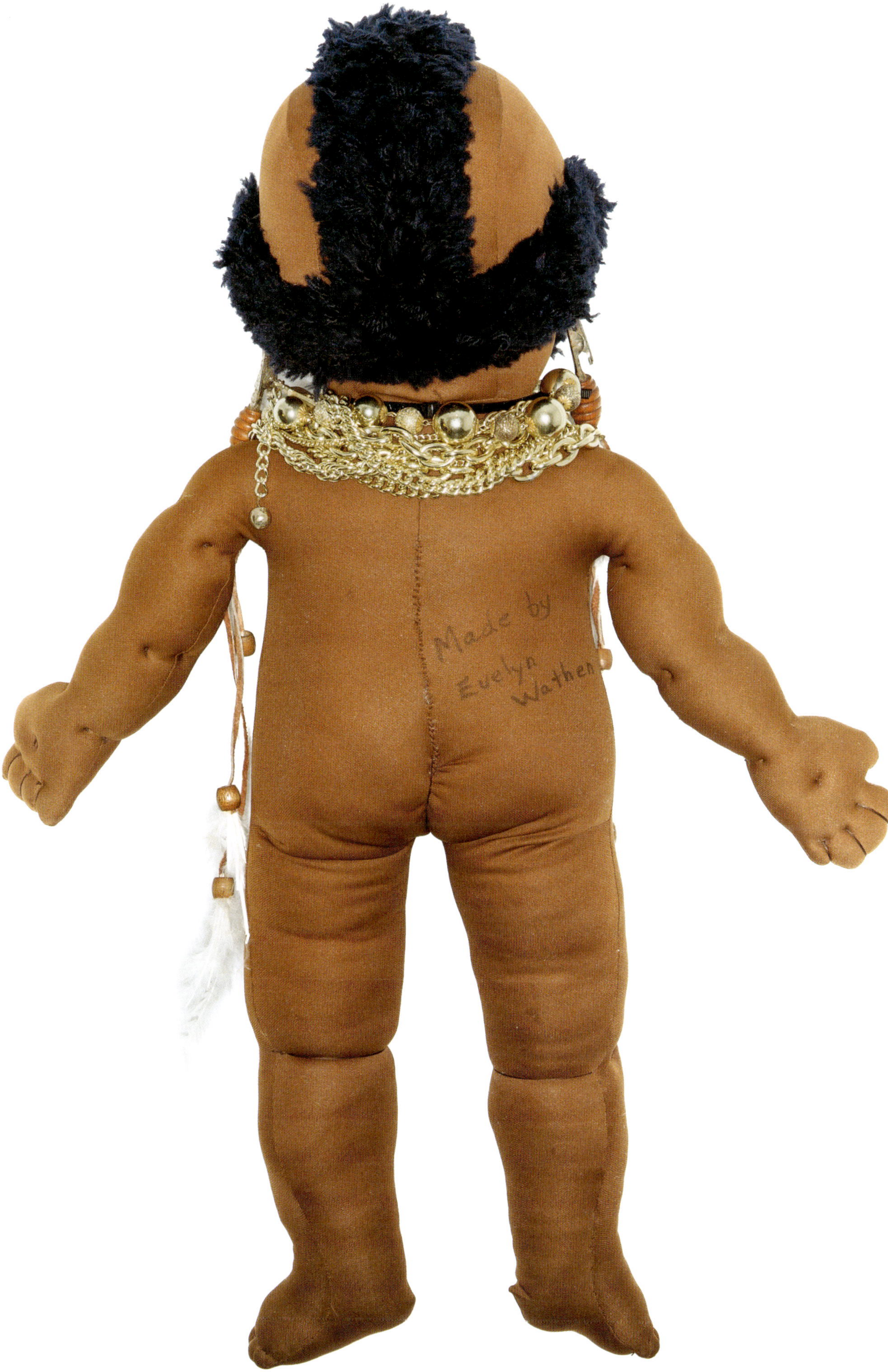
Made by
Evelyn
Wathen

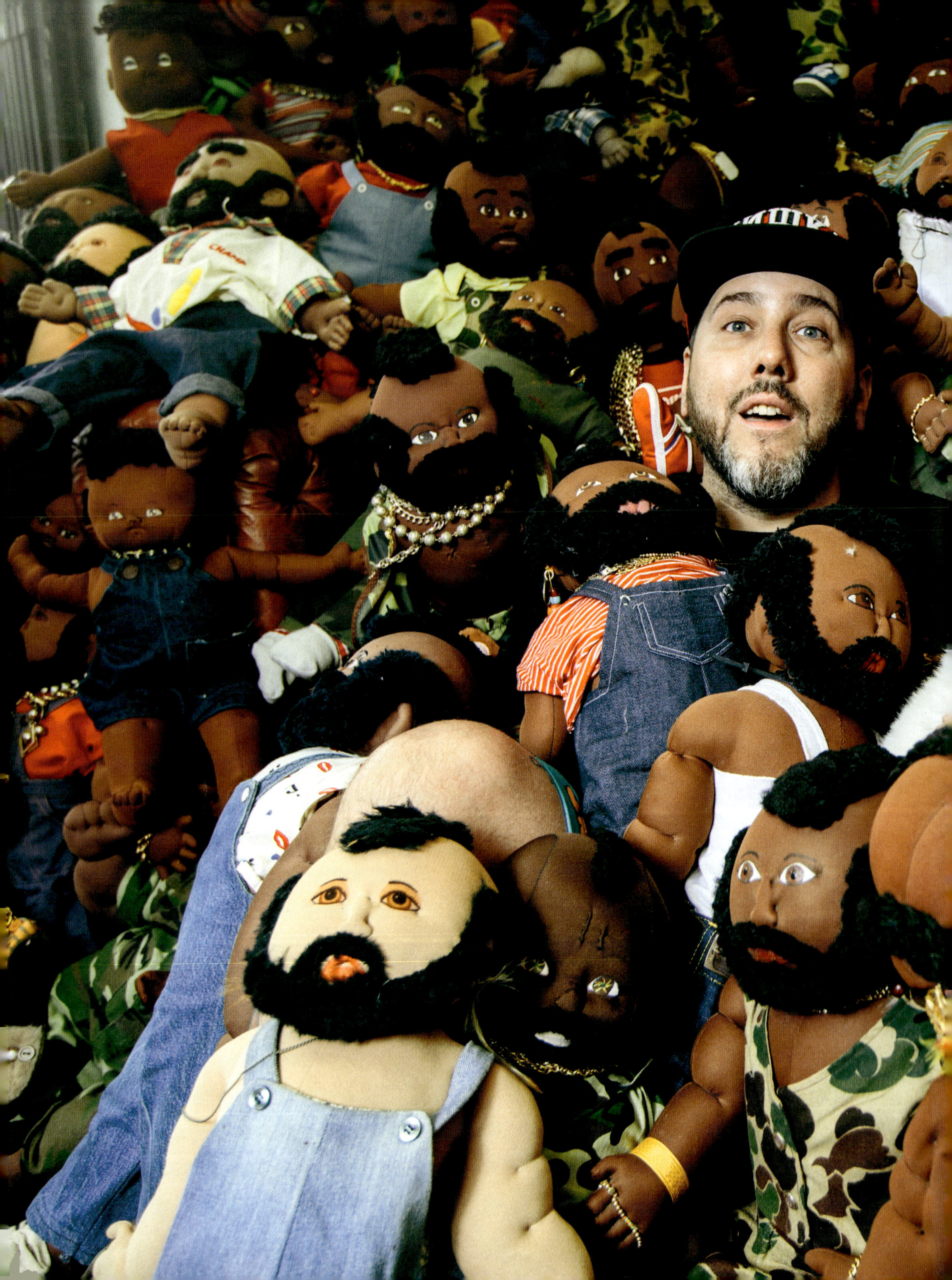

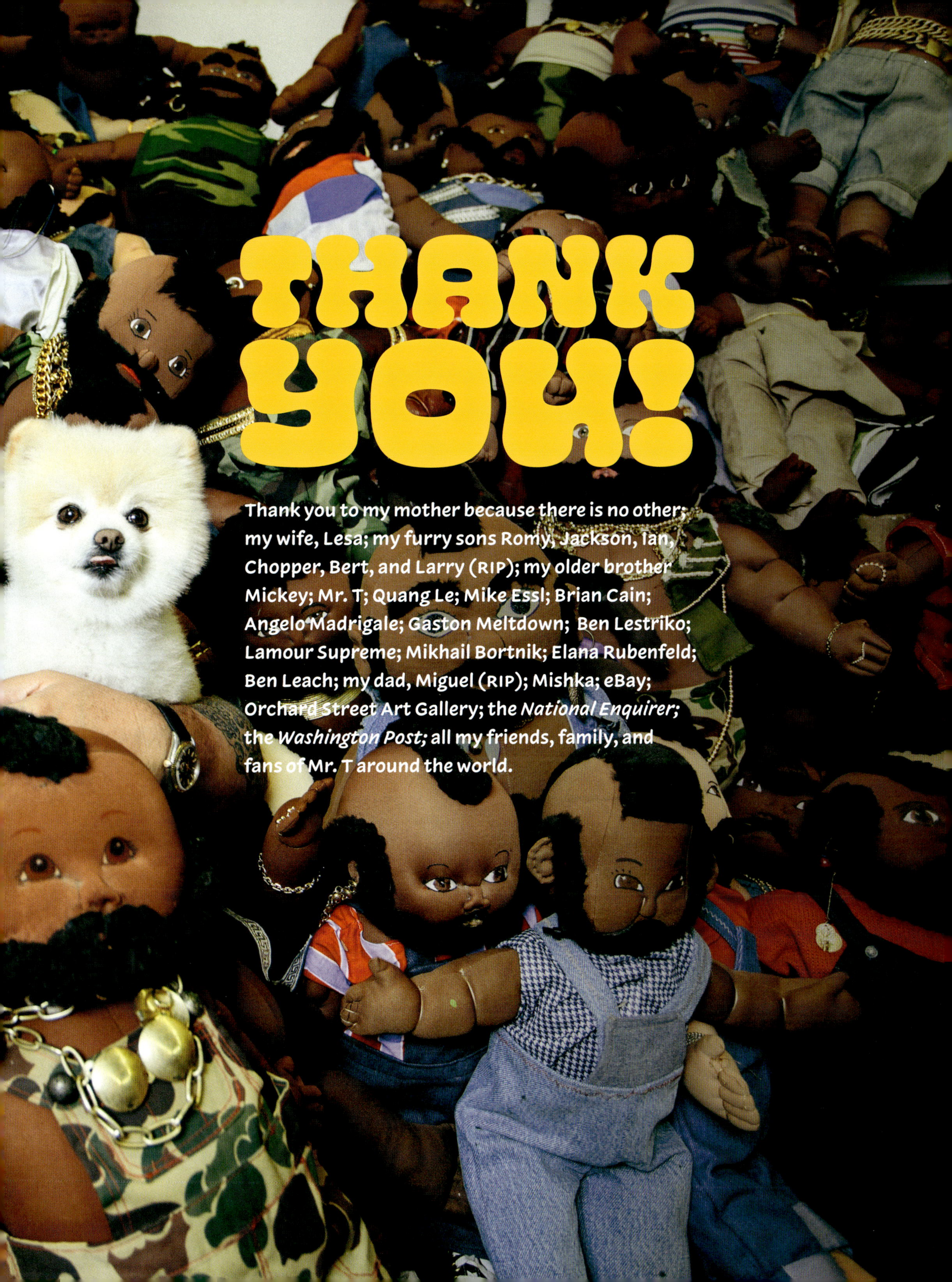

THANK YOU!

Thank you to my mother because there is no other; my wife, Lesa; my furry sons Romy, Jackson, Ian, Chopper, Bert, and Larry (RIP); my older brother Mickey; Mr. T; Quang Le; Mike Essl; Brian Cain; Angelo Madrigale; Gaston Meltdown; Ben Lestriko; Lamour Supreme; Mikhail Bortnik; Elana Rubenfeld; Ben Leach; my dad, Miguel (RIP); Mishka; eBay; Orchard Street Art Gallery; the *National Enquirer;* the *Washington Post;* all my friends, family, and fans of Mr. T around the world.

Barbara Walters: What if somebody came up to you with a gun and said, "give me all this jewelry, give me all this gold and diamonds." What would you do?

Mr. T: I would give it to them. These are material things. I tell people all the time—clients I used to work for — "it's okay to have possessions, but don't become possessed by your possessions. Don't cry over something that can't cry over you."....

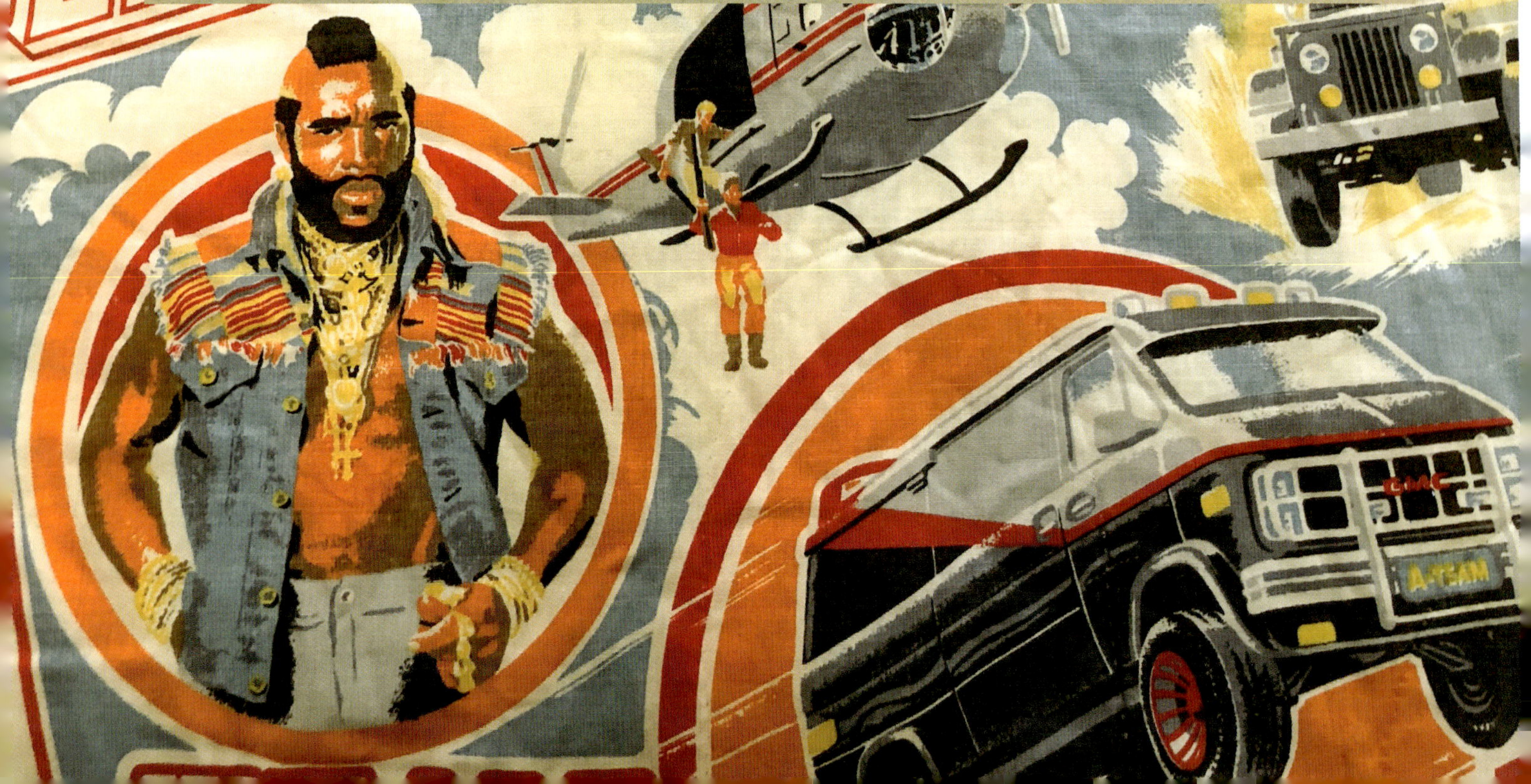

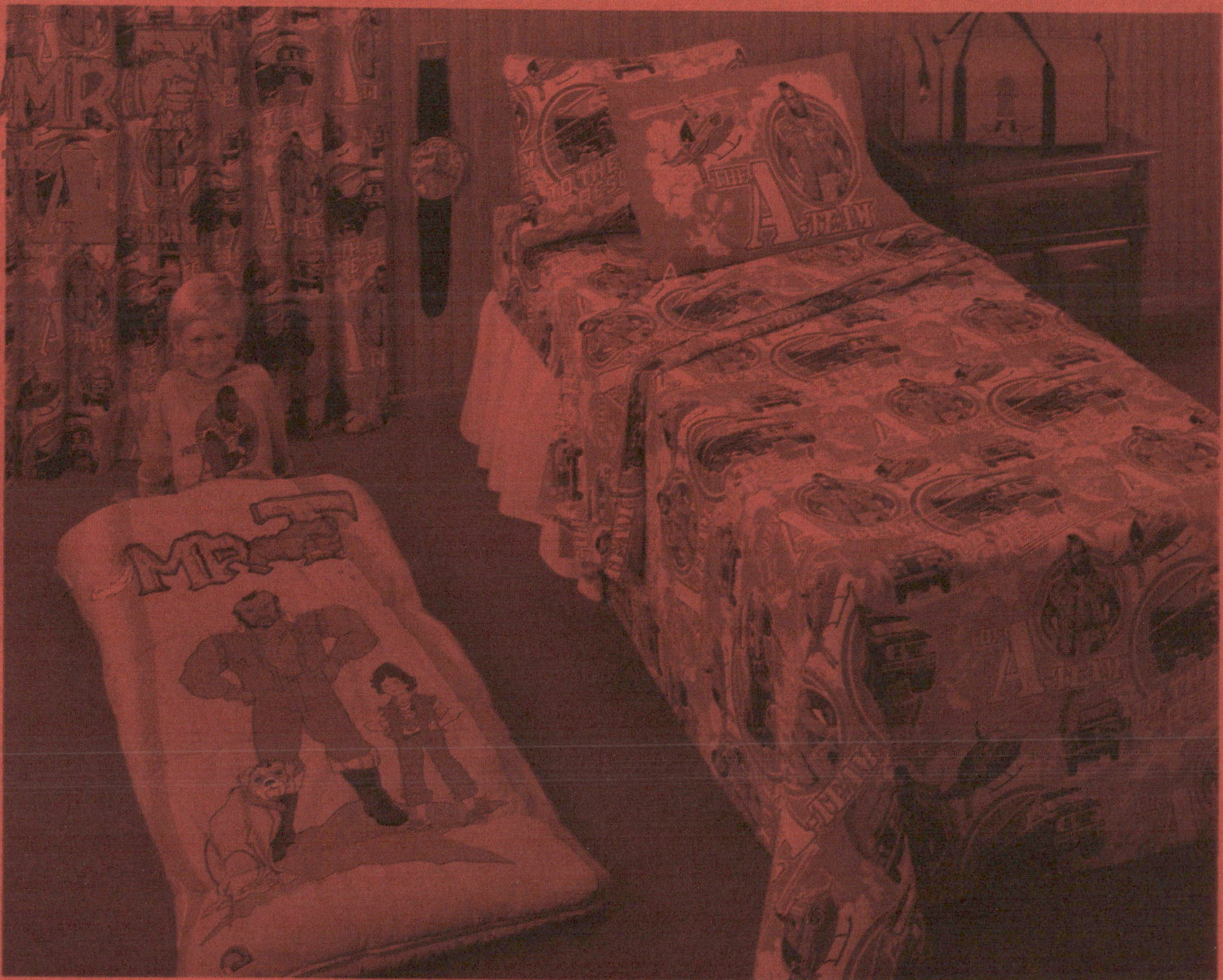
THE A-TEAM

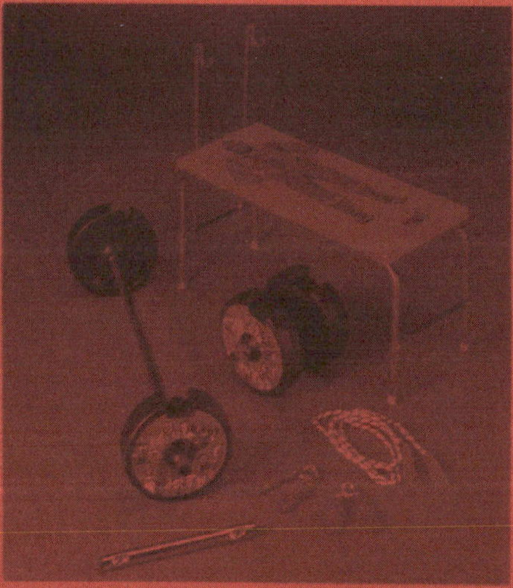

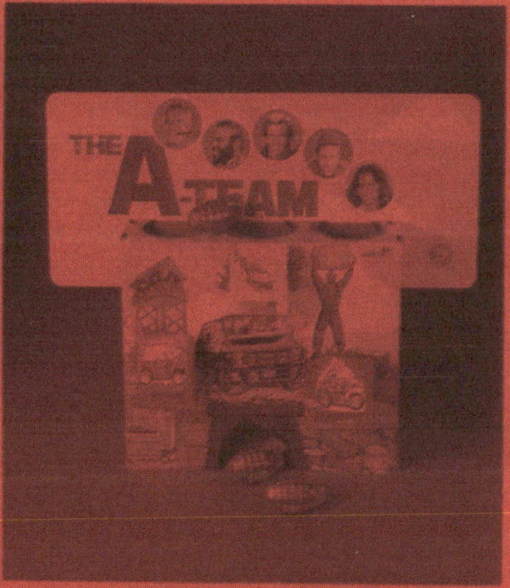
THE A-TEAM

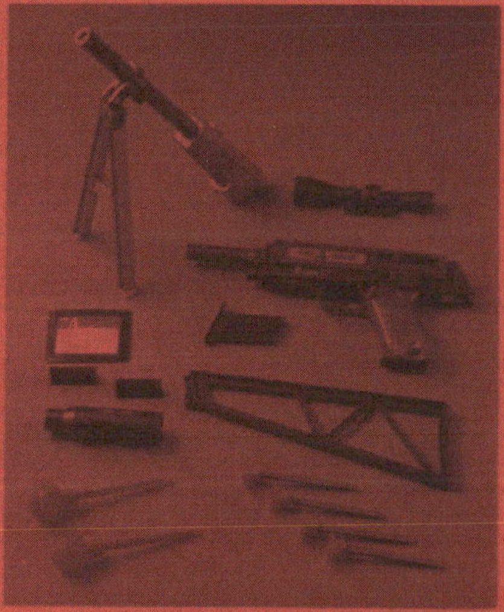

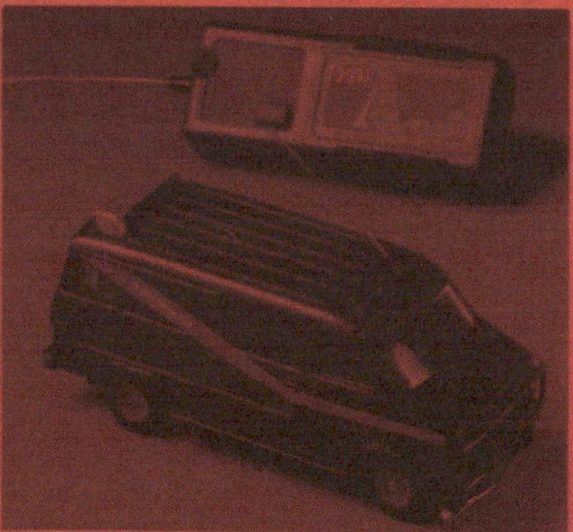

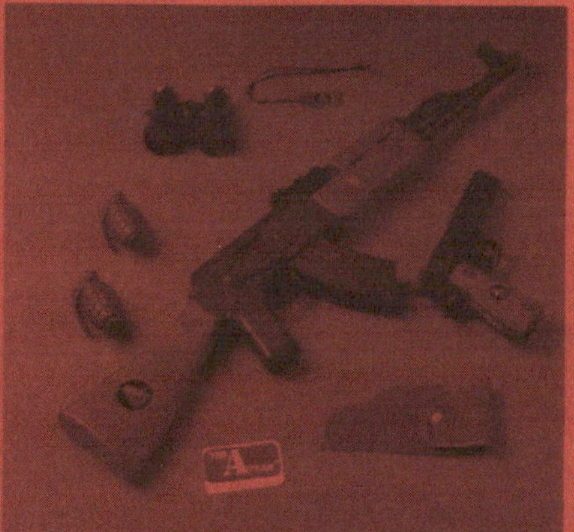

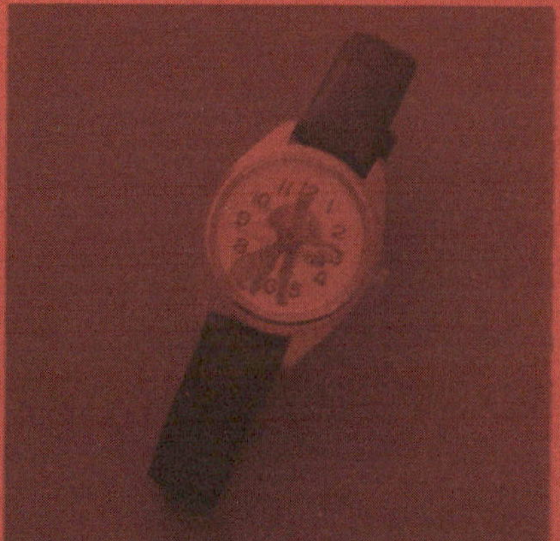